Introduction to Government and Binding Theory

984

982

9714

Blackwell Textbooks in Linguistics

Introduction to Government and Binding Theory

SECOND EDITION

Liliane Haegeman

BLACKWELL
Oxford UK & Cambridge USA

Copyright © Liliane Haegeman 1991, 1994

First edition first published 1991
Reprinted 1992 (twice), 1993 (twice)
Second edition first published 1994
Reprinted 1995 (twice)

Blackwell Publishers Ltd
108 Cowley Road
Oxford OX4 1JF
UK

Blackwell Publishers Inc.
238 Main Street
Cambridge, Massachusetts 02142, USA

British Library Cataloguing in Publication Data

A CIP catalogue record for this book is available from the British Library.

Library of Congress Cataloging in Publication Data

Haegeman, Liliane M. V.
  Introduction to government and binding theory/Liliane Haegeman.
    p.   cm.
  Includes bibliographical references and index.
  ISBN 0–631–19067–8 (pbk.)
    1. Government-binding theory (Linguistics)   I. title.
P158.2.H34   1994   90–37174
415—dc20   CIP

Typeset in 10 on 13 pt Sabon
by Graphicraft Typesetters Ltd., Hong Kong
Printed in the USA

This book is printed on acid-free paper.

Contents

Preface to the Second Edition

The second edition of this book is written very much with the same goals as the first edition, and though there are a number of changes, the book is essentially unaltered in structure and in methodology. My primary goal in writing a second edition was to make the book more user-friendly by clarifying and expanding a number of passages which were felt to be confusing and to eliminate a number of inaccuracies and inconsistencies which had been pointed out to me by various users of the book. I have also used this opportunity for increasing the number of cross-references in the book. In addition I also wanted to update the book and integrate the results of more recent research. Written in 1988–9, the first edition lacks references to a number of concepts which have become prominent in the theory and I have tried to integrate these in the book without creating an imbalance.

An important question I had to to face was that of deciding how much space I ought to devote to the Minimalist Program, which was initiated by Noam Chomsky in 1992 and which is in the process of being elaborated. Though the Minimalist Program offers many attractive aspects I feel that it is at the present stage too much of a research programme to become the object matter of a systematic introduction in a textbook, and for this reason, I have limited the discussion of the Minimalist Program. However, while this second edition has not become an introduction to the Minimalist Program I do try to highlight those concepts and elements of the theory which have become more prominent in the Minimalist Program. I have given more attention, for instance, to the role of functional heads, to specifier–head agreement relations, to reconstruction, etc. In this way I hope that the book will be useful also for those who wish to study the Minimalist Program. Whenever it seemed relevant and appropriate in the context of this book I have also briefly alluded to other concepts which are prominent in the Minimalist Program.

In order to provide space for new components without producing too large a book I have eliminated the last two chapters from the first edition. These chapters dealt with structures of Romance and Germanic languages and were felt by many to be less well integrated in the book. Some of the points dealt with in those chapters, however, have been reintegrated in the main body of the book. To mention some examples: the null object construction in Italian and in Portuguese is now discussed in chapter 8, verb movement and the head movement constraint is discussed in chapter 11, scrambling is discussed briefly in chapter 3 and is integrated in an exercise in chapter 8.

In the second edition chapter 11 focuses on functional categories and centres around the split INFL hypothesis. It also introduces the DP-hypothesis and the notion of extended projection. The chapter also offers a brief comparison between the treatment of V-movement presented in this book and that in the Minimalist Program. Chapter 12 is now devoted to a discussion of Relativized Minimality and the Empty Category Principle and to related issues such as the problem of defining A-positions in a framework which adopts the subject-in-VP hypothesis. Throughout the main body of the book I have integrated or expanded discussions of a number of concepts which did not receive due attention in the first edition: to mention perhaps the more prominent: properties of *pro*-drop languages (Introduction), the structure of small clauses (chapter 2), chain-formation (chapter 6), reconstruction (chapter 9), multiple movement (chapter 9), *wh*-absorption, (chapter 9), Full Interpretation (chapter 9), expletive replacement (chapter 9).

An objection which could be raised against the first edition is that the theory was presented perhaps too rigidly and that students might easily get the impression of a completely finished and fixed framework without any room for creativity or flexibility. For some students this could actually lead to too strong a dependence on the book and to a lack of confidence in their own independent thinking. Complications and issues for further research were largely presented in the form of exercises. In this edition I have tried to integrate some more extensive discussion of alternative issues within the main body of the text. One controversy which I have integrated in the discussion, for instance, concerns the way word-order variation should be dealt with in the theory. In so doing I hope to have shown that the theory is still evolving and should be constantly evaluated and re-evaluated in the light of new theoretical developments or empirical discoveries. I have also added additional exercises which highlight remaining problems and controversial issues and draw the students' attention to those research areas which are still an important challenge for the theory. This way I hope the book will stimulate and encourage independent and creative thinking on the part of the readers.

The work of revising the text was made much easier by the feedback I received from students and colleagues in the field. It is difficult to include all those who encouraged me by their comments and suggestions here. First I should thank Jelly Julia de Jong and Henk Verkuyl. They both sent me detailed page-by-page comments on most sections of the book; their notes were the stepping stones which guided me throughout the revision. Thanks are also due to Anna Gavarró, Wim de Geest, Arild Hestvik, David Lightfoot, Andrea Moro, Jean Rutten, Manuela Schoenenberger, Bill Turkel, Sten Vikner and Patrick Winston for comments on the book in general or on specific sections. The following colleagues were so kind as to respond to Blackwell's questionnaire and their comments helped me in making a number of decisions concerning the revisions: Andrew Barss, Frits Beukema, Wynn Chao, Sheila Dooley Collberg, Marcel den Dikken, Stanley Dubinsky, Grant Goodall, Eithne Guilfoyle, Y. Huang, Mark Johnson, Wim Koopman, Ans van Kemenade, Richard K. Larson, R. Mesthrie, Kumbirai G. Mkanganwi, Frits Stuurman and Henry Smith. I have tried to take into account their comments during the revisions. I also thank my colleagues in Geneva for creating a stimulating environment for doing generative syntax: Adriana Belletti, Corinne Grange, Teresa Guasti, Eric Haeberli, Genoveva Puskas, Manuela Schoenenberger, Ur Shlonsky and Eric Wehrli. Special thanks are due to Luigi Rizzi whose classes have inspired many of the revisions in the second edition. I wish also to thank the students whose comments made me see many shortcomings of the book and inspired the revisions. The following deserve special mention: Enoch Aboh, Carlo Cecchetto, Elisa di Domenico, Eric Haeberli, David Hodgetts, Odette Kowalski Sandra Leuenberger, Julien Musolino, Lucienne Rasetti and Michal Starke, all in Geneva, and Michael Tallon in Georgetown. Thanks to Corinne Grange for proofreading and for indexing the book and to Marguerite Nesling for the copy editing. Last but not least I also thank all the users of my book, students and teachers. I hope that this textbook will show to them that generative syntax offers us an exciting and stimulating way of thinking about language.

Thanks to Sylvie Ferioli, Corinne Grange and Raffaella Zanuttini for their never failing friendship. I also thank my parents and Johan, my brother, for their support and sympathy, and my husband, Hedwig De Pauw, for never allowing me to forget that life is not just generative syntax and for suggesting the dedication.

Liliane Haegeman
Geneva
1993

Preface to the First Edition

The purpose of this book is to provide an introduction to the mainline version of Government and Binding Theory, or GB-theory, using as a basis Noam Chomsky's more recent writings. Starting from the ideas developed in the *Lectures on Government and Binding* (1981a), the book will include the most important notions and concepts of *Some Concepts and Consequences of the Theory of Government and Binding* (1982), *Knowledge of Language* (1986a) and *Barriers* (1986b). Some of the concepts that were used earlier in the development of generative grammar but have become less relevant will occasionally be referred to and reference will also be made to some of the more recent developments of the theory. The aim of the book is not to make the reader familiar with all the literature published within the GB framework, but rather to enable him to read this literature himself, to understand it and to evaluate it independently.

The book is aimed at intermediate students in linguistics. A general introduction to generative syntax is presupposed. Roughly, the reader would be expected to be familiar with notions such as competence, performance, informants and linguistic intuition, grammaticality, acceptability, autonomy of syntax, etc. and to be able to parse sentences using the tree diagram representation and the labelled bracketing format. The book presupposes some understanding of terms such as constituent, phrase, grammatical function, lexical category, etc., but this does not mean that such concepts and terms will be taken for granted entirely. On the contrary, part of the aim of the book will be to give the concepts and terms with which the reader is familiar more precise content by offering a coherent theoretical background.

The book should be usable both in the classroom and for private study. It consists of twelve chapters each dealing with a particular component of the theory. Each chapter will contain a number of exercises which allow the reader to test the knowledge acquired in the chapter.

As a basis for the organization of the book I have chosen to start from the projection principle: i.e. the idea that all syntactic structure is projected from the lexicon. This idea is introduced in the first chapter. Starting from this initial premise the book then discusses the distribution of overt material (chapters 2 to 4) and of non-overt material (chapters 5 to 9). Chapter 10 offers an introduction to Chomsky's book *Barriers* (1986b).

Clearly, a book like this one cannot be written in a vacuum, and in this preface I can only mention a fraction of the people who have influenced the development of the book directly or indirectly.

I wish to thank my publishers for giving me the opportunity to write an introductory course book.

The manuscript of the book has developed on the basis of my own teaching at the English Department of the University of Geneva. Earlier versions of the book were used in manuscript form for students of English linguistics in the second and third year syntax programme at the University of Geneva (1988–90), as well as at the University of Bern (1988–9). The comments of my students have been of invaluable help for the rewriting of my book and I wish to use this opportunity to thank them for their enthusiastic help and patience with a manuscript that often was far from perfect.

As a teacher I owe thanks to my students, but I also owe tremendous thanks to my own teachers, especially to Neil Smith who helped me find a direction for my own research and teaching in linguistics, to Michael Brody who introduced me specifically to generative grammar, and to Henk van Riemsdijk who introduced me to the linguistic community in Europe and in the United States.

I also wish to thank the many colleagues in Geneva and elsewhere who have helped me not only by commenting on and making suggestions for parts of the book but also by being just good friends: Genoveva Puskas, Ian Roberts, Manuela Schoenenberger, Bonnie Schwartz, Andy Spencer, Sten Vikner, Richard Watts and Mariette Wauters.

Thanks are also due to Neil Smith, Noel Burton-Roberts and an anonymous reader who went painstakingly through an earlier manuscript and pointed out to me its many flaws and shortcomings. I hope that the current version of the book will not disappoint them too much.

Two friends merit special mention. Sylvie Ferioli was always willing to help me out on the practical side of typing and printing, and supported me patiently and good-humouredly at the moments when I became overwhelmed by various anxieties and worries. Corinne Grange has helped me and encouraged me throughout the whole period of my teaching in Geneva. She was one of the most enthusiastic and loyal students I have had, and she has become a colleague with whom I have been able to discuss any major or minor problems in the book. Her cheerful mood helped me across bad spots where I felt like abandoning the project entirely. I owe her special thanks for the substantial time that she invested in the rereading of the pre-final version of the text.

Thanks are also due to Ruth Kimber for the editorial work on the first edition of the book and to Philip Carpenter, who followed the development of the book and gave me valuable comments throughout.

Obviously none of the people mentioned above can be held responsible for the final version of the book, for which I assume full responsibility.

Thanks are finally due to Hedwig De Pauw for reminding me that there is more to life than generative syntax.

Liliane Haegeman
Geneva
1991

To Ferenc Czibor, Dragan Dzajic, Manoel Francisco dos Santos Garrincha, Jurgen Grabovsky, Francisco Gento, Coen Moelijn, Wilfried Puis, Antonio Simoes, Frankie Vercauteren, Branko Zebec and Sir Stanley Matthews.

Introduction:
The Chomskian Perspective on
Language Study

Contents

Introduction

The aim of this book is to offer an introduction to the version of generative syntax usually referred to as Government and Binding Theory.[1] I shall not dwell on this label here; its significance will become clear in later chapters of this book.

Government–Binding Theory is a natural development of earlier versions of generative grammar, initiated by Noam Chomsky some thirty years ago. The purpose of this introductory chapter is not to provide a historical survey of the Chomskian tradition. A full discussion of the history of the generative enterprise would in itself be the basis for a book.[2] What I shall do here is offer a short and informal sketch of the essential motivation for the line of enquiry to be pursued. Throughout the book the initial points will become more concrete and more precise.

By means of footnotes I shall also direct the reader to further reading related to the matter at hand. Much of the primary literature will be hard to follow for the reader who has not worked his[3] way through the book, but I hope that the information will be useful for future reference.

---

[1] Chomsky (1991) himself expresses reservations about the label 'Government and Binding Theory' and refers to the theory we are concerned with here as the 'Principles and Parameters Theory'. The latter term is more comprehensive in that it covers work done in the Government and Binding tradition as developed in the present book, and also work done in a recent development in the generative framework usually referred to as the Minimalist Program (Chomsky, 1992). Since the label Government and Binding Theory or its abbreviation GB-theory is widespread we continue to use it here to refer to the generative work initiated by Chomsky's book *Lectures on Government and Binding* (1981a). The term allows us to distinguish the approach developed here from the more recent approach in the Minimalist Program.

[2] For a survey of the development of the theory see van Riemsdijk and Williams (1986). This work should be accessible once chapter 7 has been covered.

The reader will find a good introduction to generative grammar in general introductions to linguistics such as Akmajian, Demers and Harnish (1979), Fromkin and Rodman (1988, 1992), Lightfoot (1982), Smith and Wilson (1979), etc. These works should be accessible at this point. For more advanced introductions the reader is referred to Chomsky (1965, 1981a, b, c, 1982, 1986a, 1988, 1991), but reading them should be postponed until after chapter 7 of this book, at which point we shall have covered most of the technical issues that are discussed.

[3] My use of the pronoun *his* for referents which may be either male and female follows the conventions of English grammar and I hope that the female readers of this book will not feel offended by it.

1   Linguistics: The Science of Language

When asked to indicate one prominent feature that distinguishes human beings
from animals, many would probably say that this feature is 'language'. Even
though animals may have communication systems, none of these systems is
as rich or as versatile as the language used by humans. Language is human-
specific.[4] This means that an understanding of the mechanisms of human
language may lead us to understand, at least partly, what it is that distinguishes human beings from animals. Linguistics, the study of language, gives
us an insight into the human mind.

Leonard Bloomfield defined linguistics as the science of language (Bloomfield, 1935). Like all scientists, linguists will aim at formulating the general
principles to account for the data with which they are faced. Linguists try to
formulate generalizations about linguistic data, i.e. language.[5]

There are various ways of approaching the study of language. I assume the
reader is familiar with the traditional view of language study, where the focus
is often on the study of one specific language, say English. A linguist studying
English will try to characterize the principles that determine the formation
of English sentences. The goal will be to provide a systematic description of
English sentence formation, the grammar of English. The description will
have to account for data such as the following:

1a   Agatha Christie has written many books.
1b   I don't like detective stories.

The sentences in (1) are **well formed**. They contrast with the sentences in
(2), which are **ill formed**.

2a   *Agatha Christie many books written has.
2b   *I detective stories like.

Well formed English sentences are constructed according to the grammar
of English: they are **grammatical**. The sentences in (2) are not formed according

---

[4]   In their introduction to linguistics Akmajian, Demers and Harnish (1979) present
a fairly comprehensive discussion of the differences between human language and
animal language.

[5]   Robins (1967) and Newmeyer (1980, 1983) offer good surveys of the development
of linguistics. These books will offer a broader background to situate the theory
we are discussing here in its historical context.

to the grammar of English: they are **ungrammatical**, as indicated by the asterisks.

When writing a grammar, the linguist will not stop at merely listing examples with the appropriate grammaticality judgements. A simple catalogue of sentences may be an interesting basis for discussion but it cannot be the ultimate goal of scientific research. In addition to describing the data, the linguist will formulate general principles which will be applicable to further data. Informally, a linguist might account for the ungrammaticality of (2), for instance, by proposing that in English verbs precede their direct objects. A first hypothesis might be that English sentences are constructed according to the SVO pattern: subject precedes verb, verb precedes object. Let us call this the SVO hypothesis. Having formulated this hypothesis on the basis of a limited set of data, the linguist will test it on the basis of further data. The SVO hypothesis will lead him to predict, for instance, that (3a) and (3b) are grammatical; but as it stands, the hypothesis also predicts that (3c) and (3d) are ungrammatical: the objects, *detective stories* and *which stories* respectively, precede the subjects:

3a   Jeeves is baking a cake.
3b   John has bought a new car.
3c   Detective stories, I don't like.
3d   Which stories do you like?

Either the SVO hypothesis itself will have to be modified in the light of the data in (3c) and (3d) or one or more extra principles are needed which interact with the original hypothesis to account for the grammaticality of (3c) and (3d). We might, for example, formulate a rule of topicalization which moves a direct object to the beginning of the sentence to account for (3c). In addition we might formulate a rule for question formation which (i) moves the questioning element (*which stories*) to the initial position of the sentence, and (ii) inverts subject and auxiliary (*do*) (cf. (3d)).

The total of all the rules and principles that have been formulated with respect to a language constitutes the grammar of that language. A grammar of a language is a coherent system of rules and principles that are at the basis of the grammatical sentences of a language. We say that a grammar **generates** the sentences of a language.

A first requirement for any grammar is that it provides a characterization of the language it describes, i.e. the grammar must be able to distinguish those strings of words which are sentences of the language from those which are not sentences of the language in question. Such a grammar will be **observationally adequate**.

2 The Native Speaker: Grammaticality and Acceptability

2.1 Descriptive Adequacy

Not only linguists have the ability to judge English sentences. Every native speaker of English knows intuitively that the sentences in (1) and (3) are acceptable and that those in (2) are not. Moreover, every native speaker of English produces a large number of grammatical sentences and understands the English sentences that he comes across. The native speaker may not be able to formulate the general principles that underlie the sentences he produces, but he has an unconscious or tacit knowledge of such principles; he has internalized a grammar of the language. The native speaker's tacit knowledge of the grammar of his language is the focus of enquiry for the linguist working in the Chomskian tradition. We say that a grammar reaches descriptive adequacy if, in addition to describing the data, it provides an account for the native speaker's intuitions.

    Let us consider some examples. We have proposed that (3c) and (3d) could be generated by a process that moves the direct object leftward to the beginning of the sentence. Now consider the examples in (4), which are not acceptable (hence the asterisk):

4a   *Detective stories, I wonder if he likes.
4b   *Where do you wonder if he lives?

To account for the unacceptability of (4a) we might propose that the process which moves the direct object in (3c) must be constrained: the direct object cannot move across *if*.

    Similarly, when we consider (4b) we might propose that the rule of question formation must also be constrained: the questioning element (*where*) must not move across *if*. At this point we have reached **observational adequacy**: we provide a description of the facts. However, if we stop at this point we are missing a significant **generalization**. The ungrammaticality of (4a) and (4b) is due to the same constraint. A **descriptively adequate** grammar will not simply provide an analysis for (3c) and (3d) and for the deviance of (4a) and (4b), but it will try to capture the relation between (4a) and (4b) and formulate a general principle to explain why both (4a) and (4b) are felt to be unacceptable. Such a principle may be that no element in English must be moved across *if*. This general principle will also lead us to predict that the examples in (5) are ungrammatical, whereas those in (6) are grammatical:

5a   *Where* do you wonder *if* Emsworth has hidden the Empress?
5b   *Which detective* do you wonder *if* Emsworth will invite for Sunday lunch?
5c   *To Bill*, I wonder *if* he will give any money.

6a   *Where* has Emsworth hidden the Empress?
6b   *Which detective* will Emsworth invite for Sunday lunch?
6c   *To Bill*, he won't give any money.

The general constraint which blocks movement of an element across *if* will be taken to be part of the native speaker's internal grammar.

A descriptively adequate grammar will not only describe the linguistic data, but it will contain the general principles and processes that enable the native speaker to produce and interpret sentences in his language and decide on the acceptability of sentences. Such a grammar is an explicit formulation of the tacit linguistic knowledge of the native speaker, his internal grammar.

The shift of focus from language itself to the native speaker's knowledge of language is the major feature of the Chomskian tradition. Both the generative linguist and the traditional linguist will be constructing grammars, i.e. general systems that underlie the sentences of a language. But the generative linguist conceives of his grammar as a reflex of the native speaker's competence. The grammar is a representation of the speaker's internal linguistic knowledge.

2.2   Grammaticality and Acceptability

At this point we turn to the notions of 'grammaticality' and 'acceptability'. 'Grammaticality' is a theoretical notion. A sentence is grammatical if it is formed according to the grammar of English as formulated by the linguist. 'Acceptability', on the other hand, is the term which characterizes the native speaker's intuitions about the linguistic data. Consider (7):

7a   Bill had left. It was clear.
7b   [That Bill had left] was clear.
7c   It was clear [that Bill had left].
7d   Once that it was clear [that Bill had left], we gave up.
7e   Once that [that Bill had left] was clear, we gave up.

(7a) contains two independent sentences. In (7b) the bracketed sentence *Bill had left* is the subject of the complex sentence *that Bill had left was clear.*

We say that *Bill had left* is a subordinate clause. It is introduced by *that*, a subordinating conjunction. Similarly, in (7c) *that Bill had left* is a subordinate clause. In (7d) the sentence (7c) is a subordinate clause in a complex sentence. A grammar must generate complex sentences in which one clause is part of another one.

Let us turn to (7e). The sentence is odd for most native speakers: it is not acceptable. However, this sentence is formed according to the same principle that we posited to account for the formation of (7b)–(7d), i.e. that one sentence may become part of another sentence. Hence (7e) would be **grammatical**, though it is not acceptable.

Faced with intuitions such as that for (7e) the linguist might decide to modify the grammar he has formulated in such a way that sentence (7e) is considered to be ungrammatical. He may also decide, however, that (7e) is grammatical, and that the unacceptability of the sentence is due to independent reasons. For instance, (7e) may be argued to be unacceptable because the sentence is hard to process. In the latter case the unacceptability is not strictly due to linguistic factors but is due to the more general mechanisms used for processing information.

The native speaker who judges a sentence cannot decide whether it is grammatical. He only has **intuitions** about **acceptability**. It is for the linguist to determine whether the unacceptability of a sentence is due to grammatical principles or whether it may be due to other factors. It is the linguist's task to determine what it is that makes (7e) unacceptable. This entails that there may be disagreement between linguists as to whether certain unacceptable sentences are grammatical or not. The disagreement is not one of conflicting judgements of the sentence (although these may also exist), but it is one of analysis. The linguist will have to determine to what degree the unacceptability of a sentence is to be accounted for in terms of the grammar. All the linguist has to go by, though, is the native speaker's intuitions about language, and these, as argued above, are the result of the interaction between his internal grammar and other factors.

In this book we focus on the linguistic knowledge of the native speaker. We restrict our attention to his internal grammar. Obviously, the interaction between the grammar and other mental processes is also an interesting area of research, but it is not the topic of this book.

2.3 *The Grammar as a System of Principles*

One approach to formulating a grammar of a language would be to suppose that the speaker's internal knowledge of English, i.e. his internal grammar, is no more than a huge check-list of grammatical sentences. Speakers could be thought to 'check' any sentence they come across against this internal inventory. Sentences which match a sentence in the list would be said to be grammatical, those that do not are ungrammatical. Depending on the degree of deviance of such ungrammatical sentences we could rank the sentences for ungrammaticality. A grammar of a language would then be simply a list of sentences. But it must be immediately obvious that listing all the grammatical sentences of a language is an impossible task and also that it misses the point.

Cataloguing all the grammatical sentences of English is first of all impossible because there is an infinite number of English sentences. In addition, there are other objections to such a listing enterprise. We stated above that linguistics is the scientific study of language. From such a perspective the listing of linguistic data is not enough. We expect general principles to explain the data.

For the generative linguist who tries to provide a representation of the native speaker's internal knowledge of a language a mere listing of sentences would never achieve descriptive adequacy: it could never account for the native speaker's knowledge of the language. Human beings – in our example speakers of English – have finite memories: we often forget things we have heard. Given that the capacity of our memories is finite, it would be absurd to claim that human beings are able to store all potential sentences of the language, an infinite set. It is thus inconceivable that the native speaker's internal linguistic knowledge is an inventory of sentences. We must assume that human beings are somehow equipped with a finite system of knowledge which enables them to construct and interpret an infinite number of sentences. This finite system of principles is what we referred to loosely above as the internal grammar of the language. The generative linguist will try to render explicit the finite system of principles that make up the native speaker's competence. In our example, the principle which prohibits moving elements across *if* will be able to account for the unacceptability of (4) and (5).

3   Knowledge of Language

3.1   *The Poverty of the Stimulus*

A speaker's knowledge of a language is largely unconscious. It is formally represented as a grammar. The grammar of a language generates the sentences of a language and assigns to each sentence a set of representations which provide the formal characterization of some of the properties of the sentence (semantic, syntactic, morphological, phonological, etc.). It is the linguist's task to render explicit the internal grammar of the speaker of a language. In order to construct such an explicit grammar of a language, the linguist can rely to some extent on data taken from usage, the output of the speakers. However, usage data are inevitably an incomplete source of information. The sentences actually produced by a speaker are only a fragment of the sentences he *could* have produced. In order to arrive at a characterization of the speaker's potential, the linguist can also rely on the speaker's knowledge of the language, i.e. on his capacity to evaluate linguistic expressions in that particular language. For instance, speakers of English intuitively know that (8a) is an acceptable sentence and that (8b) is not:

8a   She has invited Louise to her house.
8b   *Has invited Louise to her house.

Informally we will say that (8b) is unacceptable because the subject is missing. For some reason, to which we return in more detail in chapter 8, the grammar of English requires that finite sentences like (8a) have an overt subject. The grammar of Italian differs from that of English, as seen in (9). In (9a) the subject of *ha invitato* is expressed, in (9b) it is not realized:

9a   Lei ha invitato Louisa a casa.
     she has invited Louisa at home
9b   Ha invitato Louisa a casa.

We will achieve descriptive adequacy if our grammar is able to provide an explicit characterization of the general principles of sentence formation in English. This grammar will, for instance, impose the overt realization of the subject pronoun in (8b).

Now another important and fascinating question arises: we would like to understand how native speakers of a language, in our example English, come to possess the knowledge of their language. We say that a theory reaches **explanatory** adequacy if it can account for the fact that the principles of the internal grammar can get to be known by the speakers, i.e. if it can account for language acquisition.

The problem of language acquisition has often been summarized in terms of the problem of the **poverty of the stimulus**. Our linguistic capacity, for instance our knowledge of English, goes beyond the evidence we have been exposed to in our childhood. The linguist wants to account for the fact that the linguistic competence is attained in spite of important inadequacies in the stimulus, the linguistic experience. Three types of inadequacies are standardly referred to in the literature. First, we do not just come across grammatical sentences: everyday use of language contains slips of the tongue, hesitations, incomplete sentences, etc. Second, the experience, i.e. the stimulus, is finite, and we end up being able to produce and process an infinite number of sentences. Third, we acquire knowledge about our language for which we have no overt or **positive** evidence in the experience. For instance, consider the following sentences:

10a   I think that Miss Marple will leave.
10b   I think Miss Marple will leave.

11a   This is the book that I bought in London.
11b   This is the book I bought in London.

12a   Who do you think that Miss Marple will question first?
12b   Who do you think Miss Marple will question first?

On the basis of the examples in (10)–(12) the child learning English might well conclude that the conjunction *that* is optional; the data in (10)–(12) suggest that *that* can always be present and that it can always be absent. However, this conclusion would not be correct:

13a   *Who do you think that will be questioned first?
13b   Who do you think will be questioned first?

In the sentences in (13), the conjunction *that* must not be present. It is hard to see how the child can infer this from evidence to which he is exposed. Observe also that children are not explicitly taught that (13a) is ungrammatical. The problem can be summarized by saying that there is a gap between the data we are exposed to, the **input,** and our knowledge we achieve, the **output;** the stimulus underdetermines the knowledge we ultimately attain. This means that we cannot simply represent the acquisition of knowledge of language in terms of the schema (14a). The **triggering experience,** i.e. exposure to linguistic data, is not sufficient to allow a child to construct the grammar of his language.

14a   Exposure
      Triggering experience ⟶ Grammar of X

3.2 Universal Grammar

Given that neither formal teaching nor overt evidence seems to be the source
of the native speaker's intuitions, it is proposed that a large part of the native
speaker's knowledge of his language, i.e. the internal grammar, is innate. The
idea is that human beings have a genetic endowment that enables them to
learn language. It is this innate capacity for language learning common to all
human beings that the generative linguist tries to characterize. Of course, it
would be unreasonable to posit that some individuals – those that will become native speakers of English – are born with a specific grammar of English
and that others – those that will end up speaking Italian as their first language – are born with the grammar of Italian readily stored in their minds.
Human beings with normal mental faculties are able to learn any human
language. The innate linguistic endowment must be geared to any human
language and not to just one.

Let us discuss some examples informally in order to provide an outline of
the proposal. We have introduced one generalization about English: the SVO
hypothesis. The data in (7) lead us to formulate another hypothesis: any
grammatical English sentence can apparently be embedded and become a subordinate clause in a complex sentence. Let us refer to this as the embedding
principle.

15 **Embedding principle**[6]
    A grammatical sentence can become a subordinate clause in a complex
    sentence.

The embedding principle tries to render explicit part of the tacit knowledge
of the native speaker. This principle would be taken to be part of the grammar of English, hence available to the native speaker. But this principle is not
one that is particular to the grammar of English, it is not **language-specific**.
Rather, the embedding principle is part of the grammar of all human languages. Thus in French too we find sentences such as (16a) embedded in
(16b):

16a Maigret a abandonné l'enquête.
     Maigret has abandoned the enquiry.
16b Lucas a annoncé que Maigret a abandonné l'enquête.
     Lucas has announced that . . .

[6] As the reader will see later, the embedding principle is not in fact part of our
     grammar. The fact that sentences can be embedded can be deduced from the
     principles of sentence formation discussed in chapters 1 and 2.

Readers familiar with other languages will be able to check that the embedding principle applies in those languages too.

The embedding principle is a **universal** principle. Principles that hold of all languages are said to be part of **universal grammar**, or **UG** for short. Informally, UG is a system of all the principles that are common to all human languages, this means languages as different as English and Italian or Japanese.

A hypothesis adopted by generativists of the Chomskian tradition is precisely that universal grammar is innate to the human species. UG is a genetic endowment: we are born equipped with a set of universal linguistic principles. To quote Chomsky himself: 'Universal grammar may be thought of as some system of principles, common to the species and available to each individual prior to experience' (1981b: 7).

If we assume that there is such an innate linguistic endowment the task of attaining the knowledge of a specific grammar, say English, is facilitated. Someone learning English would not have to learn the embedding principle. It is innate; it is part of the genetic endowment.[7]

Universal grammar is the basis for acquiring language. It underlies all human languages. All and only human beings are equipped with UG and they are all able to learn languages. Other systems (say, dogs or television sets) are not equipped with UG and therefore will not be able to learn human languages. The linguistic endowment characterized as UG is species-specific.

3.3 Parameters and Universal Grammar

The innate linguistic endowment UG is not sufficient to enable us to speak a language. If all that is needed was UG then human beings would be able to speak any language wherever they were born and in whatever circumstances they grew up. The native language is that spoken by the child's immediate environment. It would be inconceivable, for instance, that a child growing up in a community where only English is spoken could become a native speaker of Japanese. Human beings usually master one language with native competence and they have a hard time learning other languages later in life. It is a well-known fact that achieving complete mastery of second or third languages in adulthood is exceptional.

While certain grammatical principles are universal, there is also a lot of variation between different languages. The grammar of English differs in

---

[7]   The reader may wonder why, if the principle is innate, children do not start using complex sentences straight away. However, it is conceivable that the development of the internal grammar interacts with a general maturation process. We leave this problem aside here.

important respects from that of, say, Japanese. Hence, if you 'know' the grammar of English, this will not entail that you 'know' the grammar of Japanese. In (1) we illustrated some simple English sentences and we saw that English sentences exhibit SVO word-order. In Japanese, on the other hand, the object precedes the verb; Japanese is SOV:

17 John-ga   Mary-o   but-ta.
    John-particle   Mary-particle   hit-past
    (Kuno, 1973: 3)

English and Japanese are similar in that sentences contain elements such as subjects, objects and verbs. But they differ in the way these elements are ordered linearly. The SVO hypothesis, which we postulated as part of English grammar, cannot be an absolute linguistic universal: it is part of the grammar of English (and of other languages) but not of that of Japanese. It is language-specific. How does a child learn that English has the SVO pattern? We could envisage the following scenario. The linguistic endowment UG makes available, among other things, the notions 'subject', 'object', 'verb'. Let us propose for the sake of the argument (cf. chapter 2, for a different view, though) that these are universal concepts, available in all human languages. Subject, verb and object will have to be linearly ordered. When learning a language the child will have to decide which is the word-order characteristic of his language. One option is to say that in fact word-order variation between languages is due to a primitive difference between these languages: it is a **parameter** along which English and Japanese vary. Languages could be said to vary with respect to the word-order parameter: UG provides the binary choice OV or VO, and individual languages opt for one **setting** of the parameter or another. We might say that the different word-orders of English and Japanese are directly correlated with the word-order parameter: English has the setting where the object precedes the verb, Japanese has the opposite setting for the parameter. The child learning English will have to fix the parameter for the VO setting, the child learning Japanese will have to fix the parameter for the OV setting. For each case exposure to transitive sentences in the language should enable the child to perform the setting.

Other ways of accounting for word-order variation may come to mind. The reader may recall that we suggested that the sentence-initial position of the direct object in (3c) and in (3d) above were due to a fronting operation which moves the object leftward. It is then in fact conceivable that the same kind of leftward movement could be invoked to account for the word-order found in Japanese. Say, for instance, that we propose that UG initially makes only one order available for a verb and its objects, namely the VO order. It could then be said that in Japanese a movement operation can shift the object to the left across the verb, resulting in the ordering OV. We have seen that we need such movement operations independently. The parameter distinguishing English and Japanese would then be expressed in terms of the availability of a particular leftward movement which can move the object to a position between the subject and the verb. Again the child who is learning Japanese will have to determine that the movement is available in Japanese, while the child learning English would assume that it is not.

Whichever option is chosen to account for word-order variation – and the debate is still very much open, we return to it in chapter 2 – the child learning a language must construct an internal grammar for that language. To achieve this task he uses, on the one hand, the universal notions and principles of UG and the choices that it makes available, and on the other hand he uses the data of his linguistic experience, in our example the English sentences he hears. Sentences such as those in (1) will provide evidence to the child that in English subject precedes verb and verb precedes object. A sentence such as that in (17) will enable the child exposed to Japanese data to decide that Japanese has SOV.

Exposure to linguistic material is an essential ingredient in the child's learning process. The child will need the linguistic experience to start constructing the internal grammar of his language and thus to attain the knowledge of a language. Without exposure the child would not be able to construct his internal grammar. UG is crucial in the organization of the primary linguistic experience. UG guides the way the child will interpret and organize the language he is exposed to. We have now postulated two properties of UG:

(i)   UG contains a set of absolute universals, notions and principles which do not vary from one language to the next.
(ii) There are language-specific properties which are not fully determined by UG but which vary cross-linguistically. For these properties a range of choices is made available by UG.

Absolute universal principles are rigid and need not be learnt. But even with respect to the mastery of language-specific properties very little 'learning' is involved under the hypothesis outlined above. For those principles that are parametrized, the options available are determined by UG. Attaining linguistic knowledge consists in fixing the parameters.

From this point of view, we conclude that the mastery of a language is not really the result of learning. Rather, being equipped with UG (with its parameters) and exposed to a language, the child cannot but construct the grammar of the language he is exposed to. For this reason the term 'learning' is often replaced by the term 'acquisition'.

In addition, the exposure to language will also equip us with a vocabulary, the words of the language to which we are exposed. Even if we have an innate knowledge of the principles of language we must inevitably learn the lexicon of the language, the words and their meaning, in order to be able to put this knowledge into operation. Thus an English child will have to learn all the words in the sentences above, and indeed many more. And we go on learning new words throughout our lives. Similarly a French child will learn the French lexicon, etc.[8]

To sum up: human beings are born equipped with some internal unconscious knowledge of grammar: UG. UG is a set of universal principles of language, some of which are rigidly fixed, some of which parametrized. Via the input of the experience of one particular language this knowledge can be implemented. The acquisition process is 'triggered' by the exposure, the child's linguistic experience.

Exposure will also enable the child to learn the vocabulary of the language.[9] The view of language acquisition in terms of parameter setting is the basis of current work in the generative tradition. The theory is sometimes referred to as the 'Principles and Parameters Theory' (cf. fn. 1).

3.4 Language Learning and Language Acquisition

Our ability to speak a language is based partly on the innate principles and parameters available in UG, partly on the triggering experience of exposure to a specific language. On the basis of these components we develop a grammar of one (or more) specific languages: the **core grammar** of such a language.

Schematically we can represent the generative view of language acquisition as follows:

14b
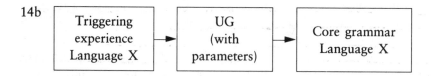

[8] The acquisition of the vocabulary of a language is also a matter of interest. For some introductory discussion the reader is referred to Lightfoot (1982: 121–2).

[9] The reader will find interesting discussion of language acquisition for instance in Deprez and Pierce (1993), Hermon (1992), Lightfoot (1981, 1982, 1989, 1991, 1993), Radford (1990), Wexler and Manzini, (1987). For more general discussion see also Chomsky (1981a, b, c), and the literature cited there. Most of these references might be hard to read at this stage and the reader is advised to postpone reading these works until he has worked through chapters 1–7 of this book.

The exposure to some language, say English, will activate the innate principles of universal grammar. The child will fix the choices to be made for the language in question, for instance, that the object follows the verb. He will also learn the vocabulary of the language. To quote Chomsky:

> Endowed with these principles, a system provided with adequate experience will develop a grammar of the peculiar and specific sort characteristic of human language . . . Lacking these principles, a system will develop no grammar or some different system. The telephone exchange, for example, has 'heard' much more English than any of us, but lacking the principles of universal grammar . . . it develops no grammar of English as part of its internal structure. (1981b: 8)

By the age of six a child exposed to English will have constructed the grammar of his language. This does not mean that no further development of his knowledge of language is possible. For instance, we go on learning new words throughout our lives. In addition we also learn certain less usual constructions of the language. These exceptional or marked patterns of the language are not taken to be part of the core grammar of the language, they belong to the **marked periphery** of the grammar and may be acquired later. The native speaker will also have to learn all of the social or cultural conventions associated with his language, for instance, that certain words belong to a very high style whereas others are informal. These conventions are not part of the grammar, they belong to the more general domain of human behaviour.

The aim of generative syntacticians is to develop a theory of language that is a model of the acquisition of language. Linguists want to provide an explicit formulation of the three components of (14b): (i) the principles of UG and the parametric variation across languages; (ii) the triggering experience needed to activate the principles of UG; and (iii) the core grammar of specific languages as it derives from these interacting components. A theory that can account for these three components will be said to have reached explanatory adequacy.

3.5 *The Generative Linguist*

The research programme as sketched here briefly and roughly is one that has been motivating linguistic research for the past thirty years and has given rise to many challenging results. The programme is indeed still developing.

It may be useful to repeat that the ultimate aim of generative linguistic theory is not to describe the details of one specific language, but rather to formulate the underlying principles that determine the grammars of human languages. These grammars are seen as representations of the native speaker's knowledge. In the course of their enquiry, linguists will examine data drawn from individual languages, of course, but the investigator will always bear in mind the interacting components in (14b).

The generative linguist who tries to characterize knowledge of a language, say English, will wish to do two things: (i) he needs to determine what properties of English are universal; and (ii) what properties are English-specific and how these relate to the parameters of UG.

It must by now have become clear that by simply looking at English and only that, the generative linguist cannot hope to achieve his goal. All he can do is write a grammar of English that is observationally and descriptively adequate but he will not be able to provide a model of the knowledge of the native speaker and how it is attained. The generativist will have to compare English with other languages to discover to what extent the properties he has identified are universal and to what extent they are language-specific choices determined by universal grammar. Even when his main concern is some aspect of the grammar of English the linguist will have to go outside this one language and engage in contrastive work.

Work in generative linguistics is therefore by definition comparative. Generative linguists often do not focus on individual languages at all: they will use *any* human language to determine the general properties of UG and the choices it allows. Data from a dialect spoken by only a couple of hundred people are just as important as data from a language spoken by millions of people. Both languages are human languages and are learnt in the same way.

4   The New Comparative Syntax

4.1   *Principles and Parameters: A Recapitulation*

When we look at the development of generative syntax in the last twenty-five years one important tendency that can be isolated is a marked return to comparative approaches. The comparative approach is obviously not the creation of generative grammar: it finds a clear precedent in the nineteenth-century comparative approaches to language study (cf. Robins, 1967).

The main goal of nineteenth-century comparative grammar was historical, i.e. that of establishing relations of parenthood and kinship across languages. The goal of the comparative approach in the generative tradition is psychological, i.e. that of accounting for the knowledge of language. As we have already seen, the following questions are asked: (i) What is knowledge of language? (ii) How is it acquired? The latter question focuses on the issue of how much of our linguistic knowledge is determined by experience and how much is due to a predetermined mental mechanism (cf. (14b)).

In order to determine how a specific language (say English) is acquired and how language in general is acquired we have to determine to what extent the properties of languages vary from one language to another, i.e. to what extent the properties are language-specific, and to what extent they are invariant across languages. Properties of language that vary cross-linguistically will be learnt by the speaker as a result of exposure to some specific linguistic environment: the fact that Italian allows the subject pronoun to be absent can be learnt through exposure to this language, for instance. Speakers who are repeatedly confronted with subjectless sentences such as (9b) will be able to infer that in the language they are exposed to the subject can be omitted. On the other hand, properties which are shared by all languages might well be taken to be part of UG, the predetermined linguistic competence of the human mind. Comparative studies of languages will play a crucial role towards providing us with answers to these questions, i.e. what is a universal and what is language-specific. In the present section we focus on the parametric variation between languages and try to clarify the notion of parameter.

Parameters are postulated to explain cross-linguistic variation. We should not assume, though, that each observed difference between one language and another corresponds to one parameter. The comparative study of languages has revealed that the properties with respect to which languages vary tend to organize themselves in clusters which are stable across languages and which allow us to arrive at a typology of languages. If a language has property X, it will also have property Y and property Z. The parametric approach will have to explain why certain properties co-occur.

4.2 *The* Pro-*drop Properties*

In order to illustrate this let us look at one of the better known parameters which has been postulated to account for the difference between English (8) and Italian (9). Recall that Italian differs from English in that the former, though not the latter, allows the subject of a finite clause to remain unexpressed. The parameter which distinguishes languages like English which do not allow a subject pronoun to be omitted and those like Italian which do is referred to as the *pro*-**drop parameter.** (For detailed discussion see, among others, Rizzi, 1982a, 1986a; Jaeggli and Safir, 1989.) Italian is a *pro*-**drop language,** English is not. That the subject pronoun can be omitted is not the only property to distinguish *pro*-drop languages like Italian from non-*pro*-drop languages like English. In Italian, the overt subject can occupy a post-verbal position; this option is not available in English:

18a È arrivato Gianni.
     is arrived Gianni
     'Gianni has arrived.'
18b *Is arrived John.

19a Ha telefonato sua moglie.
     has telephoned your wife
     'Your wife has phoned.'
19b *Has telephoned your wife.

In Italian a subject of a subordinate clause can be moved to the main clause domain across the overt conjunction *che*, corresponding to *that*; in English this is not possible: if a subject is moved then the clause from which the subject has been moved cannot be introduced by a conjunction (cf. the discussion of (13) above). The correlation between the data in (20) and the *pro-drop* phenomenon is due to Perlmutter (1971).

20a Chi credi che abbia telefonato?
     who believe (2sg) that have (subj) telephoned
     'Who do you think has called?'
20b *Who do you think that has telephoned?
20c Who do you think has telephoned?

In Italian subjects of weather verbs such as *rain* are necessarily omitted, in English such subjects must be realized by a pronoun.

21a (*Ciò) piove.
     (it) rains (3sg)
     'It is raining.'
21b *(It) is raining.

Consider now the following:

22a Che Louisa non partirà è chiaro.
     that Louise not will leave is clear
     'That Louisa will not leave is clear.'
22b That Louise will not leave is clear.

In (22) the subordinate clauses *che Louisa non partirà* and *that Louise will not leave* function as the subjects of the sentences. The sentences can be paraphrased if we move the subordinate clause to a final position: in Italian the position vacated by the moved sentence remains empty, it cannot be blocked up by a pronominal element as illustrated in (23a). In contrast, in English we must stick in a pronoun *it* to fill the vacated subject position, as shown in (23b).

23a (*Ciò) è chiaro che Louisa non partirà.
     it is clear that Louisa will not leave
23b *(It) is clear that Louisa will not leave.

These contrasts listed above are not autonomous properties of the languages in question, all can be related to the option which allows the subject pronoun to be omitted in Italian.

4.3 Relating the Properties

We started from the empirical observation that the subject pronoun can apparently be omitted. Observe that in Italian, the pronominal subject *can* also be overt; the overt realization of the subject pronoun has some semantic or pragmatic effect: for instance it signals contrast or it focuses on the subject:

24 *Lei* parte e *lui* arriva.
    she leaves and he arrives

When no contrast or no special focus on the subject is needed the pronoun is absent. This could be derived from some general consideration of **economy**: we might say that the non-expression of the subject pronoun requires less effort than when the pronoun is present, and that therefore the subject will only be present when the added effort of the overt expression has some yield. Subject pronouns appear only when it is impossible to leave them out.

The obligatory absence of the subject pronoun of weather verbs in (21a) can be related to the principle of economy suggested above: it is hard to see how a subject of a weather verb could have a contrastive function. This means that there will never be a reason to use the pronoun in Italian. A similar approach can be suggested for (22). When we move the subject clause in Italian the vacated position can be empty and it has to remain empty. Why should this be? We have already seen that the subject position in Italian need not be filled, it can be empty. In English the subject position cannot be empty so we stick in a pronoun. *It* in the English example (23b) does not contribute anything to the meaning of the sentence, *it* cannot be contrasted or focused. But in Italian, subject pronouns are only used with a contrastive or emphatic function, so there will never be any motivation for inserting a pronoun in the Italian equivalent of (23b), (23a).

Let us turn to the examples with post-verbal subjects, (18) and (19). All English sentences must have subjects. This does not mean, though, that the subject must necessarily be a referential expression, as the following example illustrates:

25   There arrived three more students.

In (25) the subject position is occupied by the element *there*. *There* is related to an indefinite post-verbal subject. Let us say that *there* fills up the position vacated by an indefinite subject (we return to this in chapters 2 and 9). The essential point is that *there* cannot be contrastive or emphatic in (25). In the Italian examples in (18a) and (19a) we also have a post-verbal subject. Since in general Italian does not need a full pronoun to occupy the vacated subject position (23a), we do not need a filler for the subject position in such examples as (18) and (19).

The data in (20) might at first sight seem puzzling. It is generally accepted that one cannot move a subject from the position to the immediate right of the conjunction (*that* in English); (20b) suggests that this is possible in Italian. However, we cannot base our judgements on a superficial comparison of two sentences in two languages. We need to consider the way these sentences are formed, their **derivation**. On the basis of the data in (18) and (19) we are led to conclude that the subject NP in Italian may appear either pre-verbally or post-verbally. Hence (20b) has two possible derivations, schematically represented in (26):

26a   Chi credi che —— abbia telefonato?
26b   Chi credi che abbia telefonato ——?

In the representation (26a) *chi* originates in the position to the immediate right of *che*, in (26b) it originates in the post-verbal position, a position also available for subjects, as seen in (20b). Now it is known that in Italian, as in English, nothing bans the leftward movement of post-verbal material across a conjunction.

27a Who do you think that John will invite ——?
27b Chi credi che Gianni inviterà ——?

The general principle which bans extracting material from a position to the immediate right of a conjunction can now be maintained for the grammar of English AND for the grammar of Italian. In the Italian sentences where this principle would appear to have been violated, the language uses the alternative derivation whereby the subject is moved from a post-verbal position.

The correlations established here for the contrast between a *pro*-drop language like Italian and a non-*pro*-drop language like English can extend straightforwardly to Spanish, for the first group (28), and French for the second (29);

28   *Spanish*
28a   Baila bien.
      dances (3sg) well
      'He dances well.'
28b   Llego Maria ayer a los doce.
      arrived Maria yesterday at noon
      'Mary arrived at noon yesterday.'
      (Jaeggli, 1981: 139)
28c   ¿Quién dijiste que vino.
      who did you say that came
      'Who did you say came?'
      (Jaeggli, 1981: 145)
28d   Me parece que Juan tiene hambre.
      me seems that Juan has hunger
      'It seems to me that Juan is hungry.'
      (Jaeggli, 1981: 146)

29   *French*
29a   *(Elle) dance bien.
      (she) dances well
      'She dances well.'
29b   *Arrivait Marie hier a midi.
      arrived Marie yesterday at noon
29c   *Qui dis-tu que viendra?
      who say you that will come
29d   *(Il) me semble que Jean a faim.
      (it) me seems that Jean has hunger
      'It seems to me that Juan is hungry.'

4.4 Agreement and Pro-drop

The reader may observe that the possibility of omitting a pronoun subject correlates with another property of the languages examined and which is particularly obvious when we compare English and Italian. If we look at the present tense paradigms for the verb inflection for these languages we observe a striking contrast:

30		*English*		*Italian*
1sg	I	speak	io	parlo
2sg	you	speak	tu	parli
3sg	she	speaks	lei	parla
1pl	we	speak	noi	parliamo
2pl	you	speak	voi	parlate
3pl	they	speak	loro	parlano
		2 forms		*6 forms*

In the case of Italian, every number/person combination has a different ending; as a result the inflectional paradigm distinguishes all six persons uniquely. There is no possibility of confusion: the ending of the verb immediately identifies the subject. One could say that such inflectional systems are **rich**. In contrast, the English system has only one distinctive form, that for the third person singular; all other persons are unmarked morphologically, the bare stem is used, which is also identical to the imperative and to the infinitive. In the literature, an attempt is made to correlate the inflectional paradigm of the language with the *pro*-drop parameter (cf. Jaeggli and Safir (1989)), Rizzi (1986a), Taraldsen (1980). Languages which have rich inflection are often *pro*-drop languages.[10] Intuitively this correlation is expected: when the verb inflection is rich we can recover the content of the subject by virtue of the inflection and the pronoun would not add information. In languages with poor inflection the verb inflection does not suffice to recover the content of the subject and the pronoun is needed. We return to this issue in chapter 8. The inflectional system of French is relatively poor and French is not a *pro*-drop language; Spanish is a *pro*-drop language and has rich inflection.

The approach above suggests that a number of properties of languages and

---

[10] Gilligan (1987) studies a sample of 100 languages from various language families and reports 76 languages with agreement which allow for the subject pronoun to be absent, against 17 languages without agreement and which allow the subject to be absent.

language types can be reduced to a unique elementary difference between their grammatical systems. The analysis of the *pro*-drop parameter, originally developed on the basis of Romance languages in the late 1970s, has led to what we can refer to as the new comparative syntax. A related development is the study of dialect variation, which has become strongly prominent in the 1980s; another promising line of research is that in the area of historical syntax. Diachronic developments of languages are interpreted again in terms of the Principles and Parameters model, diachronic changes consisting in re-settings of one or more parameters (cf. Lightfoot, 1979, 1991). In this book, the comparative approach is more prominent in chapter 8, which discusses non-overt elements; in chapter 9, where we discuss cross-linguistic variation in question formation, and in chapter 11, which concerns verb movement.

5 Purpose and Organization of the Book

5.1 *General Purpose*

In this book I provide a survey of some of the main results of generative research over the past thirty years. The book is not meant for the absolute beginner. The reader is expected to have some background in linguistics, specifically in syntax. He should, for instance, be able to parse sentences and be familiar with the tree diagram representation, and with the basic terminology of syntax. Notions such as sentence, clause, noun, verb, subject, object, etc., are presupposed. I assume therefore that the reader has had some introductory course to syntax or that he has read some introductory works.[11] However, in order to guarantee that we have a common starting-point, I shall often recapitulate the basic notions. It will also be shown how traditional concepts are used and reinterpreted within the generative framework.

The aim of the book is to offer a general introduction. I shall not go into all the complexities and details of ongoing research. Rather, I wish to familiarize the reader with the basic concepts used. I hope that the book will encourage the reader to turn to the primary literature himself and discover some of the more intricate problems. The references in the footnotes will provide indications for further reading.

Although the examples in the book will be taken primarily from English,

---

[11] I am thinking of works such as Akmajian and Heny (1975), Akmajian, Demers and Harnish (1978), Burton-Roberts (1986), Fromkin and Rodman (1988), Huddleston (1976), Jacobs and Rosenbaum (1970), Smith and Wilson (1979), Wekker and Haegeman (1985) to mention only a few.

this book is not a grammar of English. English is used as just one example of human language and we shall often discuss other languages. We shall try to decide what sort of internal grammar native speakers of English have at their disposal and to determine what it is that makes a sentence acceptable or unacceptable, what sort of grammatical principles can be advocated and to what extent these are universal or language-specific. In some sense we are like linguistic detectives. The linguistic data are like the clues a detective is given when starting his enquiry. He has to piece these data together, construct hypotheses, check these and ultimately he may discover the explanation for the evidence he has assembled. To remind the reader of this task I have chosen to illustrate the data with examples in which literary detectives play a prominent role. At the end of the book I hope that the reader will have become a competent linguistic detective himself.

5.2   Organization

The book is divided into twelve chapters. The first ten chapters provide the basic outline of the theory. The last two chapters highlight some recent developments of the theory. Each chapter is followed by a one-page summary and by a set of exercises. The exercises have a dual purpose. First, they will enable the reader to check if he has understood and assimilated the basic concepts introduced in the chapter. The empirical range of the discussion is broadened: many exercises will include a discussion of data drawn from languages other than English.

Second, the exercises will be used to draw the reader's attention to theoretical or empirical problems not touched upon in the chapter. Often a problem introduced by way of an exercise in an earlier chapter is then picked up in the discussion of a later chapter. Alternatively, the exercises will direct the reader to areas for further reading or for further research.

Footnotes will mainly be used to direct the reader to further reading. The footnotes will also indicate at which point in the book the reader should be able to tackle the literature in question.

6   Exercises

Exercise 1

Consider the following sentences. None of them is fully acceptable but they vary in their degree of deviance. If you are a native speaker of

English try to rank the sentences for acceptability. Wherever you can, try to construct an acceptable sentence modelled on the one you are judging. If you are not a native speaker of English you may attempt to carry out the task described above but it may be difficult. Another way of approaching this exercise is to ask some native speakers to do the exercise and compare their answers.

1   Which man do you know what John will give to?
2   Which man do you wonder when they will appoint?
3   Who do you wonder which present will give?
4   Which present do you wonder who will give?
5   Which man do you wonder whether John will invite?
6   Which man do you wonder whether will invite John?
7   Which man do you wonder what will give to John?
8   Which man do you wonder when will invite John?

Native English speakers are basically in agreement on the ranking of sentences 1–8. The judgements formulated are not the result of formal tuition. English grammar classes do not pay attention to sentences like 1–8. It is quite likely that speakers have never come across such sentences. In other words, they have not acquired the intuitions on the basis of overt evidence. On the contrary, given that the sentences above are judged as unacceptable, one does not expect them to be part of the linguistic data that we are exposed to.

On the basis of the judgements, try to classify the examples and formulate some principles that might account for the relative acceptability. You may find the discussion of examples (3), (4), (5) and (6) in the text of some help. In chapter 7 and following we shall discuss the sentences above and similar ones. We shall assume that they are ungrammatical and we shall attempt to formulate the rules and principles at work.

Exercise 2

If you are a native speaker of a language other than English translate the sentences in exercise 1 in your own language, keeping as close to the English models as you can, and rank them for acceptability. Try to formulate some principles to explain the degree of acceptability.

If you have access to judgements on the English data and on data in other languages, try to check if the same degree of acceptability of the examples could be explained by the same principle(s).

Exercise 3

When reading section 3 the reader will have noted that there are certain uses of English which allow the omission of the subject and in which text example (8b) would have been grammatical. The following are attested examples.

1a A very sensible day yesterday. *Saw* no one. *Took* the bus to Southwark Bridge. *Walked* along Thames Street; *saw* a flight of steps down to the river. . . . *Found* the strand of the Thames, under the warehouses. . . . *Thought* of the refugees from Barcelona walking 40 miles, one with a baby in a parcel. . . . *Made* a circuit: *discovered* St Olave's Hart Street.
    (Woolf, 1985: 203–4)
1b The poor little boy wont say whats the matter. He takes no interest in anything. *Wont* turn and wave to her . . . *drudges* on at Latin.
    (Woolf, 1985: 117)
1c Brilliant *could* have stayed all day.
    Brill – *must* come again.
    Could see everything from wheelchair.
    (Quotes from Visitors book 1991, The Green, Beaumaris, Anglesey North Wales)

Even a superficial glance at these examples shows us that all of the italicized verbs have one property in common: the subject is missing. In (1a) and (1c) the first person subject is omitted, in (1b) it is the third person. The omission of the subject in certain types of English is observed in traditional descriptions (Quirk, et al. 1985: 896–7). Such examples are relatively easy to come by in certain **registers** of English, which we could roughly characterize as belonging to abbreviated writing. We do not have to look for attested examples of usage to discuss such data; every native speaker of English will be able to think of relevant examples and even non-native speakers will quickly pick up this type of ellipsis in the appropriate register.

   All the attested examples are instances where the subject of a **root** clause is omitted. By root clause we mean a clause which is not subordinate to another clause. The following variants on sentences drawn from Virginia Woolf's diary are unacceptable:

2a I must work, as *(I) told Sally G . . . (Woolf, 1985: 38)
2b I don't think *(I) need lie quaking at night . . . (Woolf, 1985: 38)
2c I find this morning that *(I) interrupted the crisis of that London
      Group meeting . . . (Woolf, 1985: 9)

Another property that we find is that attested examples never occur in questions. In the examples in (3) drawn from usage data, the subject pronoun cannot be omitted.

3a And what could *(we) do . . . (Woolf, 1985: 19)
3b What can *(I) say . . . (Woolf, 1985: 3)
3c Now who is *(she) . . . (Woolf, 1985: 15)
3d What shall *(I) write . . . (Woolf, 1985: 40)

The absence of such examples in subordinate questions is expected if the omission of the subject is a root phenomenon.

4   and this will show how hard *(I) work . . . (Woolf, 1985: 13)

The subject also never is and in fact cannot be omitted when it is preceded by a non-subject:

5a The next book *(I) think of calling Answers to
      Correspondents . . . (Woolf, 1985: 3)
5b Such twilight gossip *(it) seemed . . . (Woolf, 1985: 8)
5c This story *(I) repeated to Duncan last night . . . (Woolf, 1985: 9)
5d And there *(I) was in the rush of an end . . . (Woolf, 1985: 11)

When a negative constituent is preposed, resulting in a word-order where the auxiliary precedes the subject, the subject pronoun cannot be omitted:

6a Seldom have *(I) been more completely miserable than I was
      about 6.30 last night . . . (Woolf, 1985: 8)
6b Never have *(I) worked so hard at any book . . . (Woolf, 1985: 16)
6c Nor do *(I) wish even to write about it here . . . (Woolf, 1985: 44)

Finally observe that only subject pronouns are omitted: objects are not omitted. There is not a single example in Woolf's diary of the omission of an object and the omission of *me* in (7) leads to an unacceptable sentence.

7 This led *(me) to imagine any number of catastrophes . . . (Woolf, 1985: 9)

At first sight one might be tempted to conclude that this variety of English exhibits a manifestation of the *pro*-drop phenomenon discussed in section 4. Evaluate this proposal. You should draw on the English data given above, on the Italian data given in (8) and (9), and on your own intuitions. Using the argumentation introduced in section 4 try to state your argument as systematically and as explicitly as possible.

8 Credo che sia già partito.
I believe that be (subj) already left
'I think that he has already left.'

9a Dove è?
where is (3sg)
'Where is he?'
9b Che vuoi?
what want (2sg)
'What do you want?'
9c Questo libro non lo voglio.
this book *non* it want (1sg)
'This book, I don't want it.'

Readers whose first language is another non *pro*-drop language are encouraged to consider the question of the omissibility of the subject in abbreviated registers (diaries, informal notes) in their native language.

For a discussion of the omission of the subject in English the reader is referred to Haegeman (1990) and to Rizzi (1992a). The latter paper relates the phenomenon of omission of the subject in the diary register to data drawn from acquisition.

1 The Lexicon and Sentence Structure

Contents

Introduction and Overview

In the Introduction we saw that a grammar of a language is a coherent system of principles which determines the formation of the sentences of a language. The basic unit with which a grammar is concerned is the sentence. A grammar will specify what the components of the sentence are, how they interact, in which order they occur, etc. Partly, the principles formulated will be of a universal nature; partly, they will have to be parametrized to bring out language-specific properties of individual languages.

Grammars have nothing to say about units higher than the sentence, such as the paragraph, the discourse exchange, the text, etc. Such higher units will be the object of another type of enquiry.[1]

In this chapter we consider the relation between the structure of the sentence and the words that make up the sentence. We shall see that sentence structure is to a large extent determined by lexical information. As pointed out in the Introduction, it is assumed that the reader is familiar with the basic techniques and terminology of sentence parsing.

Chapter 1 is organized as follows: section 1 provides a brief discussion of the central concepts of sentence structure; section 2 focuses on the relation between lexical items and sentence structure; section 3 discusses the predicate–argument structure of sentences and introduces theta theory; section 4 sums up the link between lexical items and sentence structure and introduces the projection principle; section 5 explores the application of theta theory, concentrating on clausal arguments, expletive (non-argument) pronouns and auxiliary verbs; section 6 discusses the general constraint that sentences must have subjects; and in section 7 we consider the properties of the subject theta role.

1 The Units of Syntactic Analysis

In this section we briefly recapitulate the basic notions of syntactic structure that will be the starting point for our discussion. Consider the following example:

[1] For an interesting approach to the study of sentences in discourse see Sperber and Wilson (1986) and Kempson (1988a, 1988b), who examines the link between Sperber and Wilson's theory of utterance interpretation and formal syntax.

1   Jeeves will meet his employer at the castle.

(1) is a grammatical English sentence. When we look for its component parts, the **constituents**, the units that perhaps come to mind first are the words of the sentence: sentence (1) contains eight words. But, as anyone familiar with traditional techniques of sentence parsing knows, words are not the imme- diate constituents of a sentence. Rather, they are the ultimate constituents. The words of the sentence are organized hierarchically into bigger units called phrases. In the framework of generative syntax the constituent structure of a sentence is represented in one of the following formats: by means of the **tree diagram** format as in (2a), by means of **phrase structure rules** or **rewrite rules** as in (2b), or by means of **labelled brackets** as in (2c).[2]

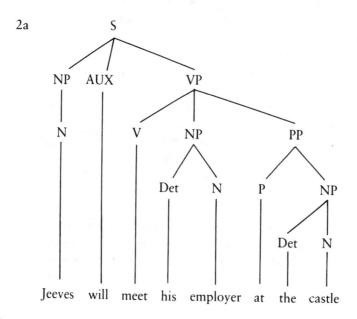

2b   (i)   S ⟶ NP – AUX – VP
     (ii)   NP ⟶ (Det) – N
     (iii) VP ⟶ V – NP – PP
     (iv)   PP ⟶ P – NP
     (v)   N ⟶ *Jeeves, employer, castle*
     (vi)   V ⟶ *meet*

---

[2] For an introduction to parsing see Burton-Roberts (1986), Fromkin and Rodman (1988), Guéron and Haegeman (in preparation), and Wekker and Haegeman (1985).

(vii) AUX ⟶ *will*
(viii) P ⟶ *at*
 (ix) Det ⟶ *the, his*

2c [$_S$ [$_{NP}$ [$_N$ Jeeves]] [$_{AUX}$ will] [$_{VP}$ [$_V$ meet] [$_{NP}$ [$_{Det}$ his] [$_N$ employer]] [$_{PP}$ [$_P$ at]
  [$_{NP}$ [$_{Det}$ the] [$_N$ castle]]]]]].

Representations such as those in (2) give us information concerning the structure of (1). They indicate, for instance, that the string *his employer* is a syntactic unit, a **constituent**. It is a **noun phrase** (NP), a constituent whose main element or **head** is the noun (N) *employer*. Analogously, the constituent *at the castle* is a **prepositional phrase** (PP); the head of this PP is the preposition *at*, which is followed by an NP, *the castle*. The constituent *meet his employer at the castle* is a **verb phrase** (VP), whose head is the verb *meet*, which is followed by the NP *his employer* and the PP *at the castle*.

The structural representations in (2) allow us also to describe syntactic operations that may affect sentence (1). Consider (3):

3a At the castle, Jeeves will meet his employer.
3b His employer, Jeeves will meet at the castle.
3c Meet his employer at the castle, Jeeves will (indeed).

The sentences in (3) are intuitively felt to be variations upon sentence (1); they are all paraphrases of (1). In order to capture the similarity between the sentences in (3) and that in (1) we assume that all these sentences have the same **underlying structure**, represented in (2). In each of the sentences in (3) one of the constituents identified in (2) has been **moved** to the beginning of the sentence, or **preposed**. Thus in (3a) the PP *at the castle* has been moved, in (3b) the NP *his employer* is moved, in (3c) the VP, *meet his employer at the castle*, is moved. The possibility for preposing elements of a sentence is structure-based: only constituents of the sentence such as NP and VP can be preposed; one cannot indiscriminately prepose any random string of words in the sentence:[3]

3d *Employer at the, Jeeves will meet his castle.
3e *Meet his, Jeeves will employer at the castle.

---

[3] For a formal discussion of operations such as preposing, see chapters 6 and 7.

Another operation that affects sentence constituents is the one that forms questions. If we form questions on the basis of (3) we see that again the constituent structure represented in (2) plays a crucial role.

We distinguish two types of questions: **yes–no questions** and **constituent questions.** The classification adopted is based on the type of answer expected. (4a) is a *yes–no* question: in normal circumstances we expect *yes* or *no* as an answer. The other questions in (4) are **constituent questions**: the answer to the question will be a constituent.

4a   Will Jeeves meet his employer at the castle?
4b   Who will Jeeves meet at the castle?
4c   Where will Jeeves meet his employer?
4d   What will Jeeves do?
4e   Who will meet his employer at the castle?

Non-embedded *yes–no* questions are formed by moving the auxiliary (here, *will*) to the left of the subject. This process is usually referred to as **subject auxiliary inversion,** or **SAI.** In non-embedded constituent questions, SAI also applies and in addition a sentence-initial question word (such as *who, where, what*) substitutes for the constituent which is being questioned. In (4b), for instance, *who* substitutes for the subject NP.[4]

Operations such as preposing and question formation thus provide evidence for the role of phrase structure in syntax.

2   Words and Phrases

Although words are not the immediate constituents of the sentence, they play an important role as the ultimate building blocks of the sentence.

Words belong to different **syntactic categories,** such as nouns, verbs, etc., and the syntactic category to which a word belongs determines its **distribution,** that is, in what contexts it can occur. Normally, one cannot easily interchange words of one category for words of another. If you were to replace the verb *meet* by the semantically related noun *appointment* in (1) you would no longer obtain a grammatical sentence:

5   *Jeeves will appointment his employer at the castle.

[4]   Chapter 7 contains a detailed discussion of the formation of questions.

The grammar of English, and indeed of any language, will have to contain the categorial information associated with lexical items since this information plays a part in the formation of sentences.

We assume that the categorial information is also available to the native speakers of the language: they will agree that (5) is unacceptable and that the unacceptability is due to the inappropriate use of the N **appointment**. We postulate that speakers of a language are equipped with an internal 'dictionary', which we shall refer to as the mental lexicon, or **lexicon**, which contains all the information they have internalized concerning the words of their language. As seen above, this mental lexicon will have to contain, among other things, information on syntactic categories. We assume that each word of the language known by a speaker will be listed in his mental lexicon with its categorial specification. For instance, a native speaker of English will presumably have a lexicon containing the following information:

6a	*meet*:	verb
6b	*employer*:	noun
6c	*castle*:	noun
6d	*at*:	preposition
6e	*the*:	determiner
6f	*his*:	determiner
6g	*appointment*:	noun

As we suggested in the Introduction, it would not make sense to claim that the native speaker's lexical knowledge, i.e. the mental lexicon, is innate. If lexical knowledge were completely innate, then human beings would have to be born equipped with the lexicons of all known or possible human languages. Rather, we assume that the lexicon of a language is learnt by each native speaker. The speaker learns the words of the language and what category they belong to. But this does not imply that he comes to this learning process totally unprepared. We assume that UG, our innate knowledge of language, contains, for example, the notion of syntactic category. When exposed to the words of a particular language, speakers will have some expectation as to which categories to discover. We shall not speculate further here as to the sort of knowledge this involves.

Lexical information plays a role in sentence structure because the syntactic category of a word determines its distribution. Let us take as an example sentence (1) and consider its syntactic representation (2a). In the tree diagram (2a) the word *appointment* will not be inserted in a position dominated by the node V because only verbs can be inserted under a node V, the same observation would apply to the other words in the sentence. Looking at the tree diagram from top to bottom we can say that the **terminal category labels** such as N, V, etc., restrict which lexical elements can be inserted.

Looking at the tree from bottom to top, we see that the words that are inserted at the bottom of the tree determine the structure of the sentence. The inserted words will determine the syntactic category of the **head** of the phrase and hence they will ultimately determine the category of a phrase, the **phrasal category**. For instance, in our example (2a) the inserted N *employer* will be the head of a phrase of the type NP and not of a VP. Chapter 2 provides a more detailed discussion of the principles that regulate sentence structure.

Clearly, the mere matching of lexical and phrasal categories is not sufficient to produce a good sentence. For instance, the random insertion of nouns in the slots provided for them in (2) produces odd results in (7b) and (7c):

7a   Jeeves will meet his employer at the castle.
7b   ?Jeeves will meet his castle at the meeting.
7c   ?Jeeves will meet his castle at the employer.

The question arises whether (7b) and (7c) are ungrammatical: is their oddness due to a violation of a grammatical principle? A native speaker might say that (7b) is bizarre because the verb *meet* is followed by the string *his castle*. The oddness is due to the fact that the concept 'meet' usually involves an interaction between two animate participants, while 'his castle' refers to an inanimate entity which does not normally qualify to take part in an action of the type 'meet'. But if we were to endow the concept 'castle' with animacy the oddness would be removed. In a fairy tale where castles take a walk (7b) would become acceptable. What is wrong with (7b) is not a grammatical issue; its strangeness relates to our general knowledge of the world. Issues of language use which hinge on the interaction of the grammar with extra-linguistic information such as that just described must not be integrated in a grammatical description. Grammars do not contain principles about our beliefs about the world around us. (7b) may therefore be seen as grammatical but as bizarre in view of our encyclopaedic knowledge of castles as inanimate objects.

Let us return to sentence (1), repeated here as (8a), and its tree diagram representation (2a) repeated here as (8b):

8a   Jeeves will meet his employer at the castle.

8b

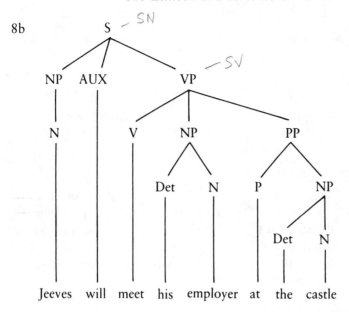

It is clear that some of the phrasal constituents of this sentence are more essential to the sentence than others. The PP *at the castle*, which specifies the place of the event, can be left out without any harm, but the NP *his employer* cannot.

8c   Jeeves will meet his employer.
8d   *Jeeves will meet at the castle.

In the next section we shall try to account for the obligatory nature of certain constituents in a sentence.

3   Predicates and Arguments

In this section we explain which constituents of a sentence are minimally required, and why. We first provide an informal discussion and then develop a formal approach known as theta theory.

3.1 Subcategorization

Consider the following sentences:

9a   Maigret will [$_{VP}$ imitate [$_{NP}$ Poirot] [$_{PP}$ with enthusiasm]].
9b   Bertie will [$_{VP}$ abandon [$_{NP}$ the race] [$_{PP}$ after the first lap]].
9c   Miss Marple will [$_{VP}$ reconstruct [$_{NP}$ the crime] [$_{PP}$ in the kitchen]].

The labelled bracketing in (9a), (9b) and (9c) shows that these sentences are structurally similar to sentence (8a) with its representation in (8b). In (8a) and in each of the sentences in (9) the VP contains a V, the head of the VP; an NP, the direct object; and a PP. In each of these the PP is optional (as illustrated in (8c) and in (10)): it provides information as to the manner, time or place of the event expressed in the sentence:

10a   Maigret will imitate Poirot.
10b   Bertie will abandon the race.
10c   Miss Marple will reconstruct the crime.

In the traditional literature on parsing, optional phrasal constituents such as the PPs in (8a) and (9) are called **adjuncts**.[5] While the PPs in the examples above are optional, we see that the VP-internal NPs are not:

11a   *Maigret will imitate.
11b   *Bertie will abandon.
11c   *Miss Marple will reconstruct.
11d   *Jeeves will meet.

This does not mean, however, that each English sentence contains just one VP-internal NP, as (12) shows:

12a   Hercule is dithering.
12b   Wooster gave Jeeves the money.

Inserting an NP into the VP of (12a) renders the example ungrammatical:

---

[5]   In chapters 7, 8 and 9 we shall turn to a technical definition of the notion adjunct, as it is used in the Government and Binding literature.

13a   Hercule is dithering *the crime/*Agatha.

On the other hand, in (12b) the verb *give* must be followed by two NPs, or alternatively by an NP and a PP:

13b   *Wooster gave Jeeves.
13c   Wooster gave [NP the money] [PP to Jeeves].

In traditional grammar the requirement that there should be or not be one or more NPs inside the VP is seen as a property of the verb involved. At least three classes of verbs are traditionally distinguished: transitive, ditransitive and intransitive verbs.[6] If a VP has a transitive verb as its head, one NP (the direct object) is required: the verb takes an NP **complement**. If a VP has a ditransitive verb as its head, two NPs or an NP and a PP (the direct object and the indirect object) are required. If a VP contains an intransitive verb as its head then no NP-complement is allowed. Whether a verb belongs to the group of transitive, ditransitive or intransitive verbs is treated as an idiosyncratic property of the verb.

Native speakers of English would agree on the judgements given for the sentences in (12) and (13). This means that they too must have internal knowledge of the principles that decide on the type of VP in which a verb may appear; the subclassification of verbs must constitute part of their lexical knowlege. Let us therefore integrate the information on verb classes in the mental lexicon which we have posited as part of the internal knowledge of the native speaker.

One way of encoding the information on the complement structure of the verb is by associating it directly with the lexical entry of the verb in question. This would lead to the following (partial) lexicon:

14a   *meet*:   verb; transitive
14b   *imitate*:   verb; transitive
14c   *reconstruct*:   verb; transitive
14d   *abandon*:   verb; transitive
14e   *dither*:   verb; intransitive
14f   *give*:   verb; ditransitive

[6] For discussion of the classification of verbs in the traditional literature, see Aarts and Aarts (1982), Burton-Roberts (1986), Huddleston (1984) and Quirk, et al. (1985).

The child acquiring English will have to learn not only the
egory of the words of his language, but also the subcategory the
to. Exposure to English sentences containing these verbs will o,
evidence of this information: the verb will occur in the appropriat
environment. The child exposed to a sentence like (15a) will thus ι
conclude that *sleep* is intransitive and will assign it the property 'intr
in its lexical entry (15b):

15a Mummy is sleeping.
15b *sleep*: verb; intransitive.

In the Chomskian tradition the notions transitive, intransitive, etc., are
encoded in distributional frames. Verbs are classified according to the type of
VP in which the verb typically occurs. For example, the verb *meet* requires
an NP complement; its VP will contain an NP. This requirement can be
represented as follows:

16 *meet*: V, [——NP]

(16) shows in which syntactic frame the verb *meet* can and must be inserted:
meet is inserted in front of an NP. The verbs are characterized on the basis
of the frames in which they occur. *Dither*, for instance, does not take any
complement; *give* takes either two NPs (12b) or an NP and a PP (13c):

17a *dither*: V, [——]
17b *give*: V, [——NP, NP] or V, [——NP, PP]

The frames that identify subcategories of verbs are called **subcategorization
frames**. We say that *meet* **subcategorizes for** or **selects** an NP.

3.2 Argument Structure and Thematic Structure

All we have done so far is classify verbs according to whether they require
any VP-internal NP. We have not really attempted to explain anything. On
the contrary, we have implied that the subcategorization frame of a verb,
i.e. whether it is transitive or intransitive, etc., is an unexplained **primitive**
property of the grammar, i.e. a property which does not follow from anything else. However, this seems intuitively wrong. Whether a verb is transitive

or not is not a matter of mere chance; it follows from the type of action or state expressed by the verb, from its meaning.

A verb like *imitate* expresses an activity that involves two participants: the active participant, the person who imitates, and the passive participant, the person or thing that is imitated. This notion of 'participants in an activity' has been formalized on the basis of the approach commonly adopted in logic. In this section we first look briefly at the logical system of representation, then we apply it to language in terms of the general notion of argument structure and of the more refined notion of thematic structure.

3.2.1 ARGUMENT STRUCTURE IN LOGIC

Logicians have long been concerned with formulating representations for the semantic structure of sentences, or more correctly propositions.[7] In the notation of formal logic, (18a) is assigned the representation (18b):

18a   Maigret imitates Poirot.
18b   A (mp)
       where A = 'imitate', m = 'Maigret' and p = 'Poirot'.

(18a) contains the NPs *Maigret* and *Poirot*, two referring expressions, i.e. expressions which serve to pick out an entity, a person, a thing, from those things we are talking about, the **universe of discourse**. It also contains a predicate *imitate*. The predicate does not refer to a person or thing but rather defines some relation between the referring expressions. In the logical notation in (18b) we see that the **predicate** 'imitate' takes two **arguments**, represented by m (for Maigret) and p (for Poirot). Predicates that require two arguments are **two-place** predicates. The transitive verbs of traditional syntax correspond approximately to the two-place predicates of logic. The arguments of a predicate are realized by noun phrases in our example: in (18a) the subject NP is one argument and the object NP is the second argument of the verb *imitate*.

Intransitive verbs correspond to **one-place** predicates: they take only one argument.

19a   Maigret stumbled.
19b   S (m)
       where S = 'stumble' and m = 'Maigret'.

---

[7] For an introduction to logic written specifically for the linguist see Allwood, Dahl and Dahl (1977), McCawley (1981).

3.2.2　ARGUMENT STRUCTURE IN NATURAL LANGUAGE

Using the basic idea of formal logic outlined above, we can say that every predicate has its **argument structure**,[8] i.e. it is specified for the number of arguments it requires. The arguments are the participants minimally involved in the activity or state expressed by the predicate.

We could use a metaphor to summarize this: predicates are like the script of a play. In a script a number of roles are defined and will have to be assigned to actors. The arguments of a predicate are like the roles defined by the script of a play. For an adequate performance of the play, each role must be assigned to an actor. It will not do either to miss out on a part in the play or to have actors on the stage who have no part to play. Adjuncts might be compared to the parts in the script which are not central to the play.

We first discuss the argument structure of verbs and its relation to sub-categorization frames. Then we also turn briefly to the argument structure of adjectives, nouns and prepositions.

The argument structure of the verb determines which elements of the sentence are obligatory. If a verb expresses an activity involving two arguments, there will have to be at least two constituents in the sentence to enable these arguments to be expressed. This conceptually defined argument structure can partly replace the classification of verbs in terms of either transitivity labels or subcategorization frames described above. If a speaker knows the meaning of the verb *meet*, in other words if he knows what activity is expressed, he will also know how many participants are involved and hence how many arguments the verb takes. 'Meet' involves two participants, and hence will be expected to take two arguments. If one argument is realized as the subject of the sentence (cf. section 6 for discussion), it follows that *meet* will select one VP-internal complement.

This does not mean that we can conclude that the verb *meet* necessarily subcategorizes for an NP. After all, the arguments might have been realized by categories other than NP.[9] The argument structure of the verb predicts the number of constituents needed but not necessarily their type. Let us assume for the moment that the type of constituent which realizes the argument must be lexically encoded. We can improve the lexical representation of verbs by specifying their argument structure, which is derived from their meaning, and the specification of the realization of the arguments. This notation replaces the labels transitive, intransitive and ditransitive, or the subcategorization

---

[8]　For a more careful statement see section 5.3 where we discuss the difference between auxiliaries and main verbs.
[9]　We return to this point in sections 5.1 and 7.1.

frames illustrated in (14) and (16)–(17) respectively.[10] We shall represent the arguments the verb takes by arabic numerals.

20a	*meet*:	verb;	1	2	
			NP	NP	
20b	*imitate*:	verb;	1	2	
			NP	NP	
20c	*reconstruct*:	verb;	1	2	
			NP	NP	
20d	*abandon*:	verb;	1	2	
			NP	NP	
20e	*give*:	verb;	1	2	3
			NP	NP	NP
			NP	NP	PP[11]
20f	*dither*:	verb;	1		
			NP		
20g	*smile*:	verb;	1		
			NP		

Recall that in addition to the arguments of the verb, sentences may also contain adjuncts, constituents providing additional information, for instance with respect to manner, place, time, etc.

[10]   There is an important distinction between subcategorization frames and argument structure. Subcategorization frames only specify the complements of the verb, i.e. the constituents that are obligatory inside the VP. The subject NP need not be mentioned in the subcategorization frame because all verbs have subjects, hence the property of having a subject does not create a subcategory of V, whereas the presence of objects does.

The argument structure lists all the arguments: it also includes the subject argument which is realized outside the VP. The thematic structure of the verb (see section 3.2.3) also lists *all* the arguments.

[11]   *Give* allows for two types of realizations of its arguments:

(i)   I gave Bill the money.
(ii)   I gave the money to Bill.

The representation in (20e) in the text serves to indicate that the second argument of *give* is either realized as an NP (i) or as a PP (ii). As (ii) and (iii) show, a PP must follow the VP-internal NP. We turn to the relative order of VP-internal constituents in chapter 3.

(iii)   *I gave to Bill the money.

In some cases it is less easy to determine the argument structure of predicates. Consider the following pairs of sentences:

21a Hercule bought Jane a detective story.
21b Hercule bought a detective story.

(21a) contains the verb *buy* with apparently three arguments. The argument *Jane* can be omitted, but as a result the meaning of the sentence changes subtly: in the unmarked context (21b) will be taken to mean that Hercule bought the detective story for himself. The action expressed in (21b) still implicitly involves someone for whom the book is bought. (21b) seems to contain an unexpressed or **implicit** argument. We shall encode the fact that some arguments may be left implicit by putting them in parentheses.

22 *buy*: verb;   1   (2)   3
                    NP   NP   NP

So far we have only illustrated the argument structure of verbs. Other lexical categories too have an argument structure. Consider (23):

23a Poirot is restless.
23b Jeeves is envious of Bertie.
23c Jeeves envies Bertie.

In (23a) the predicate *restless*, an adjective, takes one argument. *Restless* is a one-place predicate. The adjective *envious* in (23b) takes two arguments analogously to the verb *envy* in (23c), which is semantically and morphologically closely related to the adjective. (23b) and (23c) are near-paraphrases. The respective arguments of the verb *envy* in (23c) are realized by the two NPs *Jeeves* and *Bertie*. The arguments of *envious* are realized by an NP and by a PP headed by *of*. At this point we merely note that the second argument of the adjective cannot be realized by a straight NP but that it requires the presence of the preposition *of*. The reason why this should be so is treated in chapter 3.

23d *Jeeves is envious Bertie.

We cannot freely add new referring expressions to the sentences in (23):

24   *Poirot is restless of the case.

Unlike verbal arguments, the arguments of adjectives can often be left
implicit:

25a   *Poirot envies.
25b   Poirot is envious.

We shall again encode the argument structure of adjectives in the lexical ‖
information:

26a *envious*: adjective;   1   (2)
                              NP   PP
26b *restless*: adjective;   1
                               NP

   The argument structure of lexical items is not always uniquely fixed. Take ‖
for instance the adjective *conscious* in the following examples:

27a   Miss Marple is conscious of the problem.
27b   Sir Galahad is conscious.

We distinguish two argument structures for the adjective *conscious*. *Conscious* is either a two-place predicate (27a) or a one-place predicate (27b). It
would not do to say that the second argument of *conscious* is left implicit in
(27b) in the way that we argued that the second argument of *envious* in (25b)
was implicit. In (25b) the adjective *envious* has the same meaning as in (23b),
whereas there is a semantic difference between (27a) and (27b). In (27a) *be
conscious* is near-synonymous with *know, be aware*. In (27b) it means 'not
be in coma'. Depending on the meaning of the predicate we assume that a
different argument structure is associated with it:

28a *conscious$_1$*: adjective;   1   2
                                     NP   PP
28b *conscious$_2$*: adjective;   1
                                     NP

*Conscious*₁ will be parallel to *know* or *aware*:

29a *know*: verb;   1   2
                         NP   NP
29b *aware*: adjective; 1   2
                           NP   PP

Let us turn to nouns. Consider the following groups of examples:

30a Poirot will analyse the data.
30b *Poirot will analyse.
30c *There will analyse the data.

31a Poirot's analysis of the data was superfluous.
31b The analysis of the data was superfluous.
31c The analysis was superfluous.

In (30) the verb *analyse* requires two arguments. The noun *analysis* is semantically and morphologically related to the verb *analyse* and on the basis of (31a) we assume it has the same argument structure.

32a *analyse*: verb;   1   2
                          NP   NP
32b *analysis*: noun; (1) (2)
                          NP   PP

The two arguments of *analysis* are realized overtly in (31a); in (31b) the agent of the activity is left unexpressed and in (31c) both arguments are unexpressed. It is a typical property of nouns that both their arguments may be unrealized.

Prepositions too can be argued to have argument structure. The preposition *in*, for instance, will have two arguments; the preposition *between* will have three:

33a John is in London.
33b *in*: preposition;   1   2
                               NP   NP
33c Florence is between Milan and Rome.
33d *between*: preposition; 1   2   3
                               NP   NP   NP

3.2.3 THETA THEORY

Let us consider the argument structure of the verb *kill*.

34a Maigret killed Poirot.
34b *kill*: verb;   1   2
                     NP   NP

In (34a), the two argument-NPs *Maigret* and *Poirot* are intuitively felt to stand in different semantic relationships with the verb. The argument-NP *Maigret* in the subject position refers to the entity that is the **AGENT** of the activity of killing. The argument NP *Poirot*, the direct object, expresses the **PATIENT** of the activity. We used the metaphor of the script of a play when discussing argument structure of predicates. A script of a play defines not only the number of parts to be assigned, hence the number of actors involved, but also what characters are involved, it specifies which roles these actors have to play. The more specific semantic relationships between the verb and its respective arguments may be compared with the identification of the characters in a play script. In the literature these relations between verbs and their arguments are referred to in terms of **thematic roles** or **theta roles (θ-roles)** for short. We say that the verb *kill* takes two arguments to which it assigns a theta role: it assigns the role **AGENT** to the subject argument of the sentence, and the role **PATIENT** to the object argument. The verb **theta-marks** its arguments. Predicates in general have a **thematic structure**. The component of the grammar that regulates the assignment of thematic roles is called **theta theory**.

   Although many linguists agree on the importance of thematic structure for certain syntactic processes, the theory of thematic roles is still very sketchy. For example, at the present stage of the theory there is no agreement about how many such specific thematic roles there are and what their labels are. Some types are quite generally distinguished. We discuss them informally here.

35a AGENT/ACTOR: the one who intentionally initiates the action expressed by the predicate.
35b PATIENT: the person or thing undergoing the action expressed by the predicate.
35c THEME: the person or thing moved by the action expressed by the predicate.
35d EXPERIENCER: the entity that experiences some (psychological) state expressed by the predicate.

35e BENEFACTIVE/BENEFICIARY: the entity that benefits from the action expressed by the predicate.

35f GOAL: the entity towards which the activity expressed by the predicate is directed.

35g SOURCE: the entity from which something is moved as a result of the activity expressed by the predicate.

35h LOCATION: the place in which the action or state expressed by the predicate is situated.

The inventory above is very tentative. Other authors amalgamate the roles PATIENT and THEME under the one role of THEME.

35i THEME$_2$: the entity affected by the action or state expressed by the predicate.

We usually use the term THEME in this second interpretation.
  The thematic roles are illustrated in (36):

36a Galahad gave the detective story to Jane.
    AGENT   THEME   BENEFACTIVE/GOAL
36b Constance rolled the ball towards Poirot.
    AGENT   THEME GOAL
36c The ball rolled towards the pigsty.
    THEME   GOAL
36d Madame Maigret had been cold all day.
    EXPERIENCER
36e Maigret likes   love stories.
    EXPERIENCER THEME
36f Love stories please Maigret.
    THEME   EXPERIENCER
36g Poirot bought the book from Maigret.
    AGENT   THEME SOURCE
36h Maigret is in London.
    THEME   LOCATION

  The identification of thematic roles is not always easy, as the reader can see for himself. However, intuitively the idea should be clear, and we shall be drawing on this rather intuitive approach to theta theory in subsequent discussion.

The information as to the semantic relationship between the predicate and its arguments is part of the lexical knowledge of the native speaker and should hence also be recorded in the lexicon. Rather than merely specifying the number of arguments of a predicate, one may envisage a representation which specifies the type of semantic roles of these arguments. In Government and Binding Theory this is represented by means of a **thematic grid**, or **theta grid**, which is part of the lexical entry of the predicate. *Kill* would be given the lexical representation in (37a):

37a   *kill*:   verb

AGENT	PATIENT

(37a) specifies that *kill* **assigns** two thematic roles (AGENT and PATIENT). We deduce that the verb is a two-place predicate, which requires two arguments to which these roles can be assigned. Some linguists propose that the syntactic category realizing the thematic role should also be specified in the theta grid of a predicate (cf. section 7.1 for discussion).

37b   *kill*:   verb

AGENT NP	PATIENT NP

Consider some examples:

38a   Maigret killed the burglar.
38b   *Maigret killed.
38c   *Maigret killed the burglar the cellar.

We see that two arguments and no more than two are needed. In (38b) the absence of the second NP renders the sentence ungrammatical: the second theta role cannot be assigned. In (38c), conversely, one extra NP is added to the sentence. This NP cannot be assigned a thematic role because *kill* only assigns two roles, which are already assigned to the subject NP and to the object NP respectively. In (38d) we have inserted the preposition *in*. The sentence is grammatical: the preposition *in* assigns the thematic role of LOCATION to the NP *the cellar*.

38d   Maigret killed the burglar in the cellar.

One criterion for judging whether a sentence is grammatical is that the thematic roles associated with its predicate(s) must be assigned to arguments, these arguments must be structurally realized. Conversely, the referring NPs in the sentence must bear some semantic relation to a predicate. This semantic relation can be established via the assignment of thematic roles.

Each syntactic representation of a sentence is scanned for the predicate(s) it contains. Each predicate is tested with respect to its argument structure. Its arguments must be realized. More specifically the predicate is tested for its thematic roles: each role must be assigned to an argument.

Let us take as an example a sentence containing the predicate *kill*. *Kill* assigns the thematic roles of AGENT and PATIENT, hence it requires two arguments. When the theta roles can be assigned to arguments we say that they are **saturated** and we mark this by checking off the theta role in the thematic grid of the predicate. In order to identify the assignment of the respective thematic roles to the corresponding arguments, NPs are identified by means of an index, a subscript:

39a   Maigret$_i$ killed the burglar$_j$.
39b   *Maigret$_i$ killed.
39c   *Maigret$_i$ killed the burglar$_j$ the cellar$_k$.

We shall not discuss the subscripting convention here. We hope that the intuitive idea is clear: an NP refers to an individual or an object and is identified by the referential index. Two NPs with the same index are said to be **coindexed**: they are interpreted as referring to the same entity.[12]

40a   Maigret$_i$ said that he$_i$ was ill.
40b   Maigret$_i$ hurt himself$_i$.

[12]   We return to coindexation in chapter 4 and in chapter 12.

In order to show how the theta roles of a predicate are assigned we enter the index of the argument to which the thematic role is assigned in the appropriate slot in the theta grid. For (39a) the saturation of the thematic roles can be represented as in (41):

41 *kill*: verb

AGENT	PATIENT
NP	NP
i	j

If we try to do the same for (39b) we see that one of the slots in the thematic grid will remain unfilled: one thematic role is not assigned. Conversely, in (39c) there is one referential index which cannot be entered on the grid, hence cannot be assigned a thematic role.

42a *kill*: verb

AGENT	PATIENT
NP	NP
i	?

42b *kill*: verb

AGENT	PATIENT	
NP	NP	
i	j	k?

In (42a) corresponding to (39b) the thematic role of PATIENT is not assigned or not saturated. In (42b), corresponding to (39c), the argument-NP *the cellar* with the referential index *k* fails to be assigned a thematic role.

The requirement that each thematic role of a predicate must be assigned and that there must be no NPs that lack a thematic role is summed up in the **theta criterion**:

43   Theta criterion
43a   Each argument is assigned one and only one theta role.
43b   Each theta role is assigned to one and only one argument.

So far we have only discussed NP arguments. But other constituents may also be arguments: consider, for instance, (44a) and (44b):

44a   The police announced the news.
44b   The police announced that the pig had been stolen.

In (44a) *announce* is associated with two arguments, which will be assigned their thematic roles. The role AGENT is assigned to *the police*; THEME to *the news*. In (44b) the THEME role is assigned to a subordinate clause: *that the pig had been stolen*. Clauses too can thus be arguments of the predicate. We return to the issue in more detail in section 5.1.

Given the wide diversity in the labelling of thematic roles and their definitions it would be a difficult enterprise to fix the types of roles and their exact number. Even if we are unable to pin down the exact nature of the different roles involved we are usually quite clear as to how many arguments a predicate requires in a given reading. Hence, instead of specifying the exact type of thematic role for each predicate, we shall often merely list the number of arguments, identifying their roles by numbers rather than by role labels. Thus for the verb *kill* we shall use the following lexical representation, unless we need to refer explicitly to the thematic label.

45   *kill*:   verb

1 NP	2 NP

The numerals 1 and 2 represent the thematic roles assigned by the verb whose labels need not concern us.

Research in this area suggests that it might not be necessary or desirable to refer to the thematic labels in the syntax,[13] and that indeed the representation

---

[13]   For discussion, see Grimshaw (1979, 1981).

in (45) is the one we need. We do not go into that discussion here and we refer the reader to chapter 3, section 6.3 and to the literature.

4 The Projection Principle

Let us sum up what we have done so far. We have seen that the lexical items which are the ultimate constituents of a sentence play an important part in its syntactic representation. Section 2 shows that the lexical category of the head of a phrase determines the category of the phrase. Second, we have seen in section 3 that the thematic structure of a predicate, encoded in the theta grid, will determine the minimal components of the sentence. This idea that lexical information to a large extent determines syntactic structure is summed up in the projection principle:

46 **Projection principle**
Lexical information is syntactically represented.

The projection principle will play an important role throughout this book. For a discussion of the role of the lexicon in syntax see also Stowell and Wehrli (1992) and the references cited there.

5 The Assignment of Thematic Roles

In this section we look at the assignment of thematic roles in the syntax. We focus on three areas: section 5.1 discusses clausal arguments; section 5.2 discusses expletive pronouns; and section 5.3 considers the difference between lexical verbs, or main verbs, and auxiliaries.

5.1 Clausal Arguments

We have seen that the obligatory constituents of a sentence are determined by the semantic properties of the predicates (verbs, adjectives) and we have mainly discussed examples with NP-arguments. Sentences too may be arguments of a predicate.

47a   Miss Marple has announced the news.
47b   Miss Marple has announced that Poirot had left.

In (47a) the verb *announce* takes two arguments, realized by the NPs *Miss Marple* and *the news* respectively. In (47b) the arguments are realized by an NP and by the clause [*that Poirot had left*]. Consider also the following examples:

48a   The robbery surprised all the inhabitants of Blandings.
48b   [That the pig was stolen] surprised all the inhabitants of Blandings.

49a   Jeeves' decision is very unfortunate.
49b   [That Jeeves should be leaving] is very unfortunate.

50a   Poirot asked three questions.
50b   Poirot asked [whether anyone had seen the pig].

51a   Maigret believes the story about the burglary.
51b   Maigret believes [that the taxi driver is lying].

52a   Constance is aware of the problem.
52b   Constance is aware [that the pig is in danger].

The verb *surprise* takes two arguments. In (48a) both arguments are realized by NPs; in (48b) one argument is realized by a clause. Similarly, in (49a) the one argument of the adjective *unfortunate* is realized by an NP and in (49b) it is realized by a clause. In (50) and (51) we find further alternations between NPs and clauses as realizations of arguments. In (52) one of the arguments of the adjective *aware* is realized by an NP contained in a PP in (52a) and by a clause in (52b).

We conclude that the theta grid of predicates will not always specify a unique category to which a theta role can be assigned but will allow for a choice. We return to this point in section 7.1.

Let us consider clausal arguments a little more closely:

53a   [That Galahad had left] is very surprising.
53b   [For Galahad to have left] is very surprising.

54a   Maigret_i believes [this story]_j.

54b   Maigret_i believes [that the taxi driver is innocent]_j.

54c   Maigret_i believes [the taxi driver to be innocent]_j.

54d   Maigret_i believes [the taxi driver innocent]_j.

In (53) we see that the adjective *surprising* takes one argument, to which it assigns a thematic role. The argument is realized by a **finite** clause in (53a): the verb *had* is finite, it is inflected for the past tense and the clause is introduced by the **complementizer** *that*. In (53b) the argument of the main predicate is realized by a non-finite clause: *have* is in the infinitive and the sentence is introduced by the complementizer *for*. We return to the general principles of sentence structure in chapter 2.[14]

[14]   Koster (1978b) argues that what looks like a clausal subject in (48b) and in (49b) is not in the subject position. Observe for instance that (48b) cannot be embedded as such.

(ia)   I wonder whether the robbery surprised all the inhabitants of Blandings

(ib)   *I wonder whether [that the pig was stolen] surprised all the inhabitants of Blandings.

(ib) can be made grammatical if we move the clausal subject to a final position and replace it by the pronoun *it*. As mentioned in the introduction, the pronoun *it* in examples such as (ic) seems to make no contribution to the semantics of the sentence. We return to this use of *it* in section 5.2.1.

(ic)   I wonder whether it surprised all the inhabitants of Blandings [that the pig was stolen].

   Similarly, Stowell (1981) suggests that object clauses also do not occupy the same position as the object NP. Observe, for instance, that in English the object-NP *the situation* in (iia) can, and indeed must (cf. (ib)) precede the adverbial adjunct *very carefully*, while an object clause must follow it.

(iia)   He explained the situation very carefully.

(iib)   *He explained very carefully the situation.

(iic)   *He explained that he was not going to leave very carefully.

(iid)   He explained very carefully that he was not going to leave.

There is further support for these observations from Dutch. In this language subordinate clauses have the SOV pattern: in (iiia) the direct object NP *de waarheid* ('the truth') precedes the verb *zegt* ('tells'), the reverse order is not possible (iiib):

(iiia)   Ik verwacht dat Jan [de waarheid] zegt.
       I expect that Jan the truth tells
       'I expect Jan to tell the truth.'

In (54a) both arguments of *believe* are realized by NPs. In (54b) one of the arguments of *believe* is realized by a finite clause. As the bracketing indicates, the corresponding argument is realized by a non-finite clause in (54c).

The bracketing in (54c) is meant to show that we consider *the taxi driver* to form a constituent with *to be innocent*. The justification for this analysis is essentially one of analogy. If we compare the sentences (54b) and (54c) we see that they are very similar in meaning. In (54b) the verb takes two arguments: one argument which is realized by the subject NP, and one argument which is realized by a sentence. On the basis of examples like (54a) and (54b) we deduce that the lexical entry of *believe* has the following theta grid:

55 *believe*: verb

1 NP	2 NP/S

In (54a) the arguments are saturated as in (56), where *j* is the index of an NP. In (54b), similarly, the saturation of the arguments can be represented as in (56), with *j* now seen as the index of a subordinate clause.

56 *believe*: verb

1 NP	2 NP/S
i	j

(iiib)   *Ik verwacht dat Jan zegt [de waarheid].
         I expect that Jan says the truth
(iiic)   *Ik verwacht dat Jan [dat hij ziek is] zegt.
         I expect that Jan [that he ill is] says
(iiid)   Ik verwacht dat Jan zegt [dat hij ziek is].
         I expect that Jan says that he ill is

For further discussion we refer the reader to the texts cited. However, these texts will not be accessible until we have covered the material in chapter 7.

Given the close similarity in meaning between (54b) and (54c), the minimal assumption is that the verb *believe* in (54c) is the same as that in (54b) and has the same theta grid. While in (54b) the second argument is associated with a finite clause, in (54c), the second argument is associated with a non-finite clause.[15] The theta roles in (54c) are saturated as in (56), with *j* standing for the non-finite clause.

(54d) is also very close in meaning to (54b) and (54c) , so we postulate that the verb *believe* is unaltered and has the theta grid in (55). Given this assumption, we need to assign to (54d) a structure that allows the saturation of the argument roles 1 and 2. The bracketing in (54d) will do that adequately.

It is not immediately obvious how to label the structure [*the taxi driver innocent*]. In the traditional literature on parsing, the term 'verbless clause' is sometimes used. This term serves to indicate that we have a constituent which has a propositional meaning, i.e. the same sort of meaning as a full clausal structure has, but it lacks any verb forms. In (54d) the constituent [*the taxi driver innocent*] corresponds to the sentence [*the taxi driver to be innocent*] in (54c). In both sentences the NP *the taxi driver* is the subject of the predicate expressed by the AP *innocent*. In the Government–Binding literature, constituents such as [*the taxi driver innocent*] are called **small clauses**. We return to their structure throughout the book.

Non-finite clauses and small clauses are not normally[16] found as independent clauses: they can only be subordinate to some other main predicate. The italicized constituents in (57) are all small clauses:

---

[15] Note, however, that in this particular example, the non-finite clause cannot be introduced by the complementizer *for*. We shall return to this issue in chapters 2 and 3.

[16] Small clauses seem to be in frequent use in certain registers, such as informal notes or telegrams (i) or newspaper headlines (ii):

(i) Mother in hospital.
(ii) Hijackers under arrest.

Register-specific syntactic properties have not often been studied in the generative framework (see Haegeman, 1987, 1990; and Massam and Roberge, 1989).
We also find small clauses in colloquial expressions such as:

(iii) What? Me angry?

For small clauses in acquisition see Radford (1990).

57a   I consider *John a real idiot.*
57b   The chief inspector wants *Maigret in his office.*
57c   Emsworth got *Galahad in trouble.*

It is evident that the small clauses are of different types. In (57a) the small clause consists of an NP *John* and a second NP *a real idiot.* The first NP acts as a subject to the second one. In (57b) and (57c) the small clause is composed of an NP and a PP, where the NP is the subject with respect to the PP predicate.[17] That the italicized strings in (57) are constituents is supported by the fact that other material associated with the main verb of the sentence cannot occur internally to what we have called the small clause:

58   *The chief inspector wants [Maigret [very much] in his office].

In (58) the degree adjunct *very much*, which modifies the verb *want*, cannot intervene between the subject and the PP predicate of the small clause.

5.2   *Expletives*

Section 5.1 shows that not all arguments of a predicate are necessarily realized as NPs. In this section we shall see that the reverse also holds: some NPs in the subject position of the sentence are not assigned a thematic role, hence are not arguments of the predicate.

5.2.1   *IT* AND EXTRAPOSITION

The obligatory presence of certain constituents in a sentence can be accounted for in terms of the argument structure of the predicate of a sentence. Let us now extend our analysis to some further data:

59a   The burglary surprised Jeeves.
59b   That the pig had been stolen surprised Jeeves.
59c   It surprised Jeeves that the pig had been stolen.

---

[17]   For a discussion and further motivation of the analysis of small clauses, see Stowell (1983), Hornstein and Lightfoot (1987). However, these texts will only become accessible once chapter 8 has been covered.

From (59a) and (59b) we infer that *surprise* takes two arguments. Neither of
these can be omitted:

60a   *The burglary surprised.
60b   *Surprised Jeeves.
60c   *That the pig had been stolen surprised.

Surprise will be associated with the thematic grid (61):

61   *surprise*: verb

1 NP/S	2 NP

We cannot insert another NP in these sentences since this would not be
assigned a theta role by *surprise*.

62a   *The burglary surprised Jeeves *it*.
62b   *That the pig had been stolen surprised Jeeves *it*.

In (62a) or (62b) the NP *it* cannot be assigned a thematic role and thus the
sentence violates the theta criterion (43). The theta criterion specifies that
theta roles are assigned uniquely. Hence one could not, for instance, propose
that in (62a) theta role 1 is assigned both to the subject NP *the burglary* and
to the NP *it*.

   Now let us look at (59c) repeated here as (63a):

63a   It surprised Jeeves that the pig had been stolen.

(63a) is a paraphrase of (59b). We deduce that *surprise* in (63a) has the theta
grid given in (61) with two theta roles to be associated with two arguments.
How are these arguments realized? If we capitalize on the equivalence between
(63a) and (59b) then the easiest thing would be to say that in both (59b) and
(63a) one theta role, say 1, is assigned to the clause [*that the pig had been
stolen*] and the other one, 2, to *Jeeves*. This hypothesis leaves us with the NP-
constituent *it* in the subject position of (63a) unaccounted for. This NP is not
optional:

63b   *Surprised Jeeves that the pig had been stolen.

On the other hand, *it* cannot be assigned a thematic role since *surprise* only assigns two thematic roles already saturated as described above.

One element in the discussion is that the choice of a filler for the subject position in (63a) is very limited: indeed no other NP (pronominal or not) can fill the position:

64a   *This* surprised Jeeves that the pig had been stolen.
64b   *He* surprised Jeeves that the pig had been stolen.

Moreover it is not possible to question the element *it* in (63a), nor can *it* receive focal stress:

64c   *What* surprised Jeeves that the pig had been stolen?
64d   *IT* surprised Jeeves that the pig had been stolen.

In fact, the pronoun *it* in (63a) contributes nothing to the meaning of the sentence, (63a) being a paraphrase of (59b). *It* is not a referring expression: it does not refer to an entity in the world, a person or an object; it cannot be questioned; it cannot receive focal stress.

On the basis of these observations we formulate the hypothesis that *it* plays no role in the semantic make-up of the sentence and that its presence is required in (63a) simply for some structural reason. The relevant explanation for the presence of *it* in the subject position in (63a) will be argued to be that English sentences must have an overt subject (see section 6 and chapter 2 for more discussion). The pronoun *it* in (63a) acts as a mere slot-filler, a dummy pronoun without semantic contribution to the sentence; it is a place-holder for the otherwise unfilled subject position. In the literature such a dummy pronoun is often called an **expletive** pronoun. The term **pleonastic** *it* is also used. Expletives are elements in NP positions which are not arguments and to which no theta role is assigned.[18] Note that, unlike adjuncts, expletives contribute nothing to the sentence meaning.

---

[18]   The reader will recall from the Introduction that in *pro*-drop languages such as Italian the subject pronoun can be omitted (ia) and that in such languages there are no expletive pronouns (ib):

(ia)   (Io) parlo Italiano.
       (I) speak (Isg) Italian

In an example like (63a) it is sometimes said that the sentential subject is **extraposed** and that it is **in construction with** an expletive. (65) contains some more examples of extraposition patterns. The extraposed clause and the expletive are italicized:

65a *It* worries Maigret *that Poirot should have left.*
65b *It* is unfortunate *that Poirot should have said that.*
65c *It* is out of the question *that Jeeves should be fired.*
65d I consider *it* odd *that Poirot should have left.*

The expletive *it* cannot just appear in any type of sentence. Consider for instance the following pair:

66a An announcement about the robbery worried Maigret.
66b *It worried Maigret an announcement about the robbery.

(66b) shows that the expletive *it* cannot become the place-holder for an extraposed NP.[19]

5.2.2 *THERE* AND EXISTENTIAL SENTENCES

Now let us turn to another sentence pattern which poses problems for our theory outlined so far.

67a Three pigs are escaping.
67b There are three pigs escaping.

(ib) (*Ciò) è chiaro che Louisa non partirà.
      (*it) is clear that Louisa not leave (fut, 3sg)
      'It is clear that Louisa won't go.'

In *pro*-drop languages the subject pronoun is only present when it receives stress (for instance when contrasted or focalized):

(ic) *Lei* parte e *lui* arriva.
      she leaves and *he* arrives

Since expletive pronouns cannot receive focal or contrastive stress it follows that they will not be used in *pro*-drop languages.

[19] A good survey of the literature on extraposition can be found in Williams (1980). For different views see also Bennis (1986), Grange and Haegeman (1989) and Postal and Pullum (1988).

In (67a) the verb *escape* has one argument, realized by the NP *three pigs*. In (67b) the sentence contains one more element: the pronominal *there*, which occupies the subject position. First note that *there* is not an adjunct of place. In (67b) *there*, unlike place adjuncts, cannot be questioned:

68a　I saw Bill there last week.
　　　Where did you see Bill last week?
　　　There.
68b　*Where are three pigs escaping? There.

Also, unlike the place adjunct, *there* in declarative (67b) cannot be omitted freely:

69a　I saw Bill last week.
69b　*Are three pigs escaping.

But *there* does not really contribute anything to the meaning of (67b), which has the same meaning as (67a). Again the data suggest that *there* is required for structural reasons: it fills up the subject position. Unlike the place adjunct *there*, *there* in (67b) cannot receive focal stress:

70a　I saw him (right) *there*.
70b　**There* are three pigs escaping.

As was the case with the pronominal *it* discussed before, we call *there* an expletive. In contrast with *it*, *there* is associated with NP-subjects which have been moved to the right in the sentence, and it cannot be associated with clausal subjects:

71a　*There surprised Jeeves [that the pig had been stolen].

The construction with *there* has many intriguing properties. For instance the *there*-construction is only allowed if the moved subject NP is indefinite. There are also heavy restrictions on the type of verb that can occur in this construction. Transitive verbs, for instance, are disallowed.[20]

---

[20]　For the discussion of the *there*-construction, see Belletti (1988), Milsark (1974, 1977) Moro (1989) and Stowell (1978). These texts will be accessible after chapter 6 has been covered.

71b   *There are the three pigs escaping.
71c   *There saw three children the pigs.

5.2.3   CONCLUSION

We have seen that there are two pronouns in English, *it* and *there*, that can
be used without being assigned a thematic role. They are expletives filling the
subject position for structural reasons. We turn to those structural reasons in
section 6.

Expletives always turn up in the subject position of the sentence, i.e. the
NP position for which the verb does not subcategorize. Indeed the theory
outlined so far predicts that expletives will never turn up in subcategorized
positions. Expletives are elements lacking a theta role. The positions a verb
subcategorizes for are determined by the thematic structure of the verb. Whenever a verb requires a complement NP, this is because the verb has a theta
role to assign to the NP. Inserting an expletive NP in an object position would
miss the point, because the expletive element would not be able to receive the
theta role. In (72) we find a pronoun *it* as the object of *believe*, but this pronoun
is not an expletive: it is assigned a thematic role by the verb. In such examples
it can substitute for other NPs:

72   Poirot believes it/this/this story/the announcement.

The prediction of the theory outlined is thus that expletives can only occur
in NP positions that are not subcategorized for, i.e. the subject position of the
sentence.[21]

5.3   *Main Verbs and Auxiliaries*

So far we have implied that all verbs assign thematic roles. However, it is
well known that the class of verbs can be divided into two sets: (a) lexical
verbs or main verbs like *eat*, *sleep*, *walk*, and (b) auxiliaries: *be*, *have*, *do*, and
the modal auxiliaries *will*, *shall*, *can*, *may*, *must*, *ought*. All these elements are
inflected for tense:[22]

---

[21]   See Postal and Pullum (1988) for a different view.
[22]   In the present tense, verbs and the auxiliaries *have* and *be* are also inflected for
person and number. Modals are not inflected for person and number. For discussion cf. chapter 11. For the development of modals see Lightfoot (1979).

73	Verb	Present tense		Past tense
a	*eat*	eat	eats	ate
b	*sleep*	sleep	sleeps	slept
c	*walk*	walk	walks	walked
d	*be*	am/are	is	was/were
e	*have*	have	has	had
f	*can*	can	can	could
g	*do*	do	does	did

Auxiliary verbs have some special properties distinguishing them from lexical verbs. In (74) and (75) we have paired sentences containing a lexical verb in (a) and an auxiliary in (b). The reader can check that auxiliaries and main verbs behave differently in negative and interrogative patterns:

74a John eats chocolate.
    *John eatsn't chocolate.
    John doesn't eat chocolate.
74b John has eaten chocolate.
    John hasn't eaten chocolate.
    *John doesn't have eaten chocolate.

75a John eats chocolate.
    *Eats John chocolate?
    Does John eat chocolate?
75b John has eaten chocolate.
    Has John eaten chocolate?
    *Does John have eaten chocolate?

The negation element *n't* follows the auxiliaries (cf. (74b)), whereas it must precede the lexical verb (cf. 74a)). In a *yes–no* question the auxiliary and the subject of the sentence are inverted (see chapter 2 for discussion). Lexical verbs do not invert with their subjects: in both negative sentences and in questions the auxiliary *do* is needed. We return to the positions of lexical verbs and of auxiliaries in chapter 7 and especially in chapter 11. Now let us consider the thematic structure of auxiliaries and main verbs.

76a Poirot accuses Maigret.
76b Poirot has accused Maigret.
76c Poirot is accusing Maigret.
76d Poirot does not accuse Maigret.

In (76a) the assignment of the thematic roles of *accuse* is straightforward: one thematic role will be assigned to the NP *Poirot* and the other one to *Maigret*. In addition to the lexical verb *accuse*, (76b) contains the perfective auxiliary *have*. The sentence is grammatical, which must mean that all thematic roles of the predicate(s) are assigned and that all referring NPs in the sentence have a thematic role assigned to them. Given that there are just as many NPs present in (76b) as in (76a), we are led to conclude that the auxiliary *have*, though morphologically like a verb in that it is inflected for tense, person and number, does not assign any thematic roles of its own. If *have* did assign any thematic roles then we would expect (76b) to contain one or more NPs in addition to those in (76a), which would be assigned the thematic roles of the auxiliary. The same argument can be applied to the auxiliaries *be* in (76c) and *do* in (76d). We conclude that auxiliaries do not assign thematic roles.

A related problem appears in connection with the copula *be* in (77) (cf. example (54)).

77a   Maigret$_i$ believes [that the taxi driver is innocent]$_j$
77b   Maigret$_i$ believes [the taxi driver to be innocent]$_j$
77c   Maigret$_i$ believes [the taxi driver innocent]$_j$

In (77) *believe* assigns one theta role to *Maigret* and it assigns the second one to the bracketed clausal constituents. We are concerned with the internal predicate argument structure of the clausal argument. In the discussion above we have argued that the finite complement clause in (77a), the non-finite one in (77b) and the small clause in (77c) all basically mean the same thing: in all of them the property *innocent* is ascribed to the referent of the NP *the taxi driver*. We have also seen that adjectives, like verbs, have an argument structure. Let us first turn to (77c). Inside the small clause *the taxi driver innocent* the NP *the taxi driver* must have been assigned a thematic role, by virtue of clause (43a) of the theta criterion. We deduce that the NP is assigned a thematic role by *innocent*. The adjective will have the thematic grid (78):

78   *innocent*: adjective

1

In the small clause in (77c) the theta role is assigned to the NP *the taxi driver*. With respect to (77a) and (77b) *innocent* must also be able to assign its thematic role and by analogy with (77c) we assume that it assigns it to the NP *the taxi driver* and hence we conclude that the copula *be*, like auxiliaries, does not assign any thematic roles. Interestingly, the copula *be* also has the other syntactic properties of the auxiliaries:

79a The taxi driver is innocent.
79b The taxi driver isn't innocent.
79c Is the taxi driver innocent?

The formal differences between main verbs on the one hand and auxiliaries and the copula *be* on the other are matched by a semantic property: neither auxiliaries nor the copula *be* assign thematic roles.[23]

6   The Extended Projection Principle (EPP)

Our discussion reveals that sentence constituents may be required for two reasons.

In the first place, the argument structure and the theta grid of the predicate determine the minimal composition of the sentence. Sentence structure is thus partly lexically determined. This property of syntactic representations is summed up in the projection principle ((46), section 4).

Second, expletive elements are required to fill the subject position in certain constructions (section 5.2). The structural requirement which necessitates the insertion of expletives is that the subject position of a sentence must be filled, i.e. sentences must have subjects.[24] This requirement is not one that is specific to individual lexical items, but it is a general grammatical property of all sentences. In this respect the structural requirement that sentences have sub-

---

23 See Pollock (1989) for an explanation.
24 In chapters 5–8 we shall see that the subject may be non-overt. The reader will recall that in *pro*-drop languages the subject pronoun can be omitted:

(i) Parlo italiano.
     speak (1sg) Italian

This might seem in contradiction with the subject requirement discussed in the text. For sentences lacking an overt subject we will propose that there is a non-overt pronoun in the subject position. We discuss this type of non-overt subject in *pro*-drop languages in chapter 8.

jects is an addition to the projection principle. Not only must lexical properties of words be projected in the syntax, but in addition, regardless of their
argument structure, sentences must have subjects. The latter requirement has
come to be known as the **extended projection principle (EPP)** (80). The phrase
structure rules of our grammar (cf. (2b)) will specify that every sentence has
a subject. (We return to a discussion of phrase structure in chapter 2.)

80 **Extended projection principle**
    S ⟶ NP – AUX – VP

Consider (81):

81a Maigret accused Poirot.
81b *Accused Poirot Maigret.

In both (81a) and (81b) the two arguments of *accuse* are realized by the NPs
Maigret and *Poirot*. The ungrammaticality of (81b) follows from the extended projection principle (80): the subject position is not filled. Insertion of
the expletive *there* is not possible because *there* cannot be associated with
definite NPs and also it cannot be used with transitive verbs. Similarly, *it* cannot
be inserted since this expletive cannot be in construction with an NP.

82a *There accused Maigret Poirot
82b *It accused Maigret Poirot.

7 Thematic Roles: Further Discussion

7.1 *The Canonical Realization of Theta Roles*

Syntacticians do not agree about the question whether the lexical information
associated with a lexical item must specify the categorial realization of the
thematic roles, i.e. whether it must specify by which syntactic categories the
thematic roles such as AGENT, THEME etc., are realized. It has been noted,
for instance, that thematic roles such as AGENT are always realized by an
NP. It is then said that the **canonical** realization of AGENT is NP, i.e. that
this theta role is normally realized by NP. This means that the theta grid of
a verb which assigns a theta role AGENT will not need to specify by which
syntactic category the theta role is realized. In other words, this view proposes

that categorial selection or **c-selection** follows from semantic selection or **s-selection**. However, there is not always a perfect match between certain types of thematic roles and the corresponding syntactic realization. Compare, for instance, the examples in (83) (from Rothstein 1992):

83a I asked   what the time was.
                  the time.
83b I inquired what the time was.
                  *the time.

Ask and *inquire* are near-synonymous: both take a semantic complement of the type which we could informally describe as 'Question'. We could say that questions are canonically realized by interrogative clauses, and thus we expect that both *ask* and *inquire* take a clausal complement. However, the verb *ask* can also select an NP-complement (*the time* in (83a)), while *inquire* cannot. In (83a) the NP *the time* is interpreted as equivalent to a question ('what the time was'); NPs interpreted as questions are called **concealed questions**. Grimshaw (1981) uses data as those in (83) to propose that there are predictable relations between the semantic characteristics of the complement of a lexical item and the canonical realization, which she labels **canonical structural representations (CSR)**. Categorial information concerning the syntactic representation of an argument of a certain head will only be required in those cases where this argument is realized by a non-predictable category. For instance, categorial information is needed to specify that the complement of *ask* may be realized by an NP, though not to specify that it may be a clause. The latter information is derived from the semantic information that the complement of *ask* is a question. Grimshaw stresses that we cannot eliminate c-selection from lexical information because we need to specify the non-canonical realizations. We briefly return to this point in Chapter 3 (section 6.3).

In our discussion we often omit the specification of the syntactic category to which a thematic role is assigned and use representations as (83c). This convention is adopted for convenience' sake and implies no decision with respect to the relation between categorial selection and thematic roles.

83c *inquire*: verb

1	2

7.2   The Subject Theta Role

With respect to the assignment of thematic roles we have treated arguments in the subject position in the same way as arguments in the object position. For instance in (84) we would have said that both the NP *Maigret* and the NP *the taxi driver* are assigned a theta role by the verb *accuse*.

84   Maigret accused the taxi driver.

Two related observations are often advanced in the literature for treating subject arguments as different from object arguments. On the one hand, the choice of the object affects the thematic role of the subject while the choice of the subject argument does not affect the role of the object, and on the other hand, there exist 'object idioms' with the subject as a free argument while there are no subject idioms with a free object.[25] In (85) we see how the choice of the object may determine the theta role of the subject:

85a   John broke a leg last week.
85b   John broke a vase last week.

In both (85a) and (85b) the verb *break* takes an NP complement. The choice of the complement determines the thematic role of the subject: while in (85b) *John* could be considered AGENT, in (85a) this is not the case: John is the one who undergoes the event. Consider also (86). While in (86a) the literal meaning of the verb *kill* is intended, the other three examples are idioms with free subjects. The idiomatic interpretation of the sentence depends on the combination of the verb *kill* and its object.

86a   kill an insect
86b   kill a conversation
86c   kill a bottle (i.e. empty it)
86d   kill an audience (i.e. wow them)
      (examples from Bresnan, 1982: 350)

The theta role assigned to the subject is assigned **compositionally**: it is determined by the semantics of the verb and other VP constituents. Roughly,

[25]   A discussion of the grammatical functions in the Government and Binding framework is found in Marantz (1981). For a discussion of some problems raised by the approach, see Bresnan (1982).

the verb assigns an object role first, the resulting verb–argument complex will assign a theta role to the subject. The subject argument is as if it were slotted in last.

If a predicate assigns a thematic role directly to some constituent we shall say that the predicate **theta-marks** the constituent **directly**. If the predicate theta-marks an argument compositionally we call this **indirect theta-marking**.

As mentioned above, there is no agreement as to whether the difference between the types of theta roles should be considered as syntactically relevant. However, most linguists agree that the thematic role assigned to the subject must somehow be set apart from the other thematic roles. One quite popular proposal due to Edwin Williams (1981)[26] is that the argument which must be realized in the subject position and hence will be theta-marked indirectly is singled out lexically. The lexical entry for the predicate signals explicitly which argument must be outside the VP. Given that this argument is projected onto an NP outside the VP, it is referred to as the **external argument** and conventionally the external argument is indicated in the thematic grid by underlining:

87   *accuse*:   verb

1	2

Theta roles assigned to internal arguments will be referred to as **internal** theta roles; that assigned (indirectly) to the external argument is often referred to as the **external** theta role. (Cf. chapter 6, sections 3 and 5 for further discussion.)

8   Summary

In this chapter we have considered the extent to which sentence structure is determined by lexical properties. As a basis for the formation of sentences we have adopted the projection principle:

[26] Williams (1981) shows the relevance of the distinction between external and internal theta role for the domain of morphology. See also exercise 6.

In chapter 6 we shall discuss an alternative approach to the status of the subject NP.

1   **Projection principle**
    Lexical information is syntactically represented.

The type of lexical information with which we have been mainly concerned in this chapter is the thematic structure of the predicate, i.e. the number and types of arguments which the predicate takes. The thematic structure associated with lexical items must be saturated in the syntax, as stated in the theta criterion:

2   **Theta criterion**
2a   Each argument is assigned one and only one theta role.
2b   Each theta role is assigned to one and only one argument.

The theta roles of a predicate are represented in a grid-format. The assignment of thematic roles is registered by means of referential indices which are associated with thematic roles.

Independently of the argument structure of the main predicate, it is a general property of sentences that they must have subjects. This property is stated in the extended projection principle (EPP):

3   **Extended projection principle (EPP)**
    S $\longrightarrow$ NP – AUX – VP

In order to satisfy the EPP, so-called expletives may have to be inserted in the subject position of a sentence. Expletives are pronouns such as *it* and *there* in English which are not assigned a thematic role.

9   Exercises

Exercise 1

We have seen that lexical verbs are specified for the number and types of theta roles they assign: *work* assigns one thematic role (AGENT), *destroy* assigns two (AGENT, THEME) and *give* assigns three (AGENT, THEME, BENEFICIARY). Provide five more examples for each type of verb.

Exercise 2

Discuss the argument structure of the verbs in the following sentences:

1 Poirot promised Maigret the job last week.
2 Emsworth is walking the dogs.
3 That Poirot had left disappointed the crowd immensely.
4 The huge pig frightened the spectators.
5 I have received the books this morning.

Exercise 3

The following examples illustrate how arguments of predicates can be realized in different ways. Discuss the syntactic realization of the arguments in the examples.

1a I prefer very much that the students should leave first.
1b I prefer very much for the students to leave first.
1c I prefer the students out of the way.
1d I prefer the students to leave first.

2a I want hot chocolate.
2b I want my coffee to be piping hot.
2c I want my coffee piping hot.
2d I want the students out of my office.

Exercise 4

Sentences 1–10 below are all grammatical. On the basis of the examples establish the theta grid for the main verb of each sentence:

1 Mary is eating an apple.
2 John is washing the dishes.
3 The baby is drinking a glass of whisky.
4 John has never met Mary.
5 The President is kissing his wife.
6 The professor is writing a book on syntax.

7 The new secretary pleases all the students.
8 This analysis leads us to an unexpected conclusion.
9 Poirot smokes cigars.
10 Louise is expecting a visitor.

It is not necessary to give the label for each role identified; the number of arguments is the most important property to establish.

Now consider the following examples. They are also all grammatical. What problems do they raise for your treatment of the examples 1–10?

11 The children are eating.
12 Mary is washing.
13 John drinks.
14 These two students have never met.
15 The professor and his wife were kissing.
16 My father writes.
17 The students are easy to please.
18 This analysis led to quite unexpected conclusions.
19 Poirot is smoking.
20 Louise is expecting.

Exercise 5

From sentences 11–20 in exercise 4 we conclude that certain thematic roles can be implicit. In (a) below, for instance, *eat* has an understood object, which would correspond to the explicit object in (b):

a The children are eating.
b The children are eating lunch.

This is not a general property of transitive verbs, though:

c The children are devouring their food.
d *The children are devouring.

Consider the following paired examples. Again in variant (a) there seems to be one more argument present than in variant (b). Try to characterize the semantic relation between the two sentences. You are not asked to give a very technical discussion, but simply to provide a description of the difference and/or similarity between the examples:

1a Mary is cooking dinner.
1b Dinner is cooking.
2a Maigret opened the door.
2b The door opened.
3a Poirot does not grow artichokes.
3b The artichokes are not growing.
4a Maigret has arrested the criminal.
4b The criminal has been arrested.
5a Mary is eating too much cake.
5b Mary is overeating.
6a Poirot was smelling the envelope.
6b Your feet smell.
7a Maigret is washing his shirts.
7b These shirts wash well.
8a They are already closing down the new cinema.
8b The new cinema is already closing down.
9a Poirot is reading the announcement.
9b Poirot is reading.
10a The guard marched the prisoners round the square.
10b The prisoners marched round the square.

Provide a classification of the examples above according to the variation in their thematic structure.

Exercise 6

It is generally accepted that morphological processes may affect thematic structure.[27] Consider the following examples:

1a I understand his position.
1b His position is understandable.
2a This shirt is too wide.
2b He has widened the shirt.
3a They arrest the criminal.

---

[27] Williams (1981) contains an important discussion about the interaction of morphology and thematic structure.

3b The criminal has been arrested.
4a Their activities are not regular.
4b They are regularizing the activities.
5a He read the book.
5b He reread the book.

Discuss the impact, if any, of the affixation of *-able, -en,-ed, -ize*, and *re-* on the thematic structure of the stems to which they attach. For each affix, provide five more examples of the affixation process and check whether your conclusion holds.

Exercise 7

The following text belongs to the **register** of instructional writing: it is a recipe. Consider the thematic structure of the verbs in the text and try to identify which syntactic properties characterize this register:

> Beat two eggs and leave for three minutes. Add milk and mix thoroughly. Cover with grated chocolate. Bake in a moderate oven for 20 minutes. Serve immediately.

The sentences below are other examples of the register of instructional writing. Do they pattern like those in the preceding text?

1 Cross now.
2 Shake well before using.
3 Open here.
4 Push.

As you can see it is typical of the register of instructional writing that complements of verbs can be left implicit. Consider the interpretation of the implicit objects in the preceding examples. Discuss what enables people using this register to leave the objects of verbs implicit and how the reader can interpret these sentences correctly.[28]

---

[28] For discussion see Haegeman (1987) and Massam and Roberge (1989). Both articles will be accessible after reading chapter 8.

Exercise 8

Discuss the assignment of thematic roles and the problems, if any, raised for the theta criterion by the following examples:

1   John, I really don't like him.
2   Which detective will Lord Emsworth invite?
3   Which book do you think Poirot will read first?
4   Which assistant do you think will reveal the secrets?
5   The new assistant appears to have revealed the secrets.
6   Which articles did Poirot file without reading?
7   *Italian*
      Ho   visto Maria.
      have (1sg, pres) seen Maria
      'I have seen Maria.'
8   *Spanish*
      Lo   vimos   a Juan.
      him see (1pl, pres) to Juan
      'We see Juan.'
9   *French*
      Quel livre a-t-il   acheté?
      which book has-he bought
10 Quel livre Poirot a-t-il   acheté?
      which book Poirot   has-he bought
      'Which book has Poirot bought?'

Exercise 9

Although it is not always possible to define the nature of the thematic roles assigned by the verbs, the role of AGENT is one that is fairly well understood. In (1) below, for instance, the subject NP *Poirot* is assigned the AGENT role and in its passive variant (2) AGENT is assigned to an NP inside a PP introduced by *by*:

1   Poirot bought the pigs.
2   The pigs were bought by Poirot.

There are certain adjuncts which seem to require the presence of an AGENT in the sentence:

3 Poirot bought the pigs deliberately.
4 Poirot bought the pigs to annoy his mother.
5 *Poirot liked England deliberately.
6 *Poirot liked England in order to annoy his mother.

Adjuncts such as *deliberately* and *in order to annoy his mother* cannot modify predicates such as *like*. This is because these adjuncts imply intentionality, a notion which is not easily compatible with involuntary activities or states such as 'liking'. Consider the following examples: what conclusions can you draw with respect to the thematic structure of the predicates in the sentences?[29]

1a The enemy sank the ship deliberately.
1b The ship was sunk by the enemy deliberately.
1c The ship was sunk deliberately.
1d The ship sank.
1e *The ship sank deliberately.

2a We sold the books to raise money.
2b These books will be sold by the schools to raise money.
2c These books will be sold to raise money.
2d These books sell well.
2e *These books sell well to raise money.

We discuss passive sentences in chapter 3 and especially in chapter 6.

Exercise 10

In the text we suggest that there are only subject expletives and that there are no object expletives. Do you think that the examples in (1) and (2) provide counterevidence for this claim?

1 I consider it likely that Louisa will not leave.
2 I thought it stupid that she should have gone out in the rain.

---

[29] For discussion see Hale and Keyser (1986, 1987) and Roberts (1987). These texts presuppose the contents of chapter 6.

Now consider the following Italian sentence.

3a   Ritengo probabile che Maria rimanga.
     I consider likely that Maria stay (subj)
3b   (*Ciò) è strano che Maria sia venuta.
     it is strange that Maria be (subj) come
     'It is strange that Maria should have come.'

If we assume that in (1) and in (2) *it* is the subject expletive of a small clause (cf. section 5.1) then we deduce that such expletive subjects are unavailable in Italian small clauses. We might then be tempted to conclude that the absence of an expletive subject in (3a) is another effect of the *pro*-drop parameter discussed in the Introduction (section 4). Recall that Italian does not have expletive subjects in finite clauses (3b). On the basis of the following French example, discuss whether the unavailability of an expletive in (3a) should be made to follow directly from the *pro*-drop parameter:

4a   Je trouve bizarre qu'elle soit là.
     I find strange that she be there
     'I find it strange that she is there.'
4b   *Est étrange qu'elle soit là.
     is strange that she be there

We return to the structure of small clauses in chapter 2, section 3.5.

2 Phrase Structure

Contents

Introduction and overview

Introduction and Overview

In chapter 1 we established that the lexical properties of words, the ultimate constituents of the sentence, determine to a large extent the composition and the structure of the sentence. In this chapter we shall be looking more closely at the structural properties of syntactic representations.

We discuss a theory of phrase structure, X'-theory ('X-bar theory'), which aims at bringing out the common properties of the different types of syntactic constituents such as NP, VP, etc. The theory applies both to phrasal constituents and to clausal constituents.

In section 1 we give an overview of the basic notions of phrase structure which we have been assuming so far. In section 2 we develop X'-theory on the basis of phrasal categories VP, NP, AP, PP. In section 3 we extend the application of X'-theory to the clausal constituents S and S'. In section 4 we deal with the structural relation c-command and define the notion government in terms of c-command. In section 5 we introduce the binary branching hypothesis and its relevance for acquisition. In section 6 we discuss the idea that syntactic features rather than lexical categories are the syntactic primitives.

1 Syntactic Structure: Recapitulation

Consider (1a) with its tree diagram representation (1b):

1a Poirot will abandon the investigation.

1b

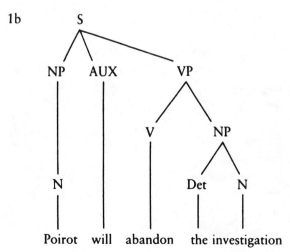

In (1a) the presence of the NPs *Poirot* and *the investigation* is required by the argument structure of the predicate *abandon*:

2   *abandon*: V

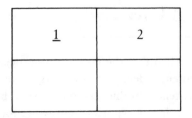

The presence of the subject NP is also required by the extended projection principle (chapter 1 (80)) which requires that sentences have subjects.

The syntactic categories of phrasal constituents such as VP, NP, etc., are also lexically determined: the VP is a constituent whose **head** is a V or which is **headed by** a V, NP is headed by an N, a PP is headed by a P and an AP is headed by an A. The different types of phrases are illustrated by means of rewrite rules in (3), where the head of the phrase is italicized. For each phrasal category we provide a tentative phrase structure rule. The asterisk to the right of a constituent indicates that one or more such constituents are possible, parenthesized constituents are not always present. Obviously, the presence of a constituent may be required because of the argument structure of the head, as discussed in chapter 1.

3a   VP ⟶ V – (NP) – (PP*)
    abandon the investigation after lunch
    work in the garden
    leave his house
    return
3b   NP ⟶ (Det) – (AP*) – N – (PP*)
    Poirot
    the *investigation*
    the Belgian *detective*
    the *detective* with the funny accent
3c   AP ⟶ (Adv) – A – (PP*)
    interested
    very *interested*
    conscious of the problem
    entirely *aware* of the circumstances
3d   PP ⟶ (Adv) – P – NP
    in France

immediately *after* the investigation
on the Orient Express

When talking about tree diagrams it is useful to have a number of technical terms available to describe the relations between the elements in a tree. We shall briefly recapitulate the basic technical terminology which will be used throughout the book to describe structural relations.

First we can think of the vertical relations between the elements in a tree. We use the term **dominance** to characterize such relations.

4   Dominance

Node A dominates node B if and only if A is higher up in the tree than B and if you can trace a line from A to B going only downwards.

In (1b) S dominates the NP *Poirot*, AUX, the VP, and indeed all other material inside the sentence. VP dominates the NP *the investigation*, but it does not dominate the NP *Poirot*, since it is not possible to trace a line from VP to the NP *Poirot* going only downwards.

It is sometimes useful to distinguish a more specific type of dominance. Consider the relationship between S and AUX, for example. S dominates AUX, and moreover, there is no intervening node between S and AUX: this is called **immediate dominance**. S also dominates the NP *the investigation* but it does not immediately dominate this NP.

We can also look at the tree diagram from a horizontal perspective and describe the left–right ordering of constituents in terms of **precedence**.

5   Precedence

Node A precedes node B if and only if A is to the left of B and neither A dominates B nor B dominates A.

In (1b) AUX, for instance, precedes VP. VP does not precede AUX, since VP is to the right of AUX. Also, even though S is to the left to VP in our tree diagram, S does not precede VP because it dominates it.

Again we can distinguish precedence from **immediate precedence**: if a node A precedes a node B and there is no intervening node, then A immediately precedes B. AUX immediately precedes VP, the NP *Poirot* precedes the VP, but does not immediately precede it.[1]

---

[1]   It has been proposed that all relations in tree diagrams must be able to be described in terms of dominance and precedence. For some formal discussion, see Lasnik and Kupin (1977). Alternative proposals are found in Goodall (1987), Haegeman and van Riemsdijk (1986) and Zubizarreta (1985). These works are very advanced. Kayne (1993) proposes a restrictive theory of phrase structure.

In (1b) the NP node dominating *Poirot* is **non-branching**: there is only one line which starts at NP and goes downwards (in our example to N). The node S is **branching**, three lines originate from S and go downwards to NP, AUX and VP respectively. We return to a discussion of branching nodes in section 5.

Let us now focus on the structure of VP. VP immediately dominates V and NP. If we compare the tree diagram representation of syntactic structure with genealogical trees, then it is as if both V and NP are children of the same parent. Linguists refer to this relationship as one of **sisterhood**: V and the object NP are **sisters**. Similarly, we can say that VP is the **mother** of the NP *the investigation*.

The verb *abandon* has a close connection with its object, witness the fact that the object cannot be omitted. In languages with rich case systems the choice of verb may sometimes determine the morphological case of the following NP. In German, for instance, *helfen* ('help') takes a DATIVE complement while *sehen* ('see') takes an ACCUSATIVE:[2]

6a Ich helfe dem Mann.
     I help the-DATIVE man
6b Ich sehe den Mann.
     I see the-ACCUSATIVE man

Using terminology from traditional grammar we shall say that the verb **governs** the object, and more generally that the head of a phrase governs the complement. The element which governs is called the **governor**; the element that is governed is called the **governee**.

At this point we shall not try to give a very precise definition: government by a head is based on sisterhood.[3]

7 **Government** (i)
   A governs B if
   (i)   A is a governor;
   (ii) A and B are sisters.
   Governors are heads.

In (1b) *abandon*, the governor, is the head of the VP and the direct object, the governee, is its sister. V does not govern the subject NP *Poirot*: V is not

---

[2] We discuss the notion of case in chapter 3.
[3] Throughout the book we shall offer more and more refined definitions of government. In addition to government by a head, as discussed here, we shall also introduce government by a phrase in chapter 8.

a sister of the NP. If X is a head and it governs Y then X **head-governs** Y.[4]
All the constituents governed by a node constitute the **governing domain** of
that node. In our example VP is the governing domain of V.

In our discussion of external and internal arguments in chapter 1 (section
7.2), the question might have been raised why arguments of a verb should be
realized inside the VP. One possible answer is that the verb can only assign
an internal theta role to NPs or clauses that it governs. Hence an NP attached
somewhere outside the governing domain of the verb would not be able to
receive an internal theta role from the V.[5] When a V governs an element and
assigns an internal theta role to it we say that it **theta-governs** this element.
In (1b) the V *abandon* **theta-governs** the object *the investigation* though not
the subject *Poirot*.

2   The Structure of Phrases

In this section we examine the structure of the phrases, VP, NP, AP and PP.
Our aim is to discover the common properties of these four phrase types. On
the basis of our analysis we shall be able to replace the four phrase structure
rules in (3) by one simplified and general rule. We start the discussion with
the VP and then extend it to NP, AP and PP.

2.1   The Verb Phrase

2.1.1   LAYERED VPs

So far we have discussed phrases in terms of two components: the head, a
lexical category, and the projection, a phrasal category. Phrasal categories are
headed by lexical categories. Schematically, VPs, for example, are constituents with the following structure:

8a   VP

V   . . .

8b   VP $\longrightarrow$ V – . . .

[4]   We refine the notion government in section 4 below and in subsequent chapters.
[5]   The assignment of theta roles will turn out to be more complex than is suggested
in this section. The reader is referred to chapter 6.

where ... stands for non-head material in the VP, obligatory or optional. Consider (9):

9 Miss Marple will [$_{VP}$ read the letters in the garden shed this afternoon].

Along the lines of the representation in (3a) sentence (9) will be represented as in (10):

10

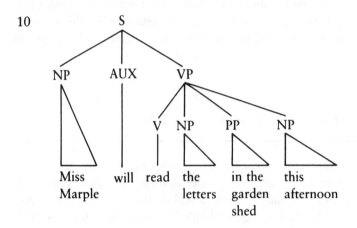

The structure of the VP in (10) is **flat**: there is no internal hierarchy between the constituents of V: all VP-internal constituents are treated as being on an equal footing. Such a flat structure might not be the best representation of the VP, however. Consider, for instance, the following examples, which are all intuitively felt to be related to (9):

11a Miss Marple will read the letters in the garden shed this afternoon and Hercule Poirot will do so too.

11b Miss Marple will read the letters in the garden shed this afternoon and Hercule Poirot will do so tonight.

11c Miss Marple will read the letters in the garden shed this afternoon and Hercule Poirot will do so in the garage tonight.

In (11), *do so* in the second conjunct substitutes for some part of the first conjunct. In (11a) *do so* substitutes for the entire VP *read the letters in the garden shed this afternoon*. In chapter 1 we have adopted the idea that substitution is structure-based: only constituents can be substituted for by an element. From this point of view, the representation in (10) is unproblematic: *do so* replaces the entire VP, a constituent.

In (11b) *do so* substitutes for only part of the VP: *read the letters in the garden shed*, and in (11c) it picks up an even smaller part of the VP: *read the letters*. If we maintain the hypothesis that substitution is structure-based, then it will be hard to reconcile the data in (11b) and (11c) with the representation in (10). On the basis of (10) substitutions affecting VP could be expected to affect either the top node VP, i.e. the entire VP (as in (11a)), or each of the VP-internal constituents, that is to say V or NP or PP. But the structure does not represent the strings *read the letters in the garden shed* or *read the letters* as constituents. There is no node which exhaustively dominates *read the letters*, for example. In order to maintain our hypothesis that substitution affects constituents only we need to redesign the tree diagram in (10) and elaborate the structure of its VP:

12

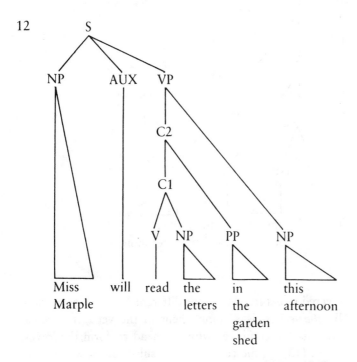

The VP in (12) has more internal structure than that in (10): it is hierarchically organized. The string *read the letters* is represented as a constituent, provisionally labelled C1, and can serve as a unit to be substituted for by *do so*. The same holds for *read the letters in the garden shed*, labelled C2. Unlike (10), (12) is compatible with the substitution data in (11).

We may wonder about the category of C1 and C2 in (12). Following our informal analysis above, we are tempted to say that, being headed by a V (*read*), they are projections of V, i.e. a type of VP. But on the other hand, they do not constitute the full VP or the **maximal VP** of the sentence. The projections of V, C1 and C2 are themselves dominated by verbal projections. C2 is dominated by VP and C1 is dominated by C2 and by VP. Projections of V that are dominated by more comprehensive projections of V are called **intermediate projections** of V. The highest projection of V, the node labelled VP in our diagram, is the **maximal projection**. The maximal projection is not normally dominated by a projection of the same category.[6] The intermediate projections of V, are labelled **V-bar**, or **V′**.

13

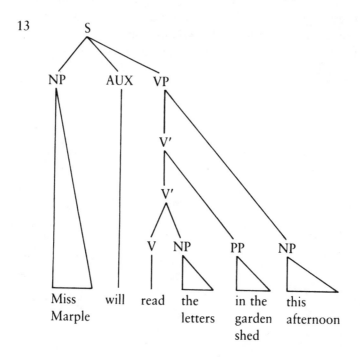

In (13) VP has a **layered** structure. There are different levels of projection. The direct object NP, *the letters*, is a complement of the verb, it is theta-governed by the verb. This NP combines with the head to form the lowest V′, the first projection in (13). In the case of *do so* substitution we see that the minimal unit affected by substitution is the first projection of the type V′. *Do so* cannot simply replace V without the direct object:

---

[6] We return to the notion of maximal projection in chapters 7, 9, 10, and 11.

14   *Miss Marple will read the letters in the garden shed this afternoon and
     Hercule Poirot will do so the diaries in the garage after dinner.

In (13) the verb projections that dominate the lowest V' are also labelled
V'. The PP *in the garden shed* and the NP *this afternoon* are adjuncts; they
combine with a V' to form another V'. Adjuncts are optional constituents and
they can be repeated: the level V' is **recursive**. The node labelled VP in (13)
is in fact another V': it dominates V' and an adjunct. (13) suggests that the
maximal projection of V is thus the highest V' which is not dominated by
another V-projection. This, however, turns out to be inadequate. Consider
(15):

15a   The detectives have all read the letters in the garden shed after lunch.
15b   All the detectives have read the letters in the garden shed after lunch.
15c   They have?
15d   *They have all?
15e   The policemen have all done so too.

In (15a) the VP is similar to that of our earlier examples, but it is preceded
by the quantifier *all*. *All* relates to the subject NP *the detectives*: (15a) is closely
related to (15b). (15c) is an example where the VP of the sentence is deleted.
Interestingly, VP-deletion affects *all*, and *all* cannot be stranded, witness
the ungrammaticality of (15d). We conclude that *all* is part of the VP. On
the other hand, in (15e) *do so* substitutes for the string *read the letters in the
garden shed this afternoon*, a V'. This means that *all* must be structurally
independent from this V'. *All*, the quantifier, is not an adjunct of time or
place like the post-verbal PPs. It is not recursive, there can only be one
quantifier to the left of V. In order to distinguish VP-adjuncts, which combine
with V' to form V', from the quantifier which combines with the highest V'
to form the full VP, we identify the position occupied by the quantifier *all* as
the specifier position. The specifier dominated by VP is represented as [Spec,
VP].[7] [Spec, VP] combines with V' to form the highest V-projection, VP.

---

[7]   The analysis of *all* as occupying the VP specifier position is based on work by
      Sportiche (1988a). Sportiche's account introduces further modifications of phrase
      structure which we shall discuss in chapter 6 (section 5).

16

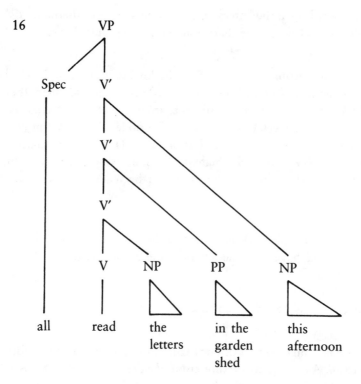

Schematically, English VPs are formed according to the following format:

17a

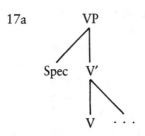

17b   VP ⟶ Spec – V'
      V' ⟶ V' – . . .
      V' ⟶ V – . . .

A complement combines with V to form a V'. An adjunct combines with a V' to form a higher V'. A V-projection may hence contain several V'-nodes. The specifier combines with V' to form VP. VP is the maximal projection of V.

Let us consider some further examples of VP structures. We must point out that often there may be no overt specifier in the VP of a given sentence, as seen in our earlier examples, or the VP may contain no adjuncts or no complements. We shall assume that the three levels, V, V' and VP are available for *any* VP in English, even if there is no overt material to attach to the different levels; the structure in (17) applies to every VP.[8]

Let us first return to example (9), which lacks the pre-verbal specifier. The representation (13) will be revised as in (18): there is no pre-verbal specifier; VP is non-branching.[9]

18

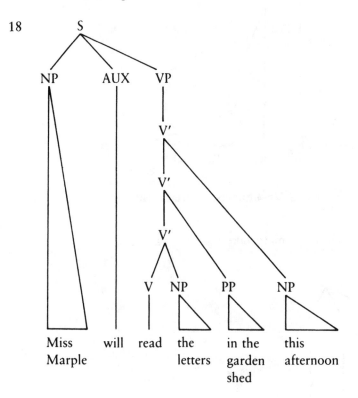

In (19a), there is again no specifier and also there is no direct object NP, *sleep* being intransitive. The lowest V' is non-branching. *After lunch* is an adjunct, which combines with the lowest V' to form another V'. VP is also non-branching. The representation of (19a) will be as in (19b):

---

[8] For some discussion of this problem the reader is referred to Chomsky (1986b: 2–4).

[9] Another option would be to say that [Spec, VP] dominates a node which is non-overt. This option will follow from our discussion of VP in chapter 6, section 5.

19a   Miss Marple will sleep after lunch.

19b

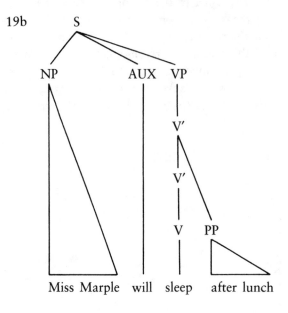

(20a) lacks a specifier and VP-adjuncts, we represent its structure in (20b):

20a   Poirot will clean his motorbike.

20b

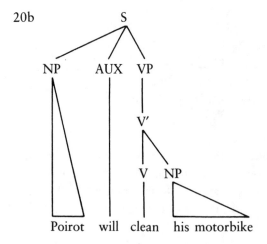

Finally, it is also possible that a VP simply dominates a verb and that there are no specifiers, adjuncts or complements. This is illustrated in (21a) with the representation in (21b):

21a Miss Marple will return.

21b

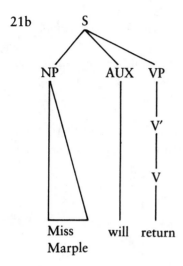

In chapter 6 we return to the internal structure of VP and we suggest an important modification.

2.1.2 PARAMETRIC VARIATION AND WORD-ORDER

The projection schema for VPs developed so far is based solely on English examples; it is too rigid to apply universally. We have already seen that the word-order in Japanese differs considerably from that in English, for instance. Consider the following examples:

22a John-ga   Mary-o   but-ta.
     NOMINATIVE   ACCUSATIVE   past
       particle   particle
     John   Mary   hit
     'John hit Mary.'
22b John-ga   Mary-ni   hon-o   yat-ta.
       NOM   DATIVE   ACC   past
     John   Mary   book   give
     'John gave Mary a book.'
22c John-ga Mary to kuruma de   Kobe-ni it-ta
     John   Mary with car   by   Kobe to go-past
     'John went to Kobe by car with Mary.'
     (from Kuno, 1973: 3, 5)

Japanese is an SOV language: the verb follows the complement and the adjuncts (Kuno, 1973: 3). Clearly, if (17) is part of UG we need to account for the ordering variation between SVO languages like English and SOV languages like Japanese. As it stands, (17) only generates verb–complement orders.

As already suggested in the Introduction to this book, one way of accounting for the different surface word-orders is to relax (17) and adopt the schema in (23). The format for phrase structure in (23) leaves the relative order of V and its complements open. The rewrite rule V′ → V; XP for instance, can then be instantiated as either V′ → V – XP or as V′ → XP – V. The semicolon separating the constituents serves to indicate that their linear order is not fixed.

23a

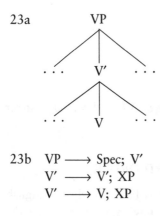

23b   VP ⟶ Spec; V′
       V′ ⟶ V′; XP
       V′ ⟶ V; XP

In (23a) the ellipses dominated by VP stand for the potential specifier, those dominated by V′ for adjuncts or for complements. In (23b) Spec stands for the specifier, XP stands for adjuncts or complements. Under this view UG determines hierarchical relations between constituents. Phrase structure rules do not determine linear ordering: *V′ → V; XP* can result in both *XP – V* and *V – XP* orders. The word-order differences between say English and Japanese remain then to be accounted for. One option is to say that in fact the word-order variation is an instance of parametric variation, it is determined by the fixing of a parameter of UG. This means that UG makes both the orders OV and VO available and the child has to set the word-order parameter for his language.

Recall that we pointed out in the Introduction, section 4, that we need not postulate one parameter to account for every observed difference between languages. For instance, the fact that the subject NP can appear post-verbally in Italian is said to follow from the *pro*-drop parameter. It could be proposed that the parameter 'P' which determines the word-order variation between

SOV languages and SVO languages, is not directly associated with linear order of constituents as such but relates to another component of the grammar. Word-order variation would then be one of the properties determined by the relevant parameter P. One might, for instance, argue that in SVO languages verbs assign their theta roles to the right, and that in SOV languages verbs assign their theta roles to the left. Under this assumption the OV order in English would be ungrammatical not because of a word-order parameter as such, but rather because the verb would not be able to theta-mark the complement to its left, hence this would result in a violation of the theta criterion: on the one hand, the verb would not be able to assign all its theta roles, and on the other hand, the object which precedes the verb would not receive a theta role.

Recently a more radical alternative has been proposed (Kayne, 1993; Zwart, 1993). Kayne (1993) proposes that the phrase structure rules of UG only determine the ordering V–complement (and also specifier–verb), i.e. he proposes that UG does contain (17) above rather than (23). In this proposal divergent orders, where O precedes V, would then be derived by a leftward movement of the object across the verb. Under this view the relevant parameter distinguishing VO languages from OV languages is related to the application of the leftward movement rule. In the remainder of the book we will stick to the more conservative position which assumes that UG only specifies hierarchical relations between V and its complements and that the linear ordering derives from a parametric setting. However, Kayne's proposal that phrase structure rules are rigidly of the format given in (17) is giving rise to important research into the nature of SOV languages (Zwart 1993).

2.1.3 EXTENDING THE PROPOSAL

One question that immediately comes to mind is whether the hierarchical structure of VP proposed in section 2.1 can be extended to the other phrasal categories. If this were possible, we might be able to replace the four phrase structure rules in (3) by a single schema. Clearly, for reasons of economy, a theory which has one generalized schema for phrasal categories of various types is to be preferred to one in which distinct phrases are constructed on the basis of different schemata. If we are able to develop one general format, this will mean that we have brought out the common properties between the phrases, a generalization which is lost if we adopt four unrelated phrase structure rules.

In the following sections we turn to the other lexical categories. In section 2.2 we discuss noun phrases, in section 2.3 adjective phrases and in section 2.4 prepositional phrases. We shall see that the projection schema developed for VP can be applied to all the categories examined.

2.2 *Noun Phrases*

Consider (24a):

24a   the investigation of the corpse after lunch

Tentatively we might draw a flat structure for (24a) along the lines suggested
by phrase structure rule (3b):

24b

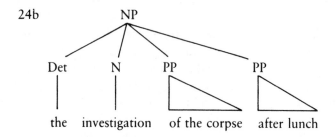

But (24b) is observationally inadequate since it fails to throw light on the
one-substitution data in (25).

25   The investigation of the corpse after lunch was less horrible than the one
     after dinner.

In (25) *one* substitutes for the string *investigation of the corpse* but this string
is not a constituent in the representation (24b): it is not exhaustively dominated by one node. A closer look at the data argues for a layered structure
of NP by analogy with that of VP. On the one hand, *one* in (25) substitutes
for the string *investigation of the corpse*, strongly suggesting that this string
should be exhaustively dominated by one node in the syntactic representation. On the other hand, we can compare the NP (24a) with the VP of (26):

26   The police will [_VP_ investigate the corpse after lunch].

It is attractive to argue that the relationship between the N *investigation* and
the PP *of the corpse* in (24a) is like that between the verb *investigate* and its
object NP *the corpse* in (26). Both the V *investigate* and the N *investigation*
have a thematic relation with the NP *the corpse*. We return to the role of *of*

in chapter 3. If the relation between the V *investigate* and its complement NP *the corpse* is intuitively felt to be like that between the N *investigation* and the NP *the corpse*, then we would miss a generalization if we were to treat the NP structure as unrelated to the VP structure. One way of integrating NPs in the format established so far is to propose the following structure for the NP (24a):[10]

27

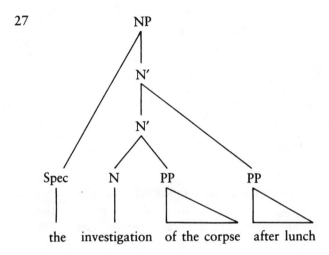

The lowest N′ projection dominates N, the head of the phrase and its complement.[11] An adjunct combines with N′ to form another N′. Adjuncts are typically PPs as in (24a) or relative clauses, as in (28) below.[12] The specifier of NP, a determiner, combines with the topmost N′ to form the maximal projection, NP.

---

[10] In recent work it has been proposed that the head of NP is not N but rather the determiner. NP is reinterpreted as DP. This analysis has come to be known as the DP-hypothesis. The reader is referred to Abney (1987) and to chapter 11 for motivation. Abney's work should only be tackled after this book has been worked through.

[11] As mentioned before, the reason why complements of N must be realized as PP will be discussed in chapter 3.

[12] We address the structure of relative clauses in chapters 7 and 8.

28a   a book [that I wrote]

28b

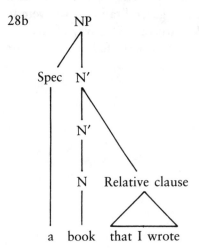

Like VPs, NPs may lack overt specifiers, complements or adjuncts, but we still generate the three levels of projection. In (29a), for instance, there is neither a complement nor an adjunct. In the syntactic representation (29b) N' is non-branching.

29a   this book

29b

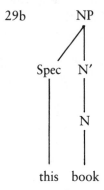

In English, the head noun precedes its complement and adjuncts, but again this is not a universal property.[13] To give but one example: in Japanese, relative clauses precede the head N:

30a *English*:
a book [that I wrote]
30b *Japanese*:
[watakusi ga kaita] hon
I wrote   book
(Kuno, 1973: 234)

Demonstrative pronouns, i.e. specifiers, also precede the head N in Japanese:

31   kono hon
this book
(Kuno, 1973: 235)

In order to allow for cross-linguistic variation in word-order we could adopt a very general phrase structure schema along the lines of (23b) for VP, which does not impose a linear order on the constituents of the phrase:

32   NP $\longrightarrow$ Spec; N'
N' $\longrightarrow$ N'; XP
N' $\longrightarrow$ N; XP

For each of the phrase structure rules the order is fixed according to the language in question (cf. section 1.2.1).

[13]   Indeed in English too the complement NP may appear before the head noun:

(i)   the painting of Saskia
(ii)   Saskia's painting

We can compare the relation between (i) and (ii) to that between an active sentence (iii) and its passive parallel (iv):

(iii)   Rembrandt painted Saskia.
(iv)   Saskia was painted by Rembrandt.

We discuss passivization in chapters 3 and 6.

2.3   Adjective Phrases

Looking at APs it seems entirely reasonable to extend the layered analysis of VP and NP above and to distinguish different levels of projection:

33a   Jeeves is [$_{AP}$ rather envious of Poirot].

33b

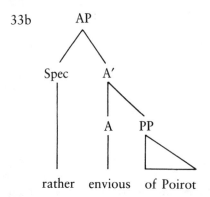

Like the verb *envy*, the adjective *envious* is a two-place predicate. In (33a) the subject NP *Jeeves* realizes one argument, the PP *of Poirot* contains the second argument. We discuss the role of the preposition *of* in chapter 3. The projection A′ dominates the lexical head *envious* and its complement.

As was the case for VP, the order of the AP constituents varies cross-linguistically: adjectives may precede their complements as in English, or they may follow them, as in German:[14]

34a   Er ist   des   Französischen   mächtig.
       he is   the   French (GEN)   able
       'He has a command of French.'
34b   Er ist   seinen   Grundsätzen   treu.
       he is   his   principles (DAT) faithful
       'He is faithful to his principles.'

---

[14]   For a discussion of the GENITIVE the reader is referred to chapter 3, specifically section 3.2.1.2.

For word-order variation in the AP see also section 2.1.2 above.

2.4 *Prepositional Phrases*

PPs too can be assimilated to the schema proposed so far. Prepositions usually require an NP complement:

35a across [$_{NP}$ the bridge]
    with [$_{NP}$ a knife]
35b right across [$_{NP}$ the bridge]

   Using the pattern adopted for VP, NP and AP as a model, we can propose the following structure:

36

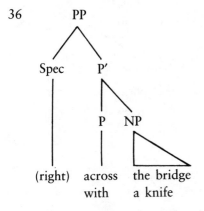

   Again the ordering of P and the complement is not universally fixed. In Japanese, elements corresponding to English prepositions follow their complements and are referred to as postpositions (see (22c); cf. section 2.1.2). Let us use the label P to indicate both pre- and postpositions.

2.5 *X-bar Theory*

From the discussion above it appears that for all lexical categories (N, V, P, A) the format of phrasal projection can be represented by means of the layered representation. (37) summarizes the discussion:

37a   VP   37b   PP

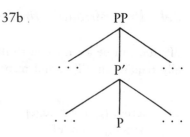

... V' ...   ... P' ...

... V ...   ... P ...

37c   AP   37d   NP

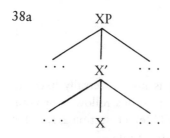   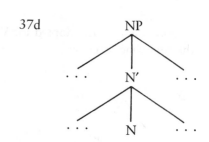

... A' ...   ... N' ...

... A ...   ... N ...

This means that we no longer need four different phrase structure rules, as suggested in (3). Abstracting away from the category of the head we arrive at the following schema:

38a   XP

... X' ...

... X ...

where X stands for N, V, A or P. Our grammar need not contain four schemata, but only one. The general format for phrase structure is summarized in the following PS-rules:

39a XP ⟶ Spec; X'
39b X'* ⟶ X'; YP
39c X' ⟶ X; YP

The part of the grammar regulating the structure of phrases has come to be known as X'-theory ('X-bar theory').[15] X-bar theory brings out what is

[15] The theory has developed as a result of proposals by Chomsky (1970).

common in the structure of phrases. According to X-bar theory, all phrases are headed by one head. In the terminology of traditional linguistics we say that all phrases are **endocentric**. The head of the projection is a **zero projection** (X^0). Heads are terminal nodes: they dominate words. X′ theory distinguishes two further levels of projection. Complements combine with X to form X′-projections (39c); adjuncts combine with X′ to form X′ projections (39b). The specifier combines with the topmost X′ to form the maximal projection XP (39a).[16]

While it is assumed that the layered projection schema in (39) is universal, we have already seen that the linear order of constituents with respect to the head of the projection is not universally fixed. One proposal has been that some other principle of the grammar accounts for the various constituent orders.[17] The specific phrase structure of one language, say English, can be derived from the interaction between the general schema in (39) and the, as yet to be specified, principle which fixes the relative order of head, complements, adjuncts and specifiers. Language-specific phrase structure rules need not be stated separately since they follow from other, more general, principles.

For English, for instance, phrases will have the structure in (38b):

38b

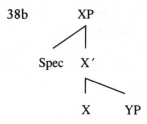

As mentioned in section 2.1.2, it is also conceivable that UG fixes the base order as in (38b) and that divergent orders are generated by additional movement. Complement-head patterns would then be the result of moving YP to the left across the head.

[16] For an early discussion of the theory and its application to English, cf. Jackendoff (1977). Many of Jackendoff's proposals have been subject to major revisions. For a survey of the origins and development of X′-theory the reader is referred to Borsley (1991) and Stuurman (1985). Further important modifications are to be found in Grimshaw (1991), which we discuss in chapter 11. Kayne (1933) argues that the properties of X′-theory can be derived from more elementary notions of the geometry of tree diagrams. Most of these authors should only be tackled after the reader has worked his way through this book.

[17] It is often proposed that there is a correlation between the ordering of the head and its complement and adjuncts in VP, PP, AP, etc. For instance, it is often proposed that languages which have OV order also have postpositions and adjectives that follow their complements. This is by no means a universal property. See Greenberg (1963, 1978) for some discussion.

We see that the head of the projection X is related to two maximal projections: its specifier and its complement (YP in (38b)). The relations between X and its complement on the one hand, and its specifier on the other hand, can all be defined within the maximal projection XP. We say that these relations are **local**. We will see throughout this book that locality plays an important role in the theory.

We have also seen that there are differences between the internal structures of the phrases. For instance, V and P take NP complements, while N and A do not take NP complements. Such differences will be explained by independent mechanisms of the grammar. In chapter 3, for instance, we shall see that case theory explains that nouns and adjectives cannot take NP complements.

As the reader will observe, the result of our discussion is that the construction-specific phrase structure rules in (3) are broken down into several separate general principles which capture what is common between the different phrases. If we can treat phrase structure universally in terms of the general projection schema (39), then we may further assume that the child learning a language need not construct this schema as part of its grammar. The principles of X′ theory will be part of UG, they are innate.[18] The ordering constraints found in natural languages vary cross-linguistically and they thus have to be learnt by the child through exposure. Very little data will suffice to allow the child to fix the ordering constraints of the language he is learning. A child learning English will only need to be exposed to a couple of transitive sentences to realize that in English verbs precede their complements.

3 The Structure of Sentences

3.1 Introduction

So far we have achieved quite an interesting general approach to phrase structure: we have developed the hypothesis that all the phrasal categories are

[18] There is a lot of discussion as to whether (39) is indeed universal. It is sometimes argued that certain languages are not subject to the hierarchical organization in (39). Languages which are not subject to the hierarchical organization are called **non-configurational** languages. If we adopt the view that certain languages are not hierarchically organized but are basically 'flat', then we must give up the idea that (39) is universal and we must introduce some parameter to distinguish configurational languages subject to (39) from non-configurational languages.

One example of a language which has been claimed to be non-configurational is Hungarian (see Kiss, 1981) and another is Warlpiri (see Hale, 1983). Maracz and Muysken (1989) contains a series of recent papers on the configurationality issue in various languages.

structured according to the X'-schema (39). Nothing has been said about the larger unit of syntactic analysis, the sentence.

We start our discussion on the basis of the bracketed clause in (40):

40   They will wonder [whether Poirot will abandon the investigation].

In (40) the bracketed string is a constituent composed of sentence (1) of this chapter preceded by the **complementizer** *whether*. Assuming that the string *Poirot will abandon the investigation* is a syntactic unit, a sentence, the bracketing in (40) can be refined to set this sentence off from the complementizer. In earlier versions of generative syntax, the simple sentence *Poirot will abandon the investigation* was labelled S and this S together with the complementizer was labelled S'.[19] Omitting details of the internal structure of VP (hence the triangle), (41a) has the representation in (41b):

41a   They will wonder [$_{S'}$ whether [$_S$ Poirot will abandon the investigation]].

41b

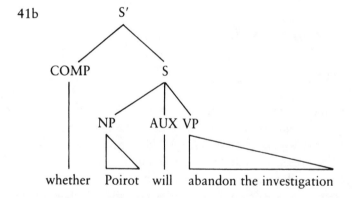

whether   Poirot   will   abandon the investigation

As it stands, this representation is not an instantiation of the X'-schema (39). If S', as the name suggests, is a projection of S, then this is an odd projection. In the X'-schema, phrasal projections project from their heads, units of the type N, V, etc. Heads are typically terminal nodes. In (41) the labelling suggests that S' is a projection of S, a non-terminal node. A similar problem arises with respect to the structure of S. S does not look like a projection of a head either. S has three immediate constituents: two are phrasal themselves (NP and VP) and one is an auxiliary.

One possibility would be to say that S' and S are not endocentric categories

[19]   The PS rule S' ⟶ COMP – S is due to Bresnan (1970). ||

but **exocentric** ones: they are not projections of heads but are composed of several units next to each other. This would mean that our grammar will have to include the projection schema (39) and in addition one or more schemata to account for the structure of S and S'. Such a move implies that there is little or nothing in common between the structure of the phrasal constituents such as NP, VP, etc., and that of clausal constituents. This will also entail that the child learning the language will have to differentiate the two types of structures and apply each to the relevant categories. It would, of course, be more attractive if the structure of clauses could be assimilated to the schema in (39), thus generalizing the X'-schema to all types of constructions. If this were possible, X'-theory would apply both to phrases and to clauses and the child would operate with one schema rather than several.

A closer look at the structure of clauses will allow us to extend the schema in (39) to sentence structure. In section 3.2 we discuss the structure of S. We shall see that it is reasonable to argue that S is headed by the constituent indicated by AUX and relabelled I for INFL and that it is organized along the lines in (39). In section 3.3 we turn to S' for which we shall argue that it is headed by the complementizer, C, and again follows the schema in (39).

3.2   S as a Projection of INFL

3.2.1   AUX AND TENSE

In (41b) S has three immediate constituents: the subject NP (*Poirot*), the VP (*abandon the investigation*) and AUX (*will*). Looking at the X'-format in (39) we can ask ourselves first which of these three could in principle qualify as a head. One possibility presents itself: AUX is a terminal node. This observation might tempt us to adopt the hypothesis that AUX is the head of S.[20] The analysis will extend automatically to sentences containing other modal auxiliaries such as *can, may, must, shall* and to sentences containing the auxiliaries *have* and *be*.

One problem for this proposal arises immediately: if AUX is the head of S, then what do we do with sentences without overt auxiliary such as (42)?

---

[20]   Jackendoff (1977) proposed that S is a projection of V. This proposal was replaced by the proposal developed in this text that the head of S is I. More recently Jackendoff's analysis has been reinterpreted: Grimshaw (1991) proposes that S is indeed a projection of I, but that it is an **extended** projection of V. To put it differently, she proposes that clauses are projections of V extended with the appropriate functional projections. We return to the notion of extended projection in chapter 11.

42 Poirot abandoned the investigation.

At first glance we might adopt the following syntactic representation:

43

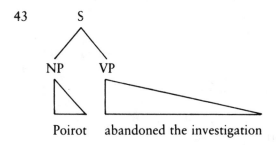

In (43) it would not be at all clear which terminal node is the head of S. It turns out that there are empirical arguments against the representation (43). Consider the examples in (44):

44a Abandon the investigation, Poirot did indeed.
44b What Poirot did was abandon the investigation.

In (44a) the verb *abandon* and its direct object NP *the investigation* have been preposed and the past tense morpheme (here *-ed*) is left behind on an auxiliary (*did*). If we assume that only constituents can move, we must conclude that *abandon the investigation* is a constituent which is relatively independent from the past tense morpheme. Such an interpretation of the structure of the sentence is difficult to reconcile with (43) where tense is an integral part of the VP. The pseudo-cleft construction in (44b) illustrates the same phenomenon: *abandon the investigation* is separated off from its past tense morpheme.

These data suggest strongly that at a more abstract level of representation the inflectional element tense cannot be part of the VP, but must be generated separately from it. In (41) the tense specification of the sentence is separate from VP and it is associated with the AUX node (*will* is the present tense of the auxiliary, *would* is the past tense). AUX in (41b) is the site on which tense is realized.

Let us capitalize on this observation and posit that in all sentences, with or without overt auxiliaries, the tense morpheme is dominated by a separate terminal node from now on label **INFL**, for **inflection**. We return to the label in the section below. In sentences with an auxiliary which is inflected for tense (such as (41)) the tensed auxiliary is dominated by INFL. INFL replaces AUX. In sentences without overt auxiliary we propose that tense is an independent category dominated by INFL. Under this analysis, the relevant part of (41a) will have the structure (45a) and (42) will have the structure (45b):

45a

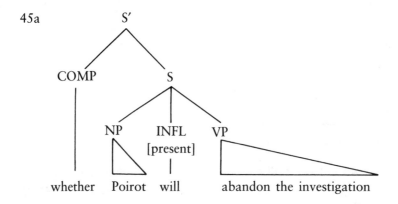

45b

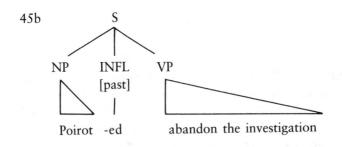

In (45b) INFL is specified for past tense and dominates the *-ed* morpheme.[21] VP is a constituent separate from the past tense. Hence we expect that VP may move independently of the tense ending. Being an affix, the past tense ending cannot be left unattached, it must be attached to the verb. We shall assume that in (45b) the past tense morphology is lowered on to the verb. We return to this issue in chapter 11.

3.2.2 AGREEMENT

We have proposed that there is a separate node INFL. As the label suggests, INFL is a node which is taken to contain all verbal inflection, i.e. including person and number properties.

---

[21] Observe that the past tense morpheme is *-ed* for regular verbs only and that irregular verbs form their past tenses differently (compare *walk–walked*, vs. *eat–ate*, or *think–thought*). The morpheme *-ed* is one realization of the abstract INFL with the feature [+past]. For irregular verbs the combination of this abstract INFL with the relevant verb gives rise to irregular forms.

In English the inflectional properties of verb conjugation are minimal, but other languages have richer paradigms of conjugation. Person and number agreement, which is present in other languages, often does not have any morphological realization in English. Compare the following data from English, French and Italian. For each language we give the conjugation for present and past tense and at the bottom of each column we indicate the total number of distinct forms:

46a *English*

Present tense	*Past tense*
I speak	I spoke
you speak	You spoke
he speaks	he spoke
we speak	we spoke
you speak	you spoke
they speak	they spoke
2 forms	*1 form*

46b *French*

Present tense	*Past tense*
je parle	je parlais
tu parles	tu parlais
il parle	il parlait
nous parlons	nous parlions
vous parlez	vous parliez
ils parlent	ils parlaient
5 forms	*5 forms*[22]

46c *Italian*

Present tense	*Past tense*
io parlo	io parlavo
tu parli	tu parlavi
lui parla	lui parlava
noi parliamo	noi parlavamo
voi parlate	voi parlavate
loro parlano	loro parlavano
6 forms	*6 forms*

[22] In French there are five forms if we take orthography into account. However, for many verbs (such as *parler* in (46b)), first person singular, second person singular and third person verb forms sound the same in many contexts.

The overt agreement properties of English verbs are heavily reduced: regular verbs have in fact only two distinct forms for the present and one form only for the past tense. The verb *be* shows some more overt inflection:

47 *Present tense*   *Past tense*
    I am   I was
    you are   you were
    he is   he was
    we are   we were
    you are   you were
    they are   they were

    3 forms   *2 forms*

Though the overt realization of agreement for person and number is restricted in English, we assume that there is **abstract** agreement, **AGR**, which is often not morphologically realized. The difference between English and French or Italian is not taken to be that English lacks AGR, but rather that the abstract AGR has fewer morphological realizations. It is sometimes said that Italian and French AGR are richer than English AGR. Recall from the Introduction that rich inflectional systems are characteristic of *pro*-drop languages, i.e. languages like Italian and Spanish in which subject pronouns can be omitted. We return to this issue in chapter 8. We propose that INFL dominates the tense feature and the agreement features (AGR) associated with V.[23]

48

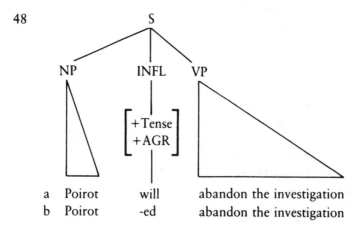

    a   Poirot   will   abandon the investigation
    b   Poirot   -ed   abandon the investigation

[23] Pollock (1989) proposes that INFL should be split up into two components, Tense and AGR, which each head one projection. The reader is referred to chapter 11 for discussion.

3.2.3 INFINITIVAL CLAUSES

In the previous sections we have examined finite or tensed clauses. Let us now turn to infintival clauses.

Tensed clauses are specified as having an INFL containing the features [+Tense] and [+AGR]. Infinitives typically lack tense marking and agreement. They are [–Tense] and [–AGR]. We can represent the subordinate clause in (49a) by the structure in (49b).[24] We assume that *to* in infinitives corresponds to the verb inflection.

49a   I did not expect [Poirot to abandon the investigation].

49b

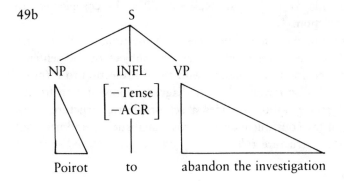

---

[24]   If we analyse the content of INFL in terms of the features (±AGR] and [±Tense] there ought to be four combinations:

[+AGR]
[+Tense]

[+AGR]
[–Tense]

[–AGR]
[+Tense]

[–AGR]
[–Tense]

So far, we have illustrated only the combination [+AGR, +Tense] in finite clauses and [–AGR, –Tense] in infinitivals. Raposo (1987) discusses agreeing infinitivals in Portuguese, a case of [+AGR, –Tense]. Stowell (1982) argues that certain infinitives in English are [–AGR, +Tense]. We refer the reader to the literature for discussion.

3.2.4 THE STRUCTURE OF IP

We have based the distinction between finite and infinitival clauses on the content of the node INFL, the features [±Tense] and [±AGR]. In other words, the type of clause is determined by the type of INFL. We propose that INFL, a category of the zero level (cf. section 2.5), is the head of S. If we assume that S is headed by INFL it follows that S, like other phrasal categories such as VP, is endocentric: it is a projection of **I, IP**.

The next question to ask is whether we can fully assimilate IP to the X'-schema in (39). The category INFL dominates material such as verbal inflection, infinitival *to*, aspectual auxiliaries and modals. Tense endings will end up on V; auxiliaries and infinitival *to* are followed by a verb. Since V heads VP, it seems reasonable to argue that I takes a VP as its complement to constitute the I' projection.

In (39) the specifier of the phrase combines with the topmost X' to form XP. In the case of sentences we propose that the subject of the sentence occupies the specifier position, it combines with the I' projection to form IP. (50a) illustrates this idea by means of a tree diagram representation for the sentences discussed above. (50b) provides a set of phrase structure rules. Again the ordering of the constituents varies cross-linguistically and need not be stated in the phrase structure rules.

50a

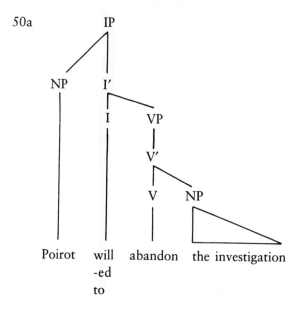

50b   IP ⟶ Spec; I'
     I' ⟶ I; VP

In many approaches to syntax **grammatical functions** such as subject and object play an important role: they are **primitives**, i.e. unanalysed and elementary concepts of the theory, and the syntactic relations are defined in terms of grammatical functions. In the approach to syntax developed here, grammatical functions are not primitive concepts of the theory; they are derivative concepts, defined in configurational terms. The subject is defined as the specifier of IP, [Spec, IP], for instance. The grammatical function subject is defined in terms of phrase structure relations, the more elementary concepts of the theory.

In the theory of syntax developed here we distinguish two types of positions: **A-positions** and **A'-positions** ('A-bar positions'). A-positions are potential theta positions, positions to which a theta role *can* be assigned, i.e. positions such as [Spec, IP], and the NP dominated by V'; [NP, V']. Observe that A-positions are not necessarily assigned a theta role: the subject position may be occupied by an expletive element. Still it counts as an A-position. In more traditional terms we might say that A-positions correspond to the positions which are associated with grammatical functions. A'-positions are often defined negatively: A'-positions are positions which are not A-positions. [Spec, CP] for instance, is standardly considered as an A'-position. Adjuncts are also taken to occupy A'-positions. In chapter 6 we will see that the definition of A-positions as proposed here raises problems. We return to the definition of A-positions and A'-positions in chapter 12.

There is a distinction to be drawn between phrasal projections of lexical categories and a projection of I. N, V and the other lexical heads we have encountered, belong to what are called open classes. Open classes do not only have a large number of members, but new members may be freely added.[25] Closed classes are groups of a restricted number of elements to which new elements cannot be added.

We have proposed that the head of S is INFL. INFL is the terminal node which dominates the inflectional morphology of the verb, affixes and infinitival *to*, which are not independent lexical categories or 'words'. The only lexical elements, 'words', that can be dominated by INFL are the aspectual auxiliaries *have* and *be* and the modals. The latter constitute a closed class composed of the following elements: *will, can, may, shall, must* and possibly *dare, need, used* and *ought*. The aspectual and modal auxiliaries in English often correspond to inflectional affixes in other languages. The English perfect is formed with the auxiliary *have*, but Latin uses an inflection (51a). While English uses the modal *shall* or *will* for expressing futurity, Latin again uses a tense ending (51b):

---

[25] Prepositions constitute a relatively closed class too, but new prepositions or complex prepositions may be added to the language (cf. *because of*, *in spite of*). We shall continue treating prepositions as part of the lexical categories.

51   *English*   *Latin*
51a I have loved   amavi
51b I shall love   amabo

INFL does not dominate open class lexical heads: it is a non-lexical head or a **functional** head. Projections of lexical heads are lexical projections; projections of functional heads are **functional projections**. We discuss the role of functional projections in the grammar in chapter 11.

3.3 S′ as a Projection of C

3.3.1 C AS THE HEAD OF CP

We have now assimilated the structure of S to the X′-format. In this section we extend the format to S′.

Observe that the nature of this unit as a whole, the type of sentence, is determined by the nature of the complementizer:

52a I will ask [**if** [Poirot will abandon his investigation]].
52b I will say [**that** [Poirot will abandon his investigation]].

The subordinate clause in (52a) is interrogative, that in (52b) is declarative. The difference between the two is signalled by the choice of complementizer introducing the clause, *if* vs. *that*. In other words, the complementizer determines the type of clause. This suggests that we treat the complementizer, represented as C, as the head of S′. Complementizers do not constitute an open class: the four complementizers that introduce subordinate clauses in English are *that, if, whether, for*. Analogously to the discussion of I, we say that the projection of C is a projection of a functional head. CP is a **functional projection**.

Complementizers such as *whether, if, that* and *for* introduce a sentence (IP): C selects an IP-complement. The choice of the type of IP is determined by the choice of C. The complementizers *that* and *if* select a finite clause as their complement; *for* selects an infinitival clause and *whether* selects either type of clause:

53a I think [that [Poirot   abandoned the investigation]].
                            *to abandon
53b I expect [for [Poirot   to abandon the investigation]].
                            *abandoned

53c Jane wonders [whether [Poirot abandoned the investigation]].
                          [to abandon the investigation]].

Among embedded clauses, we distinguish interrogative clauses from declarative clauses by virtue of their complementizer. Interrogative clauses are characterized by a complementizer, or C which has the feature [+WH], non-interrogative or declarative clauses are CPs whose head C has the feature [–WH]. Certain verbs, such as *think*, require a non-interrogative clause as their complement, they **select** non-interrogative complement clauses (cf. (53a)); other verbs, like *wonder*, select interrogative clauses (cf. (53b)). If we assume that the relevant distinction between interrogative and non-interrogative clauses is determined by the feature composition of C, the head of the clause (CP), then we can in fact describe the selection of interrogative or non-interrogative clauses in terms of head selection.

The bracketed clauses in (53a) and (53b) have the structure in (54a):

54a

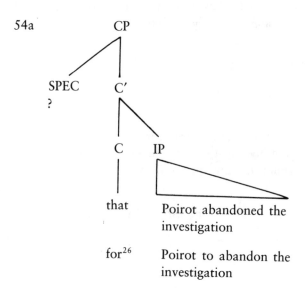

---

[26] In standard English *for* must be absent when the infinitival clause lacks an overt subject NP:

(i) *It was hard for to abandon the investigation.

Other dialects of English, though, allow *for to* sequences to some degree (see Carroll, 1983; Henry, 1989).

As a first approximation, let us assume that the bracketed interrogative clauses in (53c) have the structure (54b):

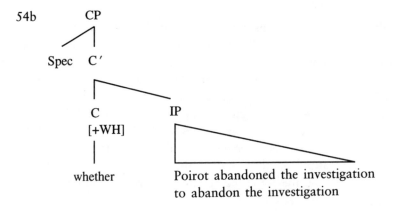

We shall reconsider the status of *whether* in chapter 5.

At this point we have no material to insert in the specifier position of CP, [Spec, CP]. We consider this point in the next section.

3.3.2 HEAD-TO-HEAD MOVEMENT

Let us consider the following examples:

55a   Poirot will abandon the investigation after lunch.
55b   Will Poirot abandon the investigation after lunch?
55c   When will Poirot abandon the investigation?

(55a) is a declarative sentence which will be assigned the structure (56a):

56a

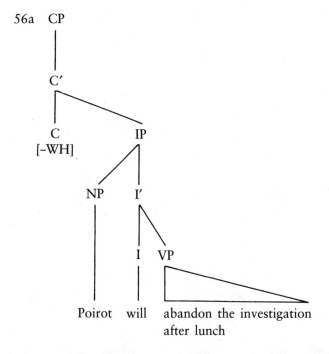

There is no overt complementizer in the sentence and we assume that the head of CP has the feature [–WH].[27]

(55b) is a direct *yes–no* question characterized by the inversion of subject and auxiliary. How can this order be derived? Various possibilities come to mind. An option that we shall explore here, and that will be elaborated in chapter 7 is that the auxiliary *will* moves from its position in I to the position C. In other words, we assume that (55b) has two syntactic representations. In one, the **underlying** structure, the modal *will* occupies the position dominated by I, as in (56a). In the second representation, the **derived** structure, the modal is moved from under I to the position dominated by C. Movement from one head position (in our case I) to another one (C) is called **head-to-head movement** and will be illustrated more extensively in chapter 7.

---

[27] We discuss the different types of questions in chapter 7. The representation in (56a) is a simplification. It is proposed that the [+WH] feature is associated with the head of embedded interrogative clauses, such as the bracketed clauses in (53c), which are selected by a higher verb, but that in case of root clauses the [+WH] feature is associated with I (cf. Rizzi forthcoming). We refer the reader to the literature.

56b

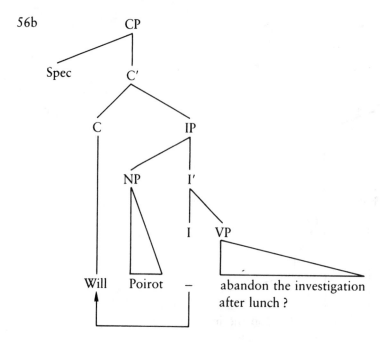

(55c) is a constituent question or *wh*-question. The auxiliary *will* precedes the subject. We assume again that, as was the case in (56b), it has moved under C. In addition, the interrogative constituent *when*, which corresponds to the time adjunct *after lunch* in (55a) and (55b), precedes the auxiliary. We assume that *when* is moved from the sentence-internal position occupied by time adjuncts in (56a) and (56b) to a position preceding C. Without going into the details of the analysis here (see chapter 7), it is clear that the X′-schema as set up offers us a position for *when* to move to: it can be inserted under the specifier node of CP, [Spec, CP] for short, a position left unoccupied in the earlier examples:

56c

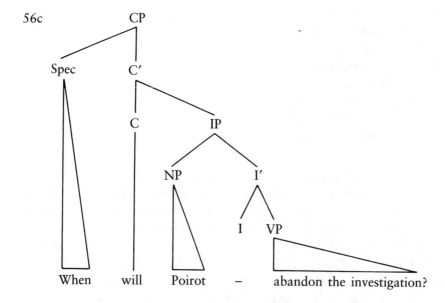

The question might be asked whether there are additional arguments for the hypothesis that the auxiliary in (55b) and (55c) moves to C, the position occupied by the complementizer in subordinate clauses.

One argument in favour of this analysis is that it predicts that the complementizer and the inverted auxiliary can never co-occur since they would have to occupy the same slot. This prediction is borne out:

57a *I wonder $\begin{Bmatrix} \text{will whether} \\ \text{whether will} \end{Bmatrix}$ Poirot abandon the investigation.

57b *When that will Poirot abandon the investigation?

A parallel question is whether it is reasonable to propose that question words such as *when* move to [Spec, CP]. In main clause questions they overtly precede the inverted auxiliary, but in subordinate clauses in English *wh*-phrases do not co-occur with the complementizer *that*.

Information from languages other than English and information from the earlier stages of English provide some evidence here. In some French and Italian dialects, subject–auxiliary inversion is not obligatory in direct questions. When the auxiliary has not inverted with the subject, C is available and we predict that the complementizer is free to occupy the C position. This prediction is borne out.

58a *Quebec French*
     Quoi que tu as fait?

what that you have done
'What have you done?'
(Cf. Koopman, 1983: 389)

58b   *Italian Romagnolo dialect*
Chi che t'è vest?
who that you have seen
'Whom have you seen?'
(Koopman, 1983: 389)

In (58a) *quoi* is in [Spec, CP], and *que* is dominated by C. The auxiliary *as* does not invert with the subject. Similarly *chi* in (58b) is in [Spec, CP], and the complementizer *che* appears under C. The auxiliary *è* is again in the IP-internal position. While the overt complementizer may co-occur with the moved *wh*-element in the dialects cited above, it cannot co-occur with an inverted auxiliary. This is predicted if we assume that both complementizer and the inverted auxiliary are dominated by C and if we also assume that a head position is normally occupied by one head only.[28]

Consider also the subordinate clauses in (59):

59a   Je me demande [quoi que tu fais].
      I wonder   what that you do
      (Quebec French; cited by Koopman, 1983: 389)

59b   Men shal knowe [who that I am]
      (1485, Caxton R 67, in Lightfoot, 1979: 322)

59c   *Men shall know who that I am.

Quoi in (59a) precedes *que*, the complementizer. We again assume that *quoi* is in [Spec, CP] and that *que* is dominated by C. The same pattern is found in earlier stages of English as shown in (59b). (59c), the word for word translation of (59b), is ungrammatical in modern English. We return to the syntactic structure of questions in chapter 7.

3.3.3   THE STRUCTURE OF CP

We have proposed that the structure of S' can be assimilated to the X'-format in (39) in the following way:

---

[28]   In certain languages a V head may incorporate a head N, thus creating a complex lexical unit dominated by V and consisting of V and N. This is apparently not possible in the case of *that* and V. For a discussion of incorporation the reader is referred to Baker (1988).

60a CP ⟶ Spec; C′
60b C′ ⟶ C; IP

C dominates the complementizer or an auxiliary (in sentences with subject–auxiliary inversion). C combines with IP to form C′. C′ in turn combines with a specifier to form the maximal projection **CP**. The position [Spec, CP] is the position to which interrogative constituents are moved.

3.4 Summary: X′-theory and Functional Categories

In section 3 of this chapter we have applied the X′-format, developed in section 2 for phrasal constituents, to the clausal constituents, S (IP) and S′ (CP). The X′-format will allow us to describe the structure of main and dependent clauses and of various types of questions.

We have now reached the important conclusion that all syntactic structure is built on the basis of the X′-format (39). This means that no special phrase structure rule needs to be stated for specific constituents and that when acquiring the language, the child will only need access to (39) to be able to assign a structure to both phrasal and clausal constituents.

3.5 Small Clauses

In chapter 1 we introduced another clause type in addition to tensed clauses and infinitival clauses: small clauses.

61a I consider [Maigret very intelligent].
61b Maigret considers [the taxi driver an important ally].
61c I consider [your proposal completely out of the question].

The bracketed strings are constituents, as shown in chapter 1. The idea was that in (61a), for instance, *Maigret* is the subject of the predicate *very intelligent* exactly like in sentence (62):

62 Maigret is very intelligent.

We raised the question as to the category label of these constituents. In the traditional literature they are called verbless clauses; we called them **small**

clauses. Let us consider the syntactic representation of the bracketed strings. We choose (61a) but the discussion also applies to the other two examples. Consider (63a):

63a

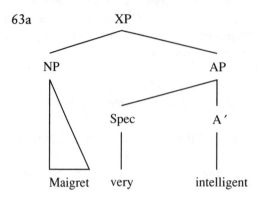

The question arises as to the status of XP in (63a). As a first observation, note that (63a) does not seem to conform to the requirements of X'-theory. X'-theory does not provide structures where two maximal projections are sister nodes. One option would be to say that the small clause XP is in fact a maximal projection of a functional head F, an abstract head which does not dominate overt material.

63b

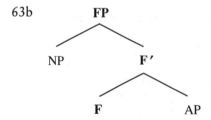

NP is the specifier of FP, the projection of F. Recall that NP is the subject of the small clause: 'Maigret is very intelligent'. Let us just speculate for a moment on this kind of representation for the small clause. Consider the following French examples:

64a Je considère   le garçon très intelligent.
     I consider   the boy very intelligent

64b   la fille très intelligente.
                      the girl very intelligent

64c   les garçons très intelligents
                      the boys very intelligent

64d   les filles très intelligentes.
                      the girls very intelligent

The adjective *intelligent* in the predicate of the small clause has overt agreement morphology in French: each number and gender combination has a different form. *Intelligent*, for instance, is masculine singular, *intelligente* is feminine singular. The adjective agrees with the subject. We could then assume that in fact small clauses contain an AGR head which dominates agreement morphology:

63c

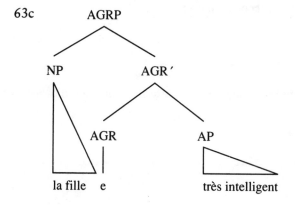

The agreement morphology would be lowered on to the adjective. Observe that it is not possible to argue that the adjective moves towards AGR since this would lead to the order *intelligente très*. The AGR node could also be posited for English small clauses as those given in (61). Unlike French, English lacks the overt forms for adjectival AGR. Observe that adjectival AGR as in (63c) differs from verbal AGR: the agreement of verbs combines person and number features, that of adjectives combines number and gender features. Under the analysis proposed here, the subject of the small clause now occupies the specifier position of AGRP, [Spec, AGRP].

Additional support for postulating an AGR head in small clauses comes from English examples such as (64b) and French examples such as (64c):

64b I consider him **as** my best friend.
64c Je considère Louisa **comme** ma meilleure amie.
'I consider Louisa as my best friend.'

In (64b) *as* seems to spell out the head of the small clause. The same applies to French *comme* in (64c).

4 Structural Relations

We discussed the structural relations dominance, precedence, and government in section 1. In this section we discuss the structural relation c-command. We shall also return to the notion of government and try to define it in terms of c-command. To illustrate the role of the notion c-command in the theory, we first consider agreement patterns.

4.1 *Agreement Patterns*

Let us examine some examples of agreement patterns. Consider the NP in (65a):

65a

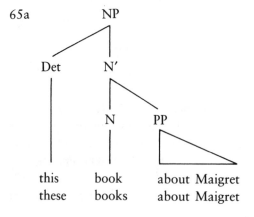

this   book   about Maigret
these   books   about Maigret

It is well known that demonstrative pronouns in English agree in number with the head of the immediately dominating NP. Agreement is overtly realized: *this* is singular, *these* is plural. Other determiners such as the definite article or possessive pronouns do not exhibit overt morphological agreement:

65b the book/the books
     my book/my books

In languages other than English specifier–head agreement between determiners and the head nouns in NPs is more extensively realized morphologically:

66a *French*

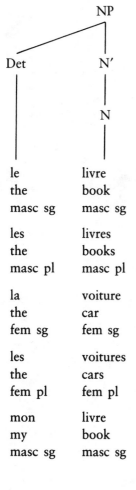

le	livre
the	book
masc sg	masc sg

les	livres
the	books
masc pl	masc pl

la	voiture
the	car
fem sg	fem sg

les	voitures
the	cars
fem pl	fem pl

mon	livre
my	book
masc sg	masc sg

mes	livres
my	books
masc pl	masc pl
ma	voiture
fem sg	fem sg
mes	voitures
fem pl	fem pl

66b   *German*

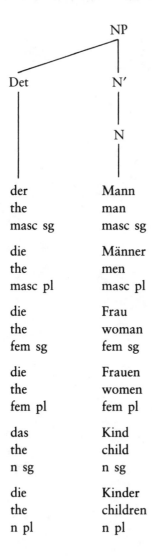

der	Mann
the	man
masc sg	masc sg
die	Männer
the	men
masc pl	masc pl
die	Frau
the	woman
fem sg	fem sg
die	Frauen
the	women
fem pl	fem pl
das	Kind
the	child
n sg	n sg
die	Kinder
the	children
n pl	n pl

The cross-linguistic variation of the overt inflection of NP determiners displayed in (65) and (66) is reminiscent of that discussed with respect to verbal and adjectival inflection. In French and German NP determiners have rich overt agreement for the nominal features gender and number. The English system is impoverished, though there are traces of overt agreement. Even in the absence of overt agreement, English head nouns and their specifiers agree in number and gender. The difference between French and English does not lie in the presence or absence of agreement as such, but rather in the morphological realization of this agreement.

Let us turn to subject–verb agreement. Consider some French examples first:

67a Poirot abandonne l'affaire.
      'Poirot abandons the case.'
67b Les inspecteurs abandonnent l'affaire.
      'The inspectors abandon the case.'
67c Nous abandonnons l'affaire.
      'We abandon the case.'

In French the verb ending is determined by the person and number of the subject. I and [Spec, IP] agree with respect to the relevant features.

67d

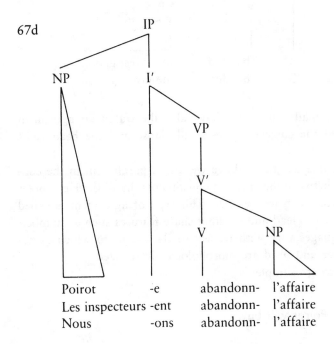

Poirot	-e	abandonn-	l'affaire
Les inspecteurs	-ent	abandonn-	l'affaire
Nous	-ons	abandonn-	l'affaire

In English there is little overt agreement, but again we have adopted the assumption that INFL is specified for abstract [AGR] in (68):

68a Poirot abandons the investigation.
68b The inspectors abandon the investigation.
68c We abandon the investigation.

Tree diagram (69) is the English analogue of (67d):

69

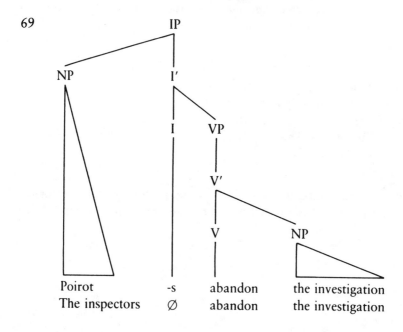

In our discussion of small clauses we have also illustrated an agreement configuration between the subject of the small clause and the head AGR (cf. 63c).

If we compare the tree diagrams above we find a parallelism in the configurational relations between the agreeing constituents. In all three examples the phrasal head agrees with its specifier. This type of agreement is called **specifier–head agreement**. Head and specifier share features such as number, gender, person. Languages vary with respect to the extent to which agreement between specifier and head are morphologically realized.

Consider the following example:

70a I wonder what Poirot will buy.

We have proposed that the C of embedded interrogative clauses contains the feature [+WH]. In (70a) the direct object of *buy* is an interrogative phrase, or a *wh*-phrase, *what*. Such an interrogative phrase could be said to also contain the feature [+WH]. In our example the *wh*-phrase occupies the specifier of CP. This means that (70a) has the structure (70b):

70b

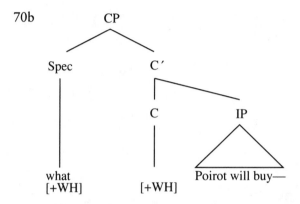

In interrogative clauses, specifier of CP and C agree with respect to the feature [+WH].[29]

The reader might conclude from the discussion above that agreement only affects the pair specifier–head, and also that it must necessarily affect this pair. Both these conclusions would be too rash.

It is not true that agreement only affects the specifier–head relation. Consider the following example from West Flemish, a dialect of Dutch:

71a ...[CP [C' da [IP den inspekteur da   boek gelezen eet]]].
            that   the inspector   that book read   has
71b ...[CP [C' dan [IP d' inspekteurs da   boek gelezen een]]].
            that   the inspectors that book read   have

In (71) the perfective auxiliary *eet/een* agrees in number and person with its subject *den inspekteur/d'inspekteurs*, illustrating specifier–head agreement. Furthermore, the complementizer *da* agrees in number and person with the subject and with the inflection: *da* is third person singular, *dan* is third person plural. The head of the CP, C, agrees with the head (and the specifier) of its complement IP.

---

[29] Cf. May (1985) and Rizzi (forthcoming) for discussion. See also chapter 12.

4.2   C-command and Government

4.2.1   C-COMMAND AND THE FIRST BRANCHING NODE

Consider the following representations where co-subscripted nodes indicate agreement:

72a   *French*

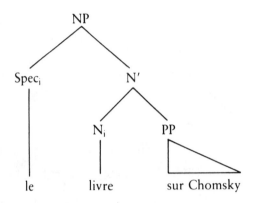

72b

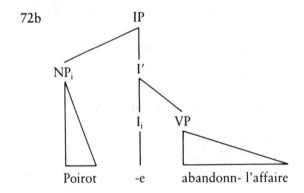

72c *West Flemish*

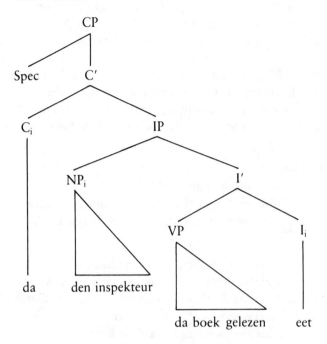

In (72a) and (72b) we have specifier–head agreement as discussed above, but the agreement of C and the lower constituents in (72c) cannot be defined in terms of specifier–head agreement. When we consider the geometrical relations between agreeing pairs of elements it appears that one agreeing element is always higher in the tree than the element it agrees with.

72d

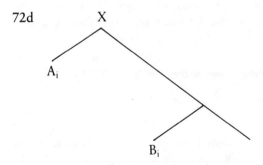

In all the representations in (72) X, the first branching node dominating A, the highest member of the agreeing pair, also dominates B, the lowest member of the agreeing pair. A itself does not dominate B and B does not dominate A. In (72a) the first branching node dominating the determiner is NP and this node also dominates N. Similarly, in (72b) the first branching node dominating the subject NP is IP and IP also dominates I. Finally, in (72c) the first branching node dominating C is C', which also dominates the subject NP and I. The relation which is schematically represented in (72d) is one that has been labelled **c-command** (as first discussed and defined by Reinhart, 1981):

73 **C-command** (i)

Node A c-commands node B if and only if

(i)   A does not dominate B and B does not dominate A; and

(ii) the first branching node dominating A also dominates B.

Given a node A it is easy to determine which nodes it c-commands. The procedure is as follows: starting from A we move upward till we reach the first branching node dominating A; then we move downwards following the branches of the tree and every node that we find on our way is c-commanded by A, regardless of whether we move rightward or leftward.

In diagram (72a), for instance, [Spec, NP] c-commands all the nodes dominated by NP. The total of all the nodes c-commanded by an element is the **c-command domain** of that element. In (72a) the NP is the c-command domain of the determiner. In (72b) the subject NP c-commands the entire IP; IP is the c-command domain of the subject. In (72c) C c-commands all the material dominated (cf. (4)) by C'. C' is the c-command domain of C. The c-command domain of an element is of necessity a constituent, given that it consists of all the material dominated by one node, hence the term c (= constituent)-command. Note in passing that under the definition in (73) a node A always c-commands itself: it will always be possible to start from node A, go up to the first branching node and return then to node A. Nothing in the definition prevents one from returning via the same route.[30]

4.2.2 GOVERNMENT

At this point let us return to our definition of government (7) in terms of sisterhood. Recall that we restrict our attention to government by heads. According to (7) A, a head, governs B in (74).

---

[30] Chomsky (1986b: 92, n. 12) discusses some other ramifications of the definition of c-command. The reader is referred to this work for discussion.

74   W

A   B

From our discussion of c-command above it follows that A, the governor, c-commands B, the governee; and conversely, B, the governee, c-commands A, the governor. Government could be defined as a relationship of 'mutual c-command'.

75   **Government** (ii)
     A governs B if and only if
     (i)   A is a governor; and
     (ii) A c-commands B and B c-commands A.

We assume that governors are heads. Below and in later chapters we shall refine the notion of government considerably.

4.2.3 M-COMMAND AND GOVERNMENT

Let us consider the following VP structures:

76a   VP

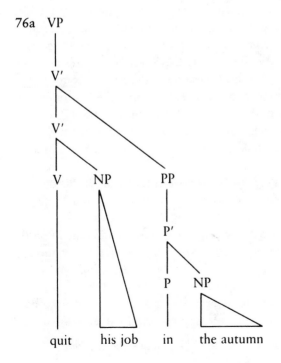

```
      VP
      |
      V'
     / \
    V'   \
   / \    \
  V   NP   PP
  |   /\    |
  |  /  \   P'
  |  |   | / \
  |  |   | P   NP
  |  |   | |   /\
 quit his job in the autumn
```

76b   VP

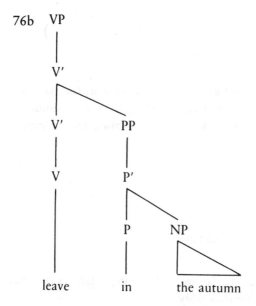

leave   in   the autumn

If we adopt our definitions of c-command (73) and government (75) above the relation between V and the PP *in the autumn* in (76a) is quite different from that between V and the PP *in the autumn* in (76b), although in both cases the PP is a time adjunct.

In (76a) the V *quit* c-commands the NP *his job*, which it governs and indeed theta-governs. Following our definitions, the V *quit* does not c-command or govern the time PP *in the autumn*. V does not c-command the PP because the first branching node that dominates it is the lower V', which does not dominate the PP. V does not govern PP because it does not c-command it.

In (76b), the V *leave* c-commands the PP *in the autumn*: the first branching node dominating V is the topmost V', which also dominates the PP. PP also c-commands V since the first branching node dominating PP is the higher V', which also dominates V. We conclude that in (76b) V and the PP *in the autumn* c-command each other. If government is defined in terms of mutual c-command, V will govern the PP. V will not govern P or the NP *the autumn* since there is no mutual c-command relation. V c-commands P and NP; P and NP do not c-command V.

We are thus led to conclude that V governs and c-commands the PP *in the autumn* in (76b) and it fails to do so in (76a). This seems a rather unsatisfactory state of affairs: intuitively one feels that both verbs, *quit* and *leave*, have the same relation to the PP *in the autumn*.

In the literature the definitions of government and c-command have been discussed extensively.[31] On the basis of various empirical and theoretical

[31] Aoun and Sportiche (1983) discuss examples like those discussed here.

considerations which we shall not go into here, it has been proposed that in configurations like those in (76) the V should uniformly govern the PP in both (a) and (b). This will capture our intuition that the relation between V and PP is the same in the VPs in (76a) and (76b). In order to arrive at this conclusion, both the notions of c-command and of government have been reformulated in terms of maximal projections.

In *Barriers*, a work to which we return in chapter 10, Chomsky (1986b: 8) proposes the following definition of c-command:

77 **C-command** (ii)
    A c-commands B if and only if A does not dominate B and every X that dominates A also dominates B.

For the choice of X in (77) two options are considered. When X is equated with the first branching node we obtain the c-command definition given in (73). This structural relation is sometimes referred to as **strict c-command**. Alternatively, X is interpreted as a maximal projection. Under the latter interpretation of (77), A **m-commands** B.

Let us apply this definition to (76). V c-commands the NP *his job* in (76a) but not the PP *in the autumn*. On the other hand, V m-commands both the NP *his job*, the PP *in the autumn* and also the preposition *in* and the NP *the autumn*. P c-commands the NP *the autumn*, and P also m-commands the NP *the autumn*. However, P does not c-command V: P', the first branching node dominating P, does not dominate V. P does not m-command V either: there is a maximal projection PP which dominates P and does not dominate V.

In (76b) V c-commands PP (unlike in (76a)), and it also m-commands the PP, the head P and the NP inside the PP. The relation between V and PP is identical to that in (76a).

Using the notion of m-command Chomsky (1986b: 8) proposes that government be defined as follows:

78 **Government** (iii)
    A governs B if and only if
    (i)   A is a governor; and
    (ii) A m-commands B; and
    (iii) no barrier intervenes between A and B.
    Maximal projections are barriers to government.
    Governors are heads.[32]

---

[32] At this point we only look at government by heads. In chapter 8 government by a maximal projection will also be considered.

In both (76a) and (76b) the verbs, *quit* and *leave* respectively, govern the PP *in the autumn*. PP being a maximal projection, the V will not be able to govern into PP. Hence, the verbs in (76a) and in (76b) m-command the NP *the autumn* but they do not govern it.

Our new definition of government (78) is intuitively more satisfactory since it allows us to establish the same relation between V and the PP (76a) and (76b). We adopt (78) from now on. The definition will be further modified in chapter 3. We return to the notion barrier in subsequent chapters and especially in chapter 10. As before, when a head governs a constituent and assigns it a thematic role, we say that the head **theta-governs** the constituent.

5 Learnability and Binary Branching: Some Discussion

In this chapter we have looked at the geometry of tree diagrams. We started out from a tree like (79) which we later replaced by (80) for various empirical and theoretical reasons.

79

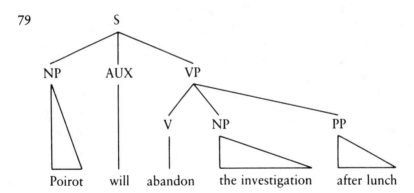

80

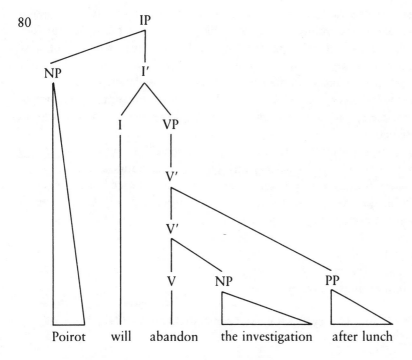

If we look at the configurational properties of the two trees there is one important contrast to which we have not paid much attention. In (79), with its flat structure, branching nodes are of different types: there are binary branching nodes, such as PP, which dominate two elements, and there are ternary branching nodes, such as VP or S, which dominate three constituents. If we added more constituents to VP we could end up with four-way or five-way branching nodes. In (80) all branching nodes are **binary branching**.

In the course of this chapter the change from the first type of structure to the second was motivated on empirical and theoretical grounds, but there are further advantages to adopting a grammar which allows only the second type.

The reader may notice that such a grammar is more aesthetically satisfying, though aesthetics may be a minor preoccupation for linguists.

A grammar which allows only binary branching nodes is more **constrained** than a grammar which freely allows any type of branching node: in the former type of grammar lots of imaginable representations are ruled out in principle. A more constrained grammar is preferred for reasons of economy and elegance and it will also be preferred if we think of the ultimate goal of linguistic theories in the generative tradition (as discussed in the Introduction).

Remember that linguists wish to account for the fact that children acquire language very fast and at an early age. In order to explain their fast acquisition we posit that children are genetically prepared for the task, that they have an innate set of principles which enable them to construct the core grammar of their language on the basis of the data they are exposed to. One component of the child's internalized knowledge of the language, the internal grammar, will concern phrase structure. Theories of phrase structure such as X'-theory attempt to represent the native speaker's internal knowledge of phrase structure.

Let us now compare two theories of phrase structure which differ in one respect. Theory A liberally allows any type of branching (binary, ternary, etc.). Theory B allows only binary branching. A child faced with linguistic data will have to decide on their phrase structure. Here are a few sentences that a child learning English might hear:

81a   Daddy sleeps.
81b   Mummy is working.
81c   Mummy must leave now.

Theory A and Theory B assign the same structure to (81a):

82

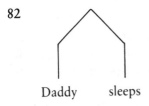

For the structure of (81b) Theory A offers three options:

83a

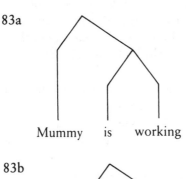

83b

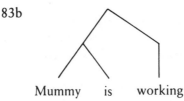

83c

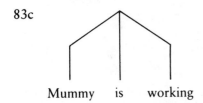

Mummy is working

Theory B only allows (83a) and (83b).

For (81c) Theory A offers eight possibilities:

84a

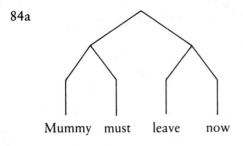

Mummy must leave now

84b

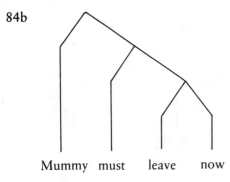

Mummy must leave now

84c

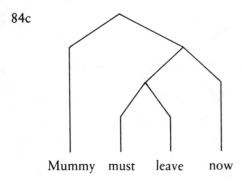

Mummy must leave now

84d

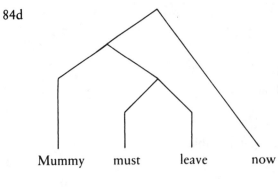

Mummy   must   leave   now

84e

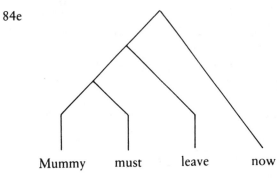

Mummy   must   leave   now

84f

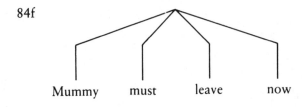

Mummy   must   leave   now

84g

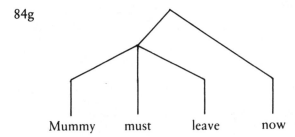

Mummy   must   leave   now

84h

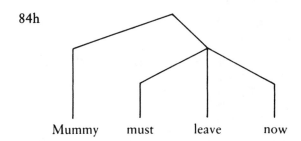

Mummy   must   leave   now

Theory B, which only allows binary branching, excludes the last three options (84f, g, h).

A child equipped with a UG that implements only binary branching will have fewer decisions to make when assigning syntactic structure to the data he is exposed to than a child equipped with a less constrained UG which allows ternary or four-way branching. It is easy to see that the more elements are involved the more choices are available. The unconstrained theory will consistently offer more choices than the binary branching theory and hence will make the child's task of deciding on the structure harder. For structuring three elements Theory A offers 50 per cent more possibilities than Theory B (three for A, two for B). For four elements Theory A offers 60 per cent more choices, with eight structures as opposed to five. The more elements there are the larger the discrepancy between the choices offered by Theory A and those offered by Theory B. You are invited to check for yourself what options would be available in the case of there being five elements.

If the ultimate goal of our grammar is to account for language acquisition, then it will be natural to aim for the more restricted type of grammar in which fewer decisions have to be made by the child. Fewer choices will automatically mean more speed in the construction of the core grammar of the language acquired. Nowadays most linguists working in the generative tradition tend to adopt some version of the binary branching framework.[33]

---

[33] Readers interested in theoretical and empirical implications of the binary branching hypothesis should consult work by Kayne (1984), who is one of the first proponents of the strict binary branching approach in the Government and Binding framework.

The binary branching hypothesis raises some important questions which we shall not go into here. One concerns the structure of double object patterns. Consider (i):

(i) John gave Mary the money.

A representation like (ii) is compatible with the binary branching hypothesis:

(ii)

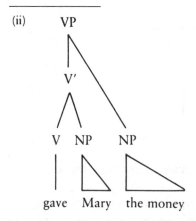

See Kayne (1984) and Larson (1988) for very influential proposals. Larson (1988) also offers a survey of the recent discussion.

Another issue is the structure of coordinate phrases such as (iii), where two constituents are linked by a conjunction *and*:

(iii)   the man and the woman

Often these are assigned a ternary branching structure:

(iv)

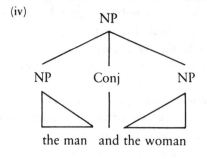

For a discussion of coordinate patterns, see Goodall (1987), who also offers a survey of the literature. Kayne (1993) develops a more restrictive theory of phrase structure.

Given the high degree of technicality the works listed above should only be consulted after chapter 8 has been covered.

6 Features and Category Labels

So far we have been assuming that the building-blocks of sentences are lexical categories such as N, V, etc., and that these are syntactic **primitives**. Primitives are 'simple', they cannot be further decomposed with respect to their syntactic behaviour.[34] However, not all linguists agree that the simplest syntactic units are words or lexical categories such as N, V, etc.

An analogy with phonology is in order. One might say that phonology is concerned with the study of phonemes, such as /b/ and /d/. Phonologists have proposed, however, that the simplest units, the primitives, at the phonetic/ phonological level are not the phonemes. If we restrict our discussion to the level of phonemes we cannot bring out the commonality between the different sounds. For instance, we cannot capture the fact that both /b/and /d/ are voiced and that both are plosives. It is proposed that the phonemes can be decomposed into smaller component parts, the distinctive **features**. The features bring out the commonality between the sounds and allow us to set up classes of phonemes. For example, the sounds /b/ and /d/ are composed of the following features:[35]

85   /b/   /d/

$$
\begin{bmatrix} + \text{ voice} \\ + \text{ plosive} \\ + \text{ bilabial} \end{bmatrix} \begin{bmatrix} + \text{ voice} \\ + \text{ plosive} \\ + \text{ alveolar} \end{bmatrix}
$$

The features listed in (85) make up a **feature matrix**. The commonality between /b/ and /d/ is brought out by the fact that their feature matrices share the features [+voice] and [+plosive]. Their difference is related to the third feature.

Following the example of phonologists, who consider the distinctive features as the primitives of phonology, syntacticians propose that the lexical categories N, V, etc., are not syntactic primitives but should be seen as complexes of syntactic features. These syntactic features themselves will be the basic building blocks, the primitives of syntactic structure.

The features that are often taken to constitute the lexical and phrasal

---

[34] We are not concerned here with the analysis of words into phonemes. Such a decomposition is not syntactically relevant and concerns the phonological component of the grammar. Apart from the identification of verb inflection, we shall not be concerned with the decomposition of words into morphemes either.

[35] For some introductory literature to the notion of features in phonology, see Fromkin and Rodman (1988).

categories are [±noun] ([±N]) and [±verb] ([±V]). The lexical categories can be decomposed into their features:

86a noun: [+N, −V]
86b verb: [−N, +V]
86c adjective: [+N, +V]
86d preposition: [−N, −V]

As in (85), the features in (86) bring out the commonality between the categories which contain the same feature. Anticipating the discussion in chapter 3, it is, for instance, argued that the fact that both verb and preposition may assign case to their complement would be related to their feature [−N]. Conversely, the fact that neither N nor A can assign structural case would be due to their shared feature [+N].

There is no clear agreement about the feature composition of C and I at this point. With respect to I we have already mentioned that it contains the features [±Tense] and [±AGR]. We shall not go deeper into this issue. We have proposed that C may contain the feature [+WH], when it heads an interrogative embedded clause, and it has the feature [−WH] when it heads a non-interrogative embedded clause.[36]

7   Summary

In this chapter we have concentrated on syntactic structure. In section 2 we propose that a uniform projection schema, the X′-format, can be developed for all phrasal categories. Phrases are hierarchically structured projections of their heads.

1 XP ⟶ Spec; X′
   X′ ⟶ X′; YP
   X′ ⟶ X; YP

[36] The reader interested in the theory of features should consult the literature. For the decomposition of the lexical categories, see Chomsky (1970) and Stowell (1981). Muysken (1983) extends the use of features to include the levels of projection X^0, X′ and XP. Muysken and van Riemsdijk (1986a) offer a survey of some of the problems containing syntactic features and projections. For some further modifications of the structure of clauses see Grimshaw (1991) and chapter 11.

The X'-format allows us to bring out the commonality between the different types of phrases. The traditional phrase structure rules for specific phrases, say VP, are reduced to more elementary notions. The hierarchical organization of the phrase is captured by X'-theory, the linear order of constituents will have to be related to some other principle of the grammar.

Section 3 shows that the X'-schema can be extended to the clausal constituents: S is reinterpreted as a projection of INFL, with the subject NP in the specifier position. S' is reinterpreted as a projection of C.

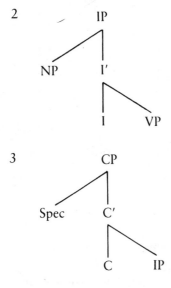

In section 4 we introduce the structural relations c-command and m-command, and we redefine government in terms of these notions.

4 C-command

A c-commands B if and only if A does not dominate B and every X that dominates A also dominates B.

When X is equated with the first branching node, A **c-commands** B. When X is interpreted as a maximal projection, A **m-commands** B.

5 Government

A governs B if and only if
(i) A is a governor;
(ii) A m-commands B; and

(iii)   no barrier intervenes between A and B.
Maximal projections are barriers to government.
Governors are heads.

We consider the importance of the binary branching hypothesis especially in the light of language acquisition (section 5) and we look at the proposal that syntactic features should replace lexical categories as syntactic primitives (section 6).

8   Exercises

Exercise 1

Using the X'-model draw a tree diagram for the following sentences:

1   Poirot will meet the new governess in the foyer of the opera.
2   Miss Marple cleaned the knife carefully with a handkerchief.
3   Maigret is quite fond of his assistant.
4   The announcement of the news on local radio surprised all the students of linguistics from England.
5   She has decided that owners of big cars without children should pay tax.

Exercise 2

In this chapter we have defined structural notions such as government, c-command and m-command. Consider the tree diagram below. Try to decide which elements are c-commanded by I, C and V, and which elements are m-commanded by them. Try to determine which elements are governed by I, by C and by V (a) when government is defined in terms of sisterhood, and (b) when government is defined in terms of m-command.

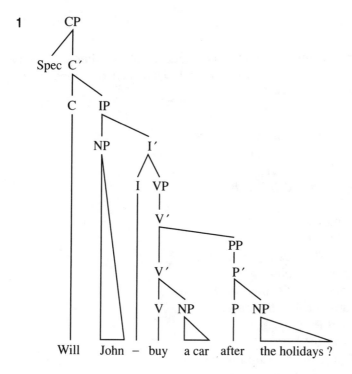

1

Will John – buy a car after the holidays ?

Exercise 3

On the basis of the tree diagram in exercise 2 decide which of the following statements are true and which are false:

1   IP dominates CP.
2   IP immediately dominates the subject NP.
3   IP is a sister of C.
4   V and the NP *a car* are sisters.
5   V head-governs the PP *after the holidays.*
6   The NP *the holidays* is a constituent of IP.
7   The NP *the holidays* is an immediate constituent of VP.
8   VP and I are sisters.
9   VP precedes I.
10 V theta-governs the NP *a car.*

Exercise 4

Using the technical terminology introduced in this chapter describe the structural relations between the following sets of nodes in the tree diagram in exercise 2.

1   V and PP *after the holidays.*
2   PP *after the holidays* and NP *a car.*
3   NP *John* and VP.
4   NP *John* and NP *a car.*
5   IP and C′.
6   C and I.
7   C and NP *John.*
8   I and NP *a car.*
9   V and NP *John.*
10 V′ and the PP *after the holidays.*
11 P and the NP *the holidays.*
12 V and P.
13 C and VP.
14 VP and the NP *the holidays.*
15 I and the NP *the holidays.*

For each pair, try to find as many structural relations as possible (precedence, dominance, sisterhood, c-command, etc.).

Exercise 5

Consider the following examples, taken from exercise 10 in chapter 1:

1   I consider it likely that Louisa will not leave.
2   I thought it stupid that she should have gone out in the rain.
3   Ritengo probabile che Maria rimanga.
    I consider likely that Maria will stay
4   Je trouve bizarre qu'elle soit là.
    I find strange that she be there

Does the discussion of the structure of small clauses in section 3.5 throw any light on the contrast between the English sentences, where a pronoun is obligatory (cf.(5)), and the French and Italian sentences where it is not?

5a *I consider likely that Louisa will not leave.
5b *I thought stupid that she should have gone out in the rain.

For the discussion you might wish to refer to section 4 of the Introduction.

3 Case Theory

Contents

Introduction and overview

Introduction and Overview

In chapter 1 we discussed the component of the grammar that regulates the assignment of thematic roles to arguments, theta theory. Chapter 2 deals with the component of the grammar that regulates phrase structure, X'-theory. The grammar we are building has a modular structure: it contains distinct interacting components or **modules**. In this chapter we consider another module of the grammar: **case theory**.

Case theory accounts for some of the formal properties of overt NPs and integrates the traditional notion of case into the grammar. Though the discussion focuses on case in English we occasionally refer to examples from German.

In section 1 we introduce the notion abstract case as distinct from morphological case. Abstract case is a universal property, while the overt realization of abstract case by means of morphological case varies cross-linguistically. Section 2 is concerned with the distribution of NOMINATIVE and ACCUSATIVE case in English. In this section we introduce the case filter, the requirement that all overt NPs be assigned abstract case. In section 3 we introduce the difference between structural case and inherent case. In section 4 we consider the adjacency requirement on case assignment. Section 5 describes the properties of passive sentences. Section 6 discusses the relation between case, theta theory and subcategorization.

1 Morphological Case and Abstract Case

Consider the examples in (1):

1a The butler attacked the robber.
1b [That the butler attacked the robber] is surprising.
1c [For the butler to attack the robber] would be surprising.

(1a) is a simple sentence, containing two NPs, *the butler* and *the robber*. In (1b) the simple sentence (1a) is used as the subject clause of an adjectival predicate (*surprising*). In (1c) we find the non-finite parallel of (1a) used as the subject of the adjectival predicate.

In chapter 1 we saw that NPs realize the arguments of the predicate of the sentence and are theta-marked, directly or indirectly. In (1) the verb *attack* assigns two theta roles. This information is encoded in the lexical entry of *attack*. Following our convention adopted in chapter 1, we indicate the relevant theta roles by numbering and ignore for the most part the specific label. Occasionally, we consider the thematic relations more carefully.

2   attack: verb

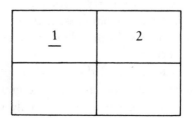

Let us replace the argument NPs in (1) by the corresponding pronouns:

3a   *He* attacked *him*.
3b   That *he* attacked *him* is surprising.
3c   For *him* to attack *him* would be surprising.

Depending on their positions in the sentences, the third person pronouns appear in different forms. When the pronoun is the internal argument of *attack* it takes the form *him*. Adopting the terminology of traditional grammar we call this form the **ACCUSATIVE** case. When the third person pronoun is the external argument of *attack* it takes either the form *he* or the form *him*. The latter form is again the ACCUSATIVE case of the pronoun; the form *he* will be called the **NOMINATIVE** case. Pronouns thus can be seen to have different case forms: *he* is NOMINATIVE, *him* is ACCUSATIVE. A third case form found in English NPs is the **GENITIVE**, illustrated in (4a) and (4b).

4a   *The butler*'s coat was too big.
4b   *His* coat was too big.

In English, the overt morphological realization of case in full lexical noun phrases is restricted to the GENITIVE case. As seen in (1), NOMINATIVE and ACCUSATIVE are not realized overtly in modern English full NPs, though these case forms were overtly marked in earlier stages of the language.[1] Adjectives and determiners, which used to have case forms in earlier stages of the language, have also lost distinct overt case forms.

The overt distinction of NOMINATIVE and ACCUSATIVE forms in modern English is still to be found in the pronoun system, though even there we find several examples of **case syncretism**: two case forms having the same morphological realization. Table (5) illustrates the overt realization of the case forms in NPs: in (a) we find the full lexical NPs, in (b) we list the pronouns. As can be seen NOMINATIVE and ACCUSATIVE are the same for the pronouns *you* and *it*.

5   English case forms

	NOMINATIVE	ACCUSATIVE	GENITIVE
a Lexical NPs:			
	the man	the man	the man's
	the good man	the good man	the good man's
b Pronominal NPs:			
1 sg	I	me	my
2 sg	you	you	your
3 sg masc	he	him	his
3 sg fem	she	her	her
3 sg neut	it	it	its
1 pl	we	us	our
2 pl	you	you	your
3 pl	they	them	their

Other languages, like Latin or German, have a morphologically rich case system where distinct cases are overtly marked on nouns, adjectives, determiners, etc., as well as on pronouns. Consider, for instance, the following Latin examples:

6a   Caesar Belgas   vincit.
      Caesar Belgians beats
      'Caesar beats the Belgians.'

---

[1]   An interesting discussion of the development of the English case system is found in van Kemenade (1986), Lumsden (1987) and Roberts (1983). These works should be accessible when chapter 7 has been covered.

6b Belgae   Caesarem timent.
    Belgians Caesar   fear
    'The Belgians fear Caesar.'

In (6a) the NP *Caesar* is in the NOMINATIVE case and the NP *Belgas* is ACCUSATIVE. Conversely, in (5b) *Belgae* is NOMINATIVE and *Caesarem* is ACCUSATIVE.

From German we give the following examples:

7a Der   Mann/Student hat den Lehrer   gesehen.
    the   man/student   has the teacher seen
    NOMINATIVE   ACCUSATIVE
7b Der   Lehrer hat den Mann/Studenten gesehen.
    the   teacher has the man/student   seen
    NOMINATIVE   ACCUSATIVE

In German, case forms are overtly realized on the determiner system of NPs and also on a certain class of nouns (cf. the ACCUSATIVE form *Studenten* in (7b)).

Although English does not have the overt case-marking that we find, for example, in Latin and in German, it has the remnants of an overt case system, as seen in the pronominal system. We therefore do not wish to say that English lacks case. Rather, following our discussion of agreement in chapter 2, section 3.2.2, we postulate that English has a fully-fledged system of **abstract case**, similar to that in Latin or German. We assume that abstract case is part of universal grammar. In English the abstract case-marking is often not morphologically realized. The degree of morphological realization of abstract case varies parametrically from one language to another.

The concept of abstract case is an important part of Government and Binding Theory. Based on work by Vergnaud (1985), Chomsky and his followers have developed a theory of case, **case theory**. As we shall see (section 6) attempts have been made to relate case theory to other components of the grammar, notably theta theory. We first look at some examples of English case forms and try to show how case theory can be developed on the basis of those.

2 Structural Case: NOMINATIVE and ACCUSATIVE

In this section we concentrate on the distribution of NOMINATIVE and ACCUSATIVE case forms. We discuss GENITIVE case in section 3.

As can be seen in (3), the NOMINATIVE case (*he*) is reserved for the NP in the subject position of finite clauses. The ACCUSATIVE case (*him*) is used both for the object NP of a transitive verb ((3a), (3b) and (3c)) and for the subject NP of an infinitival subordinate clause (3c).[2] We also find ACCU-SATIVE case realized on the NP complement of a preposition.

8   Jeeves moved towards him/*he.

Adopting the concepts of traditional grammar, we can say that subjects of finite clauses have NOMINATIVE case and that NPs that are complements of prepositions or verbs as well as NPs that are subjects of infinitival clauses appear in the ACCUSATIVE. But this informal system needs some discussion. At this point we have provided a list of occurrences without trying to relate the distribution of the case forms to other properties of the sentences in question. Recall that we argued in the Introduction that lists offer no insight into the phenomena that are listed.

2.1   Complements: ACCUSATIVE

2.1.1   V AND P AS CASE ASSIGNERS

Let us first look at the complements of transitive verbs and prepositions. Following traditional accounts of case we might say that transitive verbs and prepositions **assign** ACCUSATIVE case to the NP they govern. They **case-mark** an NP which they govern. Thus in (9) the V and the P will case-mark the complement NPs. In this view, heads assign case.

---

[2]   The subject of infinitival clauses used as main clauses is assigned either NOMINA-TIVE (i) or ACCUSATIVE (ii):

(i)   He go there? Impossible.
(ii) Him attack Bill? Never.

Sentences such as (i) and (ii) are clearly marked. They cannot be used to start a conversation, rather they will be used to echo a preceding utterance. The source of the case on their subjects is a matter for further research.

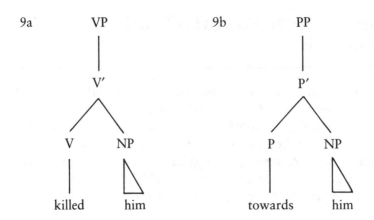

The conditions of case assignment are partly structural: ACCUSATIVE case is assigned under government. A verb cannot assign ACCUSATIVE case to an NP outside the VP such as the subject:

10   *Him found the evidence.

Consider the definition of government given in chapter 2:

11a   Government (chapter 2 (78))
      A governs B if and only if
      (i)   A is a governor;
      (ii) A m-commands B; and
      (iii) no barrier intervenes between A and B.
      Maximal projections are barriers to government.
      Governors are heads.

(11b) spells out the various components of the definition in more detail:

11b   **Government**
      A governs B if and only if
      (i)   A is a governor;
      (ii) A m-commands B;
      (iii) no barrier intervenes between A and B.
      where
      (a)   governors are the lexical heads (V, N, P, A) and tensed I;
      (b)   maximal projections are barriers.

In (10) the V *find* does not govern the subject NP.

The possibility of case assignment is also a function of the type of verb, i.e. the governor. Only transitive verbs and prepositions assign case. Intransitive verbs like *wander* or *overeat* cannot assign case to a complement NP:

12a   *He wandered them.
12b   *He overate them.

Nouns and adjectives also do not assign ACCUSATIVE case (see discussion in section 3).

13a   *Poirot's attack him.
13b   *Poirot is envious him.

We shall classify transitive verbs and prepositions as ACCUSATIVE case assigners.[3]

2.2.2   A NOTE ON MINIMALITY AND GOVERNMENT

In section 2.1.1 we propose that both V and P are ACCUSATIVE case assigners. In the configuration (14a) V case-marks the direct object NP, [NP, V'], and in (14b) P case-marks its complement, [NP, P'].

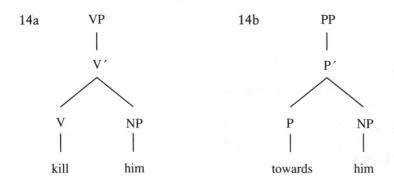

14a   VP   14b   PP

Consider though, the representation in (15):

---

[3]   In chapter 2, section 7, we pointed out that the ability of a category to assign case has sometimes been related to the presence of the feature [−N]. Prepositions and verbs are [−N], nouns and adjectives are [+N] (see Stowell, 1981).

15

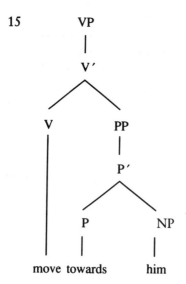

The reader may wonder which element is the case assigner in (15): is *him* case-marked by the preposition or is it case-marked by V? Under our definition of government in (11) it is P which case-marks the NP *him*, PP being a maximal projection, hence a barrier. This is also confirmed if we consider German data such as those in (16). The advantage of German is that V and P may assign distinct cases; in our example: the V *schreiben* assigns ACCUSATIVE and the P *mit* assigns DATIVE. Consider the following examples from German:[4]

16a dass er einen Roman scheibt
     that he a novel (ACC) writes
     'that he writes a novel'
16b dass er mit einem Bleistift schreibt
     that he with a pencil (DAT) writes
     'that he writes with a pencil'
16c *dass er mit einen Bleistift schreibt
     that he with a pencil (ACC) writes

In (16a) the direct object NP *einen Roman* is assigned ACCUSATIVE case by the transitive verb *schreiben*. In (16b), the complement of *mit* is assigned

---

4 (16) illustrates subordinate clauses to avoid the specific word-order problems of Germanic languages (cf. Haegeman 1992).

DATIVE. It cannot be assigned ACCUSATIVE, as seen in (16c). The structure of the VP in (16b) will be (16d), and PP is a barrier for government.

16d

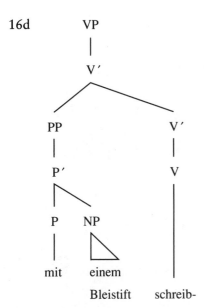

Schreiben, though potentially an ACCUSATIVE case assigner, does not assign ACCUSATIVE to the NP inside the PP.

There is an alternative way of ensuring that P case-marks its complement in (16d) and one which will become more relevant in chapters 10 and 12. We introduce it here for completeness' sake. Consider (16d) again. Both V and P c-command, and m-command, the NP; we might wish to say that V cannot assign case to NP because P is 'closer', P **intervenes** between V and NP. We could say that if there are two potential governors, the closer governor wins out. This idea is expressed in terms of a minimality condition on government (17). Observe that government is defined in terms of m-command but that the intervening Z is computed in terms of c-command.

17 **Minimality**

    A governs B if and only if

  (i)   A is a governor;

  (ii) A m-commands B;

  (iii) there is no node Z such that

      (a) Z is a potential governor for B;

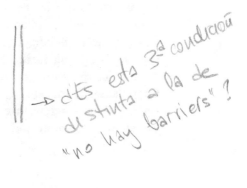

(b)   Z c-commands B;
(c)   Z does not c-command A.
(Cf. Rizzi, 1990a: 7)

(18) gives a schematic representation.

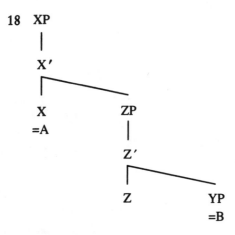

18 XP

By the Minimality condition, (17) has the effect of excluding the possibility that V govern YP, the complement of the PP in (16). The minimality condition will become important in the second half of the book, especially in chapters 8, 10 and 12.

2.2   Subjects: NOMINATIVE and ACCUSATIVE

2.2.1   NOMINATIVE SUBJECTS

Subjects of finite clauses have NOMINATIVE case (cf. (3a)). Let us try to link the assignment of NOMINATIVE case to a governing head just as we have linked the assignment of ACCUSATIVE case to V or to P in 2.1.1. One important element in the discussion is the contrast between the subjects of finite clauses and those of infinitivals; subjects of finite clauses are NOMINA-TIVE, subjects of infinitivals are ACCUSATIVE (cf. (3c)). In chapter 2 we claimed that the distinction between finite and non-finite clauses can be drawn in terms of the feature composition of the head of the clause, INFL or I. In finite clauses INFL is [+Tense, +AGR]; in non-finite clauses INFL is [−Tense, −AGR]. This suggests that the assignment of NOMINATIVE case can be associated with finite INFL. We leave it open at this point whether it is

Tense or AGR or a combination of Tense and AGR which is responsible for the NOMINATIVE case. Consider the tree diagram in (19):

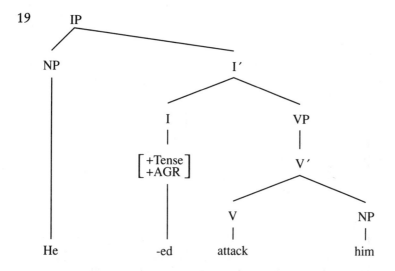

19

In order to ensure that I can case-mark [Spec, IP] under government we are forced to adopt the definition of government in terms of m-command (11). A definition in terms of c-command would not suffice: I does not c-command [Spec, IP]. On the other hand, for case assignment by V (or by P) both a definition in terms of c-command and one in terms of m-command would do: in the example above V c-commands the object NP.

It has been proposed (Sportiche 1988b) that the subject NP in [Spec, IP] is assigned NOMINATIVE case not by virtue of government by I but rather by virtue of the specifier–head agreement between the subject NP and INFL. It could thus be argued that case-marking is achieved either via government or via specifier-head agreement.[5]

2.2.2 THE SUBJECT OF INFINITIVAL CLAUSES

2.2.2.1 *For as a Case-marker* We repeat (3c) with its tree diagram representation in (20):

20a [For him to attack him] would be surprising.

---

[5] The role of agreement in determining case relations has become more prominent in more recent developments of the theory. In Chomsky (1992), it is proposed that indeed that all case assignment is licensed via specifier–head agreement relations. Such an account clearly will imply serious modifications to the discussion in section 2.2.1.

20b

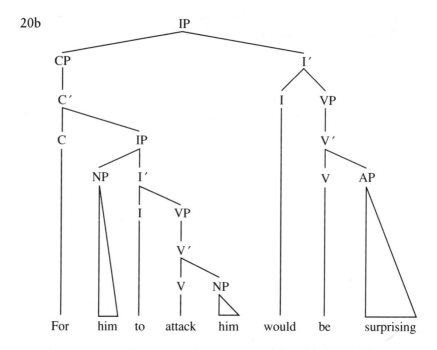

How do we account for the ACCUSATIVE case of the subject NP of the infinitival clause? One possible answer would be to argue that it is the infinitival I (*to*) that is responsible for case-marking the NP subject. This is unlikely in view of the following examples.

21a   *[Him to attack Bill] would be illegal.
21b   [That he should have attacked Bill] was surprising.

22a   *I prefer very much [him to go now].
22b   I prefer very much [that he should go now].

(21a) and (22a) each contain an infinitival subordinate clause. In each example the infinitive marker *to* is present but the sentence is not grammatical. In contrast, (21b) and (22b) contain a finite subordinate clause; the head of the clause, I, assigns NOMINATIVE case to the subject NP. Potentially, there might be different ways of explaining the ungrammaticality of (21a) and (22a), but a significant point to take into consideration is that the sentences are saved by the insertion of *for* as the complementizer of the non-finite clause:

23a [For him to attack Bill] would be illegal.
23b I prefer very much [for him to go now].

Alternatively, the sentences are rescued by the omission of the overt subject of the infinitival clause. In chapter 5 we discuss the status of the subject position (indicated with a dash) in the infinitival clauses in (24).

24a [—To attack Bill] would be illegal.
24b I prefer very much [—to go now].

Let us try to relate these groups of examples. It is the presence of the element *for* under C that enables the overt NP subject *him* to survive. When *for* is absent the subject pronoun must also disappear (24). Which property of *for* could be used to explain these phenomena?

In (23), the preposition *for* occupies the head position of CP. We call *for* in such examples a **prepositional complementizer**. *For* is a preposition, hence an ACCUSATIVE case assigner (see sections 2.1 and 2.2.1). We shall argue that the role of *for* is indeed to case-mark the subject *him*. The next question is why there should be any need for such a case on the NP.

Let us postulate that there is a universal requirement that all overt NPs must be assigned abstract case, the **case filter**.

25 Case filter
Every overt NP must be assigned abstract case.

This requirement is called a filter because it 'filters out' any construction containing an overt NP which is not assigned case. We assume, from now on, that the case filter applies to *all* overt NPs. The reader may observe that a filter such as (25) does not explain anything. It merely states that a certain type of construction is ungrammatical, without attempting to explain why this should be so. In section 6 we shall try to link the case filter to other principles of the grammar.

(21a) and (22a) are ungrammatical, but can be saved either by insertion of the case assigner *for* or by omission of the overt subject. Our hypothesis will be that (21a) and (22a) are ungrammatical because *to*, the non-finite I of the infinitival clause, cannot assign case to the [Spec, IP]. Finite I, which is [+Tense, +AGR], assigns NOMINATIVE case and contrasts with non-finite I which is [−Tense, −AGR] and does not assign case. (21a) and (22a) are ungrammatical because they violate the case filter.

The case filter has nothing to say about the subject of the infinitives in (24) since these sentences lack an overt NP subject (see chapters 5 and 8 for the discussion of infinitival clauses without overt subject).

The prepositional complementizer *for* in (23) case-marks the subject NP of the infinitival clause: (23) passes the case filter and is grammatical. However, caution is needed with respect to such an analysis of (23). We have said that case is assigned under government. Hence we would like to be able to say that the case assigner *for* governs *him*, the subject of the clause which it introduces. Consider (26):

26

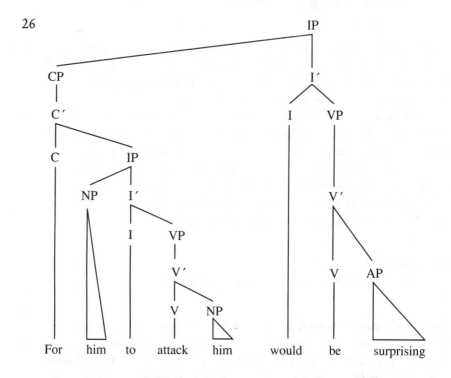

The question could be raised how come *for* can case-mark the NP in [Spec, IP]. If maximal projections are barriers for government (cf. (11)) then *for* should not be able to govern into its complement IP. We will assume that IP is not a barrier. Observe that I, the head of the infinitival IP, is a functional head which has the feature composition [-AGR, -Tense]. In (11b) we did not list non-finite I among the governors. As a first approximation, let us say that non-finite I is 'weak', it is not a governor and that its projection IP cannot block outside government. Hence *for* can govern into non-finite IP and case-mark its subject. Observe that we should ensure that in (26) the finite inflection of the matrix clause (past tense, third person singular) will not be able to govern into the lower clause to assign nominative case to the subject:

27 [CP *For he to attack Bill] was illegal.

We shall assume that while the infinitival IP is not a barrier for outside government, CP, whose head is *for*, is a barrier for government. In chapter 10 we return to the definition of barriers. If NOMINATIVE case is assigned by virtue of specifier–head agreement between the subject NP and a finite INFL, then (27) will also be excluded. The NP *he* does not have the required specifier–head relation with the matrix I, rather *he* is the specifier of *to*, the subordinate non-finite I.

2.2.2.2 *Exceptional Case-marking* Continuing the examination of subjects of infinitives in English, we turn to (28):

28 John believes [him to be a liar].

In (28) *believe* takes an infinitival clause as its internal argument. The first question we may ask is which label to assign to the bracketed string: is the relevant constituent an IP or a CP? One argument in favour of the IP hypothesis is that it is not possible to insert the complementizer *for*, which is typical for infinitival clauses, in front of the subordinate clause:[6]

29a *John believes for him to be a liar.
29b *John believes very much for him to be a liar.

(28) will have the syntactic representation (30):

---

[6] *Believe* may also take a finite CP as its complement:

(i) I believe [CP that [IP he is a liar]].

30

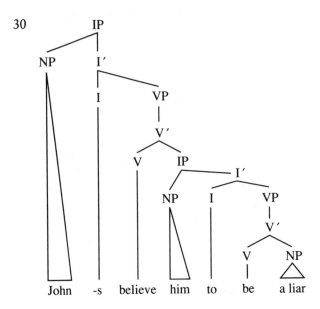

The question we address here is how *him* can satisfy the case filter, i.e. be assigned (ACCUSATIVE) case. Our hypothesis (see the discussion of (21) and (22)) was that infinitival I is not a case assigner. The obvious candidate for case-marking *him* in (30) is the transitive verb *believe*:

31 I believe this story.

In (31) *believe* case-marks the NP *this story*. On the basis of our previous discussion it is plausible that *believe* can assign case to *him*, the subject of the complement IP. *Believe* is separated from *him* by a maximal projection, infinitival IP. By assumption, infinitival IP will not constitute a barrier for outside government and hence *believe* can assign case to the relevant NP.

The situation in which a verb like *believe* can govern into an IP and assign case to its subject NP is often referred to as **exceptional case-marking** abbreviated as **ECM**.

As a final illustration consider the following examples:

32a I know [IP John to be the best candidate].
32b I don't know [CP whether [IP —to go to the party]].
32c *I don't know [CP whether [IP John to go to the party]].

(32a) is parallel to (30). *Know* takes an IP complement, governs into the maximal projection IP and case-marks *John*. In (32b), the presence of *whether* indicates that we have an infinitival clause of the type CP. In this example, there is no overt subject in the infinitival clause (see chapter 5 for non-overt subjects in infinitival clauses), thus the case filter (25) does not come into play with respect to the subject NP of the lower clause. In (32c) *know* again takes a clausal CP complement (witness the presence of *whether*). In this example the infinitival clause contains an overt NP subject *John*. The sentence is ungrammatical because it violates the case filter. Infinitival *to* is assumed to be unable to assign case. The potential case assigner *know* is separated from the relevant NP by the maximal projection CP, which is a barrier (see also the discussion in chapter 10).

2.2.2.3 Small Clauses In chapters 1 and 2 we have briefly discussed the structure of small clauses, illustrated in (33).

33a   Maigret considers [the taxi driver [entirely innocent]].
33b   I consider [Maigret [an inspector of great value]].
33c   I consider [your proposal [completely out of the question]].

Given the case filter the subject NPs of the small clauses in (33) must be case-marked. The small clauses themselves do not contain a case-marker. Consider, for instance, the simplified syntactic representation of (33a):

33d

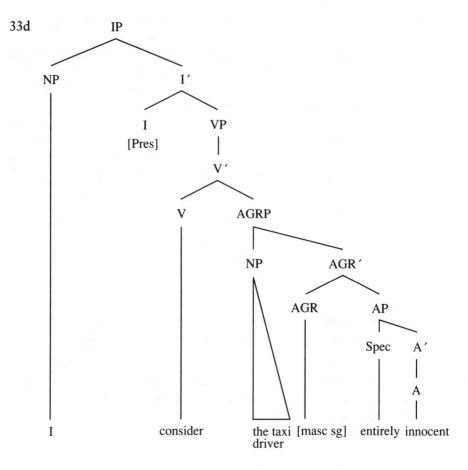

We adopt the hypothesis discussed in chapter 2 that small clauses are projections of a functional head AGR. By analogy with the argumentation used in section 2.2.2.2 we deduce that the AGR head of a small clause fails to assign case. This assumption would account for the ungrammaticality of (34a) in contrast with the grammatical example (34b):

34a   [*The taxi driver entirely innocent] was believed by everyone.
34b   [That the taxi driver is entirely innocent] was believed by everyone.

(34a) is ungrammatical because the subject of the small clause, *the taxi driver*, lacks case. In (34b) the finite INFL on *is* assigns NOMINATIVE case to its subject. Let us say that, like non-finite I, small clause AGR is too weak to case-mark its subject. We propose that in (33d) it is the verb *consider* which case-marks the subject of the small clause. Witness the fact that if we replace the small clause subject by a pronoun it will have the ACCUSATIVE form. If V can case-mark the subject of the small clause this implies that the small clause AGRP also is not a barrier for an outside governor.[7]

2.3 Summary

To sum up this section: we have argued that overt NPs are subject to the case filter: they must be assigned abstract case. We have discussed two instances of abstract case: NOMINATIVE and ACCUSATIVE. ACCUSATIVE case is assigned by a governing V or P, NOMINATIVE case is assigned by I, under government, or by specifier–head agreement. In order to account for case assignment to the subjects of infinitival clauses we have adopted two hypotheses: (i) non-finite I is not a case assigner; (ii) infinitival IP is not a barrier to outside government. Subjects of small clauses are also case-marked by an outside governor. Again we assume that (i) the small clause AGR is not a case assigner, and (ii) the AGRP which constitutes the small clause is not a barrier for government.

3 Adjectives and Nouns

3.1 Of-insertion

So far we have looked at case assignment by finite I – NOMINATIVE – and by verbs and prepositions (including *for*) – ACCUSATIVE. Nouns and adjectives are not case assigners in English:

35a Poirot envies Miss Marple.
35b *Poirot is envious Miss Marple.
35c Poirot is envious of Miss Marple.
35d *Poirot's envy Miss Marple
35e Poirot's envy of Miss Marple

All the examples in (35) contain a main predicate morphologically and semantically related to the verb *envy*. In (35a) *envy*, the verb, is used; in (35b)

---

[7] The reader will observe that the data discussed here will also be subject to important revisions if we assume with Chomsky (1992) that all case assignment (or case-checking as it is called) is done under specifier–head relations (cf. footnote 5).

and (35c) we find the related adjective *envious*; in (35d) and (35e) the noun *envy*.

Let us consider how the case filter (25) applies to these examples. In (35a) case assignment is straightforward: *Poirot* is assigned NOMINATIVE by the finite inflection and *Miss Marple* is assigned ACCUSATIVE by the transitive verb *envy*.

(35b) is ungrammatical. If we compare it with the grammatical (35a) the only difference is that we have replaced the verb *envy* by the adjective *envious*. Apparently (35b) can be rescued by the insertion of the preposition *of* as seen in (35c). How can we account for these data?

This situation is reminiscent of that discussed in section 2.2.2.1. We saw there that the prepositional complementizer *for* rescued sentences (21a) and (22a) and we argued that *for* was needed in order to guarantee that the subject NP of the infinitival clause would receive case.

We shall try to explain the ungrammaticality of (35b), without *of*, and the grammaticality of (35c), with *of*, also in terms of the case filter. If adjectives like *envious* cannot case-mark their complement then (35b) is ruled out by the case filter since the NP *Miss Marple* will not be assigned case.

We also posit that English has a default procedure to rescue sentences like (35b) which consists of inserting the preposition *of* in front of the NP. We refer to this procedure by the term ***of*-insertion**. Like any other preposition, *of* can assign ACCUSATIVE case and thus will avoid a case filter violation: in (35c) *Miss Marple* is case-marked by *of*.

Let us turn to (35d) and (35e). First of all we see that these NPs contain a GENITIVE NP, *Poirot's*, in front of their head N. We shall not discuss GENITIVE assignment in the pre-nominal position. Let us assume that there is an element POSS in the specifier position of NPs which is able to assign GENITIVE to the NP in that position.[8]

We turn to the post-nominal complement of *envy*, the NP *Miss Marple*. Analogously to (35b) and (35c), we shall try to account for the ungrammaticality of (35d) and the grammaticality of (35e) in terms of case theory. If nouns fail to assign case to their complements (35d) violates the case filter. *Of*-insertion in (35e) enables the complement NP to receive case.

3.2   *Failure of* Of-*insertion*

We consider case assignment as a structural property of verbs, prepositions and INFL. We assume that these heads are case assigners and will case-mark

---

[8]   The interested reader is referred to the discussion in Chomsky (1986a: 190) and the references cited there. See also Abney (1987).

any NP they govern. We also postulate that infinitival I is not a case assigner and that infinitival IP is transparent for outside government, hence for outside case-marking.

Let us now again turn to predicates with clausal complements.

36a I believe [that [John is honest]].
36b my belief [that [John is honest]]
36c I believe [John to be honest].
36d *my belief [John to be honest]
36e *my belief [of John to be honest]

37a Emsworth is proud of [the pig].
37b *Emsworth is proud [the pig].
37c Emsworth is proud [that [the pig has won]].
37d *Emsworth is proud [the pig to have won].
37e *Emsworth is proud [of the pig to have won].

In (36a) the verb *believe* takes a tensed CP as its complement. The subject of the lower clause *John* is assigned NOMINATIVE case by the finite INFL. In (36b), similarly, the noun *belief* takes a finite CP complement and the same mechanism of case assignment applies. (36c) exemplifies ECM: the verb *believe* governs into the complement IP and assigns ACCUSATIVE to *John*. In (36d) we see that ECM is not possible with nouns. The ungrammaticality of this example is expected if we assume that nouns are not case assigners. However, we have seen that in other examples in which noun heads fail to assign case, a default mechanism of *of*-insertion applies to rescue NPs which would otherwise end up caseless (see (35) above). As (36e) shows, *of*-insertion cannot rescue (36d).

A similar pattern is found with the adjectival complementation in (37). (37a) illustrates obligatory *of*-insertion (cf. (37b)). In (37c) the subject of the finite complement clause will be assigned NOMINATIVE by the finite inflection. In (37d) the adjective takes an IP complement. By assumption, infinitival IP is not a barrier for government by the adjective *proud* but this is not sufficient to save the construction since adjectives are unable to assign case. Again, as was the case for noun complements, the default mechanism of *of*-insertion (operative in (37a)) can apparently not be used to save (37d).

In *Knowledge of Language* Chomsky (1986a) offers an explanation for the fact that *of*-insertion is not allowed in (36e) and (37e). Chomsky's solution uses a contrast between two types of case assignment. So far we have assumed that all case was dependent on purely structural relations. Specifically we assumed that the structural relation government is a sufficient condition for case-making. Chomsky distinguishes two types of case assignment: **structural** case assignment, which depends solely on government, a configurational property, and **inherent** case assignment, which is dependent on two conditions: (i) theta role assignment, and (ii) government:

38 **Inherent case condition**
    If A is an inherent case assigner, then A assigns case to an NP if and only if A theta-marks the NP.
    (Chomsky, 1986a: 194)

Chomsky proposes that nouns and adjectives assign GENITIVE case inherently and that rather than assigning structural case, as we implied previously, *of* is the overt reflex of an inherent GENITIVE case. In English an inherent GENITIVE in the complement of NP or AP is realized by means of a preposition *of* which assigns ACCUSATIVE case. There is thus a mismatch between the abstract GENITIVE case assigned inherently by the noun or the adjective, and the overt realization by means of a preposition which assigns ACCUSATIVE.[9]

The inherent case condition (38) entails that nouns such as *envy* or *belief* and adjectives such as *proud* will only be able to assign the inherent GENITIVE to NPs which they also theta-mark. The NP *the pig* can be assigned inherent case in (37a) because it is theta-marked by the A *proud*. On the other hand, in the examples where the noun *belief* and the adjective *proud* take a sentential complement the noun or adjective cannot assign GENITIVE case to the subject of the complement clause since the noun or adjective does not assign a theta role to the relevant NPs. In (36d), for instance, the noun *belief* assigns a theta role to the entire clausal complement and not to the NP *John*.

The distinctive property of inherent case is that it is sensitive to thematic relations and to the structural condition of head-government. Structural case, in contrast, is merely subject to structural requirements and is blind to thematic relations. If a structural case assigner governs an NP it can case-mark it whatever its thematic relation with that NP. We return to inherent case in the next section and in section 5.4.

3.3 *Inherent Case in German: Some Examples*

It is generally assumed that inherent case is rather restricted in English (see Kayne, 1984), but other languages have a more developed system of inherent

---

9   The interested reader is encouraged to read Chomsky (1986a: 186–204), which contains an accessible discussion of GENITIVE in English.

case. The DATIVE and GENITIVE in German are also assumed to be instances of inherent case. In this section we briefly illustrate DATIVE and
GENITIVE in German:

39a Sie hilft ihm.
     she helps him (DAT)
39b Er ist seinen Grundsätzen   treu.
     he is his   principles (DAT) faithful.
     (Haider, 1984: 68)
39c Er schreibt mit   einem Bleistift.
     he writes   with a   pencil (DAT)

40a Sie gedachte   vergangener Freuden.
     she remembered past   joy (GEN)
40b Dieser Mann muss des Französischen mächtig   sein.
     this   man   must French (GEN)   in command be
     (Haider, 1984: 68)
40c das Lied des   Kindes
     the song of the child (GEN)

Whether a verb, adjective or preposition assigns DATIVE or GENITIVE
has to be learnt for each individual item. Hence this property is arguably part
of its lexical entry. We shall assume DATIVE and GENITIVE are assigned
inherently. This means that these cases are associated with internal theta role
assignment. Let us try to be a little more precise. Suppose we say that the
inherent DATIVE case of *helfen* ('help'), for instance, is associated with the
internal theta role in the lexicon. The lexical entry for *helfen* is then as in
(41):

41 *helfen*: verb

1	2 DATIVE

In our discussion of passivization below (section 5) we shall provide some
support for the distinction between inherent case and structural case.
We have already mentioned that languages vary with respect to the overt

morphological realization of abstract case. Another distinction to be made between languages is in terms of the extent to which heads assign inherent case.

4 Adjacency and Case Assignment

Consider the following examples:

42a Poirot speaks [NP English] fluently.
42b *Poirot speaks fluently [NP English].
42c Poirot sincerely believes [IP English to be important].
42d *Poirot believes sincerely [IP English to be important].
42e Poirot believes sincerely [CP that English is important].

In (42a) the verb *speak* takes an NP complement *English* and VP further includes an adjunct *fluently*. The NP *Poirot* is case-marked by the finite INFL; the NP *English* is case-marked by the transitive verb. In (42b) the constituents of the sentence are not altered and yet the sentence is ungrammatical. The only contrast with (42a) is that the V *speak* and the complement NP *English* are no longer next to each other or **adjacent**.

A similar pattern is found in (42c) and (42d). In both sentences *believe* takes an IP complement. In (42c) the verb *believe* case-marks the subject NP of the lower clause (*English*) and the sentence is grammatical, while in (42d) the non-adjacency of the verb and the NP to which it should assign structural case leads to ungrammaticality.

The data in (42) have led linguists to propose that government is not a sufficient condition for case assignment in English and that a further structural requirement is that the case assigner and the element to which case is assigned should be adjacent.[10] By the adjacency requirement case assigners must not be separated from the NPs which they case-mark by intervening material and hence (42b) and (42d) are ungrammatical. In (42b) the verb *speak* would not be able to case-mark the NP *English* because there is

10 The adjacency condition on case assignment was first proposed by Stowell (1981). Recent developments of the theory cast some doubt on the application of this principle. On the one hand, it is being proposed (Chomsky, 1992) that all case assignment relations depend on specifier head agreement rather than on government by a case assigning head. On the other hand, we shall see in chapter 11 that the ungrammaticality of an example such as (42b) may well be due to other factors.

intervening material; the NP *English* will violate the case filter (25). In (42d) the verb *believe* must case-mark the subject of the non-finite clause, hence ought not be separated from it; again the NP *English* violates the case filter.

The adjacency requirement has nothing to say about (42e). On the one hand, a finite clause does not need to be case-marked. The case filter applies to NPs, not to clauses. On the other hand, the subject of the finite clause, the NP *English*, will satisfy the case filter because it receives NOMINATIVE from the finite I.

In the examples in (43) the interaction of the case filter and the adjacency requirement on case assignment will again account for the judgements given. We leave the reader to work out these examples.

43a   I prefer [the boys to leave first].
43b   *I prefer very much [the boys to leave first].
43c   I prefer very much [for [the boys to leave first]].
43d   I prefer very much [that [the boys should leave first]].

It might appear as if the adjacency requirement on case assignment cannot be a linguistic universal. Consider, for example, the following German[11] example:

44a   dass Poirot diesen Roman gestern gekauft hat
       that Poirot this novel yesterday bought has

[11]   At first sight the French examples in (i) might seem to illustrate the same phenom-
       enon:

       (ia)   Jean mange souvent du chocolat.
              Jean eats often chocolate
       (ib)   Jean mange tous les jours du chocolat.
              Jean eats every day chocolate

       (ib) can be assimilated to the text examples (44). Again there is a variant for this
       sentence, (ic), where the object NP is adjacent to the verb and hence one could
       assume that (ib) derives from (ic) by movement of the direct object:

       (ic)   Jean mange du chocolat tous les jours.

       But there is no such variant for (ia):

       (id)   *Jean mange du chocolat souvent.

       We consider the position of *souvent* in chapter 11.

In (44a) the direct object NP *diesen Roman* is not adjacent to the transitive verb *gekauft* ('bought'); if the direct object NP is assigned case by the transitive verb then (44a) should lead to a violation of the adjacency condition on case assignment. (44a) has a variant where the direct object is adjacent to the verb.

44b   dass Poirot gestern diesen Roman gekauft hat
      that Poirot yesterday this novel bought has
      'that Poirot bought this novel yesterday'

One possibility that we can pursue is to propose that (44a) is related to (44b). In fact we could say that (44a) can be derived from (44b): the idea would be that the object NP *diesen Roman* has been moved leftward in (44a). The movement of the object NP within a clausal domain is referred to as **scrambling**. We do not go into this point in any detail here. We shall return to movement operations in more general terms in chapters 6 and 7.

Another problem arises for examples such as (45):

45   John really did go there.

In (45) we assume that the finite INFL on *did* will assign NOMINATIVE to the subject NP *John*. If there is an adjacency requirement on case assignment then it is surprising that *John* can be separated from *did* by the intervening adverb *really*. One strategy would be to assume that in (45) too, *John* in fact originates in the position to the immediate left of *did* and is moved across the adverb. Another possibility is to restrict the adjacency condition on case assignment to case assignment under government and to say that NOMINATIVE case assignment in (45) is not dependent on government but rather that it depends on the specifier–head relation between [Spec, IP] and INFL. We could then say that when case is assigned in a specifier–head agreement configuration the adjacency condition is not relevant.

5   Passivization: Preliminary Discussion

This section contains an introductory description of passive sentences. We return to the discussion of passive in chapter 6. At this point we mainly wish to alert the reader to the salient features of passive and their relation to case theory.

5.1 *Passivization and Argument Structure*

Let us return to some of the earlier examples of case assignment.

46a Italy beat Belgium in the semi-finals.

According to the case filter (25) all overt NPs in the sentence above must be assigned case. The reader can verify that the case filter is satisfied in (46a). Now consider (46b), the passive pendant of (46a).

46b Belgium were beaten in the semi-finals.

The effects of passivization will be familiar from the traditional literature. First, passivization affects the morphology of the verb: in (46b) the verb *beat* turns up in its participial form and is accompanied by the auxiliary *be*.

Furthermore, in the passive sentence the AGENT of the activity is not expressed by an NP in an A-position. If we wish to refer to the AGENT of the action we need to use an adjunct PP headed by the preposition *by*, which itself carries the notion of AGENTIVITY.

47 Belgium were beaten *by Italy* in the semi-finals.

In (47) *by* assigns the theta role AGENT to the NP *Italy*. That the AGENT role need not be expressed in (46b) is rather puzzling. In chapter 1 we introduced the projection principle which posits that syntactic structure is determined by lexical properties. We also adopted the theta criterion requiring that each theta role associated with a predicate be assigned to some argument (an NP or a clausal complement). In (46a) the main predicate is the verb *beat* whose argument structure is given in (48):

48 *beat*: verb

1	2

(46a) satisfies the theta criterion and the projection principle. The NP *Italy* is assigned the external theta role (1) – AGENT – and the direct object NP *Belgium* is assigned the internal theta role (2) – PATIENT.

The situation in (46b) is less clear. We clearly have the same predicate *beat* which has the same meaning as in (46a) and thus should have the theta grid (48). In (46b) there is only one argument to theta-mark, the NP *Belgium*, the subject of the sentence. Intuitively, it seems wrong to assign the external AGENT role to the NP *Belgium*. In (46b), just as in (46a), the NP *Belgium* does not refer to the AGENT of 'beat', i.e. the entity that initiates the activity, but rather to the one that undergoes it, i.e. this NP is assigned the PATIENT role. Thus we conclude that the AGENT role (1) is not assigned to an NP in an A-position. It will be taken as a crucial property of passive verbs that they fail to assign the external theta role to an NP in an A-position.

However, in (46b) we 'feel' that there is an implied AGENT, 'someone beat Belgium'. Jaeggli (1986) and Roberts (1987) propose that the AGENT role is not absent in passive sentences, rather, they claim, it is **absorbed** by the passive morphology on the verb. The external theta role cannot be assigned to an NP in an A-position because it is absorbed by the passive ending. When the AGENT needs to be expressed overtly, it is expressed by means of an adjunct PP with *by*, as in (47).

Let us look at some more examples:

49a   Everyone believes that Bertie is a liar.
49b   It is widely believed that Bertie is a liar.

The properties associated with passivization and discussed with respect to (46b) also obtain in (49):

(i)   the verb occurs in a participial form (*believed*) with *be*;
(ii) the external theta role is not assigned to an NP.

In (49b) the subject position is occupied by *it*, an expletive, i.e. an element lacking a theta role (cf. the discussion of expletives in chapter 1). The expletive is allowed in the subject position precisely because the external theta role of *believe* is not assigned to an NP in this position.

5.2   Case Absorption

If we compare (46) and (49b), the question arises why we could not also introduce an expletive in the subject position of a passive sentence like (46) and leave the complement NP in the VP-internal position:

50a *It was beaten Belgium.
50b *There was beaten Belgium.

The difference between (50) and (49b) is minimal: in the ungrammatical (50), the verb assigns the internal theta role to the NP *Belgium*, in (49b) the internal theta role is assigned to a clausal complement *that Bertie is a liar*. But what could explain their different status? The ungrammaticality of (50a) may be explained because *it* as an expletive has to be in construction with clauses and not with NPs (see chapter 1). Let us turn to (50b). In our account NPs have one crucial property that distinguishes them from clauses: NPs need case. We capitalize on this difference and try to explain the ungrammaticality of (50b) in terms of case theory. We shall assume that a passivized verb loses the ability to assign structural ACCUSATIVE case to its complement.[12] In chapter 6 we link the absorption of the external theta role to the absorption of structural case.

Given the assumption that passive verbs absorb structural case the ungrammaticality of (50b) follows. The object NP *Belgium* will not be able to receive ACCUSATIVE case from the verb *beaten*. Hence (50b) violates the case filter: the object NP fails to be case-marked. Given this assumption, (50a) will also be ruled out for case reasons: here too the NP *Belgium* cannot be assigned ACCUSATIVE case.

The only way to rescue these sentences is to allow the complement of the verb to receive case in another position in the sentence. The obvious candidate is the [Spec, IP] position to which NOMINATIVE case is assigned by the finite INFL. The [Spec, IP] position is available in passive sentences because the external argument of the predicate, which is associated with the [Spec, IP] position in active sentences, is not assigned to an NP in an A-position. The object NP is thus moved to the subject position. Movement of the clausal complement of *believe* to the subject position is also possible:

51 [CP That Bertie is a liar] is widely believed.

This movement is not obligatory, given that clausal arguments are not subject to the case filter.[13] Movement of an NP from the object to the subject position

[12] We have said that in passive sentences the external theta role is implicit. Following Jaeggli (1986) and Roberts (1987) we say that the external theta role is absorbed by the verb morphology. This means that it is 'present' in the sentence. Some evidence for this proposal is that the adverbial *widely* in (49b) seems to modify the implicit external theta role of *believed*. Jaeggli (1986) and Roberts (1987) propose that the passive morphology absorbs the case because it also absorbs the thematic role. The absorbed case in fact is associated with the absorbed theta role.
[13] Koster (1987) provides important evidence that the clause in (51) is not in the specifier position of IP. See also chapter 1 above, footnote 14.

in passive sentences is obligatory because this is the only way that such NPs can pass the case filter.[14]

Consider the examples in (52):

52a   I believe [Emsworth to have attacked Poirot].

52b   I believe [Poirot to have been attacked].

52c   *It was believed [Emsworth to have attacked Poirot].

52d   It was believed [that [Emsworth had attacked Poirot]].

(52a) illustrates ECM. In the non-finite subordinate clause the external argument of *attack* is assigned ACCUSATIVE by *believe*, and the internal argument *Poirot* is assigned ACCUSATIVE by the active V *attacked*. In (52b) the verb *attacked* is passive. The external argument is not expressed. We have proposed that passive verbs cannot assign ACCUSATIVE. Hence, in order to pass the case filter the NP *Poirot* must be **moved** to the [Spec, IP] position of the non-finite clause where it can be assigned ACCUSATIVE case by the

[14]   The reader may have observed that one may find passive sentences where the NP which receives the internal theta role is not in [Spec, IP]:

(i)   There were attacked [NP no fewer than three robbers].

If the passive verb is unable to assign case, how then does the bracketed NP pass the case filter? The answer to this question is complex and involves a discussion of the existential construction with *there*. One approach would be to adopt Belletti's (1988) account. Belletti proposes that passive verbs absorb the capacity to assign structural case, but that they may nevertheless assign an inherent PARTITIVE case. She argues further that the fact that only indefinite NPs are allowed in patterns such as (i) is related to the fact that such NPs would have PARTITIVE case. The reader is referred to Belletti's own work for discussion.

verb *believe*. We return to movement operations in section 6.2 and in chapters 6 and 7. The ungrammaticality of (52c) is due to the same reason as that in (50b): the passive verb *believed* is unable to assign case, hence the NP *Emsworth*, subject of an infinitival clause, violates the case filter. The reader can verify for himself that (52d) passes the case filter.

5.3 The Properties of Passivization

Let us summarize the major syntactic properties of passivization so far established. We return to them at length in chapter 6 where we discuss the movement of the object NP in much greater detail. Passivization has the following properties:

(i)   the verb morphology is affected;
(ii) the external theta role of the verb is absorbed;
(iii) the structural case of the verb is absorbed;
(iv) the NP which is assigned the internal theta role of the passive verb moves to a position where it can be assigned case;
(v)   the movement of the NP is obligatory in view of the case filter;
(vi) the movement of the NP is allowed because the subject position is empty.

The question arises whether these properties are in any way related, i.e. if one property can be said to be dependent on, i.e. explained by, another property. If this is not the case then we would have to assume that a child acquiring a language will have to learn all six properties above one by one. As mentioned above, Jaeggli (1986) and Roberts (1987) have proposed that properties (i) and (ii) can be linked by saying that the external theta role of the passivized verb is absorbed by the passive morphology. In chapter 6 we shall see that property (iii) can be linked to property (ii). The reader can check that (iv) is a consequence of the combination of (i), (ii) and (iii) and the case filter. Similarly, (v) and (vi) follow from property (iii), the case filter and the fact that the subject position is empty because there is no external argument (ii). The connection between the properties listed above is important. It means that a child acquiring a language will not have to learn all the properties above. Once (i) and (ii) are established, for instance, all the other properties can be deduced. If we adopt the proposal, due to Jaeggli (1986) and to Roberts (1987), that (i) and (ii) are also related, then all a child needs to do is identify the passive morphology (i).

As it stands we have treated the properties listed above as specific to the passive construction. Chapter 6 will show that these properties are not only found in passive sentences, they are not construction-specific, but they can be found in other types of sentences.

5.4 Passive and Inherent Case

5.4.1 GERMAN

We have introduced the contrast between inherent and structural case in section 3. In this section we provide some further illustration of the difference between the two types of case. We shall see that passivization of a verb affects its potential for assigning structural case but does not have any effect on the inherent case assigning properties.

Consider the following examples:

53a Sie sieht ihn.
    ACCUSATIVE
  She sees him.
53b Er   wird gesehen.
  NOMINATIVE
  He   is seen.
53c *Ihn   wird gesehen.
  ACCUSATIVE
  Him   is seen.
54a Sie hilft ihm.
     DATIVE
  She helps him.
54b *Er   wird geholfen.
  NOMINATIVE
  He   is helped.
54c Ihm wird geholfen.
  DATIVE
  him is helped

55a Sie gedachte vergangener Freuden.
     GENITIVE
  she remembered past   joy
55b Vergangener Freuden wurde gedacht.
  GENITIVE
  past   joy was remembered
(from Haider, 1985: 68)

The examples in (53) are predicted by the properties of passivization discussed above: passive *gesehen* absorbs the external theta role assigned to *Sie* in (53a) and it cannot assign ACCUSATIVE case. Hence (53c) is out: there is no ACCUSATIVE to assign. In (53b) the internal argument NP of *gesehen* is assigned NOMINATIVE by INFL.

(54) and (55) show that apparently only ACCUSATIVE is absorbed: DATIVE and GENITIVE survive under passivization. In order to explain this property of German we shall use our hypothesis (section 3.3) that the DATIVE and GENITIVE in German (54) and (55) are instances of inherent case. Passivization alters the theta grid for the verb in that it absorbs the external theta role. But, crucially, this need not affect the properties of the internal theta role. We assume that inherent case, which is associated with the internal theta role, is unaffected by passivization. If DATIVE is an inherent case then the pattern in (54) is accounted for. If GENITIVE case is inherent then the pattern in (55) follows.[15]

5.4.2 THE DOUBLE OBJECT CONSTRUCTION IN ENGLISH: DISCUSSION

If it is a property of inherent case that it survives passivization then it could be argued that GENITIVE is not the only inherent case in English. Consider (56).

56a I gave John a book.
56b John was given a book.

In this chapter, we have not said anything about verbs like *give* in (56a) which appear to take two internal arguments. These are subject to much discussion. The question we address here is how both VP-internal NPs in (56a) are assigned case.

From passive (56b) we deduce that the NP *John* must receive structural case in the active sentence (56a): in the passive sentence it loses its ACCUSATIVE and is assigned NOMINATIVE. English contrasts in this respect with many other languages where the indirect object cannot be nominativized in the passive.

57 *German*
57a Ich gab ihm   ein Buch.
     I   gave him (DAT) a   book

---

[15] For a discussion of the German case system, see Haider (1985) and the references cited there.

57b *Er   wurde ein Buch gegeben.
     he (NOM) was   a   book given
57c Ihm   wurde ein Buch gegeben.
     him (DAT) was   a   book given

58   *French*
58a Je donne un livre   à   Jean.
     I give   a   book   to   Jean
58b Je lui   donne un   livre.
     I to-him give   a   book
58c *Jean/Il est donné un livre.
     Jean/he is   given a   book

Kayne (1984) argues that English has lost inherent DATIVE case and that the indirect object in (56a) is assigned a structural ACCUSATIVE through the intermediary of the verb. In French and German the idea would be that the indirect object receives DATIVE and that passivization does not affect DATIVE.

The direct object *a book* in (56) is a problem, though. If it is assigned a structural ACCUSATIVE by the active verb *give* in (56a) then it is not obvious why the ACCUSATIVE is not affected by the passivization. If the NP *a book* is not assigned ACCUSATIVE by the verb, then what is its case? One approach would be to say that in (56a) the direct object is inherently case-marked. Inherent case is not lost under passivization.[16]

6   Visibility

6.1   *Explaining the Case Filter*

The case filter (25) applies to all overt NPs and filters out those overt NPs that lack abstract case. Remember that case can be either structural or inherent. Linguists have tried to explain this filter by relating it to other properties of the grammar. One hypothesis is based on the observation that, following

[16]   The issue of the double object construction is a very interesting one and we cannot go into all the details of the discussion here. The reader is referred to work by Chomsky (1981a: 170–1), Czepluch (1982), Haegeman (1986b), Kayne (1984), Larson (1988), Roberts (1983) and the literature cited by these authors. Most of these texts will be accessible once we have covered chapter 6.

the theta criterion, argument NPs must be assigned a theta role. The idea is then that a predicate can only assign a theta role to NPs that are **visible**. Abstract case renders an NP visible.[17]

Under this view, the case filter is no longer an independent property of the grammar. Rather it **derives** from the **visibility requirement** on NPs. This property in itself is related to theta theory: in order to be recognized as an argument of some predicate an NP must be made visible. Invisible NPs cannot be assigned a theta role. Hence, sentences in which we have argument NPs without case violate the theta criterion. Returning to our metaphor of the play, we could say that the argument NPs must be made visible by means of case in the way that the characters playing a part in a performance must be made recognizable by their outward appearance. If all actors looked identical we would not be able to tell who is playing which part. NPs are **licensed** by virtue of their case properties.

6.2 Movement and Chains (Introduction)

The visibility hypothesis sketched in section 6.1 raises further questions with respect to passive sentences. We shall introduce the issue here and return to it in chapter 6.

Consider:

59   [IP Poirot   [I′ will [VP be attacked—]]].

   ↑NOM

The major properties of passivization are listed in section 5.3. However, on closer inspection there remain important problems.

Our hypothesis developed so far is that in (59) *Poirot* is assigned NOMINATIVE case by the finite INFL. We assume that it is theta-marked by the (passive) verb *attacked*, the head of VP. In chapter 1 we postulated, though, that internal theta roles are assigned under government. In (59) there is no way that we can claim that the verb *attacked* governs the NP *Poirot* in the subject position. The question is how the verb *attacked* can theta-mark *Poirot*.

---

[17]   Chomsky (1981a: 170–83) discusses the link between visibility and case. This section will be accessible once we have read chapter 8.
   Baker (1988) proposes that the visibility requirement be replaced by a requirement of morphological identification, or m-identification. This can be achieved by case-marking. Baker also suggests other ways of m-identifying an NP. See Baker's work for discussion. The book presupposes most of the content of this book.

We have introduced the idea that abstract case is a condition on theta-marking. In (59) *Poirot*, the internal argument of *attacked*, cannot remain inside the VP because it would fail to be assigned case, the passive verb having lost its capacity for assigning the structural ACCUSATIVE case. If *Poirot* lacks case, it is not visible and therefore cannot receive a theta role from the verb. Hence *Poirot* must move in order to be case-marked and become visible. We conclude that the NP *Poirot* is forced to move to [Spec, IP] and thus to leave the VP-internal position in which it can receive its (internal) theta role.

We seem to be in a dilemma: on the one hand, *Poirot* should sit inside the VP to receive the internal theta role from *attacked*, and, on the other hand, it must move out of the VP to become visible and to be able to be theta-marked. What we seem to want to say is that the NP *Poirot* must be present inside the VP headed by *attack*, in order to be assigned the internal theta role, and that it also must be moved out of the VP to the subject position where it can be assigned NOMINATIVE case. This looks like a desperate situation: we want *Poirot* to be in two positions simultaneously: a position in which it can be theta-marked, or a **theta position** for short, and a position in which it can be case-marked, a **case position**. However, the situation can be rescued. We sketch the solution informally below and return to it in greater detail in chapters 6 and 8.

In order to maintain the idea that the internal theta role is assigned under government and the hypothesis that NPs are visible by virtue of being assigned case, we shall capitalize on the fact that the NP is moved. *Poirot* starts out as the object of *attacked*. In a way, *Poirot* IS the object of *attacked*. Then the NP *Poirot* is moved to the subject position. At this point *Poirot* IS the subject of the sentence. As will be shown extensively in chapter 6, we are led to conclude that there are two levels of syntactic representation for (59): one before the movement and one after. When *Poirot* has left the object position there remains an unfilled position or a gap inside the VP of (59).

We shall assume that the moved NP and the gap remain linked. *Poirot* is, as it were, chained to the VP-internal slot which it has deserted. The sequence of the two positions is referred to as a **chain**. We shall provisionally represent the vacant position by an *e*, for empty. We indicate that two positions are part of a chain by **coindexation**. In chapter 6 we return to representations such as (60) and to the concept chain.

60   [$_{IP}$ Poirot$_i$ [$_{I'}$ will [$_{VP}$ be attacked e$_i$]]]

We now propose that the internal theta role of *attacked* is not assigned to the NP *Poirot* as such, nor to the vacated position indicated by *e* in (60), but that it is the chain consisting of the vacant position *e* and the subject NP which will be assigned the theta role. The chain of two elements is represented as follows: $<NP_i, e_i>$.

In order to incorporate the ideas of visibility and chain formation we reformulate the theta criterion (chapter 1) in terms of chains.

61   **Theta criterion**

61a   Each argument A appears in a chain containing a unique visible theta position P, and each theta position P is visible in a chain containing a unique argument A.
(Chomsky, 1986a: 97)

61b   A position P is visible in a chain if the chain contains a case-marked position.
(Chomsky, 1986a: 96)

Let us assume that theta roles are assigned to positions, theta positions. One possibility is that an argument A appears in the theta position P. In this case it picks up the theta role in its position. We could say there is a one-member chain. This situation is illustrated in (62):

62   [$_{IP}$ The robber$_j$ [$_{I'}$ -ed [$_{VP}$ attack Poirot$_i$].

Theta role

ACCUSATIVE

In (62) *Poirot$_i$* is governed by *attack*. The NP is in its theta position and can pick up the theta role directly. The NP *Poirot* is in a chain with only one element, *<Poirot$_i$>*.

Alternatively, an argument NP has been moved out of P. It will form a chain with the vacated position and it will pick up the theta role assigned to the position P via the chain. This is illustrated in (60). In this example, the relevant argument NP is *Poirot*. The NP is the internal argument of *attack*, but it has left the theta position in order to pick up NOMINATIVE case in the subject position. The moved NP forms a chain with the vacated position: *<Poirot$_i$, e$_i$>*. The chain is visible thanks to the NOMINATIVE case assigned to the highest position and is thus able to receive the internal theta role from *attacked*.

63 [IP Poirot_i   [I' will [VP be attacked   e_i]]].

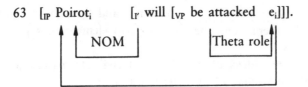

From this first, admittedly sketchy, discussion, the reader can see that 'empty positions' count as much in our theory as positions that are filled. This issue will become central from chapter 5 onwards. In chapter 6 we return to passivization and to chain formation.

6.3 *Case and NP-licensing*

Recall that we discussed the question as to whether the lexical information associated with a head should specify the categorial properties of its arguments in chapter 1, section 7.1. We considered examples such as the following:

64a I asked what the time was.
64b I asked the time.

65a I inquired what time it was.
65b *I inquired the time.

66a I wondered what time it was.
66b *I wondered the time.

It was proposed that we do not need to specify that verbs like *ask*, *inquire* and *wonder* select a CP, since CP is the canonical structural representation of questions. However, following Grimshaw (1979, 1981) we suggested that perhaps non-canonical realizations of arguments should be specified lexically, so that the lexical information associated with *ask* could specify that this verb selects an NP complement. *Wonder* and *inquire* would lack that specification. NP complements which receive a question interpretation are called concealed questions. (65b) and (66b) are ungrammatical because they violate the categorial selection properties of the verbs, *inquire* and *wonder* respectively.

However, using the notions of case theory developed in the present chapter, we might argue that in fact no categorial specification is needed in the lexical entries of predicates such as verbs. What could be said is the following: *ask*, *inquire* and *wonder* all select a complement which is interpreted as a question. In principle, questions can be realized both by CPs and by NPs. But if an argument is realized as an NP, then the NP will have to be assigned case. If we then specify that only *ask* can assign case, and that *inquire* and *wonder* are not case assigners, then it will follow that only *ask*, and not *inquire* or *wonder*, can actually take an NP complement. (65b) and (66b) would then not be excluded because they violate categorial selection but rather because the NP complement lacks case.[18]

7 Summary

Case theory is the module of the grammar concerned with the distribution of NPs. The case filter imposes a requirement on the licensing of NPs:

1 **Case filter**
Every overt NP must be assigned abstract case.

We distinguish abstract case from morphological case and we distinguish two types of abstract case: structural case (NOMINATIVE and ACCUSATIVE) and inherent case (the English GENITIVE and the German DATIVE and GENITIVE). V and P assign structural ACCUSATIVE under government. Finite I assigns NOMINATIVE case, either under government or by virtue of specifier–head agreement. Inherent case assignment depends also on theta role assignment.

In our discussion we have used the following definition of government:

2 **Government**
A governs B if and only if
  (i)   A is a governor;
  (ii) A m-commands B;
  (iii) no barrier intervenes between A and B;
where
  (a) governors are the lexical heads (V, N, P, A) and tensed I;
  (b) maximal projections are barriers

---

[18] The proposal that c-selection can be made to follow from case theory is due to Pesetsky (1982). For an evaluation of Pesetsky's proposal see Rothstein (1992). This article will be accessible after we have studied the material in Chapter 6. See also exercise 8 below.

A further requirement on case assignment is the adjacency condition.

It is a property of passive verbs that they do not assign the external theta role to an NP in an A-position and that they lose the ability to assign structural case. However, passive verbs retain their capacity to assign case inherently (section 5).

The case filter is not an independent principle of the grammar but can be related to theta theory via a visibility condition: in order to be theta-marked, an NP needs to be visible; in order to become visible an NP needs to be case-marked. In order to maintain the requirement that an NP can only be theta-marked if visible, i.e. when case-marked, we need to introduce the notion chain, which establishes a link between a theta position and a case position. The theta criterion is now defined in terms of chains.

3 **Theta criterion**
Each argument A appears in a chain containing a unique visible theta position P, and each theta position P is visible in a chain containing a unique argument A.
(Chomsky, 1986a: 97)

8 Exercises

Exercise 1

Consider the examples below. How do the NPs acquire case?

1 John left the university at noon.
2 I expect him to have written the letter by Friday.
3 For Jane to have bought the house is rather remarkable.
4 It is odd that Bill should have refused the offer.
5 Rembrandt's picture of Saskia is remarkably well preserved.
6 I want my coffee boiling hot.
7 For him to have agreed to the proposal is surprising.
8 Children should not treat their parents in this way.
9 I want these demonstrators in jail by tomorrow.
10 She thinks that Poirot will abandon the investigation.
11 Poirot is anxious for the children to return to town soon.
12 Miss Marple is aware of the problems.

13 Miss Marple has been contradicted by the inspectors.
14 Maigret gave his pipe to Janvier.
15 The book was given to the best student in the class.

Exercise 2

Consider the examples below. To what extent does case theory explain the contrasts in grammaticality?

1 Poirot preferred very much for the detectives to destroy the evidence.
2 Poirot believed Watson to be incompetent.
3 Poirot preferred the police to destroy the evidence.
4 *Poirot preferred very much the police to destroy the evidence.
5 *Anyone to destroy the evidence would be regrettable.
6 *I consider very much John to be a good candidate.
7 They consider Maigret entirely incompetent.
8 *It is considered Maigret entirely incompetent.

Exercise 3

It has been proposed (see section 6.1) that NPs need case because they need to be visible in order to receive a theta role. Discuss the problems raised for this approach by the following examples.[19]

1 It is regrettable that John has left.
2 I consider it to be regrettable that John has left.
3 *I consider very much it to be regrettable that John has left.
4 It is thought that it is regrettable that John has left.
5 They thought it regrettable that John had left.
6 *It is thought it regrettable that John has left.
7 There won't be many people at the meeting.
8 I don't expect there to be many people at the meeting.
9 *I expect very much there to be many people at the meeting.

[19] For discussion see Davis (1986).

Exercise 4

In section 4 we propose that structural case assignment is subject to an adjacency condition. This requirement will cause problems for the examples below. Discuss these problems.

1   You should drink after every meal a glass of boiling hot milk with honey.
2   Which detective would you like to invite?
3   On the wall was hanging a large picture of Napoleon.
4   *French*
    Quels   livres   a   acheté   Jean?
    which   books   has   bought   Jean
    'Which books has John bought?'
5   *Dutch*
    Jan koopt   altijd   oude   boeken.
    Jan buys   always   old   books
6   *Dutch*
    Jan heeft waarschijnlijk   die   oude   boeken gisteren   gekocht.
    Jan has   probably   those old   books   yesterday bought
7   *Dutch*
    Oude   boeken   heeft   Jan   nog   nooit   gekocht.
    old   books   has   Jan   yet   never   bought
8   *German*
    Diesen Studenten   hat   er   nicht   gesehen.
    this   student   has   he   not   seen
9   *German*
    Diesem Studenten   hat   er   nicht   geholfen.
    this   student   has   he   not   helped
    DATIVE
10 I really will help you.

Exercise 5

Discuss the assignment of case in the examples below. Which problems, if any, do they raise for case theory, discussed in chapter 3? Try to provide a classification of the types of problems that arise. As you can see, the problems are often not language-specific. In subsequent chapters some of the problems that you identify here will be solved very easily. Others, though, are a persistent problem for the theory.

1 John being in hospital, his wife has signed the cheques.
2 Poirot is coming back this week.
3 You should hold the pen this way.
4 The detective and his wife are coming back soon.
5 I saw him in the courtyard, his hands in his pockets.
6 Detective stories, I have never liked them.
7 Agatha Christie I have never liked.
8 Poirot smokes cigars and Maigret a pipe.
9 There remain different problems.
10 *French*
   Quand Pierre est-il   arrivé?
   when   Pierre is-he   arrived
   'When did Pierre arrive?'
11 *West Flemish* (a dialect of Dutch)[20]
   Jan peinst da-ze   zie   dienen boek a   gelezen eet.
   Jan thinks that-she she   that   book already read   has
   'Jan thinks that she has already read that book.'
   (*Zie* is the stressed form of the third person singular pronoun. The form *ze* is a weak form of the third person singular pronoun which attaches to the complementizer.)
12 Mee   zie   dat   hus   te verkopen is alles   veranderd.
   With she   that house to sell   is everything changed
         NOMINATIVE
   'Everything has changed because she has sold that house.'
13 *German*
   Ich weiss dass es   Hans gestern   gekauft hat.
   I   know that it (dir. obj.) Hans yesterday bought has
   I   know that   Hans bought   it   yesterday
14 *French*
   Il est arrivé un accident grave hier.
   it is   arrived an accident bad   yesterday
   'Yesterday there occurred a bad accident.'
15 Il a   voulu   acheter le   livre hier.
   he has   wanted   buy   the book   yesterday
   'He wanted to buy the book yesterday.'

---

[20] For a description of West Flemish, see Haegeman (1992).

16 Il l'avait déjà   acheté hier.
    he it-had already bought   yesterday
    'He had already bought it yesterday.'

17 *Italian*
    Gianni aveva voluto comprare il   libro ieri.
    Gianni had   wanted buy   the book yesterday
    'Gianni had wanted to buy the book yesterday.'

18 Gianni aveva voluto comprarlo ieri.
    Gianni had   wanted buy-it   yesterday
    'Gianni had wanted to buy it yesterday'.

19 Gianni l'aveva voluto comprare ieri.
    Gianni it-had   wanted buy   yesterday
    (= 18)

20 Comprati gli   stivali, Maria è   partita.
    bought   the   boots,   Maria is gone
    'Having bought the boots, Maria left.'

Exercise 6

In descriptive grammars the terms NOMINATIVE case and ACCUSA-TIVE case have sometimes been replaced by 'subject-form' and 'object-form' respectively. On the basis of our discussion in chapter 3, consider whether these labels are appropriate.

Exercise 7

In this chapter we have assumed that both infinitival IP and the small clause boundary do not constitute barriers for outside government and hence allow for their subjects to be case-marked by a governing verb:

1 I expect [$_{IP}$ you to be in my office at four].
2 I expect [you in my office at four].

What problems do the following sentences pose for treating small clauses and non-finite clauses identically with respect to case-marking.[21]

---

[21] For a discussion of small clauses, see Stowell (1983). This paper will be accessible once we have covered chapter 8.

3 For workers to be angry about pay is really undesirable.
4 *Workers to be angry about pay is really undesirable.
5 Workers angry about pay is a situation which we must avoid.

Exercise 8

In the discussion we have proposed that certain verbs are case assigners and others are not. We also propose that passivization entails absorption of structural case. This means that passivization would be restricted to transitive verbs which can case-mark their NP complement. In section 6.3 we also examined the idea that categorial selectional features of verbs partly derive from case properties. Consider the data below and evaluate the proposals:

1a I asked what the time was.
1b It was asked what the time was.
1c I asked the time.

2a I inquired what the time was.
2b *It was inquired what the time was.
2c *I inquired the time.

3a I wondered what the time was.
3b It was wondered what the time was.
3c *I wondered the time.

4a I hope that you will learn from this.
4b It is to be hoped that you will learn from this.
4c *I hope a good result.

5a They claimed that this construction is ungrammatical.
5b It has been claimed that this construction is ungrammatical.
5c *They claim the ungrammaticality of this construction.

Do you think we can maintain that passivization is restricted to verbs which case-mark their objects? For discussion of these and other examples the reader is referred to Rothstein (1992). Consider the following Dutch sentences in the light of the discussion of passivization:

6a Er werd de hele nacht gelachen en gepraat.
there was the whole night laughed and talked
'They laughed and talked the whole night.'

6b Er werd plots geschoten.
there was suddenly shot
'Suddenly shots were fired.'

Dutch, unlike English, can passivize intransitive verbs. Speakers of German can verify that this kind of passivization is also possible in German.

Ship To:

Enrique Trevino
12016 Windsor Manor Rd
Upper Marlboro, MD 207727917 USA

Ship From:

TEXTBOOKSNOW-AMAZON
8950 W PALMER ST
RIVER GROVE, IL 60171

TEXTBOOKSNOW-AMAZON   Order #: 112-4398686-6457043
8950 W PALMER ST
RIVER GROVE, IL 60171

(Attn: Returns)

DE98431

Order #: 112-4398686-6457043

SKU	Qty	Condition	Date: 01/31/2013	Title	Price	Total
23676047U	1			UsedIntro to Government & Binding Theory	$ 35.68	$ 35.68
				2 9780631190677 Refund Eligible Through= 3/5/2013		

Sub Total	$	35.68
Shipping & Handling	$	3.99
Sales Tax	$	0.00
Order Total	**$**	**39.67**

Refund Policy: All items must be returned within 30 days of receipt. Pack your book securely, so it will arrive back to us in its original condition. To avoid delays, please use the return section and label provided with your original packing slip to identify your return. Be sure to include a return reason. For your protection, we suggest using a traceable, insured shipping service (UPS or Insured Parcel Post). We are not responsible for lost or damaged returns. Item(s) returned must be received in the original condition as sold and including all additional materials such as CDs, workbooks, etc. We will initiate a refund of your purchase price including applicable taxes within 5 business days of receipt. Shipping charges will not be refunded unless we have committed an error with your order. If there is an error with your order or the item is not received in the condition as purchased, please contact us immediately for return assistance.

Reason for Refund/Return:
Condition: Incorrect Item Received   Incorrect Item Ordered   Dropped Class   Purchased Elsewhere   Other
Contact Us: For customer service, email us at customerservice@textbooksnow.com.

Page 1 of 1

Order #: 112-4398686-6457043

We are in the process of relocating to our new Aurora Illinois Distribution Facility. You may receive orders shipped from one or both River Grove and Aurora locations until our move is complete. Some orders may be split with a portion fulfilled from our two locations - generating two shipments, each having its own packing slip, but consolidated into a single invoice or charge to your account, whichever is applicable.

4 Anaphoric Relations and Overt NPS

Contents

Introduction and overview

Introduction and Overview

So far we have been looking at formal properties of sentences. We saw that the obligatory constituents of a sentence are required by the projection principle, the extended projection principle and theta theory (chapter 1). We have formulated an articulated theory of phrase structure, X′-theory (chapter 2), and we have discussed the distribution of NPs as regulated by case theory (chapter 3).

In this chapter we turn to some aspects of the interpretation of noun phrases. The module of the grammar regulating NP interpretation will be referred to as the **binding theory**. The reader will by now see why the particular theory we are presenting here is often referred to as Government and Binding Theory. In this chapter the concept binding comes in. Government has already been shown to be a structural property which is involved in syntactic processes such as theta-marking and case-marking, and in the present chapter too, government will be of primary importance. The version of the binding theory that we shall develop here is mainly based on work by Chomsky.[1]

The binding theory is the module of the grammar that will be responsible for assigning an appropriate interpretation to the italicized NPs in sentences like the following:

1a *Poirot* admires *him*.
1b *Bertie* hurt *himself*.
1c *Bertie* said that *he* felt rather ill.
1d *Bertie* expected *him* to feel a little better.
1e *He* expected *Bertie* to feel a little better.
1f *He* said that *Bertie* felt a little better.

Three types of NPs are distinguished:

(i)   full noun phrases such as *Poirot, Bertie*, etc.;
(ii) **pronouns** such as *he* and *him*, etc.;
(iii) **reflexive** elements such as *himself*, etc.

---

[1] For an accessible introduction see Chomsky (1988a). Chomsky has developed the theory in work published throughout the eighties (1980, 1981a, 1982, 1986a). Most of these studies are very advanced. Higginbotham (1980, 1983, 1988) and Burzio (1991) offer alternative proposals for the binding theory. Again these works are very advanced and should not be tackled until the reader has worked his way through this book.

A full nominal expression such as *Poirot* refers independently. Such an NP selects a referent from the **universe of discourse**, the things we know and talk about. The use of the full NP indicates that there is, or is thought to be, an entity which is identifiable by the NP. We can say informally that a lexical NP is able to select a referent by virtue of its inherent properties. It is a referential expression.

Pronouns, on the other hand, do not select a referent from the universe of discourse. Consider, for instance, the interpretation of the pronoun *he/him*. In (1a) all we know is that *him* refers to an entity that is characterized by its nominal features [+ Singular] and [+ Male]. The features of gender and number restrict the entities picked out by a pronoun, but they do not allow us to identify a uniquely specified referent from the universe of discourse. The pronoun *him* will merely select a subgroup from the wider domain of entities which we might want to talk about. On the other hand, we cannot freely choose any entity which is male as a referent for *him* in (1a): *him* cannot be used to refer to Poirot.

At this point we are talking about the interpretation of a pronoun in a sentence without any context. As soon as (1a) is contextualized we have a clearer idea as to the referent of the pronoun *him*. For instance, in the context (2) the most natural interpretation will be for *him* to refer to the same entity as that referred to by *Jeeves*.

2   A   And what about Jeeves?
    B   Poirot admires him.

Our grammar need not account for the fact that *him* in (2) will probably be taken to refer to the entity denoted by *Jeeves*. This interpretation is not a function of the properties of sentence (1a), rather it derives from the use of the sentence for communicative purposes and it arises in a specific context. Interpretive matters which depend on the context outside the sentence are not regulated in a sentence grammar but are dealt with in the domain of study that is concerned with utterance interpretation. This area of study is often referred to as pragmatics.[2]

On the other hand, the fact that *him* and *Poirot* cannot be coreferential in (1a) is a matter of the grammar. It is the natural interpretation of the sentence independently of context.[3] (1b) contains two NPs: *Bertie* and the reflexive

---

[2]   For an interesting account of the interpretation of utterances in context the reader
      is referred to work by Kempson (1988a, b) and by Sperber and Wilson (1986).
[3]   The grammatical principle that *him* and *Poirot* cannot be coreferential in (1a) may
      be overridden in special discourse contexts. Consider:

(i)   Everyone admires Poirot. I admire him, you admire him and Poirot certainly
      admires him.

Examples such as these are referred to as accidental coreference and are discussed
in Evans (1980).

element *himself*. In this sentence the interpretation of the reflexive is apparently determined independently of the context: regardless of the context chosen, *himself* must be interpreted as dependent on the subject NP *Bertie*. An interesting contrast appears when we compare (1c) and (1d). In (1c) the pronoun *he* can be interpreted as coreferential with the subject NP *Bertie* in the higher clause; in (1d) this is not the case. The contrast between (1c) and (1d) is determined by syntactic principles: in (1c) the pronoun *he* is the subject of a finite clause, in (1d) *him* is the subject of a non-finite clause. Finally compare (1c) with (1f). In (1c) the main clause subject NP *Bertie* can be coreferential with the subject of the lower finite clause, *he*. In (1f) we have reversed the positions of the lexical NP *Bertie* and the pronoun *he*, and coreference is no longer possible. Regardless of the context, the interpretation where *he* and *Bertie* are coreferential in (1f) is excluded (cf. footnote 3 though), while it is very natural in (1c).

The examples above already illustrate that the interpretation of NPs is, at least partly, constrained by grammatical principles. In the case of pronouns as in (1a) the grammar delimits the interpretation of the pronoun *him* in that whatever the context the pronoun *him* cannot be coreferential with the subject NP *Poirot*. In the case of the reflexive interpretation illustrated in (1b) the grammar determines that the reflexive *himself* must be dependent on the subject NP *Bertie*. In (1c) the grammar allows the interpretation where *he* and *Bertie* are coreferential; in (1f) this interpretation is blocked.

In this chapter we introduce the grammatical principles which determine the interpretations of NPs. The module of the grammar that regulates the referential properties of NPs is called the binding theory. The binding theory provides an explicit formulation of the grammatical constraints on NP. The binding theory essentially examines the relations between NPs in A-positions, it is a theory of **A-binding**.[4]

We will see that the binding theory contains three principles, each of which will regulate the distribution and interpretation of one specific type of NP. **Principle A** is the principle that regulates the interpretation of elements which are referentially dependent, such as reflexives. Principle A imposes that reflexives are linked to, or **bound by**, an NP in an A-position within a certain domain, the **binding domain**. We shall define this domain as carefully as

---

[4] This means that we shall not be looking at the interpretation of NPs in A'-positions. For example, we have nothing to say about topicalized NPs such as *Jeeves* in (i) and (ii):

(i) *Jeeves*, Poirot doesn't like.
(ii) *Jeeves*, nobody likes him.

Jeeves occupies an A'-position, a non-argument position. We deal with the role of A'-positions in chapter 7.

possible in the present chapter. In (1b), for instance, the reflexive *himself* must be bound by the subject NP *Bertie*. **Principle B** constrains the interpretation of pronouns: pronouns should not be linked to an NP in an A-position within the binding domain. Thus while the reflexive element *himself* must be bound by the subject NP *Bertie* in (1b), the pronoun *him* must not be bound by the subject *Poirot* in (1a). **Principle C**, finally, is the principle which determines the distribution and interpretation of referential expressions like the NP *Poirot*. Principle C says that referential expressions must not be bound by NPs in A-positions: in (1e), for instance, *Bertie* cannot be interpreted as being coreferential with *he*.

The chapter is organized as follows. Section 1 deals with the interpretation of reflexives and also defines the concepts binding, subject/SUBJECT, accessibility and governing category, which we shall need throughout the chapter. Section 2 shows that reciprocals obey the same constraint as reflexives. Reciprocals and reflexives will be grouped under the label **anaphor**. Section 3 deals with the interpretation of pronouns. Section 4 deals with referential NPs. Section 5 is a summary of the principles of NP interpretation: the binding theory. The formulation of the binding theory in this section is essentially that of Chomsky (1981a). In section 6 we discuss some problems for the binding theory. In section 7 we reinterpret the classification of NPs in terms of the binary features [± Anaphor, ± Pronominal] and we reformulate the binding theory in terms of these features, following proposals in Chomsky (1982). In section 8 we discuss the problem of circularity of coindexation.

1   Reflexives

In this section we formulate the rule of interpretation of reflexives such as *himself*.

1.1   *Binding and Antecedent*

Consider (3):

3a   Poirot hurt himself.
3b   *Miss Marple hurt himself.

In (3a) the reflexive picks up its reference from the subject NP *Poirot*. The NP on which a reflexive is dependent for its interpretation is the antecedent of the reflexive. We use coindexation[5] to indicate that *himself* and *Poirot* have the same referent:

4a Poirot$_i$ hurt himself$_i$.

The reflexive and its antecedent must agree with respect to the nominal features of person, gender and number. Lack of agreement leads to ungrammaticality in (4b), (4c) and (4d).

4b *Poirot$_i$ hurt herself$_i$.
4c *Poirot$_i$ hurt themselves$_i$.
4d *Poirot$_i$ hurt myself$_i$.

The requirement that a reflexive and its antecedent agree with respect to their nominal features follows from the fact that the reflexive depends for its interpretation on the antecedent, i.e. the reflexive and its antecedent share their referent. It would be rather odd to find that a reflexive has the property [+Male], for instance, thus constraining the selection of the referent to a male entity, and is coindexed with an antecedent which itself has the property [−Male]. There would be a contradiction in the specification of the relevant properties for the selection of the referent. The agreement constraint explains the ungrammaticality of (3b).

5a = 3b *Miss Marple$_i$ hurt himself$_i$.

In order to circumvent the agreement constraint one might think of an interpretation in which the reflexive and the subject NP are independent in reference as illustrated in (5b), but such an interpretation is unavailable:

5b *Miss Marple$_i$ hurt himself$_j$.

---

[5] The reader will recall that in chapter 3 we used co-indexation to link the elements in a chain:

(i) Poirot$_i$ was attacked e$_i$

In (i) *Poirot* and the empty element *e* form a chain, $<Poirot_i, e_i>$. The internal theta role of *attacked* is assigned to the chain. In the text example (4a) *Poirot* and *himself* each have their own theta role. We have here two one-member chains: *<Poirot>* and *<himself>*. For a discussion on some constraints on coindexation see section 8 of this chapter. In chapter 6 we return to chain formation. In chapter 12 we return to the role of indices in the grammar. We will consider work by Rizzi (1990a), who proposes that referential indices should be reserved for binding relations and that the antecedent and the non-overt element in (i) are related by another device.

Because reflexives lack independent reference they must have an anteced-ent. Reflexives must be **bound by an antecedent**. The antecedent is the **binder** of the reflexive. Throughout this section we shall make the notion 'binding' more precise.

In all our examples so far, the antecedent of the reflexive has been a full lexical NP. Pronouns may also function as antecedents for reflexives, as indi-cated in (5c): *he* is the antecedent of the reflexive:

5c He$_i$ has hurt himself$_i$.

1.2 *Locality Constraints*

Let us consider in more detail the relation between the reflexive and its antecedent.

6a Poirot$_i$ hurt himself$_i$.
6b *Poirot$_i$ thinks that Miss Marple hurt himself$_i$.

In (6a) *himself* is bound by *Poirot*, as indicated by coindexation. In (6b) binding is apparently not possible. The problem seems to be that the distance between *himself*$_i$ and its antecedent *Poirot*$_i$ is too large: *Poirot* is too far away from the reflexive. Consider the grammatical (6c) where *Poirot* and the reflexive are closer to each other and where the NP *Poirot* can bind the reflexive:

6c Miss Marple thinks that Poirot$_i$ has hurt himself$_i$.

We conclude that reflexives need an antecedent (with which they agree with respect to the features of person, gender and number) and that the antecedent must not be too far away from the reflexive. In a sense to be made more precise, the antecedent must be found in some **local domain**, the bind-ing domain. The reflexive must be **locally bound**. Needless to say, we must now try to define what this local domain for reflexive binding can be, i.e. what it means to say that a reflexive must be locally bound.

From the examples in (6) we might provisionally conclude that reflexive and antecedent must be in the same clause.[6] In the literature a condition which specifies that two elements, the reflexive and its antecedent, must be in the same clause is often referred to as a **clause-mate condition**. The binding domain for reflexives would thus be said to be the clause. In (6a) and in (6c) the antecedent

---

[6] Following chapter 2, the term clause is used to refer to IP, both embedded and non-embedded.

is sufficiently local; in (6b) the NP *Poirot* is outside the clause which contains the reflexive and cannot function as an antecedent.

Let us extend our data base now to check whether the locality constraint we have set up is adequate to account for all the data. Following our discussion in the introduction of this book, we shall adopt the following procedure. Having formulated a **hypothesis** – the clause-mate condition on reflexive interpretation–on the basis of a limited set of **data**, we **test** the hypothesis by applying it to different data. If the hypothesis fails we try to improve it, either by modifying the hypothesis itself, or by adding to it auxiliary hypotheses which take care of the problematic issues. Consider (7a):

7a   *I expect [$_{IP}$ himself$_i$ to invite Poirot$_i$].

(7a) shows that the clause-mate condition is not sufficient to allow for binding of a reflexive. In (7a) both the reflexive and the antecedent appear in the non-finite clause (IP), but the reflexive cannot be bound. We might propose that in addition to being a clause-mate, the antecedent must (as the name suggests) precede the reflexive. This would entail that (7a) is ungrammatical and (7b) is grammatical. But this also predicts that (7c) is grammatical, contrary to fact:

7b   Poirot$_i$ invited himself$_i$.
7c   *Poirot$_i$'s sister invited himself$_i$.

In both (7b) and (7c) the reflexive and the antecedent are clause-mates, they are inside the same local domain of the clause. But the reflexive *himself* in (7c) cannot be successfully bound by the presumed antecedent *Poirot*, which occupies the specifier position of the subject NP *Poirot's sister*. Compare the ungrammatical (7c) and the grammatical (7d):

7d   [$_{IP}$ [$_{NPj}$ [$_{NPi}$ Poirot]'s brother] invited himself$_j$].

As shown by the indexation the antecedent of *himself* in (7d) is not NP$_i$, *Poirot*, but rather NP$_j$, *Poirot's brother*, which contains NP$_i$.

We must refine our rule for the interpretation of reflexives to account for the examples above. In order to establish the structural relations between antecedent and reflexive we shall analyse the tree diagram representations corresponding to the above examples. Before reading the discussion below, try to draw the representations for the examples in (7) as an exercise. For each tree, examine the configurational relations between the antecedent and the reflexive and try to determine which relation is the one that allows binding.

1.3 *Structural Relations between Antecedent and Reflexive*

(8) gives the tree diagram representations for the examples in (7). For each of the examples above circle the reflexive and the antecedent in preparation of the discussion.

8a

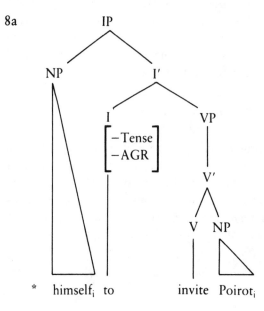

8b

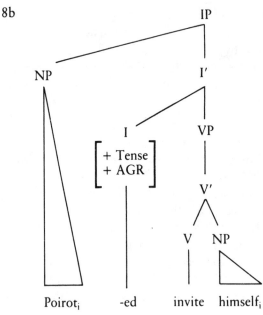

8c

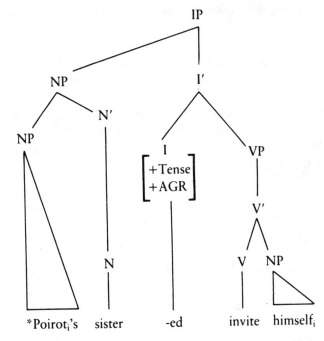

8d

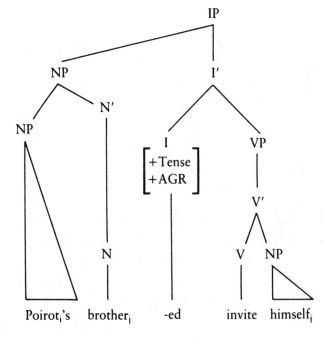

If we compare the ungrammatical (8a) with the grammatical (8b) a first observation is that in the latter the antecedent is somehow 'higher' up in the tree than the reflexive. The reader can check that this observation also applies to the other examples. But the fact that an antecedent is somehow higher in the tree is not sufficient. In (8c) *Poirot* is higher than *himself* and still it cannot serve as its antecedent.

A careful comparison of the structural relations between antecedents and reflexives in the sentences above leads us to the conclusion that the relation is one that we have described as c-command in chapter 2: <u>the antecedent must c-command the reflexive</u>.

9   **C-command**
    A node A c-commands a node B if and only if
    (i)   A does not dominate B;
    (ii)   B does not dominate A;
    (iii) the first branching node dominating A also dominates B.

The reader can verify for himself that in all of the grammatical examples in (8) the relevant relation holds.

Let us now try to formulate the constraint on the interpretation of reflexives.

10   **Principle of reflexive interpretation** (1)
    A reflexive must be bound by a clause-mate antecedent.

Binding is defined in terms of c-command as in (11):

11   **Binding**
    A binds B if and only if
    (i)   A c-commands B;
    (ii)   A and B are coindexed.

(10) says that a reflexive must be coindexed with an antecedent NP, i.e. a reflexive cannot have independent reference but depends for its reference on the binder. Remember that we focus on the binding by antecedents in A-positions, or **A-binding**. Binding from A'-positions is discussed in chapter 7.

1.4   *The Domain of Reflexive Binding*

1.4.1   GOVERNORS

An examination of further examples with reflexives shows that principle (10) is too powerful. It rules out grammatical sentences such as (12):

12   Poirot$_i$ believes [$_{IP}$ himself$_i$ to be the best].

It is easy to see that the relation between *himself* and *Poirot* does not satisfy
(10). *Poirot*, the antecedent, does indeed c-command *himself* (cf. (9)), but they
are not clause-mates. While *himself* is contained in the lower infinitival clause,
Poirot is outside it. In order to accommodate examples such as (12), we shall
need to extend the domain in which a reflexive can be bound. However, we
should be careful not to extend the domain too much given (13):

13a   *Poirot$_i$ believes [$_{CP}$ that [$_{IP}$ himself$_i$ is the best]].
13b   *Poirot$_i$ believes [$_{NP}$ Miss Marple's description of himself$_i$].

In (13a) the reflexive does not have a clause-mate antecedent and the sentence
is ungrammatical. As predicted by (10), we cannot link the reflexive *himself* to
the NP *Poirot*. The domain in which the reflexive must be bound apparently
IS the clause containing it. On the other hand, in (13b) the reflexive *himself*
cannot be linked to the antecedent *Poirot* even though they are clause-mates.

Let us look at (12) first. This is an example of an ECM construction
described in chapter 3, section 2.2.2.2. Recall that an essential property of
ECM constructions is that the subject of a lower clause is governed (and case-
marked) by an outside governor. In (12) *himself* is case-marked by the verb
of the matrix clause, *believe*. Precisely the fact that the reflexive is governed
by the verb *believe* apparently allows us to extend the domain in which we
may look for an antecedent. Let us attempt a reformulation along these lines:

14   **Principle of reflexive interpretation** (2)
     A reflexive X must be bound inside a clause that contains X and X's
     governor.

The reformulation extends the local domain in which we find an antecedent for a reflexive in those cases in which the reflexive is governed from a
higher clause.

Unfortunately, our new formulation (14) is now too weak: as the reader
can check for himself (14) fails to exclude (13b). The binding domain for the
reflexive should be the entire clause, but apparently *himself* cannot be bound
by the subject of the clause, the NP *Poirot*.

1.4.2   SUBJECTS

It looks as if the domain for binding of the reflexive in (13b) ought to be
restricted to the NP *Miss Marple's description of himself* which contains a

governor (the preposition *of*) for the reflexive. However, a general restriction of the binding domain to NPs would in turn be too powerful: it would give the correct result in (13b) but at the same time it would exclude the grammatical (13c):

13c   Poirot believes [$_{NP}$ any description of himself].

The difference between (13b) and (13c) lies in the composition of the NP which contains the reflexive. In (13b), the bracketed NP contains an NP in its specifier position: *Miss Marple*. This NP receives a theta role from the N *description*. Indeed, when we compare (13b) with (13d) we see that the NP is analogous to a subject NP:

13d   Miss Marple has described herself.

Recall that the subject NP of a clause occupies the specifier position of IP, [Spec, IP]. Analogously, we shall say that the NP in [Spec, NP] is the subject of an NP. In (13c) the specifier position of the NP is not occupied by an NP but rather by *any*. This suggests that the fact that there is a subject inside an NP determines the domain in which the reflexive can be bound. Consider furthermore that in (13e) the subject of the NP itself binds the reflexive:

13e   Miss Marple believes [$_{NP}$ Poirot$_i$'s description of himself$_i$].

1.4.3 COMPLETE FUNCTIONAL COMPLEX

At this stage there are several ingredients to incorporate in our rules for the binding of reflexives. Apart from the c-command constraint we need to determine exactly how far away we allow ourselves to look for an antecedent, i.e. what constitutes its binding domain. The major factors that come into play are the following:

(i)   clauses and NPs containing a reflexive may but need not serve as binding domains for the reflexive;
(ii)   the presence of a subject serves to delimit a binding domain;
(iii) the governor of the reflexive plays a role in defining the binding domain.

The factors listed in (i) and (ii) are not independent: both NPs and clauses have subjects, the latter obligatorily. Let us try to amalgamate all the conditions above into one formulation:

15 Principle of reflexive interpretation (3)

A reflexive X must be bound in the minimal domain containing X, X's governor and a subject.

Observe in passing that the domain defined by (15) is 'complete' in the sense that it contains all the functions determined by the projection principle. It contains the head of a projection, the predicate which assigns the theta roles, the complements, to which the internal theta roles are assigned, and the subject, to which the external theta role is assigned. For this reason Chomsky (1986a: 169–72) refers to the domain defined by (15) as a **complete functional complex (CFC)**.[7]

At this stage we ought to verify whether our third hypothesis (15) is still adequate for the examples treated so far. We repeat them here and invite the reader to check:

16a = 7a   *I expect [$_{IP}$ himself$_i$ to invite Poirot$_i$].
16b = 7b   Poirot$_i$ invited himself$_i$.
16c = 3b   *Miss Marple$_i$ hurt himself$_i$.
16d = 5c   He$_i$ has hurt himself$_i$.
16e = 6b   *Poirot$_i$ thinks [$_{CP}$ that [$_{IP}$ Miss Marple hurt himsef$_i$]].
16f = 7c   *Poirot$_i$'s sister invited himself$_i$.
16g = 7d   Poirot's brother$_i$ invited himself$_i$.
16h = 12   Poirot$_i$ believes [$_{IP}$ himself$_i$ to be the best].
16i = 13a   *Poirot$_i$ believes [$_{CP}$ that [$_{IP}$ himself$_i$ is the best]].
16j = 13b   *Poirot$_i$ believes [$_{NP}$ Miss Marple's description of himself$_i$].
16k = 13c   Poirot$_i$ believes [$_{NP}$ any description of himself$_i$].
16l = 13e   Miss Marple believes [$_{NP}$ Poirot$_i$'s description of himself$_i$].

In order to determine the binding domain for the reflexive you should proceed as follows: (i) find the governor of the reflexive, (ii) find the closest subject. The smallest IP or NP containing these two elements will be the binding domain in which the reflexive must be bound, i.e. coindexed with a c-commanding (and agreeing) antecedent.

As can be seen the principle in (15) can account for the data in (16). The importance played by the subject NP in defining the binding domain is also illustrated in the examples in (17), where the binding domain for the reflexive is the lowest IP containing the governing V (*like*) and a subject, the NP *Miss Marple*.

---

[7]   For discussion of CFC see Giorgi (1987).

17a   *Poirot$_i$ believes [$_{IP}$ Miss Marple to like himself$_i$ too much].
17b   Poirot believes [$_{IP}$ Miss Marple$_i$ to like herself$_i$ too much].

In the next section we consider some problematic examples with reflexive elements and we shall try to improve our characterization of the binding domain in order to be able to capture these examples too. The reader should be warned that the argumentation is rather complex and that the solutions proposed here are provisional and often controversial.

1.4.4   SUBJECT AND BIG SUBJECT

Let us return to example (16i), repeated here as (18).

18   *Poirot$_i$ believes [$_{CP}$ that [$_{IP}$ himself$_i$ is the best detective]].

(15) states that the reflexive *himself* must be bound in its governing category and this principle is clearly violated in (18): within the lower finite clause the reflexive does not have a binder. We might be tempted to conclude from examples such as (18) that tensed clauses are always binding domains and that reflexives which are contained in tensed clauses can never be bound outside them. However, this generalization is not adequate. Additional data show that restricting the binding domain to the immediately dominating finite clause would exclude grammatical sentences such as (19), where the reflexive *himself* is bound outside the finite clause IP: *himself* is successfully bound by the subject of the matrix clause.

19   Poirot$_i$ believes [$_{CP}$ that [$_{IP}$ a picture of himself$_i$ will be on show at the exhibition]].

Data such as (19) mean that we cannot always equate the binding domain with the tensed clause. Observe that (19) contrasts minimally with (18); while we can account for the ungrammaticality of (18), (19) is problematic for principle (15). It is hard to see how (15) can both exclude (18) and include (19). In (18) the binding domain is defined as the lower finite clause: the subject NP *Poirot* of the higher clause cannot bind the reflexive in the lower finite clause; in (19) the binding domain of the reflexive must be extended to comprise the higher clause: *Poirot*, the subject NP in the higher finite clause successfully binds *himself* in the lower finite clause.

In order to solve this problem Chomsky (1981a: 209) proposes to reconsider the notion subject when used to define binding domains. In our discussion so far, we have used the term informally to refer to subjects of clauses, tensed and infinitival, and to the subject of NPs. We have assumed that both an NP in [Spec, IP] and an NP in [Spec, NP] are subjects. It turns out that a distinction must be drawn between the subjects of finite clauses and those of non-finite ones and NPs.

In chapter 2 we saw that different clause types are characterized by the feature composition of their inflection, I, the head of the projection. The I node of tensed clauses is specified for the features [+ Tense] and [+ AGR]. [+ AGR] encodes the agreement properties of the subject: it contains the number and person features of the subject. Consider the paradigm for Italian verb conjugation given also in the Introduction and in chapter 2:

20a (io)   parlo
    I   speak
20b (tu)   parli
    you   speak
20c (lei)   parla
    she   speaks
20d (noi)   parliamo
    we   speak
20e (voi)   parlate
    you   speak
20f (loro)   parlano
    they   speak

As discussed in the Introduction, (20a) *parlo* will be understood as 'I speak'; the pronoun *io* is usually left unexpressed.[8] This is related to the fact that Italian has a rich inflectional system which allows us to recover the subject from the verbal inflection. The AGR features on the verb pick up the features of the subject. The absence of rich morphology in English does not allow the subject pronoun to remain unexpressed.

Although the inflectional endings in English are morphologically impoverished, we have adopted the idea that in English AGR is also specified abstractly for the agreement features of the subject. For both Italian and English we propose that subject and verb agree, as shown by coindexation:

---

[8] Recall from the Introduction that overt pronouns are present in Italian when they receive focal stress. When no contrast or no special focus on the subject is needed the pronoun is absent. This follows from some general consideration of **economy**: the omission of the subject pronoun requires less effort than the overt expression of the pronoun, and therefore subject pronouns will only be present when the added effort of overtly expressing them has some yield. Subject pronouns appear only when it is impossible to leave them out. Chomsky (1981a: 65) refers to this constraint on overt pronouns as the **Avoid Pronoun Principle**.

21a   io$_i$ parlo$_i$.
21b   I$_i$ speak$_i$.

In other words, AGR in I picks up the nominal features of the subject. This equation between AGR and the subject has led Chomsky to propose that AGR is 'like the subject'. In order to distinguish AGR with its subject-like properties from the NP in the subject position (the NP position dominated by IP), Chomsky refers to the AGR of finite clauses as **SUBJECT**, the **big subject**.

On the basis of this proposal Chomsky then argues that for the definition of the binding domain for a reflexive SUBJECT can count as the 'subject' mentioned in (15). This means that in (18) the finite subordinate clause contains the reflexive, its governor (I) and a SUBJECT (AGR) and will constitute the binding domain in which the reflexive must be bound. We return to (19) below.

The reader may wonder about the validity of this step which looks like a makeshift device to rescue the principle developed so far. One argument in favour of the proposal of treating AGR as a SUBJECT is that intuitively what we have been calling the 'subject' is the 'most prominent' NP-position in IP (Chomsky, 1981a: 209). The subject NP c-commands the entire clause. But AGR itself is a bundle of nominal features (person, number) contained in INFL or I, the head of IP. AGR can in this way be argued to be at least as 'prominent': even if it is not an NP position, AGR can be identified as a SUBJECT. Non-finite sentences also contain an I node, but their inflection is negatively specified for AGR. The absence of the nominal agreement features on infinitives entails that there will be no SUBJECT in infinitivals. Only an NP subject, an NP dominated by IP, can qualify. Hence:

22a   *Poirot$_i$ believes [$_{IP}$ Miss Marple to like himself$_i$ too much].
22b   Poirot$_i$ believes [$_{IP}$ himself$_i$ to be the best detective].

In (22a) the binding domain for the reflexive *himself* must be restricted to the lower clause which contains a governor *like* and a subject, the NP *Miss Marple*. In (22b) the binding domain is the main clause which contains a governor – the verb *believe* – and a subject *Poirot*. In contrast with (18) the lower I is [–AGR] hence cannot count as SUBJECT.

Now let us consider small clauses for a moment:

23a   Poirot$_i$ considers [$_{AGRP}$ Watson$_j$ entirely responsible for himself$_{i/*j}$].
23b   Poirot$_i$ considers [$_{AGRP}$ himself$_i$ responsible for the damage].

In chapter 2, we propose that small clauses are projections of an abstract functional head AGR, which is specified for the features number and gender. In chapter 3 we show that such small clause AGRPs are transparent for outside government; in other words the AGR head of a small clause is like a non-finite I, it is not strong enough to define a domain of government. In (23a), for instance, the NP *Watson* is assigned ACCUSATIVE case by the verb *considers*. The NP which is dominated immediately by the small clause AGRP, or, to put it differently, the NP in [Spec, AGRP], is the subject of the small clause; in (23a) *Watson* is the subject of the small clause *Watson entirely responsible for himself*. Let us turn to the binding relations of the elements in a small clause. In (23a) *himself* can only take *Watson* as an antecedent. This is predicted by our approach: *himself* is governed by *for*, the closest subject is *Watson*, the subject of the small clause. Hence the small clause is the relevant binding domain. In (23b) we see that the binding domain of the reflexive *himself*, which occupies the subject position of the small clause, is the matrix clause: *Poirot* binds *himself*. On the basis of our earlier discussion we conclude from this that the AGR of the small clause, though specified for the features number and gender, does not count as a SUBJECT to define a binding domain. It is not obvious what the crucial factor is that distinguishes the small clause AGR, which cannot be a SUB-JECT, from the finite AGR, which can be. One possibility is that the presence of person features play a crucial role in establishing AGR as a SUBJECT. With respect to binding possibilities small clauses behave like non-finite clauses: for both kinds of clauses the subject can be bound from outside.

According to our discussion so far, all finite clauses seem to function as binding domains for reflexives, since they all contain a SUBJECT, by definition. (19) raises a problem for this generalization. Recall that in this example *himself*, which is contained inside the subject of the embedded finite clause, can be bound by the subject in the matrix clause. We turn to these kinds of examples in the next section.

1.4.5 ACCESSIBLE SUBJECT AND THE *i*-WITHIN-*i* FILTER

Let us start from examples (18) and (19), repeated here as (24) for convenience' sake, for our final revision of the rule of reflexive interpretation.

24a *$Poirot_i$ believes [$_{CP}$ that [$_{IP}$ $himself_i$ is the best detective]].
24b $Poirot_i$ believes [$_{CP}$ that [$_{IP}$ [$_{NP}$ a picture of $himself_i$] will be on show]].

In (24a) the binding domain for the reflexive can be defined on the basis of the notions governor and SUBJECT. The inflection on *is*, third person singular, serves as the SUBJECT for the reflexive *himself*.

However, being a SUBJECT is not sufficient. Chomsky proposes that in order for an element to be able to count as a subject/SUBJECT to determine the binding domain of a reflexive it must be an **accessible** subject/SUBJECT for that reflexive. A subject/SUBJECT is accessible for a reflexive if it is possible to coindex it with this reflexive.

25   **Accessible subject/SUBJECT**

A is an accessible subject/SUBJECT for B if the coindexation of A and B does not violate any grammatical principles.

Chomsky (1981a: 211–12) proposes that one of the grammatical principles that should be considered is the *i-within-i* filter:

26   **The *i-within-i* filter.**
   $*[_{A_i} \ldots B_i \ldots]$

The goal of the filter is to avoid circularity in reference. In section 8 we discuss some examples of circularity.[9]

In (24a) the coindexation of the reflexive and the SUBJECT is unproblematic: *himself* and AGR in *is* can be coindexed without violating (25).[10] Thus AGR is an accessible SUBJECT. Moreover I is the governor of *himself*. The binding domain of *himself* will be the lower clause.

In (24b) matters are different. The reflexive *himself* is contained within the subject of the lower clause. In order to find its binding domain we need (i) a governor and (ii) an accessible subject/SUBJECT. The governor of *himself* is *of*, the preposition. Now we need an accessible subject/SUBJECT. The first element to try would be the NP subject of the lower clause: [$_{NP}$ *a picture* of *himself*]. In order for this NP to be accessible we must be able to coindex it with the reflexive:

27 [$_{NPi}$ a picture of [$_{NPi}$ himself]]

This coindexation is banned because it would violate the *i-within-i* filter (26).

Let us see if the AGR of the lower clause could count as an accessible SUBJECT. Given that the entire NP in (24b) is the subject NP of the sentence it is coindexed with AGR by virtue of its person and number agreement. The coindexation of *himself* with AGR would again violate the *i-within-i* filter. *Himself* would be coindexed with AGR and AGR in turn is coindexed with

[9]   For some discussion of accessibility and the problems it raises the reader is referred to Bouchard (1985) and Lasnik (1986). An alternative approach for examples like (24b) is found in Williams (1982).

[10]   *Himself* and SUBJECT (AGR) are co-indexed by virtue of subject–verb agreement.

the NP *a picture of himself*. Coindexation is transitive: if A is coindexed with B, and B is coindexed with C, then A is also coindexed with C. In our example *himself* would be coindexed with AGR, AGR is coindexed with the NP *a picture of himself*, hence *himself* ends up being coindexed with the NP:

28   $[_{NPi}$ a picture of $[_{NPi}$ himself]] AGR_i

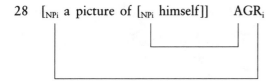

In other words, no accessible subject/SUBJECT is available inside the finite lower clause. We need to extend the binding domain of the reflexive to the next clause up: here the subject *Poirot* or the SUBJECT, AGR, can qualify: coindexation with *himself* would not lead to a violation of the *i*-within-*i* filter. The binding of the reflexive is a result of the constraint on subject/SUBJECT accessibility. Given that the finite lower clause does not contain an accessible subject/SUBJECT the binding domain is enlarged to comprise the next higher clause.

One word of caution is in place here. The coindexation proposed to determine whether a subject/SUBJECT is accessible is not to be taken as an actual coindexation. Rather, what Chomsky means is that a subject/SUBJECT is accessible if coindexation would not give rise to any violations. He obviously does not wish to imply that one must coindex the reflexive with the subject NP and therefore assume that they have the same referent.[11]

On the basis of the discussion we need yet again to modify our principle for the interpretation of reflexives:

29   **Principle of reflexive interpretation** (4)
     A reflexive X must be bound in the minimal domain containing X, X's governor and an accessible subject/SUBJECT.

In the literature the binding domain defined in (29) is often referred to as the **governing category (GC)**.[12]

---

[11]   Aoun (1986) extends the notion of accessibility to propose a modification of the binding theory. This work should be accessible as soon as chapter 8 has been covered.

[12]   For further discussion and modification of the binding theory, see Aoun (1986), Brody (1985) and Manzini (1983). For a discussion of the cross-linguistic variation with respect to the definition of the governing category and with respect to possible antecedents, see work by Burzio (1991), Hermon (1992) and Manzini and Wexler (1987). These works also attempt at providing an explanation of how the cross-linguistic variation is acquired. For the literature mentioned here it will be best to wait until we have finished chapter 8 before attempting to read the texts.

1.5 Reflexive Interpretation: Summary

Throughout this section we have been trying to elaborate a set of principles that regulate the interpretation of reflexives. Starting from a small set of data which we have extended throughout the discussion, we have gradually arrived at a more complex proposal with maximal coverage. Let us summarize the results of our findings here:

30 **Principle of reflexive interpretation**
A reflexive X must be bound in the minimal domain containing X, X's governor and an accessible subject/SUBJECT.

31 **(A-) binding**
A A-binds B if and only if
   (i)   A is in an A-position;
   (ii)   A c-commands B;
   (iii) A and B are coindexed.

32 **C-command**
A node A c-commands a node B if and only if
   (i)   A does not dominate B;
   (ii)   B does not dominate A;
   (iii) the first branching node dominating A also dominates B.

33 **Subject/SUBJECT**
   a   Subject: NP in [Spec, XP].
   b   SUBJECT corresponds to finite AGR.

34 **Accessible subject/SUBJECT**
A is an accessible subject/SUBJECT for B if the coindexation of A and B does not violate any grammatical principles.

35 **The *i*-within-*i* filter**
$*[_{A_i} \ldots B_i \ldots]$

2 Anaphors: Reflexives and Reciprocals

Up till now we have concentrated exclusively on the interpretation of reflexives such as *himself*. Reflexives cannot refer independently, they receive their referential interpretation by virtue of being bound by an antecedent. **Reciprocals** such as *each other* are also referentially dependant and are subject to the same interpretative constraints as reflexives.

36a   The students$_i$ attacked each other$_i$.
36b   *The student$_i$ attacked each other$_i$.
36c   *Each other are ill.

Reciprocals are inherently plural and hence need a plural antecedent for their interpretation. In (36b) the singular NP *the student* cannot act as the relevant binder for the reciprocal. In (36c) there is no binder available. In (36a) the reciprocal *each other* is bound by the subject NP and this sentence is grammatical. A survey of a number of examples with reciprocals shows that their interpretation is parallel to that of reflexives (cf. the examples listed in (16) for parallel constructions with reflexives):

37a   *I expect [$_{IP}$ each other$_i$ to invite the students$_i$].
37b   The students$_i$ invited each other$_i$.
37c   *The student$_i$ invited each other$_i$.
37d   They$_i$ have invited each other$_i$.
37e   *The students$_i$ think [$_{CP}$ that [$_{IP}$ Miss Marple invited each other$_i$]].
37f   *The students$_i$' sister invited each other$_i$.
37g   Poirot's brothers$_i$ invited each other$_i$.
37h   The students$_i$ believe [$_{IP}$ each other$_i$ to be the best].
37i   *The students$_i$ believe [$_{CP}$ that [$_{IP}$ each other$_i$ are the best]].
37j   *The students$_i$ believe [$_{NP}$ Miss Marple's description of each other$_i$].
37k   The students$_i$ believe [$_{NP}$ any description of each other$_i$].
37l   Miss Marple believes [$_{NP}$ the students$_i$' description of each other$_i$].

We leave it to the reader to check the application of the principle of binding for reflexives to the examples above. From now on we use the general label **anaphor** to refer to the referentially dependent NP types: reflexives and reciprocals. We can then generalize the principles and definitions established for reflexives to cover all anaphoric NPs.

38   **Interpretation of anaphors**
     An anaphor X must be bound in the minimal domain containing X, X's governor and an accessible subject/SUBJECT.

If we use the term **governing category** to refer to the binding domain described above then we can abbreviate (39):

39   **Interpretation of anaphors**
     An anaphor must be bound in its governing category.

3 Pronouns

So far we have not achieved a great deal with respect to the inventory of NPs given in the introduction to this chapter. Only anaphors have been dealt with. In this section we turn to the second type of NP: pronouns. Consider the interpretation of the pronoun in (40a):

40a   Poirot had hurt him.
40b   Poirot had hurt himself.

It is obvious that the interpretation of pronouns differs from that of reflexives. The pronoun *him* in (40a) must refer to an entity different from the subject NP *Poirot*, while a reflexive in the same position (40b) must refer to the entity denoted by *Poirot*. Whereas the reflexive must be bound in (40b), the pronoun must be **free**. The question arises whether the domain in which pronouns must be free is identical to that in which anaphors must be bound, i.e. the governing category – from now on GC – defined above.

If the binding domains were identical, we would expect that whenever we find a reflexive bound by some antecedent X we should find that a pronoun in the same position must not be bound by an NP in the position X. Moreover in those cases where reflexives are ungrammatical because no antecedents are available in their binding domain, pronouns should still be possible since the pronoun does not need an antecedent. Reflexives and pronouns should be in complementary distribution.

Let us return to the data for reflexives in (16) and check whether the prediction sketched above holds. In each of the examples in (16) we replace the reflexive by a pronoun.

41a   I expect [$_{IP}$ him$_j$ to invite Poirot$_i$].
41b   Poirot$_i$ invited him$_{j/*i}$.
41c   Miss Marple$_i$ hurt him$_j$.
41d   He$_i$ has hurt him$_{j/*i}$.
41e   Poirot$_i$ thinks [$_{CP}$ that [$_{IP}$ Miss Marple hurt him$_{i/j}$]].
41f   Poirot$_i$'s sister invited him$_{i/j}$.
41g   Poirot$_i$'s brother$_j$ invited him$_{j/*i}$.

41h Poirot$_i$ believes [$_{IP}$ him$_{j/*i}$ to be the best].

41i Poirot$_i$ believes [$_{CP}$ that [$_{IP}$ he$_{i/j}$ is the best]].

41j Poirot$_i$ believes [$_{NP}$ Miss Marple's description of him$_{i/j}$].

41k Poirot$_i$ believes [$_{NP}$ any description of him$_{j/*i}$].

41l Miss Marple believes [$_{NP}$ Poirot$_i$'s description of him$_{j/*i}$].

We shall not go through all the examples here. The reader is invited to compare the sentences above with the treatment of the examples with reflexives in (16). Let us just consider some examples.

In (41a) the pronoun is possible in the subject position of the non-finite clause. The corresponding example with the reflexive (16a) was ungrammatical because reflexives must be bound and there is no binder in the main clause of (16a). It appears from this example that pronouns need not be bound. In (41b) we see that indeed pronouns must not be bound, i.e. pronouns must be **free** where reflexives must be bound. *Him* is only possible in (41b) when there is no binder in the clause. Comparing (16b) and (41b) we see that where a reflexive and a pronominal are possible, their interpretations differ. The same point is illustrated in (41d). (41e) shows that the delimitation of the binding domain for pronouns corresponds to that of reflexives: pronouns must be free in their governing category, but they may freely be coindexed with NPs outside that domain. Thus in (41e) coindexation of *him* and *Poirot* is acceptable. (41f) illustrates that binding must be defined in terms of c-command. The pronoun *him* in this example can be coindexed with *Poirot* in the same sentence because the NP *Poirot* does not c-command the pronoun. Remember that, according to our definition, binding is not merely coindexation but it is coindexation plus c-command.

We encourage the reader to go through the remaining examples himself. It will become clear that the constraint on the interpretation of pronouns is the converse of that on anaphors. Let us formulate the constraint as follows:

42 **Interpretation of pronouns**

A pronoun must be free in its governing category;
where
(i) the **governing category** is the minimal domain containing the pronoun, its governor and an accessible subject/SUBJECT;
(ii) **free** is not bound.

It may not be superfluous to remind the reader that the principles we are setting up here concern A-binding. Consider for instance (43):

43 Poirot$_i$, Miss Marple doesn't like him$_i$.

Nothing prevents the pronoun *him* from being bound by the NP *Poirot*. In (43) *Poirot* is not in an A-position, but in an A'-position. The binding between *Poirot* and the pronoun *him* is not A-binding but A'-binding.[13]

In section 6 we return to the distribution of pronouns and reflexives in English.[14]

4   Referential Expressions

So far we have discussed two types of NPs: anaphors and pronouns. Both of these lack inherent reference; anaphors need an antecedent for their interpretation and pronouns do not require an antecedent. Pronouns inherently specify certain properties of the referent; for a complete determination of the referent contextual information is needed.[15]

Referential expressions, or *R-expressions*, constitute the third class of NPs. As the label indicates these elements are inherently referential: expressions such as *Poirot* and *the detective* select a referent from the universe of discourse. Given that R-expressions have independent reference, they do not need an antecedent; in fact they do not tolerate binding from another element. Let us look at some examples:

44a   Poirot$_i$ attacked him$_{j/*i}$.
44b   Poirot$_i$ says that he$_{i/j}$ is leaving.
44c   He$_i$ says that Poirot$_{j/*i}$ is leaving.
44d   His$_i$ brother$_k$ likes Poirot$_{i/j*k}$ very much.

For by now familiar reasons the pronoun *him* in (44a) and the R-expression *Poirot* must have different referents: both are free. In (44b) the pronoun *he* may be bound by *Poirot* since *Poirot* is outside the GC of *he*, the domain in which pronominals must be free. While the NP *Poirot* binds the pronoun *he* (outside its GC), the reverse does not hold: *he* does not c-command *Poirot*, so even if the two NPs are coindexed *he* does not bind *Poirot* according to our definition of binding: *Poirot* is free.

---

[13]   The construction in (43) has come to be known as left-dislocation: a constituent (here the NP *Poirot*) is adjoined to the left of IP and is picked up by a coindexed pronoun. We return to adjunction in chapter 7.

[14]   For cross-linguistic variation, the reader is referred to Burzio (1991), Hermon (1992) and Manzini and Wexler (1987).

[15]   For a discussion of the role of context in the interpretation of pronouns the reader is referred to Ariel (1988), Kempson (1988a, 1988b).

In (44c) the order of pronoun and R-expression is reversed compared to (44b). In this example *he* and *Poirot* must not have the same referent: *he* selects an entity distinct from that referred to by *Poirot*. If *he* and *Poirot* were to be coindexed in this example then the NP *Poirot* would be bound by the pronoun and this is not allowed.

A further extension of (44c) shows that no matter how far the potential binder is located with respect to the R-expression, binding is prohibited.

44e *He$_i$ says [$_{CP}$ that Miss Marple thinks [$_{CP}$ that Jeeves claimed [$_{CP}$ that Poirot$_i$ is leaving]]].

In (44e) three clause boundaries intervene between the R-expression *Poirot* and the pronoun, but still coindexation is not possible. This is predicted: in (44e) too the pronoun *he* would bind the NP *Poirot* if it were coindexed with it and this would violate the constraint which we have postulated above. Note in passing that the pronoun must not be coindexed with the NP *Jeeves* for the same reasons.

In (44d) both pronoun (*his*) and R-expression occur in the same sentence and coreference is possible. As the reader can verify for himself, the grammaticality of the example is predicted: the pronoun *his* does not bind the R-expression since it does not c-command it. The NP *his brother* as a whole must, obviously, not bind the NP *Poirot*.

From the examples above we conclude that R-expressions do not tolerate any A-binding: they must be free. In contrast to pronouns which must be free locally, but may be bound outside their GC, R-expressions must be free everywhere.

45 Principle of interpretation of R-expressions[16]
R-expressions must be free everywhere.

---

[16] Evans (1980: 356–7) provides examples where Principle C apparently can be overridden by conversational principles:

(i)   I know what John and Bill have in common. John thinks that Bill is terrific and Bill thinks that Bill is terrific.
(ii) Who loves Oscar's mother? I know Oscar loves Oscar's mother, but does anyone else?
(iii) Everyone has finally realized that Oscar is incompetent. Even Oscar has realized that Oscar is incompetent.

For discussion of such examples the reader is referred to Evans' own work (see also Evans 1982).

5   The Binding Theory

In this chapter we have considered in some detail the interpretation of the three types of NP: anaphors, pronouns and R-expressions. Anaphors need a local antecedent; pronouns may have an antecedent, but must be free locally; R-expressions must be free. The three principles of NP interpretation that we have established are commonly referred to as the binding theory.

46   **Binding theory**[17]
     Principle A
     An anaphor must be bound in its governing category.[18]

Jackendoff (1992) discusses examples of so called **reference shifters**, in which one phrase is used to denote a related entity:

(iv)   While he was driving to the studio, a truck hit Ringo in the left front fender. (*Ringo* denotes his car)
(v)   (One waitress to another:)
       The ham sandwich in the corner needs another cup of coffee. (*ham sandwich* denotes a person contextually related to ham sandwich)
(vi)   Plato is on the top shelf. (*Plato* denotes book(s) by Plato)
(vii) (In a wax museum:)
       Here's Mae West and here are the Beatles. This one's John, and this one's Ringo.

Jackendoff (1992) discusses how the binding theory applies to examples as those in (vii). The reader is referred to his paper for more information.

[17]   An alternative formulation for the binding theory is developed in Higginbotham (1983) who uses linking rather than coindexation to show referential dependence.

(i)

John said he thought Mary liked him.

(Higginbotham, 1983: 401)

One advantage of the arrow notation is that it is directional. In (i) the arrows show that *him* depends on *he*, and that *he* depends on *John*.
   Coindexation is not directional:

(ii) $John_i$ said that he_i thought that Mary liked him_i.

[18]   In its present format (46) Principle A says nothing about what happens if an anaphor lacks a GC. Consider:

(i)   *Each other's pictures upset Mary.
(ii)   *Each other's pictures would please their professors.

The ungrammaticality of these examples is accounted for by Chomsky (1981a: 220) who stipulates that the root sentence will count as the GC for a governed element. Hence in (i) and (ii) above Principle A will be violated.

Principle B
A pronoun must be free in its governing category.
Principle C
An R-expression must be free everywhere.

In the literature the terms Principle A, etc. are always used to refer to these principles of the binding theory.

6   Discussion Section: Problems in the Binding Theory

The binding theory predicts that pronouns and anaphors are in complementary distribution. If both a pronoun and an anaphor are possible in a position they have different readings: the pronoun will be free and the anaphor will be bound. There are some problems with this prediction; we illustrate some of them in this section.

6.1   Implicit Arguments

Consider the application of the binding theory in the following examples (taken from Chomsky, 1986a: 166ff.):

47a   They$_i$ told [$_{NP}$ stories about each other$_i$].
47b   *They$_i$ told [$_{NP}$ my stories about each other$_i$].
47c   *They$_i$ told [$_{NP}$ stories about them$_i$].
47d   They$_i$ told [$_{NP}$ my stories about them$_i$].

48a   They$_i$ heard [$_{NP}$ stories about each other$_i$].
48b   *They$_i$ heard [$_{NP}$ my stories about each other$_i$].
48c   They$_i$ heard [$_{NP}$ stories about them$_i$].
48d   They$_i$ heard [$_{NP}$ my stories about them$_i$].

The data in (47) are accounted for by the binding theory. In (47a) and (47c) the sentence is the GC for the anaphor *each other* and the pronoun *them* respectively. The anaphor is bound by the subject NP *they* in (47a), hence the sentence is grammatical. In (47c) the pronoun is bound, hence violates Principle B of the binding theory, and the sentence is ungrammatical. In (47b) and (47d) the bracketed NP is the GC for the reflexive and the pronoun respectively.

Recall that it is the presence of the subject *my* in the specifier position of NP in (47b) and (47d) which determines that the object NP is the GC. In (47b) the anaphor is not bound in its GC, hence the sentence is ungrammatical. Conversely the pronoun is free in the grammatical (47d).

(48a), (48b) and (48d) are analogous to (47a), (47b) and (47d) respectively and follow from the binding theory. (48c) raises a problem: the pronoun *them* is coindexed with a c-commanding NP. If the GC of the pronoun is the entire sentence, as suggested by (48a) and the structurally parallel (47c), then the grammaticality of the sentence is unexpected.

An explanation suggests itself on the basis of the interpretation of (48c) in comparison with (47c), specifically in terms of who does the story-telling. In (47c), 'they', referred to by the subject NP, tell the stories. In (48c) someone else tells the stories. Let us assume, following Chomsky (1986a: 167), that there is an **implicit subject** inside the NPs. We shall represent this by the abbreviation SU.

49a = 47c   *They$_i$ told [SU$_i$ stories about them$_i$].
49b = 48c   They$_i$ heard [SU$_j$ stories about them$_i$].

If the implicit subject counts as a subject to determine the GC for the pronoun, then the pronoun in (49a) is bound in the GC, while that in (49b), is free. (49a) violates the binding theory. The reader will no doubt remark that the analysis introduces another problem. In order to account for the grammaticality of (48a) we must assume that Principle A of the binding theory is respected. In other words *each other* must be bound in its GC, and the GC must be the entire sentence. Clearly, in this example we cannot propose that the implicit subject of *stories* counts as a subject to determine the GC:

50 = 48a   *They$_i$ heard [$_{NP}$ SU$_j$ stories about each other$_i$].

The asterisk in (50) refers to the syntactic representation of the sentence. If we postulate an implicit subject SU$_j$ for the NP *stories about each other*, then this NP will be the GC for *each other* and (48a) ought not to be grammatical, contrary to fact. Chomsky concludes that the 'presence of the implicit argument as subject is optional' (1986a: 167). Clearly the issue raised here is still subject to research.[19]

[19]   A similar type of example is illustrated in (i):

(ia)   They$_i$ saw a snake near them$_i$.
(ib)   They$_i$ saw a snake near themselves$_i$.

If the pronoun *them* in (ia) has the same GC as the reflexive *themselves* in (ib), then it is unexpected that they may both be coindexed with *they*. It is sometimes

6.2 Possessive Pronouns and Anaphors

Consider (51):

51a The children$_i$ like [$_{NP}$ each other$_i$'s friends].
51b The children$_i$ like [$_{NP}$ their$_{i/j}$ friends].

Contrary to expectation the anaphor *each other's* and the possessive pronoun *their* can both be bound by the NP *the children* in (51). *Their* seems to act both as the possessive form of a pronoun (when not bound by *the children*) and as that of a reflexive.

Let us first try to determine the GC for the application of the binding theory. In (51a) and in (51b), the anaphor and the pronoun are governed by the head N of the NP (*friends*). The GC needs to contain a governor and a subject. One possibility would be to say that the specifier of the NP is the subject. This means that the GC is the bracketed NP itself. On this assumption the binding theory is violated in (51a) since the anaphor would not be bound in its GC. An alternative is to discount the subject of the NP as the relevant subject, since it is itself occupied by the item to be considered (anaphor or pronoun) and to extend the GC to the clause. On this assumption, (51a) is as expected but the grammaticality of (51b) is not explained. The problem is that in the two sentences above two different types of GC are needed: in (51a) we need to refer to the entire clause as the GC; in (51b) we need to refer to the NP as the GC.

Chomsky (1986a) proposes that the binding theory should be modified slightly to accommodate the phenomena above. The discussion will be kept rather informal here.[20] Chomsky proposes that the binding domain of an NP is the domain containing a governor and a subject in which the NP COULD satisfy the binding theory.

---

proposed that in (ia) the PP *near them* is the predicate phrase of a small clause whose subject is non-overt. In (iia) we represent the non-overt subject as PRO (cf. chapter 5). (iia) is roughly analogous to (iib):

(iia) They$_i$ saw a snake$_j$ [PRO$_j$ near them$_i$].
(iib) They saw a snake which was near them.

In (iia) PRO, the subject of the small clause, is co-indexed with *a snake* (cf. (iib)). The bracketed small clause is the GC for the pronoun which will duly be free in its GC and may be bound by *they*.

[20] For further details the reader is referred to Chomsky's own discussion (1986a: 170ff.).

Let us apply this to (51b) first. The first potential binding domain for the pronoun is the NP. It contains a governor and a subject (the pronoun itself in [Spec, NP]). And indeed the NP will be the actual binding domain since the pronoun can be free in this NP. Binding from outside will thus be permitted.

In (51a) matters are different. In the first potential binding domain, the NP, Principle A could not be satisfied since there is nothing inside the NP that could potentially bind the anaphor. Needless to say, the anaphor cannot bind itself. Given that the NP does not contain a position that could potentially bind the anaphor, we must take the next category up that satisfies the definition of GC: the sentence.[21] Chomsky's proposal thus explains that both an anaphor and a pronoun may appear in [Spec, NP] with the same type of coindexation.

Although this seems a plausible solution to the problems raised for the English data in (51) it will not be possible to generalize it since not all languages pattern like English.

52a *Chinese*
Zhangsan$_i$ kanjian-le [ziji$_i$/ta$_i$ de shu].
Zhangsan   see-aspect self/him of book
'Zhangsan$_i$ saw his$_i$ book.'
(from Huang (1983), cited in Burzio, 1989: 1)

52b *Malayalam*
Mohan$_i$ [tante$_i$/awante$_i$ bhaaryaye] nulli.
Mohan self's/he's   wife   pinched
'Mohan$_i$ pinched his$_i$ wife.'
(from Mohanan (1982), cited in Burzio, 1989: 1)

53a *Latin*
Ioannes$_i$ sororem suam$_i$/eius$_{i/*i}$ vidit.
Ioannes$_i$ sister   self$_i$'s/his$_{i/*i}$ saw
'Ioannes saw his sister.'
(from Bertocci and Casadio (1980), cited in Burzio, 1989: 1)

53b *Russian*
On$_i$ uze   rasskazal mne o   svoei$_i$/ego$_{i/*i}$ zizni.
he$_i$ already tell   me   about self$_i$'s/his$_{i/*i}$ life
'He had already told me about his life.'
(from Timberlake (1979), cited in Burzio, 1989: 1)

[21] Further and more extensive modifications of the binding theory are discussed in Chomsky's own work (1986a: 174–7). The discussion presupposes chapters 5 and 6 of this book.

53c *Danish*
  Jorgen$_i$ elsker sin$_i$/hans$_{j/*i}$ kone.
  Jorgen$_i$ loves self$_i$'s/his$_{j/*i}$ wife
  'Jorgen loves his wife.'
  (from Pica (1986b), cited in Burzio, 1989: 1).

The languages illustrated in (52) and (53) have both a possessive reflexive
and a possessive pronominal. As we have seen (51b) English lacks a possessive reflexive (see Burzio (1991) for discussion).
 Languages which have a possessive reflexive show two patterns. One group
of languages behaves like Chinese in (52): both the reflexive possessive and
the pronominal possessive can occur in the [Spec, NP] position and be locally
bound. This would be accounted for under Chomsky's modification of the
binding theory discussed above. On the other hand, in the Indo-European
languages illustrated in (53) the possessive reflexive and the pronominal reflexive in a [Spec, NP] have distinct interpretations: the reflexive possessive
will be locally bound, the pronominal possessive will be locally free. In (53a),
for instance, only *suam* can be used to refer to the subject NP *Ioannes*.
Chomsky's modified binding theory referred to above will not account for the
data in (53). But the binding theory as discussed in this chapter and summarized
in (46) will.

7 NP Types and Features

7.1 *NPs as Feature Complexes*

In section 5 the binding theory was formulated as (46), repeated here as (54):

54 **Binding theory**
  Principle A
  An anaphor must be bound in its governing category.
  Principle B
  A pronoun must be free in its governing category.
  Principle C
  An R-expression must be free everywhere.

 Chomsky (1982: 78–89) proposes that the typology of NPs should be re-
considered. In chapter 2, section 7, we discussed the problem of determining

the simplest units, the primitives, of syntactic theory. We proposed that syntactic categories such as N, V, P and A were to be replaced by features matrices. The category N, for instance, would be reinterpreted as composed of two features: [+N] and [−V].

Analogously, Chomsky proposes that the three types, anaphor, pronoun and R-expression, are not syntactic primitives. Rather they can be broken down into smaller components. Categories which are subject to Principle A are characterized by the feature [+Anaphor]. Categories subject to Principle B are [+**Pronominal**]. Reflexives and reciprocals are specified positively for the feature [±Anaphor] and negatively for the feature [±Pronominal] and can thus be represented by the following feature matrix:

55a **Reciprocals and reflexives**
    [+Anaphor, −Pronominal]

Conversely pronouns are specified as in (55b):

55b **Pronouns**
    [−Anaphor, +Pronominal]

R-expressions are neither pronominal nor anaphoric:

55c **R-expressions**
    [−Anaphor, −Pronominal]

The features bring out commonalities between types of NP. Anaphors and pronouns share no features at all. Pronouns (55b) and R-expressions (55c) are both [−Anaphor]; anaphors (55a) and R-expressions (55c) are both [−Pronominal].

7.2 The Binding Theory in Terms of Features

The binding theory can be reformulated in terms of the feature specifications of NPs.

56 **Binding theory**
    Principle A
    An NP with the feature [+Anaphor] must be bound in its governing category.

Principle B
An NP with the feature [+Pronominal] must be free in its governing category.

R-expressions will not be subject to these principles since they are negatively specified for the features in question. That they have to be free need not be stated in the binding theory since binding by another referential element would contradict the fact that they are independently referential.

7.3   The Last NP

The treatment of NPs in terms of features leaves us with an interesting problem. The features proposed for NP types are **binary** features: an NP is either positively or negatively specified for the two features. If we have two features each specified either positively or negatively we expect to find four NP-types:

57a   [+Anaphor, −Pronominal]
57b   [−Anaphor, +Pronominal]
57c   [−Anaphor, −Pronominal]
57d   [+Anaphor, +Pronominal]

The first three have been associated with anaphors (reflexives and reciprocals), pronouns and R-expressions respectively. What about the fourth category (57d)?

Consider (57d) with respect to the revised binding theory in (56). An element which is [+Anaphor] must be bound in its GC. An element which is [+Pronominal] must be free in its GC. (57d) is thus subject to contradictory requirements: it must at the same time be bound and free in its GC. This seems impossible. One way out would be to find an element that lacks a GC. If there is no GC, then neither Principle A nor B will apply.

In what circumstances could an element lack a GC? The obvious possibility that comes to mind is for an element to be generated in a position where the definition of GC cannot be met. An element might lack a GC if it does not have a governor. This seems at first sight impossible. If an overt NP lacks a governor then this NP will not be able to be case-marked either. Hence an ungoverned overt NP is predicted to be ruled out by virtue of the case filter (see chapter 3). It follows that there will be no overt NP corresponding to (57d), the feature matrix [+Anaphor, +Pronominal].

Note that we are here talking only about overt NPs. If we were to admit non-overt elements then it is conceivable that an element corresponding to (57d) could be found. A non-overt NP would not be subject to the case filter which applies to overt NPs. If an NP could be allowed to be caseless, the absence of a governor would not be problematic.[22] In such a situation a GC could not be established and there would not be any contradictory application of Principle A and Principle B. In chapter 5 we will argue for the existence of non-overt NPs with the feature specification in (57d). Anticipating the discussion, these elements will be labelled PRO. However, as soon as we admit that there are non-overt NPs of the type (57d), we are led to the question: what about (57a)–(57c): are there any non-overt correlates to anaphors, pronouns and R-expressions? We return to this issue in chapters 6, 7 and 8.

8   Appendix: Circularity

In the discussion we make use of the *i*-within-*i* filter (26), following Chomsky (1981a: 212), to deal with certain binding facts. As it stands, the filter may sound like an *ad hoc* device to solve residual problems. In this section we try to give some content to the filter.

Consider the interpretation of the NPs in (58):

58a   Hercule Poirot likes Agatha Poirot very much.
58b   He likes her very much.
58c   Hercule Poirot likes his wife very much.
58d   Her husband likes Agatha Poirot very much.
58e   Her husband likes his wife very much.
58f   His wife saw Hercule, her husband.
      (cf. Higginbotham, 1983: 405)

Let us assume the following situation: the person referred to by the NP *Hercule Poirot* is married to the referent of the NP *Agatha Poirot*.

In (58b) we have replaced the full lexical NPs occurring in (58a) by their pronominal substitutes. *He* replaces *Hercule Poirot*; *her* replaces *Agatha Poirot*. The interpretation of (58b) is straightforward. In order to establish the referent of the pronouns we need to know with which NP they are coreferential. The

---

[22]   See exercise 5 for another complication though.

context, linguistic or otherwise, should provide us with the necessary information to recover these NPs.

In (58c) we replace the NP *Agatha Poirot* by the NP *his wife*. Continuing to assume that Hercule is married to Agatha the interpretation of (58c) is also unproblematic. When faced with an utterance like (58c) we need to determine what the referent of the NP *his wife* will be. In order to establish the referent of *his wife* we need to determine the referent of *his*, the pronoun. In this example *his* is coreferential with *Hercule Poirot*. Let us, following by now standard procedures, indicate this interpretation by coindexation:

59   Hercule Poirot$_i$ likes [his$_i$ wife]$_j$ very much.

In this annotated sentence *his* and *Hercule Poirot* both bear the index *i*, indicating coreference. Obviously, the NP *his wife* has a distinct index, *j*, since the referent of this NP is different from the referent of *Hercule Poirot*. The arrow linking *his* and *Hercule Poirot*[23] is supposed to indicate the referential dependency.

In (58d) we replace the NP *Hercule Poirot* by the NP *her husband*, with an effect similar to that in (58c). In order to establish the referent of *her husband* we need to establish the referent of *her*. Analogously, we can express the referential relations inside (58d) by means of coindexation:

60   [Her$_i$ husband]$_j$ likes Agatha Poirot$_i$ very much.

The interpretation of sentence (58e) raises an interesting problem. In (58b) two NPs had been replaced by a pronoun: *he* = *Hercule Poirot, her* = *Agatha Poirot*. In (58c) one NP is replaced by another coreferential NP, containing a possessive pronoun, similarly in (58d). The interpretation of (58e) suggests that we cannot apply the substitutions used in (58c) and (58d) simultaneously. (58e) is grammatical but it can only have the interpretation where one person's husband likes another person's wife. In other words the coindexation in (61) is excluded.

61   *[Her$_i$ husband]$_j$ likes [his$_j$ wife]$_i$ very much.

The question is why this should be? A related question is why (58f) is grammatical.

---

[23]   The linking arrows are introduced for expository reasons.

Let us return for a moment to (60) (= 58d). There are two NPs for which we need to establish the referent: *her husband* and *Agatha Poirot*. To establish the referent of the NP *her husband* we need to establish who *her* refers to. In order to interpret *her* we look for a possible antecedent, in this case *Agatha Poirot*.[24]

62   Her$_i$ husband   Agatha Poirot$_i$

Let us try to apply the same procedure to (58e): here there are two NPs, both containing a possessive pronoun in their specifier: *her husband* and *his wife*. The interpretation of the first NP follows the strategy described above. Let us assume that *her* refers to the second NP. The second NP in turn contains a pronoun. In order to determine what the referent of the second NP is we need to determine what the pronoun *his* refers to. For the interpretation of this pronoun, we could try to link it to the first NP:

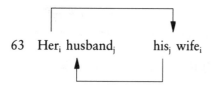

63   Her$_i$ husband$_j$ his$_j$ wife$_i$

As (63) shows, this leads to a vicious circle. In order to determine the referent of the first NP we need to turn to the second one; in order to determine the referent of the second one we need to turn to the first one, etc. Such circularity is apparently not tolerated in natural language. Hence the specific reading imposed on (58e).

(58f) is grammatical since there is no vicious circularity: the NP *his wife* depends for its interpretation on the NP *Hercule* (Higginbotham, 1983: 405):

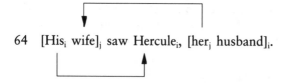

64   [His$_i$ wife]$_j$, saw Hercule$_i$, [her$_j$ husband]$_i$.

Another instance of circularity is found in (65c):

24   We leave aside the irrelevant interpretation where *her* refers to someone different from Agatha Poirot.

65a She$_i$ took her$_i$ suitcase from the rack.
65b She$_i$ is [my$_j$ cook]$_i$.
65c *She$_i$ is [her$_i$ cook]$_i$.

In (65a) the pronoun *her* refers to the entity denoted by the subject. In (65b) the predicate NP *my cook* shares the index *i* of its subject: *She = my cook*. In (65c) it is not possible to coindex both the possessive pronoun *her* and the entire NP *her cook* with the subject. In other words, we cannot interpret the predicate NP *her cook* as being coreferential with the possessive pronoun *her* in its specifier. This reading can only be rendered by the alternative in (66), where the coindexed pronoun *her* is itself contained inside another phrase (*her own*).

66 She$_i$ is [[[her$_i$] own] cook$_i$].

In order to express the coreference between *her* and the containing NP *her cook* in (65c) we would use coindexation:

67a [her$_i$ cook]$_i$

The circularity is clear. In order to establish the reference of *her* we need to establish the reference of the entire NP; in order to establish the referent of the entire NP we need to know who *her* refers to.

67b

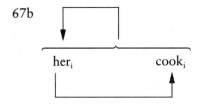

As the reader can check, the *i*-within-*i* filter (26), repeated here as (68), rules out the circular coindexation in (67a), since it rules out a construction where A contains B and where A and B share the same index.

68 **The *i*-within-*i* filter**
     *[$_{Ai}$ . . . B$_i$ . . .]

However, care must be taken when we formulate the filter. Consider (69) (example from Higginbotham, 1980: 706).

69   Mary$_i$ is [$_{NPi}$ [$_{NPj}$ [$_{NPi}$ her] cook's] best friend].

In (69) the subject NP *Mary* and the predicate NP *her cook's best friend* are coindexed. Inside the predicate NP the NP *her cook* bears the index *j*, distinct from the index of the predicate NP as a whole. But the pronoun *her* itself is coindexed with *Mary* and hence with the predicate NP without resulting in ungrammaticality. We conclude that if (B) in (68) is embedded inside another maximal projection the filter is not valid. This explanation can also be used to explain the grammaticality of (66).

9   Summary

This chapter formulates the binding theory, the module of the grammar which regulates the interpretation of NPs. In its first formulation the binding theory contains three principles each of which regulates the interpretation of one NP-type.

1   **Binding theory**
    Principle A
    An anaphor must be bound in its governing category.
    The term anaphor covers reflexives and reciprocals.
    Principle B
    A pronoun must be free in its governing category.
    Principle C
    An R-expression must be free everywhere.

We have defined the following concepts which are used extensively in the binding theory:

2   **A-binding**
    A A-binds B if and only if
    (i)   A is in an A-position;
    (ii)   A c-commands B;
    (iii) A and B are coindexed.

3 **C-command**
A node A c-commands a node B if and only if
 (i)   A does not dominate B;
 (ii) B does not dominate A;
 (iii) the first branching node dominating A also dominates B.

4 **Governing category**
The governing category for A is the minimal domain containing it, its governor and an accessible subject/SUBJECT.

5 **Subject/SUBJECT**
 a Subject: NP in [Spec, XP].
 b SUBJECT corresponds to finite AGR.

6 **Accessible subject/SUBJECT**
A is an accessible subject/SUBJECT for B if the coindexation of A and B does not violate any grammatical principles.

7 **The *i*-within-*i* filter**
*$[_{A_i} \ldots B_i \ldots]$

We have also proposed an alternative typology of NPs on the basis of their feature composition.

8a Anaphors: [+Anaphor, −Pronominal]
8b Pronouns: [−Anaphor, +Pronominal]
8c R-expressions: [−Anaphor, −Pronominal]

We have proposed a reformulation of the binding theory in terms of these features:

9 **Binding theory**
Principle A
An NP with the feature [+Anaphor] must be bound in its governing category.
Principle B
An NP with the feature [+Pronominal] must be free in its governing category.

10   Exercises

Exercise 1

Illustrate Principles A, B and C of the binding theory with examples of your own, providing three examples for each principle.

Exercise 2

Consider example (16a) in the text in the light of the binding theory developed in this chapter. How do you explain its ungrammaticality?

*I expect [himself$_i$ to invite Poirot$_i$].

Exercise 3

Consider the following examples. Does the binding theory explain the judgements we indicate?

1   *I arranged for myself to win.
2   *They would be happy for themselves to win.
3   *They recognized the necessity for themselves to leave.
4   *John requests that himself leave soon.
5   *For himself to win will amuse John.
6   *John longs for Mary to date himself.
7   We hate it for pictures of ourselves to be on sale.
8   *They expected that discussion about themselves would take place later.
9   My mother$_i$ says that for her$_i$/*herself to read so many comic books is a waste of time.
10   A picture of himself astonished John.
11   This is a picture of myself which was taken years ago.
12   John showed Mary pictures of themselves.
13   Unflattering descriptions of himself have been banned by our president.
14   *Himself astonished John.
15   Joan$_i$ recognized the necessity for her$_i$ to leave.

Discuss each example separately. Then try to classify the examples according to the problems they raise, if any. The examples and judgements indicated are taken from Nakajima (1984). This author reformulates the binding theory using COMP (C) as a subject. The reader is referred to his work for discussion and interpretation.[25] Discuss to what extent Nakajima's approach can account for the data above.

The examples (10)–(13) pose problems for our theory as well as for a theory which counts COMP as a SUBJECT. NPs like those in (10)–(13) which are headed by an N like *picture, rumour, story*, etc., are referred to as *picture*-NPs.

Recall that *picture*-NPs were used extensively in the discussion of the binding domain for reflexives. Mohanan (1985: 641) points out the following contrast:

16 The boys thought that each other's pictures were on sale.
17 *The boys thought that each other's girlfriends were pretty.

The binding theory (46) will account for (16) using the notion of accessible subject, but has no way of accounting for the structurally parallel (17). Mohanan (1985: 642, n. 5) considers it a weakness of the binding theory (46) that the *i*-within-*i* filter is introduced for the definition of accessible subject/SUBJECT and GC to deal specifically with examples with *picture*-NPs, which are in many ways exceptional (1985: 641–2).[26]

Exercise 4

Consider the interpretation of the R-expressions in the following sentences.

1 I saw the President on TV last night and the poor fellow looked tired.
2 The President said that the poor fellow was tired.
3 I met Bill and the guy looked desperate for company.
4 Bill believes the guy to be desperate for company.

---

[25] It will be preferable to postpone reading Nakajima's article until chapters 5, 6 and 7 have been covered.
[26] Mohanan (1985: 641) refers to Prewett (1977) for a detailed description of *picture*-NPs.

NPs such as *the poor fellow* and *the guy* seem to act like pronouns. In (1) the NP *the poor fellow* can be replaced by *he*. Such NPs are often referred to as **epithets**. On the basis of the examples above and further examples which you will construct yourself, decide which binding principles, if any, these epithets obey. For some discussion see Huang (1991), Lasnik (1991).

Exercise 5

In the final section of this chapter we tentatively suggest that there might be non-overt NPs which are not subject to the case filter. Discuss the implications for such a proposal in the light of the visibility principle discussed in chapter 3.

Exercise 6

Chinese offers some intriguing data for the binding theory. Consider the examples below and discuss the problems that they raise:

1 Zhangsan$_i$ shuo ziji$_i$ hui lai.
          say   self will come
  'Zhangsan said that he himself would come.'

2 Zhangsan$_i$ shuo ziji$_i$ you mei you qian mei guanxi.
          say self have not have money not matter
  'Zhangsan said that whether himself has money or not didn't matter.'
  (examples from Aoun, 1984: 16–17)

3 Yuehan$_i$ renwei Mali xihuan ziji$_i$.
  John   think Mary like self
  'John thinks that Mary likes him.'
  (example from Lasnik and Uriagereka, 1988: 122)

Would the binding theory as described above predict these data?
  Chinese lacks verb inflection for person and number. One might propose that INFL in Chinese does not contain AGR. Huang (1982) uses this observation to explain the data above. A reflexive in the

subject position of a clause will never have an accessible SUBJECT in its own clause: the GC is automatically extended to the higher clause.

Exercise 7

In his description of Japanese Kuno (1973) presents the following examples. The reflexive *zibun* in Japanese is invariant for person and number, but it can be used in a genitive form. On the basis of the examples try to decide whether the reflexive *zibun* is subject to the same constraints as an English reflexive. Discuss any problems you meet.

1　*John ga Mary$_i$ o zibun$_i$ no　　uti　　de korosita.
　　John　　Mary　'herself'-GEN house in　killed.
　　'John killed Mary in her own house.'

2　John ga Mary$_i$ ni zibun$_i$ no　　uti　　de hon o yom-asase-ta.
　　John　　Mary　　herself-GEN house in　book　read causative
　　'John made Mary read books in her own house.'

3　Jonh$_i$ wa, Mary ga zibun$_i$ o korosoo to sita toki,　Jane to nete ita.
　　John　　Mary　himself kill-try　　did when Jane with sleeping wa:
　　'John was sleeping with Jane when Mary tried to kill him (lit. himself)'.

4　Zibun$_i$ ga baka na koto ga John$_i$ o kanasimaseta.
　　　　　　fool　is　that　　　　　saddened
　　'The fact that he (himself) is a fool saddened John.'

5　Mary ga zibun$_i$ o aisite inai　koto ga John$_i$ o gakkarisaseta.
　　Mary　　　　　　loving is not that　John　distressed
　　'The fact that Mary does not love him distressed John.'

6　John$_i$ wa Mary ga zibun$_i$ o aisite iru koto o sitte ita.
　　　　　　　　　　　　is loving that　knowing was
　　'John knew that Mary loves him ('himself').'
　　(examples: Kuno, 1973: 293–313)

Observe that we proposed that like Chinese, Japanese lacks AGR. Will this help in explaining the data above?[27]

Exercise 8

Consider the following examples: what problems, if any, do they raise for the binding theory as developed in this chapter?

1   *Icelandic*
    Jon$_i$ segir [ad   Maria   elski   sig$_i$/hann$_i$].
    Jon says that   Maria   loves (subj)   self/him
    'Jon$_i$ says that Maria loves him$_i$.'
    (from Anderson (1986), cited in Burzio (1989: 1))

2   *Dutch*
    Hij$_i$ hoorde [mij over   zich$_i$/hem$_i$ praten].
    He heard   me about self/him   talk
    'He$_i$ heard me talk about him$_i$.'
    (from Everaert (1986), cited in Burzio (1989: 1))

As the reader can check, the sentences above contain anaphors which are apparently bound outside what, according to our definition, would be their GC (the bracketed string). Anaphors which allow this type of binding are referred to in the literature as **long-distance anaphors**.[28]

Exercise 9

The following example illustrates the problem of referential circularity. (Haik, 1983: 313). Discuss its interpretation:

1   His wife told her daughter that her father was angry.

---

[27] For a description of the Japanese data the reader is referred to Kuno's own text (chapter 5). For a comparison between Japanese and other languages see also Manzini and Wexler (1987). The latter text presupposes familiarity with chapters 5–8.

[28] For discussion of long-distance anaphora the reader is referred to Anderson (1986), Cole, Hermon and Sung (1990), Everaert (1986), Giorgi (1984), Hermon (1992), the papers in Koster and Reuland (1991), Pica (1986a), Wexler and Manzini (1987).

Exercise 10

The binding theory distinguishes three types of NPs: reflexives, pronouns and R-expressions, exemplified by English *himself, him* and *John* respectively. Consider the following examples from West Flemish, a dialect of Dutch, and discuss the interpretation of the object elements *ze* and *eur* in terms of the binding theory as developed in this chapter.

1   Marie$_i$ wast eur$_{i/j}$.
    Marie washes her
    'Marie washes herself.'
    'Marie washes her.'

2   Marie$_i$ wast ze$_{j/*i}$.
    Marie washes her
    'Marie washes her.'
    *'Marie washes herself.'

3   Marie$_i$ peinst da Valère ze$_{j/*i}$ kent.
    Marie thinks that Valère her knows
    'Marie thinks that Valère knows her.'
    (*her* cannot be coreferential with *Marie*)

4   Marie$_i$ peinst da Valère eur$_{i/j}$ kent.
    Marie thinks that Valère her knows
    'Marie thinks that Valère knows her.'
    (*eur* may but need not be coreferential with *Marie*)

5   Marie$_i$ zei da Godelieve$_j$ peinst da Valère eur$_{j/i/k}$ kent.
    Marie said that Godelieve thinks that Valère her knows
    'Marie said that Godelieve thinks that Valère knows her.'
    (*eur* may, but need not, be coreferential with *Marie/Godelieve*)

6   [De zuster van [Marie$_j$]$_i$] ee ze$_{j/*i}$ gezien.
    the sister of Marie has her seen
    'Marie's sister has seen her.'
    (*ze* may be coreferential with *Marie*, it may not be coreferential with *Marie's sister*)

7   Vuoda Valère ze$_{j/i}$ erkende moest Marie$_i$ euren zonnebril ofdoen.
    before that Valère her recognized must Marie her sunglasses off
    take 'Before Valère recognized her Marie had to take off her
    sunglasses.' (*ze* and *Marie* can be coreferential)

Now consider the following examples where *ze* appears in subject
position. Does subject *ze* have the same binding properties as object
ze?

8   Marie$_i$ peinst da ze$_{j/i}$ ziek is.
    Marie thinks that she sick is
    'Marie thinks that she is ill.'
    (*ze* and *Marie* can but need not be coreferential)

9   Marie$_i$ peinst da Godelieve$_j$ gezeid eet da ze$_{j/i}$ ziek was.
    Marie thinks that Godelieve said has that she ill was
    'Marie thinks that Godelieve said that she was ill.'
    (*Marie* or *Godelieve* can be coreferential with *ze*)

The examples above illustrate that the properties of one element do
not carry over directly to its closest parallel in another language: *her*
in English is quite different from *eur* or *ze* in West Flemish. Moreover, even within one language an element may behave differently
depending on the grammatical function: object *ze* seems to be subject
to different constraints from subject *ze*.

Exercise 11

Consider the following examples. What kind of problems do they
raise for the binding theory developed in this chapter?

1   [To teach oneself linguistics] is exciting.
2   It is not always easy [to defend yourself in public].
3   Protecting oneself from injury is crucial for survival.
4   *Italian*
    La buona musica riconcilia con se stessi.
    the good music reconciles with oneselves
    'Good music can reconcile you with yourself.'
    (cf. Rizzi, 1986a)

5   *Italian*
    Vede se stesso nello specchio.
    sees himself in the mirror
    'He sees himself in the mirror.'

The reader will observe that the above sentences all lack an overt antecedent for the reflexives. In the next chapters we shall propose that sentences may also have a non-overt subject. Non-finite sentences like (1)–(3) are discussed in chapter 5. The Italian examples are discussed in chapter 8.

Now also consider the following examples: do they raise any problems for the binding theory?

6   John seems to be able to take care of himself.
7   Which student do you expect will present himself first at the exam?

In (6) and in (7) it would appear as if the antecedent of the reflexive is too far removed to bind the reflexive. In (6), for instance, *John*, the subject of the matrix clause, seems to be relatively far removed from the reflexive *himself*. In (7) the subject of the matrix clause, *you*, intervenes between *which student* and *himself*. And yet, the sentences are grammatical. We return to examples such as (6) in chapter 6, and to examples such as (7) in chapter 7.

5 Non-overt Categories: PRO and Control

Contents

Introduction and overview

Introduction and Overview

So far we have been dealing mainly with the NP constituents of sentences. Their occurrence, distribution and interpretation are regulated by various principles and modules of the grammar such as the projection principle (chapter 1), the theta criterion (chapter 1), the extended projection principle (chapter 1), X'-theory (chapter 2), case theory (chapter 3) and the binding theory (chapter 4).

In this chapter we turn to a non-overt NP, i.e. an NP which is syntactically active, hence syntactically represented, but which has no overt manifestation. This non-overt NP will be represented as PRO and is characterized by the feature composition [+ Anaphor, + Pronominal]. We alluded to this NP in chapter 4 (section 7.3). Other types of non-overt NPs will be discussed in chapters 6, 7 and 8.

In section 1 we show that the non-overt subject of infinitival clauses is syntactically active. We represent it as PRO. In section 2 we show that the non-overt NP PRO has the features [+ Anaphor, + Pronominal]. PRO may be referentially dependent on, or controlled by, another NP in the sentence. The distribution and interpretation of PRO is regulated by the module of the grammar known as control theory. Section 3 examines the distribution of PRO. We see that it occurs in ungoverned positions and we derive this property from its feature composition as discussed in section 2. In section 4 we discuss some properties of control structures. In section 5 we illustrate control patterns.

1 The Non-overt Subject of Infinitivals

1.1 Theta Roles and Understood Arguments

For each of the following examples, consider how the different modules of the grammar discussed so far determine the distribution and interpretation of NPs.

1a This$_i$ would be regrettable.
1b [$_{CP}$ That Poirot$_j$ should abandon the investigation$_k$]$_i$ would be regrettable.
1c Poirot$_j$ should abandon the investigation$_k$.

Regrettable is a one-place predicate: it requires the presence of one argument, realized in (1a) by the NP *this*. In (1b) the argument of *regrettable* is realized as a finite clause: *that Poirot should abandon the investigation*. The predicate *abandon* in the subordinate clause in (1b) – and in the corresponding main clause (1c) – is a two-place predicate with an external argument, the AGENT of the activity, realized by *Poirot* in both (1b) and (1c), and an internal argument, realized here by the NP *the investigation*. (2a) represents the argument structure of *regrettable*; (2b) that of *abandon*.

2a   *regrettable*: adjective

<u>1</u>
i

2b   *abandon*: verb

<u>1</u>	2
j	k

By the extended projection principle (EPP), the subject positions in the sentences in (1) must be syntactically represented. The theta criterion requires that the arguments of a predicate should be syntactically represented. Both *regrettable* and *abandon* have an external argument which will have to be realized in a position outside the VP. With predicates which select an external argument one cannot satisfy the EPP by inserting an expletive in the subject position:

1d   *There abandoned the investigation.

The insertion of *there* in the subject position makes it impossible to realize the external argument of *abandon* in the same position: (1d) violates the theta criterion since one theta role of *abandon* fails to be assigned. Now let us turn to (3):

3 [_{CP} [_{IP} To abandon the investigation]] would be regrettable.

(3) is a complex sentence containing a non-finite subordinate clause. The infinitival clause to *abandon the investigation* in (3) realizes the external argument of *regrettable*. We now focus on the structure of the bracketed infinitival clause.

The subordinate clause has as its main predicate the verb *abandon*. On the basis of (1b) and (1c) we have established that *abandon* is a two-place predicate with an external and an internal argument (cf. (2b)). Even though the external argument of *abandon* is not overtly realized, we will interpret the bracketed sentence in (3) as if there were an external argument; we will argue that the bracketed clause in (3) contains a non-overt subject. *Abandon* assigns two thematic roles: one to an internal argument, here the NP *the investigation*, one to an external argument, here the non-overt subject. Various arguments can be advanced to support the idea that infinitival clauses like the bracketed clause in (3) contain a non-overt subject, i.e. an implicit subject which is syntactically 'present' in the sentence and which interacts with the other constituents of the sentence.

1.2 The Extended Projection Principle

We first consider an argument based on the theory of phrase structure which we have been elaborating so far. Recall that the extended projection principle (EPP) says that all projections of IP have a subject, i.e. [Spec, IP] must be projected. So all projections of I have the structure in (4a):

4a
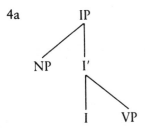

If the EPP is applied to the non-finite clause in (3) then we are forced to conclude that its syntactic representation will be like in (4b), with a non-overt [Spec, IP].

4b

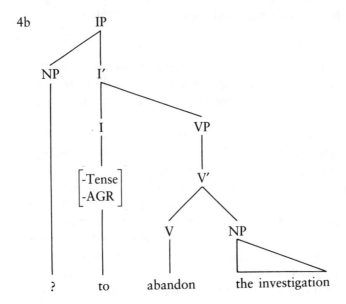

(3) is closely similar in structure to (5a) which contains an infinitival clause with an overt subject (5b/5c).

5a For Poirot to abandon the investigation would be regrettable.
5b [CP For [IP Poirot [I' to [VP abandon the investigation]]]].

5c CP

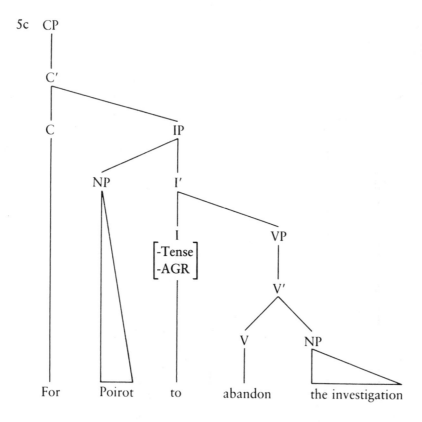

In (5a) the subject of *abandon* is the R-expression *Poirot*. This NP has a specific referent, an individual known by the name *Poirot*. In (3), though, the non-overt subject of *abandon* does not have inherent reference. Its interpretation is like that of a pronoun, either a specific pronoun (which would be recovered from the context) or generic *one*:

5d For $\left\{ \begin{array}{l} \text{you} \\ \text{him} \\ \text{them} \\ \text{one} \end{array} \right\}$ to abandon the investigation would be regrettable.

In the literature the non-overt subject of the infinitival clause is represented by the element PRO:[1]

---

[1] PRO is often called 'big PRO', in contrast with 'small *pro*' which we discuss in chapter 8.

6 CP

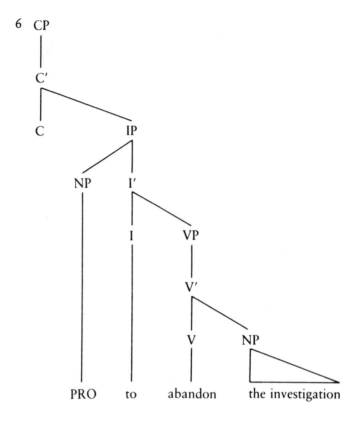

The difference between PRO and the pronouns in (5d) is that the latter have phonetic content and the former does not. PRO is a non-overt NP. This means that the EPP can be satisfied by non-overt material. By analogy with (5c), we also assume that the complementizer position in (6) is present though not filled by any overt element.

1.3   *Local Relations*

There are a number of additional arguments that support the idea that an infinitival clause without an overt subject has a non-overt subject. These arguments all have the same structure. We establish that within the clausal domain there is a local relation between the overt subject NP and another constituent. Then we show that even when the subject is not overtly realized such a local relation can be established and we propose that in such cases there is a non-overt subject.

1.3.1 PURPOSE CLAUSES

Consider (7a):

7a We will abandon the investigation [in order for you to save money].

In (7a) we have bracketed the infinitival purpose clause *in order for you to save money*. The subject of the purpose clause is *you*, and this is the AGENT of *to save money*. Now let us turn to the examples (7b)–(7d). These also contain an infinitival purpose clause, *in order to save money*. But the non-finite purpose clause lacks an overt subject.

7b [$_{CP}$ [$_{IP}$ Poirot abandoned the investigation [in order to save money]]].
7c [$_{CP}$ For [$_{IP}$ Poirot to abandon the investigation [in order to save money]]] would be regrettable.
7d [$_{CP}$ [$_{IP}$ To abandon the investigation [in order to save money]]] would be regrettable.

We focus on the interpretation of the infinitival purpose clauses.[2] In (7b), just as in (7a), the purpose clause is embedded in a finite clause. The AGENT of *to save money* is understood to be the same as the AGENT of *abandon the investigation*, i.e. it is the subject of the immediately dominating clause: *Poirot*. In (7c) the infinitival purpose clause is embedded in a non-finite clause. Again the AGENT of *to save money* will be understood to be the same as the AGENT of the immediately dominating clause, i.e. *Poirot*. In (7d) the non-finite clause *to abandon the investigation* appears not to have an overt subject; again the AGENT of the purpose clause *to save money* is identical to the AGENT of *to abandon the investigation*. The external argument of *to abandon the investigation*, though not overt, is understood and it interacts with other elements in the structure in the same way that the overt subject interacts in (7b) and (7c): it determines the interpretation of the subject of the purpose clause. Hence (7d) will have the partial representation (7e):

7e [$_{CP}$ [$_{IP}$ PRO To abandon the investigation [in order to save money]]] would be regrettable.

A similar argumentation can be developed on the basis of the following examples:

[2] See also sections 2 and 5.3.

8a	Poirot abandoned the investigation [without giving an explanation].

8b	[For Poirot to abandon the investigation [without giving an explanation]] would not be justified.

8c	[To abandon the investigation [without giving an explanation]] would not be justified.

In (8a) and in (8b) the AGENT of *giving an explanation* is interpreted as identical to the subject of the immediately dominating clause, i.e. it is interpreted as *Poirot*. In (8c) the AGENT of *giving an explanation* is interpreted as identical to the understood AGENT of *abandon the investigation*. We say again that the subject of *abandon the investigation* is syntactically represented and that it plays a role in the interpretation of the subordinate clause.

8d	[PRO to abandon the investigation [without giving an explanation]] would not be justified.

### 1.3.2	TOGETHER

Consider the distribution of *together* in the following sentences:

9a	The boys left together.

9b	*The boy left together.

The grammaticality of (9a) as opposed to the ungrammaticality of (9b) suggests that *together* needs to be related to a plural NP in an A position. This is confirmed by the contrast (9c) vs. (9d):

9c	I saw the boys together.

9d	*I saw the boy together.

Adopting a term from the previous chapter we can say that *together* requires a plural antecedent. The relation between *together* and the antecedent is local:

9e	*The boys said [$_{CP}$ that [$_{IP}$ Mary left together]].

There is no way in which *together* in the subordinate clause in (9e) could be related to the subject NP of the higher clause, *the boys*. Now consider the examples in (10):

10a   [CP For [IP the boys to leave together]] would be stupid.
10b   [CP [IP To leave together]] would be stupid.

In (10a) *together* is related to the subject of the infinitival clause, *the boys*. In (10b) it seems to have no antecedent. If we wish to retain our generalization formulated above then we could account for the grammaticality of (10b) by proposing that the non-finite clause contains a non-overt subject. It is this non-overt subject which can function as the antecedent of *together*. The infinitival clause will be represented with a non-overt subject PRO:

10c   [CP [IP PRO to leave together]] would be stupid.

1.3.3   PREDICATES

The interpretation of the predicative AP in the sentences in (11) also provides evidence for postulating PRO as the subject of the infinitival clause in (11c):

11a   Mary arrived exhausted at the party.
11b   [CP For [IP one's guests to arrive exhausted at a party]] is terrible.
11c   [[To arrive exhausted at a party]] is terrible.

In (11a) the predicate *exhausted* is predicated of the subject NP *Mary*. In (11b) similarly *exhausted* is predicated of the subject of the infinitival clause, *one's guests*. The interpretation of (11c) is that *exhausted* is predicated of the non-overt subject of *to arrive at a party*. Once again we assume that the understood subject of the infinitival clause in (11c) is represented as PRO. It interacts with other elements in the clause.

11d   [[PRO to arrive exhausted at a party]] is terrible.

We briefly return to predicates like *exhausted* in (11) in section 3.4.

1.3.4   BINDING

Finally consider (12)

12   [To identify oneself here] would be wrong.

Following our discussion above we assume that the subject of *to identify oneself* is the non-overt NP PRO. The direct object of *identify* is realized as an anaphor, the reflexive *oneself*. As discussed extensively in chapter 4, Principle A of the binding theory (chapter 4, (46)) requires that an anaphor must be bound in its governing category. Given that (12) is grammatical, we deduce that Principle A is not violated. If we postulate that the infinitival clause has a non-overt subject, PRO, this subject can act as the binder of the reflexive. The governing category of *oneself* will be the lower non-finite clause. The clause contains the governor of *oneself*, the verb *identify*, and it contains a subject, PRO. It is clear that without the assumption that there is a non-overt subject in the lower clause, it will be hard to see how Principle A of the binding theory could be satisfied in the sentence.

Let us from now on adopt the hypothesis that in infinitival clauses without an overt subject NP, the subject is represented syntactically as PRO. In the remainder of this chapter we look in some more detail at the properties of PRO.

2   The Features of PRO

2.1   *[+ Anaphoric] and [+ Pronominal]*

We have posited that infinitival clauses without overt subjects have a non-overt subject represented as PRO. Using the arguments outlined in section 1, the same element will be taken to occupy the subject position in the infinitival clauses in (13). The reader is invited to consider for himself the motivation for the presence of PRO:

13a   Poirot is considering [$_{CP}$ whether [$_{IP}$ PRO to abandon the investigation]].
13b   Poirot needed a lot of courage [$_{CP}$ [$_{IP}$ PRO to abandon the investigation]].
13c   Poirot was glad [$_{CP}$ [$_{IP}$ PRO to abandon the investigation]].

In (13a) the infinitival clause is the complement of the verb *consider*. In (13b) an infinitival clause is used as an adjunct; the clause is a purpose clause. In (13c) the infinitival clause is the complement of an adjective *glad*.

As the reader will have been able to verify, the projection principle, the theta criterion and the EPP, offer arguments for postulating PRO. However, the interpretation of PRO in (13) differs from that in the (3), repeated here for convenience's sake as (13d):

13d [$_{CP}$ [$_{IP}$ PRO to abandon the investigation]] would be regrettable.

In (13d) PRO is roughly equivalent to a pronoun. Let us say that PRO is 'pronominal'. Depending on the context PRO may be taken to refer to a specific referent ('you', 'they', etc.) or it may be interpreted as equivalent to the arbitrary pronoun *one*. In (13a), (13b) and (13c) on the other hand, PRO, the subject of the infinitive, will normally be understood as 'Poirot'. In these examples PRO is like an anaphor: it is dependent on another NP for its interpretation. Using the feature system elaborated in chapter 4 (section 7) and on the basis of the interpretations which are assigned to PRO in (13) we will propose that PRO is both pronominal (13d) and anaphoric (13a)–(13c): PRO is an NP with the feature matrix [+Anaphoric, +Pronominal].

When PRO is interpreted as referentially dependent on another NP in the same sentence, as is the case in (13a), (13b) and (13c), we say that it is **controlled** by that NP.

> The term **control** is used to refer to a relation of referential dependency between an unexpressed subject (the **controlled** element) and an expressed or unexpressed constituent (the **controller**). The referential properties of the controlled element . . . are determined by those of the controller. (Bresnan, 1982: 372)

In (13a)–(13c) PRO is **controlled** by the main clause subject NP *Poirot*. As has become our practice, we indicate the referential dependency between controller (*Poirot*) and controlled element (PRO) by coindexation:

14a Poirot$_i$ is considering [$_{CP}$ whether [$_{IP}$ PRO$_i$ to abandon the investigation]].
14b Poirot$_i$ needed a lot of courage [$_{CP}$ [$_{IP}$ PRO$_i$ to abandon the investigation]].
14c Poirot$_i$ was glad [$_{CP}$ [$_{IP}$ PRO$_i$ to abandon the investigation]].

In the cases where PRO is not controlled by another NP and refers freely, as in (13d), PRO can also have an arbitrary reading: this is **arbitrary** PRO. This occurrence of PRO is sometimes represented as follows: PRO$_{arb}$.

14d [[PRO_{arb} to abandon the investigation]] would be regrettable.

PRO may also be dependent on implicit arguments:

15a The operation was abandoned [PRO to save money].
15b [PRO to control yourself] is very advisable.

In (15a) PRO is not arbitrary in reference. Rather it is controlled by the implied AGENT of *abandoned*. In (15b) PRO is controlled by the implied BENEFACTIVE, which may be overt or implicit:

15c PRO to control yourself is very advisable (for you).

We assume that the non-overt subject NP of infinitival clauses is syntactically represented as PRO, with the feature matrix [+Anaphor, +Pronominal]. We now have to determine what the conditions of the occurrence of PRO are, in which contexts it is admitted or **licensed** and how its content, its interpretation, is determined. The module of the grammar which regulates the distribution and the interpretation of PRO is called control theory. We turn to some aspects of control theory in section 3.

2.2 *Nominal Features*

The question arises whether other grammatical features should be associated with PRO. If PRO is a non-overt NP, it will also have the categorial features [+N, −V], which are characteristic of NPs (cf. chapter 2, section 6). Overt NPs are also characterized by nominal agreement features such as person, number, and gender. In some languages such features have an overt reflex, realized on nouns, adjectives and determiners, in others the features are abstract. Italian illustrates the first type of language:

16a La ragazza è contenta.
     the girl   is contented
     fem sg   fem sg
16b Le ragazze sono contente.
     the girls   are contented
     fem plural   fem plural
16c Il ragazzo è contento.

the boy is happy
masc sg   masc sg
16d I ragazzi sono contenti.
the boys are happy
masc pl   masc pl

In the above sentences the subject NPs are all third person. The NPs are differentiated with respect to gender and number: *la ragazza* is feminine singular, *le ragazze* is feminine plural, *il ragazzo* is masculine singular, *i ragazzi* is masculine plural. The form of the article varies according to the gender and number features of the noun it is associated with. Also, the head of the AP agrees with the subject with respect to number and gender features: *contenta* is singular feminine, for instance, etc. In English, articles and adjectives do not vary morphologically with respect to number and gender features. However, we can detect person, number and gender features in certain types of sentences. Recall from chapter 4 that reflexives agree in person, number and gender with their antecedents:

17a John has hurt himself/*herself/*myself/*themselves.
17b The boys have hurt themselves/*himself/*myself.

In (17) the choice of the reflexive is determined by the grammatical features of its binder: *John* is third person masculine singular and hence it will bind a reflexive with the same features: *himself*. Similar observations apply to (18):

18a I can do this on my/*your/*his own.
18b You can do this on your/*my/*his own.
18c The boys have to do this on their/*his own.

The expression *on . . .'s own* behaves like an anaphor in that it has to be bound. The possessive pronoun in this construction matches the subject NP with respect to the features person, number and gender. The binder for the relevant phrase is local.[3] The above examples serve to show that we can identify the features of the subject NP by looking at the features of an anaphor which it binds. Now consider what happens in sentences with a

---

[3] Observe for instance that in (i) the phrase *on their own* cannot be related to the NP *the boys* because this NP is outside the immediately dominating clause.

i.   *The boys thought [CP that [IP Mary had to do this on their own]].

subject realized as PRO. In a control structure, PRO picks up the agreement features of the controller:

19a Poirot wondered [$_{CP}$ whether [$_{IP}$ PRO to invite himself/*herself to the party]].

19b Poirot wondered [$_{CP}$ whether [$_{IP}$ PRO to go to the party on his/*her own]].

Uncontrolled or arbitrary PRO is singular in English, and it can have either third person or second person features:

19c It is not always easy [$_{CP}$ [$_{IP}$ PRO to control oneself in public]].

19d It is not always easy [$_{CP}$ [$_{IP}$ PRO to control yourself in public]].

In Italian, as is to be expected, controlled PRO also picks up the features of the controller:

20a Gianni ha promesso [$_{CP}$ di [$_{IP}$ PRO parlare di se stesso]].[4]
Gianni has promised of talk of himself
'Gianni has promised to talk about himself.'

20b Gina ha promesso [$_{CP}$ di [$_{IP}$ PRO essere pronta]].
Gina has promised of be ready
'Gina has promised to be ready.'

But unlike in the case in English, arbitrary or uncontrolled PRO has the features [+ Plural] and [+ masculine]: in (20c) *se stessi*, the reflexive, has to be masculine plural, similarly in (20d) the participle *amati* is also masculine plural.

20c È difficile [$_{CP}$ [$_{IP}$ PRO parlare di se stessi/*se stesso]].
is hard talk of oneselves/*oneself
'It is difficult to talk about oneself.'

---

4 For the status of Italian *di* cf. Kayne (1991: 668).

20d È bello [CP [IP essere amati/*amata da te]].
   is nice be loved (masc pl)/loved (fem sg) by you
   'It is nice to be loved by you.'

The data sketched above suggest that in addition to the features [+N, –V, + anaphoric, + pronominal], PRO has nominal agreement features, which, in the case of arbitrary PRO vary cross-linguistically. Finally consider the following examples:

21a   [[PRO to roll down a hill]] is dangerous.
21b   Mary rolled down a hill.
21c   Stones rolled down a hill.

22a   [CP [IP PRO Essere efficienti]] è importante.
     be efficient (pl) is important
     'It is important to be efficient.'
22b   Gli professori sono efficienti.
     the teachers are efficient
22c   Quelle macchine sono efficienti
     these cars are efficient

When its subject is realized overtly the predicate *roll down a hill* may take either an animate (21b) or a non-animate (21c) argument, but when its subject is arbitrary PRO, only the animate argument is possible. Similarly in Italian the predicate *efficiente* ('efficient') may be predicated of persons (22b) or of things (22c) but when it is predicated of arbitrary PRO then the latter must have a animate interpretation. The feature [± Animate] is yet another feature to be associated with arbitrary PRO.

3   The Distribution of PRO

3.1   The Data

In this section we study the distribution of PRO. We shall examine whether this element is necessarily restricted to subject positions of infinitivals. Would it be possible to find PRO as the subject of a finite clause? Can PRO be found in a direct object position? We may also wonder whether every infinitive could have a PRO subject. A glance at the data in (23)–(25) suggests that the answer to all three questions is negative:

23a *Poirot_i wondered [_{CP} whether [_{IP} PRO_i to invite PRO]].
23b *Poirot wondered [_{CP} whether [_{IP} he should invite PRO]].

24a *[_{IP} PRO should invite the sergeant].
24b *Poirot_i wondered [_{CP} whether [_{IP} PRO_i should invite someone]].

25a *Poirot_i preferred very much [_{CP} for [_{IP} PRO_i to destroy something]].
25b *Poirot_i believed [_{IP} PRO_i to be the best detective]].

(23) shows that the non-overt element PRO cannot be used as a direct object.[5] The ungrammaticality of the sentences is due to the presence of PRO in the object position of *invite*. If we replace PRO by an overt NP the sentences become grammatical:

26a Poirot_i wondered [_{CP} whether [_{IP} PRO_i to invite her]].
26b Poirot wondered [_{CP} whether [_{IP} he should invite her]].

(24) suggests that PRO cannot appear as the subject of finite clauses, whether they be main clauses (24a) or subordinate ones (24b). If we replace PRO by an overt NP the sentences in (24) become grammatical:

27a [_{IP} You should invite the sergeant].
27b Poirot_i wondered [_{CP} whether [_{IP} he should invite someone]].

(25) finally provides evidence that although PRO may be the subject of some infinitival clauses, not every infinitival construction allows PRO as its subject.

These facts need to be explained. Recall that the ultimate goal of linguistic theory is to provide an explanation for language acquisition. We assume that the child acquiring a language will have to construct a grammar which allows for sentences containing the non-overt NP represented as PRO. The child will also have to construct a grammar which is constrained enough so as to allow

---

[5] For non-overt NPs that may occur in object position the reader is referred to chapters 6, 7, and 8.

only grammatical sentences. The grammar should not generate, for instance, (23), (24) and (25).

One can, of course, try to think of many hypotheses why PRO should not be able to turn up in the examples above. One approach would be to devise three separate statements banning PRO from (i) being the object of a transitive verb (23), (ii) being the subject of a finite clause (24); and (iii) being the subject of certain, yet to be determined, infinitivals (25). But this would be merely providing three descriptive stipulations and this would not explain anything. Listing these stipulations would also suggest that these three constraints on the occurrence of PRO are three independent principles of UG which a child must learn one by one. It would clearly be preferable if we could explain the three properties mentioned in terms of one or more other properties which are independently established. We turn to an explanation for the restrictions on the distribution of PRO in the next section.

3.2 PRO and Overt NPs

Let us see if we can find a property common to the illegitimate occurrences of PRO in (23), (24) and (25) and oppose these examples to legitimate occurrences of PRO such as those in (28).

28a Poirot₍ᵢ₎ preferred very much [PRO₍ᵢ₎ to invite the sergeant].
28b [PRO to invite the policeman] would be regrettable.

One characteristic that sets off the illegitimate occurrences of PRO in (23)–(25) from the legitimate ones in (28) is that in the former an overt NP can replace the illegitimate PRO and lead to grammaticality (as shown in (29)–(31) while this is not possible for the legitimate occurrences of PRO (32).

29a cf. 23a Poirot₍ᵢ₎ wondered [CP whether [IP PRO₍ᵢ₎ to invite *anyone*]].
29b cf. 23b Poirot wondered [CP whether [IP he should invite anyone]].

30a cf. 24a *You* should invite the sergeant.
30b cf. 24b Poirot₍ᵢ₎ wondered [CP whether [IP *he*₍ᵢ₎ should invite someone]].

31a cf. 25a Poirot₍ᵢ₎ preferred very much [CP for [IP *the detectives*₍ⱼ₎ to destroy something]].
31b cf. 25b Poirot₍ᵢ₎ believed [*Watson*₍ⱼ₎ to be the best detective].

32a cf. 28a   *Poirot$_i$ preferred very much [$_{CP}$ [$_{IP}$ *the police$_j$* to invite the sergeant]].

32b cf. 28b   *[$_{CP}$ [$_{IP}$ *Anyone* to invite the policeman]] would be regrettable.

The ungrammaticality of the examples in (32) follows from case theory (see chapter 3). In (32a) the NP *the police* will not be case-marked by the verb *prefer*, because it is not adjacent to the verb. In (32b), there is no case assigner to case-mark the NP *anyone* in the subject position of the infinitival clause. The insertion of the prepositional complementizer *for* saves the sentences:

33a   Poirot preferred very much [$_{CP}$ for [$_{IP}$ the police to invite the sergeant]].

33b   [$_{CP}$ For [$_{IP}$ anyone to invite the policeman]] would be regrettable.

The overt NP subject of the infinitival clause in (33) cannot be replaced by PRO:

33c   *Poirot preferred very much [$_{CP}$ for [$_{IP}$ PRO to invite the sergeant]].

33d   *[$_{CP}$ For [$_{IP}$ PRO to invite the policeman]] would be regrettable.

In (33a) and (33b) *for* governs the relevant NPs and will assign ACCUSA-TIVE case. We deduce from these observations that PRO in (28) occurs in an ungoverned position. From the ungrammaticality of (33c) and (33d) we conclude that PRO must not be governed.

If PRO must be ungoverned, then it cannot alternate with overt NPs and the ungrammaticality of the examples in (23)–(25) follows. Consider the italicized NPs in (29)–(31). We know from our discussion of case theory in chapter 3 that overt NPs must be case-marked and that case is assigned under government. We conclude that the relevant NPs in (29), (30) and (31) are governed. In (29) the object NP is governed by the verb *invite*. In (30) the subject NP of the finite clause is governed by INFL. The subject of infinitival clause in (31) is case-marked by the prepositional complementizer *for* in (31a) and by the verb *believe* (ECM) in (31b). In (28) PRO is legitimate and it does not alternate with overt NPs. Being ungoverned, overt NPs would not be able to be case-marked.

Let us briefly return to example (12), repeated here as (34a) with its syntactic representation (27b):

34a   To identify oneself would be wrong.

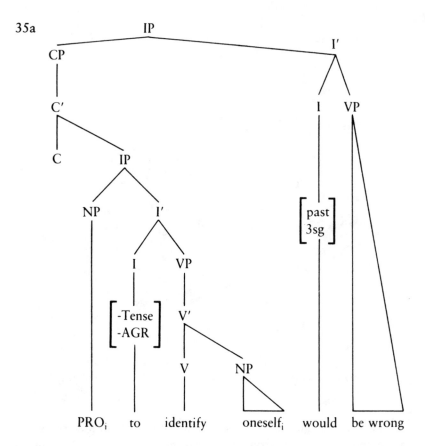

35a

If we want to say that PRO is ungoverned we must assume that the head of IP, I, does not govern PRO. Note that this is a case of a 'weak' I, i.e. one that is negatively specified for both [Tense] and [AGR] features. I is not strong enough to govern PRO (cf. chapter 3).

In our representation in (35a) we also posit that there is a C-projection. We may wonder whether the C-projection is needed. Suppose that there were no C-projection and that the representation of (34) were (35b).

35b

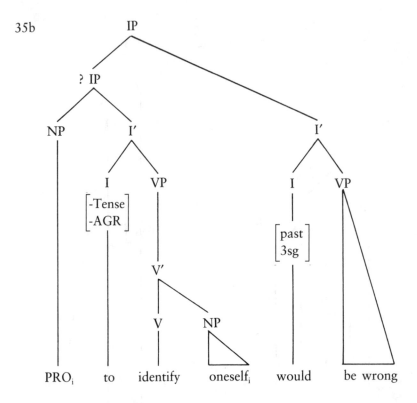

PRO is the subject of an infinitival clause. We have just adopted the hypo-thesis that infinitival I is not strong enough to govern PRO. Recall that we also assume that the projection of this 'weak' infinitival I is not a barrier for outside government [see the discussion in chapter 3). In the representation (35b), PRO, the subject of the lower IP, will be governed by an external governor, specifically the finite inflection of the higher clause, which is a governor (see chapter 3). We conclude that representation (35b) is inadequate and must be rejected in favour of (35a). In (35a) PRO is ungoverned: infinitival I is not a governor, by assumption, and CP is a barrier to government, being a maximal projection.[6]

3.3   *PRO must be Ungoverned: the PRO Theorem*

Our hypothesis with respect to the distribution of PRO is that its occurrence is restricted to ungoverned positions. PRO is admitted or **licensed** if it is ungoverned. It follows that PRO is in complementary distribution with overt

[6]   At this point we are operating with a provisional definition of the notion barrier. We return to the notion extensively in chapters 9 and 10.

NPs. Where PRO is allowed, overt NPs are excluded; where overt NPs are allowed, PRO is excluded.

This analysis is an improvement on the previous one in which we simply stipulated that PRO does not occur (i) in object positions, (ii) as the subject of finite clauses, and (iii) as the subject of certain infinitival clauses. Three properties of PRO can be derived from one general constraint: PRO must be ungoverned. But what we have achieved so far is still only a generalization which describes the restricted occurrence of PRO. It does not follow from anything. In comparison with our earlier discussion, all we have obtained is a more general stipulation: we have replaced three separate constraints by a single one. The remaining question is why PRO should be constrained to appearing only in ungoverned positions.

In the discussion of the interpretation of PRO in section 2.1 we assumed that PRO is specified as [+ Anaphor, + Pronominal]. Given our discussion in chapter 4 we expect this element, like all NPs, to be subject to the binding theory. In chapter 4, section 7 the binding theory was reformulated in terms of the features [± Anaphor], [± Pronominal]:

36 **Binding theory**
    Principle A
    An NP with the feature [+ Anaphor] must be bound in its governing category.
    Principle B
    An NP with the feature [+ Pronominal] must be free in its governing category.

According to its feature composition, PRO should be subject to both Principle A (it is [+ Anaphor]) and to Principle B (it is [+ Pronominal). In other words, as discussed in chapter 4, section 7.3, PRO is subject to contradictory requirements: it must be both bound and free in its GC. We hinted at a solution for this paradox in our earlier discussion in chapter 4, section 7.3. NPs with the features [+ Anaphor, + Pronominal] will survive if they are ungoverned. If an NP is not governed, then it will not have a GC. We had developed the hypothesis that PRO is licensed when ungoverned. The requirement that PRO be ungoverned **derives** from the binding theory as set up independently and from the characterization of PRO as [+ Anaphor, + Pronominal]. The proposition that PRO must be ungoverned is referred to as the PRO theorem:[7] it is not a self-evident truth, but it is deduced by a chain of reasoning on the basis of other accepted propositions.

---

[7] In this book we show how the PRO theorem can be derived from the binding theory. However, not all syntacticians agree on this. For other viewpoints see, for instance, Brody (1985). Kayne (1991) offers important modifications.

Consider also the following contrast:

37a *John prefers [_CP_ for [_IP_ PRO to leave]].
37b *John doesn't know [_CP_ if [_IP_ PRO to leave]].
37c John doesn't know [_CP_ whether [_IP_ PRO to leave]].

The ungrammaticality of (37a) is related to the PRO theorem: *for*, the prepositional complementizer, governs PRO. The same explanation could be used to explain why (37b) is ungrammatical: *if* is the complementizer of indirect questions and governs PRO. However, the grammaticality of the apparently analogous (37c) is surprising. One possibility is simply to stipulate that *whether* is not a governor. Another possibility (suggested in Borer, 1989: 76) would be to assign the structures (38a) and (38b) to the infinitival clauses in (37b) and (37c) respectively:

38a

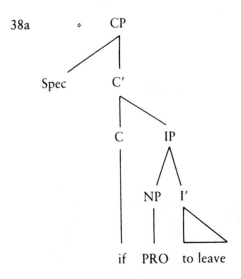

38b

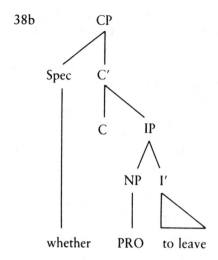

Contrary to our proposals in chapter 2, (38) differentiates between *if* and *whether*. *If* is a head, dominated by C; in (37b)/(38a) *if* will govern PRO. *Whether*, on the other hand, would not be dominated by C but is generated under [Spec, CP]. This analysis would mean that *whether* is a maximal projection. Recall that we have seen in chapter 2 that [Spec, CP] is occupied by maximal projections. *Whether* will not govern PRO in (38b)[8] according to our definitions.

3.4 Other Non-finite Clauses and PRO

So far we have seen that PRO occurs as the subject of infinitival clauses. It also occurs in other types of non-finite clauses:

39a Poirot$_i$ remembers [PRO$_i$ abandoning the investigation].
39b I$_i$ left [without [PRO$_i$ giving an explanation]].
39c Poirot$_i$ died [[PRO$_i$ waiting for Miss Marple]].
39d Poirot$_i$ arrived [PRO$_i$ angry].

---

[8] As we will see in chapter 8 and following, *whether* would also not be an ante-cedent-governor of PRO.
   The contrast between *if* and *whether* is also developed in Kayne (1991). This paper also offers important comparative discussion on the status of *if*, *whether*, and their equivalents in Romance languages. We suggest that this paper should only be tackled at the end of the present introduction. Exercise 6 at the end of this chapter provides some illustrations of the problems discussed by Kayne.

In (39a) the verb *remember* has a gerundival clause as its complement, a clause headed by the gerund of the verb *abandon*. The structure of such clauses is notably complicated.[9] Suffice it to say that, following earlier discussion, the verb *abandon* assigns two thematic roles and thus requires two arguments. We assume that the external argument is PRO. PRO is interpreted as referentially dependent on the main clause subject *Poirot*.

In (39b) we find a gerundival clause as the complement of a preposition (*without*). We do not discuss the structure of the PP headed by *without* or of the gerundival constituent. However, on the assumption that *give an explanation* needs an external argument we posit that the subject of the gerund is also PRO.

In (39c) the gerundival clause is an adjunct and is not governed by either a verb or a preposition. As the reader can see, PRO may again function as its subject. In (39d) we find PRO as the subject of a small clause. From (40) we deduce that *angry* assigns a theta role: the NP *Poirot* is assigned a theta role by the predicate *angry*. The bracketed string is a small clause complement of *thought*.

40   We thought [Poirot angry].

For (39d) we assume that the small clause has a non-overt subject. At this point the reader may well become suspicious. In chapter 3 we argued that small clauses are not barriers to outside government. In an example like (40) the subject of the small clause *Poirot* must be case-marked. In (40) the verb *think* case-marks the subject of the small clause. On the other hand, we have argued that PRO is ungoverned. How can the subject of a small clause be governed in one context (40) and ungoverned in another (39d)? We return to this issue in chapter 10. At this point we merely draw the reader's attention to the fact that the small clause in (40) is a **complement** of *think*: *Poirot angry* is assigned a theta role by the lexical head *think*. The small clause *PRO angry* is an **adjunct** in (39d), it may be omitted.[10]

4   Properties of Control

So far we have not dealt in any detail with the interpretation of PRO. We have merely established (in section 1.3) that sometimes PRO is controlled by

---

[9]   There is a vast literature on gerunds. The reader is referred for example to work by Abney (1987), Johnson (1988), Milsark (1988), Reuland (1983) and to the references cited there.

[10]   For a different interpretation of the adjunct small clause the reader is referred to Williams (1980).

an NP, sometimes it is controlled by an implicit argument, and sometimes it is not controlled at all and its interpretation is 'arbitrary'. In this section we give a brief survey of some of the central issues which control theory should deal with.[11] We describe the contrast between obligatory and optional control (section 4.1), between subject control and object control (section 4.2). We also discuss the c-command requirement on control patterns (section 4.3) and we deal with the type of NP that can act as a controller (section 4.4).

4.1 Obligatory Control and Optional Control

In the literature on control two types are often distinguished: **optional control** as in (41), and **obligatory control**, as in (42):

41a John thought that it was important [[PRO to behave oneself/himself]].
41b John asked [how [PRO to behave oneself/himself]].
41c John wonders [how [PRO to behave oneself/himself]].
41d John and Bill discussed [[PRO behaving oneself/themselves in public]].
     (examples (41c–41d) adapted from Huang (1989)).

42a John tried [[PRO to behave himself/*oneself]].
42b John was reluctant [[PRO to behave himself/*oneself]].
42c John promised Mary [[PRO to behave himself/*herself/*oneself]].
42d John told Mary [[PRO to behave herself/*himself/*oneself]].
42e John abandoned the investigation [[PRO to keep himself/*oneself sane]].
42f John arrived [PRO pleased with himself/*oneself]].

In (41) control is optional. PRO may be controlled by *John* but it may also have an arbitrary interpretation as shown by the fact PRO may bind either *himself* or *oneself*. In (42), on the other hand, PRO, must be controlled and cannot be arbitrary, as shown by the ungrammaticality of *oneself*. We return to the contrast between obligatory control and optional control in section 5.5.

4.2 Subject Control vs. Object Control

In the examples of obligatory control in (42) we see that sometimes the controller must be the subject (42a, b, c, e, f) sometimes the object NP (42d).

---

[11] This section relies heavily on Chomsky (1986a: 124–31), on Manzini (1983) and on Williams (1980). Manzini (1983) integrates the theory of control into a revised version of the binding theory. Williams (1980) relates control to the more general notion of predication, i.e. the relation between subject and predicate.

The former type is **subject control**, the latter is **object control**. Verbs like *try* and *promise*, which impose subject control, are called verbs of subject control. Verbs like *tell* are verbs of object control. Other examples of subject control are given in (43a)–(43c) and object control is further illustrated in (43d)–(43f). The phrase *on his/her/one's own* is linked to the PRO subject. We can infer which NP is the controller of PRO from the choice of possessive.

43a   Poirot$_i$ decided finally [[PRO$_i$ to go on his/*one's own]].
43b   Poirot$_i$ was willing [[PRO$_i$ to go on his/*one's own]].
43c   Poirot$_i$ was eager [[PRO$_i$ to go on his/*one's own]].
43d   Poirot$_i$ ordered Miss Marple$_j$ [[PRO$_j$ to go on her/*his/*one's own]].
43e   Poirot$_i$ instructed Miss Marple$_j$ [[PRO$_j$ to go on her/*his/*one's own]].
43f   Poirot$_i$ allowed Miss Marple$_j$ [[PRO$_j$ to go on her/*his/*one's own]].

4.3   C-command and Obligatory Control

Consider the examples of obligatory control in (44):

44a   Poirot's sister promised Miss Marple [[PRO to behave herself/*himself]].
44b   Poirot told Watson's sister [[PRO to behave herself/*himself]].

In (44a) only the NP *Poirot's sister* can control PRO in the subordinate clause. The NP *Poirot* in its specifier position cannot function as a controller of PRO. Similarly, in (44b), only the entire NP *Watson's sister* can be a controller for PRO. There appears to be a configurational constraint on control similar to the constraints that define the antecedent for binding: in the case of obligatory control the controller must c-command the controlled element. The reader can verify that *Poirot* in (44a) or *Watson* in (44b) do not c-command PRO.

In the case of optional control the situation is different, as illustrated in (45):

45a   [[PRO not to behave myself/himself/oneself]] would be wrong.
45b   [[PRO to behave myself]] would be my pleasure.

In (45a) PRO is not controlled by anything in the sentence: it may be taken to have an arbitrary reading or it may be taken as referring to a specific referent which will have been established in the context. In (45b) PRO will be taken to be controlled by the specifier *my* of the NP *my pleasure*. The controller *my* in (45b) does not c-command PRO. Williams (1980) argues that the c-command requirement distinguishes obligatory control from optional control.

4.4 The Controller: Argument Control

Consider the following examples:

46a Three accidents occurred after lunch.
46b There occurred three accidents after lunch.
46c No medical help was available on the premises.
46d There was no medical help available on the premises.
46e Three more accidents occurred without there being any medical help available on the premises.
46f There occurred three more accidents without there being any medical help available on the premises.
46g *There occurred three more accidents without PRO being any medical help available on the premises.

In (46a) *occur* takes one argument. In (46b) we have an example of an alternative sentence pattern in which the subject position of *occurred* is occupied by the expletive element *there*. Expletives are non-argument elements which fill an NP position. The expletive subject is required for structural reasons (EPP).

Similarly in (46c), the subject of the sentence is the NP *no medical help* and in the paraphrase in (46d) the subject position is taken up by the non-argument *there*.

As can be seen in (46e) and (46f) *there* may also be the subject of a gerundival clause. However, (46g) shows that it is not possible for PRO to be controlled by an expletive *there* in the higher clause. We conclude from the examples that control by an expletive is not allowed: PRO must be controlled by an argument.

5 Control Patterns: Further Examples

In this section we illustrate and discuss some types of control sentences. The following topics are discussed: (i) sentences with PRO as the subject of a complement clause (5.1), (ii) passivization and control (5.2), (iii) adjunct clauses with PRO subjects (5.3), (iv) subject clauses with PRO subjects (5.4), (v) the contrast between obligatory control and optional control (5.5).

5.1   PRO *in Complement Clauses*

Consider examples (43) repeated here as (47):

47a   Poirot$_i$ decided finally [[PRO$_i$ to go on his/*one's own]].
47b   Poirot$_i$ was willing [[PRO$_i$ to go on his/*one's own]].
47c   Poirot$_i$ was eager [[PRO$_i$ to go on his/*one's own]].
47d   Poirot$_i$ ordered Miss Marple$_j$ [[PRO$_j$ to go on her/*his/*one's own]].
47e   Poirot$_i$ instructed Miss Marple$_j$ [[PRO$_j$ to go on her/*his/*one's own]].
47f   Poirot$_i$ allowed Miss Marple$_j$ [[PRO$_j$ to go on her/*his/*one's own]].

When PRO is the subject of a declarative complement clause it must be controlled by an NP. Arbitrary PRO is excluded in (47). However, different properties obtain when the complement clause is interrogative. In (48) either subject control (48a) or arbitrary control (48b) is possible:

48a   John asked [$_{CP}$ how [$_{IP}$ PRO to behave himself]].
48b   John asked [$_{CP}$ how [$_{IP}$ PRO to behave oneself]].
      (from Manzini, 1983: 127)

As the term suggests, a controller must be present in the case of obligatory control. Certain verbs in English may take arguments optionally rather than obligatorily:

49a   This analysis led the students to the wrong conclusion.
49b   This analysis led to the wrong conclusion.

The direct object *the students* in (49a) is optional. We do not go into the discussion of this example here (see Rizzi, 1986a). Interestingly, *lead* may also act as an object control verb. In (50a) PRO, the subject of the complement clause of *lead*, must be controlled. As expected, the direct object of *lead* cannot be omitted (50b).

50a   This analysis led the students, [[PRO, to conclude for themselves/*oneself that Poirot was Belgian]].

50b   *This analysis led [[PRO to conclude for oneself that Poirot was
Belgian]].

Lead contrasts with *promise* which is a verb of subject control. In (51b) we
see that the complement NP of *promise* can be omitted.

51a   Poirot, promised Miss Marple, [[PRO, to go]].

51b   Poirot, promised [[PRO, to go]].

Because *lead* is a verb of object control, the direct object must be present in
order to control the subject of the infinitival clause. In the case of *promise*,
the direct object is not required as a controller.[12]

5.2   Passivization and Control

The interaction between passivization and control is complex. In this section
we describe some of the effects. Unfortunately, no full account is available at
this stage of development of the theory.

   In sentences which have object control patterns, passivization is generally
possible. The object of the active sentence becomes the subject of the passive
sentence (see the discussion of passivization in chapter 3 and also chapter 6)
and controls PRO:

52a   Miss Marple, was ordered [$_{CP}$ [$_{IP}$ PRO, to go on her/*one's own]].

52b   Miss Marple, was instructed [$_{CP}$ [$_{IP}$ PRO, to go on her/*one's own]].

52c   Miss Marple, was allowed [$_{CP}$ [$_{IP}$ PRO, to go on her/*one's own]].

Subject control verbs do not pattern uniformly with respect to passivization,
as the following sets of sentences illustrate.

53a   They preferred to go.

53b   They wanted to go.

53c   They tried to go.

53d   They decided to go.

---

[12]   That an object controller cannot be omitted is known as **Bach's generalization**. We
return briefly to the data in chapter 8.

54a   *It was preferred to go.
54b   *It was wanted to go.
54c   *It was tried to go.
54d   It was decided to go.

That matters are very complex can be illustrated when we look at the behaviour of the verb *promise*. In (55a) *promise* takes an NP complement and a clausal complement. The subject of *promise* controls the PRO subject in the non-finite clause and passivization is not possible:

55a   They promised Miss Marple to go.
55b   *Miss Marple was promised to go.

The ungrammaticality of (55b) cannot be explained by saying that the verb *promise* does not passivize at all, as can be seen in (56) and (57).

56a   Emsworth promised Miss Marple a new bicycle.
56b   Miss Marple was promised a new bicycle.

57a   Emsworth promised Miss Marple that she would get a new bicycle.
57b   Miss Marple was promised that she would get a new bicycle.

In (55b) *promise* is a verb of subject control and it fails to passivize. Consider (58), though, taken from Bresnan (1980: 404) where *promise* is a control verb and does passivize:

58a   Mary was never promised [[PRO to be allowed to leave]].
58b   It was never promised to Mary [[to be allowed to leave]].
58c   [PRO to be allowed to leave]] was never promised to Mary.

The sentences in (58) which involve control are parallel to those in (59) which do not involve control. At this point it is hard to formulate a coherent theory to account for the patterns illustrated here (cf. Bresnan 1980). One point that favours passivization appears to be that in (58) the complement clause of (passive) *promise* itself also is passivized.

59a Mary was never promised that she would be allowed to leave.
59b It was never promised to Mary that she would be allowed to leave.
59c That she would be allowed to leave was never promised to Mary.

5.3 PRO in Adjunct Clauses

PRO as the subject of adjunct clauses is also obligatorily controlled:

60a John abandoned the investigation [[PRO to save money for himself/
     *oneself]].
60b John arrived [PRO exhausted].
60c John hired Mary [[PRO to fire Bill]].
     (Manzini, 1983: 428)

In (60a) and (60b) PRO is controlled by the subject *John*, in (60c) either subject control or object control is possible.

5.4 PRO in Subject Clauses

In declarative complement clauses and in adjunct clauses PRO is obligatorily controlled. This is not the case when PRO appears in subject clauses. In (61a) we have an example of arbitrary control, in (61b) PRO is controlled by *Bill* which does not c-command it. In (61c) an NP from a higher clause (*Mary*) controls PRO. (61d) shows again that c-command is not obligatory (data from Manzini, 1983: 424, (36)–(39)):

61a [[PRO to behave oneself in public]] would help Bill.
61b [[PRO to behave himself in public]] would help Bill.
61c Mary knows that [[PRO to behave herself in public]] would help Bill.
61d [[PRO to behave himself in public]] would help Bill's development.

Various proposals have been formulated to deal with the data described in this section. However, at this stage no completely satisfactory control theory has been developed to cover all the complexities involved.[13]

---

[13] The reader is referred to the literature for further discussion. See, for example, Borer (1989), Bouchard (1984), Chomsky (1981a: 74–9, 1986a: 119–31), Huang (1991), Koster (1984a), Manzini (1983) and the criticism in Mohanan (1985) and Williams (1980).

5.5   *Obligatory Control is not a Lexical Feature*

Let us return for a moment to the contrast between obligatory control and optional control, introduced in section 4.1. Optional control is found in examples like (62)–(64) (from Huang, 1989: 199–200):

62a   [PRO smoking] is harmful.
62b   [PRO to behave oneself] is important.

63a   John and Bill discussed [PRO behaving oneself].
63b   John said [PRO to behave oneself].

64a   John wonders [how [PRO to behave oneself]].
64b   It is unclear [whether [PRO to go there]].

In all the examples above PRO is uncontrolled. In (62) it appears in a sentential subject, in (63) and in (64) it appears in a complement.
    Obligatory control is illustrated in (65):

65a   John tried [[PRO to behave himself/*oneself]].
65b   John was reluctant [[PRO to behave himself/*oneself]].
65c   They forced John [[PRO to identify himself/*oneself]].

One question that remains is what it is that makes control optional/obligatory. Is it a lexical property associated with a specific verb or adjective, or is it a configurational property of the syntax of the sentence? In subject clauses, control is optional. In complement clauses control can be optional (as in (63) and (64) or it can be obligatory as in (65). This contrast might lead us to the conclusion that obligatory control is an idiosyncratic property of lexical items which could be given a specific feature, say [+ Obligatory control]. This feature would then be associated with the non-finite complement. The PRO subject of the infinitival complements of verbs with the relevant feature would be subject to obligatory control. The PRO subject of infinitival complements of verbs which lack the relevant feature would not be subject to obligatory control. Non-finite subject clauses, not being the complement of the verbs of the specific class, would not be subject to obligatory control. An approach in terms of a lexical feature would capture the idiosyncratic nature of control pattern with complement clauses. However, this lexical approach would not account for instances of obligatory control which cannot be reduced to a lexical property of individual verbs. One instance in point is illustrated in (66): PRO subjects of the adjuncts are subject to obligatory control. As Huang (1989: 202) points out 'this obviously has nothing to do with the lexical properties of their main verbs'. Verbs like *arrive* in (66a) or *leave* in (66b) are not associated with the property [+ Obligatory control]:

66a John arrived [PRO pleased with himself/*oneself].
66b John left the band [PRO to start working on his/*one's own].

6 Summary

This chapter focuses on a non-overt NP, represented as PRO, which occurs as the subject of non-finite clauses. After providing empirical and theoretical arguments for postulating such an empty category, we examine its distribution and its interpretation. The module of the grammar that regulates the occurrence and interpretation of PRO is called control theory.

The feature composition of PRO is argued to be [+Anaphor, +Pronominal], from which we derive the PRO theorem:

1 **PRO theorem**
    PRO must be ungoverned.

We say that PRO is **licensed** when it is ungoverned. This property allows us to predict that PRO does not alternate with overt NPs.

With respect to the interpretation of PRO we see that it is either controlled by an argument NP or it is arbitrary in interpretation. In some sentence patterns control is obligatory, in others it is optional. Both subject and object NPs may be controllers. In the case of obligatory control the controller must c-command the controlled element.

In the final section of the chapter we illustrate the occurrence of PRO in three syntactic environments: in complement clauses, in adjunct clauses and in subject clauses.

Throughout the chapter we have described a number of properties of PRO. However, the discussion has often been rather descriptive and fragmentary. At this stage of the theory it is not possible to offer a coherent and fully developed theory of control.

7   Exercises

Exercise 1

In this chapter we have shown that the complementary distribution of PRO and overt NPs can be related to considerations of case theory and binding theory. Hence a pattern such as that in (1) and (2) is expected:

1a   *I tried Bill to go.
1b   I tried to go.
2a   I believed Bill to be innocent
2b   *I believed to be innocent.

For each of the above examples provide a detailed syntactic representation and discuss the contrast in grammaticality between the paired examples. Consider which verb is a control verb and which an ECM verb. On the basis of examples such as those above one could conclude that a verb is *either* a control verb *or* an ECM verb.
Now consider the following examples:

3a   I expect John to go first.
3b   I expect to go first.
3c   I want John to go first.
3d   I want to go first.

How could one account for the grammaticality of all four examples? Would it be possible to maintain that a verb is either a control verb or an ECM verb?
Consider the following examples from West Flemish, a dialect of Dutch. We have provided syntactic annotations. Which problems do the examples pose for the theory?

4a   [Me [$_{IP}$ Marie da   te   zeggen]] is   et   al   utgekommen.
      with   Marie that to   say   is   it   all outcome
      'Because Marie said that, everything was revealed.'
4b   [Me [$_{IP}$ zie da   te   zeggen]] . . .
      with   she that to   say
      'Because she has said that, . . .'

Zie is the third person feminine singular NOMINATIVE pronoun.

4c [Me [PRO_i da   te zeggen]] ee Jan_i t   al   verroan.
   with   that to say   has Jan it all betrayed
   'By saying that, John has given away everything.'

Exercise 2

Consider again the idea that PRO is ungoverned. What problems does this raise for our discussion of the visibility requirement on theta-marking discussed in chapter 3?[14]

Exercise 3

Consider the syntactic structure of the following sentences. Try to provide arguments for positing PRO whenever needed:

1 Cinderella needs time to clean the chimney.
2 Snow White ate the apple to please the witch.
3 The dwarfs intend to take a cleaner.
4 The dwarfs need a man who will do their washing.
5 The dwarfs need a man to do their washing.
6 Cinderella suggested going to the party.
7 Prince Charming asked Cinderella to come along.
8 While waiting for the coach, Cinderella fell ill.
9 When in doubt, ask a policeman.
10 Cinderella was happy to accept the offer.
11 I shall give you the examples, whenever relevant.
12 Moving house often means buying new furniture.
13 To err is human, to forgive divine.
14 Cinderella was anxious to try the shoes.
15 To know you is to love you.

[14] The reader will see that explaining the case filter in terms of visibility is problematic. One possible way out is to argue that PRO is inherently case-marked. PRO would have a case specification as part of its feature composition (cf. section 2.2). We shall not explore this possibility here. The occurrence of PRO is one issue that raises questions for reducing the case filter to visibility. See also Davis (1986).

Exercise 4

Consider the following pairs of sentences. The (b) sentences suggest a syntactic representation for the (a) sentences. Which arguments could be advanced against the representations?

1a   I have eaten.
1b   I have [vp eaten PRO].
2a   This analysis led to a remarkable conclusion.
2b   This analysis [vp led PRO [pp to a remarkable conclusion]].
3   *Italian*
3a   Ho visto Luigi.
3b   [ip PRO ho [vp visto Luigi]].
        (Cf. chapter 8 for discussion of such Italian examples.)
4a   Take three eggs and boil for two minutes.[15]
4b   Take three eggs and [vp boil PRO for two minutes]].
5a   They met after a party.
5b   They met PRO after a party.
6a   This book is too difficult for me to read.
6b   This book is too difficult [cp for [ip me to read PRO]].
7a   He is a man whom you like when you see.
7b   He is a man [cp whom [ip you like PRO] [cp when [ip you see
        PRO]]].
        (See chapter 8 for discussion.)
8a   John is ill. I know.
8b   John is ill. [ip I [vp know PRO]].
9a   John opened the door and left.
9b   John opened the door and [ip PRO left].
10   *Italian*
10a Questo conduce la gente a concludere che . . .
        This   leads   people to conclude   that . . .
10b Questo conduce PRO   a concludere che . . .[16]

Exercise 5

So far we have illustrated cases of PRO being controlled by one antecedent NP. Identify the controller of PRO in the following examples.

---

[15]   The examples in (4) are from the register of instructional writing. See Haegeman (1987) and Massam and Roberge (1989) for discussion.
[16]   For a discussion of examples such as (10) see Rizzi (1986a) and chapter 8 of this book.

1 Mary told John that it would be nice [PRO to go to the pictures together].
2 Mary told John that [PRO going to the pictures on their own] was out of the question.
3 Bill wanted Tom to approve the decision [PRO to swim across the pond together].
4 Bill wanted Tom to agree that it was time [PRO to swim across the pond together].
5 Bill's mother wanted Tom to agree that it was time [PRO to swim across the pond together].
((3), (4) and (5) from Chomsky, 1986a: 126 (147))

As suggested by the presence of *together* and *on their own*, PRO in the examples above must have a plural controller. The plurality is obtained by combining two NPs. The examples illustrate what are known as **split antecedents**. Do the split antecedents in these examples c-command PRO? Williams (1980) argues that split antecedents are only possible in the case of optional control. Using examples of your own, check whether this hypothesis can be maintained. You may base your examples on section 4.1.

Exercise 6

In the text we have discussed the difference in status between English *if*, which we take to be C^0, and *whether*, which we take to be in [Spec, CP]. This difference would account for the contrast between (37b) and (37c), repeated here as (1a) and (1b) respectively:

1a *John doesn't know if to leave.
1b John doesn't know whether to leave.

Observe that *if* and *whether* can also be used to introduce a conditional clause:

1c If John goes, we will all be sad.
1d Whether John goes or not, things will have to change anyway.

The French equivalent of English *if/whether* is *si*. On the basis of the examples below try to decide whether *si* is C^0, like English *if*, or [Spec, CP], like English *whether*:

2a   Marie ne sait pas si elle devrait aller au cinéma.
Marie does not know *si* she should go to the movies
'Marie does not know if she ought to go to the movies.'
2b   *Marie ne sait pas si aller au cinéma.
Marie does not know *si* to go to the movies
2c   *Marie ne sait pas si ou non elle devrait aller au cinéma.
Marie does not know *si* or not she ought to go to the movies
2d   *Marie ne sait pas si Jean aller au cinéma.
Marie does not know *si* Jean go to the movies
(Examples from Kayne, 1991: 666–7)
2e   Si Marie va au cinéma, Jean restera seul.
si Marie goes to the movies, Jean will remain alone
'If Marie goes to the movies, Jean will remain alone.'

What about the status of Italian *se*?

3a   Gianni non sa se dovrebbe andare al cinema.
Gianni does not know *se* should-go-3sg to the movies
'Gianni does not know if he should go to the movies.'
3b   Gianni non sa se andare al cinema.
Gianni does not know *se* go to the movies
'Gianni does not know whether to go to the movies.'
3c   Se Gianni avesse fatto questo, Paola . . .
if Gianni had done that, Paola . . .
(Examples from Kayne, 1991: 671–2)

Italian *se*, though similar to French *si*, can introduce a non-finite clause with a non-overt subject, suggesting that like English *whether* it might occupy [Spec, CP]. If this were indeed the case, then *se* should behave exactly like other elements in [Spec, CP]. We have seen in chapter 2 that interrogative constituents such as *what*, or to *whom*, occupy [Spec, CP]:

4a   I don't know what to say.
4b   I wonder to whom to tell this.

Consider the sentences (5) and (6). Such sentences are marginally acceptable in colloquial Italian. As shown in the (a) sentences, the italicized pronominal element is an argument of the lower bracketed infinitival clause. The (b) sentences show that it can be associated with the matrix verb. In (5) *ti* ('you') is the complement of *dire* ('say') but it can also precede the finite verb of the matrix clause *saprei* ('would know'). In (6a) *lo* is the complement of *affidare* ('entrust') but it can also be associated with finite *saprei* ('would know'). We do not go into the structure of these sentences in more detail here.[17]

5a Su questo punto, non saprei che dir*ti*.
      on this point, *non* would-know (1 sg) what tell-you
      'On this point, I would not know what to tell you.'
5b Su questo punto, non *ti* saprei che dire.
      on this point, *non* you would-know (1sg) what say
      'On this point I would not know what to tell you.'
      (Rizzi, 1982a: 36, (136a))
6a Mario, non saprei a chi affidar*lo*, durante le vacanze.
      Mario, *non* would-know (1sg) to whom entrust-him, during the
         holidays
      'Mario, I would not know to whom to entrust him during the
         holidays.'
6b ?Mario, non *lo* saprei a chi affidare, durante le vacanze.
      Mario *non* I would-know to whom entrust during the holidays
      'Mario, I would not know to whom to entrust during the holidays.'
      (Rizzi, 1982a: 36 (136b))

As the reader can verify, the unacceptability of (7a) would pose a problem for those analyses which propose that Italian *se* is in [Spec, CP], analogously to *che* in (5) or *a chi* in (6).

7a Questo libro, non saprei comprar*lo*.
      this book, *non* would-know (1sg) *se* (if) buy-it
      'This book, I would not know whether to buy it.'
7b *Questo libro, non *lo* so se comprare.
      this book I don't know *se* buy

These data show that it is not always clear which items are to be treated as occupying C and which are in [Spec, CP]. For discussion of this point and of the contrast between French *si* and Italian *se* the reader is referred to Kayne's study (1991).

---

[17] For a discussion of these patterns the reader is referred to Rizzi (1982a: 1–48) and also to Kayne (1989) and (1991).

6 Transformations: NP-Movement

Contents

Introduction and Overview

In this chapter we discuss NP-movement, which plays a part in the derivation of passive sentences and raising structures. We examine the characteristics of NP-movement and of the verbs that induce it. From our analysis it follows that each sentence is associated with two levels of syntactic representation: D-structure and S-structure. The relation between these levels will be discussed in this chapter.

In section 1 we give a general survey of movement transformations. In section 2 we concentrate on NP-movement as instantiated in passive sentences and in raising sentences. We discuss the arguments in favour of the assumption that a moved NP leaves a trace in its base position. We also discuss raising adjectives. Section 3 focuses on the verbs which induce NP-raising. It will be argued that the case assigning properties of a verb depend on its argument structure. We discuss the distinction between two types of one-argument verbs: those with only an external argument ('intransitives') and those with only an internal argument ('unaccusatives'). In section 4 we examine the relation beween D-structure and S-structure and we discuss how the principles of grammar posited so far apply to these levels. In section 5 we consider the hypothesis that subject NPs are base-generated VP-internally.

1 Movement Transformations

We have already touched upon the movement of constituents in interrogative and in passive sentences (cf. chapters 2 and 3). In this section we give a general survey of the movement transformations posited so far.

1.1 Passivization: Recapitulation

In chapter 3 we discussed the properties of passivization illustrated in (1a):

1a This story is believed by the villagers.
1b The villagers believe this story.

(1a) contains the passive form of the verb *believe*. Comparing (1a) with its active counterpart (1b), we see that the subject NP of the passive sentence, *this story*, corresponds to the internal argument of the active verb. In chapter 3 we proposed that in both (1a) and (1b) the NP *this story* is assigned the internal theta role by the verb. Internal theta roles are by definition assigned directly under government by the head. Hence, the NP *this story* in (1a) ought to be assigned its theta role under government by the verb *believe*, exactly as in (1b). As it stands, *believe* obviously does not govern the NP *this story* in (1a).

In order to maintain the parallelism between (1a) and (1b) and our hypothesis that internal theta roles are assigned directly by a governing head we developed a movement analysis relating the patterns in (1a) and (1b). We proposed that at some level of syntactic representation the NP *this story* IS the direct object of the verb *believe*:

2a   [IP e [I' is [VP [V' believed [NP this story]] by the villagers]].

(2a) is called the **D-structure** of (1a). It encodes the basic thematic relations in the sentence as determined by the argument structure of the predicate, passive *believed*. In (1a) the external theta role of *believed* is not assigned to an NP in the subject position, but it is assigned to an NP in a *by*-phrase. Because of the extended projection principle the subject position in (2a) is generated but is not filled by an argument NP. The empty subject position is indicated by the symbol *e* for 'empty'. In the D-structure (2a) the object NP *this story* is VP-internal and is assigned an internal theta role directly by the governing verb.

In addition to the D-structure representation which reflects lexical properties, a sentence is associated with a second level of representation, **S-structure**. The S-structure of (1a) is (2b):

2b   [IP This story$_i$ [I' is [VP believed [e$_i$]] by the villagers]].

NOMINATIVE

In (2b) the NP *this story* has been moved from the VP-internal position to the subject position of the sentence. This movement is called **NP-movement**. As a result of movement, the VP-internal D-structure position of *this story* is left vacant or empty: it is a **gap** represented provisionally by *e*. We turn to a discussion of such empty positions in section 2. The link between the gap and the moved NP is indicated by coindexation. The coindexation encodes the derivational history of the sentence.

The word-order of (2a) is referred to as the **underlying order**. The S-structure order in (2b) is called the **derived order**: it is an order which results from modifications of the D-structure. Similarly, the NP *this story* in (2b/1a) is referred to as a **derived subject**: it is not a D-structure subject of the sentence (2a). The D-structure position of the NP, i.e. the object position, is called the **base-position**. We say that the NP *this story* is **base-generated** in the object position of the passive V *believed*.

In our discussion in chapter 3 we derived the movement of the NP from the object position to the subject position from case theory. For some reason (to which we return in section 3) passive verbs do not assign structural case to their complements. If the NP *this story* were to stay in the object position, it would violate the case filter, as seen in (2c):

2c   *There is believed this story by the villagers.

In (2b), *this story* occupies the subject position, where it is assigned NOM-INATIVE case by INFL. Our analysis implies that the case filter must apply at S-structure (2b). At the level of D-structure (2a) the NP *this story* is in its base-position where it cannot be assigned case.

When discussing the syntactic structure of a sentence we shall from now on assume that there are two **levels of syntactic representation**: D-structure and S-structure. Both levels of representation encode syntactic properties of the sentence. D-structure encodes the predicate–argument relations and the thematic properties of the sentence. The S-structure representation accounts for the surface ordering of the constituents. We return to the relation between the two levels in section 4.

1.2   *Questions*

1.2.1   SURVEY

In this section we briefly discuss the representation of the sentences in (3), concentrating on the questions (3b)–(3f).

3a   Lord Emsworth will invite Hercule Poirot.
3b   Will Lord Emsworth invite Hercule Poirot?
3c   Lord Emsworth will invite whom?
3d   Whom will Lord Emsworth invite?

3e   I wonder [whether Lord Emsworth will invite Hercule Poirot].
3f   I wonder [whom Lord Emsworth will invite].

(3a) is a declarative sentence. (3b) is a direct *yes–no* **question** (to be discussed in 1.2.2), (3c) is an **echo question** (to be discussed in 1.2.3), (3d) is a direct *wh*-**question** also referred to as a **constituent question** (to be discussed in 1.2.4). For completeness' sake (3e) and (3f) have been added. The bracketed strings in these examples are **indirect questions**: (3e) contains an indirect *yes–no* question; (3f) an indirect *wh*-question. Indirect questions will be discussed in chapter 7, where we return to a full discussion of questions.

From (3a) we infer the argument structure of the verb *invite*:

4   *invite*: verb

<u>1</u>	2

In (3a) the external argument of *invite* is realized by the NP *Lord Emsworth* and the internal argument is realized by the NP *Hercule Poirot*. The D-structure of (3a) is given in tree diagram format in (5). The external argument of *invite* is syntactically represented by the NP in the subject position of the clause; the internal argument is syntactically represented by the direct object of the V, the NP dominated by V'.

5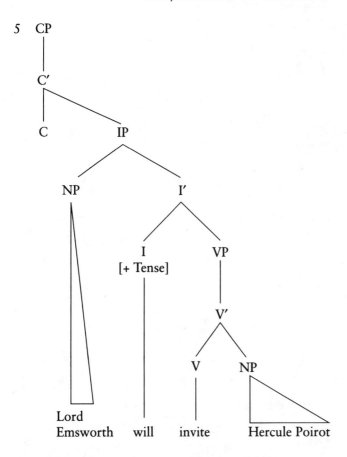

The S-structure representation of example (3a) is given in (6). It does not differ substantially from its D-structure (5). Recall that S-structure is the level at which structural case is assigned: I assigns NOMINATIVE to the subject NP and the verb assigns ACCUSATIVE to the direct object NP.

6   CP

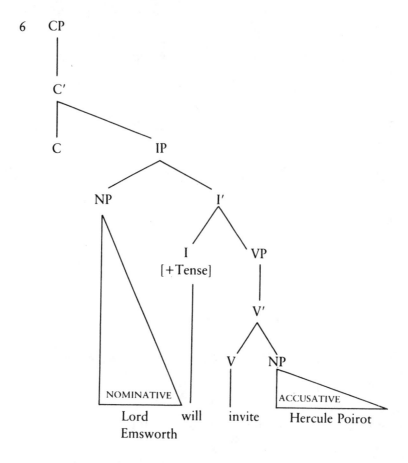

A word of caution is in order at this point. We assume that ALL sentences have two levels of syntactic representation: D-structure and S-structure. In passive sentences such as (1a) discussed above, the D-structure (2a) differs clearly from the S-structure (2b): a constituent has been moved. But, as indicated in (5) and (6), the difference between D-structure and S-structure may be minimal: in this example no movement has taken place and the two levels of representation will not differ in word-order.

1.2.2   *YES–NO QUESTIONS*

Questions such as (3b) are called *yes–no* questions for the obvious reason that one expects an answer such as 'Yes' or 'No'. Let us try to work out the syntactic representation of this question, bearing in mind that we need to consider both D-structure and S-structure.

In chapter 2 we saw that sentences are projections of I which in turn are complements of C. Because they are always specified for tense we assume that modal auxiliaries like *will* are base-generated in the position dominated by I, as illustrated in (5) and (6) above (cf. chapter 11). One potential problem for the representation of (3b) concerns the surface position of the modal auxiliary *will*, which in our example precedes the subject NP. We assume that the order exhibited in (3b) is not the underlying order of the sentence but a derived order, an order obtained as the result of moving an element. The D-structure position of *will* in (3b) will be as in (7). *Will* is dominated by I, the position which it also occupies in (5):

7

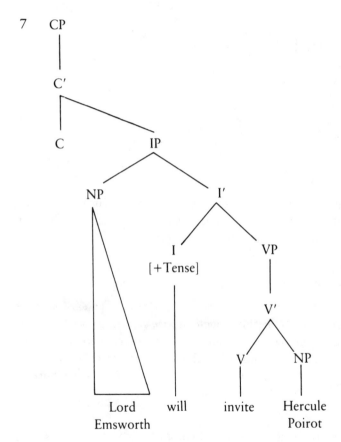

In our discussion in chapter 2 we proposed that the inverted order auxiliary – subject (cf. (3b)) arises from the fact that the modal auxiliary has been moved out of the base-position, where it is dominated by I, to the vacant position dominated by C. Under this analysis, the S-structure of (3b) is as in (8).

8   CP

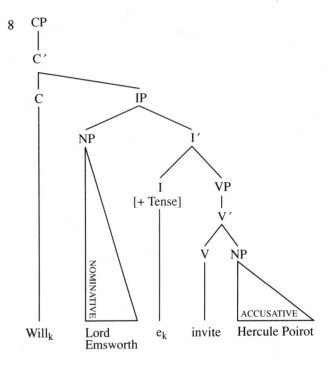

In (8) the gap resulting from moving *will*$_k$ is indicated by e_k. The link between the position vacated by *will* and the moved element is again indicated by coindexation. We discuss verb movement in chapter 11.

1.2.3   ECHO QUESTIONS

(3c) is an echo question. It will be used as a reaction to a sentence such as (3a) by a speaker who wishes the interlocutor to repeat (part of) (3a). Echo questions are formed by simply substituting a **question word** (here *whom*) for a constituent. Interrogative constituents such as *whom* are called **wh-constituents**. *Whom* realizes the internal argument of *invite*. The D-structure of (3c) is as follows:

9   [$_{CP}$ [$_{IP}$ Lord Emsworth will [$_{VP}$ invite [$_{NP}$ whom]]]]?

Given that there is no reordering of constituents in echo questions the S-structure of (3c) will be like its D-structure:

10   [$_{CP}$ [$_{IP}$ Lord Emsworth will [$_{VP}$ invite [$_{NP}$ whom]]]]?

1.2.4 *WH*-QUESTIONS

Finally we turn to (3d), a *wh*-question. Unlike echo questions, which are used in the rather specific circumstances discussed above, ordinary *wh*-questions are freely used when a speaker needs some information. The *wh*-constituent *whom* questions one constituent. To (3d) one might expect answers such as 'Hercule Poirot', 'Lord Peter Wimsey', 'Bertie Wooster', 'his mother-in-law', etc. Let us again try to provide the D-structure and the S-structure representations of (3d).

The first question that we need to address here is how the arguments of *invite* are realized. As was the case in the preceding examples, the external argument is realized by the NP *Lord Emsworth*. By analogy with (3c) we would like to say that the internal argument of *invite* is the NP *whom*.

Two problems arise with respect to the internal argument NP. If internal theta roles are assigned directly under government, then, like (1a), (3d) raises the question of how *invite* assigns a theta role to *whom*, which it plainly does not govern. A second and related question concerns the form of *whom*. It is an ACCUSATIVE case. In chapter 3 we argued that ACCUSATIVE case is assigned at S-structure by a governing verb.

The D-structure of (3d) is no different from the D-structure of the echo question (3c) discussed in 1.2.3:

11   [$_{CP}$ [$_{IP}$ Lord Emsworth will [$_{VP}$ invite [$_{NP}$ whom]]]]?

At S-structure we assume that, as is the case in (3b), the modal *will* in (3d) is moved to the position dominated by C. As discussed in chapter 2, we further assume that *whom* is moved to the specifier position immediately dominated by CP, [Spec, CP]. The symbol e_i indicates the position vacated by *whom$_i$*. Coindexation establishes the link between *e* and the moved constituent. Movement of question words is referred to as **wh-movement**.

12

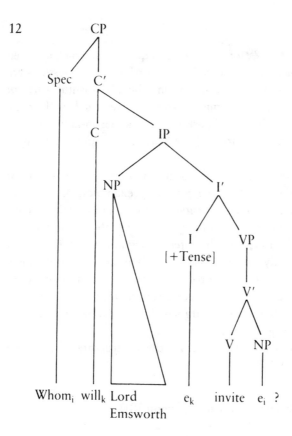

The problems raised concerning the theta-marking and case-marking of *whom* can now be solved. We will assume that the verb *invite* assigns its internal theta role to the VP-internal position e_i and that it also assigns ACCUSATIVE to this position. In chapter 7 we return in detail to the properties of *wh*-movement.

1.3   Syntactic Representations

Throughout the discussion in this chapter we have been assuming that sentences have two levels of syntactic representation:

(i)   **D-structure**

This level encodes the lexical properties of the constituents of the sentence. It represents the basic argument relations in the sentence. External arguments are base-generated in the subject position relative to their predicate;[1] internal arguments are governed by the predicate in their base-position.

(ii) **S-structure**
This level reflects the more superficial properties of the sentence: the actual ordering of the elements in the surface string, and their case forms.

The two levels of syntactic representation are related to each other by means of movement transformations: elements which originate in some position at D-structure may be moved elsewhere at S-structure. Schematically our grammar thus looks as follows:

13 D-structure

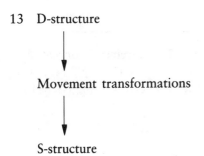

Movement transformations

S-structure

Section 4 considers the relation between D-structure and S-structure in more detail.

In the discussion above, we have distinguished three types of movement: (i) **head-movement**: the movement of auxiliaries from I to C; (ii) ***wh*-movement**: the movement of *wh*-constituents to the specifier of CP (or [Spec, CP]); and (iii) **NP-movement**: the movement associated with passive in which an NP is moved to an empty subject position.[2] In this chapter we discuss NP-movement in more detail. In chapter 7 we turn to *wh*-movement. Head-movement is discussed in chapters 11 and 12.

Even at this preliminary stage of the discussion the reader can see that the three types of movement have a lot in common. In each of the movements

---

[1] See section 5 for an alternative analysis of the NP in the canonical subject position, though.

[2] For different proposals concerning the levels of representation see for instance van Riemsdijk and Williams (1981), who posit a level between D-structure and S-structure, Zubizarreta (1987), who introduces a level of lexical structure; and Brody (1993b) and Koster (1987), who argue that only one level of representation is needed. Chomsky (1992) proposes a different approach to phrase structure.

you take an element and move it somewhere else. In the literature this operation is often referred to in general terms as '**move-α**', **move alpha**, that is 'move something'. The types of movements discussed can be differentiated on the basis of the element which is moved, and on the basis of the **landing site**, the position to which an element moves. Either we move a head of a projection to another head position: in (3b) and in (3d) *will*, the head of IP, moves to C, the head of CP. Alternatively, a maximal projection is moved, as illustrated by NP-movement in (1a), and by *wh*-movement in (3d). Chomsky (1986b) argues that in fact movement must be restricted to just these types: either we move a head or we move a full phrase. We discuss landing sites of movement in the following chapters.

2   NP-movement

In this section we consider the mechanisms of NP-movement, concentrating mainly on the position vacated by movement: the trace (2.2). NP-movement is triggered not only by passive verbs but also by so-called raising verbs (2.1) and by raising adjectives (2.3).

2.1   *Introduction: Passive and Raising*

As a starting point let us consider the syntactic representations of passive sentences:

14a   This story was believed by the villagers.
14b   Poirot was believed to have destroyed the evidence.

We have already discussed (14a). The D-structure of (14a) is given in (15a) and the S-structure in (15b):

15a $[_{IP}$ e $[_{I'}$ was $[_{VP}$ believed $[_{NP}$ this story] by the villagers]]]].
15b $[_{IP}$ $[_{NP}$ This story$_i$] $[_{I'}$ was $[_{VP}$ believed $[e_i]$ by the villagers]]].

In (15a) the NP *this story* is theta-marked directly by the verb *believed*. The subject position is empty since passive verbs do not assign an external theta role. In (15b) *this story* is moved to the subject position and case-marked by the finite inflection.

Let us consider (14b) which also contains passive *believed*. (14b) can be paraphrased by means of (16):

16 It was believed [CP that [IP Poirot had destroyed the evidence]].

In (16) the subject position of the main clause is occupied by an expletive, *it*, which is not assigned a theta role. Passive *believed* takes a sentential complement (the bracketed CP) as its internal argument.

Inside the subordinate clause, the verb *destroy* assigns an internal theta role to the NP *the evidence* and the NP *Poirot* is the external argument which is assigned the AGENT role: 'Poirot is the person who is engaged in the activity of destroying.' Note specifically that the verb in the main clause, *believed*, does not have a thematic relation with *Poirot*, the subject of the subordinate clause.

The thematic relations in (14b) are identical to those in (16). *Believed* takes as its internal argument a clausal complement, here infinitival. *Poirot*, the surface subject of the main clause, has a thematic relation (AGENT) with the predicate *destroy* in the lower infinitival clause. Again, *Poirot* has no thematic relationship with *believed*. We conclude that in (14b) *Poirot* is a derived subject which is assigned the external theta role of the lower verb *destroy*. On this assumption, the D-structure of (14b) will be (17a), where *Poirot* is base-generated as the subject NP of the infinitival clause:

17a [IP e [I' was [VP believed [IP Poirot to have destroyed the evidence]]]].

Believed directly theta-marks the lower IP. *Poirot* is the external argument of *destroy*, the predicate of the lower infinitival clause. *Believed*, being passive, fails to assign structural case. If the NP *Poirot* were left in the subject position of the lower clause at S-structure it would not be case-marked. This explains the ungrammaticality of (17b) and (17c):

17b *It was believed this story.
17c *It was believed Poirot to have destroyed the evidence.

A way of enabling the NP *Poirot* to pass the case filter in (17a) is by moving it from the subject position of the lower clause to the subject position of the higher clause, leaving a coindexed gap:

17d [IP Poirot_i [I' was [VP believed [IP e_i to have destroyed the evidence]]]].

Consider now (18). The relation between (18a) and (18b) is exactly parallel to the relation between (16) and (14b).

18a   It seems [that [Poirot has destroyed the evidence]].
18b   Poirot seems to have destroyed the evidence.

(18a) shows that *seem* is like passive *believe*: it is a one-place predicate which takes a clausal complement. The subject position is not assigned a theta role and it is filled by the expletive *it*. We infer from (18a) that the thematic structure of *seem* is (18c):[3]

18c   *seem*: V

1

In the complement clause, the NP *Poirot* in (18a) is the external argument of *destroy*.

The thematic relations in (18b) are identical to those in (18a). Again *seem* has the argument structure in (18c). The NP *Poirot* is the external argument of *destroy*. At D-structure *Poirot* is the subject of *destroy*, and the subject position of *seem*, which receives no theta role, is empty. (19a) is parallel to (17a) the underlying structure of (14b).

19a   [$_{IP}$ e seems [$_{IP}$ Poirot to have destroyed the evidence]].

Apart from its argument structure, *seem* shares another property with passive *believe*: it cannot assign structural case:

19b   *It/*There seems Poirot to have destroyed the evidence.

(19b) is ungrammatical for the same reason that (17b) is ungrammatical: the external argument of the verb *destroy* is caseless. In order to be able to be

---

[3]   To indicate that 1 is an internal argument it is not underlined. Recall that we adopted the convention that the external argument is underlined.

theta-marked by *destroy* the NP must be visible, and in order to be visible *Poirot* needs to be case-marked. Movement to the subject position of the main clause brings rescue. (19c) is the S-structure representation of (18b): *Poirot* is a derived subject. (19c) is again parallel to (17c).

19c [$_{IP}$ Poirot$_i$ [$_{I'}$ -s [$_{VP}$ seem [$_{IP}$ e$_i$ to have destroyed the evidence]]]].

(19c) is another example of NP-movement. Because the subject of the lower clause is raised out of the clause and moved into a higher clause, this movement is sometimes referred to as **NP-raising** or **raising**. Verbs such as *seem* which induce raising are called **raising verbs**.[4]

2.2 Traces

We have now discussed three examples of NP-movement. The relevant S-structures are given in (20):

20a [$_{IP}$ This story$_i$ [$_{I'}$ was [$_{VP}$ believed [e$_i$] by the villagers]]].
20b [$_{IP}$ Poirot$_i$ [$_{I'}$ was [$_{VP}$ believed [$_{IP}$ [e$_i$] to have destroyed the evidence]]]].
20c [$_{IP}$ Poirot$_i$ [$_{I'}$ -s [$_{VP}$ seem [$_{IP}$ [e$_i$] to have destroyed the evidence]]]].

In each of these examples we assume that there is a null element in the position vacated by the NP. Coindexation is used to indicate that the null element and the NP in the matrix subject position are linked. In chapter 3 we introduced the term **chain** to refer to this link and we shall return to this notion in 4.6. An empty category which encodes the base-position of a moved constituent is referred to as a **trace** and will be indicated from now on by *t*:

21a [$_{IP}$ This story$_i$ [$_{I'}$ was [$_{VP}$ believed t$_i$ by everyone]]].
21b [$_{IP}$ Poirot$_i$ [$_{I'}$ was [$_{VP}$ believed [$_{IP}$ t$_i$ to have destroyed the evidence]]]].
21c [$_{IP}$ Poirot$_i$ [$_{I'}$ -s [$_{VP}$ seem [$_{IP}$ t$_i$ to have destroyed the evidence]]]].

The moved element is called the **antecedent** of the trace. In the remainder of this section we go through the arguments for positing traces in syntactic representations.[5]

---

[4] For an early discussion of raising, see Postal (1974).
[5] The reader will no doubt observe that the argumentation used in 2.2 is similar to that used to justify the presence of PRO in chapter 5, section 1. However, note that PRO does not result from movement. We return to a comparison of PRO and trace in section 4.6 and in chapter 8.

2.2.1 THETA THEORY

A first argument for postulating traces of NP-movement was advanced in chapter 3 and is used in the discussion above. It is based on the projection principle and theta theory on the one hand, and on case theory on the other hand.

In chapter 3 we introduced the idea that the case filter is not an independent principle of the grammar but that it derives from the visibility requirement for NPs: in order to be assigned a theta role an NP must be visible. Visibility of overt NPs is achieved via case-marking. Remember that internal theta roles are directly assigned to the NPs by the governing head. An external theta role is assigned indirectly to the subject of the clause containing the predicate.

In each of the S-structures in (21) the moved NP is visible: it is assigned NOMINATIVE. But the position to which the theta role is assigned is not the derived position but the base-position. In other words, for theta role assignment both the D-structure position and the S-structure position of the NPs in (21) are relevant. The D-structure position is indicated by the trace, it is the position to which the theta role is assigned. The S-structure position is case-marked. This analysis allows us to maintain theta theory and the visibility principle as discussed in chapter 3. In chapter 3 (section 6.2 (61)) we cited Chomsky's reformulation of the theta criterion as in (22):

22 **Theta criterion**

22a Each argument A appears in a chain containing a unique visible theta position P, and each theta position P is visible in a chain containing a unique argument A.
(Chomsky, 1986a: 97)

22b A position P is visible in a chain if the chain contains a case-marked position.
(Chomsky, 1986a: 96)

The reader will be able to verify that the conditions for theta role assignment are fulfilled in the S-structures in (21). Consider, for example, (21b). The argument *Poirot* appears in a chain <*Poirot$_i$*, t_i>. The position occupied by *Poirot* is called the **head** of the chain; that occupied by the trace is called the **foot** of the chain. The subject position of the non-finite clause, to which the external theta role of the lower verb is assigned, is a theta position. It is visible in the chain <*Poirot$_i$*, t_i> because the chain contains a case-marked position: the subject position of the main clause is assigned NOMINATIVE by the finite I. The reader can check that the same conditions obtain in (21a) and in (21c).

2.2.2   THE EXTENDED PROJECTION PRINCIPLE

In chapters 1 and 2 we discussed general principles of phrase structure and we introduced the requirement that sentences must have subjects (the EPP). The EPP requires that the non-finite IPs in (21b) and (21c) have a subject position. In the S-structures in (21b) and (21c) the subject position of the lower clause is occupied by the trace, an empty category (see also section 4.3 below).

2.2.3   LOCAL RELATIONS

In the following examples we find further evidence for positing a trace in the subject position of non-finite clauses such as (21b) and (21c). For all the examples the reasoning is identical. It is the same type of argumentation that we used for postulating the non-overt subject PRO in non-finite clauses in chapter 5, section 1.3. As a first step of the argumentation we consider sentences with overt subjects and we observe that there is some syntactic relation (say agreement, or binding) which obtains between the subject and another constituent in the clause. This relation is subject to a locality condition. Then we turn to sentences which lack an overt subject. We observe that the same syntactic relation obtains in spite of the fact that there is no overt subject. In order to maintain the locality condition in its simplest form we postulate that there is a non-overt subject and that this non-overt subject is syntactically active. In the examples in chapter 5 the relevant non-overt subject was represented as PRO; in the present chapter the non-overt subject is a trace of a moved NP. Consider the following sets of examples:

23a   [$_{IP}$ It seems [$_{CP}$ that [$_{IP}$ Poirot has been the best detective/*detectives]]].

23b   *[$_{IP}$ Poirot thinks [$_{CP}$ that [$_{IP}$ these schoolchildren are a lousy detective]]].

23c   [$_{IP}$ Poirot seems to have been the best detective].

23d   [$_{IP}$ These schoolchildren seem to have been the best detectives].

24a   It seems [that [the schoolchildren have left together]].

24b   *The schoolchildren thought [that [Poirot had left together]].

24c   The schoolchildren seem to have left together.

24d   *Poirot seems to have left together.

25a   It seems [that [Poirot has done the job his/*her/*my own way]].

25b   *I thought [that [Poirot would do the job my own way]].

25c   Poirot seems to have done the job his own way.
25d   *Poirot seems to have done the job her own way.

26a   It seems [that [Poirot has hurt himself/*herself]].
26b   *I thought [that [Poirot had hurt myself]].
26c   Poirot seems to have hurt himself.
26d   *Poirot seems to have hurt herself.

In (23a) the predicate NP *the best detective* must be singular rather than plural. It agrees in number with the subject *Poirot*. (23b) shows that agreement is clause-bound: *a lousy detective* cannot agree, for instance, with the subject of a higher clause. Without going into the details of agreement rules, let us assume that there is a **clause-mate condition on agreement**.

If we now turn to (23c) and (23d) it appears that the predicate of the infinitival clause agrees in number with the subject of the higher clause. Clearly, one might wish to modify the rule of agreement to allow for this possibility. But on the assumption that there are empty categories we do not need to change our agreement rule at all:

27   [$_{IP}$ Poirot$_i$ [$_{I'}$ -s [$_{VP}$ seem [$_{IP}$ t$_i$ to be the best detective]]]].

We assume that the NP *the best detective* agrees with the subject of the lower clause, t_i. This means that the trace carries the relevant properties of the antecedent NP, that is, for our example, number. As seen before (chapter 5, section 2), 'empty' categories such as PRO or trace are not devoid of properties: they are specified for syntactic features. The term 'empty' refers to the fact that these categories are not associated with phonetic material.

The discussion of the examples in (24)–(26) follows the same lines as that of (23). In (24) the adjunct *together* in the lower clause has to be linked to a clause-mate plural NP (cf. the ungrammaticality of (24b)).[6] For (24c), we assume that the moved NP *the schoolchildren* is related to *together* via its trace in the lower clause:

28   [$_{IP}$ The schoolchildren$_i$ [$_{I'}$ I [$_{VP}$ seem [$_{IP}$ t$_i$ to have left together]]]].

In chapter 5, section 2.2, we saw that there is a clause-mate constraint on the interpretation of the phrase *his/her . . . own way*. The possessive pronoun

[6]   Cf. the discussion of PRO in chapter 5, section 1.3.2.

in this phrase is like an anaphor in that it is referentially dependent on an antecedent NP in the same clause with which it agrees in person, number and gender (cf. (25a,b)). By positing a trace in the position vacated by the NP *Poirot* we can relate the phrase *his own way* to a clause-mate in (25c).

29 Poirot$_i$ seems [$_{IP}$ t$_i$ to have done the job his$_i$ own way].

(29) also shows that, like PRO, traces are fully specified for all the nominal features such as person, number and gender.

The examples in (26) should look familiar to the reader. (26b) illustrates a binding theory violation: the reflexive *myself* in the lower clause is not bound in its GC. If we maintain that *seem* takes a clausal complement whose subject position is occupied by a trace in (26c) then we can maintain the binding theory as formulated in chapter 4.

30 Poirot$_i$ seems [$_{IP}$ t$_i$ to have hurt himself$_i$].

2.3 Some Properties of NP-movement

In this section we sum up our discussion of NP-movement so far. In section 2.3.1 we give a catalogue of properties which we have already established, in section 2.3.2 we examine the configurational relation between the antecedent and the vacated position.

2.3.1 PROPERTIES OF A-CHAINS

(31) provides the typical examples of NP-movement which were the basis for our discussion.

31a [$_{IP}$ This story$_i$ [$_{I'}$ was [$_{VP}$ believed t$_i$ by the villagers]]].
31b [$_{IP}$ Poirot$_i$ [$_{I'}$ -s [$_{VP}$ seem [$_{IP}$ t$_i$ to have destroyed the evidence]]]].

As suggested above, a distinction is sometimes made between examples such as (31a), which are instances of **passivization**, and examples such as (31b), which are referred to as **NP-raising**.[7] Passivization moves an object NP to the subject position of the same clause; in raising patterns a subject NP is raised

---

[7] The term subject-to-subject raising is also used (cf. Postal, 1974).

from a lower clause to a higher clause. The terms raising and passivization are useful descriptive labels but the reader should not have the impression that passivization and raising are mutually exclusive. In (32a), discussed in section 2.1 as (14b), passive *believed* is a raising verb: the subject NP *Poirot* is moved from the lower infinitival clause to a higher clause. (32b) combines passivization in the lower infinitival IP and raising. This example will be discussed below (see (35b)).

32a [$_{IP}$ Poirot$_i$ [$_{I'}$ was [$_{VP}$ believed [$_{IP}$ t$_i$ to have destroyed the evidence]]]].
32b [$_{IP}$ This story [$_{I'}$ -s [$_{VP}$ seem [$_{IP}$ t$_i$ to be believed t$_i$ by everyone]]]].

Let us make a provisional inventory of the properties common to all the examples of NP-movement illustrated here.

a   The moved element is an NP.
b   Movement is obligatory.
c   The landing site of movement is an empty position.
d   The landing site is an A-position.
e   The landing site is an NP-position.
f   The landing site of movement is a position to which no theta role is assigned. Let us call this a θ' (theta-bar) position by analogy with an A'-position.
g   The landing site of the movement is a position to which case is assigned. In our examples the landing site is the subject position of a finite sentence.
h   The site from which the element is moved is an NP-position to which no case is assigned.
i   Movement leaves a **trace**.
j   The trace is coindexed with the moved element, the **antecedent**, with which it forms a chain. Because the head of the chain is an A-position, the chain created by NP-movement is called an **A-chain**.
k   The chain is assigned one theta role.
l   The theta role is assigned to the lowest position of the chain: the **foot** of the chain.
m   The chain is case-marked once.
n   Case is assigned to the highest position of the chain: the **head** of the chain.

The characteristics of A-chains listed above are not all independent. Let us consider some of them here.

That the NP moves obligatorily ((a) + (b)) in the examples discussed is due to the fact that it would otherwise be caseless and violate the case filter. NP-movement is said to be **case-driven**.

Both statements (a) and (b) need some qualification. Consider (33):

33a Everyone believed [$_{CP}$ that Poirot would give up].
33b It was believed by everyone [$_{CP}$ that Poirot would give up].
33c [$_{CP}$ That Poirot would give up] was believed by everyone.

In (33a) active *believed* takes a clausal complement. In (33b) the verb is passivized; the complement has not moved. In (33c) the clausal complement is moved.[8] In this example movement affects CP rather than NP. We see that it is not obligatory: CPs, unlike NPs, are not subject to the case filter, hence CP may remain in its base-position in (33b).

Movement is to an empty position (c). Intuitively this is reasonable. Suppose an NP were to move into a position already occupied by another NP. Clearly this would result in some sort of a clash. The principles we have established so far enable us to account for this property.

Let us assume that there were a putative verb *HIT* which takes an external and an internal argument but which, unlike English *hit*, does not assign ACCUSATIVE case. We will project a D-structure like (34a):

34a [$_{IP}$ John [$_{VP}$ HIT Mary]].

In (34a) *Mary* is assigned the internal theta role of *HIT* and *John* is assigned the external theta role. The NP *Mary* will be caseless if left in place at S-structure. Suppose it were to move into the position occupied by *John*:

34b [$_{IP}$ Mary$_i$ [$_{VP}$ HIT t$_i$]].

Mary is assigned NOMINATIVE case and forms a chain with its trace. At S-structure *HIT* will assign its internal theta role to the visible chain <*Mary$_i$*, t$_i$>.

What about the external theta role? If *HIT* were to assign it to *Mary$_i$* then the chain <*Mary$_i$*, t$_i$> would have two theta roles in violation of the theta criterion (22). If *HIT* failed to assign its external theta role then again the theta criterion is violated since one theta role is now unassigned. We conclude that it is not possible for an NP to move into a position already occupied by another NP. This means that there can be no verb like *HIT*, which

---

[8] We assume here that CP is moved to [Spec, IP]. Koster (1978b) argues against this hypothesis. See chapter 1, footnote 14.

assigns both an external and an internal theta role and fails to assign case to its complement. We return to types of verbs in section 3 below.

The reader can work out for himself that movement of an NP will also have to be to a θ′ position (cf. property (f)).

Do NPs always move to positions in which case is assigned? (See property (g).) Yes and no. Consider:

35a   It seems [that [this story is believed by everyone]].
35b   This story seems to be believed by everyone.

(35a) is straightforward: *seem* takes an internal clausal argument and lacks an external argument. *Believed* in the lower clause is passivized and assigns its internal theta role to the NP *this story*. We invite the reader to provide the D-structure and S-structure representations for (35a).

(35b) is a paraphrase of (35a). *This* story is the internal argument of *believed*. The subject position of *believed* is unoccupied at D-structure, though it must be present because of the EPP. *Seem* also lacks an external theta role (cf. (35a)): the subject position of the higher clause is empty at D-structure:

36a   [$_{IP}$ e [$_{I'}$ -s [$_{VP}$ seem [$_{IP}$ e to be believed this story ...]]]]

In its VP-internal base-position, *this story* cannot be assigned case. Hence it will move. The subject position of the lower IP cannot serve as the ultimate landing site for the movement since this is also a caseless position: we have proposed that *seem* does not assign ACCUSATIVE case.

We might propose that the NP *this story* moves in one fell swoop to the subject position of the higher clause. This would mean that it can cross an IP. We shall see in section 4.5.2 that this is not possible for independent reasons. Consider (37a) with the S-structure (37b):

37a   *John seems that it is believed by everyone.
37b   *John$_i$ [$_{I'}$ -s [$_{VP}$ seem [$_{CP}$ that [$_{IP}$ it is believed t$_i$ by everyone]]]]].

In (37b) the lower subject position is filled by an expletive, and the NP *John*, the internal argument of *believed*, is moved directly to the subject position of the higher clause where it receives NOMINATIVE case. The ungrammaticality of (37a) suggests that NPs cannot cross the subject NP of their own clause and move to the subject position of a higher clause. Movement of an NP must be 'local' in a way yet to be made precise. Let us adopt this descriptive statement for the moment and assume that the NP *this story* in (35b) moves first to the subject position of *be believed* and then to the subject position of the higher clause. There are two stages or **cycles** for the movement transformation. The first cycle for the operation of move-alpha (cf. section 1.3 for the term) is the lowest clause. The second cycle includes the next higher clause, and so on. We assume that each of these movements leaves a trace in the vacated site and that all traces are coindexed with the antecedent, and thus with each other:

36b This story$_i$ seems [$_{IP}$ t$_i'$ to be believed t$_i$ by everyone].

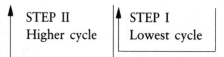

STEP II	STEP I
Higher cycle	Lowest cycle

Movement of *this story* is **cyclic**: it goes step by step creating **intermediate traces** until we arrive at the final landing site. We indicate the intermediate trace with a prime notation. The chain created by NP movement in (36b) has three members: <*this story$_i$, t'$_i$, t$_i$*>. The head of the chain is *this story$_i$*, the foot is the trace t$_i$.

Returning to our question concerning the landing site of NP-movement, we conclude that NP-movement ultimately moves the NP into a position which is case-marked: the head of the chain is case-marked (properties (m) and (n)). Indeed, this is only natural since we saw that the NP must move precisely to become case-marked (properties (a) and (b)).

The discussion of the properties of movement developed in this section is important from the point of view of language acquisition. We have proposed that a speaker of the language has an internal grammar. If our grammar is a representation of this internal knowledge then the properties of NP-movement which we have postulated must be 'known' to the native speaker. From the discussion it follows that the properties listed above do not have to be learnt one by one. They are descriptive statements which can be deduced from more general principles of the grammar. If a child has the general principles (theta theory, case theory, the projection principle, X'-theory, etc.) at his disposal, the individual descriptive statements listed above follow. As an exercise we invite the reader to try to derive the remaining properties listed above on the basis of the theory established so far.

When we turn to other types of movement we see that some of the properties listed above are maintained, others differ, where the differences are related to the nature of the moved element. Consider, for instance, *wh*-movement, as illustrated in example (3d), repeated here as (38a):

38a   Whom will Lord Emsworth invite?

Anticipating the discussion in chapter 7, it is clear that *wh*-movement is not restricted to moving NPs (property(a)) but it can also move PPs or APs:

38b   At what time will Lord Emsworth arrive?
38c   How big was the pig?

The landing site of *wh*-movement is not an A-position (property (d)): [Spec, CP] is an A′-position. The landing site of *wh*-movement is also not an NP position: [Spec, CP] is not specified with respect to the features [±N, ±V]: PPs (38b) and APs (38c) also move to [Spec, CP]. In addition, [Spec, CP] is not a position to which case is assigned (property (g)). Unlike NP-movement, *wh*-movement is not case-driven: *wh*-movement does not affect a constituent in order to avoid a case filter violation: in (3d) *whom* originates in the [NP, V′] position, which is case-marked by V. This means that case is not assigned to the landing site of movement (property (n)).

On the other hand, we shall see in chapter 7 that the remaining properties listed above hold of NP-movement and of *wh*-movement: the landing site of movement is an empty position (property (c)), the landing site of movement is a theta-bar position (f), we will argue that *wh*-movement leaves a trace (i), which is coindexed with the moved element, the antecedent with which it forms a chain (j). In the case of *wh*-movement, which moves a constituent to [Spec, CP], an A′-position, the chain is an A′-chain. The chain is associated with one theta role (k) which is assigned to the foot of the chain (l). The chain contains one case position (m). For further discussion of the relation between chains and movement see also section 4.6.

2.3.2   C-COMMAND

In section 2.3.1 we have looked at several examples of NP-movement for which we have identified a set of common properties. We have discussed examples in which NPs move from a VP-internal position to the subject position of a sentence, or instances where an NP is moved from a subject position of a lower clause to the subject position of a higher clause. Schematically NP-movement operates as in (39):

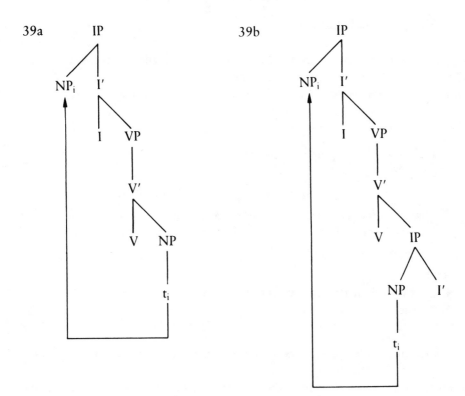

NPs are moved upwards. If we examine the configurational relationships between the antecedent and the trace in these representations we see that the antecedent **c-commands** the trace. We return to this property of movement in section 4.5.1.

2.4 Raising Adjectives

So far we have only looked at examples of NP-movement **induced** by raising verbs or passive verbs. Adjectival predicates too may induce raising. Consider (40):

40a It is likely [CP that John will leave].
40b John is likely to leave.

The main clause subject position in (40a) is occupied by the expletive *it*, hence we conclude that *likely* takes one argument, realized here by a CP, and fails to assign an external theta role. In (40a), *John* is assigned a theta role by the lower verb *leave*. *John* has no thematic relation with the adjective *likely*.

(40b) is a paraphrase of (40a). *John* is again an argument of *leave*, and has no thematic relation with the adjective *likely*; in (40b) *John* is in a derived position. Its base-position is the subject position of the lower clause: (41a) is the D-structure representation of (40b) and (41b) its S-structure:

41a [$_{IP}$ e is likely [$_{IP}$ John to leave]].
41b [$_{IP}$ John$_i$ is likely [$_{IP}$ t$_i$ to leave]].

We have treated the adjective *likely* in exactly the same way as the raising verb *seem*. *Likely* is referred to as a **raising adjective**. Another example of raising adjectives is *certain* in (42).

42a It is certain that the weather will change.
42b The weather is certain to change.

One might infer that all modal adjectives are raising adjectives. This conclusion would be wrong, though. *Probable*, for instance, which is near-synonymous to *likely*, does not allow the subject of the lower non-finite clause to raise to the higher subject position:

43a It is probable that John will leave.
43b *John is probable to leave.

3 Burzio's Generalization

3.1 *Case-Marking and Argument Structure*

In the preceding section we mentioned two properties of passive constructions in English.

(i) Absorption of the case assigning properties of the verb: a passive verb fails to assign structural case to the complement NP; this NP has to move to a position in which it can be case-marked.
(ii) Absorption of the external argument of the verb: the D-structure subject position is generated empty.

We have postulated that raising verbs are like passive verbs in that they (i) fail to assign structural case and (ii) lack an external argument.

Burzio (1986) has related these two properties by the descriptive generalization in (44a) which is schematically summarized in (44b):

44a **Burzio's generalization**
   (i)   A verb which lacks an external argument fails to assign ACCUSA-TIVE case.
       (Burzio, 1986: 178–9)
  (ii)   A verb which fails to assign ACCUSATIVE case fails to theta-mark an external argument.
       (Burzio, 1986: 184)

44b T ⟷ A
    (Burzio, 1986: 185)
    T represents the external theta role, assigned indirectly. A stands for ACCUSATIVE.

In this section we look at Burzio's general classification of verbs. (45) gives a survey of three possible argument structures for verbs.

45a VERB 1:

<ins>1</ins>	2

45b VERB 2:

<ins>1</ins>

45c   VERB 3:

$$\begin{array}{|c|}\hline 2 \\ \hline \\ \hline \end{array}$$

A verb with the theta grid in (45a) is traditionally called a transitive verb: it is a verb which has two arguments and assigns two theta roles, e.g. *abandon* (which assigns the roles of AGENT and THEME). Such a verb must be able to case-mark its complement NP. If a transitive verb failed to case-mark the object, then it would be like the putative verb *HIT* discussed in 2.3.1 above. We have seen that such verbs do not exist.

(45b) is the thematic grid of an intransitive verb: a verb which has only an external argument, such as *work* (which assigns the external role of AGENT). The D-structure and S-structure representations of sentences containing such intransitive verbs will be, schematically, as in (46a) and (46b) respectively:

46a $[_{IP}$ NP $[_{I'}$ $[_{VP}$ V]]]
46b $[_{IP}$ NP $[_{I'}$ $[_{VP}$ V]]]

We see that the S-structure is isomorphic in the relevant respects to the D-structure. According to Burzio's generalization, verbs of this kind could case-mark a complement NP. Since these verbs lack an internal argument, they will not take an NP-complement, though, and their case-marking potential will not need to be activated.[9]

The third class of verbs with the theta grid (45c) is the one that we shall look into now. This class contains verbs which only have an internal argument. The most obvious examples of such verbs that we have already come across are passive verbs. We have seen that as a result of passivization the external argument gets suppressed. Verbs of the third class will be generated in a D-structure like (47a):

47a $[_{IP}$ e $[_{I'}$ $[_{VP}$ VERB NP]]]

Following Burzio's generalization, the VERB in (47a) cannot assign ACCUSATIVE case to its complement. This is in line with our discussion: we have

---

[9]   Cf. the discussion of this point in Burzio's own work (1986: 184).

said that passive verbs fail to assign structural case. At S-structure the NP to which the internal theta role is assigned will have to move to the subject position to be case-marked:

47b $[_{IP}$ NP$_i$ $[_{I'}$ $[_{VP}$ VERB t$_i]]]$

Verbs which lack an external argument and therefore cannot assign ACCUSATIVE case to their complement-NP will from now on be referred to as **unaccusative** verbs. We shall see presently that not only passive verbs belong to this class.

The surface strings of the S-structures (46b) and (47b) will be similar, the trace in (47b) having no phonetic content. On the surface a sentence with an unaccusative verb of class 3 will look like a sentence with an intransitive verb of class 2. One of the important consequences of this analysis is that verbs that are one-place predicates are to be divided into two groups: intransitive verbs with only an external argument (VERB 2) and unaccusative verbs with only an internal argument (VERB 3). We turn now to some empirical motivation from Italian for this claim.

3.2   Unaccusatives in Italian

Burzio's research relied initially on the study of Italian verbs and we shall discuss some of the essential data in this section. For further discussion the reader is referred to Burzio's own work (1986).

Consider the following examples:

48a   Giacomo telefona.
       'Giacomo telephones.'
48b   Giacomo arriva.
       'Giacomo arrives.'

Both *telefonare* and *arrivare* are one-argument verbs, but a cluster of properties distinguishes them and suggests that *arrivare* is more like a passive verb. We look at two of these properties here, *ne*-cliticization and auxiliary selection.

3.2.1   NE-CLITICIZATION

3.2.1.1   Introduction: extraction from objects.   The basic facts of *ne*-cliticization in Italian are illustrated in the following examples:

49a   Giacomo ha insultato due studenti.
      'Giacomo has insulted two students.'
49b   Giacomo ne   ha   insultati due.
      Giacomo of-them   has   insulted   two
      'Giacomo has insulted two.'

50a   Giacomo ha parlato a due studenti.
      'Giacomo has spoken to two students.'
50b *Giacomo ne   ha   parlato a due.
      Giacomo of-them   has   spoken   to two
      'Giacomo has spoken to two.'

A noun head of an NP can become attached to a higher verb as *ne*, leaving its specifier behind. *Ne* is a clitic: a pronominal element which must be associated with a head. The attachment of *ne* to a verb head is referred to as **ne-cliticization**.[10] (50) shows that this is only possible if *ne* is extracted from a post-verbal NP: extraction from a PP produces ungrammaticality. (51) and (52) show that the conditions on *ne*-cliticization are more stringent:

51a   Giacomo passa tre settimane a Milano.
      'Giacomo passes three weeks in Milan.'
51b   Giacomo ne passa tre a Milano.

52a   Giacomo resta tre settimane a Milano.
      'Giacomo stays three weeks in Milan.'
52b *Giacomo ne resta tre a Milano.

Ne-cliticization from the NP *tre settimane* is allowed in (51b) and disallowed in (52b). The contrast between these two sentences correlates with another distinction: in (51a) *tre settimane* is a complement of the verb, in (52a) it is not:

51c   Tre settimane sono state passate a Milano.
      three weeks are been passed in Milan
52c *Tre settimane sono state rimaste a Milano.
      three weeks are been remained in Milan

---

[10]   For a discussion of *ne*-cliticization see also Belletti and Rizzi (1981).

Ne-cliticization is restricted to NPs which are complements of V. Such NPs appear in the structure (53):

53   V'

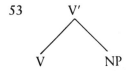

V   NP

3.2.1.2 *Transitive sentences and free inversion*   Now recall another property of *pro*-drop languages like Italian, already discussed in section 4 of the Introduction to this book. In Italian the subject NP may appear post-verbally in the so-called free inversion patterns. First consider transitive sentences:

54a   La ragazza/lei l'ha comprato.
      the girl it-has bought
      'The girl/She has bought it.'
54b   L'ha comprato la ragazza/lei.
      it-has bought the girl/she (NOM)
      'The girl/She has bought it.'

In (54b) the post-verbal subject *la ragazza/lei* is assigned NOMINATIVE case. Since the direct object is realized by the element *l'*('it'), it is unlikely that the post-verbal subject occupies the direct object position. This is confirmed on the basis of *ne*-cliticization:

54c   L'hanno comprato tre ragazze.
      it have bought three girls
      'Three girls have bought it.'
54d   *Ne l'hanno comprato tre.

In (54d) we cannot extract *ne* from the post-verbal subject in a transitive sentence. We conclude that the post-verbal subject NP in (54b) and in (54d) is in a position outside the lowest V'. Let us assume it is adjoined to VP (for discussion of adjunction cf. section 4.1 below and also chapter 7).[11]

---

[11] Various proposals have been formulated to account for the NOMINATIVE case assignment to the post-verbal subject in (54b). See, for instance, Belletti (1988), Burzio (1986), Rizzi (1982a, forthcoming). Cf. section 4.1 below.

3.2.1.3 Post-verbal subjects of passive verbs The free inversion pattern associated with transitive sentences (54) is also found with passive verbs:

55a Molti studenti furono arrestati.
    many students were arrested
    'Many students were arrested.'
55b Furono arrestati molti studenti.
    were arrested many students
    'Many students were arrested.'

As the internal argument of the verb, the NP *molti studenti* originates in the [NP, V'] position. In (55a) the NP is a derived subject which has been moved to the [Spec, IP] position. Data from *ne*-cliticization suggest that the post-verbal subject in (55b) is in [NP, V'], i.e. the base object position:[12]

56 Ne furono arrestati molti
    of them were arrested many
    'Many of them were arrested.'

The VP of (55b) would have the structure (57):

---

[12] Belletti (1988) proposes that the post-verbal indefinite NP in the passive sentence in (55b) is assigned an inherent PARTITIVE case by the passive verb. Her general thesis is that while passive verbs do not assign structural case they assign a PARTITIVE case inherently. Semantically PARTITIVE case is only compatible with indefinite NPs. For examples such as (ia), where a definite NP *il professore* appears post-verbally, Belletti adopts the analysis suggested for (54b):

(i) Fu arrestato il professore.
    was arrested the professor
    'The professor was arrested.'

Belletti proposes that the definite NP *il professore* is not in the object position [NP, V']. Rather it is adjoined to VP, where it receives NOMINATIVE case (cf. section 4.1):

(ii) Fu arrestata lei.
    was arrested she

If we adopt Belletti's approach we conclude that only indefinite post-verbal subjects of passive verbs occupy the [NP, V'] position. This analysis will also apply to the post-verbal subjects of verbs of VERB 3 type.

57 V'

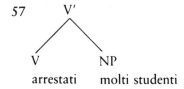

V   NP

arrestati   molti studenti

3.2.1.4 Post-verbal subjects and one-argument verbs An important contrast appears when we consider the application of ne-cliticization to the post-verbal subjects of one-argument verbs:

58a Molti studenti telefonano.
many students telephone
'Many students are calling.'
58b Telefonano molti studenti.
telephone many students
58c *Ne telefonano molti.

59a Molti studenti arrivano.
many students arrive
'There arrive many students.'
59b Arrivano molti studenti.
arrive many students
59c Ne arrivano molti.

Consider first *telefonare* ('telephone') in (58). The subject may appear either post-verbally or pre-verbally. From the impossibility of *ne*-cliticization (58c), we conclude that the inverted subject in (58c) does not occur in the position dominated by V', but is outside V'.

The situation for *arrivare* is quite different. Again both pre-verbal and post-verbal subjects are allowed but *ne*-cliticization from the post-verbal subject is possible (59c). This leads us to conclude that the NP *molti studenti* in (59b) occupies the position dominated by V'. In other words, the structure of (59b) is like that of passive (56):

60   [IP e I [VP [V' arrivare [NP molti studenti]]]].

Burzio proposes to assimilate verbs such as *arrivare* to the class of passive verbs. These verbs lack an external argument and their sole argument is

internal. Both passive verbs and verbs such as *arrivare* have the argument
structure of VERB 3 above:

61   VERB 3:

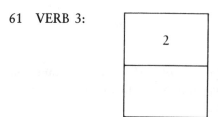

At D-structure the subject position of sentences with these verbs remains
unfilled:

62a   [_IP_ e furono [_VP_ [_V'_ arrestati [_NP_ molti studenti]]]].
62b   [_IP_ e I [_VP_ [_V'_ arrivare [_NP_ molti studenti]]]].

At S-structure there are two possibilities:

(i)   Either the complement of the verb is moved to the subject position to
      be assigned NOMINATIVE case. The subject is then a derived subject.

63a   [_IP_ Molti studenti_i_ furono [_VP_ [_V'_ arrestati [_NP_ t_i_]]]].
63b   [_IP_ Molti studenti_i_ I [_VP_ [_V'_ arrivare [_NP_ t_i_]]]].

Movement of the NP to the subject position leaves a coindexed trace in the
vacated position inside V'.

(ii) Alternatively, the object NP remains in its base-position. The null
      subject in (64) is non-thematic, it is a non-overt expletive.[13]

---

[13]   Recall from the Introduction that non-overt expletives are not allowed in English:

(i)   *Arrived three students.
(ii) *Seems that John is ill.

The ungrammaticality of (i) and (ii) is due to the fact that pronominal subjects in
English must be overt. In Italian a pronominal subject may be non-overt:

(iiia) *Speaks English.
(iiib) Parla inglese.

We discuss the nature of the non-overt subject in Italian in chapter 8.

64a [$_{IP}$ e furono [$_{VP}$ [$_{V'}$ arrestati [$_{NP}$ molti studenti]]]].
64b [$_{IP}$ e I [$_{VP}$ [$_{V'}$ arrivare [$_{NP}$ molti studenti]]]].

Telefonare has a different argument structure. It has only an external argument.

65 VERB 2:

The D-structure of sentences (58a) and (58b) will be:

66a [$_{IP}$ Molti studenti [$_{I'}$ I [$_{VP}$ telefonare]]].

Two S-structures are possible. Either the NP *molti studenti* stays in its base-position:

66b [$_{IP}$ Molti studenti [$_{I'}$ I [$_{VP}$ telefonare]]].

Alternatively, the subject appears in a post-verbal position outside V'. The [NP, IP] position is again occupied by a non-overt expletive.

66c [$_{IP}$ e I [$_{VP}$ [$_{V'}$ telefonare] molti studenti]].

3.2.1.5 Conclusion On the basis of *ne*-cliticization data we have concluded that there are two types of verbs which are traditionally called intransitive. Verbs like *telefonare* have an external argument; verbs like *arrivare* have just an internal argument. For the latter class of verbs Burzio's generalization predicts that although they have an internal argument they do not assign ACCUSATIVE case, exactly in the way that passive verbs fail to assign ACCUSATIVE. Verbs of the *arrivare* class are **unaccusatives**.

We have seen that whenever a verb allows *ne*-cliticization from what looks like an inverted subject NP, this NP must occur in the object position, the position dominated by V'. Such a verb will lack an external argument and will not assign ACCUSATIVE case. In (67) we give some more examples.

67a	Ne	vengono	molti.		
	of-them	come	many		
67b	Ne	vanno	molti	al	concerto.
	of-them	go	many	to-the	concert
67c	Ne	tornano	molti.		
	of-them	return	many		
67d	Ne	partono	molti.		
	of-them	leave	many		
67e	Ne	muoiono	molti.		
	of-them	die	many		
67f	Ne	cadono	molti.		
	of-them	fall	many		
67g	Ne	entrano	molti.		
	of-them	enter	many		

Though the class of unaccusative verbs is not easily defined (see Burzio's own work for discussion), it appears that it contains primarily verbs of movement and verbs that indicate some state or a change of state.

3.2.2   AUXILIARY SELECTION

We have seen that certain one-argument verbs have only an external argument, while others have only an internal argument to which they cannot assign ACCUSATIVE case. *Ne*-cliticization distinguishes these verbs. Another distinction is the choice of perfective auxiliary:

68a   Giacomo ha telefonato.
68b   Giacomo è arrivato.

Burzio proposes that the selection of the perfective auxiliary *essere* is dependent on the following condition:

69   ***Essere* selection**
      There is a chain between the subject position and the complement position of the verb.
      (cf. Burzio, 1986: 55)

Following our discussion in 3.2 the S-structure representations of the examples in (68) will be as in (70):

70a [$_{IP}$ Giacomo [$_{I'}$ ha [$_{VP}$ telefonato]]].
70b [$_{IP}$ Giacomo$_i$ [$_{I'}$ è [$_{VP}$ arrivato t$_i$]]].

In (70b) *Giacomo* has moved to the subject position and has left a coindexed trace. There is a chain between the moved NP and the vacated position. (70b) fulfills the condition for *essere* selection. In (70a) no movement is assumed and the condition for *essere* selection is not satisfied.

If we return briefly to the other examples of unaccusative verbs listed under (67) we see that these verbs also select *essere* as the perfect auxiliary:

71a Roberto è venuto.
71b Roberto è andato al concerto.
71c Roberto è tornato.
71d Roberto è partito.
71e Roberto è morto.
71f Roberto è caduto.
71g Roberto è entrato.

Passive verbs are also unaccusative: they also meet the condition for *essere* assignment in (69):

72 Notevoli danni sono stati arrecati alla chiesa.
    Important damage has (lit. are) been caused to the church.

3.3 One-argument Verbs in English

Let us try to see if Burzio's analysis of the one-argument verbs carries over to English. We have already discussed passive verbs. The crucial properties of these verbs are that (i) they fail to assign an external theta role, i.e. they lack an external argument; and that (ii) they do not assign ACCUSATIVE case to their complement. Can other verbs be considered unaccusatives along the lines of the Italian verbs of the *arrivare* group?

3.3.1 RAISING PREDICATES

Raising verbs also belong to the class of unaccusatives. Consider the representations in (73):

73a   [$_{IP}$ Poirot$_i$ [$_{I'}$ was [$_{VP}$ believed [$_{IP}$ t$_i$ to have destroyed the evidence]]]].
73b   [$_{IP}$ Poirot$_i$ [$_{I'}$ -s [$_{VP}$ seem [$_{IP}$ t$_i$ to have destroyed the evidence]]]].

We have discussed the derivation of (73a) and (73b) in section 1.1. The verbs *believed* and *seem* take one internal clausal argument and do not assign an external theta role to the subject position. For both verbs we have also said that they cannot assign an ACCUSATIVE case to the subject position of the lower infinitive.

   We now see that the properties attributed to these verbs are captured by Burzio's generalization: passive and raising verbs lack an external argument and they consequently fail to assign ACCUSATIVE case.

3.3.2   VERBS OF MOVEMENT AND (CHANGE OF) STATE

We may wonder whether the English verbs of movement and (change of) state are like their Italian counterparts of the *arrivare* class. Remember two crucial features of verbs of the *arrivare* class: they allow *ne*-cliticization from the post-verbal subject and they select *essere* as a perfect auxiliary. In present-day English there is no choice of auxiliary for the perfect, this being invariably *have*, and there is no equivalent to *ne*-cliticization, so the diagnostics introduced are not immediately applicable.

   A consideration of the history of the language throws some light on the issue. While modern English uses only *have* as a perfective auxiliary, older stages of the language had both *have* and *be*. At those earlier stages verbs of movement and change of state like *come, go, return, grow, die, fall* formed their perfective forms by means of *be*:

74a   Se halga faeder *waes* inn agan.
      the holy father   was   in gone
      'The holy father had gone in.'
      (Quirk and Wrenn, 1957: 78)
74b   *Is* nu   geworden.
      is   now   become
      'It has happened.'
      (Quirk and Wrenn, 1957: 79)

Present-day English still allows the form in (75) (cf. 74a):

75   Poirot is gone.

From earlier stages of the language we obtain indirect support for the idea that verbs of movement and change of state are unaccusative verbs like their Italian counterparts of the *arrivare* class.

Another argument can be obtained from present-day English and concerns the use of the expletive *there*. We have briefly discussed existential sentences such as (76) and (77) in chapter 1:

76a Three men arrived at the palace.
76b There arrived three men at the palace.

77a Three students came to the party.
77b There came three students to the party.

In (76a) the subject precedes the verb *arrived* while in the existential pattern (76b) it follows it and the expletive *there* occupies the [Spec, IP] position. It is clear, though, that the existential pattern cannot be used with every verb in English.[14]

78a Three men bought a book.
78b *There bought three men a book.

79a Three men slept in the room.
79b *There slept three men in the room.

Transitive verbs are excluded (78b). Only a subset of one-argument verbs allows the construction, as indicated by the ungrammaticality of (79b). A closer look at these and other examples suggests the following descriptive generalization: the *there*-construction is restricted to one-argument verbs of movement and (change of) state. In addition to the verbs given above, Burzio (1986: 159) mentions: *arise, emerge, ensue, begin, exist, occur, follow*. The Italian counterparts of these verbs (*sorgere, emergere, succedere, cominciare, esistere, accadere, seguire*) all pattern like *arrivare*.[15] We follow Burzio in assuming that the English verbs of movement and of (change of) state listed above are also unaccusatives, i.e. fail to assign ACCUSATIVE case and lack an external theta role.

---

[14] See Belletti (1988) and Moro (1989) for a discussion of the existential construction.
[15] See Burzio (1986: 160–1) for discussion though.

3.3.3 ERGATIVE-CAUSATIVE PAIRS

Some English verbs have properties which have led some linguists to treat them as unaccusatives.

80a The enemy$_i$ sank the boat$_j$.
80b The boat$_j$ was sunk.
80c The boat$_j$ sank.

The argument structure for active *sink* is given in (81a). We have specified the theta roles and we have entered the relevant indices in the theta grid of the verb to indicate which NP realizes which argument:

81a *sink*: verb

1 AGENT	2 THEME
i	j

In (80b) passive *sink* has the argument structure (81b):

81b *sunk*: verb

2 THEME
j

For by now familiar reasons we propose (82a) as the D-structure and (82b) as the S-structure of (80b):

82a [$_{IP}$ e [$_{I'}$ was [$_{VP}$ [$_{V'}$ sunk [$_{NP}$ the boat]]]]].
82b [$_{IP}$ The boat$_j$ [$_{I'}$ was [$_{VP}$ [$_{V'}$ sunk [$_{NP}$ t$_j$]]]]].

In (80c) the NP *the boat* has the same thematic relation to the verb as in (80b): *the boat* is the THEME, the thing that is affected by the activity. One might assume that *sink* in (80c), although active, has an argument structure similar to that of a passive verb, i.e. that *sink* in (80c) is an unaccusative verb.

82c   *sink*: verb

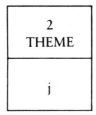

2
THEME

j

On this assumption, (80c) would have the D-structure (83a) and the S-structure (83b):

83a   [IP e [I' past [VP [V' sink [NP the boat]]]]].
83b   [IP The boatj [I' past [VP sink [NP tj]]]].

In (83a) the NP *the boat* is base-generated as the object of *sink*; at S-structure it becomes a derived subject. The two argument structures correlate with a semantic difference between two uses of *sink*. (80c) encodes that some object (the boat) is engaged in some activity (the sinking). In (80a) the external argument specifies who is responsible for the sinking: (80a) is equivalent to 'the enemy made the boat sink' or 'the enemy caused the boat to sink'. In view of the element of causation involved in the interpretation of *sink* in (80a), this use of the verb is referred to as the **causative** pattern.

There are two reasons for not referring to *sink* in (80c) as an unaccusative verb. First, unlike *arrive*, *sink* has a transitive pendant which does assign ACCUSATIVE:

84a   The enemy sank the ship.
84b   *I arrived the baby to the crèche.

Second, unlike the unaccusative verbs of movement and (change of) state mentioned above, *sink* does not appear in the *there*-construction:

85a   There came three new sailors on board.
85b   *There sank three ships last week.

On the basis of these two criteria it seems reasonable to argue that *sink* (and verbs which pattern like it) is not an unaccusative verb. Other verbs that pattern like *sink* are *open, close, increase, break, drop*:

86a Poirot opened the door.
86b The door opened.

87a Poirot closed the door.
87b The door closed.

88a The police have increased the activities.
88b The activities have increased.

89a Poirot broke the vase.
89b The vase broke.

90a The boy dropped the vase.
90b The vase dropped.

Rather than claiming that these verbs have the theta structure in (82c) we propose that they are intransitive verbs which project their THEME argument in the subject position at D-structure:

91 *sink*: verb

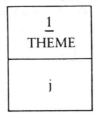

The D-structure of (80c) will not be as in (83a) but will be:

92 [$_{IP}$ The boat$_j$ [$_{I'}$ past [$_{VP}$ sink]]].

In this book the term unaccusative is used for passive verbs, raising verbs and verbs of movement and (change of) state, and we refer to one-argument verbs like *sink* as **ergatives**.[16] The classification of verbs as unaccusative/ergative is a matter of ongoing research. Many authors do not make any distinction between the terms, or consider verbs with transitive pendants like *sink*, which we label ergatives, as unaccusatives. The reader is referred to the literature for details.

4 Levels of Representation and Principles of the Grammar

In this chapter we have developed the hypothesis that all sentences are associated with two syntactic representations: D-structure and S-structure. In this section we discuss the relation between these levels and we shall give an overview of how the principles of grammar established in previous chapters apply to them.

4.1 The Structure Preserving Principle

There is an important constraint on the relation between syntactic representations: structures established at D-structure must be preserved at S-structure: transformations are **structure preserving**.

If a syntactic position is required at D-structure it will be present at S-structure as well. For instance, a position required by the projection principle at D-structure will also be present at S-structure. A position projected as a certain category at D-structure cannot change its category at S-structure: NP-positions remain NP-positions, I remains I, etc. A D-structure NP-position, for example, cannot be turned into a PP-position at S-structure. If we adopt the hypothesis briefly alluded to at the end of chapter 2 that syntactic category labels represent bundles of features ([±N], [±V]) then we conclude that features assigned at D-structure are preserved, i.e. they do not change. If NPs are also assigned the features [± anaphor; ± pronominal] then these features too are expected to be invariant between D-structure and S-structure. This point becomes relevant in chapter 8.

The structure preserving principle also has consequences for movement. One constraint which it imposes on movement is that phrasal projections

---

[16]   In so doing we depart from Burzio's own analysis (1986) and we follow a suggestion in work by Belletti (1988: 4, 14), based on Hale and Keyser (1986, 1987). Obviously, the same type of analysis will also apply to the equivalents of the ergatives in other languages.

must move into positions which are themselves labelled as phrasal projections. NPs, for example, must not move into positions dominated by lexical
categories (such as N) or intermediate phrasal categories (N'). Heads such as
I must move into other head positions.

Second, movement will have to respect syntactic categories. For example,
NPs can move into NP-positions without problem, but they will not be able
to move into a position labelled AP. This does not mean that NPs must move
to NP-positions. Provided all other principles of the grammar are respected,
NPs will also be allowed to move to positions which are not specified for a
syntactic category (see the discussion of *wh*-movement in section 2.3.1 and
in chapter 7). The structure preserving principle does not prevent that a
moved element is given a new position at S-structure, a position that does not
exist at D-structure, as long as the new position created respects the principles of phrase structure. Such a move would not violate the principle that
structure must be preserved.

Consider, for instance, the example of free subject inversion in Italian:

93a Il ragazzo ha   telefonato.
        the boy   has   telephoned.
93b Ha telefonato il ragazzo.

The VP of (93a) is as in (93c); *il ragazzo* is in [Spec, IP].

93c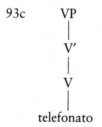

In (93b) the subject NP occurs post-verbally. We assume that the D-structure
(93b) is like that of (93a). At S-structure the subject NP *il ragazzo* is post-
verbal. Recall from (58c) that *ne*-cliticization is impossible from the post-
verbal subject of *telefonare*, suggesting that the postposed subject is not in the
object position [NP, V']. It is proposed in the literature that the post-verbal
subject NP is adjoined to VP:

93d

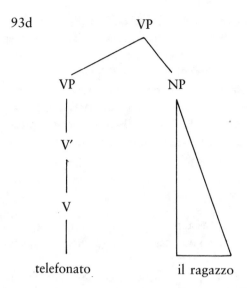

The S-structure in (93d) is not incompatible with the structure preserving principle: all structure assumed at D-structure (93c) is preserved. We return to adjunction structures in chapter 7.

4.2 The Theta Criterion

In 2.2.1 we discussed the application of theta theory to the two levels of representation.

D-structure is a representation of lexical properties. D-structure representations are subject to the theta criterion: all syntactic arguments of the predicates must be realized. Moreover we must not randomly generate arguments (say NPs) which cannot be associated with any predicate since they will fail to receive a theta role.

S-structure encodes the result of movement transformations. The structure preserving principle will also entail that movement leaves traces since positions created at D-structure must be preserved. Traces of movement form a chain with their antecedent. If we redefine the theta criterion in terms of chains (cf. 22)) we can maintain that the theta criterion also applies at S-structure, as discussed above. (See also section 4.6.)

4.3 The Extended Projection Principle

The EPP is another principle regulating syntactic structure which applies at all levels of syntactic representation: sentences must have subject positions,

[Spec, IP] positions, at all syntactic levels. It is important to point out here that the EPP imposes that the [Spec, IP] position be generated. The EPP does not impose that this position be filled by overt elements: we have already seen that it may be filled by a trace or by PRO. Also, the EPP does not require that the [Spec, IP] position be filled by arguments: we have seen that sometimes it is filled by an expletive element. Given the structure preserving principle discussed in 4.1 it follows that if the EPP forces us to generate a [Spec, IP] position at D-structure, this position is also present at S-structure.

4.4 *The Case Filter*

Throughout this chapter we have been assuming that the case filter applies at S-structure. NPs do not need to be assigned case at D-structure. Structural case is assigned at S-structure (cf. section 1.1).

This does not mean that at D-structure NPs must be caseless. All we are saying is that case is not **checked** at D-structure. In chapter 3 we adopted the idea that inherent case is associated with theta roles as a lexical property. The German DATIVE in (94a) was taken to be an inherent case. The verb *helfen* is assumed to have the lexical structure in (94b):

94a   Poirot hilft ihm.
      Poirot helps him-DATIVE

94b   *helfen*: verb

1	2 DATIVE

If D-structure is a representation of lexical structure then we can assume that the DATIVE will be assigned to *ihm* at D-structure. As seen before, inherent case is unaffected by passivization.

94c   Ihm wurde geholfen.
      him was helped
      'He was helped.'
94d   *Er   wurde geholfen.
      he (NOM) was   helped

4.5 The Binding Theory

4.5.1 LEVEL OF APPLICATION

In chapter 4 we discussed the module of the grammar which regulates the interpretation of NPs: the binding theory. At that point in the discussion we were not worried about levels of representation. We simply looked at sentences, pretending there was a unique syntactic representation associated with them. Now life is more difficult: we have two levels of representation and we may well ask at which point the binding theory (**BT**) is supposed to apply.

In order to decide at which level the BT applies we examine the application of the BT in examples in which movement has taken place. We shall consider the application of Principle A first and then that of Principles B and C.

The standard example that is often used to illustrate the application of Principle A is (95a).

95a They seem to each other to be intelligent.

The D-structure of (95a) is (95b) and its S-structure is (95c):

95b [$_{IP}$ e seem to each other [$_{IP}$ they to be intelligent]].
95c [$_{IP}$ They$_i$ seem to each other$_i$ [$_{IP}$ t$_i$ to be intelligent]].

Principle A of the BT requires that anaphors such as *each other* be bound in their GC. The GC of *each other* is the matrix clause. In the D-structure (95a) *each other* cannot be bound in its GC since there is no NP available to bind it. The correct binding configuration arises at S-structure: the derived subject *they* can bind the anaphor:

95d [$_{IP}$ They$_i$ seem to each other$_i$ [$_{IP}$ t$_i$ to be intelligent]].

Belletti and Rizzi claim that (95a) only shows 'that Principle A can be fulfilled at S-structure, not that it cannot be fulfilled at D-structure' (1988: 313). They include in the discussion examples such as (96):

96a Replicants of themselves seemed to the boys to be ugly.
     (from Johnson, 1985, quoted in Belletti and Rizzi, 1988: 316)
96b *D-structure*
     [$_{IP}$ e seemed to the boys [$_{IP}$ replicants of themselves to be ugly]]

96c   *S-structure*

[IP [Replicants of themselves]k seemed to the boys [IP tk to be ugly]].

In (96a) the reflexive *themselves* is referentially dependent on the NP *the boys*, hence we expect it is bound by it. At S-structure (96c) the anaphor is not c-commanded by the antecedent *the boys*, hence is not bound by it. Belletti and Rizzi argue that D-structure (96b) stands a better chance of satisfying Principle A. However, even here there will be problems. It is not immediately clear how the NP *the boys*, which is a complement of the preposition *to*, can c-command the reflexive even at D-structure. The reader can verify for himself that the first branching node dominating the NP *the boys* will be the PP node dominating *to the boys*. One might try to circumvent the problem by saying that the PP node somehow does not count (but see Rizzi (1986c: 76–8) for discussion)

96d

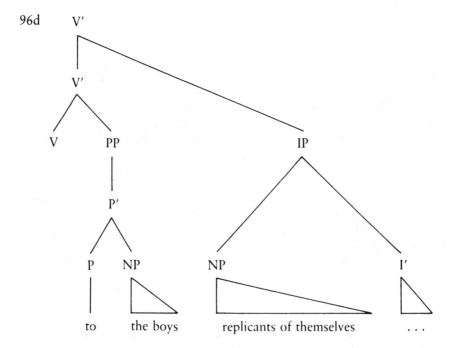

Another problem with the example is that it contains a reflexive associated with what is called a *picture*-NP. NPs are known to be problematic for the BT.[17] Consider for instance (97):

---

[17]   We have illustrated the problems with *picture*-NPs in chapter 4, exercise 3. For discussion of the data the reader is referred to work by Prewett (1977) and Jackendoff (1992). Nakajima (1984) proposes that *picture*-NPs should be kept outside the BT. Mohanan (1985) contains a similar suggestion.

97 This is a picture of myself which was taken years ago.

In (97) the reflexive *myself* lacks an antecedent and yet the sentence is grammatical. Because of their special behaviour it is sometimes proposed that *picture*-NPs be treated separately from other NPs with respect to the BT. Rizzi and Belletti's argument that Principle A can be satisfied at D-structure is weakened because it relies on *picture*-NPs, which are problematic for the binding theory anyway.

Let us consider the application of Principle C. (98a) is ruled out on the interpretation indicated by the coindexation: *Bill* must not be coreferential with *he* (Belletti and Rizzi, 1988: 318).

98a *He$_i$ seems to Bill$_i$'s sister to be the best.

Consider the syntactic representations of the sentence:

98b *D-structure*

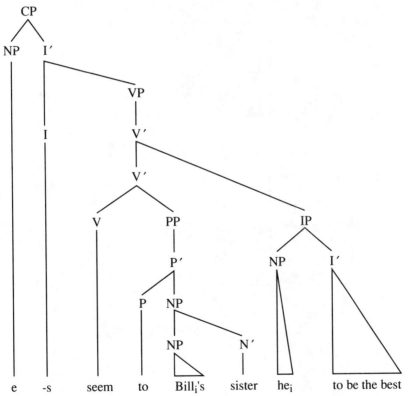

98c *S-structure*

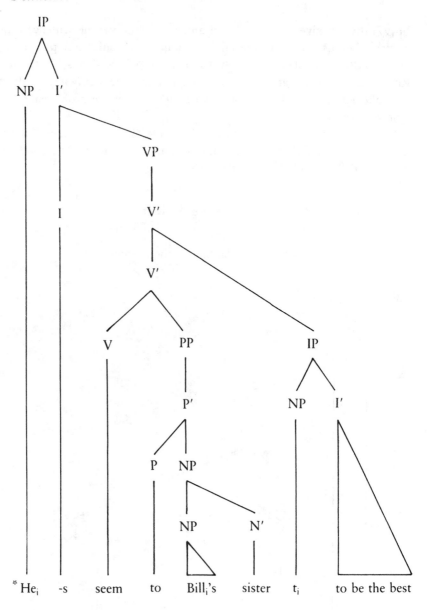

If we were to assume that Principle C can be fulfilled at D-structure it would not be possible to rule out (98a) with the intended interpretation on the basis of the BT. At D-structure (98b), *he$_i$* is coindexed with *Bill$_i$* but *Bill* does not c-command the pronoun, nor does the pronoun c-command *Bill*, as the reader can verify on the tree diagram. The D-structure configuration (98b) is identical in the relevant respects to the structure of (99) where coindexation between *Bill* and *he* is allowed:

99a It seems to Bill$_i$'s sister that he$_i$ is the best.
99b D-structure/S-structure
     It seems to Bill$_i$'s sister [that [he$_i$ is the best]].

We conclude that it is the S-structure representation (98c) which is ruled out by Principle C. *Bill$_i$*, an R-expression, is bound by *he$_i$* and this violates Principle C. This suggests that Principle C must be satisfied at S-structure.

The same reasoning can be applied to (100) to demonstrate that Principle B cannot be satisfied at D-structure either:

100 *He$_i$ seems to him$_i$ to be likely to be the best.
     (Belletti and Rizzi, 1988: 318)

We leave the reader to work out the D-structure and S-structure of this example.

On the basis of the discussion above, we conclude that Principles B and C apply to S-structure configurations. The evidence that Principle A can be fulfilled at D-structure is controversial.[18]

4.5.2 THE FEATURE COMPOSITION OF NP-TRACES

Let us return to a point left unexplained in section 2.3.1 above. It was observed that example (37a), repeated here as (101), is ungrammatical:

101 *John$_i$ seems that it is believed t$_i$ by everyone.

Let us try to explain why this should be so.

We have seen that traces of NP-movement occupy an NP-position and

---

[18] We return to the level of application of the binding theory in chapter 9, section 4.

have nominal AGR-features (gender, number and person). This means that these traces are in fact like non-overt NPs. In chapter 4 we propose that NPs are subject to the BT. The question to address is: which principle applies to traces of NP-movement, i.e. what type of NP are NP-traces? Recall that there were four types of NPs:

102a   Typology of NPs

Type	OVERT	NON-OVERT
[+Anaphor, −Pronominal]	anaphors	
[−Anaphor, +Pronominal]	pronouns	
[−Anaphor, −Pronominal]	R-expressions	
[+Anaphor, +Pronominal]		PRO (chapter 5)

The binding theory says that:

(i)   elements that are [+Anaphor] must be bound in their GC.
(ii) elements that are [+Pronominal] must be free in their GC.

Consider the typical examples of NP-movement: a passive sentence (103a) and a raising construction (103b):

103a   [John$_i$ is believed t$_i$ by everyone].
103b   [John$_i$ seems [$_{IP}$ t$_i$ to be the best]].

Which of the combinations of features listed in (102) would be appropriate to characterize the NP-traces in (103)?

Suppose the traces were considered to be R-expressions ([−Anaphor, −Pronominal]). Clearly this is not a good idea as the traces in (103) are coindexed with a c-commanding NP in an A-position. If a trace of NP-movement were an R-expression it would violate Principle C.

Suppose the trace is [−Anaphor, +Pronominal], i.e. a pronoun. Again this will not do: the traces in (103) are bound in their GC. The reader will be able to work out that in both examples in (103) the antecedent *John* is contained in the GC of the trace.[19]

---

[19]   Remember that we stipulated in chapter 3 that infinitival IP is not a barrier for outside government, hence *seem* governs the trace in the subject position of the complement IP.

Could the trace be like the non-overt element PRO, [+Anaphor, +Pronominal] discussed in chapter 5? We have seen that such NPs are subject to contradictory requirements with respect to the BT. The only context in which PRO is licensed is when it is ungoverned. Clearly, the object position of the passive verb in (103a) is governed, and similarly, infinitival IP not being a barrier, *seem* will govern the trace in the subject position of the infinitival IP (103b).

Finally, we are left with the category [+Anaphor, −Pronominal], subject to Principle A. This is rather a nice result. As the reader can verify for himself, the traces in (103) are bound in their GC: t_i is coindexed with a c-commanding antecedent in its GC. NP-traces are like anaphors.

If we treat NP-traces as anaphors the ungrammaticality of (101) follows from the BT: t_i must be bound in its GC. The GC is the lower clause, containing a governor (*believe*) and a subject (*it* or the SUBJECT, AGR). In (101) the trace is not bound in its GC.

At this point it is clear that the term 'antecedent', which we introduced to refer to the moved NP, is not accidental. The moved NP behaves like an antecedent in that it **binds** the trace. The requirement that the moved NP should bind the trace will also account for some of the properties discussed in section 2.3. Recall that antecedents of NP-movement c-command their traces (see section 2.3.2). We have defined binding in terms of coindexation with a c-commanding element in an A-position. The c-command relation between the moved NP and its trace follows if we assume that the trace must be bound by the moved element. We return to the binding relations between an antecedent and its trace in section 4.6.

On the basis of the examples discussed above we have identified NP-traces as non-overt NPs of the type [+Anaphor, −Pronominal]. This means that in our inventory of NP types (102a) we can pair them with overt anaphors:

102b Typology of NPs

Type	OVERT	NON-OVERT
[+Anaphor, −Pronominal]	anaphors	NP-trace
[−Anaphor, +Pronominal]	pronouns	
[−Anaphor, −Pronominal]	R-expressions	
[+Anaphor, +Pronominal]		PRO

There are now only three gaps in the paradigm we have set up. The absence of overt elements which are [+Anaphor, +Pronominal] was motivated in chapter 4. We have as yet no non-overt elements which are [−Anaphor,

+Pronominal] and [−Anaphor, −Pronominal]. In subsequent chapters we shall see that these latter types also exist so that we shall be able to arrive at a picture where all overt NP-types have a non-overt pendant. We return to the classification of non-overt categories in chapters 7 and 8.[20]

4.6 Chains and Movement

4.6.1 CHAINS

Section 2.3 contains an inventory of the properties of NP-movement. NP-movement creates a chain. We shall see in chapter 7 that *wh*-movement also leads to chain formation. In (104a) NP-movement creates the chain *<this story$_i$, t$_i$>*; in (104b) it creates the chain *<Poirot$_i$, t$_i$>*:

104a   This story$_i$ was believed t$_i$ by the villagers.
104b   Poirot$_i$ seems [$_{IP}$ t$_i$ to have destroyed the evidence].

In section 4.5.2 we have seen that traces of NP-movement behave like anaphors: they are subject to Principle A of the binding theory: they have to be bound in their governing category. In the chain *<Poirot$_i$, t$_i$>* in (104b), for instance, the first member of the chain, *Poirot$_i$*, locally binds the next one, *t$_i$*. (104c) is ungrammatical because *Poirot* fails to bind its trace locally.

104c   *[$_{IP_1}$ Poirot$_i$ is likely [$_{CP}$ [that [$_{IP_2}$ it appears [$_{IP_3}$ t$_i$ to be the best candidate]]]]].

Let us list the properties of chains which we have identified so far:

  (i)   the highest member of the chain, i.e. the head of the chain, is a θ′-position;
  (ii)   the foot of the chain is a theta position;
  (iii) if the chain contains more than one member, the lower members of the chain are traces;
  (iv)   the members of the chain are coindexed;
  (v)   the chain contains one argument;
  (vi)   the chain is associated with one theta role;
  (vii) the chain contains one case position;
  (viii) a member of a chain locally binds the next member.

---

[20]   The classification of NPs on the basis of the features given in (102a) is discussed at length by Chomsky (1982).

In (104a) and in (104b) the chains have two **members**, but clearly chains might have more than two members:

104d Poirot$_i$ seems [$_{IP}$ t'_i to have been arrested t_i].

In (104d) NP-movement leads to the three member chain $<Poirot_i, t'_i, t_i>$: this chain contains two NP-traces, each of which bound by an antecedent: t_i is bound by the intermediate trace t'_i, t'_i itself is bound by the NP *Poirot$_i$*. For completeness'sake also consider (104e) in which $<Poirot>$ is a one member chain:

104e I have invited Poirot.

We define a chain as follows:

105 Chains
105a $C= <x_1, \ldots x_n>$ is a chain iff, for $1 \leq i < n$, x_i is the local binder of x_{i+1}.

where

105b x is a binder of y iff, for x, y = a category, x and y are coindexed, and x c-commands y;

105c x is the local binder of y iff x is a binder of y and there is no z such that z is a binder of y, and z is not a binder of x.
(cf. Rizzi, 1986c: 66)

(22a) repeated as (105d) defines the theta criterion in terms of chains:

105d Theta criterion
Each argument A appears in a chain containing a unique visible theta position P, and each theta position P is visible in a chain containing a unique argument A.
(Chomsky, 1986a: 97)

(105d) expresses a bi-uniqueness condition between theta roles and chains containing exactly one argument. The chain formation mechanism is essentially free: a sequence of constituents meeting the definition in (105d) can form a chain, but there is no obligation. Consider (104d): the object position of *arrested* is a theta position. The subject position of the embedded clause and the matrix subject position are not theta positions. On the basis of the S-structure of (104d) we could create the following chains:

106a $\langle$Poirot$_i\rangle$, $\langle t'_i\rangle$, $\langle t_i\rangle$
106b $\langle$Poirot$_i$, $t'_i\rangle$, $\langle t_i\rangle$
106c $\langle$Poirot$_i\rangle$ $\langle t'_i$, $t_i\rangle$
106d $\langle$Poirot$_i$, t'_i, $t_i\rangle$

However, by the theta criterion as defined in (105d) (106a)–(106c) are excluded. In all of them the argument *Poirot* will belong to a chain which fails to be assigned a theta role, and a theta role will be assigned to the chain containing t_i and which fails to contain an argument. (106d) meets the theta criterion: (104d) is well formed with the chain formation in (106d). Consider now (104f):

104f   Poirot$_i$ wants [$_{CP}$ [$_{IP}$ PRO$_i$ to be arrested t_i]].

The subject position of the matrix clause is a theta position, and so is the object position of *arrested*. The subject position of the infinitival CP is non-thematic. As before, we can form a number of chains:

107a $\langle$Poirot$_i\rangle$, $\langle$PRO$_i\rangle$, $\langle t_i\rangle$
107b $\langle$Poirot$_i$, PRO$_i\rangle$, $\langle t_i\rangle$
107c $\langle$Poirot$_i\rangle$, $\langle$PRO$_i$, $t_i\rangle$
107d $\langle$Poirot$_i$, PRO$_i$, $t_i\rangle$

The theta criterion rules out (107a), (107b), and (107d). In (107a) PRO is not associated with a theta position, and the theta role assigned by *arrested* to its complement is not associated with an argument. In (107b) the chain $\langle$*Poirot$_i$*, PRO$_i\rangle$ contains two arguments, *Poirot* and PRO, and the chain $\langle t_i\rangle$ will be assigned the theta role by *arrested* and does not contain an argument. In (107d) again the chain contains two arguments. In (104f) the only option for chain formation is (107c).

4.6.2 DERIVATIONAL CONCEPTION VS. REPRESENTATIONAL CONCEPTION OF CHAINS

The reader might conclude from the discussion so far that chain formation is inevitably the result of movement and that chains cannot be created independently of movement. In this conception of chains, the so-called **derivational** conception, it is as if a constituent is provided with a derivational history which keeps track of the application of movement. Chains are built in the course of the derivation and encode all the derivational steps. There is another conception of chains (cf. Brody, 1993a, 1993b, Rizzi, 1986c), the **representational** view. In this conception, chains are read off from S-structure, and they do not necessarily reflect the derivational history of the constituent. In this section we shall consider some empirical evidence for the representational conception of chains. Consider first the following sentences from Italian.

108a   Gianni$_i$ è stato affidato t$_i$ a Maria.
       Gianni is been entrusted to Maria
       'Gianni has been entrusted to Maria.'

108b   Gianni$_i$ le è stato affidato t$_i$.
       Gianni to her is been entrusted
       'Gianni has been entrusted to her.'

In (108a) the NP *Gianni* originates as the object of passive *affidato* and moves to [Spec, IP]. This movement creates a two member chain <*Gianni$_i$, t$_i$*>. The verb *affidato* also takes a PP complement *a Maria*. In (108b) the same derivation applies as in (108a), but the indirect object is realized by the element *le*, which is a clitic associated with the finite verb *è*. These examples show clearly that *affidato* selects two complements, the indirect object and the direct object, hence it must assign two theta roles.

Now consider (109):

109a   Gianni$_i$ vede se stesso$_i$ nello speccio.
       Gianni sees himself in the mirror

109b   Gianni$_i$ si$_i$ vede nello specchio.
       Gianni himself sees in the mirror

(109a) is a transitive sentence: the verb *vede* ('sees') takes the reflexive *se stesso* ('himself') as its complement. In (109b) the reflexive is realized by a clitic element, *si*, associated with the inflected verb *vede*. In order to represent the binding relations between the reflexive and its antecedent we coindex the antecedent *Gianni*$_i$ and the reflexive, *se stesso*$_i$ and *si*$_i$, respectively. Now we turn to (108c) and (108d):

108c   Gianni$_i$ è stato affidato t$_i$ a se stesso$_i$.
       Gianni is been entrusted to himself
       'Gianni has been entrusted to himself'
108d   *Gianni$_i$ si$_i$ è stato affidato t$_i$.

(108c) again contains the passive *affidato*, the structure is the same as that in (108a) but in this example the PP complement contains a reflexive, *se stesso*. We might expect that just as was the case in (109) *se stesso* can alternate with its clitic variant *si*, but replacing *se stesso* by the clitic *si* leads to ungrammaticality (cf. Kayne, 1975; Rizzi, 1986c). The ungrammaticality of (108d) is unexpected: after all, we simply combine two patterns which are independently legitimate: (i) passivization as illustrated in the grammatical examples in (108), and (ii) reflexivization with *si* illustrated in (109). The problem cannot be that there is a binding relation with a passivized subject, since this is possible in (108c), nor can it be that the combination of passivization and the clitic construction as such is ungrammatical, since (108b) is a passive sentence containing a clitic. The problem seems to be due to the combination of passivization, which triggers movement of *Gianni*, in the presence of the reflexive clitic. Or, more precisely, the problem concerns the formation of the chain <*Gianni*$_i$, *t*$_i$> across the intervening *si*, which itself is coindexed with the members of the chain. Let us consider this issue more carefully.

There is a local binding condition on chain formation ((105a) and (105c)). This means that in (108d) we will not be able to form a chain which includes *Gianni*, the moved NP, and its trace, without also including the coindexed *si*. The two member chain <*Gianni*$_i$, *t*$_i$> violates (105c): in this chain *Gianni*$_i$ will not locally bind the trace: *si*$_i$ would be a closer binder of *t*$_i$. Apparently we must include *si*$_i$ in the chain. The three member chain <*Gianni*$_i$, *si*$_i$, *t*$_i$> is also illicit: it violates the theta criterion (105d) as defined on chains: it contain two arguments and it receives the two theta roles assigned by *affidato*: that associated with the direct object NP and that associated with the indirect object NP. Needless to say, we also cannot form two chains, the one member chain <*Gianni*$_i$> and the two member chain <*si*$_i$, *t*$_i$>, since this would mean that *Gianni* is not associated with any thematic position. and *si* is associated with two theta roles.

Data such as (108d) are important because they show that apparently chain formation is not based purely on syntactic movement: the chain <*Gianni₁*, *t₁*>, which would be a faithful record of NP-movement of *Gianni* and which would satisfy the theta criterion, cannot be formed.

Rizzi concludes from data such as (108d) and parallel data from Romance that 'chain formation cannot "skip" intervening binders' (Rizzi, 1986c: 71). Data such as these hence offer support for the representational conception of chains. Rizzi says:

> if chains were blind recordings of applications of [movement] nothing would prevent formation of a chain including only [the NP *Gianni*] and its trace . . . and the proposed explanation would be lost. (1986c: 95)

5 Subjects and Derived Subjects

So far we have assumed that unaccusative verbs induce NP-movement, hence that their subjects, i.e. NPs which occupy the [Spec, IP] position, are derived subjects. In this section we consider a proposal which has been gaining ground in the literature where it is argued that subjects of transitive and intransitive verbs are base-generated in [Spec, VP]. This section is based on Sportiche (1988a).

Consider the following French sentences:

110a Tous les garçons ont lu   ce livre.
      all   the boys   have read this book
110b Les garçons ont tous lu   ce livre.
      the boys   have all read this book

(110a) and (110b) are paraphrases. It has often been proposed that they are syntactically related, in the sense that one is derived from the other. One possibility would be that (110b) derives from (110a). In (110b) the quantifier *tous* occupies the position which we have identified as [Spec, VP] (cf. chapter 2). If (110a) were closer to the underlying order of the sentence in (105b) then we would have to assume that *tous* is moved downwards from the subject position [Spec, IP] into the VP.

Alternatively, we might assume that the NP *tous les garçons* originates in the [Spec, VP] position. Under this view both (110a) and (110b) involve movement. In (110a) the NP *tous les garçons* moves as a whole to the [Spec, IP] position, in (110b) only the phrase *les garçons* moves, leaving the quantifier in the [Spec, VP] position. Roughly, the D-structure of the sentence in (110) would be (111) and their S-structures would be (112):

111

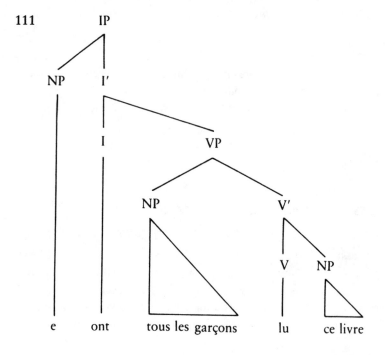

112a

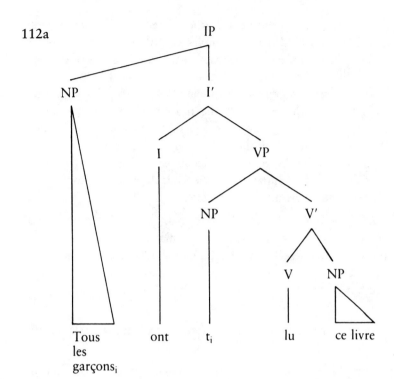

112b

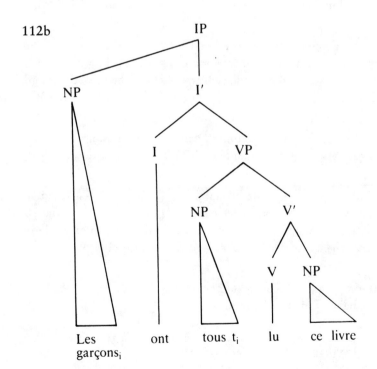

In (112b) *tous* is adjacent to the trace of the moved NP. The movements of the NPs in (112a) and (112b) are examples of NP-movement: an NP is moved to the subject position. Hence the trace of the moved NP is of the type [+anaphor, −pronominal] and subject to Principle A of the BT.

In his discussion of these sentences Sportiche (1988a) provides arguments that the relation between the trace and the moved NP is like that of an anaphor and its antecedent. In (112b) *tous* signals the position of the trace. *Tous* in (112b) is c-commanded by the related NP. The c-command relation is necessary, as illustrated by the ungrammaticality of (113b). In this sentence the NP *ces livres* does not c-command *tous*, hence it does not c-command its trace, which is assumed to be adjacent to *tous*.

113a   L'auteur de tous ces livres a acheté cette maison.
       The author of all these books has bought this house.
113b   *L'auteur de ces livres a tous acheté cette maison.
       *The author of these books has all bought this house.

Second, the quantifier must not be too far removed from the related NP:

114   *Les garçons lui   ont   demandé de [[PRO tous acheter ce   livre]].
       the boys   him have asked   all   to-buy this book

In (114) the NP *les garçons* cannot be related to the quantifier *tous* in the lower clause. Sportiche explains the ungrammaticality of (113b) and of (114) by arguing that the quantifier *tous* is adjacent to a trace of the moved NP and that the trace is a trace of NP-movement, subject to Principle A of the BT.

115a   *L'auteur de [$_{NP}$ ces livres]$_i$ a tous t$_i$ acheté cette maison.
115b   *[$_{NP}$ Les garçons]$_i$ lui ont demandé de [[PRO tous t$_i$ acheter ce livre]].

Sportiche (1988a)[21] proposes that all subject NPs are base-generated in the [Spec, VP] position. Hence a sentence such as (116a) would have the D-structure (116b) and the S-structure (116c). Similarly the English example in (117a) would have the D-structure (117a) and S-structure (117c):

116a   Les filles ont gagné le championnat.
       'The girls have won the championship.'

[21] Similar proposals are discussed in Kitagawa (1986), Kuroda (1986), Koopman and Sportiche (1991) Sportiche (1988a) and Zagona (1982).

116b

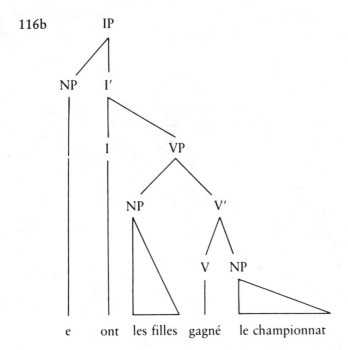

e   ont   les filles   gagné   le championnat

116c

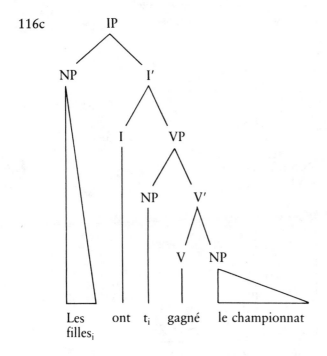

Les   ont t_i gagné   le championnat
filles$_i$

117a   The girls have won the championship.

117b

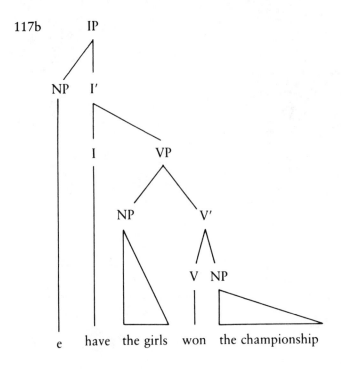

e   have   the girls   won   the championship

117c

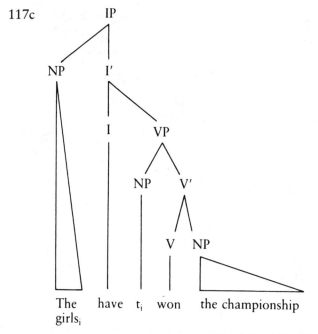

The   have   t$_i$ won   the championship
girls$_i$

The proposal that NPs in [Spec, IP] are derived subjects obviously has considerable consequences for the theory of grammar outlined so far. For instance, the proposal entails that the [Spec, IP] position is always empty at D-structure and is not theta-marked; in other words, it is a θ'-position at D-structure. In addition we can no longer define the external argument of the predicate as that realized outside VP, since all subject NPs will have traces in [Spec, VP]. The classification of verbs discussed in section 3 of this chapter will also have to be revised. If [Spec, VP] is an NP position the question can also be raised whether all NP-movement must pass through it. Finally note that the application of the binding theory as discussed in chapter 4 will also be affected by the subject-in-VP hypothesis. Recall that the definition of governing category makes crucial use of the notion subject. We assume that subjects are specifier positions of IP, AGRP (in the case of small clauses), and NP. We can now add to this the specifier position of VP. Consider, for instance, (118):

118a   John has hurt himself.

In this example the anaphor *himself* is bound by the subject NP *John*. In chapter 4 we simply assumed a representation as in (118b)

118b   John$_i$ has [$_{VP}$ hurt himself$_i$].

This representation does not take into account the subject-in-VP hypothesis developed here. Under such a hypothesis the S-structure of (118b) is (118c).

118c   John$_i$ has [$_{VP}$ t$_i$ hurt himself$_i$].

When we determine the governing category of *himself* we have to look for a governor and a subject. Based on the subject-in-VP hypothesis, these conditions are fulfilled VP-internally: *hurt* is a governor for the reflexive and the trace of the moved subject NP *John* in [Spec, VP] is a subject. Under this view, VP is the governing category for the reflexive and *himself* has to be bound inside VP. *Himself* will be bound by the VP-internal trace, which in turn is bound by *John*.

These, and many other issues are subject to future research. For expository reasons we will often ignore the subject-in-VP-hypothesis in the remaining chapters of this book, unless it substantially affects the line of argumentation. The hypothesis will be relevant, for instance, when we turn to reconstruction in chapter 9, section 3.

6   Summary

This chapter discusses the properties of NP-movement, as illustrated in passive and raising stuctures. NP-movement is case-driven: it affects NPs which cannot be case-marked in their base-position. NP-movement leaves a coindexed trace which is a non-pronominal anaphor, hence subject to Principle A of the binding theory. The moved antecedent NP and the trace form a chain.

Verbs which induce NP-movement are those which lack an external theta role and fail to assign ACCUSATIVE case. These verbs are referred to as unaccusative verbs. The link between the two properties of these verbs is expressed by Burzio's generalization:

1   **Burzio's generalization**
   (i)   A verb which lacks an external argument fails to assign ACCUSA-TIVE case.
        (Burzio, 1986: 178–9)
   (ii) A verb which fails to assign ACCUSATIVE case fails to theta-mark an external argument.
        (Burzio, 1986: 184)

The chapter also examines the relation between the two levels of representation: D-structure and S-structure. The structure preserving principle imposes severe restrictions on the effect of transformations. The theta criterion and the extended projection principle are argued to apply at both D-structure and at S-structure, while case theory and the binding theory apply at S-structure.

In the final section we discuss the proposal that all NPs in [Spec, IP] are in a derived position and are base-generated in [Spec, VP].

7   Exercises

Exercise 1

Discuss the derivation of the following sentences. For each sentence provide a D-structure representation, an S-structure representation, and discuss the assignment of theta roles and of case.

1 The prisoners have been arrested.
2 Poirot seems to like the countryside.
3 George is thought to have been invited to court.
4 They expect Bill to be arrested presently.
5 For Bill to have been arrested so soon was disappointing.
6 I expect that Poirot will be invited.
7 Not to have been invited to court was a real insult.
8 I expect to be invited.
9 John appears to have left.
10 John is likely to leave soon.

We know that subject NPs agree with INFL. At what level of representation will this agreement be determined?

Exercise 2

Consider the Italian examples below. Try to classify the italicized verbs on the basis of the selection of perfective auxiliaries (see section 3). The infinitive of the verb is given in parentheses. What problems, if any, do these examples raise?

1 Maria è già *partita*.   (partire)
  Maria is already left.
2 Maria è *stata* malata.   (essere)
  Maria is been ill
3 Maria ha *guardato* se stessa nello specchio.   (guardare)
  Maria has watched herself in the mirror
  'Maria has looked at herself in the mirror.'
4 Maria s'è *guardata* nello specchio.
  Maria herself is watched in the mirror
  'Maria has looked at herself in the mirror.'

How could the verbs in the following French examples be classified?

5 Maria est déjà *partie*.   (partir)
  Maria is already left
6 Le bateau a *coulé*.   (couler)
  the ship has sunk
7 On   a   *coulé* le   bateau.
  they have sunk   the   ship

8   Maria a *travaillé* longtemps.   (travailler)
    Maria has worked for a long time
9   Maria a *été* malade.   (être)
    Maria has been ill
10 Maria s'est   *regardée* dans le   miroir.   (regarder)
    Maria herself-is watched in   the   mirror
    'Maria has looked at herself in the mirror.'

Discuss the classification of the verbs in the Dutch examples below.

11 Maria is al   *vertrokken.*   (vertrekken)
    Maria is already left
12 Maria heeft lang *gewerkt.*   (werken)
    Maria has   long worked
    'Maria has worked for a long time.'
13 Maria heeft dat   boek   *gekocht.*   (kopen)
    Maria has   that book   bought
    'Maria has bought that book.'
14 Maria is ziek *geweest.*   (zijn)
    Maria is ill   been
    'Maria has been ill.'
15 Maria heeft zichzelf in de spiegel *bekeken.*   (bekijken)
    Maria has   herself in the mirror   watched.

Exercise 3

Discuss the derivation of the following sentences:

1   They got Bill to accept the job.
2   Bill got to accept the job.
3   They got Bill into trouble.
4   Bill got into trouble.
5   They got all their friends invited.
6   All their friends got invited.
7   The robber got himself attacked by Jeeves.

What conclusions can you draw with respect to the argument structure
of *get* in these examples?[22]

---

[22] For discussion see Haegeman (1985).

Exercise 4

We have said that both anaphors and NP-traces are assigned the features [+anaphor, –pronominal]. On the basis of examples that you will construct discuss the similarities and differences between the overt anaphor *himself* and NP-trace.

Exercise 5

Consider the following sentences. For each sentence we offer some possible syntactic representations. Which one is theoretically justified?

1a John tried to go.
1b [IP John$_i$ tried [CP [IP PRO$_i$ to go]]].
1c [IP John$_i$ tried [IP t$_i$ to go]].

2a John seems to be happy.
2b [IP John$_i$ seems [IP t$_i$ to be happy]].
2c [IP John$_i$ seems [CP [IP PRO$_i$ to be happy]]].

3a John is happy to leave.
3b John$_i$ is happy [IP t$_i$ to leave].
3c John$_i$ is happy [IP PRO to leave].
3d John$_i$ is happy [CP [IP PRO to leave]].

Exercise 6

The following sentences are ungrammatical. Why?

1 *John$_i$ seems that Mary likes t$_i$.
2 *John$_i$ seems that he$_i$ is believed t$_i$ to be happy.
3 *I$_i$ believe [IP PRO$_i$ to be happy].
4 *It is believed [IP John$_i$ to have been invited t$_i$].
5 *I$_i$ never cry when [IP PRO$_i$ watch a film].
6 *I$_i$ want [IP John to invite PRO$_i$].
7 *John$_i$ seems that [IP it appears [IP t$_i$ to be happy]].
8 *There hit John.

9   *John$_i$ invited t$_i$.
10   *Himself$_i$ seems to Bill$_i$ to be the best candidate.

Exercise 7

So far we have assumed that *seem* is a verb which selects only one internal argument. Discuss the problems raised for this hypothesis by the following example:

John seems as if he does not like Mary.

Exercise 8

In section 3.2.1 we have seen that *ne*-cliticization data are used as a diagnostic to determine that an NP is in the canonical object position [NP, V′]:

1a   Ne sono stati arrestati tre.
      ne are been arrested three
      'Three of them have been arrested.'
1b   Ne sono arrivati tre.
      ne are arrived three
      'Three of them have arrived.'
1c   *Ne hanno telefonato tre.
      ne have called three

Now consider the following data:

2a   Gianni ha messo [tre libri] [sulla tavola].
      Gianno has put three books on the table
      'Gianni has put three books on the table.'
2b   Gianni ha messo [sulla tavola] [tre libri].
      Gianni has put on the table three books
      'Gianni has put on the table three books.'

3a   ?Ho dato [un libro che mi avevano consigliato la settimana scorsa] [a Gianni].
      have given a book that me they-had suggested last week to Gianni

3b Ho dato [a Gianni] [un libro che mi avevano consigliato la settimana scorsa].
have give to Gianni a book that they me had advised last week
'I gave a book to Gianni which they had suggested to me last week.'

In each of the above pairs we find the order V – NP – PP in the (a) sentences and the order V – PP – NP in the (b) sentences. The question arises how these orders are derived. Discuss this issue using the data of *ne*-cliticization in (4) and (5):

4a Gianni ne ha messi [tre] [sulla tavola].
4b *Gianni ne ha messi [sulla tavola] [tre].

5a ?Ne ho dato [uno che mi avevano consigliato la settimana scorsa] [a Gianni].
5b Ne ho dato [a Gianni] [uno che mi avevano consigliato la settimana scorsa].

The French data in (6)–(9) parallel the Italian data: *en* is the French equivalent of *ne*:

6a Trois hommes sont venus.
three men are come
'Three men have come.'
6b Il en est venu trois.
it *en* is come three
'Three have come.'

7a Trois hommes ont téléphoné.
three men have telephoned
'Three men have called.'
7b *Il en a téléphoné trois. (* with the interpretation: 'Three have telephoned.')
it *en* has telephoned three

8a Ils ont donné [un prix] [à Jean].
they have given a prize to Jean
'They gave Jean a prize.'

8b   Ils en ont donné [un] [à Jean].
     they *en* have given one to Jean
     'They have given one to Jean.'
8c   Ils ont donné [à Jean] [un prix].
8d   *Ils en ont donné [à Jean] [un].

9a   ?Ils ont donné [un livre qu'on avait conseillé à l'Uni] [à Jean].
     they have given a book that one had recommended at the Uni-
        versity to Jean
9b   *Ils en ont donné [un qu'on avait conseillé à l'Uni] [à Jean].
     they *en* have given one that one had recommended at the Uni-
        versity to Jean
9c   Ils ont donné [à Jean] [un livre qu'on avait conseillé à l'Uni].
     they have given to Jean a book that one had recommended at the
        University
     'They gave Jean a book which had been recommended at Univer-
        sity.'
9d   Ils en ont donné [à Jean] [un qu'on avait conseillé à l'Uni].
     they *en* have given to Jean one that one had recommended at the
        University
     'They gave Jean one that had been recommended at the Univer-
        sity.'

From the data given above we are led to conclude that the surface
string V – PP – NP can apparently be generated by different derivations. For a discussion of the phenomena given here the reader is
referred to work by Belletti and Shlonsky (forthcoming) and also
Haegeman (1991).

Exercise 9

When we reconsider the discussion of chain formation in section 4.6.
in the light of the subject-in-VP hypothesis, it turns out that matters are
more complicated than implied in that section. Specifically, since the
ungrammaticality of the text example (108d), repeated here for the
reader's convenience as (1), is ascribed to the fact that the chain
between the moved NP *Gianni* and its trace cannot be established
across *si*, the grammaticality of text example (109b), repeated here as
(2), becomes problematic. Discuss.

1 *Gianni$_i$ si$_i$ è stato affidato t$_i$.
Gianni *si* is been entrusted

2 Gianni$_i$ si$_i$ vede nello specchio.
Gianni *si* sees in the mirror
'Gianni sees himself in the mirror.'

7   *Wh*-Movement

Contents

Introduction and overview

Introduction and Overview

In chapter 6, section 1 we gave a survey of various types of movement. Movement affects either heads or maximal projections. Chapter 6 discussed movement of NPs in passive and raising patterns. In this chapter we turn to *wh*-movement. We discuss the moved constituent, its landing site and the arguments for positing traces in the extraction site. We show that the subjacency condition imposes a constraint on the range of *wh*-movement and is subject to parametric variation. Using the subjacency condition as a diagnostic we show that English relative clauses are derived via *wh*-movement.

We continue to elaborate our typology of empty categories, adding *wh*-traces which are of the type [−anaphor, −pronominal]. From our discussion it follows that heavy NP-shift and PP-extraposition from NP are also instantiations of *wh*-movement.

In section 1 we illustrate *wh*-movement in questions. Section 2 concerns the moved constituent; section 3 the landing site. In section 4 we consider arguments for traces of *wh*-movement. In section 5 we describe some special properties of subject extraction. Section 6 deals with the subjacency condition on movement. In section 7 we turn to the typology of empty categories and in section 8 we discuss heavy NP-shift and PP-extraposition from NP.

1   *Wh*-movement: Some Examples

In chapter 6 section 1.2 we gave a brief analysis of *wh*-questions such as (1).

1   Whom will Lord Emsworth invite?

The *wh*-constituent *whom* is the internal argument of *invite*: it is VP-internal at D-structure. We also assume that the auxiliary *will* is base-generated under I.

2a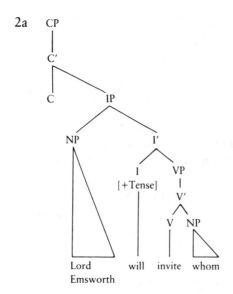

At S-structure, *will* is moved to the position dominated by C by head-to-head movement. Second, and more importantly for the present discussion, *whom* is moved to the sentence-initial position: [Spec, CP]. We postulated that, as was the case for NP-movement discussed in chapter 6, movement of *whom* leaves a coindexed trace. Using the terminology familiar from chapter 6, we call the moved element *whom*$_i$ the **antecedent** of t_i.

2b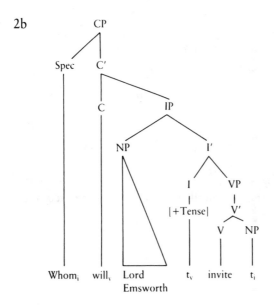

In this chapter we do not deal with the movement of the auxiliary and we concentrate on the movement of elements such as *whom*.[1]

2   *Wh*-Phrases

In this section we discuss some of the main properties of the constituent which undergoes *wh*-movement in interrogative sentences.[2] In each of the *wh*-questions in (3) a constituent is fronted:

3a   [What] will Poirot eat?
3b   [Which detective] will Lord Emsworth invite?
3c   [Whose pig] must Wooster feed?
3d   [Where] will Jeeves live?
3e   [When] will the detective arrive at the castle?
3f   [Why] must Wooster feed the pig?
3g   [To whom] will the police inspector give the money?
3h   [In which folder] does Maigret keep the letters?
3i   [How] will Jeeves feed the pigs?
3j   [How big] will the reward be?

From (3) it is clear that the moved constituent is a phrase. Various types of constituents can move: NPs (3a, b, c), adverb phrases (3d, e, f, i), PPs (3g, h) and APs (3j). As the reader can verify for himself, the moved element may be both an argument of the verb or an adjunct.[3] The moved constituent in (3) will be referred to as a **wh-phrase** or a **wh-constituent**. The motivation for the label is transparent in (3a)–(3h): the moved constituent either consists of, or contains a word beginning with *wh*-. In (3i) and (3j) the *wh*-questions are not introduced by a word which begins with *wh*-, but we can paraphrase the examples using a *wh*-phrase:

4a   [In *what* way] will Jeeves feed the pigs?
4b   [Of *what* size] will the reward be?

---

[1]   For a discussion of the movement of auxiliaries i.e. head-to-head movement, see chapters 10, 11 and 12.
[2]   In sections 6 and 8 we shall see that the range of elements that undergo *wh*-movement includes non-interrogative elements.
[3]   In chapter 9 we shall see that the distinction between arguments and adjuncts is important. We return to this distinction in chapters 10 and 12.

The term *wh*-phrase will also be used to refer to the moved phrases in (3i) and (3j).

Let us consider the structure of the *wh*-phrases more carefully. In (3a), (3d), (3e), (3f) and (3i) the *wh*-element is itself the head of the moved phrase (cf. (5a)). In (3b), (3c) and (3j) the *wh*-element is the specifier of the moved phrase (5b). We turn to the PPs in (3g) and (3h) presently.

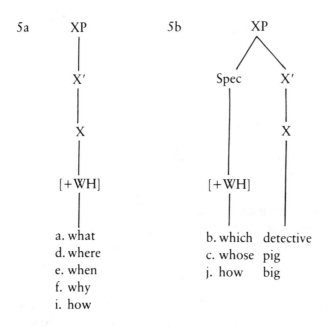

5a

a. what
d. where
e. when
f. why
i. how

5b

b. which detective
c. whose pig
j. how big

Since the nature of the phrase is determined by the nature of the head it follows that a phrase containing an interrogative element as its head will be characterized as an interrogative phrase or a *wh*-phrase for short. Let us say that an interrogative word carries a feature [+WH]. We have discussed the projection of phrases in chapter 2. The properties of the phrase are determined by the properties of the head. If a head of a phrase is specified as [+WH] the phrase will also be specified as [+WH]: the WH-feature **percolates** from the head of the phrase to the maximal projection.

In (5b) the phrase XP whose [Spec, XP] contains a *wh*-word and is interpreted as an interrogative phrase or a *wh*-phrase. We conclude that the features of the specifier also determine the features of the entire phrase. This should not surprise us too much. We have already seen (in chapter 2) that there is often agreement between head and specifier, for gender and number for instance. We can assume that features of the specifier are assigned to the head of the phrase and percolate to the maximal projection.[4]

In (3g) and (3h) the moved PPs are of the following form:

6   PP

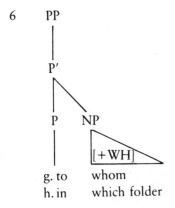

      g. to   whom
      h. in   which folder

The presence of a *wh*-phrase as the complement of the preposition apparently suffices to allow the PP to undergo *wh*-movement. We might propose that the [+WH] feature of the NP percolates to the PP.

Compare (3g) and (3h) with the examples in (7):

7a   [$_{NP_i}$ Whom] will the police inspector give the money to?
7b   [$_{NP_i}$ Which folder] does Maigret keep the letters in?

In (7) the *wh*-phrase is moved out of the PP; the head of the PP is left behind. The phenomenon in which a preposition is left behind after its complement has been moved out is called **preposition-stranding**. The phenomenon where the preposition is moved along with the complement NP is referred to as **pied-piping**: the preposition is pied-piped with the NP in (3g) and (3h). In English pied-piping of prepositions is always legitimate. Preposition-stranding is restricted, as the following examples show:[5]

8a   ?*Which party did Poirot meet Maigret after?
8b   ?*Whose office did the inspectors discuss the crime in?

---

[4]   Abney (1987) proposes that NPs should be reinterpreted as projections of the deter-miner. If this analysis were to be adopted it would obviously also follow that a phrase whose determiner is [+WH] is itself characterized as [+WH] (cf. chapter 11).
[5]   See Hornstein and Weinberg (1981) and Kayne (1984) for discussion.

The possibility of preposition-stranding is subject to cross-linguistic variation, as illustrated in the following examples:

9a *French*
    *Qui   as-tu   parlé   de?
    who   have-you   talked   about
    'Who did you talk about?'
    vs. De qui as-tu parlé?
9b *Italian*
    *Cui   hai   parlato di?
    who   have-you   talked   about
    vs. Di cui hai parlato?

The question that should be answered is what explains the difference between languages with preposition-stranding, such as English, and languages without, such as Italian and French. Ideally the difference should be related to some difference in parameter setting between the languages.[6] We do not discuss this issue here.

3   The Landing Site of *Wh*-Movement

In this section we discuss where the constituent which is affected by *wh*-movement is moved to, i.e. its **landing site.**

3.1   *Long vs. Short Movement*

Consider the following example:

10   Whom do you believe [$_{CP_j}$ that [Lord Emsworth$_k$ will invite]]?

(10) is a complex sentence. *Believe* takes two arguments: the external argument is realized by its subject *you*, the internal argument is clausal (CP_j). We have already seen that *invite* takes two arguments. The external argument is

---

[6]   Kayne (1984), for example, relates the difference between English and other languages to the fact that in English prepositions assign structural ACCUSATIVE while in other languages prepositions assign an inherent case.

realized by the NP *Lord Emsworth*. It seems natural to say that *whom* is the internal argument. On this assumption, the D-structure of (10) should be (11a).

11a

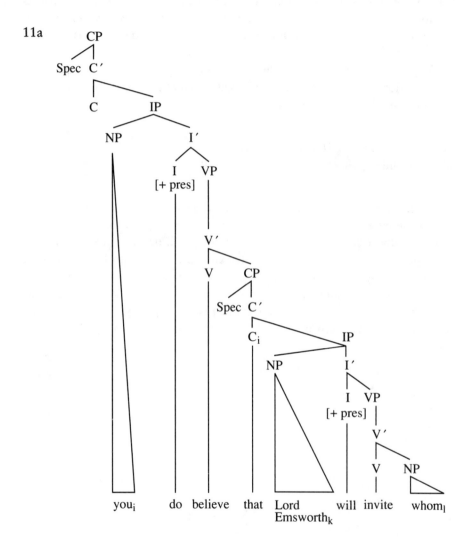

Under the subject-in-VP hypothesis, *Lord Emsworth* would originate in [Spec, VP] and move to its position in [Spec, IP]. We leave this aspect of the derivation aside for expository reasons.

At S-structure *whom* is moved from the lower clause to the [Spec, CP] of the higher clause, leaving a coindexed trace in its base-position (t_l). In addition the auxiliary *do* is moved to C.

11b   [CP Whom₁ do [IP you₁ believe [CPⱼ that [IP Lord Emsworthⱼ will invite tₗ]]]]?

The difference between our earlier examples such as (1) and (3), where a *wh*-element moves to the [Spec, CP] position of the sentence in which it is theta-marked, and examples such as (11), where it moves beyond its own clause to the [Spec, CP] of a higher clause, is often made in terms of **short vs. long movement**.

We assume that the reader is familiar with the contrast between direct or **root** questions such as the ones discussed so far and indirect or embedded questions as illustrated in (12):

12a   He wonders [if [Lord Emsworth will invite Poirot]].
12b   I wonder [whom [Lord Emsworth will invite]].

One property that distinguishes root questions from embedded questions is that in the latter the auxiliary does not move: in (12) *will* has not inverted with the subject NP. The D-structure for (12a) will be as in (13). *Wonder* is a two-place predicate, which assigns its external theta role to *he*, the subject, and the internal theta role to the interrogative clause which it governs. The realization of the arguments of *invite* is unproblematic: the external argument is the subject NP and the internal argument is the object NP. The S-structure of the sentence will also be as in (13) since no constituents are moved.

13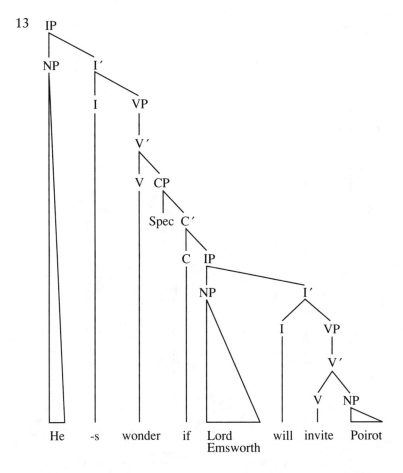

What about (12b)? Based on the preceding discussion we propose that the D-structure and the S-structure of (12b) are (14a) and (14b) respectively:

14a

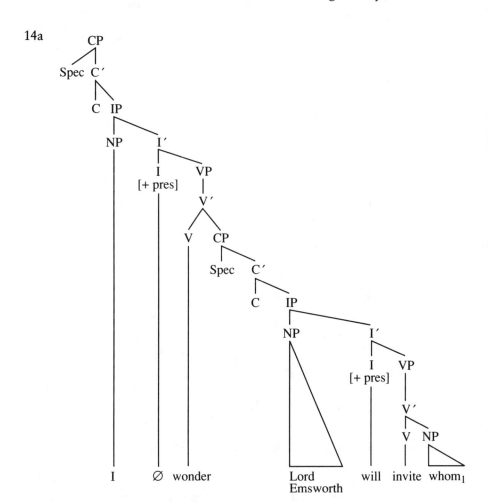

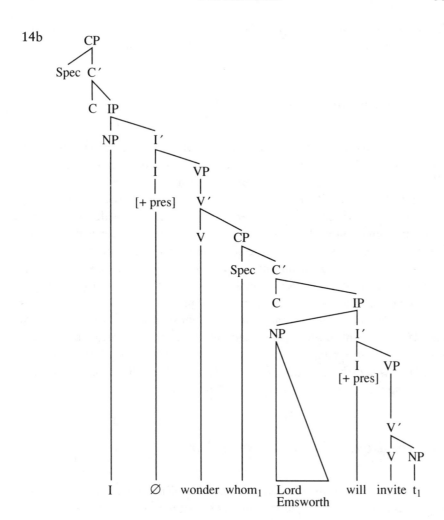

(14) exemplifies short *wh*-movement in embedded questions. The reader is invited to provide a description of the syntactic representation of (15), which is an example of long *wh*-movement in embedded questions:

15 I wonder whom they believe that Lord Emsworth will invite.

3.2 C-command

When we consider the configurational relation between the antecedent of *wh*-movement and the trace we see that, as in the case of NP-movement (cf.

chapter 6, section 2.3.2), the *wh*-antecedent c-commands its trace. We leave it to the reader to verify this in the preceding examples.

3.3   Wh-movement and Substitution

We have been assuming that the landing site of *wh*-movement is [Spec, CP]. The motivation for this proposal was discussed briefly in chapter 2.

A first and rather natural assumption is that an element moves into an unoccupied position. Remember that we adopted the structure preserving principle for transformations (chapter 6, section 4.1). Considering that *wh*-movement moves phrasal projections of different categories, it is not reasonable to claim that all these categorially distinct *wh*-constituents move to a position that is labelled for one specific category. Rather, the landing site for *wh*-movement must be a position which is not specified for the phrasal category. [Spec, CP] is just such a position: the phrase structure rules allow us to project the position but they do not identify it for a specific phrasal category. A non-filled [Spec, CP] can receive phrasal constituents of any syntactic category: NP, AP, etc. The proposal developed here treats *wh*-movement as substitution: the *wh*-phrase fills a hitherto unoccupied position. In this respect, *wh*-movement is like NP-movement.

3.4   The Doubly Filled COMP Filter

In chapter 2 we have already given empirical evidence for taking [Spec, CP], the position to the left of C, as the landing site of *wh*-movement: in many languages we find sequences of a *wh*-word followed by an overt complementizer:

16a   *Dutch*
      Ik   weet   niet   *wie*   *of*   Jan   gezien   heeft.
      I   know   not   whom   whether   Jan   seen   has
      'I don't know whom Jan has seen.'
16b   *Flemish* (a dialect of Dutch)[7]
      Ik   weet   niet   *wie*   dat   Jan   gezien   heeft.
      I   know   not   whom   that Jan   seen   has
      'I don't know whom Jan has seen.'

---

[7]   For discussion see Haegeman (1992).

16c *Bavarian German*[8]

    I woass ned *wann dass* da Xavea kummt.

    I know not when that Xavea comes

    'I don't know when Xavea is coming.'

    (Bayer, 1984a: 24)

16d *Early English*:

    men shal wel knowe *who that* I am

    'Men will know well who I am.'

    (Caxton, 1485, R 67, in Lightfoot, 1979: 322)

In modern English there appears to be a restriction barring the occurrence of a *wh*-phrase in [Spec, CP] when the head of this CP is filled by an overt complementizer. In the literature this constraint is formulated as a filter: the **doubly filled COMP filter**.

17 **Doubly filled COMP filter**[9]

    When an overt *wh*-phrase occupies the Spec of some CP the head of that CP must not dominate an overt complementizer.

The label doubly filled COMP was associated with the earlier analysis of clauses as S'. In this type of analysis the positions [Spec, CP] and C were not clearly distinguished. It was assumed that both the complementizer and the moved element in (16) were dominated by the node COMP. For (16a), for instance, the relevant S-structure would have been as in (18).[10]

18

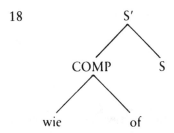

---

[8] For discussion of the Bavarian data, see Bayer (1984a, 1984b).

[9] The doubly filled COMP filter was first formulated in Chomsky and Lasnik (1977).

[10] There are a number of alternative analyses for the structure of the data in (16). (18) is only one example. We leave these divergencies out of the discussion here since they have become obsolete.

Following the convention in the current literature, we maintain the label doubly filled COMP filter here and reinterpret it according to the CP-analysis of clauses as suggested in (17).[11]

The hypothesis that the landing site of *wh*-movement is the position [Spec, CP], leads us to expect that only one element can be moved to occupy this position:

19a   John wondered which book Bill bought for whom.
19b   John wondered for whom Bill bought which book.
19c   *John wondered for whom which book Bill bought.
19d   *John wondered which book for whom Bill bought.

(19c) and (19d) will be ruled out by our grammar since two phrases would have to be moved to [Spec, CP]. Recall that we cannot move a phrase under C because C is a head position. Multiple movement is not possible in English.

However, there are examples from Polish which are problematic (Lasnik and Saito, 1984: 280):

20   Maria zastanawiala się,   kto   co   przyniesie.
     Maria wondered   who   what   would-bring
     'Maria wondered who would bring what.'

(20) illustrates **multiple *wh* movement**: in this case two *wh* phrases have been moved to sentence-initial position. In the next section we shall discuss one possible derivation for (20).

3.5   *Adjunction*

3.5.1   GENERAL DISCUSSION

Recall, first of all, our discussion of the structure preserving principle in chapter 6, section 4.1. We have seen that the structure preserving principle does not allow us to destroy existing structure by movement operations, but that it does not exclude that structure be added as long as the resulting representations are compatible with the principles of our grammar. We briefly discussed one example where new structure is generated: free subject inversion

---

[11]   As it stands (17) is non-explanatory. It would, of course, be preferable if it could be derived from some general principle.

in Italian. In this section we shall discuss the proposal that *wh*-movement also sometimes creates a new position.

We first provide a general discussion of adjunction structures. Schematically D-structure representations are like (21):

21

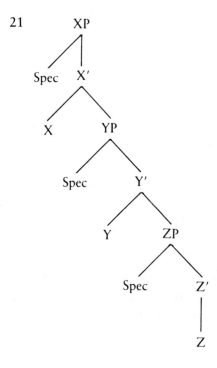

For the sake of generality, we leave aside which phrasal categories are involved and what their functions might be. Assume that the constituent ZP is going to be moved and that it cannot be moved INTO a position. This means we must create a new position for ZP. Following the discussion of *wh*-movement so far we assume that moved elements c-command their traces. Suppose ZP moves somewhere in the vicinity of the topmost node, XP.

22a

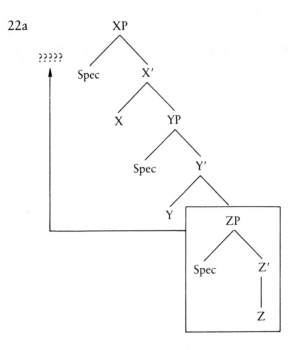

We need to create a node for the moved ZP but in doing so we must respect all the principles of the grammar, specifically the X'-format for phrase structure. One option is to attach ZP in the following way:

22b

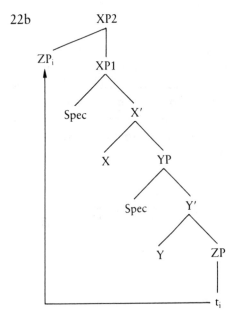

In (22b) a new node XP, identified for convenience' sake as XP2, is created, dominating the original XP, XP1, and the moved element is attached there. As mentioned briefly in chapter 6, section 4.1, this operation is referred to as **adjunction**. Adjunction respects our phrase structure theory: the new constituent XP is headed by X. The node XP created by adjunction is binary branching, etc.

Let us go into the relation between XP and ZP more carefully. There are two nodes XP. XP1 is the original maximal projection. It is sometimes called the **base maximal projection**. XP2 dominates the base maximal projection XP1 and the adjoined ZP. ZP is dominated by the topmost maximal projection XP2, but it is not dominated by the base maximal projection XP1. YP in contrast is dominated both by XP1 and by XP2. In a way, YP is completely inside the projection of X, YP is **included** in the projection of X. ZP is only partly inside the projection of X, it is not fully part of the projection of X.

In chapter 2 we proposed that syntactic representations be described in terms of dominance and precedence. We may wonder whether the maximal projection of X in our adjunction structure above can be said to dominate the adjoined ZP. Roughly speaking, the answer is 'partly'. Let us adopt the proposal formulated by Chomsky (1986b: 7) based on May (1985) to define the notion **dominance**:

23 **Dominance**
    A is dominated by B only if A is dominated by every segment of B.

A is ZP in our example, B is the maximal projection of X. The idea, informally, is that in (22b) the maximal projection of X is the combination of XP1 and XP2. ZP is not dominated by every **segment** of the maximal projection of X: ZP is dominated by the topmost XP2, but it is not dominated by the base maximal projection XP1.

Even though ZP is not dominated by the maximal projection of X, it is not entirely outside the maximal projection of X, being dominated by the topmost segment XP2. Because ZP is dominated by a segment of XP, we say that ZP is not **excluded** from XP. Following Chomsky (1986b) **exclusion** is defined as follows:

24 **Exclusion**
    B excludes A if no segment of B dominates A.

Speaking metaphorically, we could say that a position created by adjunction is like a balcony: when on a balcony you are neither completely outside the room nor completely inside. You may, for instance, easily participate in conversations going on inside while at the same time get dripping wet if it is raining outside.

A restriction imposed on adjunction by Chomsky (1986b) is that phrases can only be adjoined to maximal projections and that adjunction can only be to non-arguments.

We have gone in some detail into the notion adjunction because it will be relevant also for section 8 below and for subsequent chapters.

3.5.2 *WH*-MOVEMENT AS ADJUNCTION?

Let us return to multiple movement in the Polish example (20) repeated here as (25a):

25a   Maria zastanawiala się, [kto   co   przyniesie].
      Maria wondered   who what   would-bring
      'Maria wondered who would bring what.'

The bracketed indirect question is introduced by two *wh*-phrases *co* ('what') and *kto* ('who'). Consider also (26a) (from Lasnik and Saito, 1984: 238, (11)).

26a   Maria myśli [że co [$_{\rm IP}$ Janek kupi€ t]]?
      Maria thinks that what Janek bought
      'What does Maria think that Janek bought?'

Since *co* follows the complementizer *ze* and precedes the subject *Janek* in (26a), it obviously is not in [Spec, CP]. Let us assume that *co* is adjoined to IP. Adjoined positions are A'-positions. The relevant part of the structure of (26a) would be (26b).

26b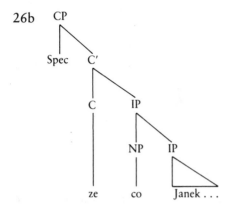

For (25a) we propose that *co* is also adjoined to IP, and that *kto*, which precedes it, has been moved to [Spec, CP]:

25b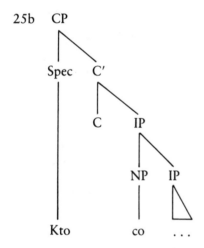

Note that neither (25b) nor (26b) violates the doubly filled COMP filter: in (26a) the position dominated by C is occupied, but [Spec, CP] is not; in (25b) [Spec, CP] dominates overt material but C does not.

An adjunction analysis of *wh*-movement in the Polish examples (25) and (26) allows us to derive sentences with multiple movement.[12] Polish differs crucially from English in that the former, though not the latter, allows for multiple movement:

---

[12] The Polish data are discussed for the purpose of exemplification. It is quite conceivable that the analysis proposed here is not the optimal analysis. For discussion of *wh*-movement in the Slavic languages the reader is referred to Rudin (1989), Toman (1981), and Wachowicz (1974).

27a   *I wonder what to whom John gave.
27b   *I wonder to whom what John gave.

In order to exclude examples of multiple movement at S-structure in English (and similar languages) we assume that in English *wh*-movement is done by substitution: the moved phrase moves into [Spec, CP].[13] We could then argue that whether *wh*-movement operates through adjunction or not is a matter of parametric variation.

3.5.3   A NOTE ON SOME ALTERNATIVE PROPOSALS

Adjunction has played an important role in a number of recent developments of the theory, as we shall also see in chapters 9 and 10. However, more recently proposals have been put forward to constrain adjunction possibilities severely (cf. Kayne, 1993). We do not go into these developments in detail. Let us just return for one moment to the problem raised in (22a), repeated here as (28a). The question we addressed above was where ZP could move to in the structure (28a). Let us assume that KP occupies [Spec, XP].

28a

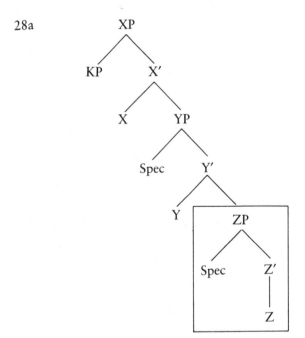

---

[13]   In earlier versions of the theory an adjunction analysis had also been adopted for *wh*-movement in English (see Chomsky, 1980, 1981a) but such an analysis has been abandoned. Lasnik and Saito (1984), which is to a large extent the basis of chapter 9 of this book, still assume an adjunction analysis for English. In chapter 9 their discussion is reinterpreted in terms of substitution.

One option, developed in section 3.5.1, is to propose that ZP adjoins to XP, creating a new segment XP. An alternative approach could be that we do not adjoin ZP to XP, i.e. the dominating projection, but rather that we adjoin it to KP, the specifier of XP. Recall that specifiers dominate maximal projections. If we can adjoin a maximal projection to another maximal projection then ZP could adjoin to KP, the specifier of XP, resulting in a structure like (28b):

28b

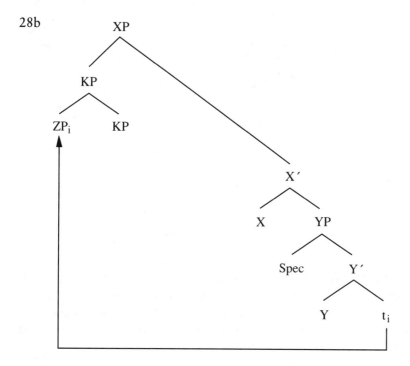

In (28b) we create an adjunction structure on KP, which would have the same properties as the adjunction structure discussed in section 3.5.1. Notably, ZP would not be dominated by KP, because it is only dominated by one segment of KP, but, on the other hand, KP does not exclude ZP, since one segment of KP dominates ZP. Structures such as (28b) have also been used in the literature.

A final more radical approach would be to propose that when we move ZP it must always move to a specifier postion, and that specifier–head relations are bi-unique, i.e. there is one specifier to one head. If such a constraint is imposed on our grammar then the leftward movement of ZP in (28a) would force us not simply to create a segment of a maximal projection to which the ZP constituent can adjoin, but rather to create a full projection, i.e. a maximal projection with its own head. The maximal projection which would have to be created would not have a lexical head. If there had been a lexical head (say, V, or P) available, then the maximal projection would have been projected at D-structure. Rather the maximal projection we create would have an abstract functional head. (28c) would be such a structure:

28c

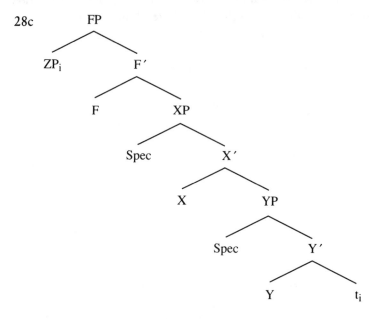

We return to the role of functional heads in chapter 11. We do not pursue the problem of the restrictions on adjunction here. Obviously the choice between the different types of structures will have conceptual and empirical implications. (Cf. Kayne 1993 for a very restrictive theory in which adjunction structures are heavily constrained.)

3.6 *Movement of Maximal Projections: A-movement vs. A′-movement*

At this point it may be useful to summarize the discussion of movement so far and to compare the landing site of NP-movement, discussed in chapter 6, and that of *wh*-movement, discussed in this chapter.

29a Poirot$_i$ will be invited t$_i$.
29b Poirot$_i$ seems t$_i$ to be the best detective.

30a Who/Whom$_i$ do you think Lord Emsworth will invite t$_i$?
30b Who$_i$ do you think t$_i$ is the best detective?

(29) illustrates NP-movement. An NP is moved to the subject postion, an A-position. (30) illustrates *wh*-movement: a *wh*-element is moved to [Spec, CP], an A'-position. Based on the distinction in landing sites, we say that the chain created by NP-movement is an **A-chain** and that created by *wh*-movement is an **A'-chain**. We distinguish the antecedents of the two types of movement in terms of A-antecedent vs. A'-antecedent. The antecedent of NP-movement c-commands its coindexed trace: we say that it **A-binds** the trace. In the case of *wh*-movement the antecedent also c-commands the coindexed trace, but it occupies an A'-position: *wh*-antecedents **A'-bind** their traces (cf. section 7). Movement to an A-position is **A-movement**; movement to an A'-position is **A'-movement**.

4   Traces and *Wh*-Movement

As was the case for NP-movement, *wh*-movement leaves a trace coindexed with its A'-antecedent. We refer to traces of *wh*-movement as *wh*-traces and to traces of NP-movement as NP-traces. In this section we provide some arguments for postulating *wh*-traces. Our reasoning in the chapter is closely parallel to that used in chapter 6 to motivate NP-traces.

4.1   *Theta Theory and the Projection Principle*

One motivation for *wh*-traces is analogy: having posited that NP-movement leaves traces it seems reasonable to also adopt this proposal for *wh*-movement. A second argument comes from theta theory. In chapter 6, section 4.2, we argued that the theta criterion applies to all syntactic levels. Internal theta roles are assigned by the lexical head under government. In an S-structure representation such as (31) *invite* will not be able to theta-mark *whom*, but it will assign the internal theta role to its trace.

31   Whom$_i$ do$_v$ you t$_v$ believe that Lord Emsworth will invite t$_i$?

4.2   *Agreement and Binding*

In chapter 6, we provided some arguments for postulating NP-traces, based on locality constraints on syntactic processes. The same type of arguments can be advanced in favour of coindexed *wh*-traces:

32a Poirot thinks [the sergeants are lousy detectives/*is a lousy detective].
32b Which sergeants$_i$ does Poirot think [t$_i$ are lousy detectives]?

33a Poirot thinks [the sergeants have left together].
33b Which sergeants$_i$ does Poirot think [t$_i$ have left together]?

34a Poirot thinks [the sergeants have done the job their/*his own way].
34b Which sergeants$_i$ does Poirot think [t$_i$ have done the job their/*his own way]?

35a Poirot thinks [the sergeants have invited them for lunch].
35b Who$_i$ does Poirot think [t$_i$ have invited them for lunch]?

In the (b) examples above a *wh*-constituent has been moved from the lower finite clause to the [Spec, CP] of a higher clause. In all cases a subject NP is moved (we return to movement of the subject in section 5).

The finite verb in the lower clause is plural and must be plural for all the sentences above. This can only be explained if the subject of the verb is plural. We assume that subject–verb agreement is a local process, i.e. that each verb agrees with its own (clause-mate) subject. Under this assumption postulating a coindexed *wh*-trace in the lower subject position enables us to state the agreement rule in a maximally simple way. Note that this again means that traces have nominal features such as number and person.

In (32) the lower clause contains the copula *be* and a predicate NP. As (32a) shows, the predicate NP agrees in number with the subject of its clause. Postulating a coindexed trace in (32b) allows us to maintain that subject–predicate agreement is constained by a clause-mate condition.

In (33) the lower clause contains the adjunct *together* which must be related to a clause-mate plural NP. The coindexed trace resulting from *wh*-movement will serve as the relevant NP.

In (34a), the antecedent for anaphoric *their* in *in their own way* is local: it is the subject of the clause. *Poirot*, for instance, cannot serve as the antecedent of *his* in *in his own way* in the lower clause. Postulating a subject trace in the lower clause of (34b) allows us to state the anaphoric relation maximally simply.

In (35a) Principle B of the binding theory predicts that *them* in the lower clause cannot be coreferential with the NP *the sergeants* (see chapter 4 and the discussion of the level of application of Principle B in section 4.5). In (35b) *who* is not inside the GC of *them*. If we assume that there is a *wh*-trace coindexed with *who* in the subject position of the lower clause then we predict that *them* must not be coreferential with *who*.

4.3 Case

4.3.1 *WH*-PRONOUNS AND CASE

We have seen that abstract case is often not morphologically realized in English. For the *wh*-element *what*, for instance, there is no overt difference between the NOMINATIVE and the ACCUSATIVE, as the following echo questions demonstrate:

36a I think that the castle will be destroyed.
36b You think that WHAT will be destroyed?

37a I think that Lord Emsworth will sell the pig.
37b You think that Lord Emsworth will sell WHAT?

The situation with *who* is different:

38a I think that Poirot will arrive first.
38b You think that WHO/*WHOM will arrive first?

39a I think that Lord Emsworth will invite Poirot.
39a You think that Lord Emsworth will invite WHO/WHOM?

In (38b) the echo question contains a *wh*-constituent in the lower subject position: only *who* is admitted, *whom* is disallowed. In (39b) the *wh*-constituent occupies the object position: both *who* and *whom* are possible in spoken English, in writing *whom* is used. Putting aside many complications with respect to the use of *who/whom* here, we assume that the NOMINATIVE case is morphologically realized as *who* and that the ACCUSATIVE is realized either as *who* or as *whom*. Given this assumption let us turn to (40):

40a Who/*Whom$_i$ do you think t$_i$ will arrive first?
40b Who/Whom$_i$ do you believe that Lord Emsworth will invite t$_i$?

In (40a) the moved *wh*-phrase is NOMINATIVE; in (40b) it is ACCUSATIVE. In English NOMINATIVE and ACCUSATIVE are assigned at S-structure and under government (see chapter 3 for discussion). Neither in (40a) nor in (40b) do the case assigners, the finite I and the transitive verb *invite* respectively, govern the moved *wh*-phrase. But the traces of *who* and *whom* are governed by the relevant case assigners. We adopt the idea that the trace of *wh*-movement is case-marked. The case on the trace will make the theta position visible and will allow the verb to assign its theta role.

4.3.2   WH-TRACE VS. NP-TRACE: MORE CONTRASTS

Let us briefly compare *wh*-traces and NP-traces with respect to the assignment of case.

41a   Poirot$_i$ will be invited t$_i$.
41b   Poirot$_i$ seems t$_i$ to be the best detective.

42a   Who/Whom$_i$ do you think Lord Emsworth will invite t$_i$?
42b   Who$_i$ do you think t$_i$ is the best detective?

   NP-traces are not assigned case. In (41a) the passive verb fails to case-mark its complement NP and in (41b) unaccusative *seem* is unable to case-mark the subject of the lower non-finite clause. The *wh*-traces in (42) are case-marked: the verb *invite* in (42a) assigns ACCUSATIVE case to its complement; the finite I in (42b) assigns NOMINATIVE to the *wh*-trace in the subject position. The situation of the antecedent of the trace is reversed: in the case of NP-movement the antecedent is assigned case. In the case of *wh*-movement the antecedent is not in a position to which case is assigned.

   (43) summarizes the comparison between NP-movement which is A-movement and *wh*-movement, which in A′-movement.

43a   A-movement; NP-movement
       A-chain
       Antecedent (head of the chain):   +Case
       Trace (foot of the chain):   −Case
43b   A′-movement; *wh*-movement
       A′-chain
       Antecedent: −Case
       Trace: +Case

   By simply inspecting the head or the foot of a chain we can identify the type of movement and its properties. Chapter 8 offers a more detailed comparison between the two kinds of movement.

4.4 Adjunct Traces

So far we have only discussed *wh*-traces of arguments. Adjunct phrases are also subject to *wh*-movement:

44   When did you tell her that Bill is coming?

In the sentence-initial position of (44) we have the temporal adjunct *when*. *When* can be related to, or **construed with,** the activity expressed in the matrix clause, i.e. 'telling', or with that in the subordinate clause, 'coming'. The trace of the moved phrase will indicate which clause the time adjunct modifies. (45b) and (45d) suggest the type of answer for each interpretation:

45a   When$_i$ did you tell her t$_i$ [that Bill is coming]?
45b   I told her yesterday that Bill is coming.
45c   When$_i$ did you tell her [that Bill is coming t$_i$]?
45d   I told her that Bill is coming tomorrow.

5   Subject Movement

In this section we turn to two problems related to *wh*-movement from subject position. Both phenomena will be described here and will be discussed in more detail in chapters 8, 9, 10 and 12.

5.1 Vacuous Movement

Let us look at sentences in which the subject is questioned.

46a   Who$_i$ do you think [t$_i$ will arrive first]?
46b   Who will arrive first?

In (46a), an example of long subject movement, *who* has been extracted from the subject position of the lower clause, leaving a coindexed trace. In (46b) matters are not so obvious. In the literature two contrasting proposals have been put forward: it is usually assumed that, by analogy with object movement and long subject movement, the subject *wh*-phrase also moves in examples such as (46b). Under this view the S-structure representation of (46b) will be (47):

47   [$_{CP}$ Who$_i$ [$_{IP}$ t$_i$ will arrive first]]?

In contrast with the long subject movement in (46a), the effect of short movement in (46b) cannot be observed on the surface string, t_i having no phonetic content. Movement transformations whose effects cannot be observed are referred to as instances of **vacuous movement**. Chomsky (1986b: 48–54) argues that the vacuous movement analysis of *wh*-questions such as (46b) may not be the optimal analysis. Apart from a number of empirical arguments which we shall not discuss here,[14] Chomsky advances an argument from language acquisition. The child who is acquiring a language uses overt evidence for constructing the grammar and the syntactic representations of sentences. The child acquiring English and faced with a sentence like (46b) has no overt evidence for assuming that the subject *who* has moved. An S-structure like (48) would be equally compatible with the evidence:

48   [$_{CP}$ [$_{IP}$ Who will arrive first]]?

We continue to adopt the vacuous movement hypothesis, but will occasionally refer to the alternative proposal (48).

5.2   The That-*trace Filter*

Consider the following examples:

49a   Whom$_i$ do you think [$_{CP}$ that [$_{IP}$ Lord Emsworth will invite t$_i$]]?
49b   Whom$_i$ do you think [$_{CP}$ [$_{IP}$ Lord Emsworth will invite t$_i$]]?

50a   *Who$_i$ do you think [$_{CP}$ that [$_{IP}$ t$_i$ will arrive first]]?
50b   Who$_i$ do you think [$_{CP}$ [$_{IP}$ t$_i$ will arrive first]]?

For most speakers[15] there is an asymmetry between the sentences in (49) where an object is extracted and those in (50) where a subject is extracted.

[14]   We return to the issue in chapter 10. See also Chomsky (1986b: 48–54) and George (1980).
[15]   There is a lot of idiolectal variation which we shall not go into here. An interesting survey of intuitions is given in Sobin (1987). This paper presupposes chapter 8.

In (49) it does not matter whether the head of the lower CP is overtly realized or not; in (50) we can only extract a subject from inside a lower clause provided there is no overt complementizer. (50a) is ruled out in Chomsky and Lasnik (1977) by means of a filter:

51   *That*-trace filter
     The sequence of an overt complementizer followed by a trace is ungrammatical.

As it stands, the filter does not explain anything: it merely states that the sequence *that* – *t* is ungrammatical. In chapters 8, 9, 10 and 12 we shall see how a more principled account for the filter can be proposed. Let us consider some data which raise problems for (51).

In Italian the complementizer *che* can introduce a sentence from which a subject has been extracted. As shown in the Introduction, this is not evidence against the *that*-trace filter. Recall that subject NPs in Italian may also occur post-verbally; it is hence conceivable that *chi* in the Italian example (52) is extracted from the post-verbal position.[16]

52   *Italian*
     Chi   credi   che   venga?
     who   you-think   that come (SUBJ)
     'Who do you think is coming?'

Like English, French does not allow the complementizer *que* to introduce sentences from which the subject has been moved. In (53a) we need to replace the complementizer *que* by the form *qui*. This has come to be known as the **que-qui rule** (Pesetsky, 1981), which we discuss in chapter 8, section 4.1.2.

53   *French*
     a   *Qui crois-tu   que   viendra?
         who think-you   that will-come

[16] For (52) we could propose the following rough S-structure:

(i)   Chi$_i$ credi [$_{CP}$ che [$_{IP}$ e [$_{VP}$ venga t$_i$]]]?
      (cf. chapter 6, section 3)

The empty subject position marked by *e* would be a non-overt expletive. See also the Introduction and chapter 8. For a full discussion of the Italian data the reader is referred to Rizzi (1982c).

b Qui   crois-tu   qui   viendra?
   who   think-you 'who' will-come
   'Who do you think will come?'.

In Dutch there is a lot of dialectal variation as indicated by the diacritic %: some dialects allow the sequence *dat*-trace, others do not.

54 *Dutch*
    %Wie denk je   dat   dat   boek gekocht heeft?
    who   think you   that that book bought   has
    'Who do you think has bought that book?'

   Leaving aside the cross-linguistic variation and returning to English, we see that the *that*-trace filter in (51) can also account for the judgements in (55):

55a I would prefer Bill to come first.
55b Who would you prefer to come first?
55c I would prefer for Bill to come first.
55d *Who would you prefer for to come first?

The ungrammaticality of (55d) can be related to the ban on a sequence complementizer-trace:

55e *Who$_i$ would you prefer [$_{CP}$ for [$_{IP}$ t$_i$ to come first]]?

6 Bounding Theory

6.1 Island Constraints: The Data

Consider (56), an example of *wh*-movement:

56 [$_{CP}$ How$_i$ did [$_{IP}$ you say [$_{CP}$ that [$_{IP}$ Jeeves thinks [$_{CP}$ that [$_{IP}$ Lord Emsworth will solve this problem t$_i$]]]]]].

The *wh*-phrase *how* is moved from inside the lowest clause and ends up in the matrix [Spec, CP]. Research initiated by Ross in the 1960s (Ross, 1967) has shown that *wh*-movement is not unconstrained. In this section we shall consider the central data. In later sections we shall provide an analysis of the data.

6.1.1 THE COMPLEX NP CONSTRAINT

Consider the data in (57). (57a) and (57b) are grammatical, (57c), which is closely similar in structure and in interpretation to (57b), is not.

57a $[_{CP}$ Who$_i$ did $[_{IP}$ he see t$_i$ last week]]?

57b $[_{CP}$ Who$_i$ did $[_{IP}$ Poirot claim $[_{CP}$ that $[_{IP}$ he saw t$_i$ last week]]]]?

57c *$[_{CP}$ Who$_i$ did $[_{IP}$ Poirot make $[_{NP}$ the claim $[_{CP}$ that $[_{IP}$ he saw t$_i$ last week]]]]]?

In the ungrammatical (57c) the *wh*-phrase, *who*, is extracted from inside a complex NP, an NP whose head N (*claim*) takes a sentential complement. Ross proposes that movement out of a complex NP is blocked. Complex NPs are **islands** for movement. The constraint which bans movement out of a complex NP is often referred to as the **complex NP constraint**, abbreviated as **CNPC**.

6.1.2 *WH*-ISLANDS

Now consider the data in (58):

58a $[_{CP1}$ How$_i$ do $[_{IP}$ you $[_{VP}$ think $[_{CP2}$ that $[_{IP}$ John could $[_{VP}$ solve this problem t$_i$]]]]]]?

58b I wonder $[_{CP}$ which problem$_j$ $[_{IP}$ John could solve t$_j$ this way]].

58c *$[_{CP1}$ How$_i$ do $[_{IP}$ you $[_{VP}$ wonder $[_{CP2}$ which problem$_j$ C^0 $[_{IP}$ John could $[_{VP}$ solve t$_j$ t$_i$]]]]]]?

58d ??$[_{CP1}$ Which problem$_j$ do $[_{IP}$ you $[_{VP}$ wonder $[_{CP2}$ how$_i$ C^0 $[_{IP}$ John could $[_{VP}$ solve t$_j$ t$_i$]]]]]]?

In (58a) we extract *how* from the lower clause and move it to the matrix [Spec, CP$_1$] analogously to the movement of *how* in (56) or *who* in (57b). This movement is unproblematic. Equally unproblematic is the movement of *which problem* in (58b): *which problem* is extracted from the VP-internal position and moves to the embedded [Spec, CP]. In (58c) we combine the two types of movement: *how* moves to the matrix [Spec, CP1] and *which problem* moves to the lower [Spec, CP2]. Though each of these movements is in itself legitimate the resulting sentence is ungrammatical. A slightly better – though not perfect – result is obtained if we move *how* to the lower [Spec, CP2] and *which problem* to the higher [Spec, CP1], as shown in (58d). The question arises how to account for the degraded status of (58d) and for the ungrammaticality of (58c). We will consider some aspects of this question in this chapter. For further discussion see also chapters 8, 9 and 12. When we compare (58c) and (58d) with the grammatical (58a), (56) and (57b), we infer that the presence of the intervening *wh*-element in the lower [Spec, CP2] poses a problem for the movement of a *wh*-phrase to a higher [Spec, CP1]. In order to account for the degraded status of examples such as (58c) and (58d) Ross assumes that *wh*-questions are also islands, i.e. that extraction out of *wh*-questions is problematic.

6.1.3   ISLANDS

On the basis of the material in 6.1.1 and 6.1.2 we have identified two types of islands for *wh*-movement: complex NPs; and indirect questions, i.e. embedded CPs introduced by *wh*-constituents. The latter are referred to as **wh-islands**. The fact that Ross uses the term **islands** for both types of structures suggests that they have something in common, though he himself did not offer a unified explanation for the island constraints. The question arises how the constructions involving complex NPs and those involving *wh*-islands can be related. We turn to this issue in 6.2.

6.2   *Subjacency*

6.2.1   THE SUBJACENCY CONDITION ON MOVEMENT

In analyses of *wh*-movement an attempt has been made to provide a more general treatment of Ross' island constraints. This has led to the formulation of the **bounding theory**, another sub-component of the grammar which defines the **boundaries** for movement and thus determines how far an element can be moved. It has been proposed (Chomsky, 1973, and later work) that the constituents S and NP are boundaries for movement. In our terminology (see chapter 2) S corresponds to IP. This constraint on the distance of movement is known as the subjacency condition:

59 **Subjacency condition**
    Movement cannot cross more than one bounding node, where **bounding nodes** are IP and NP.

Let us first consider the application of the subjacency condition in a grammatical sentence. Consider (56), repeated here as (60a):

60a [$_{CP1}$ How$_i$ did [$_{IP1}$ you say [$_{CP2}$ that [$_{IP2}$ Jeeves thinks [$_{CP3}$ that [$_{IP3}$ Lord
Emsworth will solve this problem t$_i$]]]]]]?

?

At first sight the reader might be tempted conclude that the subjacency condition (59) is violated in (60a): *how* is extracted from the lower CP and ends up in the higher [Spec, CP1], crossing, it would appear (i) the lower IP3, (ii) the intermediate IP2, and (iii) the matrix IP1. Condition (59) rules out this derivation. However, observe that there is an alternative representation possible: we do not have to move *how* in one single step from the lowest clause to the matrix domain; the *wh*-element could also move stepwise: first it moves to the lowest [Spec, CP3], then it moves to the intermediate [Spec, CP2] and finally it moves to the matrix [Spec, CP1]. We assume that at each intermediate step the movement leaves a trace. We shall refer to the traces in between the foot of the chain and its head as **intermediate** traces.

60b [$_{CP1}$ How$_i$ did [$_{IP1}$ you say [$_{CP2}$ t$_i$ that [$_{IP2}$ Jeeves thinks [$_{CP3}$ t$_i$ that [$_{IP3}$ Lord

STEP III STEP II STEP I

Emsworth will solve this problem t$_i$]]]]]]?

Each of the intermediate steps is an application of *wh*-movement. Each clause (CP) defines a domain of application for *wh*-movement, a syntactic domain in which *wh*-movement can apply, or a **cycle**. We say that the movement is **successive cyclic**: it applies in successive cycles, from bottom to top. We have seen in chapter 6 that NP movement is also cyclic and also leaves intermediate traces. In general, it is assumed that transformations are subject to cyclicity: all transformations that are restricted in application to a lower cycle will apply prior to those that involve higher cycles. As the discussion shows, a vacant [Spec, CP] serves as a sort of passway for movement: thanks to the availability of this vacant position, movement out of the lower clause is possible. [Spec, CP] is like an escape hatch. In section 6.2.3 we shall see that when the intermediate [Spec, CP] is filled this gives rise to subjacency violations, as movement would then have to cross two consecutive IPs.

6.2.2   THE COMPLEX NP CONSTRAINT

Let us first turn to the data introduced in section 6.1.1. We have seen that extraction out of a complex NP leads to an ungrammatical result. (61a) violates Ross' complex NP constraint:

61a   *[$_{CP1}$ Who$_i$ did [$_{IP2}$ Poirot make [$_{NP}$ the claim [$_{CP2}$ that [$_{IP2}$ he saw t$_i$ last week]]]]]?

The example violates the subjacency condition. Consider the representation of (61b) where we have made maximal use of landing sites available for *wh*-movement:

61b   *[$_{CP1}$ Who$_i$ did [$_{IP1}$ Poirot make [$_{NP}$ the claim [$_{CP2}$ t$_i$ that [$_{IP2}$ he saw t$_i$ last week]]]]]?

Step 1 is legitimate: only one bounding node is crossed, IP2. Step 2 is illegitimate: two bounding nodes, NP and IP1, are crossed. Violations of the complex NP constraint are violations of subjacency.

In our discussion of (61b) we represent each step of the the derivation of the sentence by means of an arrow. This is done for expository reasons, we do not need to rely on the derivational history of this example in order to check the subjacency condition. The S-structure representation of the sentences in itself records effects of movement: traces indicate the vacated positions and this includes both the D-structure position of the moved phrase, and the intermediate landing sites. By inspecting the distance between the traces in terms of bounding nodes we can detect subjacency violations.

6.2.3   *WH*-ISLANDS

Now let us turn to the examples of extraction out of *wh*-islands, illustrated in (58c) and (58d). We repeat them here as (62a) and (62b).

62a   *[$_{CP1}$ How$_i$ do [$_{IP1}$ you [$_{VP}$ wonder [$_{CP2}$ which problem$_j$ C^0 [$_{IP2}$ John could [$_{VP}$ solve t$_j$ t$_i$]]]]]]?
62b   ??[$_{CP1}$ Which problem$_j$ do [$_{IP1}$ you [$_{VP}$ wonder [$_{CP2}$ how$_i$ C^0 [$_{IP2}$ John could [$_{VP}$ solve t$_j$ t$_i$]]]]]]?

The problem with both examples is that *wh*-movement crosses more than one bounding node. In (62a), *how* must move from the position inside IP2 to the matrix [Spec, CP1]. It cannot stop in the intermediate [Spec, CP2] because that is already occupied by the NP *which problem*. [Spec, CP2] cannot serve as an escape hatch for *wh*-movement.

The reader might argue that the (62a) could have an alternative derivation which might circumvent subjacency. What if we were first to move how successive cyclically to its landing site, the matrix [Spec, CP1], and then subsequently move *which problem* to the lower [Spec, CP2]? Let us go through this derivation in some detail. We first move how to the ultimate landing site, respecting subjacency:

62a′   *[$_{CP1}$ How$_i$ do [$_{IP1}$ you [$_{VP}$ wonder [$_{CP2}$ t$_i$ C^0 [$_{IP2}$ John could [$_{VP}$ solve which problem$_j$ t$_i$]]]]]]?

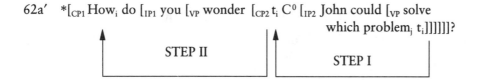

STEP II   STEP I

Now *which problem* would have to move to the intermediate [Spec, CP2]. This movement raises several problems. In (62a′) the movement of *how* involves the lower cycle (CP2) and the higher cycle (CP1) which contains the landing site. The subsequent movement of *which problem* would be restricted to the lower cycle, CP2. This means that the movement of *which problem* to the intermediate [Spec, CP2] violates the cyclicity condition. Second, consider the intended movement of *which problem*. It has to be moved to the intermediate [Spec, CP2]. If we allow this movement to take place, we will have to obliterate the intermediate trace of *how* in [Spec, CP2] and the chain between the antecedent *how* and the trace in the base position will be destroyed. Again the S-structure representation of (62a) will also register the problem: the antecedent *how* in [Spec, CP1] will not be locally related to its trace, since the *wh*-phrase in [Spec, CP2], *which problem*, will interfere and prevent the formation of the chain <*how$_i$*, t$_i$>.

One problem which we return to in later chapters is posed by the contrast between (62a) and (62b). Though (62b) is not fully acceptable, it is not as degraded as (62a). Anticipating the later discussion, consider that both sentences violate subjacency. In (62a) we extract an adjunct, *how*, from a *wh*-island; in (62b) we extract an argument, the direct object *which problem*. The subjacency violations would account for the degradation in both sentences. We return to the adjunct–argument asymmetry in chapters 9, 10 and 12, where we shall see that (62a) violates an additional principle of the grammar.

6.3 Subjacency as a Diagnostic for Movement

Wh-movement is subject to the subjacency condition. Whenever the possible linking of an empty position and its antecedent can be seen to be subject to this condition we can conclude that *wh*-movement is involved (cf. van Riemsdijk, 1978b). In this section we consider two constructions for which a movement analysis has been proposed: left dislocation (6.3.1) and relative clause formation ((6.3.2) and (6.3.3)). Using the subjacency condition as a diagnostic we show that a movement analysis is not appropriate for left dislocation but that relative clauses are derived by means of *wh*-movement. In section 6.3.4 we see that NP-movement is also subject to the subjacency condition.

6.3.1 LEFT DISLOCATION: MOVEMENT AND COPYING?

(63) illustrates **left dislocation**:

63a Simenon, I don't like him.
63b Simenon, I always wonder when I discovered him.

In (63a) the NP *Simenon* is in a sentence-initial position. Let us assume it is adjoined to IP (for adjunction see section 3.4). The pronoun *him* is coreferential with the NP *Simenon*. One might propose that the NP *Simenon* IS the D-structure object of *like* and that it has been moved to the sentence-initial position. The pronoun *him* would then be interpreted as a pronominal copy inserted at the vacated site.

64a $[_{IP}$ Simenon$_i$ $[_{IP}$ I don't like him$_i]]$.

A closer look at the examples shows that a movement analysis is in-appropriate. The distance between *Simenon*$_i$ and *him*$_i$ is not subject to the subjacency condition: in (64b) two bounding nodes (IPs) intervene; indicated by #:

64b Simenon$_i$, $[_{IP}$ I always wonder $[_{CP}$ when $[_{IP}$ I discovered him$_i]]]$.
         #   #

This leads us to the conclusion that left dislocation is not the result of movement. The sentence-initial NP *Simenon* has not been moved from inside IP. We assume that the NP is present in the adjoined position at D-structure.

This conclusion is important. So far we have suggested that adjunction structures are created by *wh*-movement. The examples above lead us to the conclusion that adjunction structures can be base-generated, i.e. that they also occur at D-structure. At this point then, we must reconsider the discussion of phrase structure in chapter 2 and include adjunction structures. The X'-schema has to be completed with the phrase structure rule in (65a), where the semicolon means that order is irrelevant, allowing both right adjunction (65b) and left adjunction (65c):

65a XP $\longrightarrow$ XP; YP
65b XP $\longrightarrow$ XP–YP
65c XP $\longrightarrow$ YP–XP

The X'-format can then be summarized as in (66):

66a XP $\longrightarrow$ XP; YP
66b XP $\longrightarrow$ Spec: X'
66c X' $\longrightarrow$ X'; YP
66d X' $\longrightarrow$ X; YP

6.3.2 RELATIVE CLAUSES AND *WH*-MOVEMENT

Consider the following example, with partial bracketing:

67 I know [$_{NP}$ the man [$_{CP}$ whom [$_{IP}$ Emsworth will invite]]].

(67) contains a complex NP with a relative clause: the head noun *man* is modified by a clause (CP). We focus on the internal structure of the relative clause here. Based on the presence of a tensed auxiliary (*will*) and a subject NP we propose that the relative clause is an IP preceded by the relative pronoun *whom*. This is strikingly similar to the structure of indirect questions. Let us assume that relative clauses are sentences, i.e. CPs, and that the relative pronoun *whom* occupies [Spec, CP]. Note that as a maximal projection *whom* could only occupy [Spec, CP], C being reserved for heads. The predicate of the relative clause, the verb *invite*, needs an internal argument. There is no overt element present but by analogy with our analysis of *wh*-questions we propose that *invite* is followed by a trace whose antecedent is *whom*. The complete S-structure of the relative clause in (67) is (68a) and its D-structure (68b):

68a   [$_{CP}$ Whom$_i$ [$_{IP}$ Emsworth will [$_{VP}$ invite t$_i$]]]?
68b   [$_{CP}$ [$_{IP}$ Emsworth will [$_{VP}$ invite whom]]]?

The hypothesis is that relative clause formation involves *wh*-movement. If this is correct then the relative clause construction should be subject to the subjacency condition on movement (59).

69a   This is the man whom Emsworth claims that he will invite.
69b   *This is the man whom Emsworth made the claim that he will invite.

In (69a) long movement is allowed in relative clauses. (69b) is a violation of the complex NP constraint. The S-structure representations of the relevant NP in the sentences in (69) are given below.

70a   [$_{NP}$ the man [$_{CP}$ whom$_i$ [$_{IP}$ Emsworth claims [$_{CP}$ t$'_i$ that [$_{IP}$ he will invite t$_i$]]]]]]

The violation of subjacency in (69b) will be signalled by means of the diacritic # on the brackets.

70b   *[$_{NP}$ the man [whom$_i$ [$_{IP}$ Emsworth made [$_{NP}$ the claim [t$'_i$ that

                    #   #

[$_{IP}$ he will invite t$_i$]]]]]]

Using the subjacency condition as a diagnostic we find confirmation that relative clause formation is indeed a result of movement. In chapter 10 we reformulate the subjacency condition in terms of the notion barrier.

As it stands the S-structure representations in (70) are not sufficient to allow us to interpret the relative clause. (70a), for example, does not indicate that *whom$_i$* is to be linked to *the man*. We assume that the interpretation of the relative pronoun is achieved through a rule of coindexation where *the man* and *whom* end up having the same index. This coindexation is used to represent the fact that the relative clause modifies or is 'predicated of' *the man*, it is a **predication rule**.[17]

---

[17]   For a discussion of predication the reader is referred to Williams (1980). It is proposed in the literature that the co-indexation rule does not apply at S-structure but at the level of logical form, LF, which is discussed in chapter 9. Further discussion of the predication rule is found in Chomsky (1982: 92–3) and Safir (1986).

6.3.3 RELATIVE CLAUSES AND RESUMPTIVE PRONOUNS

In the section above we have seen that relative clauses in English are derived by means of *wh*-movement. However, relative clauses need not be formed by means of movement. Consider the following examples from French, taken from Zribi-Hertz (1984).

71a Voici l'homme$_i$ à qui$_i$ Marie a parlé t$_i$.
     here-is the man to whom Marie has talked
71b Voici l'homme$_i$ que Marie lui$_i$ a parlé.
     here-is the man that Marie to-him has talked

72a Voici la maison$_i$ à laquelle$_i$ Marie pense encore t$_i$.
     here-is the house about which Marie thinks still
72b Voici la maison$_i$ que Marie y$_i$ pense encore.
     here-is the house that Marie of-it thinks still

73a Voici le courrier$_i$ qui$_i$ t$_i$ est arrivé ce soir.
     here-is the mail which is arrived tonight
73b Voici le courrier$_i$ qu' il$_i$ est arrivé ce soir.
     here-is the mail that-it is arrived tonight

The (a) examples above illustrate 'standard' French, the (b) examples illustrate 'popular' French. The (a) examples are straightforward illustrations of *wh*-movement: in (71a), for instance, the PP *à qui* is moved to [Spec, CP] and binds a trace in its extraction site. The (b) example illustrates an alternative strategy for the formation of relative clauses. The *relative* clause is headed by the complementizer *que* and it contains a pronoun *lui* which is coindexed (by the rule of predication) with the relativized NP *l'homme*. The pronoun which is related to the relativized NP is called a **resumptive pronoun**.

English too has a substandard resumptive pronoun strategy for the formation of relative clauses. Zribi-Hertz (1984: 27) gives the following example (from Chomsky, 1982: 11, his (8b)).

74 the man who$_i$ John saw him$_i$

(74) differs from the French examples in that the resumptive pronoun *him* is associated with a *wh*-element in [Spec, CP]. Given that the pronoun occupies its base-position, we must conclude that the *wh*-element must be

base-generated in [Spec, CP], i.e. it does not move to that position.[18] An important consequence of this analysis is that because no *wh*-movement is involved, the subjacency condition should not come into play:

75   the man who$_i$ [$_{IP}$ they think [$_{CP}$ that [$_{IP}$ [$_{CP}$ when [$_{IP}$ Mary marries him$_i$]] then everyone will be happy]]]

The resumptive pronoun *him* is inside a clause introduced by *when*. As (76) shows, such clauses are *wh*-islands; we assume *when* is in [Spec, CP]:

76   *the man who they think that [$_{CP}$ when [$_{IP}$ Mary marries]] then everyone will be happy

For many speakers of English, the resumptive pronoun strategy is a way of overcoming subjacency violations.[19]

77   I am looking for those documents which I can never remember where I put them.

6.3.4 NP-MOVEMENT

If the subjacency condition is a constraint on movement, then we expect it will also apply to NP-movement. In (78) the subjacency condition is respected: in (78a) no bounding nodes are crossed; in (78b) one bounding node is crossed.

78a   John$_i$ was invited t$_i$ at Mary's house.
78b   John$_i$ seems [$_{IP}$ t$_i$ to have lost].

Now consider the ungrammatical (79a):

79a   [$_{IP1}$ *John$_i$ seems [$_{CP2}$ that [$_{IP2}$ it is likely [$_{IP3}$ t′$_i$ to [$_{VP}$ t$_i$ win]]]]].

John originates as the subject of the lowest clause, IP3, and moves to [Spec, IP1] in the matrix domain. For completeness' sake we add the trace in the

---

[18]   For French we shall assume that the resumptive pronoun is related to a non-overt element in [Spec, CP]. Such non-overt elements will be discussed in chapter 8, section 4.
[19]   For further discussion see Sells (1984) and Zribi-Hertz (1984: 27–8).

lower [Spec, VP] (cf. the subject-in-VP hypothesis developed in chapter 6, section 5), though this will play no role in the discussion: the movement from t_i to t'_i does not violate any principles of the grammar. Following the discussion in this chapter, the ungrammaticality of (79a) could be interpreted as a subjacency violation: the movement from t'_i to [Spec, IP1] crosses two bounding nodes: IP2 and IP3. There is an additional problem with (79a), though, which is independent of the subjacency condition. Consider (79b), where we have eliminated the subjacency effect:

79b   *[$_{IP1}$ John$_i$ seems [$_{CP2}$ that [$_{IP2}$ it is believed t_i by everyone]]].

The movement of *John* in (79b) does not violate subjacency and the sentence remains ungrammatical. In chapter 6, section 4.5.2. we saw that (79b) is ungrammatical because the trace of *John* is not bound in its governing category, IP2. In chapter 6 we argued that NP-traces are subject to Principle A of the binding theory. In (79a): the governing category of t'_i is IP2: IP2 contains the trace itself, its governor *likely*, and a subject, the NP *it* in [Spec, IP2]; t'_i is not bound in its governing category. According to our definition of chains (chapter 6 (105a)) the chain <*John$_i$*, t_i> cannot be formed in (79a): *John$_i$* does not locally bind t_i.

6.4   The Subjacency Parameter

Consider the following Italian NPs (Rizzi, 1982b: 50):

80a   tuo   fratello,   a   cui   mi   domando che   storie
      your brother,   to whom myself I-ask   which stories
      abbiano   raccontato
      they-have told
      'your brother, to whom I wonder which stories they told'
80b   il   solo   incarico   che   non   sapevi   a   chi
      the   only   charge   that not   you-knew to whom
      avrebbero   affidato
      they-would-have   entrusted
      'the only charge about which you did not know to whom they would
      have entrusted it'
80c   la   nuova idea   di Giorgio, di cui   immagino che cosa pensi
      the new   idea   of Giorgio, of which I-imagine what   you-think
      'Giorgio's new idea, of which I imagine what you think'

The English equivalents of (80) are far less acceptable:

81a   *your brother, to whom I wonder which stories they told,
81b   *the only task which you ignore to whom they'd entrust
81c   *George's new idea, of which I can imagine what you think,

The reader will probably be able to identify the English examples in (81) as violations of the subjacency condition. In (81a), for instance, *to whom* has been extracted out of an embedded question introduced by *which stories*, crossing IP$_2$ and IP$_1$:

82   your brother [$_{CP}$ to whom$_i$ [$_{IP1}$ I wonder [$_{CP}$ which stories$_j$ [$_{IP2}$ they told t$_j$
                                        #   #

     t$_i$]]]]

Apparently this type of extraction is allowed in Italian: omitting irrelevant details the S-structure of (80a) is (83). *A cui* has crossed IP$_2$ and IP$_1$, without any harm.

83   tuo fratello [$_{CP}$ a cui$_i$ [$_{IP1}$ mi domando [$_{CP}$ che storie$_j$ [$_{IP2}$ abbiano raccontato
     t$_j$ t$_i$]]]]

One possibility would be to claim that the subjacency condition is language-specific, like the doubly filled COMP filter, and does not apply in Italian. If this were true one would equally expect that extraction out of any type of indirect question and out of complex NPs is freely possible, contrary to fact (example from Rizzi, 1982b: 51):

84   *tuo fratello, [$_{CP}$ a cui$_i$ [$_{IP}$ temo [$_{NP}$ la   possibilità   [$_{CP}$ t'$_i$
     your brother   to whom I fear   the possibility
     che [$_{IP}$ abbiano   raccontato t$_i$ tutto]]]]]
     that   they-have told   everything

Rizzi's proposal to account for the example given here is NOT that subjacency is irrelevant for Italian. Rather he proposes that the bounding nodes are parametrized, i.e. that different languages may have different bounding nodes. While we assume that in English NP and IP are the relevant bounding nodes, for Italian bounding nodes would be NP and CP. On the basis of this proposal the grammaticality of (80) follows: in each of the examples only one CP has been crossed (see (83)). The ungrammaticality of (84) is also predicted. In (85) we indicate the relevant bounding nodes by the diacritic #:

85   *tuo fratello, [$_{CP}$ a cui$_i$ [$_{IP}$ temo [$_{NP}$ la possibilità [$_{CP}$ t′$_i$ che [$_{IP}$ abbiano
                                         #   #

     raccontato t$_i$ tutto]]]]]]

In (85) the PP *a cui* ('to whom') originates in the lowest clause: it is the complement of *raccontare* ('tell'). It is first moved to the lowest [Spec, CP], and then it has to move across CP and across NP, crossing two bounding nodes.

   The subjacency parameter is one of the earliest formulated in the present theory.[20]

7   Binding Theory and Traces of *Wh*-Movement

7.1   Typology of NPs

In the discussion of *wh*-movement it has become clear that some of the *wh*-traces (86) have the status of NPs:

86a   Whom$_i$ will Lord Emsworth invite t$_i$?
86b   Which detectives$_i$ do you expect [t$_i$ to admire themselves most]?

The trace in (86a) occupies a position normally taken by an NP, it is case-marked by the verb and it is assigned a theta role. In (86b) the trace binds a reflexive with which it shares features of person, number and gender. If these *wh*-traces are NPs,[21] the next question is how they behave with respect to the BT. Or to put it differently: what type of NPs are those traces? In chapter 4 we identified four NP types based on the features [± Anaphor] and [± Pronominal]:

---

[20]   For a discussion of the subjacency parameter in French the reader is referred to Sportiche (1981). Further discussion of the Italian data is found in Rizzi (1982b). For various modifications of the parameter see also Chomsky (1986b) and chapters 9 and 10.

[21]   Clearly, traces of PPs, for example, will not have the status of NPs but rather that of PPs.

87   Typology of NPs

Type	OVERT	NON-OVERT
[+Anaphor, –Pronominal]	anaphors	NP-trace (chapter 6)
[–Anaphor, +Pronominal]	pronouns	?
[–Anaphor, –Pronominal]	R-expressions	?
[+Anaphor, +Pronominal]	– – – – –	PRO (chapter 5)

We have assimilated NP-traces with anaphors. Could we do the same for *wh*-traces? At first glance one might wish to say yes. After all, *wh*-traces need a c-commanding antecedent. But a more careful analysis shows that the answer is 'No'. The moved *wh*-constituent is coindexed with its trace and c-commands it. Since the *wh*-constituent is in an A'-position, it does not A-bind its trace. We have said (section 3.5) that the moved *wh*-constituent A'-binds its trace. The binding theory developed in chapter 4 is about A-binding, i.e. binding from an A-position, and says nothing about A'-binding. The reader can verify for himself that the *wh*-trace is not A-bound by anything in its GC in the examples above.

We do not dwell too long on the question whether the *wh*-trace is like the null element PRO, discussed in chapter 5. It must be clear that the *wh*-trace is governed and PRO must not be governed.

Is the *wh*-trace then like a pronoun? Principle B of the binding theory says that pronominal elements must be free in their GC. In other words a pronoun may be bound by something outside the GC. If *wh*-traces were like pronouns they should have the same distribution. Let us try to construct an example:

88a   The detective$_i$ thinks [that [$_{IP}$ he$_i$ likes Bill best]].
88b   *Who$_i$ does the detective$_j$ think [t'$_i$ [$_{IP}$ t$_i$ likes Bill best]]?

In (88a) the pronoun *he* is allowed to be coreferential with the NP *the detective*, since the latter is outside its GC. In (88b) the lowest trace of *who$_i$* occupies the position filled by the pronoun *he* in (88a). But in (88b) the natural answer is not that 'the detective thinks that he himself likes Bill best', i.e. that the NP *the detective* can be coindexed with *who* and consequently with the trace of *who*; t$_i$ and the NP *the detective* must not be coreferential in (88b). If the trace of *wh*-movement were like a pronoun then the facts would be rather hard to explain.

Last but not least we turn to the final option: what if *wh*-traces were like R-expressions? Following Principle C of the binding theory they would have to be free everywhere. A brief look at the data above confirms that this is indeed the right answer. The fact that the trace of *who* in (88b) cannot be bound by *the detective* follows directly. The example is structurally parallel to (88c).

88c   *He$_i$ thinks [that [$_{IP}$ John$_i$ likes him best]].

We can now identify one more null element in the table above: *wh*-traces are like R-expressions:

89   Typology of NPs

Type	OVERT	NON-OVERT
[+Anaphor, −Pronominal]	anaphors	NP-trace
[−Anaphor, +Pronominal]	pronouns	?
[−Anaphor, −Pronominal]	R-expressions.	*wh*-trace
[+Anaphor, +Pronominal]	— — — —	PRO

In the discussion we have distinguished the concepts A′-binding from A-binding, and A′-bound from A-bound. If we wish to refer to 'any' binding we can use the terms **X-binding** or **X-bound**. Traces must be X-bound.

By way of summary, let us look at some examples of movement in order to see how the binding theory applies.

90a   Who do you think is believed to be the best detective?
90b   *Poirot seems is the best detective.

We invite the reader to provide the S-structure and the D-structure for these examples before continuing to read. The sentences in (90) have S-structures (91a) and (91b) respectively:

91a   Who$_i$ do [$_{IP}$ you think [$_{CP}$ t″$_i$ [$_{IP}$ t′$_i$ is believed [t$_i$ to be the best detective]]]]?
91b   *Poirot$_i$ seems [$_{CP}$ t′$_i$ [$_{IP}$ t$_i$ is the best detective]].

(91a) contains a combination of NP-movement and *wh*-movement. *Who$_i$* originates as the subject of the lower infinitival clause. Being caseless – *believed* is passive – *who* moves to the subject position of the higher clause where it is assigned NOMINATIVE case. (In passing we draw the reader's attention to the fact that it is quite possible, as in (91a), that a *wh*-constituent undergoes NP-movement.) From this subject position *who_i* is then *wh*-moved to the matrix [Spec, CP], via the intermediate [Spec, CP]. The trace in the subject position of the infinitival clause has all the properties of an NP-trace: it is caseless, it is A-bound and like anaphors it is bound in its governing category. The trace in the subject position of *is believed* is a trace of *wh*-movement: it has case, it is A'-bound and so, like R-expressions, it is not A-bound.

Let us turn to the ungrammatical (90b), whose S-structure is given in (91b). The idea is here that the NP *Poirot_i* moves from the lower subject position of a finite clause to the subject position of the matrix clause VIA the intervening specifier of CP where it leaves an intermediate trace. The lower trace in the subject position of *is* has case and thus to all appearances is a trace of *wh*-movement. The lower trace is A'-bound from the intermediate [Spec, CP]: it is the foot of an A'-chain. The analysis implies that NPs can undergo *wh*-movement, a possibility independently allowed as we discuss in section 8.1. Admitting this possibility for the moment without further discussion, the representation (91b) is still problematic: the lower trace, being like an R-expression, must be free. In the example it is bound by the NP *Poirot_i* in an A-position, the subject position of *seems*. (91b) violates the binding theory. Movement which goes from an A-position to an A'-position and back to an A-position is often referred to as **improper movement**.[22]

Let us briefly consider another derivation for (90b): take the S-structure representation (92), where we assume that the NP *Poirot_i* moves directly from the lowest subject position to the matrix position, leaving a coindexed trace.

92   *$[_{IP}$ Poirot_i seems $[_{CP}$ $[_{IP}$ t_i is the best detective]]].

The trace in (92) is assigned NOMINATIVE by the finite INFL of *is*, so we conclude that it is a *wh*-trace. There are two problems with this derivation. First, a *wh*-trace should have an antecedent in an A'-position, which is not the case in (92), and second, it should not be A-bound, which it is. On the other hand, suppose we were boldly to ignore the case diagnostic and assume t_i is an NP-trace. We only do this to our detriment. An NP-trace is subject to Principle A of the BT: it must be bound in its GC. The GC is the lower finite clause (see chapter 4 for the definition of the GC and for the role of AGR in particular) and clearly the trace is not bound there. Whatever syntactic representation we imagine for (90b) it will violate some principle of

[22]   The term is from May (1985).

our grammar. (90b) has no legitimate syntactic representation and is ungrammatical.

7.2 Crossover

In the literature[23] the following examples have received a lot of attention (cf. (88b)):

93a *Who$_i$ does he$_i$ think t$_i$ left?
93b *Who$_i$ does he$_i$ think you saw t$_i$?
93c *Who$_i$ does he$_i$ see t$_i$?

The ungrammaticality was at one time attributed to the fact that *wh*-movement moves a constituent across a coindexed pronoun. It was proposed that these examples are ruled out by the so-called **leftness condition**, reformulated here for expository reasons (Koopman and Sportiche, 1982: 140) and illustrated in (94b):

94a **Leftness condition**
     A *wh*-trace cannot be coindexed with a pronoun to its left.

94b *Who$_i$ does he$_i$ think t$_i$ left?

The ungrammatical examples in (93) are usually described as illustrating **strong crossover (SCO)**.[24] It is clear that such examples can also be explained in terms of the discussion in section 7.1: in all instances the *wh*-trace will be A-bound.

   Now consider the contrast in (95). An example such as (95b) is referred to as **weak crossover (WCO)**. The term is chosen because the ungrammaticality is less strongly felt than that illustrated in (93).

95a Who$_i$ loves his$_i$ mother?
95b *Who$_i$ does his$_i$ mother love t$_i$?

[23] See Koopman and Sportiche (1982: 148) and the references cited there.
[24] A first discussion of crossover is found in Postal (1971). This work is written in a pre-Government and Binding framework but it anticipates a lot of current discussion.

The contrast in grammaticality between the sentences in (95) can also be explained by the leftness condition (cf. Koopman and Sportiche, 1982: 140). The contrast in (95), however, does not follow from the BT. In (95b) the trace is not A-bound: the pronoun *his* does not c-command, hence does not bind, the *wh*-trace. We conclude that SCO follows from the binding theory but WCO does not. One proposal is to maintain the leftness condition. This will rule out both the examples in (93) and (95b). However, there is then some redundancy in our theory since (93) is ruled out both by the binding theory and by the leftness condition. The leftness condition and the BT do the same job in (93), this suggests that one of the two is superfluous. Restricting the leftness condition for WCO seems an *ad hoc* solution.[25]

8   Movement to the Right in English

So far we have discussed only leftward movement of constituents in English: NP-movement takes a constituent to a c-commanding [Spec, IP] and *wh*-movement takes an element to a c-commanding [Spec, CP]. In this section we illustrate two instances of rightward movement, known as heavy NP-shift and PP-extraposition from NP. We shall see that these two are instances of *wh*-movement. Our discussion will entail that the term *wh*-movement is to be interpreted as movement to an A'-position.

8.1   Heavy NP-shift

In chapter 3 we discussed case assignment in English. On the basis of examples like those in (96) we postulated an adjacency constraint on ACCUSATIVE assignment.

96a   Poirot speaks English badly.
96b   *Poirot speaks badly English.
96c   Bertie drinks whisky every night.
96d   *Bertie drinks every night whisky.
96e   Jeeves introduced him to the guests.
96f   *Jeeves introduced to the guests him.

---

[25]   For an alternative analysis of weak crossover, the reader is referred to Koopman and Sportiche (1982). Further discussion of crossover and relative clauses is found in Safir (1986). See also Lasnik and Stowell (1991).

Certain examples seem to provide counterevidence for the adjacency requirement on case assignment in English:

97a Jeeves introduced to the guests [$_{NP}$ the famous detective from Belgium].
97b My doctor told me to drink every night [$_{NP}$ two glasses of mineral water
with a slice of lemon].

The bracketed NPs in (97) are internal arguments of the verbs (*introduce*
and *drink* respectively); they are directly theta-marked. Theta theory specifies
that direct theta-marking is achieved under government. At S-structure the
relevant NPs should be made visible by case. In order to account for the thematic relations between the verbs and their complements we assume that the
sentence-final positions of the NPs in (97) are derived positions and that the
D-structure of these sentences is as in (98):

98a Jeeves [$_{V'}$ introduced [$_{NP}$ the famous detective from Belgium]] to the
guests.
98b My doctor told me to [$_{V'}$ drink [$_{NP}$ two glasses of mineral water with
a slice of lemon]] every night.

The S-structure of these examples will be (99):

99a Jeeves [$_{VP}$ [$_{VP}$ [$_{V'}$ introduced t$_i$ to the guests] [$_{NP_i}$ the famous detective from
Belgium]]].
99b My doctor told me to [$_{VP}$ [$_{VP}$ [$_{V'}$ drink t$_i$] every night] [$_{NP_i}$ two glasses of
mineral water with a slice of lemon]].

The question that arises is how to characterize the rightward movement
of the object NP: is it A-movement or is it A'-movement? Recall that A-
movement is movement to an A-position, and is exemplified by NP-movement
in raising and passive sentences; A'-movement is movement to an A'-position
and is exemplified by *wh*-movement in interrogative and relative clauses.

As is standard by now, we assume that movement leaves traces. At first
sight it might appear that the rightward movement of the NP in (99) is NP-
movement, i.e. A-movement, and leaves an NP-trace: after all, the moved
constituent is an NP. This would mean that the chain created by the movement of the NP in (99) is an A-chain, i.e. a chain whose head is an A-
position. Two problems arise. First, the traces which constitute the foot of
the chain in (99) are case-marked by the verb. NP traces are ordinarily not

assigned case. In addition, if the movement is A-movement, then the landing
site of the movement must be an A-position. A-positions are positions in
which arguments occur, they are positions which are assigned grammatical
functions, i.e. the object position and the subject position. On the basis of
this definition it is hard to see how the landing site of the rightwardly moved
NP could be an A-position. Another property of A-movement as instantiated
by NP-movement is that it substitutes an NP for an empty position. NP
movement in passive sentences, for instance, moves an object NP into a
subject position, raising moves a subject NP of a non-finite clause into the
subject position of a higher clause. In both cases we assume that the subject
position [Spec, IP] is generated in the base and then filled by the moved
constituent. But it is hard to see how to motivate a base-generated sentence-
final position which could become the landing site for the rightward movement
of the NP in (99). There is no motivation to postulate a sentence-final position which can host the moved NP, whether this position be categorially
specified as an NP position, or categorially unspecified. We conclude that the
NP is moved to a position created for it. In other words the moved NP is
adjoined. (See the discussion of adjunction in connection with structure
preservation in chapter 6; and also section 3.4 above.) Let us assume that the
moved NP is adjoined to VP producing a structure like in (100):

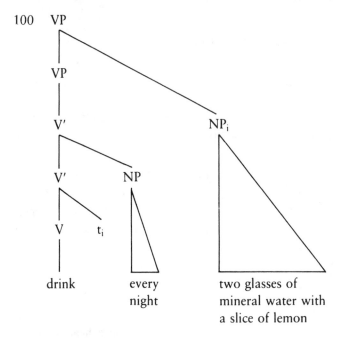

The moved NP$_i$ c-commands its trace, a desirable result since we have seen
that both NP-traces and *wh*-traces are c-commanded by their antecedents.

Obviously, the adjunction analysis is incompatible with the hypothesis that the chain <NP_i, t_i> is an A-chain. The adjoined position is an A'-position. We conclude that the chain created by the moved NP in our example is like the chain created by *wh*-movement. The trace is A'-bound. That the trace is assigned case is as expected.

If the empty category in the object position in (100) is indeed a trace created by movement – our hypothesis – then the link with its antecedent should be subject to the subjacency condition on movement. This is easy to check. In (101) we see that rightward movement of NPs must not cross more than one bounding node: NP_i crosses its containing IP and in addition an NP-node and the result is ungrammatical:

101   *[$_{NP}$ The man [$_{CP}$ who$_j$ [$_{IP}$ t$_j$ drinks t$_i$ every night]]] bothers me [$_{NP_i}$ two glasses of mineral water with a slice of lemon].

We may wonder why the object NPs in (96) cannot be adjoined to the VP. What distinguishes the grammatical examples from the ungrammatical ones is that the moved NP in the grammatical examples is rather **heavy**. Apparently the adjunction of object NPs to the VP is only admitted with heavy NPs. A precise definition of the concept of heaviness has not been formulated but the intuitive idea is clear. Rightward movement of NPs as exemplified in (97) is called **heavy NP-shift**.[26]

[26]   Not every reordering of complements is necessarily due to A'-movement of the object. For some examples the reader is referred to Belletti and Shlonsky (forthcoming). These authors show that the variation in word-order V – PP – NP in the Italian examples in exercise 9 in chapter 6 is obtained via two distinct derivations. The pattern in (ib) is derived by rightward movement of the object; while that in (iib) is derived by leftward movement of the PP.

(ia)   ?Ho dato [$_{NP}$ un libro che mi avevano consigliato la settimana scorsa] [$_{PP}$ a Gianni].
have given a book that me they-had suggested last week to Gianni

(ib)   Ho dato [$_{PP}$ a Gianni] [$_{NP}$ un libro che mi avevano consigliato la settimana scorsa]
have give to Gianni a book that they me had advised last week
'I gave a book to Gianni which they had suggested to me last week.'

(iia)   Gianni ha messo [$_{NP}$ tre libri] [$_{PP}$ sulla tavola]
Gianno has put three books on the table
'Gianni has put three books on the table.'

(iib)   Gianni ha messo [$_{PP}$ sulla tavola] [$_{NP}$ tre libri]
Gianni has put on the table three books
'Gianni has put on the table three books.'

8.2   PP-extraposition from NP

In the examples below we concentrate on the bracketed NPs:[27]

102a   I read [$_{NP}$ a description [$_{PP_i}$ of Hockney's latest picture]] yesterday.
102b   I read [$_{NP}$ a description] yesterday [$_{PP_i}$ of Hockney's latest picture].

The sentences in (102) are paraphrases. The bracketed PP is the complement of the head N *description*. We shall assume that the D-structure of the examples corresponds to (102a) and that the surface order of (102b) is derived. The PP$_i$, *of Hockney's latest picture*, has been moved out of the NP and is adjoined to the right. Movement of constituents out of NPs is referred to as **extraposition**: PP$_i$ is extraposed from the object NP.

Let us assume that extraposition leaves a coindexed trace and that the extraposed constituent must c-command its trace. Analogously to the discussion of heavy NP-shift above it would not be reasonable to argue that the moved PP is inserted in an unfilled PP position. As before we would have a hard time motivating that such a position is projected at D-structure. We conclude that the PP must be in an adjoined position.

Assuming that the extraposed PP in (102b) is in a derived position as a result of movement, we expect the subjacency effects illustrated in (103):

103   *[$_{NP_1}$ A translation [$_{PP}$ of [$_{NP_2}$ a description t$_i$]   ]   ] has appeared [$_{PP_i}$ of
                                                              #   #
       Hockney's latest picture].

If PP$_i$ is to be construed with the N *description* then it would have been extraposed out of NP$_2$ and subsequently out of NP$_1$. This is not a possible construal.

8.3   Conclusion

In this section we illustrate two types of rightward movement: heavy NP shift and extraposition from NP. Both movements are assumed to involve adjunction of the moved constituent to a maximal projection; these examples illustrate A'-movement. The moved element moves to an A'-position, its trace is

[27]   For discussion of extraposition from NPs see, among others, Coopmans and Roovers (1986), Guéron (1980) and Rochemont (1978).

case-marked and A'-bound, the moved element and its trace form an A'-chain. These data show that A'-movement does not necessarily involve *wh*-constituents, and that the movement of an NP is not necessarily A-movement.

9 Summary

This chapter discusses the properties of *wh*-movement, an instantiation of A'-movement. A'-movement moves a constituent to an A'-position, leaving a coindexed trace in the base position. Typically *wh*-movement is involved in the derivation of interrogative sentences where a *wh*-constituent moves to [Spec, CP]. It is also involved in the formation of relative clauses. We have seen that A'-movement may also affect NPs, as is illustrated in heavy NP-shift, or post-nominal modifiers as is seen in extraposition from NP. A'-movement is either done by substitution (to [Spec, CP]) or by adjunction (heavy NP-shift, extraposition from NP).

Wh-movement is subject to the subjacency condition on movement:

1 **Subjacency condition**
   Movement cannot cross more than one bounding node.

The bounding nodes are subject to parametric variation. In English IP and NP are bounding nodes; in Italian CP and NP are bounding nodes.

In addition we discuss two filters which both involve the content of C:

2 **Doubly filled COMP filter**
   When an overt *wh*-phrase occupies the Spec of some CP the head of that CP must not dominate an overt complementizer.

3 ***That*-trace filter**
   The sequence of an overt complementizer followed by a trace is ungrammatical.

These filters are language-specific.

Traces of NPs which are *wh*-moved are characterized as [−anaphor, −pronominal] and are subject to Principle C of the binding theory.

In our discussion we have also paid attention to adjunction structures, illustrated in (4):

4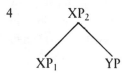

In (4) YP is adjoined to XP_1. Adjunction may arise from movement as in heavy NP-shift. Left-dislocation structures suggest that adjunction structures may also be base-generated. We have now extended our phrase structure rules to allow for adjunction:

5a XP ⟶ XP; YP
5b XP ⟶ Spec; X'
5c X' ⟶ X'; YP
5b X' ⟶ X; YP.

The relation between the adjoined element and the phrase to which it is adjoined has led us to redefine the notion **dominance** and also to introduce the concept **exclusion**:

6 **Dominance**
   A is dominated by B only if A is dominated by every segment of B.

7 **Exclusion**
   B excludes A if no segment of B dominates A.

10 Exercises

Exercise 1

Discuss the motivation for the intermediate traces in the following representations:

1a Who$_i$ does the detective think [$_{CP}$ t'$_i$ that [$_{IP}$ he likes t$_i$ best]]?
1b Who$_i$ does the detective think [$_{CP}$ t'$_i$ [$_{IP}$ t$_i$ likes him best]]?

Exercise 2

Consider the following sentences, some of which we have already given in the exercises to the Introduction of this book.

1 ?Which man do you wonder when they will appoint?
2 *Who do you wonder which present will give?
3 ??Which present do you wonder who will give?
4 ??Which man do you wonder whether John will invite?
5 *Which man do you wonder whether will invite John?
6 *Which man do you wonder what will give to John?
7 *Which man do you wonder when will invite John?

Although none of the sentences above is entirely acceptable to all native speakers, the degree of unacceptability varies. A sentence with an asterisk is worse than one with a question mark. Try to account for the relative unacceptability of these sentences using the concepts developed in chapter 7. When discussing these sentences you should first of all determine their syntactic representations, D-structure and S-structure. Then you should try to identify which principle or principles are violated.

In your analysis you will no doubt discover that the extraction of a subject *wh*-constituent is consistently more difficult than that of an object. This type of asymmetry was discussed in terms of the *that-trace* filter. From the analysis of the examples above try to check whether the filter as formulated in the chapter is adequate and if not, try to reformulate it. In subsequent chapters we shall return to examples such as those above.

If you are a native speaker of a language other than English then check how translations of examples like those above fare in this language.

Exercise 3

In section 6.3.1 we have seen that an analysis of left dislocation in terms of movement and pronoun insertion is not consistent with our present version of the grammar. A structure that closely resembles left dislocation is topicalization:

1a   Detective stories, I have never liked them.
1b   Detective stories, I have never liked.

(1a) illustrates left dislocation, (1b) topicalization. On the basis of the example above and of the examples given below try to decide whether a movement analysis would be adequate to account for topicalization:

2a   ?Detective stories, I wonder if he likes.
2b   ?Detective stories, I wonder who reads.
2c   *Detective stories, I don't believe the rumour that they will ban.
2d   *Detective stories, I don't like linguists who read.
2e   Detective stories, I expect will be quite successful.
2f   *Detective stories, I expect that will be successful.
2g   *Detective stories, I wonder if will be successful.
2h   *Detective stories, I wonder when will be successful.

Exercise 4

Discuss the derivation (D-structure, S-structure and the various principles that determine them) of the following sentences:

1   Which detective do you think will invite Miss Marple?
2   This is the author whom I like best.
3   Which detective will be invited next week?
4   These are stories which are believed everywhere.
5   Which detective do you think seems to be nicest?
6   Which ships will the enemy sink first?
7   Which ships do you think will sink first?
8   Which sailors do you think will arrive first?

Exercise 5

Compare the properties of NP-movement and *wh*-movement on the basis of section 2.3 in chapter 6, where we discuss the properties of NP-movement. Make a list of similarities and differences between A-chains and A'-chains. This exercise prepares you for the next chapter.

Exercise 6

Consider the application of the binding theory in the following examples:

1 Which pictures of himself will John sell?
2 Which pictures of each other do you think that your parents prefer?
3 Those are the pictures of himself which John likes best.
4 Every picture of him, John likes.

Do examples like these produce evidence for Belletti and Rizzi's (1988) proposal that Principle A can be satisfied either at D-structure or at S-structure? We return to these data in chapter 9.

Exercise 7

Consider the application of the binding theory in the following examples:

1 Which pictures of himself$_i$ will John$_i$ sell?
2 Which pictures of each other$_i$ do you think that your parents$_i$ prefer?
3 Which pictures of himself$_i$ does John$_i$ think that Jane will sell?
4 Which pictures of himself$_i$ does Jane think that John$_i$ will sell?
5 Criticize himself$_i$ John$_i$ never will.
6 Criticize himself$_i$ Mary never thought that John$_i$ would.
7 *Criticize himselfi John$_i$ never thought that Mary would.
8 John$_i$ wondered which pictures of himself$_i$ Mary liked.

Do the examples above provide support for Belletti and Rizzi's (1988) claim that Principle A can be satisfied either at D-structure or at S-structure? We return to examples like the ones above in chapter 9.

Exercise 8

How can the grammaticality judgements of the following English examples be accounted for?

1   **Which book did you wonder when would be published?
2   *Who did Poirot tell you why he had interviewed?

How could we account for the fact that (1) is worse than (2)?
   Consider the following data from Italian (Rizzi, 1982b: 54–6). Can the subjacency parameter discussed in section 6.4 account for them?

3   Non so   proprio chi possa avere indovinato a chi
    not know really who could have guessed   to whom
    affiderò   questo incarico
    I'll-entrust this   task
    'I really don't know who might have guessed to whom I will entrust this task.'
4   *Questo incarico, che   non so   proprio chi possa avere
    this   task,   which not know really who could have
    indovinato a chi   affiderò,   mi sta   creando   un sacco
    guessed   to whom I'll-entrust, me is   giving   a lot
    di   grattacapi.
    of   trouble
    'This task, which I really don't know who might have guessed to whom I'll entrust, is giving me a lot of trouble.'
5   Il mio primo libro, che   credo   che tu   sappia a chi
    my   first book, which I-believe that you know to whom
    ho   dedicato,   mi   è sempre stato molto caro.
    I-have dedicated, to-me is always   been very   precious
    'My first book, which I know that you know to whom I have dedicated, has always been very dear to me.'
6   *Il mio primo libro, che   so   a chi   credi   che abbia
    my   first book, which I-know to whom you-think that I-have
    dedicato mi   è stato sempre   molto   caro.
    dedicated, to-me is been always   very   dear.

   Jaeggli (1981: 170) gives the following Spanish data:

7   *el unico encargo que   no sabias   a quién iban
    the only task   which you didn't-know to whom they-would
    a dar
    give
8   *A quién no   sabias   qué le regalaron?
    to whom didn't you-know what they-had-given

9 *tu hermano, a quièn me pregunto que historias le habran
your brother, to whom I-wonder what stories they have
contado
told.

Assuming that the bounding nodes for subjacency may be parametrized (along the lines suggested by Rizzi 1982b), would the data above suggest that the bounding nodes in Spanish are like in English or like in Italian?

Exercise 9

In section 5.1 we discussed the vacuous movement hypothesis for subject extraction. Consider the following examples from Chomsky (1986b: 50, example (109)). According to Chomsky (1) is more acceptable than (2). Would this contrast in grammaticality be relevant to the discussion in section 5.1?

1 He is the man to whom I wonder who knew which book to give.
2 He is the man to whom I wonder who John told which book to give.

In chapter 5 (section 3.3) we discussed the position of *whether* as being possibly in [Spec, CP]. According to Chomsky (1986b: 50), example (3) (his (110)) is more acceptable than (2) above.

3 He is the man to whom I wonder whether John told us which book to give.

Does this throw any light on the discussion in chapter 5?

8 An Inventory of Empty Categories

Contents

Introduction and Overview

Chapters 5–7 introduced three types of non-overt NPs, PRO, NP-trace and *wh*-trace, and at this point it is useful to take stock of the various properties that we have attributed to these non-overt or null elements.

The first part of this chapter provides a survey of our discussion and extends our analysis of the properties of null elements. We introduce a principle to constrain the occurrence of traces: the empty category principle.

In the second part we complete our inventory of null elements. We discuss evidence for a fourth null element, the zero pronoun *pro*. We also discuss the null operator and illustrate its use in English and in Portuguese.

Since much of this chapter is a revision and extension of the preceding part of the book, the reader should find this a relatively straightforward chapter which enables him to consolidate his knowledge and prepares him for the subsequent part of the book in which we shall further develop the grammar which we have been elaborating.

Section 1 contains an inventory of the empty categories discussed so far. Section 2 discusses the licensing of empty categories and the empty category principle. In section 3 we deal with the null element *pro*. Section 4 discusses non-overt antecedents of *wh*-traces and section 5 deals with the parasitic gap phenomenon.

1 Null Elements in English: Recapitulation

The null elements introduced so far are exemplified in (1). (1a) illustrates PRO, (1b) illustrates NP-trace, and (1c) illustrates *wh*-trace.

1a John$_i$ would prefer very much [[PRO$_i$ to invite Bill]].
1b [$_{IP}$ Bill$_i$ will be invited t$_i$].
1c [$_{CP}$ Whom$_i$ would [$_{IP}$ John prefer [$_{CP}$ t$'_i$ for [$_{IP}$ us to invite t$_i$]]]]?

The three null elements illustrated here all have an S-structure antecedent, an NP with which they are coindexed, but the status of PRO is quite distinct from the status of traces. And similarly, NP-trace and *wh*-trace can be differentiated. Let us recapitulate some of the distinctions between the null elements here.

1.1   D-structure Representations

D-structure is a representation of the argument structure and the thematic relations of the sentence.[1] The D-structures corresponding to the S-structures in (1) will be as in (2):

2a   [$_{IP}$ John$_i$ would prefer very much [$_{CP}$ [$_{IP}$ PRO$_i$ to invite Bill]]].[2]
2b   [$_{IP}$ e will be invited Bill].
2c   [$_{CP}$ [$_{IP}$ John would prefer [$_{CP}$ for [$_{IP}$ us to invite whom]]]]?

The D-structures (2b) and (2c) encode the underlying positions of the arguments *Bill* and *whom* respectively. The S-structures (1b) and (1c) illustrate the effect of the transformation move-α: *Bill* in (1b) and *whom* in (1c) have been moved, leaving a trace. Two comments are in order with respect to the examples. In (1c) there is also an intermediate trace in the specifier position of the lower CP. We need to postulate this trace in order to guarantee that the subjacency condition is observed (see chapter 7, section 6). We discuss the status of intermediate traces in chapters 9 and 10. In the D-structure (2b) the empty subject position indicated by *e* is generated because of the EPP.

Let us turn to (1a) and (2a) which illustrate the occurrence of PRO. In (2a) we see that PRO is a D-structure null element. This is an important feature distinguishing PRO from the traces in (1b) and (1c) which arise at S-structure as a result of movement.

The reader should find it easy to work out for himself why PRO must be present in the D-structure representation (2a). Let us follow the procedure we

---

[1]   Several authors argue against the distinction between D-structure and S-structure (Brody, 1993b; Chomsky, 1992; Zubizarreta, 1987).

[2]   Under the hypothesis that all NPs in [Spec, IP] are derived subjects and that the base-position of external arguments is [Spec, VP] (chapter 6, section 5), PRO will be base generated in [Spec, VP] and moves to [Spec, IP] at S-structure. (2a) would then be replaced by (ia) and the S-structure (1a) would be represented more accurately as (ib), where PRO has undergone NP-movement and leaves a co-indexed trace in [Spec, VP]:

(ia)   [$_{IP}$ John would prefer very much [$_{CP}$ [$_{IP}$ e to [$_{VP}$ PRO invite Bill]]]].
(ib)   [$_{IP}$ John$_i$ would prefer very much [$_{CP}$ [$_{IP}$ PRO$_i$ to [$_{VP}$ t$_i$ invite Bill]]]].

Observe that the basic contrast between traces and PRO still holds: PRO is present at D-structure.

have adopted for determining D-structure. In (1a)/(2a) there are two verbs: *prefer* and *invite*. Both are two-place predicates requiring an external and an internal argument.

Given the projection principle, which holds at each syntactic level, the theta roles must be assigned, hence the arguments must be present, both at D-structure and at S-structure. At both levels of representation *prefer* theta-marks the NP *John* indirectly and the clausal complement (CP) directly. *Invite* theta-marks PRO indirectly and *Bill* directly.

PRO is present at D-structure and has its own theta role, independently from the theta role of its antecedent, *John*. The position in which PRO is generated at D-structure is a theta-position. The antecedent of PRO, *John*, also has a theta role.

1.2   Identification of Null Elements

A consideration of thematic properties of null elements helps us to identify the type of zero element we are dealing with: PRO or trace. So far our discussion suggests that D-structure null elements with thematic roles could only be PRO (but see section 3 below for a discussion of *pro*), traces being an S-structure phenomenon by definition.

At S-structure a null element with an antecedent may be either PRO or trace. If the antecedent and the non-overt element each have a theta role, the non-overt category will be identified as PRO. If the antecedent and the null element share a theta role the null element will be identified as a trace.

Since PRO has its own theta role it may also appear without an antecedent:

3a   [$_{CP}$ [$_{IP}$ PRO to invite Poirot]] would be a mistake.
3b   [$_{CP}$ [$_{IP}$ PRO to shave myself now]] would be painful.

1.3   Government

In chapters 4 and 5 we discussed the status of the null element PRO and on the basis of the binding theory we deduced that this element must be ungoverned. In both (1a) and (3) PRO is ungoverned: CP is a barrier protecting PRO from government (but see the discussion in chapters 9 and 10 for modification of this proposal).

Let us turn to the traces in (1b) and (1c). We ignore the intermediate trace in (1c), to which we return in chapter 9. The traces in (1b) and (1c) are governed by the verbs, *invited* and *invite* respectively. In section 2 below we shall argue that traces must be governed and we shall discuss this property in detail. The configurational property of government thus also distinguishes traces from PRO: traces must be governed and PRO must not be governed. Looking at S-structure zero elements we can decide on whether they are PRO or trace on the basis of their government properties: a governed empty category can only be a trace, an ungoverned one can only be PRO. In section 3 we identify another null element which is governed: *pro*.

1.4   The Binding Theory and the Typology of NPs

We have established that the three null elements posited are specified for the features [±Anaphor] and [±Pronominal] in the following way:

4   Typology of NPs

Type	OVERT	NON-OVERT
[+Anaphor, −Pronominal]	anaphors	NP-trace
[−Anaphor, +Pronominal]	pronouns	?
[−Anaphor, −Pronominal]	R-expressions	*wh*-trace
[+Anaphor, +Pronominal]	− − − − − − − − − −	PRO

The importance of a chart like (4) should not be underestimated. What such a representation means is that labels such as trace or PRO are not primitives or unanalysable concepts of the theory. A term such as PRO is a shorthand term for a null element with the feature combination [+Anaphor, +Pronominal]. Though we go on using the terms PRO and trace in our discussion, the reader should bear in mind that these are used for convenience' sake and can be analysed in terms of more elementary properties.

Depending on the feature matrices of the NPs, they are subject to different principles of the binding theory. NP-traces are subject to Principle A, *wh*-traces to Principle C, PRO is subject to both Principles A and B, hence its special distribution (cf. discussion in chapter 5). NP-trace and PRO both have the property of being [+Anaphor], in contrast with *wh*-traces.

1.5   NP-trace and PRO

1.5.1   CHAIN FORMATION

In chapter 6, section 4.6.1 we discussed the chain formation process. We recapitulate the discussion briefly here. Consider (5a):

5a   Poirot$_i$ seems [$_{IP}$ t$_i$ to enjoy the enquiry].

Enjoy assigns an external theta role; *seem*, a raising verb, does not. For expository reasons, we ignore the subject-in-VP hypothesis developed in chapter 6, section 5, which will not affect the line of argumentation here. Recall that a chain is a sequence of coindexed positions where each position locally binds the next position down (cf. discussion chapter 6, section 4.6, (105)). Chain formation is free: for (5b) we could create the chains (5b) or (5c). In (5b) the NP trace, t_i, is a member of a chain distinct from the chain of its antecedent, in (5c) t_i and *Poirot$_i$* belong to the same chain.

5b   <Poirot$_i$>, <t$_i$>
5c   <Poirot$_i$, t$_i$>

By the theta criterion as defined on chains (cf. chapter 6, section 4.6, (105d)) only (5c) is legitimate. In (5b) the argument *Poirot$_i$* belongs to a chain which fails to be assigned a theta role, and the external theta role of *enjoy* will be assigned to the chain <t_i>, which fails to contain an argument. Since it does not contain a case position, <t_i> is not visible. (5c) meets the theta criterion: the chain contains one argument, one theta-position, and it is visible by virtue of the NOMINATIVE case on *Poirot*. NP-traces and their antecedents have to be members of one chain.

 Consider now (6a) in which PRO is the subject of the non-finite clause:

6a   Poirot$_i$ wants [$_{CP}$ [$_{IP}$ PRO$_i$ to write a novel]].

Both *want* and *write* assign an external theta role. As before we ignore the subject-in-VP hypothesis, which does not alter the line of argument (see footnote 2). By the chain formation process, we can form either the chain (6b), where PRO and Poirot each head a chain, or (6c), where Poirot and PRO are part of a single chain:

6b   <Poirot$_i$>, <PRO$_i$>
6c   <Poirot$_i$, PRO$_i$>

The theta criterion excludes (6c): the chain <*Poirot$_i$*, PRO$_i$> contains two arguments, *Poirot$_i$* and PRO$_i$. *Poirot$_i$* and PRO$_i$ each have to belong to a separate chain, as in (6b).

The NP-trace and its antecedent form a single chain, while PRO and its antecedent are members of separate chains. This has consequences for the distance between the antecedent and PRO or the NP-trace respectively. Consider (5d):

5d   *[$_{IP1}$ Poirot$_i$ is likely [$_{CP}$ [that [$_{IP2}$ it appears [$_{IP3}$ t$_i$ to be the best candidate]]]].

(5d) is ungrammatical: t_i is ..ot locally bound by the antecedent. Because PRO and its antecedent do not enter into a chain, the distance between PRO and its antecedent is not subject to locality conditions: the intervention of *it* between *Poirot$_i$* and PRO$_i$ in (6d) is irrelevant:

6d   Poirot$_i$ agreed [$_{CP}$ that [$_{IP}$ it would not be easy [$_{CP}$ [$_{IP}$ PRO$_i$ to leave early]]]].

1.5.2   ANTECEDENTS

The antecedent of PRO and that of the NP-trace also differ with respect to their grammatical functions. The controller of PRO may be a subject (7a) or an object (7b), or it may be an implicit argument (7c):

7a   John$_i$ prefers very much [$_{CP}$ [$_{IP}$ PRO$_i$ to invite Bill]].
7b   I told John$_i$ [$_{CP}$ [$_{IP}$ PRO$_i$ to invite Bill]].
7c   The house was sold [$_{CP}$ [$_{IP}$ PRO to save money]].

NP-movement moves an NP into an A-position. The relevant landing site is a subject position, this follows from our theory developed so far. NP-movement cannot move an element into an object position, i.e. an NP-position immediately dominated by V', [NP, V']. This does not have to be stated as an independent principle. NP-movement is substitution: an NP is moved to a position that is empty at D-structure. Let us consider the possibility that the object position, [NP, V'], could be a landing site for NP-movement. This would involve a derivation like that in (8). The D-structure would be as in (8a) and NP-movement into [NP, V'] would derive the S-structure (8b):

8a   [$_{IP1}$ NP1 [$_I$] [$_{VP}$ [V' BELIEVE [$_{NP2}$ e] [$_{IP2}$ NP3 to VP]]]]
8b   [$_{IP1}$ NP1 [$_I$] [$_{VP}$ [V' BELIEVE [$_{NP2}$ NP3] [$_{IP2}$ t$_3$ to VP]]]]

In order for this derivation to be possible, we would have to imagine that there is a putative verb *BELIEVE* which is like English *believe* in that it takes an external argument, realized as NP_1, and a clausal complement, IP2. *BELIEVE* differs from *believe* in that it also subcategorizes for an NP, [NP, V']. In (8a), NP3 is the D-structure subject of the lower IP2; it is theta-marked by the lower V. NP3 will be caseless: it cannot receive structural ACCUSATIVE from *BELIEVE* because it is not adjacent to it. NP3 cannot receive inherent case from *BELIEVE* since it is not theta-marked by *BELIEVE* (cf. chapter 3 on case). At S-structure we propose that NP3 moves into the [NP, V'] position, in order to be assigned ACCUSATIVE by *BELIEVE*. This derivation is excluded by the principles we have been assuming so far, which make it impossible to generate a D-Structure such as (8a) and an S-structure such as (8b). The question arises what would allow the position NP2 to be generated within V'. D-structure is the representation of thematic relations. VP-internal NPs are projected to realize arguments of V. This means that in order to be projected at D-structure NP2 should be an argument of V, hence theta-marked by *BELIEVE*. In other words, with a D-structure as in (8a) *BELIEVE* assigns three theta roles: one to NP1, one to NP2 and one to IP2. If we were to generate a D-structure such as (8a) and then move NP3 into the NP2 position, then the chain <NP3, *t3*> in (8b) would be assigned two theta roles, that assigned to NP2 by *BELIEVE* and that assigned to NP3 by the verb of the non-finite clause. This chain will violate the theta criterion which requires a one-to-one relation between arguments – i.e. chains – and theta roles (cf. chapters 1, 3 and 6). If NP2 were not a theta position, i.e. if putative *BELIEVE* were like *believe* in that it has only one internal argument, realized by IP, then there could be no motivation for projecting [NP2, V'] at D-structure. We conclude that verbs such as *BELIEVE* in (8) do not exist and that NP-movement cannot move an NP into the object position [NP, V'].[3]

---

[3] Derivations such as that sketched in (8) were postulated in earlier versions of the grammar where they were referred to as subject-to-object raising (SOR), in contrast with subject to subject raising.

Recall from chapter 6, section 5, that it is currently assumed that the thematic position of the subject is VP-internal. This will not change anything to the discussion here: NP1 originates inside the VP and moves to [Spec, IP1]. (ia) replaces (8a), (ib) replaces (8b):

(ia) $[_{IP}$ e   [I] $[_{VP}$ NP1 BELIEVE $[_{NP2}$ e] $[_{IP2}$ NP3 to VP]]]
(ib) $[_{IP}$ NP1 [I] $[_{VP}$ t1   BELIEVE $[_{NP3}]$ $[_{IP2}$ t_3 to VP]]]

As mentioned before, whenever the subject-in-VP-hypothesis does not have consequences for the argumentation we ignore it in the discussion.

1.6   *Traces*

NP-trace and *wh*-trace share the feature [–Pronominal] (cf. section 1.4). During the discussion in chapters 6 and 7 and the sections above we have already identified several properties which distinguish NP-traces and *wh*-traces. These concern the moved element, its landing site and its extraction site:

9   Traces: survey of properties

	NP-trace	*wh*-trace
Moved category	NP	XP (NP, PP, etc.)
Landing site	A-position by substitution	A′-position by substitution or adjunction
	NP-position	[Spec, CP] or adjoined position
Properties of antecedent		
Case	Yes	No
Chain	A-chain	A′-chain
Properties of trace		
Features	[+Anaphor] [–Pronominal]	[–Anaphor] [–Pronominal]
Binding theory	A	C
Theta role	Yes	Yes
Case	No	Yes (when target = NP)
Governed	Yes	Yes

Needless to say, all these properties are not independent of each other. We invite the reader to try and relate them in the way that we have done in the discussion of NP-traces in chapter 6.

2   Null Elements in a Grammar

If we assume null elements as a component of the grammar of natural languages, we must assume that the language learner has the ability to postulate such null elements in the representations he assigns to sentences. He needs to have evidence for positing these categories and ways of identifying them. The discussion above has shown that not any null category can appear anywhere, in the same way that overt categories too cannot be generated randomly.

Recall from chapter 3 that overt NPs must be assigned abstract case. We proposed that the case feature on the NP makes it visible for theta role assignment. We could say that abstract case legitimates NPs, or, to put it differently, that overt NPs are **formally licensed** by case. Null elements too must be formally licensed, their presence in the structure must be legitimated. Moreover, we should also have a way of identifying the content of the non-overt elements. The learner must know, and the grammar must specify (i) how non-overt elements are licensed in the structure; and (ii) how such elements can be given content. In the preceding discussion we have already considered the distribution and interpretation of PRO. PRO can only appear in ungoverned contexts. We can say that (i) PRO is licensed in ungoverned contexts; and (ii) that its interpretation is determined by control theory. In the next section we address the licensing conditions of traces.

2.1 Formal Licensing: the Empty Category Principle

In our survey of the properties of traces we have noticed that both NP-traces and *wh*-traces are governed. Government has been identified as the formal licensing condition for traces: traces must be governed. However, simple government will not suffice to license a trace: traces must be governed in a special way.

The discussion of the government requirement of traces starts out from the **subject–object asymmetry** exhibited in (10) and (11) and already discussed in chapter 7, section 5.1.

10a   Whom$_i$ do [$_{IP}$ you think [$_{CP}$ t$'_i$ that [$_{IP}$ Lord Emsworth will invite t$_i$]]]?
10b   Whom$_i$ do [$_{IP}$ you think [$_{CP}$ t$'_i$ [$_{IP}$ Lord Emsworth will invite t$_i$]]]?

11a   *Who$_i$ do [$_{IP}$ you think [$_{CP}$ t$'_i$ that [$_{IP}$ t$_i$ will invite Poirot]]]?
11b   Who$_i$ do [$_{IP}$ you think [$_{CP}$ t$'_i$ [$_{IP}$ t$_i$ will invite Poirot]]]?

While objects can be freely extracted across overt complementizers, subjects can only be extracted from clauses without overt complementizers. This phenomenon was described in terms of the *that*-trace filter. The *that*-trace filter has been reinterpreted in the light of the government requirement for traces. The idea is that in order to be licensed, i.e. legitimated in certain positions, traces must be governed in a special way: they must be **properly governed**. Proper government can be achieved in two quite distinct ways: **theta-government** and **antecedent-government**. A head **theta-governs** a constituent if it both governs and theta-marks the constituent. Antecedent-government is government by a coindexed maximal projection. At this point we extend our range of governors: either heads or maximal projections can be governors under the right conditions. The licensing condition that traces must be properly governed is known as the **empty category principle**:

12	**Empty category principle (ECP)**
Traces must be properly governed.
A properly governs B if and only if A theta-governs B or A antecedent-governs B.
(cf. Chomsky, 1986b: 17)
A theta-governs B if and only iff A governs B and A theta-marks B.
A antecedent-governs B iff A governs B and A is coindexed with B.

The new definition of government in (13) incorporates both head- and antecedent-government and takes into account the minimality condition (14). We shall discuss the notion barrier in chapter 10.

13	**Government**
A governs B if and only if
(i)   A is a governor;
(ii) A m-commands B;
(iii) no barrier intervenes between A and B;
(iv) minimality is respected.
where governors are: (a)   heads,
(b)   coindexed XPs.

14	**Minimality** (cf. chapter 3, section 2.2)
A governs B if and only if there is no node Z such that
(i)   Z is a potential governor for B;
(ii) Z c-commands B;
(iii) Z does not c-command A.

Let us carefully consider the structures in which the relevant traces appear in the examples above on the basis of the partial tree diagram representations.

15 = 10

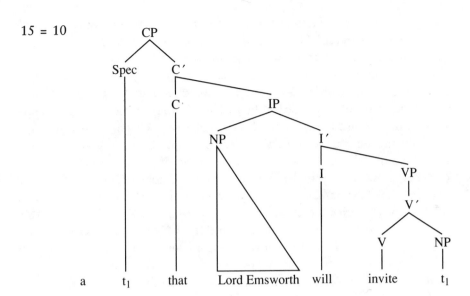

16 = 11

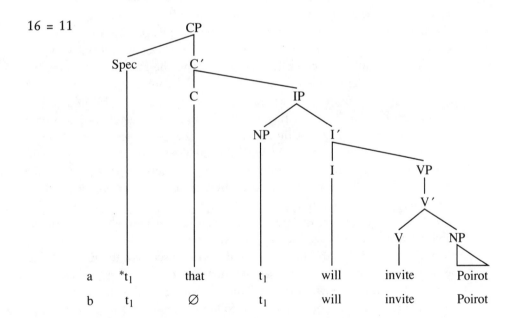

In (15a) and in (15b) the lowest trace is governed by the verb *invite* by which it is also theta-marked. This type of government is **theta-government**. We shall be looking at intermediate traces in chapter 9.

In (16a) and in (16b) the subject-trace is governed by INFL, from which it will receive NOMINATIVE case. But this trace is not theta-governed by INFL since it is not theta-marked by it. The theta role assigned to the subject of the lower clause is the external role of the verb *invite*.

Following our earlier discussion, let us adopt the hypothesis that even though finite INFL is a governor, it is defective. IP, its maximal projection, does not constitute a complete barrier for outside government (see chapter 9 and especially chapter 10, which deals exclusively with the notion barrier). If IP is not a barrier for government, the subject traces in (16a) and (16b) could be properly governed from the outside of IP. Proper government will only be possible by antecedent-government, though: there is no theta-marker for the subject outside IP, so theta-government is not available.

In (16a) the complementizer *that* intervenes between the trace in the subject position and the intermediate trace in [Spec, CP]. The complementizer is the head of CP, hence it is a potential governor. Assuming that IP is not a barrier for government, *that* governs into IP and will be able to govern the trace in the subject position. The intermediate trace in the [Spec, CP] position is coindexed with the trace in the subject position of IP and, assuming again that IP is not a barrier, the intermediate trace should thus be able to antecedent-govern the trace in the subject position. We have a construction with two potential governors: the complementizer *that* and the intermediate trace. By minimality (14) the coindexed trace in [Spec, CP] cannot govern the subject trace because the complementizer *that* is a Z in the sense of (14) and will be the governor of the trace in the subject position. But *that* is not a proper governor (12): *that* does not theta-mark the trace and hence does not theta-govern it; *that* is not coindexed with the trace so it does not antecedent-govern it either. Without a proper governor, the subject-trace violates the ECP and (16a) is ungrammatical. In (16b) there is no overt complementizer to interfere with the government from the intermediate trace. Again assuming that IP is not a barrier, the trace in [Spec, CP] can antecedent-govern the subject trace. The subject trace is properly governed.

On the basis of the subject–object asymmetries discussed, the ECP (12) has become established as a licensing condition on traces. It may be useful to point out a contrast between the ECP and the anti-government constraint for PRO. That PRO must not be governed follows from its feature specifications as already discussed. The ECP, on the other hand, is conceived as a primitive of the theory of null elements. The ECP is a principle which, at the moment, does not seem to follow from anything else in the grammar.

Having established that the ECP formally licenses traces we now turn to the question how their content is recovered. There is a rather natural answer here. We have seen that traces must have an antecedent. The properties of the trace will be able to be recovered by virtue of the coindexation with its antecedent.

In the next sections we illustrate the ECP and we turn to some problems.

2.2 Subjacency and ECP

Consider the judgements in (17) and (18).

17a ?What do you wonder when John bought?
17b *Who do you wonder when bought these books?

18a ?What do you wonder who will read?
18b *Who do you wonder what will read?

Although none of the sentences in (17) and (18) is perfectly acceptable, there is a marked decrease in the acceptability of the (b) examples. If we turn to the S-structure representations of these sentences we can explain these intuitions:

19a ?$[_{CP1}$ What$_i$ do $[_{IP_1}$ you wonder $[_{CP2}$ when$_j$ $[_{IP2}$ John bought t$_i$ t$_j$]]]]?
　　　　　　　　#　　　　　　　　　　　#

19b *$[_{CP1}$ Who$_i$ do $[_{IP1}$ you wonder $[_{CP2}$ when$_j$ $[_{IP2}$ t$_i$ bought these books t$_j$]]]]?
　　　　　　　　#　　　　　　　　　　　#

20a ?$[_{CP1}$ What$_i$ do $[_{IP1}$ you wonder $[_{CP2}$ who$_j$ $[_{IP2}$ t$_j$ will read t$_i$]]]]?
　　　　　　　　#　　　　　　　　　　　#

20b *$[_{CP1}$ Who$_j$ do $[_{IP1}$ you wonder $[_{CP2}$ what$_i$ $[_{IP2}$ t$_j$ will read t$_i$]]]]?
　　　　　　　　#　　　　　　　　　　　#

All the examples above are violations of Ross' *wh*-island constraint. In more general terms they are subjacency violations. In (19a) *wh*-movement violates subjacency: two bounding nodes, IP1 and IP2, are crossed. In (19b) the subjacency condition is violated in a similar fashion, but the sentence is markedly worse. This is due to the fact that not only subjacency is violated but in addition the ECP is violated. The subject-trace in IP2 is not properly governed: it is not theta-governed nor is it governed by its antecedent *who$_i$*. This latter statement depends on the assumption that though the lower IP2 is not a barrier to outside government, CP2, the maximal projection that intervenes between the antecedent *who$_i$* and the trace in the lower IP2, is a barrier. We return to the notion of barrier in chapter 9 and especially in chapter 10. We return to antecedent-government in chapter 12.

In (20a) only subjacency is violated. All the traces are properly governed: the object-trace is theta-governed by the verb and the subject-trace is antecedent-governed by *who$_i$*.

In (20b) an ECP violation is added to a subjacency violation. The lower subject-trace is not properly governed: it is not theta-governed for obvious reasons and *what$_i$* in [Spec, CP2] is not its antecedent, hence cannot antecedent-govern it. Again the real antecedent of the subject-trace is too far away to antecedent-govern it.

2.3 *Some Problems*

In this section we turn to some problematic examples which our theory so far cannot handle. We shall deal with properties of adjunct traces and with subject extraction. These problems will be tackled more fully in chapters 9, 10 and 12.

2.3.1 ADJUNCT MOVEMENT AND ECP

Consider (21), an example of short movement of a time adjunct:

21a   I wonder [$_{CP}$ when$_i$ [$_{IP}$ John bought it t$_i$]].

If the ECP applies generally to traces then we expect that the trace of *when* is also subject to the ECP. In this section we consider the application of the ECP to adjuncts and we shall discover that there are some problems. We return to those in chapter 9.

As an optional time adverbial, *when* is not theta-marked by the verb. So we shall not be able to claim that its trace is theta-governed by the verb. The only way for an adjunct-trace to be properly governed is by antecedent-government. In this way adjunct-traces are like subject-traces. (21b) is a partial tree diagram representation of the S-structure of (21a).

21b

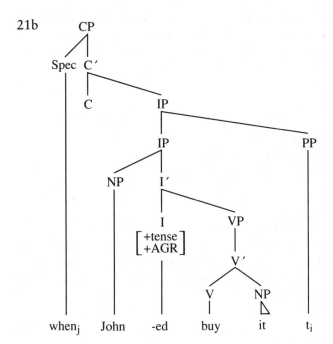

We assume that the time adjunct is base-generated in a position adjoined to IP (cf. chapter 7, section 5 and 5.1 on adjunction). That *when* should be adjoined as a modifier to IP is plausible since *when* specifies the time and INFL contains the feature [±Tense]. Given this assumption *when*$_j$ will ante-cedent-govern its trace. Hence the ECP is satisfied.

The assumption that the trace of *when* is outside VP is crucial for our discussion. If the trace of *when* had been inside the VP,[4] then it could not have been governed by its antecedent, assuming that VP is a barrier for outside government. But even if the representation of (21a) as (21b) is plausible there are other examples that cannot be handled this way. Certain adverbial phrases must have their D-structure position inside VP and still allow extraction. (This point is raised at some length in Chomsky, 1986b: 19–20.) Consider (22) which is closely analogous to (21) and is equally grammatical. The only difference is that here a manner adverbial has been moved (cf. Chomsky, 1986b: 29, (37)).

22 I wonder [$_{CP}$ how$_j$ [$_{IP}$ John will fix it t$_j$]].

---

[4] I.e. as assumed in chapter 2.

Traces of manner adjuncts are not theta-governed by the verb. Consequently they can only satisfy the ECP by antecedent-government. Concerning the D-structure position of manner adverbials like *how* and the corresponding S-structure positions of their traces there is strong evidence that these adverbs are VP constituents.

23a What John will do is [vp fix the car clumsily].
23b [vp Fix the car clumsily] is what they all do.
23c [vp Fix the car clumsily] John surely did.

In the three examples above the manner adjuncts behave as VP constituents. In the pseudo-cleft sentences (23a) and (23b) the adjunct *clumsily* is clefted with the VP. In (23c) the manner adjunct is preposed along with the verb and its object. Under this analysis the S-structure representation of (22) would be (24): the trace of *how* is inside VP.

24

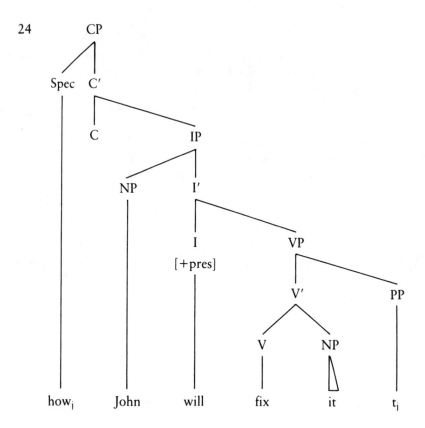

If (24) is the only representation available then the antecedent *how$_j$* should not be able to antecedent-govern the trace t_j. The antecedent is separated from the trace not only by the defective I-projection but also by VP, a barrier.

Although adjunct traces and subject traces are similar in that they can only satisfy the ECP through antecedent-government, the two types of traces pattern differently with respect to long movement. Compare long subject *wh*-movement in (25) with long adjunct *wh*-movement in (26):

25a *Who$_i$ do [$_{IP}$ you think [$_{CP}$ t'$_i$ that [$_{IP}$ t$_i$ will invite Poirot]]]?
25b Who$_i$ do [$_{IP}$ you think [$_{CP}$ t'$_i$ [$_{IP}$ t$_i$ will invite Poirot]]]?

26a When$_j$ do [$_{IP}$ you think [$_{CP}$ t'$_j$ that [$_{IP}$ Emsworth will invite Poirot t$_j$]]]?
26b When$_j$ do [$_{IP}$ you think [$_{CP}$ t'$_j$ [$_{IP}$ Emsworth will invite Poirot t$_j$]]]?

The presence of the overt complementizer *that* in (25a) is the cause of the ungrammaticality of the sentence: the complementizer prevents antecedent-government of the subject-trace by the intermediate trace. In (26a) the adjunct-trace is in exactly the same relation to its antecedent and yet the sentence is grammatical. The ECP is satisfied in (26a), an unexpected conclusion in the light of our theory so far. We return to the problem in chapter 9 and in chapter 12.

Adjunct-traces contrast with complement traces in that the latter are theta-governed, while the former are not. This was already illustrated in chapter 7, example (58), repeated here for the reader's convenience as (27):

27a [$_{CP1}$ How$_i$ do [$_{IP1}$ you [$_{VP}$ think [$_{CP2}$ that [$_{IP2}$ John could [$_{VP}$ solve this problem t$_i$]]]]]]?
27b [$_{CP1}$ [$_{IP1}$ I wonder [$_{CP2}$ which problem$_j$ [$_{IP2}$ John could solve t$_j$ this way]]]].
27c *[$_{CP1}$ How$_i$ do [$_{IP1}$ you [$_{VP}$ wonder [$_{CP2}$ which problem$_j$ C^0 [$_{IP2}$ John could [$_{VP}$ solve t$_j$ t$_i$]]]]]]?
27d ??[$_{CP1}$ Which problem$_j$ do [$_{IP1}$ you [$_{VP}$ wonder [$_{CP2}$ how$_i$ C^0 [$_{IP2}$ John could [$_{VP}$ solve t$_j$ t$_i$]]]]]]?

In (27a) we extract the manner adjunct *how* from the lower clause and move it to the matrix [Spec, CP$_1$]. This movement is unproblematic. Equally unproblematic is the movement of the direct object NP *which problem* in (27b): *which problem* is extracted from the VP-internal position and moves to the embedded [Spec, CP$_2$]. In (27c) we combine the two types of movement: *how* moves to the matrix [Spec, CP$_1$] and *which problem* moves to the lower [Spec,

CP$_2$]. In (27d) we move the adjunct to the lower [Spec, CP2] and we move the object to the higher [Spec, CP1]. As discussed in chapter 7, both (27c) and (27d) violate subjacency, but the degradation is much worse in (27c) than in (27d), suggesting strongly that adjunct-extraction should not be treated on a parallel with object-extraction. We return to the issue in chapters 9 and 12. We shall see that the degraded status of (27c) is due to an ECP violation which is added to the subjacency violation.

2.3.2 SUBJECT MOVEMENT

Let us briefly return to (20a), repeated here as (28a) for convenience' sake:

28a [$_{CP1}$ What$_i$ do [$_{IP1}$ you wonder [$_{CP2}$ who$_j$ [$_{IP2}$ t$_j$ will read t$_i$]]]]?
         #   #

We have proposed that the relative unacceptability of this example is due to a subjacency violation. However, such an analysis presupposes that the subject *wh*-element *who* is moved. An alternative S-structure of this example would be (28b) in which *who*$_j$ stays in the subject position.

28b [$_{CP1}$ What$_i$ do [$_{IP1}$ you wonder [$_{CP2}$ t$'_i$ [$_{IP2}$ who$_j$ will read t$_i$]]]]?

(28b) does not violate any principles of the grammar. *What* has moved successive-cyclically, leaving an intermediate trace in the lower [Spec, CP]. The fact that the sentence is not perfectly acceptable must be explained (cf. chapter 10, section 4.1).

3 Non-overt Subjects: the *Pro*-drop Parameter

3.1 *The Gap in the Paradigm:* pro

3.1.1 NULL SUBJECTS IN ITALIAN

Our classification of NPs is based on two features [±Anaphor] and [±Pronominal]. It is easy to see that on the basis of two features, each specified as either + or −, there are four possible combinations.

We have seen that for overt NPs only three of the four combinations are actually realized and we have discussed why the category [+Anaphor, +Pronominal] is excluded in principle (chapter 4).

For non-overt NPs we should ideally use the same typology and thus we also identify four possible combinations. So far we have only identified three and we have not discovered a non-overt corollary to the combination [−Anaphor, +Pronominal]. Indeed this was the situation that generative linguists had arrived at in the beginning of the 1980s. However, the **gap in the paradigm** of non-overt categories is not very fortunate. There is no reason why there ought not to be an empty category characterized by the features [−Anaphor, +Pronominal]. Such an element would be subject only to Principle B of the binding theory (cf. Chomsky, 1982: 78).

Turning to languages other than English, we find evidence for such an empty category. Consider the following examples from Italian:

29a Gianni ha parlato.
     Gianni has spoken.
29b e Ha parlato.
     has (3sg) spoken
29c Gianni ha detto [$_{CP}$ che [$_{IP}$ e ha parlato]].
     Gianni has said that has spoken

In (29a) *parlare* assigns its external theta role to *Gianni*. By analogy we assume that the same is true of the occurrence of *parlare* in (29b) and (29c). On the basis of the EPP we postulate that there is a subject position, [Spec, IP], in all the examples in (29). The projected subject position of *ha parlato* in (29b) is an NP-position which is not phonetically realized and in which the external theta role of the verb is realized. We postulate that the [Spec, IP] position is occupied by a zero element. The question is: what are the properties of this zero NP?

The non-overt subject of (29b) is obviously not a trace, there being no antecedent. It would also not be very reasonable to assimilate *e* with PRO. Recall that PRO must be ungoverned and the finite inflection in (29b) and (29c) will govern *e*.

The empty element in (29b) has definite reference: its interpretation is like that of an overt pronoun. Like a pronoun it may refer to an entity in the non-linguistic context (29b), or it may be coindexed with an element in the linguistic context. In (29c) one possible interpretation is that the non-overt subject of *ha parlato* is identical to that of the overt subject of *ha detto*. In other words, the non-overt subject in (29b) and (29c) is the missing non-overt NP that we have been looking for: it is a non-overt pronoun. The null element has the feature combination [−Anaphor, +Pronominal]. This final non-overt NP is represented by *pro*, 'small *pro*'. Again the label *pro* is only a shorthand label to single out the element with the specific feature combination given.

30a *pro* Ha parlato.
30b Gianni ha detto che *pro* ha parlato.

3.1.2 INFLECTION AND *PRO*

In earlier discussion (Introduction) we have already seen that any pronominal subject in Italian may remain unexpressed. We posit that the understood subject is syntactically represented by a non-overt pronominal. The subject pronoun is only overtly expressed when it is emphasized; *pro*, being a null element, can obviously not be stressed.

31a io   parlo   *pro* parlo
31b tu   parli   *pro* parli
31c lei   parla   *pro* parla
31d noi   parliamo *pro* parliamo
31e voi   parlate   *pro* parlate
31f loro parlano   *pro* parlano

Expletive pronouns in Italian are also realized as *pro*. Since they contribute nothing to the interpretation of a sentence, expletives will never be stressed, hence they will never be overt.[5]

32 *pro* Sembra che Gianni sia ammalato.
       seems   that Gianni is (subj) ill

In (32) we assume that the subject position of the matrix clause is filled by *pro*, which in this example is a non-overt expletive pronoun.

3.1.3 THE TYPOLOGY OF NULL ELEMENTS: SOME DISCUSSION

Let us complete our survey of NP-types:

---

[5] The same observation holds for weather verbs such as *rain, snow*, etc. In Italian their subject is never overt. See the Introduction.

33 Typology of NPs

Type	OVERT	NON-OVERT
[+Anaphor, −Pronominal]	anaphor	NP-trace
[−Anaphor, +Pronominal]	pronoun	*pro*
[−Anaphor, −Pronominal]	R-expression	*wh*-trace
[+Anaphor, +Pronominal]	– – – – – – – – – –	PRO

Consider (34a):

34a Ho   telefonato.
   (I) have   telephoned

The S-structure representation of (34a) is as in (34b): *pro* is the external argument of *telefonare*.

34b *pro* ho   telefonato
       have (1sg) telephoned

Empty categories with the features [−Pronominal] are traces, they are created by movement. A′-movement gives rise to a trace of the type [−Anaphor, −Pronominal], A-movement gives rise to a trace of the type [+Anaphor, −Pronominal]. In the model of the grammar we are adopting here, traces are not present at D-structure. The empty categories with the feature [+Pronominal], *pro* and PRO, are present at D-structure. In (34) *pro* must be present at D-structure since it is assigned the external theta role of *telefonare*. When it is coreferential with an antecedent, *pro* does not form a chain with the antecedent: both *pro* and the antecedent *Gianni* have their own theta role:

34c Gianni$_i$ dice che *pro*$_i$ ha telefonato.
    Gianni says that has telephoned
    'Gianni says that he has telephoned.'

The NPs *Gianni* and *pro* do not form a chain: the chain <*Gianni*$_i$, *pro*$_i$> would contain two arguments and would have two theta roles. <*Gianni*$_i$, *pro*$_i$> would violate the theta criterion. Similarly in (34d) PRO and its antecedent do not form a chain:

34d   Gianni$_i$ wants [$_{CP}$ [$_{IP}$ PRO$_i$ to telephone Maria]].

This does not mean, though, that *pro* or PRO can never be part of a chain. Consider (35):

35a   *pro$_i$* è stato invitato t$_i$.
       pro is been invited
       'He/She has been invited.'
35b   [PRO$_i$ to be invited t$_i$ at court] was a great honour.

In (35a) *pro$_i$* heads the A-chain <*pro$_i$*, t$_i$>, in (35b) PRO heads the A-chain <PRO$_i$, t$_i$>. Moreover, if we adopt the subject-in-VP hypothesis developed in chapter 6, section 5, then we will assume that all arguments in [Spec, IP] head an A-chain, this will also apply to *pro* and to PRO:

36a   [$_{CP}$ [$_{IP}$ PRO$_i$ to [$_{VP}$ t$_i$ buy a newspaper every day]]] is important.
36b   [$_{IP}$ *pro$_i$* ho [$_{VP}$ t$_i$ comprato un giornale]].
               have (1sg) bought   a   newspaper
       'I have bought a newspaper.'

According to the subject-in-VP hypothesis V (*buy* in (36a), *comprare* in (36b)) assigns its external theta role to the argument in its specifier position. We assume then that in (36a) PRO originates in [Spec, VP] and moves to [Spec, IP], leaving a trace in its base position. The external theta role of V is assigned to the chain <PRO$_i$, t$_i$>. In (36b) *pro* is the external argument of *comprare*, we assume again that it originates in [Spec, VP], where it is theta-marked, and it moves to [Spec, IP], where it will be licensed and identified via the rich INFL.

   Though they have a number of properties in common, PRO and *pro* also differ with respect to their distribution: *pro* is found in governed positions ([Spec, IP]) while PRO is ungoverned.

3.2   *Cross-linguistic Variation: the* Pro-drop *Parameter*

We have now established the existence of a fourth non-overt NP, with the features [−Anaphor, +Pronominal], *pro*. So far we have given examples from

Italian. The English analogues of the Italian examples discussed above show that *pro* subjects are not a universal property of all human languages.[6]

37a *Has spoken.
37b *John has said that has spoken.

It is intuitively clear what allows the subject to be unexpressed in Italian and disallows this in English. In Italian the verb inflection is rich. As seen above (31), there are six different present tense forms in Italian, one for each person and number combination. This will allow one to identify the person and number of the subject even when the overt pronoun is absent. In English only third person subjects in the simple present can be identified on the basis of the verb inflection, English inflection is otherwise too poor to enable one to identify person and number of the subject on the basis of verb forms only.

We say that a rich INFL can identify an empty category in the subject position while a poor INFL fails to do so. In other words the grammatical features of the subject can be recovered from those of INFL, specifically from AGR, in languages with rich verb inflection. In English these features are not recoverable because its AGR is too poor. The identification of the subject features via AGR is represented by coindexation.[7]

38 *pro*$_i$ parlo$_i$.

We have already seen that languages which allow a pronominal subject to be left unexpressed are called **pro-drop languages**, they 'drop' the subject pronoun. Italian is a *pro*-drop language, English is not. This cross-linguistic variation is referred to as the **pro-drop parameter**. A child acquiring a language will have to discover whether the language he or she is exposed to is *pro*-drop or not. Clearly not very much overt evidence is needed to establish that subject pronouns can be left unexpressed. A child will have to set the *pro*-drop parameter either positively or negatively: the positive setting means that the language is a *pro*-drop language.

Spanish is like Italian in that it allows null subjects, but French is like English in that it does not have null subjects.

---

[6] For a survey of a range of languages see Jaeggli and Safir (1989). Various articles in this volume propose alternative accounts to the one given in this book.
[7] The agreement between [Spec, IP] and [I] is sometimes represented by co-superscripting:

(i) *pro*^{i} parlo^i.

39   *Spanish*
39a *pro* Vimos a Juan.
     Ø (we) see Juan
39b *pro* Baila bien.
     Ø (he/she) dances well
39c *pro* Estamos cansadísimos.
     Ø (we) are very tired

40   *French*
40a **pro* Voyons Jean.
     Ø   (we) see Jean
cf. Nous voyons Jean.
40b **pro* Danse   bien.
     Ø   (he/she) dances well
cf. Il/elle danse bien.
40c **pro* Sommes très fatigués.
     Ø   (we) are very tired
cf. Nous sommes très fatigués.

Let us look at an interesting example from another language group: modern Hebrew also allows the subject pronoun to be dropped:

41a 'Ani 'axalti 'et   ha-tapu'ax.
     I   ate-lsg ACC   the-apple
41b 'Axalti 'et ha-tapu'ax.

The *pro*-drop possibility in modern Hebrew is restricted. Borer (1980, 1983) shows that it is not allowed in the present tense at all and that in main clauses with the future and past tenses it is restricted to first and second persons (Borer, 1986: 392):

42a Hu 'axal 'et   ha-tapu'ax.
     he ate-3sg ACC the-apple
42b *'Axal 'et ha-tapu'ax.
42c 'Ani/'ata/hu 'oxel 'et   ha-tapu'ax.
     I/you/he   eat-sg ACC   the-apple
42d *'Oxel 'et ha-tapu'ax.

Borer relates the *pro*-drop option in modern Hebrew to the richness of inflection. In the present tense, only gender and number are overtly realized, person is not. The third person is the unmarked form in the other tenses too. The idea then is that not all types of inflection are strong enough to allow *pro*-drop.[8]

3.3 *Licensing of* Pro

Following our discussion of null elements we again ask (i) how *pro* is formally licensed; and (ii) how its content is recovered.

Rizzi (1986a) proposes that in *pro*-drop languages *pro* is subject to two requirements: (i) it is licensed under head-government: in the examples above the null element in the subject position is governed by INFL, a head; (ii) the content of *pro* is recovered through the rich agreement specification.

43   The *pro*-drop parameter

43a *pro* is governed by X^0_y;

43b Let X be the licensing head of an occurrence of *pro*: then *pro* has the grammatical specification of the features on X coindexed with it.

Whether a language has any X^0 of type *y* licensing *pro* is a language-specific property. Also the choice of X^0 varies cross-linguistically. In English *I* is not a choice for X in (43a). Hence null elements cannot occur in subject positions. In Italian and Spanish *I* is a choice for X^0 in (43a).

Modern Hebrew poses a problem in that *I* can be a choice for X^0 but apparently only in a restricted way (see (42) above). In certain cases the features of the governing head of *pro* will not be sufficient and hence the content of *pro* cannot be recovered (see discussion above).

Another problem for this account is posed by languages such as Japanese and Chinese. Huang (1984) argues that Chinese allows null subjects, i.e. is a *pro*-drop language, in spite of the fact that it lacks AGR entirely. The same observation holds for Japanese and Korean. Huang's (1984) proposal is to argue that *pro* is possible either in languages with rich agreement or no agreement at all. Some languages (German and the Scandinavian languages discussed in Platzack (1987)) allow only expletive, i.e. non-referential, subjects to be non-overt. This could be related to the fact that INFL in these

---

[8]   The Hebrew data are more complicated once we also turn to subordinate clauses. With past and future tenses a null subject is obligatory in any grammatical person in a subordinate clause if this subject has an antecedent in the matrix clause. For discussion of these data and a new interpretation, see Borer (1989).

languages is richer than it is in English, though poorer than in Italian. We could say that INFL may well license null subjects in these languages, but that its AGR features do not enable us to identify a referential *pro*. The only option for a subject *pro* to survive in such languages would be when it is non-referential, i.e. an expletive *pro*.[9]

The reader will have observed that (43a) does not restrict the licenser of *pro* to inflection only and that in principle other types of heads could license *pro*.

3.4   Null Objects in Italian

3.4.1   THE DATA

Consider the data in (44):

44a   Questo conduce la gente$_i$ a [PRO$_i$ concludere quanto segue].
      this leads the people to conclude what follows
      'This leads people to conclude what follows.'
44b   Questo conduce – a [PRO concludere quanto segue].
      this leads to conclude what follows
      'This leads one to conclude what follows.'

In (44a) *condurre* takes three arguments, realized by the subject NP (*questo*), the object NP (*la gente*) and the non-finite clausal complement (*a concludere quanto segue*). (44a) is an example of a structure with object control (cf. chapter 5): the direct object NP *la gente* controls the PRO subject of the infinitival clause. In (44b) the direct object NP is absent, but the sentence remains grammatical and again there is a PRO subject in the infinitival clause. This is rather puzzling: an object controller cannot be omitted in sentences with obligatory control (chapter 5):

45a   This leads people [PRO to conclude what follows].
45b   *This leads [PRO to conclude what follows].

While our discussion predicts that (45b) is ungrammatical, it leaves the grammaticality of the Italian parallel (44b) unexplained. In spite of the absence of a direct object in this example, PRO is interpreted as being controlled by

---

[9]   For discussion see Huang (1989) and Rizzi (1986a).

the (implied) object of *condurre* ('lead'). (44b) means, roughly, 'this leads one to conclude what follows'.

3.4.2 CONTROL BY THE UNDERSTOOD OBJECT

Consider the following Italian sentences (Rizzi, 1986a):

46a L'ambizione spesso spinge – a [PRO commettere errori].
the-ambition often pushes   to make mistakes
'Ambition often makes one make mistakes.'
46b In questi casi, di solito Gianni invita – a [PRO mangiare con lui].
in these cases, usually Gianni invites to eat with him
'In these cases Gianni generally invites people for dinner.'

In the examples in (46) the object controller is understood. In English the direct object controller cannot be omitted, as can be seen from the glosses. An important feature of the interpretation of (44b) and of the examples in (46) is that the implicit object is interpreted as 'one', 'people in general', it has a non-specific or arbitrary reading. Following the reasoning adopted in this book let us postulate that the understood object in Italian is realized by a non-overt element, an empty category. Such a hypothesis allows us to maintain that the controller cannot be omitted in sentences with object control, thus accounting for the ungrammaticality of the English example (45b), while at the same time accounting for the grammaticality of (44b) and (46), which lack an overt object controller. In English, apparently the object cannot be realized as a non-overt category in examples like (45b), in such examples there simply is no object at all; in the Italian cases like (44b), there is a non-overt controller for the object, here represented as *e*:

44c Questo conduce e_i a [PRO$_i$ concludere quanto segue].

3.4.3 CONSTRAINTS ON THE INTERPRETATION OF THE NON-OVERT OBJECT

An interesting property of the non-overt object in Italian is that it consistently has the nominal features [Masculine, Plural]:

47a La buona musica riconcilia e_i con se stessi$_i$.
the good music reconciles with themselves (masc pl)
'Good music reconciles one with oneself.'

47b   Un dottore serio visita e$_i$ nudi$_i$.
      a good doctor visits nude (masc pl)
      'A good doctor examines his patients nude.'

(47a) contains a plural reflexive *se stessi*. According to Principle A of the binding theory, reflexives must be bound in their GC. Since (47a) is grammatical, we deduce that it contains an appropriate binder for the reflexive. The subject NP *la buona musica* cannot be the relevant binder: the subject is feminine singular while the reflexive is masculine plural. Also, of course, from the point of view of the interpretation, the reflexive in these examples is not dependent on the subject. As the English translation shows, it is the understood object which binds the reflexive. (47b) contains a masculine plural predicate AP (*nudi*). The plural AP again does not relate to the subject NP, which is masculine singular. Again the plural AP relates to the implicit object.

The examples in (47) thus offer further evidence for postulating a non-overt element in the object position, i.e. the position [NP, V'], in Italian: the non-overt object is not simply 'understood', it plays an active part in the sentence in that it is involved in syntactic relations such as binding or predication. Observe that the feature content of the non-overt object is restricted to [+Masculine, +Plural], the feature content which is also associated with arbitrary PRO in Italian (48) (cf. chapter 5):

48   È difficile essere sempre allegri.
     is (3sg) hard be always cheerful (masc pl)
     'It is hard always to be cheerful.'

Indeed the non-overt object can only have the arbitrary reading. (49), where we force a specific interpretation on the object, is ungrammatical:

49   *Ieri il medico ha visitato nuda.
     yesterday the doctor has examined naked (fem sg)

3.4.4   THE IDENTIFICATION OF THE EMPTY CATEGORY

Let us try to characterize the null element in the object position of the Italian sentences above in terms of the theory of empty categories developed so far. Recall that we have four empty categories, defined in terms of the features [±Anaphor] and [±Pronominal]. It is unlikely that an empty category in [NP, V'] could be PRO, i.e. [+Anaphor, +Pronominal]: the [NP, V'] position is governed by V and we know that PRO must be ungoverned. Could the empty category be an NP-trace, i.e. [+Anaphor, −Pronominal]? At first glance, this is also unlikely. Recall that NP-movement is case-driven: an NP which cannot be case-marked in its base position moves to a landing site where it can receive case. It is clear that the NP in the object position of *condurre* in (44b) can be case-marked, witness the fact that it alternates with an overt NP, *la gente*, in (44a). Similarly, overt objects would be possible in (46) and in (47). Moreover, if the non-overt category had the feature [+Anaphor] it would have to have an A-binder, clearly this is not the case. The same conclusion can be drawn with respect to *wh*-traces, which are [−Anaphor, −Pronominal]: we do not have evidence for A′-binding in the examples (cf. section 4.3. and exercise 7 below). This leaves us with one final option: *pro*, the non-overt pronominal with the feature matrix [−Anaphor, +Pronominal], which was postulated in the subject position of Italian finite clauses without overt subject. This would lead us to propose the following representations:

50a Questo conduce pro_i a [PRO_i concludere quanto segue].
50b La buona musica riconcilia pro_i con se $stessi_i$.
50c Un buon dottore visita pro_i $nudi_i$.

The properties of object *pro* differ from those of subject *pro*: object *pro* is restricted in interpretation. In Italian, subject *pro* is equivalent to a subject pronoun: depending on the finite inflection it may be first, second or third person, singular and plural, and it can have a non-specific interpretation (51a) or a specific one (51b, 51c):

51a *pro* dicono che le donne sono diventate più   indipendenti.
     pro say-3pl that the women are   become   more independent
     'They say that women have become more independent.'
51b *pro* sono   andati a Roma.
     pro are-3pl gone   to Rome
     'They went to Rome.'
51c *pro* vuole   scrivere un romanzo.
     pro want-3sg write   a novel
     'He wants to write a novel.'

We have seen that non-overt objects always have the features plural masculine (cf. (52a)) and they never have specific reference (cf. (52b)):

52a   *Ieri sera la buona musica ha veramente riconciliato *pro* con se stesso.
      last night the good music has really reconciled with himself
52b   *Ieri il dottore ha visitato *pro* nudi per la prima volta.
      yesterday the doctor has examined naked (masc pl) for the first time

We need to account for the restriction on the features and the interpretation of object *pro* in Italian. Let us relate this issue to the general question
of the licensing and identification of *pro*. We have assumed that subject *pro*
is licensed because it is governed by the relevant licenser, INFL. We have also
proposed that the feature content of subject *pro* is recovered via the AGR
features of INFL, which is rich in Italian. (43) implies, though, that heads
other than I(NFL) might also be licensers of *pro*. Rizzi proposes that 'the
licensing of *pro* in object position can now be viewed as another instantiation
of the licensing schema: in Italian, V belongs to the licensers of *pro*, in English
it does not' (1986a: 519).

In addition to being licensed, *pro* must also be identified: its content must
be recovered. In the case of subject *pro*, the AGR features of INFL identify
pro. For the identification of verb-governed *pro*, Rizzi proposes that its
content is established through a mechanism of *arb* assignment, which will
associate the arbitary interpretation with *pro*:

53   *Arb* interpretation
     Assign *arb* to the direct theta role.
     (Rizzi, 1986a: 521)

If *arb* in Italian is associated with the features [+Masculine, +Plural], as
shown in (48), then we expect that non-overt objects, which are assigned *arb*,
should have these features.

To summarize: V can license *pro* in the object position in Italian. In English
this is not possible. The recovery of the content of object *pro* in Italian is due
to a rule of arbitrary interpretation.[10]

---

[10]   Rizzi (1986a) provides a discussion of further constraints of V as a licenser of *pro*.
       For a slightly different analysis see also Authier (1989b) and (1992). Based mainly
       on French data, Authier stresses the role of Tense in determining the arbitrary
       reading of the null objects.

4 Non-overt Antecedents of *Wh*-movement

In this section we return to *wh*-movement. Based on data from English and from Portuguese we will see that sometimes the antecedent of *wh*-movement can be non-overt.

4.1 Relative Clauses

4.1.1 EMPTY OPERATORS AND OBJECT RELATIVES

In chapter 7 we discussed the derivation of relative clauses. Consider:

54a This is [$_{NP}$ the man [$_{CP}$ whom [$_{IP}$ John claims [$_{CP}$ that [$_{IP}$ he will invite]]]]].

54b *This is [$_{NP}$ the man [$_{CP}$ whom [$_{IP}$ John made [$_{NP}$ the claim [$_{CP}$ that [$_{IP}$ he will invite]]]]]].

54c ?This is [$_{NP}$ the man [$_{CP}$ whom [$_{IP}$ John wondered [$_{CP}$ when [$_{IP}$ he will invite]]]]].

Based on subjacency effects we assume that relative clauses are derived by *wh*-movement. The S-structures of the sentences in (54) are given in (55). We indicate subjacency violations by means of the diacritic # on the relevant bounding nodes:

55a This is [$_{NP}$ the man [$_{CP}$ whom$_i$ [$_{IP}$ John claims [$_{CP}$ t$'_i$ that [$_{IP}$ he will invite t$_i$]]]]]].

55b *This is [$_{NP}$ the man [$_{CP}$ whom$_i$ [$_{IP}$ John made [$_{NP}$ the claim [$_{CP}$ t$'_i$ that
 #   #
[$_{IP}$ he will invite t$_i$]]]]]]].

55c ?This is [$_{NP}$ the man [$_{CP1}$ whom$_i$ [$_{IP}$ John wondered [$_{CP2}$ when [$_{IP}$ he will
 #   #
invite t$_i$]]]]]].

But there are other types of relative clauses which we have not discussed so far. (56a) is an example:

56a This is [$_{NP}$ the man [$_{CP1}$ that [$_{IP}$ John claims [$_{CP2}$ that [$_{IP}$ he will invite]]]]]].

In (56a) CP1 is a relative clause: it modifies the N *man*. However, at first sight it is not clear that *wh*-movement is involved: there is no overt *wh*-element in the structure. On the other hand, the theta criterion forces us to postulate a non-overt element in the object position of *invite* in (56a).

56b This is [$_{NP}$ the man [$_{CP1}$ that [$_{IP}$ John claims [$_{CP2}$ that [$_{IP}$ he will invite e]]]]].

The question arises of what kind of empty category *e* could be. From the discussion so far there is not much choice. The non-overt element is governed by V, hence PRO is excluded, since PRO must be ungoverned. *Invite* is an active verb, it case-marks the NP in the [NP, V′] position. This means that *e* cannot be NP-trace either, NP-traces being typically caseless. This leaves us with two options: *pro* or *wh*-trace. The former is also excluded since V does not license object *pro* in English (cf. the preceding discussion in section 3.4). This would lead us to conclude that *e* is a *wh*-trace, and we would have to postulate that in (56) the antecedent of the *wh*-trace is non-overt. We represent the non-overt antecedent of a *wh*-trace by **OP**, for non-overt operator, or **empty operator**. The relevance of the term operator will become clear in chapter 9. OP is like an overt *wh*-constituent: it moves from the VP-internal base position to [Spec, CP1]. In order to avoid subjacency violations, it will have to move via the intermediate [Spec, CP2], where it will leave a trace t'_i.

56c This is [$_{NP}$ the man [$_{CP1}$ OP$_i$ that [$_{IP1}$ John claims [$_{CP2}$ t'_i that [$_{IP2}$ he will invite t_i]]]]].

If the non-overt element in the relative clauses in (56) is created by moving an empty operator, then we expect that this movement gives rise to subjacency effects, parallel to those encountered for the movement of overt *wh*-phrases. The data in (56d) and (56e) parallel those in (54b) and (54c) and confirm this prediction. (56d) violates the complex NP constraint, in (56e) the non-overt operator is extracted from a *wh*-island.

56d *This is [$_{NP}$ the man [$_{CP}$ OP$_i$ that [$_{IP}$ John made [$_{NP}$ the claim [$_{CP}$ t'_i that
　　　　　　　　　　　　　#　　　　　　　　#
[$_{IP}$ he will invite t_i]]]]]].

56e ?This is [$_{NP}$ the man [$_{CP}$ OP$_i$ that [$_{IP}$ John wondered [$_{CP}$ when [$_{IP}$ he will
　　　　　　　　　　　　　　#　　　　　　　　　　#
invite t_i]]]]].

OP is another non-overt element. The literature is not very explicit about its properties (cf. Authier, 1989a; Contreras, 1993; Jaeggli, 1981; Lasnik and Stowell, 1989). Below we illustrate some further uses of the zero operator. Consider the following example:

57a   This is [NP the man [CP1 [IP1 John claims [CP2 that [IP2 he will invite]]]]].

In (57a) is closely similar to (56a). The only difference is that the complementizer *that* is absent in (57a) and it is present in (56a). We do not need to say anything specific about an example like (57a). We know that the complementizer *that* can delete in English:

58a   I think that Poirot is a decent detective.
58b   I think Poirot is a decent detective.

We will assume that the analysis of (57a) is like that of (56a), except that in (57a) the complementizer is non-overt.

57b   This is [NP the man [CP OP$_i$ [C^0 Ø] [IP John claims [CP t'$_i$ that [IP he will invite t$_i$]]]]].

Under this analysis the decrease in acceptability of (57c) and (57d) is due to subjacency effects:

57c   *This is the man John made the claim that he will invite. (cf. (55b))
57d   ??This is the man John wondered when he will invite.   (cf. (55c))

4.1.2   SUBJECT RELATIVES

In section 4.1.1 we have discussed object relatives, i.e. relative clauses in which the moved element, the antecedent, is the object of the relative clause. Let us now turn to subject relatives.

59a   This is the letter which will surprise Poirot.
59b   This is the letter that will surprise Poirot.

Adopting our analysis developed so far there are two options for the S-structure of (59a) depending on whether we assume that the relative pronoun *which* moves vacuously to [Spec, CP] or not:

60a   This is the letter [CP which_i [IP t_i will surprise Poirot]].
60b   This is the letter [CP [IP which will surprise Poirot]].

We shall adopt (60a) here. Recall that traces are subject to the ECP. In (60a) the trace of the subject is governed by the antecedent *which*. Let us turn to (59b). We assume that a non-overt operator has moved to [Spec, CP]:

61a   This is the letter [CP OP_i that [IP t_i will surprise Poirot]].

The S-structure (61a) raises important questions. At first sight, the configuration in (61a) is exactly like the one which we explicitly excluded by the *that*-trace filter, and which we have shown to be ruled out by the more general ECP. According to our discussion the trace in the subject position in (61a) cannot be properly governed by its antecedent (here OP_i) because there is an intervening complementizer *that*.

   In order to account for the grammaticality of (61a), Pesetsky (1982: 306) proposes that a special coindexation mechanism be invoked for this construction. This mechanism would have the effect of collapsing the empty operator in [Spec, CP] and the adjacent complementizer into one constituent which has all the relevant features of the operator:

62   **Complementizer contraction** (English)
     OP_i that   →   that_i

As a result of the contraction (62) the S-structure of (61a) is as in (61b):

61b   This is the letter [CP that_i [IP t_i will surprise Poirot]].

By virtue of the contraction with OP_i, *that_i* will now be able to govern the trace in the subject position. (62) captures the intuition that the element *that* in relative clauses functions like a relative pronoun: it seems to unite the properties of C and of the OP in [Spec, CP]. Observe that *that* can only receive an index from the operator in [Spec, CP]. (62) does not apply when *that* has an intermediate trace as its specifier:

63a   *This is the letter that John said that would surprise Poirot.
63b   *This is the letter [CP1 OP_i that [IP1 John said [CP2 t'_i that [IP2 t_i would surprise Poirot]]]].

63c *Complementizer contraction*
   *This is the letter [$_{CP1}$ that$_i$ [$_{IP1}$ John said [$_{CP2}$ t$'_i$ that [$_{IP2}$ t$_i$ would surprise Poirot]]]].

Complementizer contraction may apply to the complementizer *that* of CP1, but this does not save the sentence. The trace in the subject position of IP2 is not properly governed. The complementizer *that* of CP2 continues to block antecedent-government from the intermediate trace in [Spec, CP2]. (62) does not apply to the sequence *t$'_i$ -that* in CP2.

Pesetsky (1981) argues that similar mechanism of complementizer contraction can be used to account for the *que/qui* alternation in the following French examples:

64a l'homme que Maigret a arrêté
   the man that Maigret has arrested
64b l'homme que je pense que Maigret a arrêté
   the man that I think that Maigret has arrested

65a *l'homme qu'a été arrêté
   the man that has been arrested
65b l'homme qui a été arrêté
   the man who has been arrested
65c *l'homme que je pense qu'a été arrêté
   the man that I think that has been arrested
65d l'homme que je pense qui a été arrêté
   the man that I think who has been arrested

Que is the French equivalent of English *that*. For the S-structure representations of (64) we adopt the null operator analysis:

66a l'homme [$_{CP}$ OP$_i$ que [$_{IP}$ Maigret a arrêté t$_i$]]
66b l'homme [$_{CP}$ OP$_i$ que [$_{IP}$ je pense [$_{CP}$ t$'_i$ que [$_{IP}$ Maigret a arrêté t$_i$]]]]

(65a) and (65c) contain ECP violations. Consider the S-structures in (67):

67a *l'homme [$_{CP}$ OP$_i$ que [$_{IP}$ t$_i$ a été arrêté t$_i$]]
67b *l'homme [$_{CP}$ OP$_i$ que [$_{IP}$ je pense [$_{CP}$ t$'_i$ que [$_{IP}$ t$_i$ a été arrêté t$_i$]]]]

The trace in the subject position of the lowest clause is not properly governed: the intervening complementizer *que* governs the subject and, being a closer governor by minimality, *que* prevents antecedent-government by the non-overt operator in [Spec, CP]. In (67) we have also indicated the trace of NP movement in the complement position of *arrêté*. Needless to say, this trace is properly governed by the verb and poses no particular problems.

(65b) and (65d), conversely, are grammatical. The only difference between these examples and the ungrammatical pendants (65a) and (65c) is that *que* is replaced by *qui*. Pesetsky (1981: 308) proposes that the replacement of *que* by *qui* is the overt reflex of the application of complementizer contraction in French:

68   **Complementizer contraction** (French)
XP_i que   → qui_i/___$[_{IP}t_i$

The effect of (68) is like that of the English contraction given in (62): it collapses a complementizer and an adjacent index-bearing element in its specifier. But (68) differs from (62) in some respects. (68) only applies to a complementizer adjacent to a subject-trace which is coindexed with a con-stituent XP in its specifier. In this sense (68) is more restrictive than (62). (68) is less restrictive in that it applies both to a sequence of an operator followed by *que* and of an intermediate trace followed by *que*. The S-structures of the grammatical sentences are given in (69).

69a   l'homme $[_{CP}$ qui_i $[_{IP}$ t_i a été arrêté $t_i]]$
69b   l'homme $[_{CP}$ OP_i que $[_{IP}$ je pense $[_{CP}$ qui_i $[_{IP}$ t_i a été arrêté $t_i]]]]$

As the reader can verify for himself, (68) applies in both examples. In (69b) the contraction applies to the lower C, the higher *que* is not adjacent to the subject-trace, hence is not affected. As a result of the application of (68) the subject-traces in (69) will be properly governed. The alternation between *que* and *qui* in French is referred to as the *que/qui* **alternation**; the complementizer contraction rule (68) is sometimes referred to as the *que/qui* **rule**.

4.2   Null Operators in Infinitivals

4.2.1   INFINITIVAL RELATIVES

Consider the following sentences:

70a   I need a man whom I can love.
70b   I need a man that I can love.
70c   I need a man to love.

The derivation of (70a) is straightforward. Its S-structure is given without discussion in (71a):

71a I need [$_{NP}$ a man [$_{CP}$ whom$_i$ [$_{IP}$ I can love t$_i$]]].

(70b) is equally unproblematic: we assume that the null operator OP$_i$ has been *wh*-moved:

71b I need [$_{NP}$ a man [$_{CP}$ OP$_i$ that [$_{IP}$ I can love t$_i$]]].

(70c) is an example of an infinitival relative. We posit that analogously to the previous examples the object of *love* is a null operator that has been moved. In addition, the infinitival clause has a null element as its subject which we identify as PRO. PRO is controlled by the main clause subject *I*.

71c I$_i$ need a man [$_{CP}$ OP$_i$ [$_{IP}$ PRO$_i$ to love t$_i$]].

4.2.2 INFINITIVAL ADJUNCTS

Another construction for which the null operator hypothesis has been advocated is given in (72):

72 John is too stubborn to invite.

The infinitival clause expresses a purpose. (72) is parallel in structure to (73):

73a John is too stubborn [$_{CP}$ for [$_{IP}$ us to invite him]].
73b John is too stubborn [$_{CP}$ for [$_{IP}$ us to invite]].

In (73a) the external argument of *invite* is *us*, the subject NP, and the internal argument is *him*, the direct object NP. For (73b) we assume that the complement of *invite* is a null element which is both governed and case-marked. The most obvious hypothesis is that it is a *wh*-trace, i.e. that it is an A'-bound zero element.

74 John$_i$ is too stubborn [$_{CP}$ OP$_i$ for [$_{IP}$ us to invite t$_i$]].

The reader can check for himself that it will not do to argue that the null element in the object position of *invite* is PRO because this would violate the anti-government condition on PRO. The NP-trace option is equally unlikely. On the one hand, the null element is assigned ACCUSATIVE case and NP-traces are caseless. On the other hand, if the null element were identified as an NP-trace it would be subject to Principle A of the binding theory: it would have to be bound in its GC. The GC for the NP in the object position of *invite* is the lower clause: it contains both a governor (*invite*) and a subject (*us*). It follows that if we identified the null complement of *invite* as an NP-trace, this trace would be A-free and hence it would violate Principle A of the binding theory. An English V does not license *pro*.

On the analogy of the sentences in (73) with that in (72) it is reasonable to postulate that both the subject and the object in (72) are non-overt categories. The subject of the infinitive is PRO; the object will be assumed to be a trace coindexed with a moved zero operator:

75   John$_i$ is too stubborn [$_{CP}$ OP$_i$ [$_{IP}$ PRO to invite t$_i$]].

The hypothesis that movement is involved in (74 = 73b) and (75 = 72) and not, of course, in (73a), can be tested if we check for subjacency effects:

76a   John is too stubborn for us to even wonder when to invite him.
76b   *John is too stubborn for us to even wonder when to invite.
76c   *John is too stubborn to even wonder when to invite.

4.2.3   PRINCIPLE C AND OPERATOR BINDING

One potential problem has to be tackled here. We have seen that traces of *wh*-movement are like R-expressions and hence subject to Principle C of the binding theory: they must be free everywhere. In fact, Principle C appears at first sight to be violated in both (74) and (75) where the trace of the moved operator is coindexed with *John$_i$*, a c-commanding NP in an A-position.

In his discussion of such examples Chomsky (1986a) proposes that Principle C be reformulated as follows:

77   **Principle C**
     a   An R-expression must be A-free in the domain of its operator.
     b   An R-expression must be A-free.
     (Chomsky, 1986a: 86)

The term operator can be taken to be equivalent to the head of an A′-chain. Principle C is now stated as a disjunction: it contains two clauses either of which will apply. First, we apply clause (77a): it will apply to all R-expressions which are operator-bound, i.e. it applies to traces of movement. If (77a) does not apply, i.e. when the R-expression is not bound by an operator, we apply (77b).[11]

4.3 Null Objects in Portuguese

Consider the following examples from European Portuguese (Raposo, 1986):

78a A Joana viu-o na televisão ontem de noite.
   Joana saw him on television last night
   'Joana saw him on television last night.'
78b A Joana viu na televisão ontem de noite.
78c José sabe que Maria o viu.
   José knows that Maria him saw
   'José knows that Maria saw him.'
78d José sabe que Maria viu.

In (78a) and in (78c) the verb *viu* ('see') takes two arguments, one realized by the subject NP, the other by the object clitic *o*, an element associated with the inflected verb. (78b) and (78d) are problematic: the external argument is realized by the subject NP, but there is no overt direct object NP. The object of *viu* is 'understood', both in (78b) and in (78d). (78b) and (78d) mean roughly the same as (78a) and (78c) respectively: the complement of *viu* is 'him', 'her', 'it' or 'them'. It is the specific entity which is salient in the context of the discourse and is sometimes referred to as the **discourse topic**. Following the reasoning adopted so far, it seems natural to assume that there is a non-overt object in (78b) and in (78d). The representation of these sentences would then be as in (79):

79a A Joana viu *e* na televisão ontem de noite.
79b José sabe que Maria viu *e*.

The question arises what kind of empty category this null object could be. PRO is an unlikely candidate: PRO must be ungoverned and the [NP, V′]

---

[11] For further revisions of Principle C the reader is referred to Chomsky's own discussion (1986a: 98).

position is governed by V. NP-trace is also unlikely. The trace of NP-movement is subject to Principle A of the binding theory: it must be bound in its
governing category. In (79a) the non-overt object of *viu* is not bound by *Joana*.
Similarly in (79b) the non-overt object is not bound by *Maria*. We might think
that the non-overt element is *pro*. Recall that *pro* is found in the subject position
of languages with rich agreement in INFL, and also in the object position (cf.
discussion in section 3 above). Again, though, it is unlikely that the non-overt
category in (79) could be equated with the non-overt pronoun. Consider, for
instance, the sentences in (80):

80a João$_i$ disse [$_{CP}$ que [$_{IP}$ *pro$_i$* viu o Pedro]].
     João said that *pro* saw-3sg Pedro
     'João said that he saw Pedro.'
80b João$_i$ disse [$_{CP}$ que [$_{IP}$ Pedro viu e$_{j/*i}$]].
     João said that Pedro saw *e*
     'João said that Pedro saw him.'

Portuguese is like Italian in that it has non-overt subject pronouns. This is
illustrated in (80a). The non-overt subject of the embedded clause can be
coreferential with the matrix subject. This is as expected. We know that *pro*
has the feature matrix [−anaphoric, +pronominal]: by Principle B of the
binding theory, it must be free in its governing category, here the embedded
clause. *João* is outside the governing category and hence can bind *pro*. In (80b)
we see that the non-overt object cannot be coreferential with the matrix
subject. This suggests strongly that the non-overt object is not subject to
Principle B, rather the non-overt object is apparently subject to Principle C:
it must be free everywhere. An empty category which is subject to Principle
C is a *wh*-trace. This leads us to propose that the non-overt object in the
Portuguese sentences we are examining is a *wh*-trace bound by a non-overt
antecedent. The examples in (78b) and (78d) are then another illustration of
the null operator construction (for additional arguments cf. Raposo, 1986;
Rizzi, 1986a).

81a [$_{CP}$ OP$_i$ [$_{IP}$ A Joana viu t$_i$ na televisão ontem de noite]].
81b [$_{CP}$ OP$_i$ [$_{IP}$ José sabe que Maria viu t$_i$]].

We assume that OP functions as a non-overt topic operator. The non-overt
topic construction is not exclusive to Portuguese. Campos (1986) shows that
the analysis proposed for Portuguese also applies to Spanish. Huang applies
a similar analysis to non-overt objects in Chinese and to certain constructions

in German (Huang, 1984: 546ff.). The non-overt topic operator is not available in English: the English equivalents of (78b) and (78d) are ungrammatical. Whether a language has a non-overt topic or not seems to be a matter of parametric variation (cf. also Huang, 1984, 1991) and Authier (1989a,b).

5 Parasitic Gaps

5.1 Description

This section deals with a quite unusual construction which has been the subject of much discussion in the literature.

82a Poirot is a man whom you distrust when you meet.
82b Poirot is a man that anyone that talks to usually likes.

We focus solely on (82a). The analysis carries over to (82b). (82c) contains a complex relative clause with two verbs: *distrust* in the higher clause and *meet* in the time clause. Both verbs are two-place predicates which assign an external and an internal theta role. The question that we ask here is: how are the internal arguments realized? Adopting our by now familiar strategy we assume that the complements of the verbs are null elements:

83 Poirot is a man [$_{CP}$ whom [$_{IP}$ you distrust e_1 [$_{CP}$ when [$_{IP}$ you meet e_2]]]].

Let us try to identify the type of null element represented by e_1 and e_2 respectively. Both *es* in (83) occur in a governed position in which they are assigned ACCUSATIVE case. The most plausible option is to say that they are *wh*-traces. For e_1 this is reasonable enough: e_1 would be a trace co-indexed with *whom* exactly like in (84):

84 Poirot is a man [$_{CP}$ whom$_i$ [$_{IP}$ I distrust t_i]].

e_2 is problematic. If it is coindexed with an antecedent relative pronoun, then where is the pronoun? As far as the meaning goes, e_2 is interpreted as coreferential with e_1. One might want to say that, like e_1, e_2 is bound by *whom*, but this hypothesis raises problems.

On the one hand, extraction from adverbial clauses introduced by *when* normally leads to subjacency effects:

85   *Poirot is a man whom I yawn [when I see].

In addition the hypothesis that *whom* is the antecedent of e_2 and of e_1 means that it is the antecedent of two empty categories. But it is not possible to argue that one element, *whom*, has been moved from the two distinct positions indicated by *e*. *Whom* should have one and only one D-structure position, either the position of e_1 or that of e_2.

An interesting observation is that e_2 in some sense depends for its existence on the presence of e_1. When we eliminate e_1 from the sentence, replacing it by a pronoun for instance, the sentence becomes less acceptable:

86   *Poirot is a man [$_{CP}$ whom$_i$ [$_{IP}$ you distrust him [$_{CP}$ when [$_{IP}$ you meet t$_i$]]]].

In (86) *whom* has been extracted from the *when*-clause, producing subjacency effects analogous to those in (85).

Non-overt elements like e_2, which depend for their existence on the presence of another null element have been labelled **parasitic gaps**. A parasitic gap is a null element whose presence must be licensed by another gap in the sentence.[12]

In the literature various proposals have been formulated to account for the occurrence of parasitic gaps and to identify the type of null element we are dealing with. It is not our purpose here to discuss all the analyses that have been proposed in detail. We shall merely introduce two different options that have been adopted in the literature.

5.2   The PRO Hypothesis

Given that *whom* in our example (83) can only be extracted from one of the empty positions, say e_1, and hence fill the corresponding position at D-structure, it is assumed that the position of the parasitic gap, say e_2, is occupied by a theta-marked empty category at D-structure. So far we have been assuming

---

[12]   Parasitic gaps were first discussed by Engdahl (1983) and Taraldsen (1981). See also Brody (1993b), Chomsky (1982, 1986b), Kayne (1989), Manzini (1993) and Safir (1987) for discussion.

that in English null elements present at D-structure are associated with the feature matrix [+pronominal, +anaphor], i.e. PRO for short.

It has been proposed in the literature that the parasitic gap e_2 is PRO. PRO in (87a) would be controlled by the object of *distrust*. We represent this referential dependency by coindexation. For our purposes it is irrelevant whether PRO is already coindexed with *whom* at D-structure, or whether it gets coindexed at S-structure only. Remember that the anti-government condition on PRO does not apply at D-structure.

87a   Poirot is a man [$_{CP}$ [$_{IP}$ you distrust whom$_i$ [$_{CP}$ when [$_{IP}$ you meet e_2]]]].

$$= PRO_i$$

At S-structure *whom* moves to [Spec, CP] and leaves a trace.

87b   Poirot is a man [$_{CP}$ whom$_i$ [$_{IP}$ you distrust t$_i$ [$_{CP}$ when [$_{IP}$ you meet e_{2i}]]]].

$$*PRO_i/t_i$$

Let us turn to e_2 in (87b). It is a null element which is governed, and which is assigned ACCUSATIVE. Being governed, e_2 cannot be PRO. Through the index i e_2 is A'-bound by *whom$_i$*. At S-structure e_2 is an A'-bound empty category, i.e. it is like a *wh*-trace. In the literature elements that are A'-bound are often referred to as **variables** as we shall see in chapter 9.

The analysis outlined here has one important property: it allows for an e to be identified as one type of NP at D-structure and as another at S-structure. At D-structure the features of e_2 would have been [+Pronominal, +Anaphor], at S-structure they are [−Anaphor, −Pronominal]. In other words, the referential features of an NP are allowed to change. One might expect, contrary to fact, that other features could change between D-structure and S-structure: agreement features, tense features or categorial features (see chapter 2), for instance. Chomsky (1986b: 17) proposes that features assigned at D-structure remain constant. This is a strong argument against the PRO hypothesis as described here.

The hypothesis that e_2 is [−anaphor, −pronominal] at S-structure predicts correctly that parasitic gaps are subject to Principle C of the binding theory and therefore must not be A-bound.

88   *Poirot is a man [$_{CP}$ who$_i$ [$_{IP}$ t$_i$ runs way [when [you see e_{2i}]]]].

(88) illustrates a property that was discovered early on in the discussion of parasitic gaps: the so called **anti-c-command condition** on parasitic gaps. The

coindexed trace must not c-command the parasitic gap (88) nor must the parasitic gap c-command the coindexed trace (89).

89   *Poirot is a man [$_{CP}$ who$_i$ [$_{IP}$ e$_{2i}$ runs way [when [you see t$_i$]]]].

(89) violates the subjacency condition on movement and in addition the trace in the lower clause, itself [−anaphor, −pronominal], violates Principle C of the binding theory.

5.3   *Parasitic Gaps are Traces*

In Chomsky (1986b: 55) examples analogous to the following are discussed.

90   Poirot is a man who$_i$ I interviewed t$_i$ before
    (a)   hiring e.
    (b)   deciding to hire e.
    (c)   ?wondering whether to hire e.
    (d)   *wondering when to hire e.
    (e)   *announcing the plan to hire e.
    (f)   *expecting the announcement that they would hire e.
    etc.

In (90) we adopt the hypothesis that *who* has been extracted from the object position of *interviewed* leaving a trace in its base-position. The gap in the object position of *hire* marked by *e* is a parasitic gap.

While (90a) and (90b) are fully acceptable, the other examples degrade in acceptability. The decrease in acceptability in (90) is strongly reminiscent of subjacency effects illustrated in (91):

91a   Which detective did you hire?
91b   Which detective did you decide to hire?
91c   ?Which detective did you wonder whether to hire?
91d   *Which detective did you wonder when to hire?
91e   *Which detective did you announce the plan to hire?
91f   *Which detective did you expect the announcement that they would hire?

We shall not go through all the examples here. The reader can verify the impact of the subjacency condition for himself. In (91) subjacency effects are entirely expected. These examples illustrate *wh*-movement in a straight-forward way.

But if parasitic gaps show subjacency effects then we are forced to con-clude that they are also traces of movement. The question stated earlier reappears: what is the antecedent of the parasitic gap? Which element has been moved from the object position of *hire* giving rise to subjacency effects in (90)?

In our earlier discussion one option that we blatantly failed to explore is that parasitic gaps are traces of empty operators, the null element represented as OP and discussed above. This is the option taken in Chomsky (1986b). (90a) is assigned the D-structure in (92a) and the S-structure (92b):

92a Poirot is a man [$_{CP}$ [$_{IP}$ I interviewed who$_i$ [before [$_{CP}$ [$_{IP}$ PRO hiring OP$_j$]]]]].

92b Poirot is a man [$_{CP}$ who$_i$ [$_{IP}$ I interviewed t$_i$ [before [$_{CP}$ OP$_j$ [$_{IP}$ PRO hiring t$_j$]]]]].

On the basis of the analysis proposed here the subjacency effects in parasitic gap constructions are entirely expected.

The proposal developed means that sentences with parasitic gaps contain two A'-chains: in (92b) one chain is composed of *who$_i$* and its trace; the second is composed of OP$_j$ and its trace. Chomsky (1986b: 63) proposes that for the correct interpretation of the parasitic gap and its operator, the two chains are united in a process of **chain composition**:

93 **Chain composition**
    If C = <x$_1$ ... x$_n$> is the chain of the real gap and C' = <b$_1$ ... b$_m$> is the chain of the parasitic gap, then the 'composed chain' <C, C'> = <x$_1$, ... x$_n$, b$_1$ ... b$_m$> is the chain associated with the parasitic gap construction and yields its interpretation.

The A'-chain containing the parasitic gap will be assigned an interpretation by virtue of entering into a composed chain with the A'-chain of the real gap. If there is no real gap in the sentence the chain containing the parasitic gap will be uninterpreted and the sentence will not be grammatical. One of the components that will be part of the licensing conditions of parasitic gaps will be to define the conditions on chain composition. This is discussed in detail by Chomsky (1986b: 54–68) and the reader is referred to the discussion there.

5.4 Conclusion

In section 5.2 and 5.3 we have compared two accounts of parasitic gaps: the PRO hypothesis and the trace hypothesis. Given that parasitic gaps show subjacency effects, the latter hypothesis is preferable.

The study of parasitic gaps is important not only because we are dealing with a rather complex phenomenon but also because of the marginal status of the data we are looking at. If we accept the account proposed here then parasitic gaps, though marginal, follow completely from principles established independently for the grammar. In other words we do not need a special component in our grammar to deal with such relatively marginal phenomena. Given that the properties of parasitic gaps are derived from principles of our grammar which are established independently, the child will not have to be exposed to actual parasitic gap sentences to acquire their properties. Rather, the properties of parasitic gap sentences follow from the grammar as it is. Indeed, given our grammar, parasitic gaps 'must' be possible.[13]

6   Summary

In this chapter we first give an inventory and description of all the null elements posited in previous chapters and their licensing conditions.

1a   PRO, characterized by the feature matrix [+Anaphor, +Pronominal], must not be governed. Its content is determined by control theory.
1b   Traces, which are [−Pronominal], are subject to **empty category principle: ECP.**

2   **ECP**
     Traces must be properly governed.
     A properly governs B if and only if A theta-governs B or A antecedent-governs B.
     A theta-governs B if and only if A governs B and A theta-marks B.
     A antecedent-governs B iff A governs B and A is coindexed with B.

[13]   For a discussion of the learnability of parasitic gaps see also Chomsky (1982: 39). This work should be accessible to the reader at this point.

Government is defined as in (3) and contains the minimality condition (4):

3   **Government**
    A governs B if and only if
    (i)   A is a governor;
    (ii) A m-commands B;
    (iii) no barrier intervenes between A and B;
    (iv) minimality is respected.
    where governors are: (a)   heads;
                           (b)   coindexed XPs.

4   **Minimality**
    A governs B iff there is no node Z such that
    (i)   Z is a potential governor for B;
    (ii) Z c-commands B;
    (iii) Z does not c-command A.

The content of traces is determined by their antecedents.

In addition we have identified the non-overt pronominal *pro*. The occurrence of *pro* is subject to parametric variation. The licensing conditions of *pro* are given in (5):

5   **The *pro*-drop parameter**
5a   *pro* is governed by X^0_y;
5b   Let X be the licensing head of an occurrence of *pro*: then *pro* has the grammatical specification of the features on X coindexed with it.

We also discuss movement of null operators in various types of clauses (relatives, infinitival relatives, purpose clauses). The final section of the chapter describes the parasitic gap phenomenon which can also be interpreted as involving a null operator construction.

7   Exercises

Exercise 1

Another example of complementizer contraction with overt reflex is found in West Flemish, a dialect of Dutch which seems to have a type of rule similar in its domain of application to the French rule but with optional overt reflex. We invite the reader to work out the syntactic representations of the sentence and the formulation of the complementizer contraction rule.[14]

1a	den	vent	da	Valère		gezien	eet		
	the	man	that	Valère		seen	has		
1b	den	vent	da	Jan	zeid	da	Valère	gezien	eet
	the	man	that	Jan	said	that	Valère	seen	has
1c	den	vent	dad	ier		geweest	eet		
	the	man	that	here		been	has		
1d	den	vent	die	ier		geweest	eet		
	the	man	who	here		been	has		
1e	den	vent	da	Jan	zei	dad	ier	geweest	eet
	the	man	that	Jan	said	that	here	been	has
1f	den	vent	da	Jan	zei	die	ier	geweest	eet
	the	man	that	Jan	said	who	here	been	has
1g	*den	vent	die	Jan	zei	dad	ier	geweest	eet
	the	man	who	Jan	said	that	here	been	has
1h	*den	vent	die	Jan	zei	die	ier	geweest	eet
	the	man	who	Jan	said	who	here	been	has

Exercise 2

In our discussion of (1) below we have assumed that the subject of the infinitival clause is PRO and that the object is a trace bound by an empty operator:

1   I_j need a man $[_{CP}$ OP$_i$ $[_{IP}$ PRO$_j$ to love $t_i]]$.

We now ask the reader to work out why it would not be possible to argue that the empty operator is in the subject position at D-structure and is subsequently moved to the [Spec, CP], while a null element PRO is generated in the object position where it remains throughout the derivation:

2   *I_j need a man $[_{CP}$ OP$_j$ $[_{IP}$ t_j to love PRO$_i]]$.

[14]   For discussion of the West Flemish data see Bennis and Haegeman (1984) and Rizzi (1990a). *Da* and *dad* are variants of the complementizer *da* ('that').

Exercise 3

Consider the representation (1) below and discuss why it is not allowed in our grammar.

1 *Poirot is a man [cp whom_i [ip you distrust t_i [cp when [ip you meet t_i]]]].

Exercise 4

Consider text example (82b), which we left undiscussed.

82b Poirot is a man that anyone that talks to usually likes.

In the light of the preceding chapter discuss the D-structure and the S-structure representations of this sentence.

Text examples (82a) and (82b) are the two typical instances of parasitic gap constructions: in (82a) the gap occurs in an adjunct clause, in (82b) it occurs inside a subject.

Exercise 5

Consider example (1). It was argued in chapter 6 section 4.5.2 that this example was a violation of the BT, the trace of *John* not being bound in its GC. Consider whether other principles of the grammar can be used to rule out the example:

1 *John seems that it is likely to resign.

Exercise 6

In the text we have proposed that the non-overt object in Italian (1a) is pro, while the non-overt object in Portuguese (1b) is a trace of a zero operator:

1a Questo conduce pro a concludere quanto segue.
     this leads to conclude what follows

1b   [_CP OP_i [IP A Joana viu t_i na televisao ontem de noite]].
      Joana saw on television last night

Consider to what extent the following data can be used in support of these hypotheses: (2) is from Portuguese, (3) is from Italian:

2a   *Quando é que João vai oferecer à Maria.
      when is João going to offer to Maria
2b   Para qual dos filhos é que Maria comprou?
      for which of the children did Maria buy it
      (cf. Rizzi, 1986a: 513)

3a   Non so come questa musica possa riconciliare con se stessi.
      non know (1sg) this music could reconcile with oneself
      'I don't know how good music could reconcile one with oneself.'
3b   Non so come queste parole possano condurre a concludere quello.
      non know (1sg) how these words could lead to conclude that
      'I don't know how these words could lead one to conclude that.'

Exercise 7

In chapter 3, section 4, we discussed the following German example, which was a problem for the adjacency requirement on case assignment:

1a   dass Poirot diesen Roman gestern gekauft hat.

                                            ((44a) of chapter 3)

      that Poirot this novel yesterday bought has

In (1a) the direct object NP *diesen Roman* is not adjacent to the transitive verb *gekauft* ('bought'); if the direct object NP is assigned case by the transitive verb then (1a) should lead to a violation of the adjacency condition on case assignment. (1a) has a variant where the direct object is adjacent to the verb.

1b   dass Poirot gestern diesen Roman gekauft hat

                                            (cf. (44b) chapter 3)

      that Poirot yesterday this novel bought has
      'that Poirot bought this novel yesterday'

We proposed that in fact (1a) is related to (1b) by movement: the object NP *diesen Roman* has been moved leftward in (1a), leaving a trace in its base position:

1c   dass Poirot diesen Roman$_i$ gestern t$_i$ gekauft hat

The movement of the object NP within a clausal domain is referred to as **scrambling**. The question arises whether the movement of the object in (1c) is A-movement, i.e. like NP-movement, or A'-movement, like *wh*-movement. Consider also the following example:

2   Ich habe diesen Roman ohne zu lesen weggeworfen.
     I have that novel without to read away thrown
     'I threw the novel away without reading it.'
     (Frank, Lee and Rambow, 1992: (47)).

To what extent can (2) offer evidence for the nature of the movement in (1c)? For discussion of scrambling the reading is referred to the literature (Bennis and Hoekstra, 1984; Frank, Lee and Rambow, 1992; Grewendorf and Sternefeld, 1989; de Haan, 1979; Haegeman, 1992; Koster, 1978a; Stechow and Sternefeld, 1988: 452–77; Uszkoreit, 1987: 151–60).

9 Logical Form

Contents

Introduction and Overview

So far we have mainly been looking at the formal properties of sentences and we have paid relatively less attention to their interpretation. This chapter focuses on matters of sentence interpretation. We shall see that for the appropriate representation of the interpretation of quantifiers and of *wh*-phrases we have to postulate a level of representation in addition to D-structure and S-structure. This level of representation is referred to as 'Logical Form' or LF. The transformation move-α maps S-structure onto LF. Quantifier raising and *wh*-raising are instantiations of move-α which map S-structure onto LF.

We shall consider in some detail the cross-linguistic variation in the implementation of *wh*-movement: in some languages it must apply as early as S-structure, in others it applies only at LF; in some languages multiple movement is allowed (and even obligatory) at S-structure, in others multiple movement is not possible at S-structure but it does apply at LF.

The level of LF is a syntactic level of representation in the sense that it is subject to the ECP, a condition which we have seen to apply also at S-structure. We will provide a more detailed account of the application of the ECP and we will offer evidence to support the hypothesis that all traces, including intermediate traces, are subject to the ECP.

Having introduced an additional level of representation, LF, we reconsider the level of application of the binding theory. It will turn out that in certain cases binding properties of the sentence can be computed directly on S-structure; in other cases, the moved constituent apparently has to be placed back in its base-position; and in a third type of example the moved constituent has to be lowered into an intermediate landing site in order to create the appropriate configuration for binding. This phenomenon of lowering a phrase to its base-position or to an intermediate landing site is referred to as reconstruction.

We also turn to the interpretation of existential constructions and to the Principle of Full Interpretation which requires that LF only should contain elements that are legitimate at that level.

Section 1 introduces the level of LF and the notion of quantifier raising. Section 2 discusses *wh*-movement and its application at LF. Section 3 focuses on the application of the ECP. Section 4 deals with reconstruction and section 5 deals with scope reconstruction, and with the interaction of the scope of *wh*-constituents and of quantifiers. Section 6 deals with the Principle of Full Interpretation.

1   The Interpretation of Quantifiers

1.1   *Some Concepts from Logic*

Consider the following sentences.

1a   George saw William.
1b   George saw everyone.
1c   George saw every policeman.
1d   George saw someone.
1e   Everyone saw someone.

The interpretation of (1a) is straightforward: the subject NP *George* and the object NP *William* each pick out a referent from the universe of discourse, and the predicate *see* establishes a relation between these entities. In the notation of formal logic the interpretation of (1a) would be represented roughly as in (2a):

2a   S (gw)

where S is the predicate 'see', and g and w represent the arguments, 'George' and 'William' respectively. We do not go into the representation of past tense.

(1b) contains a **quantifier**, *everyone*. One might try representing the interpretation of (1b) by means of (2b), by analogy to (2a):

2b   S (ge)

where e would stand for 'everyone'. However, this representation misses an important property of quantifiers like *everyone*. Quantifiers differ from R-expressions like *George* and *William* in that they do not pick out a specific entity from the universe of discourse. (1b) does not mean 'Take the entity referred to by the NP *everyone* and assign to it the property that George sees it.' Rather, (1b) means something like 'For every element x, provided that this x is human, it is true that George saw x.' The interpretation of the internal argument of *see* in (1b) is variable and depends on the domain of the quantifier. The variability of the interpretation of *everyone* in (1b) is clear if we think of two distinct situations. In one situation a teacher could be speaking about her class. *Everyone* will be taken to indicate all the people present in the class. In another situation a teacher could be speaking about her colleagues. Here *everyone* will be taken to indicate all the colleagues.

Referential NPs such as *William* or *George* are constants; they do not have a variable interpretation. Whichever situation we think of, say the first one or the second one mentioned above, the NP *George* picks out a particular person baptized with that name. Regardless of the fact that there are obviously many people called George, in a particular context the NP *George* in (1a) or in (1b) selects one such person – the one that is contextually most accessible[1] – and it will not pick out every person with that name. This distinction between quantifiers and referential expressions is not captured by the representations (2a) and (2b): (2b) fails to represent the variable component characteristic of the interpretation of quantifiers. In order to represent the meaning of (1b) logicians use representations such as (3a):

3a $\forall\ x\ (Hx \longrightarrow Sgx)$

which can be roughly paraphrased as follows:

3b $\forall\ x$ $(Hx \longrightarrow Sgx)$
    For all x it is the case that if x is human then George saw x

One of the arguments of *see* (S) is an element x which depends on the quantifier $\forall$ for its interpretation. The representation (3a) and its paraphrase (3b) contain a conditional element, represented by the arrow. The first part of the conditional, the element to its left, (Hx), restricts the range of x to humans. An alternative representation for the interpretation of the quantifier *everyone* is given in (3c). Again we add a paraphrase:

---

[1] Accessibility is not a syntactic notion but relates to the way we process utterances in a context, i.e. to what is often referred to as 'pragmatics'. Referents may be accessible because they have been mentioned in a previous utterance, because they are salient in a specific context, or because they are easily retrievable from memory. For a discussion of accessibility see Ariel (1988). For more general discusion of the role of accessibility and context in utterance interpretation see Sperber and Wilson (1986).

3c ∀x,   x = H   (Sgx)
        For all x, such that x is human,   George saw x

In the representations above, *x* is called a **variable**, its interpretation varies
with, or depends on, the quantifier; the **variable** is **bound** by the quantifier.
∀ is the **universal** quantifier and corresponds to 'all' or 'every'. Quantifiers
are also sometimes referred to as **operators**. We assume that each variable
must be bound by an operator, and each operator must bind a variable. The
interpretation of the variable depends on the operator which binds it and on
the restrictions posed on its range: the logical representation of (1c) would be
as in (3d):

3d ∀x, x = P (Sgx)

where *x* is restricted to 'policemen' (*P*).
   (1d) also contains a quantifier: *someone*. The logical representation of (1d)
would be as in (3e):

3e ∃x,   (x = H)   &   (Sgx)
        There is an x such that x is human   and George saw x

∃ is the **existential** quantifier, ∃*x* means that there exists at least one referent
for the variable *x*. In both (3c) and (3e) the quantifier binds a variable *x*, in
(3c) the variable is bound by the universal quantifier and in (3e) it is bound
by the existential quantifier.
   Now let us turn to (1e), repeated here as (4).

4   Everyone saw someone

(4) has two interpretations:

5a   For every x there is some y such that it is the case that x saw y.
5b   There is some y, such that for every x, it is the case that x saw y.

In (5a) each person may have seen someone different: Manuela saw Sten,
Corinne saw Jamal, Genoveva saw Eric; in (5b) there is one individual that
was seen by everyone, for instance, Manuela, Corinne and Genoveva all saw

Sten. In (5a) the number of persons seen, the number of *y*s, depends on the universal quantifier, i.e. on the number of persons that observe or see, the number of *x*s; in (5b) there is one person who was seen (*y*), in other words the number of persons seen is independent of the universal quantifier. The direction of dependence between the quantifiers determines their **scope**. In (5a) the existential quantifier ('someone') depends on the universal quantifier ('everyone'): the universal quantifier has **wide scope**; the existential quantifier has **narrow scope**.

Quantifiers such as *everyone* and *someone* take scope over a certain domain and they can affect the meaning of other elements in that domain; they are operators and in the logical representations they have to occupy a scope position. In representations of standard logic, scope positions are left-peripheral. The scope of the quantifier is the domain to its right. In (5a) the universal quantifier appears to the left of the existential quantifier: the existential quantifier is in the scope of the universal quantifier; in (5b) the existential quantifier is not in the scope of the universal quantifier.

1.2 Quantifier Movement and Logical Form

It is proposed in the literature that the scope properties of operators play a part in the syntax of sentences and that they must be syntactically represented. We provide support for this hypothesis in section 3. Let us assume that in addition to D-structure and S-structure, there is a level of representation which encodes logico-semantic properties such as the scope of operators. This level is called **Logical Form** or **LF**. At the level of LF the universal quantifier *everyone* in (1b) has to be represented as an operator and has to occupy a scope position. i.e. a left-peripheral position. This means that the quantifier must be moved out of its argument position to a scope position:

6a [$_{IP}$ everyone$_i$ [$_{IP}$ George saw x$_i$]].

(6a) is derived by moving *everyone* to a left-peripheral position. In the literature it is usually proposed that *everyone* is adjoined to IP. Like *wh*-movement discussed in chapter 7 and NP-movement discussed in chapter 6 we assume that the movement of *everyone* leaves an empty category in the extraction site, with which it is coindexed. We represent this empty category here as *x*, in order to highlight its similarities with operator-bound variables of logic. An adjoined position is an A'-position; *x* is a trace bound by an element in an A'-position, i.e. and A'-trace. Recall that, the scope of the quantifier *everyone* is the domain to its right, more precisely, we identify the

scope of the quantifier as its c-command domain, i.e. IP. The tree diagram
analogue of (6a) is (6b):

6b

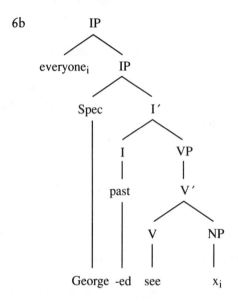

The proposal we are developing here entails that a sentence does not only
have a D-structure representation and an S-structure, but it also has a representation of its logico-semantic properties: its Logical Form or LF. LF can be
motivated as a level of syntactic representation because, as we shall see in
subsequent sections, it is subject to the principles that govern syntactic representations, such as the ECP (introduced in chapter 8, section 2). The LF
representation is not identical to the semantic representations introduced by
semanticists and formal logicians; LF is an intermediate step that mediates
between S-structure and the semantic representations. The movement of the
quantifier at LF is often referred to as **quantifier raising** (or **QR**). The reader
should not confuse this type of movement with the raising of an NP discussed
in chapter 6. QR adjoins a quantifier to IP at at LF and is an example of A'-
movement (cf. chapter 7); raising as discussed in chapter 6 moves an NP to
a subject position and is an instantiation of A-movement.

Our grammar contains a general movement operation, **move-α** ('move-
alpha') 'move something', which moves a constituent (a head or a phrase).
Move-α can apply at various levels of representation: at S-structure (as discussed in chapters 6 and 7) and at LF (as illustrated in the examples above).
Our grammar is then organized in the following way:

7a

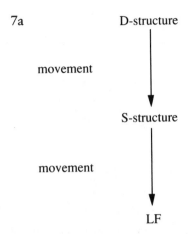

Between D-structure and S-structure move-α may move heads to head positions (as in the movement of the finite auxiliary to C), it may move NPs to A-positions (NP-movement illustrated in passive and raising sentences) and it may move maximal projections to A′-positions (*wh*-movement). Quantifier raising moves a quantifier to a scope position at LF. Movement between S-structure and LF has no overt reflex, it is non-overt movement or **covert movement**. The quantifier *everyone* does not occupy a left-peripheral position in the string (1b). (1b) does not spell out the LF representation, it corresponds more closely to the S-structure representation. In order to distinguish surface strings from the abstract LF representations, our grammar will be organized as follows:

7b

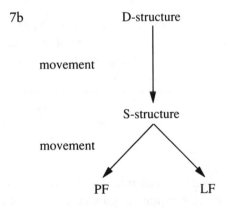

Where **PF** stands for **phonetic form**, the overt realization or the **spell-out** of the sentence, the way the sentence is spelt out.

2   *Wh*-phrases and LF Movement

2.1   Wh-*phrases as Operators*

Consider now the examples in (8).

8a   George saw William.
8b   Who did George see?
8c   Which policeman did George see?

(8a) is a declarative sentence, (8b) and (8c) are constituent questions. English constituent questions are formed by preposing a *wh*-constituent, *who* in (8b), *which policeman* in (8c). The *wh*-constituent determines the interpretation of the entire sentence, it takes scope over the sentence. The scope of a *wh*-operator is its c-command domain: a *wh*-operator in [Spec, CP] will take scope over the CP whose specifier it occupies.

   The contrast between (8a) on the one hand, and (8b) and (8c) on the other hand, is similar to that between (1a) and (1b, c, d) above. *Who* and *which policeman* in (8b) and in (8c) respectively, do not have a specific referent. (8b) and (8c) could be paraphrased as in (9):

9a   For which x, x is human, is it the case that George saw x?
9b   For which x, x is a policeman, is it the case that George saw x?

In (9a), a rough semantic representation of (8b), the *wh*-constituent *who* does not select one referent in the universe of discourse; it is an operator which binds a variable ('for which x is it the case that . . .'); (10a) is the S-structure representation of (8b): the *wh*-phrase is moved to [Spec, CP] and binds a trace.

10a   [$_{CP}$ Who$_i$ did [$_{IP}$ George see t$_i$]]?

Observe the parallelism between the S-structure representation (10a) and the semantic representation (9a): in both representations the *wh*-constituent occupies a left-peripheral position, i.e. a scope position; in both representations the *wh*-element binds a sentence-internal empty category. The LF representation of (10a) is (10b), where the *wh*-constituent is represented as an operator binding a variable by analogy with the representation of quantificational structures discussed in section 1:

10b [$_{CP}$ Who$_i$ did [$_{IP}$ George see x$_i$]]?

(8c), repeated here as (11a), has S-structure (11b) and LF (11c):

11a Which policeman did George see?
11b [$_{CP}$ Which policeman$_i$ did [$_{IP}$ George see t$_i$]]?
11c [$_{CP}$ Which policeman$_i$ did [$_{IP}$ George see x$_i$]]?

From now on, each sentence is associated with the following levels of representation: D-structure, S-structure, PF and LF.

One observation should be made concerning the notations used. In the LF representations in the literature, *wh*-traces are often replaced by *x* to indicate their status as variables, but this is not a generalized practice. In this book we often do not replace traces by *x* and we will also sometimes represent the empty category resulting from quantifier movement by *t*. In both cases it is clear that the empty category resulting from movement is A'-bound and when it is an NP it has case. *Wh*-traces and empty categories left by quantifier movement are both variables, they are both bound by an operator in a left-peripheral scope position.

2.2 Wh-*raising*

In English sentences which contain one *wh*-constituent, this must be moved to [Spec, CP] to derive a constituent question:

12a I wonder who John saw.
12b *I wonder John saw who.

Wh-movement is obligatory. On the basis of the discussion in section 1 above let us say that movement enables the *wh*-constituent to acquire sentential scope. (In chapter 12 we offer some further discussion of *wh*-movement.) In (12a) the moved *wh*-constituent occupies [Spec, CP]; its scope domain is the domain which it c-commands, i.e. the clause.

Wh-movement is not universal. In the following Japanese examples the italicized *wh*-constituent does not occupy a scope position.

13a John-wa   *naze* kubi-ni natta no?
     John-topic why   was fired   *Question marker*
     'Why was John fired?'
13b Bill-wa [_{CP} John-ga   *naze* kubi-ni natta tte] itta   no?
     Bill-topic   John-NOM why   was fired   C   said   Q
     'Why did Bill say that John was fired?'
     (from Lasnik and Saito, 1984: 244)

The *wh*-constituent *naze* occupies the same position in both (13a) and (13b),
though its scope varies as suggested by the glosses. *No* is a question marker
(*Q*). It indicates the scope of the *wh*-constituent. In (13a) *naze* and *no* are
associated with the same clause. In (13b) *no* is associated with the higher
clause and *naze* occupies a position in the lower clause. Some further examples of the same phenomenon are given in (13c)–(13e):

13c John-ga *dare-o*   butta ka siranai.
              who-ACC hit John Q   know not
     'I don't know who John hit.'
13d John-wa, Mary-ga *dare-o*   kiratte-iru to   sinzite-ita   ka?
     John   Mary   whom-ACC hating is   that believing was Q
     'Who did John believe that Mary hated?'
     (from Kuno, 1973: 13)
13e Watasi-wa John-ga   *nani-o*   katta ka sitte iru.
     I-topic   John-NOM what-ACC bought Q   know
     'I know what John bought.'
     (from Lasnik and Saito, 1984: 235)

Although in Japanese *wh*-constituents such as *naze* (13a, b), *dare* (13c, d) and
nani (13e) do not appear to undergo *wh*-movement at S-structure, it seems
natural to assume that semantically they are like their English equivalents,
why, *who* and *what*. Specifically, being question words, we would assume
that they have to take sentential scope, and that they are interpreted as
operators binding variables. For instance, (13c) means 'I don't know for
which x, x human, it is the case that John hit x', and (13d) means: 'For which
x, x human, is it the case that John believed that Mary hated x?' If the
interpretation of *wh*-constituents in Japanese is not fundamentally different
from their English counterparts then the LF representations of the sentences
in (13) should encode the fact that in Japanese too, *wh*-phrases are operators
which take scope over a clause and which bind a variable. Various possibilities

of encoding the scope of the *wh*-constituent in (13c), repeated here as (14a), come to mind. We could propose an LF representation as in (14b):

14a John-ga dare-o butta ka siranai.
     John   who   hit   Q know not
     'I don't know who John hit.'
14b [$_{CP}$ [$_{IP}$ John ga x_i butta] ka dare-o$_i$] siranai.

In (14b) we follow Lasnik and Saito (1984: 244, n. 15), who assume that Japanese *wh*-operators move rightward because overt complementizers occur sentence-finally in Japanese. This representation entails that scope positions can be left-peripheral, as in English, or right-peripheral, as in Japanese. Since we assume that the *wh*-phrases move to [Spec, CP], (14b) also implies that the specifier position is not linearly ordered with respect to the head: specifiers can precede the heads, as in English, or follow them, as in Japanese, i.e. the order of the specifier and the head is subject to parametric variation. An alternative approach is conceivable, though. If we want to have a unified definition of a scope position as a left-peripheral position, an option that is suggested, for instance in Rizzi (forthcoming), and one which we have been assuming tacitly in the preceding discussion, then it would be more natural to propose that the LF movement of *dare-o* will be leftward:

14c [$_{CP}$ dare-o$_i$ [$_{IP}$ John ga x_i butta] ka] siranai.

Let us assume that *ka* is an overt realization of the complementizer which occurs sentence-finally in (14c). Suppose that we say that the specifier of CP is to the left of C^0 in Japanese and that the complement, i.e. IP, is also to its left. On these assumptions (14c) would have the structure in (14d):

14d

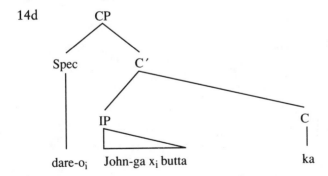

In (14d) the *wh*-phrase *dare-o* moves to [Spec, CP] at LF. Under this view scope positions and specifier positions are universally left-peripheral, and the ordering specifier – head is not subject to parametric variation.[2]

Chinese is like Japanese in that there is no overt *wh*-movement as illustrated in (15):

15a   Wo xiang-zhidao [$_{CP}$ [$_{IP}$ Lisi   mai-le   sheme]].
       I   wonder   Lisi   bought-Aspect   what
       'I wonder what Lisi bought.'
       (Lasnik and Saito, 1984: 239)
15b   Zhangsan   wen   [shei   mai-le   shu].
       Zhangsan   ask   who   buy-Aspect   book
       'Zhangsan asked who bought books.'

---

[2]   The reader may remember Kayne's (1993) hypothesis that all structural representations are of the following format:

(i)   XP

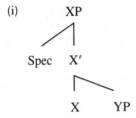

     Spec   X′

          X   YP

Kayne also proposes that all movement is leftward. His proposal entails a massive simplification of phrase structures but it raises important problems for the study of languages with sentence-final complementizers, such as Japanese, illustrated in (13) and (14). On the view that the base structure of Japanese has a head-initial CP, we would have to assume that the sentence-final position of the complementizer is derived by movement. Specifically, we would have to assume that the IP complement of C is moved into [Spec, CP] (ii). As the reader can imagine, this proposal has far-reaching consequences which go well beyond the scope of an introductory book.

(ii)   CP

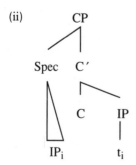

     Spec   C′

            C   IP

     IP$_i$ t$_i$

15c [Zhangsan xiangzin [shei mai-le   shu]].
     believe   who buy-Aspect book
     'Who does Zhangsan believe bought books?'
15d [Zhangsan zhidao [shei   mai-le   shu]].
     Zhangsan know who   buy-Aspect book
     (i) 'Zhangsan knows who bought books.'
     (ii) 'Who does Zhangsan know bought books?'
     (b,c,d from Aoun, 1984: 18)

Again, at LF the *wh*-phrase moves to a scope position where it can function as an operator binding a variable. The LF representations of the sentences (15a) and (15d) are given in (16:

16a Wo xiang-zhidao [$_{CP}$ sheme$_i$ [$_{IP}$ Lisi mai-le x_i]].
16b   (i) [Zhangsan zhidao [[shei]$_i$ [x_i mai-le shu]]]
      (ii) [[shei]$_i$ [Zhangsan zhidao [x_i mai-le shu]]]

Let us recapitulate the discussion. In section 1 we have proposed that in addition to D-structure and S-structure, there is a third level of representation: LF, or Logical Form, which encodes the semantic properties of clauses; LF represents the scope of operators. Operators such as quantifiers, which occupy an argument position at S-structure, move to a scope position at LF. Scope positions are left-peripheral positions. At LF quantifiers adjoin to IP.

Wh-constituents have operator-like properties and they move to attain a scope position. In English *wh*-constituents move to a left-peripheral A′-position, [Spec, CP], at S-structure as a result of *wh*-movement, and hence they attain a scope position (see the next section for refinement, though). With respect to the scope properties of the moved *wh*-phrases, nothing needs to be added or modified at LF. In Japanese and in Chinese *wh*-phrases do not undergo *wh*-movement.[3] They remain sentence-internally. We assume that

---

[3] The analysis presented here is not the only one conceivable. A very interesting alternative account is proposed by Watanabe (1992). Watanabe proposes that while there is no movement of an overt element in Japanese, there is movement of a non-overt *wh*-operator, OP, which is extracted from the *wh*-phrase. (For a discussion of non-overt operators, the reader is referred to chapter 8, section 4.) Very roughly, the text example (13c) repeated here as (ia) would have the representation (ib), where OP has been extracted from the *wh*-phrase.

(ia) John-ga dare-o butta ka siranai.
          who hit   Q know not
     'I don't know who John hit.'

in these languages too, *wh*-phrases have operator properties and move to a scope position at LF. *Wh*-movement at LF thus mimics *wh*-movement at S-structure. The application of *wh*-movement at LF is often referred to as *wh*-raising.

As discussed above, our grammar has a number of levels of representation: D-structure, S-structure and LF.[4] The movement of *wh*-phrases to derive LF representations in Chinese and in Japanese has no overt reflex. In the surface string the *wh*-elements in Japanese and Chinese do not appear in a scope position and neither do the quantifiers in English (cf. section 1). The surface form of the sentence is derived from the S-structure representation. Recall (cf. (7b) above) that in the framework adopted here, the separation of the superficial form of the sentence and its LF is obtained by positing Phonetic Form or PF, which spells out the S-structure representation and which does not encode LF movements such as the movement of quantifiers or *wh*-raising.

(ib) [OP$_i$ [John-ga [dare t$_i$] -o butta] ka] siranai.
      who   hit   Q   know not

The non-overt operator is an abstract question operator which would be extracted and moved to a scope position. We assume that the specifier of CP is left-peripheral. As mentioned in the discussion it might also be the case that the ordering of specifier and head is subject to parametric variation.

In Watanabe's account the difference between English and Japanese is not that in one language there is *wh*-movement at S-structure and in the other there is not. In Watanabe's account *wh*-movement of the *wh*-operator is universally required at S-structure: all *wh*-phrases are associated with an abstract operator OP, and minimally the abstract operator has to move at S-structure. The difference between English and Japanese is that in English the abstract question operator cannot be separated from the *wh*-constituent with which it is associated and in Japanese it can.

Watanabe's account presupposes an economy-based account in which movement is restricted to what is required. In principle it is enough if the abstract operator moves at S-structure and this is what happens in Japanese. If only the abstract operator has to move and if this is possible in the grammar of Japanese, then only the abstract operator will move: all additional movement would be superfluous, hence non-economical. For English, Watanabe assumes that the non-overt operator must also move at S-structure. Because the grammar of English does not allow the non-overt operator to be separated from the associated *wh*-phrase, the *wh*-phrase must move along with the associated *wh*-operator. The variation between Japanese and English then reduces to the question of whether or not the abstract question operator can be separated from the associated *wh*-phrase. The reader is referred to the literature for a discussion of this proposal (Brody, 1993b).

[4] Chomsky (1992) proposes another approach to syntactic structures. The static demarcation of the levels of representation in (17) is reinterpreted in terms of a more dynamic approach in which sentence structures are built up step by step. Central in the new proposal is the relation between phonetic form and interpretation (PF and LF in (17)) mediated by syntactic structures. Brody (1993b) proposes a one-level approach to syntactic representations.

17   D-structure

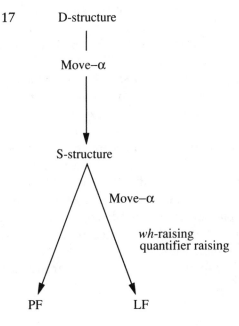

Move–α

S-structure

Move–α

wh-raising
quantifier raising

PF   LF

The model in (17) has come to be known as the **T-model**.

A terminological point is in order here. In the literature the terms **syntactic movement** or **movement in the syntax** are often used to indicate movement which takes place at S-structure, in contrast with **LF-movement**. Other authors talk about **overt** movement when referring to movement at S-structure and about **covert** movement when referring to LF-movement. In (17) we have only mentioned instantiations of A′-movement at LF: QR and *wh*-raising. The other types of movement discussed also mediate between S-structure and LF. In section 6 below we turn to an instance of A-movement at LF. In chapter 11 we discuss head movement at LF.

2.3 *Multiple* Wh-*movement*

2.3.1 *WH- IN SITU* AND MULITIPLE QUESTIONS IN ENGLISH

Languages differ with respect to the level of application of *wh*-movement. In English *wh*-movement applies as early as S-structure, in Japanese and Chinese it applies at LF. In this section we shall see that in English *wh*-movement may also apply at LF. Consider the following examples.

18a   What did George give to whom?
18b   When did George say what?

Both sentences in (18) contain two *wh*-phrases. Unlike Polish and other Slavic languages for instance, English does not have **multiple movement**: in the examples in (18) one *wh*-phrase moves to [Spec, CP] (*what* in (18a), *when* in (18b)) and the other *wh*-phrase remains within the IP domain, a *wh*-phrase which has not moved to [Spec, CP] is said to be *in situ*. In (18a), one *wh*-phrase, *what*, is in a scope position, the other one, *to whom*, is *in situ*.

We have seen that *wh*-phrases are interpretively different from NPs like *George* in that they are not referential expressions: they do not serve to pick out a referent from the universe of discourse, rather they are operators which bind variables. The *wh*-phrases in (18) are all interpreted as operators, regardless of whether they have actually been moved or not. In (18a) *what* is an operator at S-structure, but *to whom* will also be interpreted as an operator. It is desirable that at LF all *wh*-phrases be represented as operators binding variables. (18a) is not only a question about what was being given but it also questions who was the receiver. The most natural answer to (18a) will treat the *wh*-phrases as a pair. One might expect answers like (19a), for instance, but not (19b) or (19c):

19a   George gave the letter to Miss Marple and the postcard to William.
19b   *The letter.
19c   *To Miss Marple.

Recall that LF is the level that encodes interpretative properties of the sentence. We will propose that the intuition that *to whom* is an operator in (18a) should be represented at the level of LF. The *wh*-phrase *to whom*, which is *in situ* at S-structure, is moved to [Spec, CP] at LF as represented in (20). Since there is only one position in [Spec, CP] we assume that the LF movement of *to whom* creates an adjoined position: *to whom* adjoins to [Spec, CP].

20

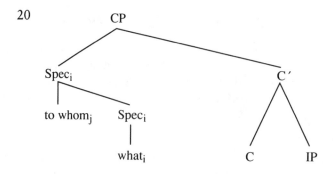

At S-structure *what* moves to [Spec, CP]. The movement of *to whom* is delayed till LF. Let us assume that the index of *what* (*i*) **percolates** to Spec and that the index of *to whom* does not. This means that *what* determines the properties of [Spec, CP].

Let us consider the interpretation of the sentences in (18) once again. A *wh*-phrase turns the sentence with which it is associated into a question. Sentence (18a) is a single question in spite of the presence of two *wh*-constituents. Recall from (19) that the two operators in (18a) are interpretively linked, question (18a) is a question about pairs of entities: receivers are paired with themes. We assume that the interpretive linking of the two interrogative constituents is achieved by merging their interrogative components: the two *wh*-operators are converted into one operator. The process by which two *wh*-operators are merged in (18a) is called **wh-absorption**. Wh-absorption converts two *wh*-operators into one operator which binds two variables. We could try to give a more general interpretation to the process of absorption. From the discussion in chapter 2 the reader will recall that the X'-format provides a specifier position for XP. Let us assume that there is one specifier for each phrase. When several constituents seem to function as specifiers to one head then these constituents have to undergo a process of absorption which converts them into one.

2.3.2 MULTIPLE MOVEMENT

We have already come across instances of cross-linguistic variation with respect to the mode of application of *wh*-movement. The level of application of *wh*-movement is subject to cross-linguistic variation. In English constituent questions, one *wh*-phrase must move at S-structure, the others remain *in situ*. In Chinese and Japanese there is no overt movement (but see footnote 3 for a different account). French seems to have a mixed system. For embedded clauses French is like English, with *wh*-movement of one phrase being forced. In root clauses, though, *wh*-phrases may also stay *in situ*:

21a Je me   demande qui tu as   vu.
    I   myself ask   who you have seen
    'I wonder who you have seen.'
21b *Je me   demande Sylvia a   vu   qui.
    I   myself ask   Sylvia has seen who
21c Qui as   tu vu?
    who have you seen?
    'Who did you see?'

21d Tu as vu qui?
   you have seen who
   'Who did you see?'

The question arises how this variation can be accounted for in a *Principles and Parameters* approach. Let us assume first that *wh*-phrases are universally interpreted as operators and that this intrinsic semantic property must be reflected by their LF representation. Analogously to the representation of operators in formal logic, let us say that *wh*-operators must occupy a scope position where a scope position is a left-peripheral A'-position. [Spec, CP] qualifies as a scope position. In some languages the *wh*-elements already occupy a scope position at S-structure: they have moved to [Spec, CP] in the syntax. In other languages they only attain the scope position at LF. Crucially, what is variable is not whether the language has *wh*-movement or not, rather what varies is the level at which *wh*-movement applies.

Languages which allow *wh*-movement at S-structure differ with respect to whether they allow multiple movement at S-structure or not. English does not allow multiple movement (22a), neither does French (22b), but Polish (22c) and Hungarian (22d) do:

22a *English*
   *Who what said?
22b *French*
   *Qui quoi fait?
   who what does
22c *Polish*
   Kto co robi?
   who what does
   (Pesetsky, 1989)
22d *Hungarian*
   Ki mit làtott?
   who what saw
   (Puskas, 1992)

For languages like English in which only one *wh*-operator can move to [Spec, CP] we assume that all remaining *wh*-constituents raise to [Spec, CP] at LF:

22e When did George give what to whom?

In (22e) the *wh*-phrase *when* has been moved to [Spec, CP] at S-structure. Following the discussion above, we assume that *what* and *to whom* both move at LF to adjoin to [Spec, CP]. Though English lacks multiple *wh*-movement at S-structure, the LF representations associated with sentences with multiple *wh*-phrases still allow all *wh*-constituents to be fronted, i.e. at LF multiple movement is possible. This means that the parametric variation does not concern the question whether or not languages have multiple movement, but rather at which level of representation multiple movement can apply. In Hungarian, multiple movement applies already at S-structure, in English only one constituent moves at S-structure and the others move at LF. In Chinese, all movement of *wh*-constituents is postponed till LF. It could be claimed that, due to their internal syntactic properties, some languages such as English do not allow multiple movement at S-structure, while other languages do allow it. In languages where multiple *wh*-fronting is syntactically possible, it is in fact obligatory: (22f), where only one *wh*-constituent has been fronted and the other one remains *in situ*, is ungrammatical in Hungarian:

22f *Ki latott mit?
     who saw what

In our discussions we have seen that languages vary with respect to the mode of application of *wh*-movement. In Chinese *wh*-movement is covert; in English it is overt and only one constituent can move, and must move; in Polish *wh*-movement is overt and in sentences with multiple *wh*-constituents all of them move. It is clear that the cross-linguistic differences we have described above ought to be accounted for.

2.3.3 EARLINESS VS. PROCRASTINATE: SOME DISCUSSION

In this section we discuss the parametric variation observed with respect to *wh*-movement. The aim of this section is to guide the reader to some of the literature. There are two positions in the debate, which can be summarized by the labels 'Earliness' and 'Procrastinate'. We briefly consider each of these approaches.

One way of interpreting the difference between languages with (multiple) movement and those without is to say (with Pesetsky, 1989) that there is an **Earliness Principle** which forces movement to apply as early as possible, i.e. based on the diagram in (17) movement which *can* apply at S-structure *must* apply at S-structure and cannot be postponed till LF. Let us see how the Earliness Principle will be implemented. We have proposed that *wh*-phrases are intrinsically operators: at LF they have to occupy a left-peripheral scope position and they bind a variable. This means that a *wh*-phrase cannot occupy an argument position at LF. When a sentence contains multiple *wh*-phrases they ultimately all have to be fronted, i.e. at LF they all must be moved and bind a variable.

In Chinese, S-structure movement is not possible; in English only one constituent can move but multiple movement is not possible; and in Polish multiple movement is possible. The availability of movement as such has to be explained; it should be related to the syntactic properties of the language in question. For instance, we might say that adjunction to [Spec, CP] is excluded in English, which means that multiple movement is excluded.

We then interpret the cross-linguistic variation with respect to *wh*-movement in terms of the Earliness Principle. If the grammar of a language *allows* syntactic *wh*-movement then *wh*-movement *must* apply at S-structure; this is the case for English. If the grammar of the language does not allow overt *wh*-movement, then there will be no S-structure movement. This would be the case of Japanese and Chinese. If the language allows for multiple fronting at S-structure, then the movement of all the *wh*-phrases will be enforced by the Earliness Principle; this would be the case in Hungarian or Polish. If the grammar of the language does not allow multiple movement, then multiple *wh*-fronting will not apply at S-structure and it will be delayed till LF.

Pesetsky's Earliness Principle (1989) offered an interesting way to account for the cross-linguistic variation with respect to *wh*-movement. In recent approaches to syntax, though, the Earliness Principle is being challenged. It has been proposed (Chomsky, 1991, 1992) that syntactic mechanisms are regulated by **economy** principles and that economy will delay movement as late as possible. This is referred to as **Procrastinate**. Obviously, this view is not compatible with the Earliness account and the cross-linguistic variation with respect to *wh*-movement has to be reinterpreted. One option is to relate the level of application of *wh*-movement to the morphological strength of the *wh*-feature on the *wh*-constituent. The idea is that when the *wh*-feature is morphologically **strong** this is reflected at the spell-out level, i.e. the surface form; this will mean that the feature induces movement of the constituent at S-structure. We could say that the *wh*-feature is strong in English and weak in Japanese. In English *wh*-movement is necessary at S-structure. In Japanese it is not. By Procrastinate we postpone movement as late as possible; since we do not have to move a *wh*-constituent at S-structure in Japanese we do not move the *wh*-constituent. We do not go into this issue here and refer the reader to the literature.[5]

---

[5]   For discussion of *wh*-movement see Aoun, Hornstein and Sportische (1981), May (1985), Rizzi (forthcoming). For discussion of multiple *wh*-movement also Brody (1993b), Pesetsky (1989), Puskas (1992), Rizzi (forthcoming), Rudin (1989). The presentation in the text is very sketchy. For discussion of *wh*-movement and parametric variation in an economy-based approach see Chomsky (1992) and Watanabe (1992). For more discussion of the Earliness Principle as opposed to Procrastinate, see Brody (1993b).

2.3.4 A NOTE ON PARASITIC GAPS

In chapter 8, section 5, we discussed the phenomenon of parasitic gaps, i.e. gaps which are licensed by their occurrence in a sentence which contains another *wh*-trace (23).

23 Which books did John file t_i without reading e_i?

If parasitic gaps are licensed by another A'-bound gap, it might be the case that such a licensing gap occurs not at S-structure but at LF. A parasitic gap might be licensed by a gap resulting from LF-movement of an operator, for example by the *wh*-raising of a *wh*-constituent which occupies its base-position at S-structure. (24a), however, shows that parasitic gaps must be licensed at S-structure:

24a *Who read which articles without filing e?

Wh-raising would give us the LF representation (24b) for the above example, but this clearly is not sufficient to license the parasitic gap indicated by *e*:

24b *[Which articles$_j$ who$_i$] t_i read t_j without filing e_j.

We conclude that parasitic gaps are licensed at S-structure.

3 The ECP

3.1 ECP Effects at LF

In this section we show that LF is subject to the ECP.

3.1.1 SUBJECT–OBJECT ASYMMETRIES

There is a subject–object asymmetry with respect to multiple questions. Consider the following examples.

25a   I don't remember who said what.
25b   *I don't remember what who said.

In our discussion in chapter 8 we saw that the ECP can account for S-structure subject–object asymmetries. Let us try to see if the ECP could also explain the difference between (25a) and (25b). The S-structure of the grammatical (25c) is given in (26a) and its LF representation in (26b). We omit irrelevant details for expository reasons:[6]

26a   I don't remember [$_{CP}$ who$_i$ [$_{IP}$ t$_i$ said what]].
26b   I don't remember [$_{CP}$ [$_{Spec i}$ what$_j$ [$_{Spec i}$ who$_i$]] [$_{IP}$ t$_i$ said t$_j$]][7]

(25b) has the following representations:

27a   *I don't remember [$_{CP}$ [$_{Spec j}$ what$_j$] [$_{IP}$ who$_i$ said t$_j$]].
27b   *I don't remember [$_{CP}$ [$_{Spec j}$ who$_i$] [$_{Spec j}$ what$_j$]] [t$_i$ said t$_j$]].

Recall the proposal that the constituent first moved to [Spec, CP] assigns its index to [Spec, CP] and that any element subsequently adjoined to the indexed specifier of CP does not transmit its index. The S-structures (26a) and (27a) do not violate any of the principles so far developed. Subjacency, theta theory, the case filter and the ECP are observed, as the reader can verify.

Let us turn to the LF representations (26b) and (27b). In order to keep our theory as general as possible we postulate that traces resulting from movement at LF are also subject to the ECP. This assumption provides us with a natural explanation for the ungrammaticality of (27b) in contrast with the grammaticality of (26b).

(28a) is a partial tree diagram to represent (26b):

---

[6]   In (26a) the assumption is that *who* is moved vacuously to [Spec, CP]. Alternatively *who* is not moved at S-structure and both *wh*-phrases move at LF, leading to LF representation in (26b).

[7]   We represent traces at LF as *t*. Recall that often such traces are represented also as *x*.

28a

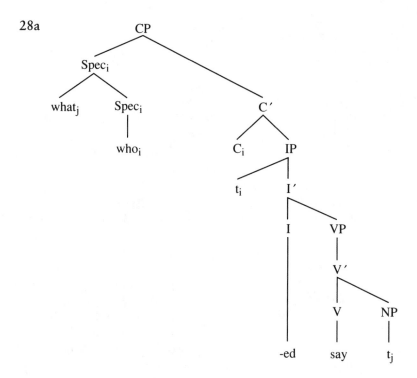

The variable coindexed with *what_j*, i.e. t_j, is properly governed by the lexical verb *say*. The variable t_i in the subject position is coindexed with *who_i* and with [Spec, CP]. Spec_i c-commands t_i. It is separated from the variable by C′, which is non-maximal and thus not a barrier, and also by IP, which we posited is not a barrier. The subject trace, t_i is properly governed: it is antecedent-governed.[8] Consider (28b), the LF representation of (25b).

---

[8] A problem remains which we shall not go into here. Strictly speaking, *what_j* in the adjoined position might be said not to c-command its trace, hence not to A′-bind it. We shall assume that the operator *what_j* can bind its trace through being associated with *who*, as illustrated in the paired reading of the question (cf. section 2.2).

28b*

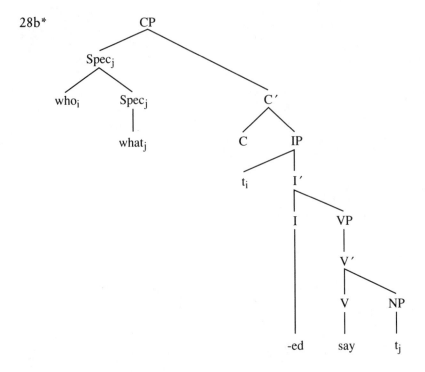

The variable t_j is properly governed by the verb; t_i, the trace of *who_i*, is not properly governed. Its antecedent is adjoined to [Spec, CP] but *who_i* cannot transmit its index to the specifier and hence it will be prevented from governing the variable.

To sum up the discussion so far. We have posited that in addition to D-structure and S-structure there is a third level of representation, LF. This level derives from S-structure by move-α. One instantiation of move-α at LF is the movement of *wh*-elements which were not moved at S-structure. Evidence for the existence of a syntactic level of representation, LF, is the fact that ECP effects are observed at LF.

3.1.2   ARGUMENT VS. NON-ARGUMENT AND THE ECP

We have been relating the ECP effects to subject–object asymmetries. This needs some further discussion.

Why do subjects differ from objects with respect to ECP? The answer is that subjects are not theta-governed, while objects are. Subject traces will always need to be antecedent-governed to satisfy the ECP.

It follows that other elements which are not theta-governed, such as adjuncts, will behave like subjects. Like subjects, they can only satisfy the ECP by antecedent-government. We expect that there will be an asymmetry between complements (theta-governed) and non-complements (antecedent-governed). Consider (29):

29a When did George do what?
29b *What did George do when?

(29a) will have an LF representation (30a):

30a [$_{CP}$ [$_{Spec_j}$ what$_i$ [$_{Spec_j}$ when$_j$]] did [$_{IP}$ George [$_{VP}$ do t$_i$]] t$_j$]]?

In (30a) the variable bound by *what$_i$* is properly governed: it is theta-governed by the verb. The variable bound by *when$_j$* is also properly governed: *when$_j$* is the head of [Spec, CP] and antecedent-governs its trace.

In (29b) *what$_i$* is the head of [Spec, CP] and *when$_j$*, which is *wh*-raised at LF, will not be able to antecedent-govern its trace. Given that this trace is not theta-governed by the verb either, it violates the ECP:

30b *[$_{CP}$ [$_{Spec_i}$ when$_j$ [$_{Spec_i}$ what$_i$]] did [$_{IP}$ George [$_{VP}$ do x$_i$]] x$_j$]]?

The ECP thus accounts for the complement–adjunct asymmetries in questions such as (29a) and (29b). Postulating a syntactic level of LF representation enables us to account for a range of data without there being a need for additional principles. We merely apply the syntactic principles we have adopted previously for S-structure representations.

3.1.3 SUBJECT–OBJECT ASYMMETRIES AND OPERATORS

In this section we shall see further evidence for LF movement of quantifiers: the asymmetries between subject and object which we identified with respect to S-structure movement and which also became apparent with respect to *wh*-movement at LF (cf. section 3.1.2) appear to play a role in determining the scope of negative constituents.

French negative existentials such as *personne* ('no one') have the property that they are accompanied by a negative clitic *ne* (at least in the standard language):

31a Je n'aime   personne.
    I   not-like no one
    'I like no one.'

In the literature it has often been assumed that the element *ne* is an overt scope-marker. The LF representation of (31a) will be:

31b   [Personne$_i$ [$_{IP}$ je n'aime t$_i$]].

In other words: 'For no person is it the case that I love him or her.' The scope of the negative existential *personne* is the entire clause.

An interesting contrast appears when we compare simple sentences with complex ones:

32a   Je n'ai invité personne.
      'I have not invited anyone.'
32b   Personne n'a téléphoné.
      'No one has telephoned.'

33a   J'ai demandé qu'on n'invite personne.
      'I have asked that they invite no one.'
33b   J'ai demandé que personne ne téléphone.
      'I have asked that no one telephones.'

34a   Je n'ai demandé qu'on invite personne.
      I have not asked that they invite anyone
      'There is no person such that I have asked that they invite him or her.'
34b   *Je n'ai demandé que personne téléphone.
      I have not asked that anyone telephone

In the simple sentences in (32) the scope of *personne* is the containing clause as can be seen from the translation. In (33) the scope of the negation in the lower clause is restricted to the lower clause. Crucially for our purposes, the negation does not bear on the verb *demander* ('ask') of the main clause. In (34) *ne* is found in the matrix clause. It indicates that *personne* should have main clause scope and thus negate the verb *demander*. This works fine when *personne* is in the object position in the lower clause, but it fails when *personne* is in the subject position. We shall consider these two examples here in some detail.

In (34a) the negative existential *personne* has scope over the main clause. Whereas (33a) means that there is a request being made that no one should be invited, (34a) means that there has not been a request to invite any person. (33a) has the LF representation (35a) and (34a) has the LF representation (35b):

35a [J'ai demandé [$_{CP}$ que [$_{IP}$ personne$_i$ [$_{IP}$ on n'invite t$_i$]]]].
35b [Personne$_i$ [$_{IP}$ je n'ai demandé [$_{CP}$ que [$_{IP}$ on invite t$_i$]]]].

Correspondingly, the LF representation of (33b) will be (36a) and that of the ungrammatical (34b) – where *personne* takes scope over the higher clause – ought to come out as (36b):

36a [J'ai demandé [$_{CP}$ que [$_{IP}$ personne [t$_i$ ne téléphone]]]].
36b *[Personne$_i$ [$_{IP}$ je n'ai demandé [$_{CP}$ que [$_{IP}$ t$_i$ téléphone]]]].

The asymmetry between the two sentences in (34) is a typical subject–object asymmetry. Such asymmetries are usually related to the ECP. The idea is that (36b) is like a *that*-trace violation: *personne* in (36b) is not able to antecedent-govern its trace in the lower subject position.[9]

3.2 The Application of the ECP

In this section we return to the general discussion of the application of the ECP. Our analysis developed so far has a number of shortcomings, also pointed out in chapter 8 (section 2.3), which we try to amend here.

3.2.1 THAT-TRACE EFFECTS

As the reader will remember from chapter 8, the ECP allows us to dispense with the unexplained *that*-trace filter: (37b) is a violation of the ECP: t_i in the [Spec, IP] position is not properly governed because *that* prevents the trace in [Spec, CP] from antecedent-governing it.

37a Who$_i$ do you think [$_{CP}$ t'$_i$ [$_{IP}$ t$_i$ came]]?
37b *Who$_i$ do you think [$_{CP}$ t'$_i$ that [$_{IP}$ t$_i$ came]]?

If we assume that adjuncts also leave traces the grammaticality of (38b) is unexplained:

38a Why$_i$ do you think [$_{CP}$ t'$_i$ [$_{IP}$ he left early t$_i$]]?

[9] For more discussion of the scope facts in French the reader is referred to Kayne (1984) which should be accessible at this point in our discussion. Rizzi (1982c) discusses similar facts in Italian. For an analysis of negation see Haegeman (in preparation).

38b   Why$_i$ do you think [$_{CP}$ t$'_i$ that [$_{IP}$ he left early t$_i$]]?
       (Lasnik and Saito, 1984: 255)

The trace of the moved adjunct *why* must be antecedent-governed, not being theta-governed. In (38a) the intermediate trace, t$'_i$, can antecedent-govern the lowest trace; but (38b) remains unexplained: how is it that the intervening *that* in C does not prevent antecedent-government? In their analysis of the ECP Lasnik and Saito (1984) offer a way of dealing with the problem. Their proposal is further modified in Chomsky (1986b). We adopt Lasnik and Saito's proposal and Chomsky's account here.[10]

3.2.2   TWO ASSUMPTIONS

In order to solve the problems discussed above, Lasnik and Saito introduce two assumptions with respect to the application of the ECP.

3.2.2.1   *ASSUMPTION I: Level of gamma-marking*   Consider (37), where the subject is extracted. Subjects are arguments and they are theta-marked by the verb. Subject argument-NPs are hence required by the projection principle.

On the other hand, *why* in (38) is an adjunct, hence not required by the projection principle: the verb *leave* does not theta-mark *why*.

Roughly speaking, the idea that Lasnik and Saito propose is that adjuncts come into full force at the level of LF only. Traces of adjuncts will be subject to the ECP only at that level and NOT at S-structure. Arguments, on the other hand, are present at S-structure where the projection principle requires them, and they are subject to the ECP at S-structure.

For determining whether the ECP is observed Lasnik and Saito propose a system of **gamma-marking**; γ, is the Greek *g*, for government. At S-structure we check argument traces for proper government. Those that respect the ECP are marked [+γ], those that violate the ECP are [−γ]. At LF we recheck all variables for the ECP. Those variables that are the reflexes of S-structure argument traces will already have a gamma-feature. An element which is [+γ] at S-structure will also be [+γ] at LF. Gamma-marking at LF will thus concern two types of variables only: (i) variables which are reflexes of S-structure adjunct traces; (ii) variables of LF applications of move-α. Positing this discrepancy for the level of gamma-marking might appear an *ad hoc* move, but it is crucial in Lasnik and Saito's (1984) proposal and we adopt it here.

---

[10]   The reader is advised to read through Lasnik and Saito's (1984) account in order to appreciate the range and complexity of the issue involved. We offer only a small fragment of the discussion.

Lasnik and Saito propose that the ECP must be satisfied at LF at the latest. This proposal comes down to a two-step procedure in the application of the ECP: (i) gamma-marking; (ii) checking the representation of a sentence at LF.[11]

The proposal that the feature assigned by gamma-marking is constant is in itself plausible. We have already seen that syntactic features do not change in the course of a derivation. For instance, a category which is a VP at D-structure is not altered at S-structure. Nominal features such as gender, person and number do not change either: once an NP is singular, for instance, it will remain so. The features [±anaphor] and [±pronominal] also do not vary from one level to the next. This last property led us to abandon the PRO analysis of parasitic gaps in chapter 8.

3.2.2.2 ASSUMPTION II: Deletion at LF Lasnik and Saito (1984) also discuss the role of *that*. In English its role is minimal: it can be deleted without semantic effect. Lasnik and Saito propose that at LF *that* is irrelevant because it does not contribute to the semantics of the sentence and may be deleted without altering the interpretation of the sentence. But when *that* is present in the surface string of the sentence, it must be present at PF and hence must be present at S-structure.

In fact Lasnik and Saito propose a slightly more general deletion process at LF: an element that does not contribute to the logico-semantic representation can be deleted at LF. To subsume move-α and delete-α they use the term **affect-α**.

3.2.3 APPLYING THE PROPOSAL

In order to get used to the new components in our, by now quite intricate, grammar we shall go through all the relevant examples:

39a   Who$_i$ do you think [$_{CP}$ t$'_i$ [$_{IP}$ t$_i$ came]]?
39b   *Who$_i$ do you think [$_{CP}$ t$'_i$ that [$_{IP}$ t$_i$ came]]?

40a   What$_i$ do you think [$_{CP}$ t$'_i$ [$_{IP}$ John likes t$_i$]]?
40b   What$_i$ do you think [$_{CP}$ t$'_i$ that [$_{IP}$ John likes t$_i$]]?

41a   Why$_i$ do you think [$_{CP}$ t$'_i$ [$_{IP}$ he left early t$_i$]]?
41b   Why$_i$ do you think [$_{CP}$ t$'_i$ that [$_{IP}$ he left early t$_i$]]?

---

[11]   This two-step procedure is perhaps reminiscent of the idea that while case-marking may apply both at D-structure (for inherent case) and at S-structure (for structural case), the case filter applies at S-structure.

In (39) and (40) arguments have been *wh*-moved. This means that there will be traces, which must be gamma-marked at S-structure (ASSUMPTION I). The object trace in (40) is theta-governed by the verb *like* and the subject trace in (39) must be antecedent-governed. This is possible in (39a) but prevented by the intervening *that* in (39b). As before we ignore intermediate traces to which we return in section 3. Gamma-marking for (39) and (40) is encoded in (42) and (43) respectively.

42a Who$_i$ do you think [$_{CP}$ t$'_i$ [$_{IP}$ t$_i$ came]]?
                         [+γ]
42b *Who$_i$ do you think [$_{CP}$ t$'_i$ that [$_{IP}$ t$_i$ came]]?
                             [−γ]

43a What$_i$ do you think [$_{CP}$ t$'_i$ [$_{IP}$ John likes t$_i$]]?
                         [+γ]
43b What$_i$ do you think [$_{CP}$ t$'_i$ that [$_{IP}$ John likes t$_i$]]?
                            [+γ]

At LF the traces are interpreted as variables bound by the *wh*-operator and they retain the gamma feature. When the ECP is checked at LF, (42b) will be rejected because it contains a trace which is [−γ].

Now we turn to (41). Adjunct traces are not gamma-marked at S-structure, but rather at LF. According to ASSUMPTION II, the complementizer *that* may be deleted. This means that the LF representations of (41a) and (41b) will be identical and the trace of *why* satisfies the ECP as desired.

41c Why$_i$ do you think [$_{CP}$ t$'_i$ [$_{IP}$ he left early t$_i$]]?
                         [+γ]

Let us return to an earlier example to see if our adjusted theory applies appropriately. After all, we should not introduce auxiliary assumptions to rescue some examples and then find that our previous good results have become undone. (29), repeated here as (44), illustrates the asymmetry between arguments and adjuncts:

44a When did George do what?
44b *What did George do when?

The structures of both examples will contain traces. In the S-structure (45a) of (44a) there will be an adjunct-trace, so we need not worry about gamma-marking yet. In (45b), the S-structure of (44b), there will be argument-trace and gamma-marking will apply.

45a [$_{CP}$ [$_{Spec_j}$ when$_j$] did [$_{IP}$ George [$_{VP}$ do what$_i$] t$_j$]]?
45b *[$_{CP}$ [$_{Spec_i}$ what$_i$] did [$_{IP}$ George [$_{VP}$ do t$_i$] when$_j$]]?
                                                         [+γ]

At LF *wh*-raising applies to the second *wh*-phrase. Gamma-marking applies to all traces not gamma-marked yet:

46a [$_{CP}$ [$_{Spec_i}$ what$_i$ [$_{Spec_j}$ when$_j$]] did [$_{IP}$ George [$_{VP}$ do t$_i$] t$_j$]]?
                                                                        [+γ] [+γ]
46b *[$_{CP}$ [$_{Spec_i}$ when$_j$ [$_{Spec_i}$ what$_i$]] did [$_{IP}$ George [$_{VP}$ do t$_i$]] t$_j$]]?
                                                                        [+γ] [−γ]

In (46a) the variable resulting from *wh*-raising *what$_i$* is theta-governed by *do*: it is properly governed and assigned [+γ]. The trace left after S-structure movement of *when$_j$* is also properly governed since it is antecedent-governed.

In (46b) the variable bound by *what$_i$* retains its [+γ] feature assigned at S-structure, but the variable resulting from *wh*-raising *when$_j$* is not properly governed: it is not theta-governed, being an adjunct-trace, and it cannot be antecedent-governed because *when$_j$* cannot govern it from its adjoined position in [Spec, CP].

Finally we discuss example (47a).

47a Why do you wonder whom John will invite?

This example is grammatical if we interpret *why* as bearing on the reason for wondering. An answer could be: 'I wonder because I am concerned about the man's knowledge of French.' But (47a) cannot have the reading in which *why* is connected with *invite*. Apparently we cannot represent this sentence as an example of long movement of *why* parallel to (47b):

47b Why do you think that Emsworth will invite George?

(47b) is ambiguous. *Why* can be interpreted with or **construed with** *think* or with *invite*.

We return to (47b) below (section 3.3.2). Let us now concentrate on (47a). The possible interpretation of (47a) will have S-structure (47c) and LF (47d):

47c Why$_i$ do [$_{IP}$ you wonder t$_i$ [$_{CP}$ whom$_j$ [$_{IP}$ John will invite   t$_j$]]]?
                                                                    [+γ]
47d Why$_i$ do [$_{IP}$ you wonder t$_i$ [$_{CP}$ whom$_j$ [$_{IP}$ John will invite   t$_j$]]]?
                   [+γ]   [+γ]

This ought to pose no problems to the reader: the argument trace is gamma-marked at S-structure and the trace of *why* is gamma-marked at LF.

(47e) is the S-structure of (47a) where *why* is construed with the lower clause:

47e *Why$_i$ do [$_{IP}$ you wonder [$_{CP}$ whom$_j$ [$_{IP}$ John will invite t$_j$ t$_i$]]]?

First of all, note that the subjacency condition has been violated: *why* has crossed two bounding nodes IP. But it appears that the sentence is more than a mere subjacency violation. In order to assess the impact of subjacency let us first look at a simple example (48a):

48a ??Whom do you wonder why John will invite?

This sentence is marginal but it can be interpreted: *whom* is the object of *invite*. (48a) is an example of a subjacency violation, but the ECP is satisfied. Gamma-marking applies to the trace of *whom* at S-structure (48b) and to the trace of *why* at LF (48c).

48b Whom$_i$ do [$_{IP}$ you wonder [$_{CP}$ why$_j$ [$_{IP}$ John will invite t$_i$ t$_j$]]]?
              #   #   [+γ]
48c Whom$_i$ do [$_{IP}$ you wonder [$_{CP}$ why$_j$ [$_{IP}$ John will invite   t$_i$ t$_j$]]]?
                                                              [+γ] [+γ]

In (47a) *why* cannot be construed with the lower clause at all. This leads us to conclude that it cannot just be that subjacency is violated. Subjacency violations do not lead to such strong effects. The S-structure and the LF representations of (47a) with their gamma-features are given in (48f) and (47g) respectively.

47f   *Why$_i$ do [$_{IP}$ you wonder [$_{CP}$ whom$_j$ [$_{IP}$ John will invite   t$_j$ t$_i$]]]?
                                                                         [+γ]
47g   *Why$_i$ do [$_{IP}$ you wonder [$_{CP}$ whom$_j$ [$_{IP}$ John will invite   t$_j$ t$_i$]]]?
                                                                         [+γ] [−γ]

In the S-structure (47f) gamma-marking applies to the trace of *whom$_j$*. In the LF representation (47g) gamma-marking applies to the trace of *why*. *Why* is separated from its trace by two IP boundaries and one CP boundary. We conclude that the antecedent is too far removed from the trace to be able to antecedent-govern it. We need to make this conclusion more precise and we return to the matter in chapter 10. Chapter 12 provides a different account.

Our discussion above illustrates a general phenomenon to which we shall return in the following sections: sentences that violate subjacency may give rise to unacceptability but those that violate ECP are much worse. We invite the reader to check the modified account here with other examples of ECP effects discussed in this and the preceding chapter.

3.3   Intermediate Traces and the ECP

3.3.1   THE PROBLEM

We have not yet discussed the status of the intermediate traces created by movement. Clearly, the formulation of the ECP would be maximally simple if we could assume that it also applies to these traces. Otherwise we have to discriminate such traces from traces in base-positions, a complication of the theory which we then would have to explain. In this section we shall see that, like adjunct traces, intermediate traces at LF are subject to the ECP and must be antecedent-governed.

3.3.2   INTERMEDIATE TRACES AND ANTECEDENT-GOVERNMENT

Consider an S-structure representation (49a) and the corresponding LF representation (49b):

49a   Whom$_i$ do [you think [t′$_i$ that [John will invite   t$_i$]]]?
                                                          [+γ]
49b   Whom$_i$ do [you think   [that [John will invite   t$_i$]]]?
                                                          [+γ]

At S-structure the trace in the base-position is [+γ]: it is theta-governed by the verb. The intermediate trace is created in order to satisfy the subjacency condition (see chapter 7). Since the intermediate trace is not in an argument position, we treat it like an adjunct trace. The trace is not theta-governed: *think* theta-marks the complement CP but not the trace in [Spec, CP]. In order to satisfy the ECP the intermediate trace would have to be antecedent-governed. According to ASSUMPTION I, the intermediate trace, which is a non-argument trace, could be gamma-marked at LF, like all adjunct traces. But recall that ASSUMPTION II allows elements which do not contribute to the logico-semantic representation of a sentence to be deleted at LF. The intermediate trace is such an element. In the LF representation (49b) the intermediate trace is accordingly deleted. As a result, (49) is in a sense a non-example: at the level where we are checking the gamma-features of intermediate traces there are no such traces left. This does not mean that the problem of intermediate traces is a non-problem, though.

Consider (50a) (= 47b), in which an adjunct is extracted, with the S-structure (50b) and the LF (50c):

50a Why do you think that Emsworth will invite George?
50b Why$_i$ do [$_{IP}$ you think [$_{CP}$ t'$_i$ that [$_{IP}$ Emsworth will invite George t$_i$]]]?
50c Why$_i$ do [$_{IP}$ you think [$_{CP}$ t'$_i$ [$_{IP}$ Emsworth will invite George t$_i$]]]?
                        [?]   [+γ]

The lowest trace of the moved adjunct *why* must be gamma-marked at LF: it must be assigned the feature [+γ], by virtue of being antecedent-governed. The question is how t_i is antecedent-governed, by t'_i or by *why*?

Compare (50) with (51). (51) was discussed in the previous section as (47a). We consider only the impossible interpretation in which *why* is construed with the lower clause. We have already established that under this interpretation the sentence violates subjacency and, more importantly, the ECP.

51a *Why do you wonder whom John will invite?
51b *Why$_i$ do [$_{IP}$ you wonder [$_{CP}$ whom$_j$ [$_{IP}$ John will invite t$_j$ t$_i$]]]?
                                                                        [+γ]
51c *Why$_i$ do [$_{IP}$ you wonder [$_{CP}$ whom$_j$ [$_{IP}$ John will invite t$_j$ t$_i$]]]?
                                                                        [+γ] [−γ]

The distance between *why* and the trace in the base-position in (51c) was said to be too great for antecedent-government. This distance is exactly the same in (50c). We conclude that antecedent-government of the trace in the base-position in (50c) is ensured not by *why* itself but by the intermediate trace, t'_i, which hence must not be deleted at LF.

If we postulate that the intermediate trace must be properly governed like any trace then in (50c) the intermediate trace must be antecedent-governed by *why*:

50d   Why$_i$ do [$_{IP}$ you think [$_{CP}$ t'_i [$_{IP}$ Emsworth will invite George t$_i$]]]?
          [+γ]   [+γ]

At this point we should perhaps dwell one moment on the LF representations (50d) and (51c), repeated here as (52a) and (52b):

52a = 51c   *Why$_i$ do [$_{IP}$ you wonder [$_{CP}$ whom$_j$ [$_{IP}$ John will invite   t$_j$ t$_i$]]]?
                                                                           [+γ] [−γ]
52b = 50d   Why$_i$ do [$_{IP}$ you think [$_{CP}$ t'_i [$_{IP}$ Emsworth will invite George   t$_i$]]]?
                                  [+γ]   [+γ]

We attributed the impossibility of construing *why* with the lower clause in (52a) to the ECP, saying that *why* would be too far from its trace to ante-cedent-govern it. The distance between *why* and its trace is two IPs and one CP. On the other hand, we assume that *why* in (52b) can antecedent-govern the intermediate trace although it is separated from it by one IP and one CP. It looks as if we shall need to be very careful about defining which categories define barriers for government since blatantly neither CP nor IP can always constitute a barrier. This intricate matter is discussed in chapter 10.

There is, of course, another way of discussing this issue. That would be by claiming that intermediate traces do not need to be governed at all. Though such a step would complicate our formulation of the ECP it would not lead to any different predictions with respect to the examples discussed so far.

3.3.3   INTERMEDIATE TRACES MUST BE ANTECEDENT-GOVERNED

In order to test whether intermediate traces are subject to the ECP, we need an example whose ungrammaticality can be attributed solely to the presence of an ungoverned intermediate trace. This is not an easy matter but let us try.

53   *Why do you wonder whom Bill thinks that John will invite?

(53) is grammatical if we interpret *why* as asking for the reason of the wondering, but *why* cannot be construed with either *think* or *invite*. As in the discussion of (47a), we assume that the impossible readings are attributed to the ECP since subjacency violations do not produce such strong effects. We shall only discuss the reading in which *why* is construed with *invite*, hence the asterisk.

The S-structure and LF representations of (53) are (54a) and (54b) respectively:

54a   *$[_{CP1}$ Why$_i$ do $[_{IP_1}$ you wonder $[_{CP2}$ whom$_j$ $[_{IP_2}$ Bill thinks $[_{CP3}$ t'$_i$ that $[_{IP3}$
        John will invite   t$_j$ t$_i$]]]]]]?
                            [+γ]
54b   *$[_{CP1}$ Why$_i$ do $[_{IP_1}$ you wonder $[_{CP2}$ whom$_j$ $[_{IP_2}$ Bill thinks $[_{CP3}$ t'$_i$ $[_{IP3}$ John
                                                                              [−γ]
        will invite   t$_j$ t$_i$]]]]]]?
                      [+γ] [+γ]

In (54a) t_j is marked [+γ], being theta-marked by *invite*. In (54b) the lowest trace of *why* is properly governed by the intermediate trace, t'_i, in [Spec, CP3]. This means that this trace must be present at LF. If the intermediate trace in [Spec, CP3] were itself not subject to the ECP the sentence would only violate subjacency and this would not explain the strong unacceptability of the reading in which *why* is construed with the lower clause (CP3). Let us assume that the intermediate trace in [Spec, CP3] is subject to the ECP. Given that it is not in an argument position, proper government will have to be achieved by antecedent-government. But the trace is separated from the antecedent *why$_i$* by two IPs and one CP. As seen above (52a), this distance is apparently too great for antecedent-government: the combination of the three maximal projections has the effect of creating a barrier.

If we assume that intermediate traces are subject to the ECP at LF then we have a way of explaining why the representation (54b) is ruled out. So far no other principle of our grammar is able to explain the strong ungrammaticality of this sentence.

An example that makes the same point is discussed in Chomsky (1986b: 11 (22d)).

55   *How did Bill wonder $[_{CP}$ who $[_{IP}$ wanted [t' [to fix the car t]]]]?

We invite the reader to work out why (55) is ungrammatical.

4   Reconstruction

4.1   *The Binding Theory and Reconstruction*

In chapter 4 we discussed the application of the binding theory. This module of the grammar regulates the interpretation of NPs.

56   **Binding Theory**
     Principle A
     An NP with the feature [+anaphor] must be bound in its governing category.
     Principle B
     An NP with the feature [+pronominal] must be free in its governing category.

Recall also that R-expressions are inherently referential and resist A-binding (Principle C).

   Consider the following examples (see also chapter 7, exercise 6):

57a   John$_i$ wondered which pictures of himself$_i$ Mary liked.
57b   Which pictures of himself$_i$ will John$_i$ sell?
57c   Which pictures of each other$_i$ do you think that your parents$_i$ prefer?
57d   Which pictures of himself$_i$ does John$_i$ think that Jane will sell?
57e   Which pictures of himself$_i$ does Jane think that John$_i$ will sell?
57f   Which pictures of himself$_{i/j}$ does John$_i$ think that Bill$_j$ will sell?
57g   Criticize himself$_i$ John$_i$ never will.
57h   Criticize himself$_i$ Mary never thought that John$_i$ would.
57i   *Criticize himself$_i$ John$_i$ never thought that Mary would.

In this section we return to some of these examples. (57a) is unproblematic: *himself*, the anaphor, is bound by the matrix subject *John*. In this example the binding theory can apply to the S-structure representation. (57b) is grammatical in spite of the fact that the reflexive *himself* is not c-commanded by the antecedent *John*. At first sight, such an example might appear to be direct support for Belletti and Rizzi's (1988) proposal that Principle A can apply at D-structure: at D-structure the *wh*-phrase *which pictures of himself* will occupy its base-position and the reflexive will be bound by the subject NP:

58 John$_i$ will sell which pictures of himself$_i$?

(57c) could be dealt with in an analogous way. We leave the reader to work it out for himself. But this approach is problematic for other examples. Consider, for instance, (57d). The example is grammatical, which means that the reflexive *himself* must be bound. The antecedent of *himself* must be an NP with the feature [+Masculine], i.e. *John* rather than *Jane* will be the antecedent. As was the case in (57b) and (57c) the antecedent *John* does not c-command *himself* at S-structure. In this example, though, the D-structure will not help us either:

59a *D-structure*
     [$_{CP1}$ [$_{IP1}$ John$_i$ does think [$_{CP2}$ that [$_{IP2}$ Jane will sell which pictures of himself$_i$]]]]?

At D-structure the only potential binder for the reflexive is *Jane*, but *Jane* does not have the relevant feature. How can we account for the grammaticality of this example? Consider the derivation of (57d): its D-structure is given in (59a); in (59b) we have given the S-structure configuration with all the relevant traces:

59b [$_{CP1}$ [Which pictures of himself$_i$]$_j$ does [$_{IP1}$ John$_i$ think [$_{CP2}$ t$'_j$ that [$_{IP2}$ Jane will sell t$_j$]]]]?

We assume that the *wh*-phrase *which pictures of himself* has moved via the lower [Spec, CP2] to reach the higher [Spec, CP1]. In (57d) the reflexive is bound by *John*, but neither the S-structure position nor the D-structure position of the *wh*-phrase can account for this kind of binding in an obvious way. We have to establish a c-command relation between *John* and *himself*, but the NP *Jane*, which is a potential binder, should not intervene as a c-commanding subject. When we consider (59b) very carefully it would appear that the position we need is the position signalled by the intermediate trace in [Spec, CP2], *t$'_j$*. It is proposed in the literature that the binding relation which is required for this sentence can be achieved by **reconstruction**. Reconstruction is a process by which a moved phrase is 'placed back' to a previous movement site. The *wh*-phrase in our example has moved through the intermediate [Spec, CP2]. As a first analysis, to be modified below, we reconstruct the *wh*-phrase to the position of the intermediate trace in order to ensure that the reflexive can be bound by the antecedent *John*:[12]

59c [$_{CP1}$ [$_{IP1}$ John$_i$ does think [$_{CP2}$ [which pictures of himself$_i$]$_j$ that [$_{IP2}$ Jane will sell t$_j$]]]].

Let us turn to (57e), repeated here as (60a):

60a [$_{CP1}$ [Which pictures of himself$_i$]$_j$ does [$_{IP1}$ Jane think [$_{CP2}$ t$_j$ that [$_{IP2}$ John$_i$ will sell t$_j$]]]]?

In this example the antecedent of the reflexive *himself* is again *John*; the position relevant for the binding of the reflexive is the lowest trace of the moved *wh*-phrase. On a reconstruction approach we could say that the relevant relation is achieved by moving the *wh*-phrase *which pictures of himself* back into the position marked by the lower trace:

60b [$_{CP1}$ Does [$_{IP1}$ Jane think [$_{CP2}$ t′$_j$ that [$_{IP2}$ John$_i$ will sell [which pictures of himself$_i$]$_j$]]]]?

However, the structure derived by reconstruction as proposed in (59c) and (60b) is also unsatisfactory: though it does allow us to account for the interpretation of the reflexives, we no longer can account for the fact that the relevant sentences are questions. Consider (60a), for instance. On the assumption that the interrogative scope of the *wh*-operator is determined by its c-command domain (cf. section 2.1. above), the interrogative component of

---

[12] Reconstruction phenomena are discussed among others in Aoun and Li (1989), Barss (1986, 1988), Brody (1993b), Chomsky (1992), Huang (1993). For a different view the reader is referred to van Riemsdijk and Williams (1981). In the text we propose that reconstruction places the relevant constituent in a lower position. Barss (1986) deals with the phenomenon in a different way: he makes crucial use of the chain created by movement. Reconstruction type phenomena are also found in the following examples:

(i)   What John saw was a picture of himself.
(ii) I saw the pictures of each other that Jane and Ann took.
(iii) The pictures that Jane and Ann admire most are each other's pictures.

(i) is an example of a pseudo-cleft construction. For an early discussion of this construction see Higgins (1972).

the *wh*-phrase *which pictures of himself* has matrix scope, it c-commands the matrix clause. On this view, the appropriate LF representation of (60a) cannot be (60b): in (60b), the *wh*-operator does not have the matrix clause in its c-command domain. The LF representation must be more like that in (60c):

60c [$_{CP1}$ [Which x]$_j$ does [$_{IP1}$ Jane think [$_{CP2}$ t$'_j$ that [$_{IP2}$ John$_i$ will sell [x pictures of himself$_i$]$_j$]]]]?

Reconstruction does not move the entire *wh*-phrase back into a lower position, but only part of it.

Finally consider the examples in (61). Both are ambiguous in that either *John* or *Bill* serves as an antecedent for *himself*:

61a [$_{CP1}$ [Which pictures of himself]$_j$ did [$_{IP1}$ John think [$_{CP2}$ t$'_j$ that [$_{IP2}$ Bill would sell t$_j$]]]]?
61b [$_{CP1}$ [$_{IP1}$ John wonders [$_{CP2}$ [which pictures of himself]$_j$ [$_{IP2}$ Bill would sell t$_j$]]]].

In (61a) *himself* can be bound either by *John* or by *Bill*. This means that in this example reconstruction can freely place the relevant section of the *wh*-phrase either in the position of the intermediate trace (t'_j) or in the position of the lower trace (t_j), i.e. the reconstruction site is freely chosen. The reconstruction process will leave the *wh*-operator in the S-structure position to garantee that it can c-command the clause to which it gives interrogative force. In (61b) the reflexive is bound either by *John* or by *Bill*. When *Bill* is the antecedent, we assume that the *wh*-phrase reconstructs in the base position; when *John* is the antecedent there is no reconstruction. We conclude as a first approximation that reconstruction is not automatic, and that apparently the site of reconstruction is fairly free. In the next sections we shall see that the apparent optionality of reconstruction can be restricted if other principles of the grammar come into play.

We turn to the other examples of (57) presently. First consider some other examples of reconstruction. So far we have looked at instances of Principle A effects, where reflexives or reciprocals require binding. Recall that the binding theory also applies to NP-traces, i.e. traces of NP-movement, as discussed in chapter 6. The binding requirement for NP-traces can also be satisfied by reconstruction. Consider (62a):

62a John$_i$ is [$_{AP}$ very likely [$_{IP}$ t$_i$ to win]].

This is an example of NP-movement, specifically NP-raising, discussed in chapter 6. We assume that *John* originates as the subject of *to win* and is moved to the canonical subject position of the matrix clause to be assigned case. The trace of *John* in the lower non-finite IP has to be bound, it is subject to Principle A of the binding theory. This is unproblematic in (62a). Consider now (62b), where the AP headed by *likely* has been *wh*-moved:

62b   [$_{CP}$ [$_{APk}$ how likely [$_{IP}$ t$_i$ to win]] is$_j$ [$_{IP}$ John$_i$ t$_j$ t$_k$]]?

In (62b) the trace in the subject position of *to win* is not bound by *John* at S-structure, but if we return the moved phrase *how likely to win* to its base-position, the desired effect will be achieved.

In (63) we see that reconstruction is also relevant for Principle B effects. In (63a) *him* cannot be coindexed with *John* in spite of the fact that *John* does not c-command *him* at S-structure.

63a   With him$_{j/*i}$, John$_i$ never talked.
       (cf. Huang, 1993: 105)

On a reconstruction approach (63a) will be ruled out in the same way as (63b). The preposed PP apparently has to reconstruct.

63b   John$_i$ never talked with him$_{j/*i}$.

Consider the interaction of reconstruction with Principle C:

64a   ??[[How many pictures of John$_i$]$_j$ does [$_{IP}$ he$_i$ think [$_{CP}$ t$'_j$ that [$_{IP}$ I like t$_j$]]]]?
64b   ?[[How many pictures of John$_i$]$_j$ do [$_{IP}$ you think [$_{CP}$ t$'_j$ that [$_{IP}$ he$_i$ will like t$_j$]]]]?

(64a) could be ruled out as a violation of Principle C, if we assume that the *wh*-phrase *how many pictures of John* is reconstructed to a lower position. We would have to conclude that reconstruction is at least preferred for (64a): if we did not reconstruct the *wh*-phrase the sentence ought to be grammatical, which it is not. Observe, though, that (64a) is not considered completely ungrammatical. We return to this point presently.

(64a) is less acceptable than (64b). This will follow again if we consider the

S-structure representation of these sentences more carefully. In (64a) there are two reconstruction sites available: the base-position and the intermediate [Spec, CP], but neither kind of reconstruction can lead to a grammatical representation. If we reconstruct the fronted NP *how many pictures of John* to the base position then the pronoun *he* will c-command the NP *John* and if the pronoun and the NP are coindexed the sentence should be ruled out be Principle C: *John* is an R-expression and it will be bound. The same will apply if we reconstruct the *wh*-phrase to the intermediate [Spec, CP]: again *he* will c-command *John*. In (64b) there are again two sites for reconstruction: the base-position and the intermediate trace in [Spec, CP]. If we reconstruct to the base-position, the sentence is ungrammatical: *he* c-commands *John*. If we reconstruct the fronted NP to the position of the intermediate trace, the pronoun *he* will not c-command *John* and thus can be coindexed with it.

The interaction of reconstruction and Principle C leaves many questions, though. We have already seen that (64a) is not entirely ruled out, contrary to what Principle C in combination with reconstruction would lead us to expect. The effect of Principle C seems to be weakened even further if the R-expression is more deeply embedded in the moved phrase as suggested by the contrasts in (65) (from Huang, 1993: (12b)–(12c)):

65a   ??Which pictures of John$_i$ does he$_i$ like most?
65b   ?Which claim that John$_i$ was a thief did he$_i$ deny?
65c   Which pictures that John$_i$ took does he$_i$ like most?

While (65a) is marginal, (65b) and (65c) are much improved, even though again the reconstruction site could only be the base position of the *wh*-phrase. Reinhart (1981) relates the contrasts in (65) to the depth of embedding of the R-expression in the moved *wh*-constituent. Another factor that might play a role (cf. Lebeaux, 1989) is the contrast between complement and adjunct:

65d   Which pictures near John did he like most?

In (65a) *John* is a complement, in (65d) it is part of an adjunct. A similar contrast is found in the pair (65e)–(65f):

65e   Which claim that John$_i$ was asleep was he$_{j/*i}$ willing to discuss?
65f   Which claim that John$_i$ made was he$_{i/j}$ willing to discuss?
      (Chomsky, 1992: (33))

In (65e) the pronoun *he* cannot take *John* as an antecedent, suggesting that reconstruction takes place; in (65f) *he* and *John* can be coindexed, suggesting that reconstruction is only an option. We leave the problems with respect to the interaction of reconstruction and the application of Principle C aside in this book. The reader is referred to the literature for discussion.

Let us summarize the above discussion and say that S-structure is relevant for the binding theory, since the intermediate traces count, but that we also have to appeal to reconstruction. Reconstruction is another process which has no overt effects on the string: there is no surface reflex of the reconstruction effects in the examples given. Apparently in some cases reconstruction is obligatory (Principle B), in some cases it is optional (Principle A, partly Principle C). The reconstruction site is the base position of the moved element or an intermediate trace of movement.

4.2 VP Fronting and Reconstruction

Now consider examples (57g)–(57i) repeated here as (66). In all these examples a VP has been preposed:

66a $[_{VP_i}$ Criticize himself$_i]$ John$_i$ never will t$_j$.

66b $[[_{VP_i}$ Criticize himself$_i]$ [Mary never thought $[_{CP}$ t$'_j$ that $[_{IP}$ John$_i$ would t$_j]]]]$.

66c *$[[_{VP_i}$ Criticize himself$_i]$ [John$_i$ never thought $[_{CP}$ t$'_j$ that $[_{IP}$ Mary would t$_j]]]]$.

In (66a) the reflexive *himself* is bound by *John*, the subject of the matrix clause. As a first approximation, to be revised below, we could say that the fronted VP reconstructs into its base-position and that *John* binds the reflexive. In (66b) the same analysis applies: the lower subject *John* binds the reflexive after the VP has been reconstructed into its base-position. The question arises whether we could also use the intermediate trace for reconstruction of the VP. In (66b) position of the intermediate trace (t$'_j$) will not be usable: if we were to reconstruct the VP into that position then there would be no c-commanding NP with the relevant properties available: *Mary*, the subject of the matrix clause, is feminine and *himself* is masculine. But (66c) shows that even with a relevant binder available in the matrix clause, the effect still is ungrammatical.[13] *John*, the subject NP of the matrix clause, cannot serve

---

[13] Examples such as the ones discussed here are dealt with in Huang (1993). This paper discusses the many problems related to reconstruction in far greater detail than we can do here.

as the antecedent of the reflexive contained in the fronted VP. Fronted VPs always have to be reconstructed to their base-positions. In general, reconstruction to the base-position is not enforced by the binding theory: in previous examples fronted NPs were reconstructed to the position of intermediate traces. What property of the fronted VP forces reconstruction to the base-position? One option, which seems rather promising, will be explored here. Recall the discussion of the base-position of the subject in chapter 6, section 5. We discussed the French examples (110) repeated here as (67):

67a   Tous les garçons ont lu ce livre.
        all the boys have read this book
67b   Les garçons ont tous lu ce livre.
        the boys have all read this book

We proposed that the quantifier *tous* in (67b) signals the base position of the subject. Both examples would have a D-structure where *tous les garçons* originates in a VP-internal position, and where the canonical subject position [Spec, IP] is empty:

67c   [IP e ont [VP [NP tous les garçons] lu ce livre]].

At S-structure, either the full subject NP *tous les garçons* moves to the subject position, as in (68a):

68a   [IP [NP_i Tous les garçons] ont [VP t_i lu ce livre]].

Alternatively, the phrase *les garçons* moves and strands the quantifier *tous*,[14] leading to sentence (68b):

68b   [IP [NP_i Les garçons] ont [VP tous t_i lu ce livre]]

Observe that the subject-in-VP hypothesis developed in chapter 6 implies that the canonical subject is in a derived subject position and has a VP-internal trace. The trace of the moved subject is an NP-trace, it is subject to Principle

---

14   The exact mechanism of the movement of *les garçons* is a question for research. Shlonsky (1991), for instance, proposes that *les garçons* is not moved out directly from its position to the right of *tous*, but rather transits to a specifier position to the left of *tous*. The reader is referred to Shlonsky's article for discussion.

A of the binding theory and has to be bound by an NP in an A-position. This hypothesis will help account for the need to reconstruct fronted VPs into their base-position.

One immediate consequence of the approach developed here is that if VP always contains the trace of the moved subject then the representation of the examples in (66) is as in (69). Accordingly, the VP-internal reflexive *himself* in the examples in (69) can be bound by the trace of the subject NP (cf. also the discussion in chapter 6, section 5, (118)).

69a $[_{VP_j}$ t_i Criticize himself$_i$] John$_i$ never will t_j.

69b $[_{VP_j}$ t_i Criticize himself$_i$] Mary never thought $[_{CP}$ t'_j that $[_{IP}$ John$_i$ would t_j]].

69c *$[_{VP_j}$ t_i Criticize himself$_i$] John$_i$ never thought $[_{CP}$ t'_j that $[_{IP}$ Mary$_k$ would t_j]].

Strictly speaking, and contrary to what we suggested above, the fronted VP does not have to reconstruct in order to allow the reflexive to be bound. However, we should not conclude that the fronted VP does not reconstruct. The VP-internal trace of the subject, t_i, is an A-trace and itself subject to the binding theory, specifically to Principle A. Reconstruction is now required to allow the VP-internal subject trace to be bound. In (69a) we will reconstruct the VP to the base-position (t_j) and t_i will be bound by *John*, the NP in the canonical subject position, [Spec, IP]; t_i binds *himself*. In (69b) we will reconstruct the fronted VP into its base-position. In this way *John* can bind t_i and t_i will bind the reflexive. In (69c) we cannot reconstruct the fronted VP to an appropriate position. If we were to reconstruct the VP to the base-position then *Mary* could bind the VP-internal trace, t_i, but if t_i binds the reflexive *himself*, *Mary* will bind *himself* by transitivity of coindexation, and there will be a clash in features between *Mary* and *himself*:

69d *John$_i$ never thought $[_{CP}$ t'_j that $[_{IP}$ Mary$_k$ would $[_{VP}$ $t_{k/i}$ criticize himself$_i$]]].

If we reconstruct the fronted VP to the intermediate position, *John*, the matrix subject, can bind t_i, and its features, [Masculine, Singular] also match those of the reflexive *himself*, but now *Mary*, the subject NP of the lower clause, is not associated with a chain any more, hence *Mary* cannot receive a thematic role:

69e $[_{CP1}$ $[_{IP1}$ *John$_i$ never thought $[_{CP2}$ $[_{VP}$ t_i Criticize himself$_{i/*k}]_j$ that $[_{IP2}$ Mary$_k$ would t_j]]]].

Moreover, in (69e) *John* is the external argument of both *thought* and of *criticize*. It will receive two thematic roles and violate the theta criterion. Consider, finally, (70)

70 $[_{VP_j}$ t$_i$ Criticize himself$_{i/*k}]$ John$_k$ never thought $[_{CP}$ t$'_j$ that $[_{IP}$ Bill$_i$ would t$_i]]$.

In (70) the fronted VP *criticize himself* contains an anaphor, *himself*. In spite of the fact that there are two potential antecedents, *John$_k$* and *Bill$_i$*, the antecedent of *himself* must be *Bill*. This follows from the discussion above: in order to satisfy the binding requirement on the VP-internal subject trace t$_i$ we must reconstruct the fronted VP into its base-position (t$_i$).

   To sum up. In order to create the configurations relevant for binding, we reconstruct constituents which have been subject to A′-movement into either their base-position or into a position occupied by an intermediate trace created by movement. Fronted VPs always reconstruct to their base-position; this follows from the hypothesis that the subject NP originates in a VP-internal position.

4.3   Reconstruction and Idioms

As a final set of data related to reconstruction consider the following examples, taken from Chomsky (1992).

71 John wonders which pictures of himself Bill took.

(71) contains a fronted *wh*-phrase *which pictures of himself* which in turn contains a reflexive, *himself*. The anaphor can be bound either by *John* or by *Bill*, depending on whether we reconstruct the *wh*-phrase or not: if we do not reconstruct then the matrix subject *John* will bind the reflexive. However, there is an additional semantic effect in this example. *Take pictures* can have an idiomatic reading, 'photograph' and a literal reading, 'remove pictures'. According to Chomsky (1992: 35ff.) the idiomatic reading is only available when the antecedent of *himself* is *Bill*. This would follow if we assume that idiomatic expressions have to be interpreted as units. The idiomatic reading of *take pictures* can only be achieved if we have a representation where the elements of the idiom constitute a unit, i.e. assuming that the interpretation if achieved at LF, we will arrive at the idiomatic reading if we reconstruct the *wh*-phrase containing the N *pictures* to the base-position.

5 Two Notes on Scope Interactions between *Wh*-operators and Quantifiers

In this section we introduce further problems in the analysis of reconstruction facts. We do not intend to provide a complete analysis, but simply wish to illustrate the kind of work that is being done.

5.1 VP Adjunction of Quantifiers

In this section we turn to more examples of quantifier interpretation. Consider the contrast between (72a) and (72b):

72a Who does everyone like?
72b Who likes everyone?

The first question is ambiguous: either there is one person liked by everyone, say Chomsky, or there are as many persons as there are entities associated with *everyone*. In the latter reading one could answer: Sten likes Tarald, Corinne likes Luigi, Ian likes Oswaldo, Bonnie likes Irene. In the first interpretation, *who* takes scope over *everyone*. In the second reading *everyone* takes wide scope. If we were to assume that QR only moves a quantifier to IP, as suggested so far, then (73a) would be the LF representation for (72a):

73a

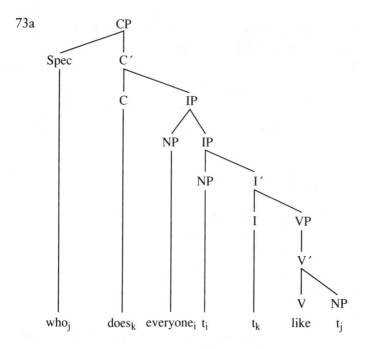

Everyone is adjoined to IP. Remember that adjunction creates a maximal projection on top of another one (see chapter 7). We have assumed that in order to be 'inside' – or dominated by – a category an element must be inside – or dominated by – ALL the maximal projections which make up that category.

In (73a) *everyone* is not dominated by IP in this sense, since it is only dominated by one segment of it, the higher IP. *Everyone* is, to use our metaphor, 'on the balcony'. *Everyone* is, however, dominated by the category CP and so is *who*. This means that in this representation *who$_j$* and *everyone$_i$* are dominated by exactly the same maximal projections. May (1985) proposes that when two quantifiers are dominated by exactly the same maximal projections either may take wide scope, hence the two readings associated with the sentence.

Adopting this analysis raises a problem for (72b). This sentence is unambiguous: *who* must have wide scope. To a question like (72b) the only possible answer is something like: 'Sten'. Sten would be an individual who likes everyone else. Suppose we apply QR as before and adjoin *everyone* to IP:

73b

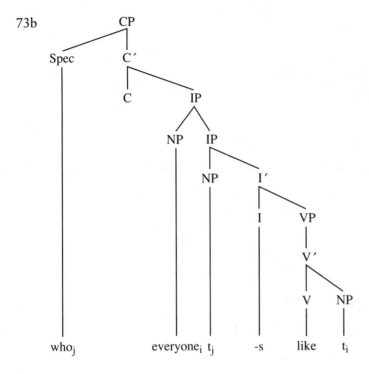

The reader can see that relation between *who$_j$* and *everyone$_i$* is identical to that in (73a). Hence (73b) should lead us to say that (72b) is ambiguous, contrary to fact.

May (1985) proposes that the LF representation of (72b) is not (73b) but (73c):

73c

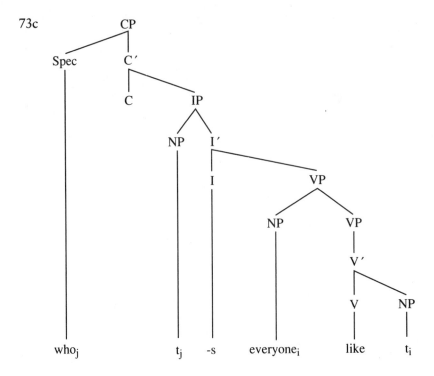

In (73c) *everyone$_i$* is adjoined to VP and not to IP. *Everyone$_i$* is not dominated by VP, being dominated by one segment only. *Everyone$_i$* is dominated
by IP. *Who$_j$* is dominated by CP and not by IP. May argues that in this
representation the scope of *who* must be wider than that of *everyone*. The
scope of a quantifier at LF will be determined by the maximal projection
which dominates it. Adjunction to VP is not new in our theory. In chapter
6 we discussed free subject inversion in Italian as an instance of VP-adjunction,
and in chapter 7 we discussed heavy NP-shift and PP-extraposition in those
terms.

5.2 Scope Reconstruction

Consider (74a):[15]

74a How many papers can you correct in one hour?

---

[15] This example is inspired by the discussion in Cresti (1993) and Longobardi (1987).

(74a) is ambiguous; depending on the interaction of the fronted *wh*-phrase and the quantificational element in *in one hour*. In one interpretation the question can be paraphrased as 'For how many papers is it the case that you can correct each paper in one hour?' The answer could be something like: 'I can correct three of the papers in an hour, the others will take longer.' The second interpretation is the one where *in an hour* has wide scope, and can be paraphrased as 'Which is the total of papers that you will manage to correct in the span of one hour?' where the answer would be something like: 'Six, I take ten minutes per paper.' The same ambiguity is found in (74b):

74b   How many papers do you think you can correct in one hour?

Following the discussion in section 1 of this chapter we assume that the scope of a quantifier is its c-command domain. If we assume the quantificational phrase *in one hour* adjoins to IP, then for (74a) we end up with a partial representation as in (75).

75

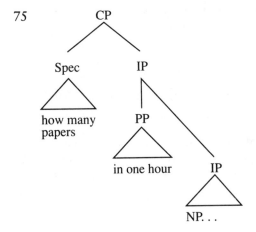

Based on the discussion of adjunction in chapter 7 (section 3.5) we say that the PP *in one hour* is not dominated by IP, since it is only dominated by a segment of IP. The first maximal projection dominating PP is not IP but CP; hence both the moved *wh*-phrase and the quantificational element *in one hour* are dominated by the same maximal projection, resulting in the ambiguity (cf. May, 1985). But if this approach is feasible for (74a) it is far less so for (74b) where *in an hour* would adjoin to the lower IP and where the *wh*-phrase occupies the matrix [Spec, CP], However, the relevant scope interaction can be achieved if we are allowed to reconstruct the fronted *wh*-phrase into the domain of the lower clause. Observe that reconstruction is blocked if a *wh*-element occupies the intermediate [Spec, CP]:

74c   How many papers do you wonder whether you can correct in an hour?

In this example *how many papers* has wide scope with respect to *in one hour*. The interpretation is: 'For how many papers is it the case that you can correct the paper in an hour?' The reconstruction involved in these examples restores scope relations and is referred to as **scope reconstruction**. Not all reconstruction is blocked by intervening *wh*-phrases:

76   [$_{CP1}$ [Which pictures of himself$_i$]$_j$ does [$_{IP1}$ Mary wonder [$_{CP2}$ whether [$_{IP2}$ Bill$_i$ likes t$_j$]]]]?

The reflexive *himself* in (76) is bound by *Bill*, suggesting that the preposed *wh*-phrase can be reconstructed into its base position regardless of the intervening *wh*-phrase *whether*. The domain of reconstruction and its properties is subject to further research (cf. Brody, 1993b).

6   Expletive Replacement and Full Interpretation

In our discussion of LF representations we have concentrated essentially on the representation of operator scope. In this section we briefly introduce the Principle of Full Interpretation. We shall illustrate this principle on the basis of the existential construction in English. Consider (77):

77   There arrived [$_{NP}$ three more candidates].

(77) contains an existential construction, in which the [Spec, IP] position is occupied by the expletive *there* and the NP *three more candidates* occupies a VP-internal position. *Arrive* is an unaccusative verb (cf. the discussion in chapter 6, section 3.2.3) and we assume that the post-verbal NP occupies its base position [NP, V']. The existential construction raises many interesting questions which we do not go into here (cf. Belletti, 1988; Hoekstra and Mulder, 1990; Moro, 1989; and Safir, 1985 for a survey of the literature). One aspect which we briefly consider is the role of *there* in the semantic

representation of the sentence. Recall that we assume that expletives do not contribute to the meaning of a sentence. If this is true, then it is not clear what part the expletive can play in the LF representation of the sentence. LF is the level of representation which encodes semantic properties of the sentence. Chomky (1986a) proposes that LF should only contain elements that are legitimate at that level, i.e. elements which contribute to the semantic interpretation. This constraint is referred to as the **Principle of Full Interpretation (FI)**. The legitimacy of an element at LF derives from the fact that it receives an appropriate interpretation at that level. By FI elements which do not receive an interpretation should be absent at LF.

In view of FI the presense of the expletive *there* at LF would be problematic. *There* is associated with the post-verbal NP. Let us call the latter NP the **associate** of the expletive. Chomsky proposes that the associate moves to the expletive at LF. One option (Chomsky, 1986a) is that the associate replaces the expletive (78a) at LF, this is referred to as **expletive replacement**; another option (Chomsky, 1991) is that the associate is adjoined to the expletive (78b) at LF:

78a $[_{IP} [_{NP_i}$ three more candidates] will arrive $t_i]$.
78b $[_{IP} [_{NP_i}$ three more candidates [there]] will arrive $t_i]$.

Either process will ensure that FI is satisfied: in (78a) the expletive is eliminated, in (78b) we could say it is given interpretive content by the associate.

The derivation of (78) illustrates another application of move-α mapping S-structure onto LF: the movement of the associate to the expletive is an instance of A-movement, i.e. movement to [Spec, IP]. Again, of course, this is covert movement without overt spell out.

7 Summary

In this chapter we have seen evidence for positing the level of Logical Form or LF. This level represents the interpretation of scope-taking elements such as *wh*-phrases and quantifiers. *Wh*-raising and quantifier raising are non-overt applications of move-α mediating between S-structure and LF.

In the discussion we have described the cross-linguistic variation in the implementation of *wh*-movement. We have seen that in some languages *wh*-movement is overt, it applies at S-structure, while in others it is covert, it applies at LF. Among the languages with overt movement, some allow multiple movement, others allow only one *wh*-constituent to move.

LF movement is like S-structure movement, specifically it leaves coindexed traces which are subject to the ECP. We have refined our notion of the ECP in order to account for the observed argument/non-argument asymmetries. Following proposals in the literature (Lasnik and Saito, 1984) we assume that gamma-marking applies to argument traces at S-structure and to other traces at LF. Furthermore there is a free deletion process at LF. We assume that the ECP is checked at LF and that intermediate traces are subject to the ECP.

We have also discussed some aspects of reconstruction, i.e. the phenomenon whereby fronted constituents are moved to their base positions or to positions of traces which have been created by prior movement. Reconstruction is often required to restore a binding configuration. In the discussion we have seen that the subject-in-VP hypothesis introduced in chapter 6 will help account for the restrictions on VP-reconstruction.

Finally we introduce the Principle of Full Interpretation and its application to existential constructions.

8   Exercises

Exercise 1

Discuss the S-structure and the LF representations of the following sentences and show how the ECP applies.

1   I told them [$_{CP}$ whom$_i$ [$_{IP}$ John will invite t_i]].
2   Whom$_i$ did you tell them [$_{CP}$ that [$_{IP}$ John will invite t_i]].
3   Where$_i$ did you tell them [$_{CP}$ [$_{IP}$ John will invite whom t_i]]?

Exercise 2

In earlier versions of Government and Binding Theory (cf. Chomsky, 1981a: 250) proper government was interpreted either as **lexical government** or as antecedent-government. A is a lexical governor for B if A head-governs B and A is a lexical category (N, V, A, P). In later versions (i.e. the one adopted here) lexical government has been replaced by theta-government. On the basis of examples (1) and (2) below, show that lexical government is not enough and that theta-government is required.

1 Why do you think Emsworth will invite Poirot?
2 Why do you wonder whom Bill thinks John will invite?

In (1) *why* can be interpreted as modifying both *think* and *invite*. In (2) *why* cannot be construed with *invite*.

Exercise 3

Discuss the contrast in grammaticality between the following sentences:

1 I don't know who said that Bill must retake which exam.
2 *I don't know which student said that who must retake the syntax exam.

Exercise 4

In the following examples the quantifier in the main clause takes scope over that in the subordinate clause. Provide the LF representations of these sentences.

1 Everyone believes that someone loves him.
2 Everyone believes that he loves someone.

On the basis of examples such as these it has been proposed that quantifier scope is clause-bound: QR does not normally raise quantifiers out of their clauses.

Does this hypothesis predict the fact that *everyone* in (3) can have scope over *someone*?

3 Someone believes everyone to be invited.

(3) contrasts with (4) where *everyone* cannot have scope outside the immediately dominating clause:

4 Someone believes that everyone will be invited.

The contrast between (3) and (4) is also found in (5) vs. (6):

5 I expect that no one will come.
6 I expect no one to come.

In (5) the negation contained in *no one* cannot take scope over the main verb *expect*. (6) may have the interpretation: 'I do not expect anyone to come' or 'For no person is it the case that I expect them to come.' Try to identify the syntactic properties of the paired sentences that may influence the interpretations outlined.

Exercise 5

Consider the following French examples:

1 Jean a   trouvé beaucoup de livres.
   Jean has found   many   of books
   'Jean has found many books.'
2 Jean n'a   pas trouvé de   livres.
   Jean *ne*-has not found   of   books
   'Jean has not found any books.'
3 *De livres n'ont   pas été   trouvés par Jean.
   books   *ne*-have not been found   by   Jean
4 Beaucoup de livres   ont   été   trouvés par Jean.
   many   books have been found   by   Jean
5 Jean ne veut   pas que tu   achètes de   livres.
   Jean *ne* wants not that you buy   books
6 *Jean ne veut   pas que de livres soient achetés.
   Jean *ne* wants not that books   be bought

Kayne (1984) proposes that constructions of the form *de ... N* be analysed as containing an empty category corresponding to the overt *beaucoup*:

7 [$_{NP}$ e de livres]

How would this proposal enable us to account for the contrasts in acceptability among the examples above?

Exercise 6

In chapter 7, section 7.2, we discussed the phenomenon known as crossover:

1a *Who$_i$ does he$_i$ see t$_i$?
1b *Who$_i$ does his$_i$ mother love t$_i$?

In both examples the pronoun (*he, his*) cannot be bound by the *wh*-phrase. The example (1a) is referred to as **strong crossover (SCO)**. We have seen that SCO can be derived from Principle C: the trace of *who* is an R-expression and if it is coindexed with *he* in (1a) it will be A-bound. (1b) illustrates **weak crossover (WCO)**: the pronoun *his* cannot be bound by the moved *wh*-phrase. This time Principle C cannot be invoked. Consider now the data below. In (2a) the pronoun *he* is coindexed with the quantifier *everyone*, and the pronoun will receive a variable interpretation. Pronouns which are bound by a quantifier are called **bound pronouns**. Similarly in (2b) the pronoun *he* is bound by the *wh*-phrase.

2a Everyone$_i$ will present his$_i$ work.
2b Who$_i$ will present his$_i$ paper first?

In what way can data such as (3) and (4) be used in support of LF, specifically in support of Quantifier Raising at LF?

3a *Who$_i$ did you say he$_i$ made you visit t$_i$?
3b *He$_i$ saw me visit nobody$_i$.
4a *Which man$_i$ did you say his$_i$ friends dislike t$_i$?
4b *His$_i$ friends should betray no man$_i$.

Exercise 7

We have seen that reconstruction sometimes uses intermediate traces. (1) illustrates such a case:

1 Which picture of himself does Bill think that Jane likes?

Discuss the application of reconstruction in the examples below; the judgements were obtained from a native speaker of British English. What kind of problems would these examples raise for the approach developed in section 4?

2 Which pictures of himself does Bill wonder whether Jane likes?
3 Which pictures of himself does Jane wonder whether Bill likes?
4 Which pictures of himself does Jane wonder whether Bill thinks that John likes?
5 *Which pictures of himself does Jane wonder whether Bill thinks that Ann likes?

Can our theory, developed so far, account for the grammaticality judgements given above?

Now consider the following sentences, the judgements given are from the same native speaker:

6 Which pictures of himself does John expect Mary to buy?
7 Which pictures of himself did John get Mary to buy?
8 Which pictures of himself did John consider Mary too proud of?

No doubt you will conclude that the data lead to many problems of analysis. For this particular matter the theory in its present stage cannot offer a clear answer. Crucially we need to appeal to intermediate traces. The exact role of intermediate traces with respect to reconstruction is subject to ongoing research. In chapter 10 we return to intermediate traces.

Exercise 8

Discuss the problems raised for the binding theory by the following examples:

1a Himself$_i$, John$_i$ does not like t$_i$.
1b *John$_i$, he does not like t$_i$.
1c *Him$_i$, he does not like t$_i$.

2a Himself$_i$ he$_i$ thinks Mary loves t$_i$.
2b Him$_i$, he$_i$ thinks Mary loves t$_i$ with all her heart.

2c *John$_i$, he$_i$ thinks Mary loves t$_i$ with all her heart.
    (Barss, 1988: 25)

The reader is referred to Barss (1988) for discussion of such examples.

Exercise 9

Consider the following sentences. How could the theory of reconstruction we have been developing account for them?

1a They wonder which pictures of each other I will prefer.
1b I wonder which pictures of each other they will prefer.

2a Criticize each other I never thought they would.
2b *Criticize each other they never thought I would.

3a They wonder how proud of each other we can be.
3b *They wonder how proud of each other I can be.

10 Barriers

Contents

Introduction and Overview

Throughout this book we have repeatedly referred to the concept of barrier. We have often talked about barriers for government, specifying at various points that certain maximal projections were or were not barriers for outside governors. We have also used the notion 'bounding node' with respect to the subjacency condition on movement: NP and IP are said to be bounding nodes; they impose limits on the distance a constituent can move.

Intuitively, it seems that the concepts barrier and bounding node are similar. Both restrict the domain of application of grammatical processes. But so far we have treated these two concepts quite independently. For instance, we argue, on the one hand, that IP is defective and does not constitute a barrier for government, while, on the other hand, we have defined IP as a bounding node for subjacency.

In this chapter we formulate a definition of the notion barrier which can be used both in the definitions of government and proper government and in the definition of subjacency. The chapter is based on Chomsky's monograph *Barriers* (Chomsky, 1986b). The aim of this chapter is to give an introduction to the general principles behind Chomsky's work and to render the related literature more accessible. For a fully-fledged account the reader should consult Chomsky's own work. Recently a number of alternative approaches to deal with locality relations have been developed (Manzini, 1992; Rizzi, 1990a). Rizzi's (1990a) proposal is one of the most influential and has come to be known as **Relativized Minimality**. This approach is discussed in full in chapter 12. The *Barriers* model is important because many of the concepts introduced there have been taken up in the literature.

Section 1 defines the notion barrier. In section 2 the subjacency condition is formulated in terms of barriers. In section 3 the ECP is reinterpreted in terms of barriers. Section 4 raises some remaining problems for *wh*-movement and section 5 introduces the extension of the barriers framework to NP-movement.

1 Maximal Projections: Transparent or Opaque?

In the course of our discussion we have explicitly or implicitly treated maximal projections as barriers for outside government, although many exceptions were allowed on what might have looked like a more or less *ad hoc* basis. Government plays an important role in many syntactic processes. NPs are case-marked under government; traces have to be properly governed, a more restricted type of government. Whenever we can show that case is assigned or that a trace is governed from outside the maximal projection, we shall have to conclude that this projection is transparent for government. The relevant data are described in section 1.1. On the other hand, PRO must be ungoverned. Whenever PRO occupies the specifier position of a maximal projection, that maximal projection must be opaque to outside governors. The relevant data are described in section 1.2. We analyse the data in sections 1.3 and 1.4.

1.1 Case-marking and Proper Government

1.1.1 INFINITIVAL IP

Consider (1).

1a I believe [$_{IP}$ him to be happy].
1b I prefer very much [$_{CP}$ for [$_{IP}$ him to leave first]].
1c John$_i$ is believed [$_{IP}$ t$_i$ to be happy].

(1a) is an example of exceptional case-marking (ECM): the subject NP of the lower infinitival clause is assigned ACCUSATIVE case by the matrix verb *believe* (see chapter 3 for discussion). This means that in (1a) IP cannot be a barrier for an outside governor. The same point applies to (1b), where *for* assigns ACCUSATIVE to *him*.

The ECP forces us to conclude that in (1c) too, the lower IP is not opaque for an outside governor. The trace of the moved NP *John* must be properly governed to satisfy the ECP. It is clear that there is no proper governor inside the lower infinitival clause: the lower IP does not contain a theta-governor or an antecedent-governor for the trace. Hence the relevant governor must be outside IP. At this point we shall not discuss which element is the relevant governor in (1c). The verb *believed* is an unlikely candidate since this verb theta-marks and hence theta-governs the clause IP and not its subject. We return to examples like (1c) in section 5 below.[1]

---

[1] For a full discussion of this example the reader is referred to Chomsky (1986b: section 11).

1.1.2 FINITE IP

Finite IP too must not be an inherent barrier given the grammaticality of (2):

2a $[_{CP}$ Who$_i$ do $[_{IP}$ you think $[_{CP}$ t$'_i$ $[_{IP}$ t$_i$ left]]]]?
2b $[_{CP}$ When$_i$ did $[_{IP}$ he leave t$_i$]]?

In both examples the lowest traces must be properly governed and neither the trace of *who$_i$* nor that of *when$_i$* is theta-governed. We conclude that in both examples the antecedent in [Spec, CP] must be able to (antecedent-) govern the trace. This means that the IP projections in (2) cannot be barriers for outside government.

1.1.3 TRANSPARENT CP

Let us try to see if there are reasons for assuming that other maximal projections too are not barriers. Consider (3a) with the LF representation (3b).

3a When do you think that Emsworth will invite Poirot?
3b When$_i$ do $[_{IP}$ you think $[_{CP}$ t$'_i$ $[_{IP}$ Emsworth will invite Poirot t$_i$]]]?
     　　　　　　　　　　[+γ]　　　　　　　　　　　　　　　　[+γ]

Because we are dealing with adjunct traces, gamma-marking will only take place at LF. We assume that the complementizer *that* is freely deleted at LF (see chapter 9, section 3.2.2.2). In (3b) the lowest trace of *when* is antecedent-governed by the intermediate trace, t$'_i$, as expected if IP is not a barrier. The intermediate trace must also be properly governed (see chapter 9) and it can only be antecedent-governed. We are forced to conclude that *when* antecedent-governs the intermediate trace. This means that neither IP nor CP can constitute a barrier to government.

1.1.4 TRANSPARENT SMALL CLAUSES

Small clauses offer further evidence that maximal projections are not necessarily opaque for outside government:

4a I thought $[_{AGRP}$ John unhappy].
4b I thought $[_{AGRP}$ John a great friend].
4c I expect $[_{AGRP}$ John in my office].

Following chapter 2, section 3.5, we assume that small clauses are AGRPS, i.e. maximal projections of a functional head, AGR. In each of the examples in (4) government from outside AGRP must be possible: the subject NP of the small clauses must be able to be case-marked by the matrix V. The small clause AGRP is transparent for outside government.

The same conclusion follows from a consideration of the examples in (5) where a *wh*-phrase has been extracted from the subject position of a small clause AGRP. The ECP requires that traces be properly governed:

5a   [$_{CP}$ Who$_i$ did [$_{IP}$ you [$_{VP}$ t$'_i$ [$_{VP}$ think [$_{AGRP}$ t$_i$ unhappy]]]]]?
5b   [$_{CP}$ Who$_i$ did [$_{IP}$ you [$_{VP}$ t$'_i$ [$_{VP}$ think [$_{AGRP}$ t$_i$ a great friend]]]]]?
5c   [$_{CP}$ Who$_i$ did [$_{IP}$ you [$_{VP}$ t$'_i$ [$_{VP}$ expect [$_{AGRP}$ t$_i$ in your office]]]]]?

The sentences in (5) are grammatical, this means the ECP must be satisfied. In each of the examples, the trace of *who* in [Spec, AGRP] is not theta-governed: AGR does not theta-mark the subject of the small clause and the matrix verb does not theta-govern it either. In each sentence, the trace in the subject position of the small clause, [Spec, AGRP], satisfies the ECP by antecedent-government. Given that the antecedent *who* is outside the small clause AGRP we again conclude that the small clause is transparent for antecedent-government.

1.1.5   CONCLUSION

On the basis of data concerning ECM and ECP we have established so far that certain maximal projections must be transparent for outside government.

1.2   PRO

1.2.1   OPAQUE SMALL CLAUSES

The PRO theorem (chapter 5), in contrast, helps identify those maximal projections that must be barriers for outside government. Consider (6):

6   John arrived totally exhausted.

In (6) there are two predicates: the V *arrive* and the A *exhausted*. Both of these need an argument to which to assign their thematic role. If we assume that *arrive* assigns its thematic role to *John* we shall need to posit a non-overt

NP to which *exhausted* may assign its own thematic role (see discussion in chapter 5). A consideration of the properties of the non-overt subject of *totally exhausted* suggests that this is the null element referred to as PRO, which must be ungoverned at S-structure. We conclude that the small clause is opaque in (7): it is a barrier for outside government (from the verb or from I).

7   John arrived [PRO totally exhausted].

In (8) the same conclusion can be reached:

8a   John came home [PRO a wiser man].
8b   John came home [PRO in a foul mood].

We conclude that maximal projections sometimes are barriers to outside government and sometimes are not. They are not barriers by definition. Barrier-hood is a relative property which apparently is determined by the syntactic position in which the maximal projection appears.

1.2.2   OPAQUE CP

As another piece of evidence that maximal projections are sometimes opaque for outside government, consider the following example:

9   John decided [$_{CP}$ [$_{IP}$ PRO to see the movie]].
    (Chomsky, 1986b: 11)

PRO must be ungoverned, so we are forced to conclude that either CP or IP is a barrier to government from the outside.

A similar conclusion is obtained when we consider (10a) which is ungrammatical when *why* is construed with *invite*. Under this interpretation (10a) has the LF (10b):

10a   *Why do you wonder whom Bill thinks John will invite?
10b   [$_{CP1}$ Why$_i$ do [$_{IP1}$ you wonder [$_{CP2}$ whom$_j$ [$_{IP2}$ Bill thinks
      [$_{CP3}$ t′$_i$ [$_{IP3}$ John will invite t$_j$ t$_i$]]]]]]?
           [$-\gamma$]   [$+\gamma$] [$+\gamma$]

Based on the discussion in chapter 9, the intermediate trace in [Spec, CP] is the offending trace: it violates the ECP (see the [$-\gamma$]). *Why$_i$* cannot antecedent-govern the relevant trace because it is too far away. We conclude that though IP or CP are not absolute barriers for outside government, the combination of IP1, CP2, IP2 and CP3 is a barrier in this example.

1.3   Conclusion: Maximal Projections May or May Not be Barriers

We arrive at a problematic situation. On the one hand, we wish to say that maximal projections are not necessarily barriers for outside government (see the discussion in section 1.1), they are not barriers intrinsically. On the other hand, we need to assume that such projections are sometimes barriers for government (section 1.2). To add to the confusion, compare (9) with (11):

11   [$_{CP1}$When$_i$ did [$_{IP1}$ John decide [$_{CP2}$ t$'_i$ [$_{IP2}$ PRO to fix the car t$_i$]]]]?

We need to assume that IP2 is not a barrier for outside government since *t$'_i$* must govern *t$_i$*. Similarly we need to assume that *when* is able to antecedent-govern *t$'_i$*. Hence in (11) the combination of IP1 and CP2 should also not be a barrier for government. But, on the other hand, we want to be able to say that PRO is ungoverned. Hence, the combination CP2 and IP2 ought to be a barrier for government.

One conclusion that appears to follow from the discussion so far is that IP is never a barrier on its own. Rather, it seems in certain circumstances to reinforce another maximal projection and form a barrier with it. In (11) the combination CP$_2$ + IP$_2$ is a barrier, whereas IP$_2$ on its own is not. On the other hand, the combination IP1 + CP$_2$ is not a barrier. Structurally the combination CP + IP seems to be a potential barrier. For (10) we could assume that the barrier for the government of the offending trace is constituted by CP2 + IP2. This hypothesis will be confirmed in our analysis below, where we shall provide a more general justification.

1.4   Defining Barriers

In this section we provide a definition of the notion barrier. We shall see that certain maximal projections are barriers themselves, intrinsically, others become barriers by inheritance.

1.4.1 L-MARKING

Let us return to some of the small clause examples discussed previously:

12a I thought [John unhappy].
12b I thought [John a great friend].
12c I expect [John in my office at five].

13a John arrived [PRO totally exhausted].
13b John arrived [PRO a wiser man].
13c John arrived [PRO in a bad mood].

We see that sometimes the small clauses are transparent (12), sometimes they are opaque (13). There is one important contrast between the two groups of examples. In (12) the small clauses are complements of the verbs *think* and *expect*; in (13) the small clauses are adjuncts: they modify the VP but they are not arguments of the verb *arrive*. In (12) the lexical verbs govern the small clauses and theta-mark them: the verbs **theta-govern** the small clauses. In order to refer to the special relation established between a lexical item and the complement which it governs and theta-marks, Chomsky introduces the term **L-marking**.

As a first hypothesis let us say that a maximal projection which is L-marked is transparent for an element contained in it, and that a maximal projection which is not L-marked is potentially opaque for an element contained in it. A maximal projection which is not L-marked is called a **blocking category (BC)**.

14a **L-marking**
     A L-marks B if and only if A is a lexical category that theta-governs B.
     (Chomsky, 1986b: 15)
14b **BC**
     C is a BC for B if and only if C is not L-marked and C dominates B.
     (Chomsky, 1986b: 14, def. (25))

From the examples in (13) we might conclude that a BC is of necessity a barrier for outside government, but this conclusion is too rash. Consider (15):

15   When$_i$ do [$_{IP1}$ you think [$_{CP}$ t$'_i$ that [$_{IP2}$ John left t$_i$]]]?

IP2 is the complement of *that*. Even if one were to argue that the complementizer assigns a theta role to IP2, it is standardly assumed that the complementizer *that* is not a lexical category. One argument for this assumption is that *that* does not have any real semantic content and in fact in English *that* can be deleted, which is not true for other lexical categories. IP2 is not L-marked by *that*. *Think* theta-marks CP, which is therefore L-marked. But *think* does not theta-mark IP_2. Hence IP_2 is not L-marked and a BC. In (15) t_i must be antecedent-governed by t'_i. We conclude that IP2, though a BC, is not a barrier for outside government.

Let us say that a maximal projection is an intrinsic barrier for an element contained in it if the maximal projection is a BC, exception being made for IP. We assume that the exception for IP is justified because IP is 'defective' in that its head is a bundle of syntactic features, [± Tense ± AGR].

1.4.2   INHERITANCE

In section 1.1 we suggested that IP on its own would never be a barrier. On the other hand, an IP dominated by a CP was said to be a barrier. This is schematically represented in (16a), which corresponds to an example like (16b):

16a $[_{CP} \ldots [_{IP} \ldots]]$
16b   John decided $[_{CP} [_{IP}$ PRO to see the movie]].

In (16b) *decide* L-marks CP. Hence CP is not a BC. IP is not L-marked; it is a BC. Remember that we argued that the BC IP on its own is not a barrier. It is the combination of IP and CP that results in the opacity. Chomsky (1986b) proposes that in our example CP becomes a barrier because it dominates a BC. CP is a barrier **by inheritance**. This leads us to the following definition for barrierhood:

17   A is a barrier for B if and only if (a) or (b):
   (a)   A is a maximal projection and A immediately dominates C, C is a BC for B.
   (b)   A is a BC for B, A is not IP.
   (cf. Chomsky, 1986b: 14)

In (16) A is CP, B is PRO, and the relevant BC, C, is IP.

The notion government can be redefined integrating the notion barrier in (17). We distinguish between government by a head and antecedent-government:

18a **Government**

X governs Y if and only if

  (i)   X is either of the category A, N, V, P, I;

      or

      X and Y are coindexed;

  (ii) X c-commands Y;

 (iii) no barrier intervenes between X and Y;

 (iv) minimality is respected.

18b **Minimality condition on government**

There is no Z such that Z satisfies (i), (ii) and (iii) and X c-commands Z.

(18a(i)) allows for the two types of government. (18b), the minimality condition on government, serves to ensure that if two potential governors compete for government of Y then the closer one wins out. (See also chapter 12.)

1.5 *Unifying Subjacency and Government*

In the theory developed in *Barriers* (Chomsky, 1986b) the notion barrier is used in the definition of government and it is also used to replace the notion bounding node in the definition of subjacency. Informally, government cannot cross a barrier and movement must not cross more than one barrier.[2] In the subsequent sections of this chapter we turn to examples to illustrate the idea. Given the relative complexity of the discussion we shall give several examples to illustrate the same point. In this way we hope that the reader can familiarize himself with the theory. It is advisable that the reader try to analyse the examples before reading our discussion. Do not get discouraged if at first your own analysis contains certain lacunae. If you go through all the sentences we discuss here you will finally get the knack.

2 Subjacency and Barriers

In this section we see how the notion barrier can be integrated in the definition of the subjacency condition on movement.

---

[2] For a more careful formulation of the notion which does not appeal to counting barriers the reader is referred to Chomksy's own discussion (1986b: 30–1).

2.1   Movement and Adjunction

2.1.1   SHORT MOVEMENT AND LONG MOVEMENT

We first look at the application of the notion barrier to the standard examples of subjacency. Let us say that movement must not cross more than one barrier.

Consider (19):

19a   When will John fix the car?
19b   When do you think John will fix the car?

We discuss the examples one by one. The S-structure of (19a) is given in (20):

20   [$_{CP}$ When$_i$ will [$_{IP}$ John fix the car t$_i$]?

BC

We assume that *when* is base-generated in a position outside VP. The movement of *when* crosses only IP. By our definitions IP is a BC (14b) but it is not a barrier (17b). In (20) *wh*-movement does not violate subjacency.

Now let us turn to (19b), whose S-structure is given in (21).

21   [$_{CP1}$When$_i$ do [$_{IP1}$ you [$_{VP}$ think [$_{CP2}$ t′$_i$ [$_{IP2}$ John will fix the car t$_i$]]]]?

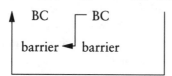

BC   BC

barrier   barrier

We do not consider the distance between the lower trace and the intermediate trace of *when*, which is the same as the distance between *when* and its trace in (20), but we concentrate on the distance between the intermediate trace and the antecedent *when*. Between *when* and t′$_i$ we find the embedded CP, a maximal projection which is L-marked hence not a BC. A second intervening XP is VP. VP is not L-marked, hence it constitutes a BC and a barrier (17b). The third maximal projection intervening between *when*$_i$ and t′$_i$ is the matrix IP1. IP1 is a BC. According to (17), IP is not a barrier intrinsically but it may become a barrier by inheritance if it dominates a BC. In (21) IP1 dominates the BC VP, hence IP1 is a barrier. In the representation

(21) the movement of *when* crosses two barriers, VP and IP1, and ought to violate subjacency. But example (19b) is a perfectly natural example of long *wh*-movement and there are no subjacency effects.

In passing, we observe that given the present analysis (21) would also violate the ECP. The intermediate trace is not theta-governed and therefore must be antecedent-governed at LF (see discussion in chapters 8 and 9). If two barriers, VP and IP1, intervene between the trace and its purported antecedent it is not clear how antecedent-government could obtain. But there are no ECP effects in this example. Our analysis as developed so far thus raises problems for this example.

Indeed, other examples of *wh*-movement would at first sight also turn out to be subjacency violations under the analysis we have sketched in this chapter. Consider (22), a perfectly normal example of short object extraction:

22 [_CP_ Who_i did   [_IP_ John   [_VP_ invite t_i]]?

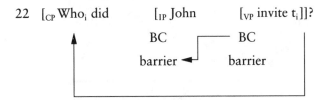

As the reader can verify, VP is a barrier (it is a BC) and IP becomes one by inheritance. But of course (22) does not violate the subjacency condition at all.

Either we shall have to abandon the formulation of subjacency in terms of barriers formulated above, or we must reconsider the definition of barriers, or we must try and think of alternative syntactic representations to replace (21) and (22).

2.1.2 VP-ADJUNCTION

The problem raised by (21) and (22) is due to the piling up of two BCs: IP, which is not an inherent barrier (by hypothesis), dominates a BC (VP) and becomes a barrier by inheritance. However the syntactic representations given in section 2.1.1 are not the only ones to consider. On the basis of previous discussions in this book it is possible to devise alternative derivations.

2.1.2.1 Heavy NP-Shift In chapter 7 we discussed examples of heavy NP-shift, an instance of A'-movement in which the moved element is right-adjoined to a maximal projection, say VP. (23a) has the partial structure (23b). We assume that the adverb phrase is VP-adjoined.

23a My doctor told me to drink very slowly [NP two glasses of mineral water
with a slice of lemon].

23b

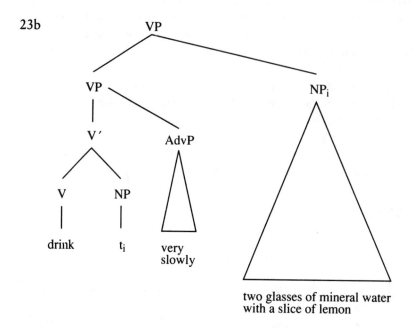

two glasses of mineral water
with a slice of lemon

2.1.2.2 *VP adjunction and quantifier raising* In chapter 9 section 5.1 we
propose that LF movement of quantifiers adjoins an operator to VP. One
example discussed there was (72b), repeated here as (24a) with the LF representation (24b).

24a Who likes everyone?

24b

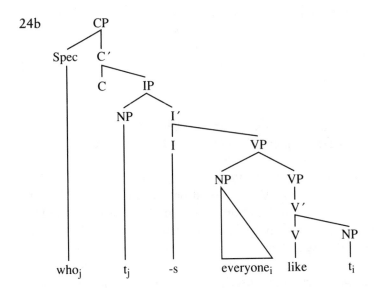

In the discussion of (24b) we adopted the idea[3] that the VP-adjoined constituent *everyone_i* in (24b) is not dominated by VP because it is not dominated by both segments of VP. The position created by adjunction is a marginal position, neither inside nor outside the maximal projection to which adjunction takes place (cf. chapter 7). We compared such a position to a balcony: when you're on a balcony you have not really left the room completely. Pursuing this idea let us say that the movement of *everyone_i* in (24b) does not cross the maximal projection VP, though it does cross one segment of it.

2.1.2.3 VP adjunction and Wh-movement Let us now return to the problematic example (22), repeated here with its initial analysis as (25a):

25a Who_i did [_IP John [_VP invite t_i]]?

If we allow for a possibility of adjoining moved constituents to VP, then nothing stops us in principle from also carrying out the movement of *who_i* to [Spec, CP] in two steps: first we adjoin *who_i* to VP and then we move it to [Spec, CP]:

---

[3] For discussion see May (1985)

25b   Who$_i$ did   [$_{IP}$ John   [$_{VP}$ t'$_i$ [$_{VP}$ invite t$_i$]]]?

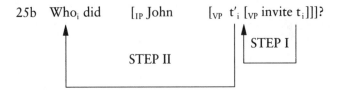

Step I is parallel to the adjunction we find in the case of heavy NP-shift in (23) and to the VP-adjunction by QR in (24). Step I does not strictly speaking cross VP: it crosses only one segment of it. No barriers are crossed and Step I does not violate subjacency. Step II does not strictly speaking 'cross' VP either: the topmost segment of VP is crossed but not the lowest VP. Again then, this maximal projection does not come into play when we determine the barriers relevant to check for violations of subjacency. Step II does cross IP, a non-L-marked maximal projection, hence a BC (see (14b)). But, by hypothesis, IP is not a barrier inherently: IP only may become a barrier by inheritance. Following our definitions, IP in (25b) cannot become a barrier by inheritance for the VP-adjoined trace: between the VP-adjoined trace and IP there is only a segment of a maximal projection (the higher VP) but not a full BC. Step II also does not violate subjacency and our sentence is grammatical, a desirable result.

By using VP-adjunction, independently justified on the basis of heavy NP-shift examples and examples of QR, we can retain our reformulation of subjacency in terms of barriers. The option of adjoining a constituent to VP is a way of circumventing the subjacency condition. The adjoined position functions as an escape hatch. We shall exploit this option maximally in the discussion of the examples below.

Let us reconsider (19b) and its problematic representation in (21) repeated here as (26a):

26a   [When$_i$ do [$_{IP}$ you [$_{VP}$ think [$_{CP}$ t'$_i$ [$_{IP}$ John will fix the car t$_i$]]]]]?

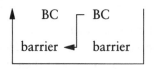

It is clear that the VP-adjunction analysis enables us to account for the grammaticality of our example in terms of subjacency:

26b [When$_i$ do [$_{IP}$ you [$_{VP}$ t"$_i$ [$_{VP}$ think [$_{CP}$ t'$_i$ [$_{IP}$ J. . . . t$_i$]]]]]]?

Step I crosses CP which is L-marked by *think* and hence not a BC. It does not 'cross' VP for reasons discussed above. Step II crosses IP which is not L-marked and thus a BC, but which on its own does not qualify for barrierhood. Hence neither step crosses a barrier and the sentence is all right for subjacency.

The ECP is also satisfied: the intermediate traces will be antecedent-governed: both t'$_i$ in the lower [Spec, CP] and the VP-adjoined trace, t"$_i$, are antecedent-governed since no barrier intervenes.

2.2 Island Violations

Let us turn to some standard examples of island violations and see if the theory developed so far is able to deal with them.

First, we consider the extraction from a complex NP in (27). We only indicate the traces relevant for the discussion. We return to the example in section 3.1 below.

27 [$_{CP1}$ Whom do [$_{IP_1}$ you [$_{VP1}$ t" [$_{VP_1}$ know [$_{NP}$ the date [$_{CP2}$ when [$_{IP2}$ Mary
                                    #   #
[$_{VP2}$ t' [$_{VP2}$ invited t]]]]]]]]]]?

In (27) *whom* first adjoins to the lower VP2 in order to avoid barrierhood; then it adjoins to the higher VP1, crossing IP2, CP2 and NP. IP2 is a BC, though not a barrier. CP2 dominates a BC and becomes a barrier by inheritance. Moreover, CP2 itself is a maximal projection which is not L-marked (it is not theta-marked by the N *date*) hence it is a BC and a barrier intrinsically. NP is L-marked by *know*, this means it is not a BC or a barrier intrinsically. But NP dominates CP2, which is a BC, and hence the NP is a barrier by inheritance. This means that the movement of *whom* from the VP2-adjoined position to the VP1-adjoined position crosses two barriers, CP2 and NP, signalled by the diacritic #. The movement from the VP1-adjoined position to [Spec, CP] crosses IP, which is a BC though not a barrier.

Compare the status of (27) with that of the *wh*-island extraction in (28). (28) is slightly deviant, though much more acceptable than (27):

28   ?[$_{CP1}$ Which man do [$_{IP1}$ you [$_{VP1}$ t″ wonder [$_{CP2}$ when [$_{IP2}$ PRO to [$_{VP2}$ t′

                                                                   #

[$_{VP2}$ meet t]]]]]]]?

In (28) *which man* first moves to adjoin to VP2, then it moves to adjoin to VP1, crossing IP2, a BC, and CP2, which will become a barrier by inheritance. The next movement to [Spec, CP] is legitimate, IP1 is a BC but not a barrier. *Wh*-movement in (28) crosses one barrier (CP2).

In chapter 7, section 6.2, we had defined the subjacency condition as (29a):

29a   **Subjacency condition** (i)
     Movement cannot cross more than one bounding node, where bounding nodes are IP and NP.

Recall that at that stage of the discussion we did not consider VP-adjunction.

In our earlier discussion in chapter 7, we would have been able to capture the difference in acceptability between (27) and (28) in terms of the number of bounding nodes which are crossed by *wh*-movement. According to (29a), and if we do not consider VP-adjunction as an option, three bounding nodes would have been crossed in (27): IP1, NP and IP2. Only two bounding nodes would have been crossed in (28): IP2 and IP1. If we maintain (29a) and if we allow VP-adjunction, a distinction can also be made: (27) remains a subjacency violation, IP2 and NP are crossed; (28) no longer violates subjacency: in each step of movement only one IP is crossed.

We reformulate the subjacency condition replacing bounding nodes by barriers:

29b   **Subjacency condition** (ii)
     Movement must not cross more than one barrier.

Barrier is defined in (17). The degree of deviance of a sentence with respect to the subjacency condition can be computed in terms of the number of barriers which are crossed. (27) is unacceptable: two barriers are crossed (CP2 and NP). Let us assume that optimally, movement does not cross any barriers at all. If one barrier is crossed, as in (28), there is a slight reduction in acceptability; we will say that when one barrier is crossed there is a **weak** subjacency violation.

3 ECP and Barriers

3.1 Degree of Grammaticality: Subjacency and ECP

In section 2 we have seen how the subjacency condition can be reinterpreted in the *Barriers* framework. In this section we consider ECP violations in the light of our definition of the notion barrier.

3.1.1 EXAMPLE 1: EXTRACTION FROM A RELATIVE CLAUSE

Consider:

30a *Whom do you know [NP the date [CP when [IP Mary invited]]]?
30b **When do you know [NP the man [CP whom [IP Mary invited]]]?

In (30a), (27) in section 2.2, the subjacency condition is violated: *whom* is extracted out of a complex NP, an NP whose head is modified by a relative clause. (30b) is ungrammatical in the reading in which *when* is construed with *invited*. (30b) is worse than (30a) – under the intended interpretation, that is – though they have a similar syntactic structure: in both extraction takes place from inside a complex NP. The S-structure of (30a), annotated to indicate movement, is

31   *[CP Whom_i do [IP you

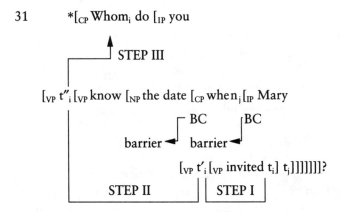

STEP III

[VP t″_i [VP know [NP the date [CP when_j [IP Mary

BC   BC

barrier ◄ barrier ◄

[VP t′_i [VP invited t_i] t_j]]]]]]]?

STEP II   STEP I

When₁ moves to the lower [Spec, CP] crossing only the lower IP. This is a BC but not a barrier inherently.

In Step I *whom* adjoins to VP. This step does not cross any BC since it only crosses one segment of VP. Step II is problematic: *whom* moves and adjoins to the matrix VP. It crosses the lower IP, the lower CP, and NP. Starting from the lowest point, the embedded IP is a BC but it is not an intrinsic barrier. CP is a maximal projection which is not L-marked, hence a BC and hence a barrier. (Being on top of the BC IP, CP would become a barrier by inheritance anyway.) NP is a maximal projection which dominates a BC (CP) hence is also a barrier by inheritance. Thus in Step II *whom* crosses two barriers. Step III is unproblematic: only one IP is crossed.

Now we turn to (30b) which is felt to be worse than (30a). The S-structure representation of (30b) is (32):

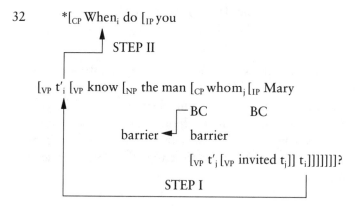

We do not deal with the movement of *whom₁* in detail, we simply adopt the analysis with VP-adjunction. We assume that *when* originates outside VP. *When* moves out of its base-position and will have to cross the lower IP, the lower CP and the NP to adjoin to the matrix VP. CP is a barrier, and so is NP, by inheritance (cf. the discussion of (31)). Step II is identical to Step III in (31) and we refer the reader to the discussion above. As far as subjacency is concerned, (32) is no different from (31). How come that (32) is intuitively felt to be so much worse than (31)?

At this point the ECP comes into play. The ECP states that traces must be properly governed. In chapter 9 we have developed a rather refined and complicated system of checking for proper government. Let us apply this to the examples above. In both examples there are two A'-chains, one headed by *when* and one headed by *whom*. Traces of arguments are subject to gamma-marking at S-structure, while traces of adjuncts are gamma-marked at LF. (33a) is the S-structure of (30a) with the relevant gamma-marking and in (33b) we produce the LF representation:

33a *[$_{CP}$ Whom$_i$ do [$_{IP}$ you [$_{VP}$ t″$_i$ [$_{VP}$ know [$_{NP}$ the date [$_{CP}$ when$_j$ [$_{IP}$ Mary [$_{VP}$ t′$_i$ [$_{VP}$ invited t$_i$]] t$_j$]]]]]]]?
$\qquad\qquad$ [+γ]

33b *[$_{CP}$ Whom$_i$ do [$_{IP}$ you [$_{VP}$ know [$_{NP}$ the date [$_{CP}$ when$_j$ [$_{IP}$ Mary [$_{VP}$ invited t$_i$] t$_j$]]]]]]?
$\qquad\qquad$ [+γ] [+γ]

In (33a) the lowest trace of the object is properly governed, being theta-governed by the verb. We do not gamma-mark any of the other traces: they are not in A-positions. At LF all traces are checked for gamma-marking. However, we may freely delete redundant material and we use this opportunity to delete the intermediate traces created by adjunction and the maximal projections which are created by the adjunctions. Now we are left with only one trace to gamma-mark: t_j. This trace is duly antecedent-governed by *when* in the lower [Spec, CP]: there are no intervening barriers.

Now let us turn to (30b). The S-structure with gamma-marking is (34a) and the LF representation (34b).

34a **[$_{CP}$ When$_i$ do [$_{IP}$ you [$_{VP}$ t′$_i$ [$_{VP}$ know [$_{NP}$ the man [$_{CP}$ whom$_j$ [$_{IP}$ Mary [$_{VP}$
$\qquad\qquad$ BC
[$_{VP}$ t′$_j$ [$_{VP}$ invited t$_j$]] t$_i$]]]]]]]?
$\qquad\qquad\qquad$ [+γ]

34b **[$_{CP}$ When$_i$ do [$_{IP}$ you [$_{VP}$ t′$_i$ [$_{VP}$ know [$_{NP}$ the man [$_{CP}$ whom$_j$
$\qquad\qquad$ BC $\qquad\qquad$ [+γ] $\qquad\qquad\qquad$ ⌐BC
$\qquad\qquad\qquad\qquad\qquad$ barrier ◂—⌐ barrier
[$_{IP}$ Mary [$_{VP}$ [$_{VP}$ invited t$_j$]] t$_i$]]]]]]]
$\quad$ BC $\qquad\qquad$ [+γ] [−γ]

(34a) raises no peculiar problems. The lowest t_j is [+γ] being theta-governed by *invited*. In (34b), we must check the proper government of the remaining traces. Being an adjunct-trace, t_i can only be antecedent-governed. The intermediate trace $t′_i$, adjoined to the higher VP ought to take care of antecedent-government but this trace cannot antecedent-govern the lowest t_i, being separated from it by two barriers, CP and NP. Needless to say deleting $t′_i$ is pointless since t_i is too far from the matrix [Spec, CP]. The intermediate $t′_i$ itself satisfies the ECP, being antecedent-governed by *when*.

The difference in grammaticality judgements between (30a) and (30b) has nothing to do with subjacency. Both examples are violations of subjacency: two barriers are crossed. But (30b) is considerably worsened because the sentence also violates the ECP. This example illustrates another aspect of the relative grammaticality of sentences. Given that there are various principles of grammar which may be violated the sentence will worsen as more than one principle is violated. It also turns out that ECP violations are a cause of strong ungrammaticality.

3.1.2 EXAMPLE 2: EXTRACTION FROM AN ADJUNCT

Consider the contrast in (35):

35a   Who did Bill go to Rome to visit?
35b   *Where did Bill go to Rome to work?

(35a) is acceptable, (35b) is unacceptable with *where* construed with the purpose clause.
    The S-structure of (35a) is (36):

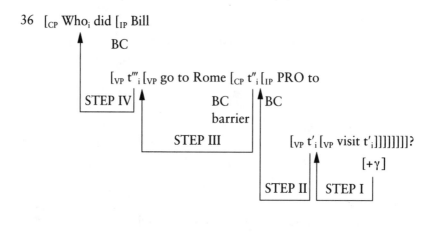

36   [$_{CP}$ Who$_i$ did [$_{IP}$ Bill

In (36) we maximally exploit the VP-adjunction option. Step I does not cross any BC/barriers, VP-adjunction provides the needed escape hatch. Step II crosses the lower IP, which is a BC but not a barrier on its own. Step III crosses the lower CP, the purpose clause. Purpose clauses are adjuncts: they are not L-marked hence they are BCs and barriers. This means that Step III crosses one barrier. Remember that Step III does not cross the higher VP because it only crosses the lower segment VP. Step IV crosses only the higher

IP, a BC but not an independent barrier. (35a) is a weak subjacency violation: one barrier is crossed. As far as ECP is concerned, we see that the trace in the object position of *visit* is properly governed: it is [+γ] since it is theta-governed by the verb. We need not be concerned with the status of the intermediate traces at S-structure. Neither will we need to worry about them at LF since we can liberally delete them all.

The S-structure of (35b) is (37a) and its LF-representation is given in (37b):

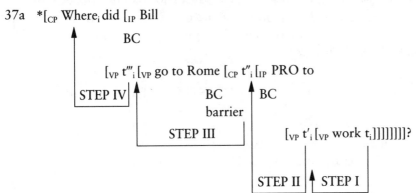

37a   *[$_{CP}$ Where$_i$ did [$_{IP}$ Bill

[$_{VP}$ t'''$_i$ [$_{VP}$ go to Rome [$_{CP}$ t''$_i$ [$_{IP}$ PRO to

[$_{VP}$ t'$_i$ [$_{VP}$ work t$_i$]]]]]]]]?

37b   [$_{CP}$ Where$_i$ did   [$_{IP}$ Bill [$_{VP}$ t'''$_i$ [$_{VP}$ go to Rome [$_{CP}$ t''$_i$ [$_{IP}$ PRO to
                        BC   [+γ]   BC [–γ]   BC
                                                                              barrier

[$_{VP}$ t'$_i$ [$_{VP}$ work   t$_i$]]]]]]]]?
[+γ]   [+γ]

We assume that the place adjunct originates inside VP but nothing hinges on this assumption. (37a) is in the relevant respects identical to (36): one barrier, the lower CP, is crossed by Step III, resulting in a weak subjacency violation. At S-structure no gamma-marking takes place since we have extracted an adjunct. Gamma-marking is done at LF, (37b). Since the lower CP is not L-marked, it is a barrier, and *t''$_i$* in the lower [Spec, CP] cannot be antecedent-governed by a governor outside CP and violates the ECP. This explains the difference in grammaticality between (35a) and (35b): both violate subjacency weakly, but (35b) also violates the ECP.

3.1.3   EXAMPLE 3: EXTRACTION FROM A SUBJECT CLAUSE

Compare the following examples: in each an element is extracted from a subject clause.

38a   *This is a book which reading would be fun.
38b   **This is a pen with which writing would be fun.

Both sentences are felt to be unacceptable but (38b) is markedly worse. We go through the derivations of these sentences below. As the reader may by now anticipate the contrasting grammaticality will be related to the fact that (38b) violates not only subjacency, as does (38a), but also the ECP.

The S-structure and LF-representations of the relevant NP in (38a) are as in (39a) and (39b) respectively. We assume without discussion that the gerund *reading* heads an NP[4]

39a $[_{NP}$ a book $[_{CP}$ which$_i$ $[_{IP}$ $[_{NP}$ PRO $[_{VP}$ t$'_i$ $[_{VP}$ reading t$_i]]]$
                  BC   BC
                  barrier barrier $[+\gamma]$
       would . . .

39b $[_{NP}$ a book $[_{CP}$ which$_i$ $[_{IP}$ $[_{NP}$ PRO $[_{VP}$ reading   t$_i]]]$
                                                                   $[+\gamma]$
       would . . .

In (39a) *which*, the object of *reading*, first adjoins to the gerundival VP and then moves to [Spec, CP]. Following Chomsky we assume (i) that adjunction to arguments is not possible; and (ii) that *wh*-movement does not adjoin to IP in English. The movement of *which* crosses two maximal projections: NP and IP. NP is not L-marked: it is assigned an external theta role, but not under direct government by the verb. Hence NP is a BC and a barrier. IP is a maximal projection and it dominates a BC. IP will become a barrier by inheritance. The movement of *which* violates subjacency: it crosses two barriers. At S-structure the trace of *which* in the base-position is theta-governed by the verb *reading*, hence properly governed and $[+\gamma]$. At LF intermediate traces can be deleted and the trace of *which* is properly governed.

In (40) we represent the S-structure and LF of (38b):

40a $[_{NP}$ a pen $[_{CP}$ with which$_i$ $[_{IP}$ $[_{NP}$ PRO $[_{VP}$ t$'_i$ $[_{VP}$ writing t$_i]]]$
                  BC   BC
                  barrier barrier
       would . . .

---

[4]   Cf. Aoun and Sportiche (1983: 219). See also Abney (1987).

40b [NP a pen [CP with which_i [IP ⠀⠀⠀⠀[NP PRO [VP t'i [VP writing ⠀t_i]]]
⠀⠀⠀⠀⠀⠀⠀⠀BC⠀⠀⠀⠀⠀⠀BC⠀⠀⠀⠀⠀⠀⠀[−γ]⠀⠀⠀⠀⠀⠀⠀[+γ]
⠀⠀⠀⠀⠀⠀⠀⠀barrier⠀barrier

⠀⠀⠀⠀would . . .

In (40a) the moved adjunct is first adjoined to the gerundival VP and then crosses NP and IP, identified as barriers above. The representation violates subjacency. At S-structure adjunct traces are not gamma-marked. At LF (40b) the intermediate trace of the moved adjunct, *t'_i*, cannot be antecedent-governed: the intervening barriers prevent the antecedent from governing the trace. Hence (40b) violates the ECP.

3.1.4 EXTRACTION FROM COMPLEMENTS

In (35) and (38) we illustrate two violations of what used to be known as the condition on extraction domains, or the CED.[5] This constraint bars movement out of subjects and out of adjuncts. In (38) the extraction is out of a subject and in (35) out of an adjunct. What unites the two examples is that an element is extracted from a category which is not directly theta-marked by a lexical head. Such extraction will always cross a BC and a barrier.

Furthermore when an adjunct is extracted from an adjunct clause or a subject clause, the ECP will be violated: the barrier(s) intervening between a trace and an antecedent will block antecedent-government. In the case of complement extraction no such ECP violation arises given that the complement will be theta-governed.

Extraction from L-marked categories is predictably better than extraction from adjuncts or subjects:

41a⠀Which book would you recommend reading?
41b⠀With which pen would you recommend writing?

The S-structure and LF representations of (41a) are (42a) and (42b) respectively:

42a⠀Which book_i would [IP you [VP t'_i [VP recommend [NP PRO
⠀⠀⠀⠀⠀⠀⠀⠀⠀⠀⠀⠀⠀⠀⠀⠀⠀⠀⠀⠀⠀⠀BC
⠀⠀[VP t'_i [VP reading⠀⠀t_i]]]]]]?
⠀⠀⠀⠀⠀⠀⠀⠀⠀⠀[+γ]

⠀⠀⁵⠀Cf. Huang (1982).

42b   Which book$_i$ would [$_{IP}$ you [$_{VP}$ recommend [$_{NP}$ PRO [$_{VP}$ reading   t$_i$]]]]?
                                                                                    [+γ]

In (42a) *wh*-movement does not cross any barriers. In contrast with the example illustrating extraction from a subject gerundival NP, (39a), the gerundival NP in (42a) is L-marked and hence not a BC. The trace of *which book* is theta-governed, hence [+γ] and at LF intermediate traces are deleted. (41b) has the representations in (43):

43a   With which pen$_i$ would [$_{IP}$ you [$_{VP}$ t″$_i$ [$_{VP}$ recommend [$_{NP}$ PRO [$_{VP}$ t′$_i$
                                                BC

      [$_{VP}$ writing t$_i$]]]]]]?
43b   With which pen$_i$ would [$_{IP}$ you [$_{VP}$ t″$_i$ [$_{VP}$ recommend [$_{NP}$ PRO
                                                BC   [+γ]
      [$_{VP}$ t′$_i$ [$_{VP}$ writing t$_i$]]]]]]?
          [+γ]   [+γ]

No additional problems arise with respect to the extraction of the adjunct. At LF all traces are antecedent-governed.

   Finally, we invite the reader to turn to (44) which contains extractions from *wh*-islands.

44a   ?Which man do you wonder when to meet?
44b   *With which pen do you wonder what to write?

(44a) is like (28) discussed in section 2.2. *Wh*-movement extracts an object NP from a *wh*-island, created by the moved *when*. (45a) is the S-structure of (44a):

45a   [$_{CP}$ Which man$_i$ do [$_{IP}$ you [$_{VP}$ t″$_i$ [$_{VP}$ wonder [$_{CP}$ when$_j$ [$_{IP}$ PRO to
                                        BC   BC
                                                                                        ↓
                                                                                     barrier

      [$_{VP}$ t′$_i$ [$_{VP}$ meet t$_i$]] t$_j$]]]]]]?
          [+γ]

The lower CP is a barrier by inheritance: it dominates the BC, IP. Thus (45a) weakly violates subjacency. Being theta-governed by *meet*, the trace of *which* *man*$_i$ is properly governed. At LF the trace of *when* is subject to gamma-marking, it is antecedent-governed, hence properly governed. Intermediate traces of *which man* can be deleted:

45b [$_{CP}$ which man$_i$ do [$_{IP}$ you [$_{VP}$ wonder [$_{CP}$ when$_j$ [$_{IP}$ PRO to
                BC   BC

                                        barrier

[$_{VP}$ meet t$_i$ t$_j$]]]]]]?
        [+γ] [+γ]

In (44b) there is a weak subjacency violation, as is the case in (44a), and in addition there is an ECP violation:

46a [$_{CP}$ With which pen$_j$ do [$_{IP}$ you [$_{VP}$ t$_j$ [$_{VP}$ wonder [$_{CP}$ what$_i$ [$_{IP}$ PRO to
                BC   BC
                                                        barrier

[$_{VP}$ t$_j$ [$_{VP}$ t$_i$ [$_{VP}$ write t$_i$ t$_j$]]]]]]]]]]?
                                    [+γ]

We assume without discussion that both the PP and the NP may adjoin to the lower VP.[6] Movement of *what*$_i$ does not cross any barriers; movement of *with which* crosses the lower CP barrier. The trace of *what*$_i$ is properly governed via theta-government by *write*. For gamma-marking of the trace of the adjunct we need to turn to LF. The intermediate trace of *what*$_i$ is deleted.

46b [$_{CP}$ With which pen$_j$ do [$_{IP}$ you
                BC

[$_{VP}$ t″$_j$ [$_{VP}$ wonder
    [+γ]
[$_{CP}$ what$_i$ [$_{IP}$ PRO to [$_{VP}$ t′$_j$ [$_{VP}$ write t$_i$ t$_j$]]]]]]]]?
        BC   [−γ]   [+γ] [+γ]
barrier

(46b) violates the ECP: *t′*$_j$, adjoined to the lower VP, cannot be properly governed. Its antecedent, the trace, *t″*$_j$, adjoined to the higher VP, is separated from it by a barrier, CP.

---

6 See discussion in Chomsky (1986b: 66).

3.2 Extraction: Summary

On the basis of the examples above we conclude that extraction from complements which are not islands is straightforward for both adjuncts and complements. On the other hand, extraction from complements which are islands leads generally to subjacency violations and in addition it results in ECP violations when adjuncts are extracted. Extraction from adjuncts will also lead to subjacency violations and in the case of adjunct extraction from adjuncts an ECP effect is added.

4   Discussion Section: Further Data

4.1   Subjects and the Vacuous Movement Hypothesis

We have claimed that extraction from *wh*-islands results in subjacency effects, with additional ECP effects if adjuncts are extracted. In previous discussion (chapter 7), however, we discussed the special problem of subject extraction. It was proposed that in questions like (47) it would be possible to assume that the subject *wh*-phrase remains *in situ*:

47a   [$_{CP}$ [$_{IP}$ Who likes John]]?
47b   I wonder [$_{CP}$ [$_{IP}$ who likes John]].

If this analysis is correct, no *wh*-islands are created: [Spec, CP] is still available for movement.

48   ?What do you wonder who saw?
     (Chomsky, 1986b: 48)

Assuming that *who* is unmoved, the S-structure of (48) is (49):

49   [$_{CP}$ What$_i$ do [$_{IP}$ you wonder [$_{CP}$ t''$_i$ [$_{IP}$ who$_j$ [$_{VP}$ t'$_i$ [$_{VP}$ saw t$_i$]]]]]]?
           BC   BC   [+γ]

At LF *who*, an operator, has to be moved to an operator position. Chomsky suggests it is moved to the lower [Spec, CP], obliterating the trace of the moved *what*.[7] That (48) is not quite perfect may be due to the fact that at LF *who* moves into a [Spec, CP] into which another constituent has already moved.

The hypothesis that subject *wh*-constituents remain *in situ* at S-structure is interesting since it accounts for the contrast in grammaticality between (50a) and (50b).[8]

50a ?This is a paper that we need someone who understands.
50b *This is a paper that we can intimidate with.

Chomsky considers (50b) as less acceptable than (50a). Consider the S-structure and LF representations of (50a):

51a ?a paper [$_{CP}$ OP$_i$ that [$_{IP}$ we [$_{VP}$ t'''$_i$ [$_{VP}$ need [$_{NP}$ someone [$_{CP}$ t''$_i$
                                                               BC
                                              barrier   barrier

[$_{IP}$ who [$_{VP}$ t'$_i$ [$_{VP}$ understands t$_i$]]]]]]]]]].
BC

51b ?a paper [$_{CP}$ OP$_i$ [$_{IP}$ we [$_{VP}$ need [$_{NP}$ someone [$_{CP}$ who$_j$ [$_{IP}$ t$_j$ [$_{VP}$ understands t$_i$]]]]]]]].

At S-structure, the zero operator, OP$_i$ can move through the lower [Spec, CP] crossing two barriers, NP and CP. (51a) violates subjacency. At LF, the subject relative *who$_j$* covers the intermediate trace of OP$_i$ in the specifier position of the lower CP.[9]

(50b) is slightly worse than (50a). (52) is its S-structure.

52 *a paper [$_{CP}$ OP$_i$ that [$_{IP}$ we [$_{VP}$ t''$_i$ [$_{VP}$ need
                              BC

[$_{NP}$ someone [$_{CP}$ OP$_j$ that [$_{IP}$ we can
                  BC   BC

   barrier   barrier

[$_{VP}$ t'$_i$ [$_{VP}$ t'$_j$ [$_{VP}$ intimidate t$_j$ with t$_i$]]]]]]]]]]]].
            [+γ]   [+γ].

---

[7] The moved *who* will have to take the place of *what* in order to be able to transmit its index to [Spec, CP]. If the moved *who* were simply adjoined to the trace of *what* then it would not be able to antecedent-govern its own trace.
[8] See Chomsky (1986b: 51) and Chung and McCloskey (1983).
[9] Cf. the discussion of (49) above.

In (52), the zero operator OP_i moves to the lowest [Spec, CP] crossing only IP. OP_i moves to the higher [Spec, CP] and crosses two barriers: CP, which is itself not L-marked and also inherits barrierhood from the lower IP, and NP, which inherits barrierhood from the CP. OP_i cannot move through the lower [Spec, CP]. The LF representation of (52) will cause no further problems: the relevant argument traces are already properly governed, and the intermediate traces can be deleted. The difference of acceptability between (50a) and (50b) could not be explained if we assume that *who* is moved at the S-structure (50a). As the reader can verify, under such an analysis both sentences would only involve identical subjacency violations.[10]

4.2 *Noun Complement Clauses*

Consider the following sentences. (53b) is unacceptable if *when* is construed with the lower clause. We only discuss this reading.

53a ?Which car did John announce a plan to steal tonight?
53b *When did John announce a plan to steal Bill's car?

Using Ross' terminology we would classify both examples above as violations of the complex NP constraint. The *wh*-constituents have been extracted from inside a clause which is the complement of an N. Let us examine these sentences in the *Barriers* framework. (54) is the S-structure of (53a):

54 ?[$_{CP}$ Which car$_i$ did [$_{IP}$ John [$_{VP}$ t$'''_i$ [$_{VP}$ announce [$_{NP}$ a
　　　　　　　　　　　　BC

　　plan [$_{CP}$ t$''_i$ [$_{IP}$ to [$_{VP}$ t$'_i$ [$_{VP}$ steal t$_i$] tonight]]]]]]]]?
　　　　　BC　　　　　　　　　　　[+γ]

In this example the complement CP is L-marked by the head N, hence the CP is not a barrier. The NP itself is not a barrier either since it is also L-marked. But intuitively the example is not perfect (cf. Chomsky, 1986b: 35).

Adjunct extraction from complex NPs is worse, as illustrated by (53b), which has the S-structure (55a):

---

[10] In *Barriers* Chomsky (1986b: 48–54) gives more examples where an analysis with a subject *wh*-constituent *in situ* at S-structure gives promising results.

55a *[$_{CP}$ When$_i$ did [$_{IP}$ John [$_{VP}$ t″$_i$ [$_{VP}$ announce [$_{NP}$ a
             BC

 plan [$_{CP}$ t′$_i$ [$_{IP}$ to [$_{VP}$ steal Bill's car] t$_i$]]]]]]]?
      BC

Again no barriers are crossed, but the sentence is still not acceptable. Chomsky suggests that there must be a barrier for movement in these examples and he proposes that the CP complement of the N *plan* may be such a barrier (see Chomsky, 1986b: 36).

Let us turn to the LF representation corresponding to the S-structure (55a). We need to consider LF because the trace of the moved *when* is an adjunct trace and can only be gamma-marked at LF.

55b *[$_{CP}$ When$_i$ did [$_{IP}$ John [$_{VP}$ t″$_i$ [$_{VP}$ announce [$_{NP}$ a
           BC   [+γ]

 plan [$_{CP}$ t′$_i$ [$_{IP}$ to [$_{VP}$ steal Bill's car] t$_i$]]]]]]]?
      [−γ]   [+γ]

The lowest trace of *when* is properly governed by the intermediate trace, t′$_i$, in the lowest [Spec, CP]. The highest intermediate trace, t″$_i$, will be antecedent-governed by *when*. This leaves us to consider the gamma-feature of t′$_i$.

56*

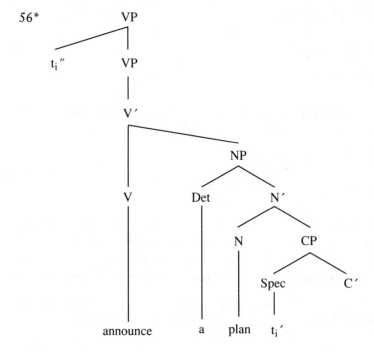

t''_i ought to antecedent-govern t'_i. It does indeed c-command t'_i but it is not the closest governor. The N *plan* governs CP and assigns it a theta role. Hence N L-marks CP. CP is neither a BC nor a barrier so N can govern inside CP and crucially it can govern the t'_i. This means that by minimality the antecedent trace, t''_i, loses out and will not be able to govern t'_i. Regardless of the status of CP with respect to subjacency, t'_i violates the ECP (cf. Chomsky, 1986b: 43). In noun complement clauses the N-head will alway govern the CP complement, thus it will always prevent antecedent-government of material inside CP from the outside. It follows that adjunct extraction from N-complement clauses is impossible.

5 A-Chains

So far we have applied the *Barriers* framework as developed by Chomsky (1986b) exclusively to examples of *wh*-movement, i.e. to A'-chains. In this section we turn to A-chains. We shall see that, as it stands, our theory faces serious problems when it comes to dealing with raising and passive constructions (cf. chapter 6). In the present section the problems will be raised and some suggestions for their solution are put forward. For extensive discussion and a complete analysis the reader is referred to Chomsky's own work (1986b: 68ff.).

(57) illustrates NP-movement:

57a John will be invited.
57b John seems to have left.

In each of these sentences the subject NP *John* is a derived subject. The S-structure representations of (57) are as in (58).[11]

58a [$_{IP}$ John$_i$ will [$_{VP}$ be invited t$_i$]].
58b [$_{IP}$ John$_i$ -s [$_{VP}$ seem [$_{IP}$ t$_i$ to have left]]].

Consider (58a). *John* originates as the direct object of *invited* and moves to the subject position. It crosses the maximal projection VP which is a BC and a barrier. This would mean that sentences such as (57a) and (58a) contain a weak subjacency violation, hardly the result we expect for sentences as

---

11 Following the subject-in-VP hypothesis we would assume that in fact the derived subject moves via [Spec, VP]. This has no bearing on the discussion.

normal as those. Assuming that *invited* theta-governs the trace of *John*, the ECP is not violated.

The situation becomes worse in the case of raising sentences such as (57b). Consider the S-structure (58b). *John* originates as the D-structure subject of the lower IP. It moves to the subject position and crosses IP, a BC though not a barrier, and VP, a BC and a barrier. Again (58b) ought to be a weak subjacency violation. The trace of *John* in (58b) can only satisfy the ECP through antecedent-government. The only potential antecedent is *John*, from which it is separated by a barrier, VP. In fact, the antecedent *John* will never be able to govern the trace in the lower infinitival clause since *seem* is always a closer governor and thus by minimality prevents *John* from governing the trace. It is hardly desirable that we should be forced to consider sentences like (57b) as ECP violations.

The reader might suggest that we use the escape hatch introduced in the case of *wh*-movement, where movement was allowed to go via VP-adjunction. However this solution is not possible in the case of A-chains. Consider, for instance, (57a/58a), the passive sentence. Suppose we allowed *John* first to adjoin to VP before moving to the subject position:

59    $[_{IP}$ John$_i$ will $[_{VP}$ t$'_i$ $[_{VP}$ be invited t$_i]]]$.

In (59) the lowest trace, t_i, is bound by the intermediate trace, t'_i, which occupies an A'-position, the position created by VP-adjunction. Hence t_i in (59) is like a *wh*-trace. It has the features [−Anaphor, −Pronominal] and is subject to Principle C of the binding theory. But t_i is also A-bound by *John*. (59) illustrates a case of improper movement: movement from an A position to an A'-position and back to an A-position.[12] In *Barriers* (1986b: 68–80) Chomsky offers a solution to the problem raised here. We give a brief indication of the direction taken. The account here is a rough approximation and the reader should also read the primary literature. The problem in the examples above is clearly the status of VP. VP is a maximal projection. It is not L-marked, hence a BC, hence a barrier.

In chapter 2 we discussed the structure of clauses and we suggested that I is the head of S, which we got to refer to as IP. As a head, I selects a V-projection, VP. I is composed of agreement features and tense features. Tense features typically associate with VP. We could say that I theta-marks VP. This means that I governs VP and theta-governs VP. It does not mean that I L-marks VP, though, since we have argued that I is not a lexical category, but rather a bundle of grammatical features.

---

[12]   See chapter 7, section 6.1 for discussion.

Another characteristic of IP is that the subject NP agrees with INFL for the features summed up as AGR: person and number. Let us say that I also 'agrees' with the head of the VP which it selects. After all, it is this verb which will finally be inflected for tense. Let us indicate the V–I agreement through coindexation. The subject NP and I also agree, we also coindex them. The chain $<John_i, INFL_i, works_i, >$, created by the coindexation in (60) is called an **extended chain**.

60   $[_{IP}$ John$_i$ $[_{I'}$ INFL$_i$ $[_{VP}$ works$_i]]]$.

In a raising construction like (57b/58b) we would end up with an extended chain: the subject NP agrees with INFL, INFL agrees with the associated V *seem*:

61   John$_i$ INFL$_i$ seems$_i$ $[_{IP}$ t$_i$ to have left].

This coindexation solves at least one of the problems raised: t_i is now coindexed with *seem*$_i$, which governs the trace. Hence the trace is governed by a coindexed element, and this could qualify as antecedent-government.[13]

6   Summary

In this chapter we have defined the notion barrier and integrated it in our theory. The definition of barrier is as follows:

1   A is a **barrier** for B if and only if (a) or (b):
    (a)   A is a maximal projection and A immediately dominates C, C is a BC for B;
    (b)   A is a BC for B, A is not IP.

Using (1) we define government as follows:

2a   **Government**
     X governs Y if and only if
     (i)   X is either of the category A, N, V, P, I;
           or
           X and Y are coindexed;

---

[13]   Antecedent-government of a trace of XP, i.e. a phrase, by a coindexed head might be unexpected. For a different approach see chapter 12.

    (ii)   X c-commands Y;
   (iii)   no barrier intervenes between X and Y;
   (iv)   minimality is respected.

2b **Minimality condition on government**
    There is no Z such that Z satisfies (i), (ii) and (iii) and X c-commands
    Z.

The subjacency condition is formulated in terms of barriers:

3 **Subjacency condition**
   Movement must not cross more than one barrier.

Barriers are defined as in (1).

We show that the ECP can also be reinterpreted in terms of the notion barrier.

The *Barriers* framework applies quite straightforwardly to *wh*-movement. For NP-movement, we see that there are additional problems which require that coindexation be extended.

7 Exercises

Exercise 1

Discuss (1) and (2) in terms of our new interpretation of the subjacency condition and the ECP:

1 Who does the detective think that he likes best?
2 Who does the detective think likes him best?

Exercise 2

Consider the following sentences from the exercises in the introduction to this book, most of which are also discussed in exercise 2 in chapter

7. Using the *Barriers* framework developed in chapter 10, try to account for the relative acceptability of the examples below as indicated by the question marks and the asterisks:

1a ?Which man do you know what John will give to?
2b ?Which man do you wonder when they will appoint?
3c *Who do you wonder which present will give?
4d ?Which present do you wonder who will give?
5e ?Which man do you wonder whether John will invite?
6f *Which man do you wonder whether will invite John?
7g *Which man do you wonder what will give to John?
8h *Which man do you wonder when will invite John?

When discussing these sentences you should first determine their syntactic representations. Then you should try to identify which grammatical principle or principles are violated.

Exercise 3

Compare (38a), repeated here as (1), with (2):

1 *This is a book which reading would be fun.
2 This is a book reading which would be fun.

How does the contrast in grammaticality fall out from our discussion?

11 Functional Heads and Head Movement

Contents

Introduction and overview

Introduction and Overview

In the first ten chapters of this book we develop the core notions of the theory known as the Government and Binding Theory. In the last two chapters we select a number of recent developments which have led to considerable modifications of the framework. We cannot hope to discuss all the developments that have been proposed, and we restrict the discussion to some of those which have initiated much recent research. Chapter 11 discusses the theory of phrase structure, chapter 12 considers locality conditions in syntax and the ECP.

We propose in chapter 2 that the clause is an endocentric category, i.e. a clause is a projection of a head. S is reinterpreted as a projection of I(nflection), and S′ is reinterpreted as a projection of C(omplementizer). C and I are functional heads. In the present chapter we look in more detail into the role of the functional heads of the clause, I in particular. On the basis of a comparative study of the distribution of the inflected verb in French and in English we shall adopt the so-called **Split INFL hypothesis** (Pollock, 1989) which proposes that I be decomposed into two separate functional heads, each with its own projection, AGR and T. IP is reinterpreted as AGRP, AGRP dominates TP. We will also consider the constraints on V-movement in more detail and show how the obligatory stepwise movement of the verb is due to the empty category principle.

After having shown how clauses are projections of functional heads which host the inflectional features of V, we turn to the structure of NPs. There are arguments for proposing that those constituents which are standardly referred to as noun phrases are in fact projections of a functional head, spelt out in English by the determiner. This proposal has come to be known as the **DP hypothesis** (Abney, 1987).

Based on the discussion of the role of functional projections and their association with lexical projections, we also look at the notion of extended projection, a notion which enables us to reconcile the traditional idea that clauses are projections of V with the more recent proposal that clauses are projections of functional heads.

Finally we briefly consider recent developments in the generative framework where an economy-driven programme is being developed referred to as **the Minimalist Program**. We look at the treatment of verb movement in this programme and compare it with our own discussion.

Section 1 discusses the notion of head movement as developed so far. Section 2 concentrates on the Split INFL hypothesis and is based on data from V-movement in French and in English. Section 3 discusses functional projections in the clausal domain. Section 4 shows how the **Head Movement Constraint** derives from the ECP. Section 5 deals with the so-called DP hypothesis. Section 6 develops the notion **extended projection** and section 7 looks at verb movement in the light of the Minimalist Program.

1   Head Movement in English: a First Survey

Let us first briefly recapitulate the notion of head movement developed in various sections of this book. We have proposed that the structure of the clause is as in (1a): clauses are projections of C, C selects IP and I in turn selects VP.

1a
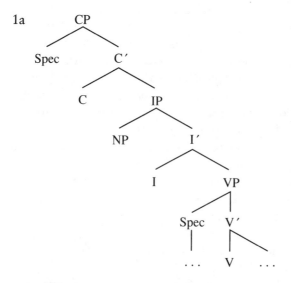

It is assumed that the English modal auxiliaries, *will, shall, can, may* and *must*, are base-generated under I. There are various considerations that bear on this issue. One is that modal auxiliaries are in complementary distribution with agreement morphology: *will*, in (2), for instance, is invariant no matter what the person and number of its subject is:

2a   Violetta will meet Alfredo.
2b   Violetta and Thelma will meet Alfredo.

Also, the modal auxiliaries lack non-finite forms: modals do not have infinitives (3a), gerunds (3b), perfect participles (3c):

3a He will be able to/*can go.
3b Being able to/*canning to pay one's debts is important.
3c Alfredo has been able/*could change the appointment.

In root interrogative sentences the modal auxiliary precedes the subject NP:

4a Will Violetta meet Alfredo?
4b Whom will Violetta meet?

We proposed in chapter 7 that sentences with subject–auxiliary inversion, as those in (4), are derived by moving the auxiliary under C:

1b

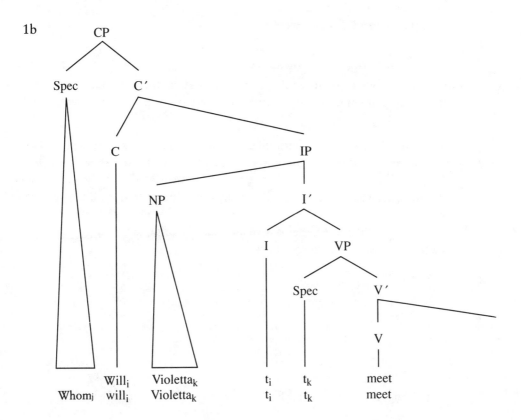

We assume that, as is the case for moved XPs, the moved auxiliary, a head, leaves a trace. Following recent proposals in the theory (cf. chapter 6, section 5) we assume that the base position of the subject NP *Violetta* is VP-internal. At S-structure the subject NP moves to [Spec, IP].

Subject–auxiliary inversion is not restricted to modal auxiliaries; as the name suggests, it applies to all auxiliaries and it fails to apply to lexical verbs.

5a   (When) was Violetta invited by Alfredo?
5b   *(When) got Violetta invited by Alfredo?[1]

We return to the ungrammaticality of subject–verb inversion (5b) below. Let us first consider (5a). The passive auxiliary *be* differs from modal auxiliaries in that it does combine with finite person and number inflection (6) and also that it has non-finite forms, such as infinitive (7a), gerund (7b), perfect participle (7c). The same applies to progressive *be* and to perfective *have*.

6a   Violetta was invited.
6b   Violetta and Thelma were invited.

7a   Violetta wants to be invited.
7b   Being invited to Alfredo's party is important for Violetta.
7c   Violetta should have been invited to the party a long time ago.

Since they are compatible with inflection we assume that the auxiliaries *have* and *be* are not base-generated under I; rather they are verbs and, as will be shown extensively below, they move to I to be associated with the inflectional morphology. The rough underlying structure of (6a) is (8a); as the reader will remember, we assume that the subject of a passive clause originates as a direct object (chapter 6), the passive auxiliary *be* originates as a V head which selects a (passive) VP-complement:

---

[1]   For a discussion of the so-called *get* passive, cf. Haegeman (1985).

8a

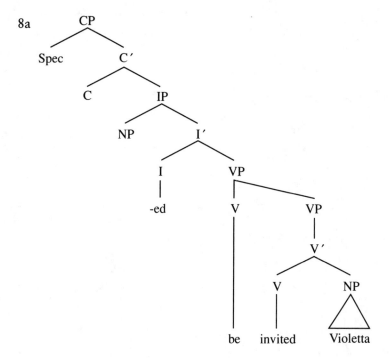

At S-structure the object NP *Violetta* moves to [Spec, IP], via [Spec, VP], in order to be able to be case-marked, by the finite I, and the auxiliary *be* moves to I to associate with the finite inflection:

8b

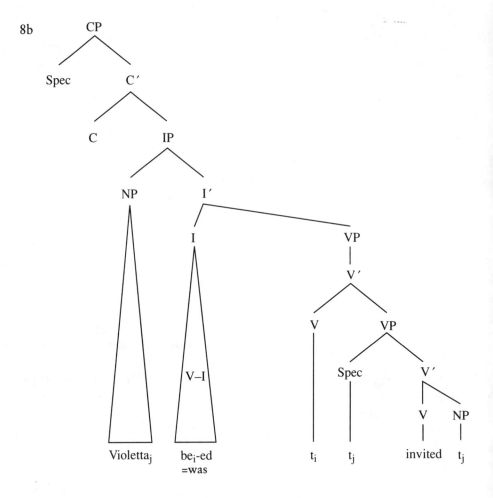

The association of a verb with its inflectional ending is a form of **incorporation:**[2] the inflectional ending is assumed to be a (functional) head, V is a (lexical) head. By virtue of the incorporation of V by I, the inflectional head and the verb become one complex head. In interrogative sentences (5a) the inflected auxiliary precedes the subject NP, we assume it moves under C:

---

[2]   For discussion of incorporation cf. Baker (1988). For a discussion of different types of incorporation by functional heads, see Rizzi and Roberts (1989).

8c

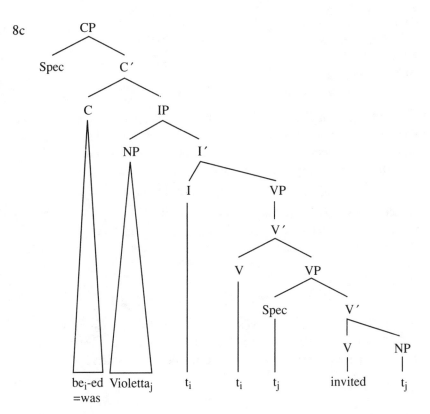

The movement of the modal auxiliary from I to C, and the movements of the perfective, progressive and passive auxiliaries from V to I and also from I to C, all instantiate movement of a category of the zero level, i.e. X^0-movement or **head movement**. Following our discussion in earlier chapters, we assume that the structure preservation constraint restricts movement by imposing that heads move to head positions. Auxiliary movement is head-to-head movement.

   In English, auxiliaries undergo subject–auxiliary inversion in root interrogatives, but lexical verbs do not do so, as seen in (5b). The impossibility of inversion with the subject is not a universal property of verbs. In many languages subject–verb inversion is grammatical. (9) illustrates some cases:

9a   *French*
       Quand viendra-t-elle?
       when come-fut-she?
       'When will she come?'

9b   *Dutch*
     Wanneer komt Marie?
     when comes Marie
     'When does Marie come?'

In French (9a) and in Dutch (9b) the inflected lexical verb (*viendra, komt*) precedes the subject (*elle, Marie*). This means that in principle nothing bans the subject–verb inversion pattern. And in fact, in earlier English, the inflected verb could also precede the subject NP:

9c   Hwæt sægest pu, yrplingc?   Hu begæst   þu weorc þin?
     what say-2sg you ploughman   how carry-out-2sg you work your
     'What do you say, ploughman? How do you carry out your work?'
     (from Ælfricos, *Grammar and Colloquy*, 20.22, cited in Closs-Traugott, 1972: 73)

In the literature this issue has given rise to important discussion (Emonds, 1970, 1976; Pollock, 1989) and has led to modifications in the structural representation of clauses. We discuss this issue in the next section.

2   The Split INFL Hypothesis

In the discussion of verb movement we focus on the contrast between French and English.[3] This section is based essentially on Pollock (1989). Recall that in French the inflected verb may precede the subject (9a): the French lexical verb can move to C: this is impossible in English. There are other differences in terms of verb positions between the two languages, which suggest that this contrast correlates with a more general contrast between French and English. Anticipating the discussion that will follow we could say that while in English lexical verbs remain under V and are not subject to head-to-head movement, lexical verbs in French do undergo head-to-head movement.

First consider (10)–(12): we pair a French sentence (a) with its English counterpart (b), comparing the relative position of the inflected verb and the sentential negation *pas* or *not*:

---

[3] For an introductory discussion to word-order in the West Germanic languages Dutch and German cf. Haegeman (1992). For Italian cf. Belletti (1990).

10	*V – Neg*	*Neg – V*

10a Violetta n'est pas invitée.   *Violetta ne pas est invitée.
     Violetta *ne* is not invited
     'Violetta is not invited.'

10b Violetta is not invited.   *Violetta not is invited.

11a Violetta n'a pas mangé.   *Violetta ne pas a mangé.
     Violetta *ne* has not eaten
     'Violetta has not eaten.'

11b Violetta has not eaten.   *Violetta not has eaten.

12a Violetta ne mange pas de chocolat.   *Violetta ne pas mange de
                                            chocolat.

     Violetta *ne* eats not chocolate
     'Violetta does not eat chocolate.'

12b *Violetta eats not chocolate.   Violetta does not eat chocolate.

In (10) and in (11) the auxiliaries *être/be* and *avoir/have* precede the negative elements *pas/not* in both languages, and in fact they have to precede them. In (12) a contrast emerges: while lexical verbs have to appear to the left of *pas* in French, they can only appear to the right of *not* in English. As a first approximation, to be modified very shortly, we could propose the following kind of base structure for both French and English:

13

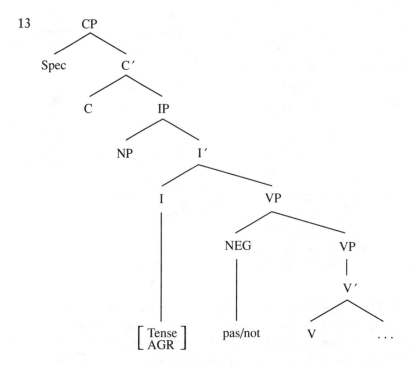

In English finite clauses, V moves to I only if V is an auxiliary, in French finite clauses all Vs must move to I.

Consider the French non-finite clauses in (14):

14   *V – Neg*   *V – Neg*

14a   N'être pas invité, c'est triste.   Ne pas être invité, c'est
                                                            triste.

      ne be not invited it is sad
      'It is sad not to be invited.'

14b   N'avoir pas reçu de cadeaux, c'est triste.   Ne pas avoir reçu de
                                                            cadeaux c'est triste

      ne have not received presents it is sad   *ne* not have received
                                                            presents it is sad

14c   *Ne manger pas de chocolat, c'est triste.   Ne pas manger de
                                                            chocolat, c'est triste.

      ne eat not chocolate it is sad   *ne* not eat chocolate it is
                                                            sad

Two differences emerge between finite and non-finite clauses in French.

(i)   Though French auxiliaries must move to the left of the negative element *pas* in finite clauses (cf. above), they optionally remain to its right in infinitival clauses (14a, 14b).

(ii) Whereas the French lexical verbs always precede *pas* in finite clauses, they remain to the right of the negation in infinitival clauses (14c).

In English infinitival clauses a similar situation obtains (examples and judgements from Pollock (1989: 376, (21–2))). English auxiliaries marginally may precede negation in non-finite clauses, but they preferably follow negation (15a), (15b), and lexical verbs must appear to the right of negation (15c), as was also the case in finite clauses.

15	*V – Neg*	*Neg – V*
15a	?To be not happy is a prerequisite for writing novels.	Not to be happy is a prerequisite for writing novels.
15b	(?) To have not had a happy childhood is a prerequisite for writing novels.	Not to have had a happy childhood is a prerequisite for writing novels.
15c	*To get not arrested under such circumstances is a miracle.	Not to get arrested under such circumstances is a miracle.

Based on the data above we conclude that the nature of INFL determines the possibility of V-movement. We return to this point below. For the moment we summarize by saying that finite lexical verbs in English never appear to the left of negation. In the representation (13) this means V never moves past Neg to I. French finite lexical verbs do move past Neg. In both languages finite auxiliaries move past Neg: obligatorily in finite clauses, optionally in infinitives.

In addition to the ordering of V and sentential negation, English and French also differ with respect to the order of verbs and adverbials such as *often/souvent*. Again we first consider finite clauses: in French all finite Vs, auxiliary or lexical, must appear to the left of such adverbials, in English finite auxiliaries appear to the left of those adverbials, finite lexical verbs appear to their right:

16	*V – Adverb*	*Adverb – V*
16a	Il arrive souvent en retard. he arrives often late	*Il souvent arrive en retard.
16b	Il est souvent invité. he is often invited	*Il souvent est invité.

| 16c | Il a   souvent mangé du chocolat. | *Il souvent a mangé du |
| | he has often   eaten   chocolate | chocolat. |

17a	*He arrives often late.	He often arrives late.
17b	He is often invited.	*He often is invited.
17c	He has often eaten chocolate.	*He often has eaten chocolate.

In finite clauses, the order of V and adverb parallels the order of V and negation: whenever V can precede negation it also can precede the adverb, whenever the inflected verb must follow the negation it must follow the adverb. As a first analysis we might propose that the negation and the adverb have the same position, i.e. both could be VP-adjoined:

18a $[_{IP}$ [NP] $[_I$ Tense/AGR] $[_{VP}$ $\begin{Bmatrix} \text{Neg} \\ \text{Adv} \end{Bmatrix}$ $[_{VP}$. . .

However, this hypothesis cannot be maintained in view of the following data:

19	*V – Adverb*	*Adverb – V*
19a	(Ne pas) arriver souvent en retard c'est triste.	(Ne pas) souvent arriver en retard . . .
	(*ne* not) arrive often late it is sad	(*ne* not) often arrive late . . .
19b	Être souvent invité . . .	Souvent être invité . . .
	be often invited	often be invited . . .
19c	Avoir souvent mangé trop . . .	Souvent avoir mangé trop . . .
	have often eaten too much	often have eaten too much

20a	*To arrive often late . . .	To often arrive late . . .
20b	?To be often invited . . .	To often be invited . . .
20c	(?) To have often eaten too much . . .	To often have eaten too much . . .

The French data in (19a) are crucial for the analysis: we see that though non-finite lexical verbs cannot precede negation, they can precede the adverb *souvent*. If the structure of the French clause were as in (18a) this would be problematic. (18a) suggests that *pas* behaves in the same way as *souvent*, contrary to fact. In fact, (19a) shows that *pas* and *souvent* must occupy distinct positions. The non-finite verb can end up between *pas* and *souvent*. Recall that verb movement is head movement: in (18a) there is no head position between the negative *pas* and the adverb. If both *pas* and the adverb were VP-adjoined, then an intervening constituent would also have to be VP-adjoined. But by the structure preservation constraint only maximal projections can adjoin to maximal projections. In (18b) a head, an X^0, would have to adjoin to VP, an XP:

18b $[_{IP}$ [NP] $[_I$ Tense/AGR] $[_{VP}$ Neg ? $[_{VP}$ Adv $[_{VP}$ ...

What we need is a head position, i.e. an X^0, located between Neg and the adverb. But we cannot simply insert a head position there, the presence of a head, i.e. X^0, implies the presence of a projection: XP. This follows from the X'-theory of phrase structure developed in chapter 2. There are apparently two head positions that V can move to: one to the left of the sentential negation and one to its right (and preceding adverbs like *souvent/often*). Before we tackle the type of heads that these could be, let us briefly consider the syntax of negation in French. As (21) shows, French negation is bipartite: it is composed of an element *ne* and an element *pas*. Observe, though, that *ne* is attached to the finite verb with which it moves along to C:

21a Elle n'a pas mangé.
     she *ne* has not eaten
     'She has not eaten.'
21b N'a-t-elle pas mangé?
     ne has she not eaten
     'Has she not eaten?'
21c *A-t-elle ne pas mangé?

Since *ne* can move to C, we assume that it is a head-like element. Following Pollock (1989) we assume that negation is expanded by a projection NegP, whose head is *ne* and whose specifier is *pas*; *ne* and the inflected auxiliary form one complex head.[4]

Now we return to the problem of V-movement. We have seen that there are two landing sites for verbs: one to the left of the negation, and one to the

---

[4] Our discussion of negation in French in this chapter cannot do justice to all the problems involved. Further discussion would be beyond the scope of an introductory text. For a discussion of negation in French, see also Hirschbüler and Labelle (1993), Moritz (1989), Muller (1991), Pearce (1990a, 1990b, 1991), Rowlett (1993). For a discussion of negation in Romance the reader is also referred to Zanuttini (1991, 1993). For a discussion of Italian and French negation see also Haegeman (in preparation).

right of the negation and to the left of adverbs like *souvent*. What kind of head positions could these be? Pollock proposes that the two head positions are both inflectional positions, and that they represent the two components that we have till now associated with INFL: Tense, and AGR. (18b) will be modified in that (i) we add a NegP; (ii) the head I is reinterpreted as one functional head and the position '?' is interpreted as another functional head. The question arises where to locate AGR and T respectively. Pollock himself (1989) identifies I with T for Tense and '?' with AGR. However, following Belletti (1990) and others, we propose the opposite: AGRP dominates TP, the projection of T. Based on this assumption, a French negative clause has the structure (18c):

18c

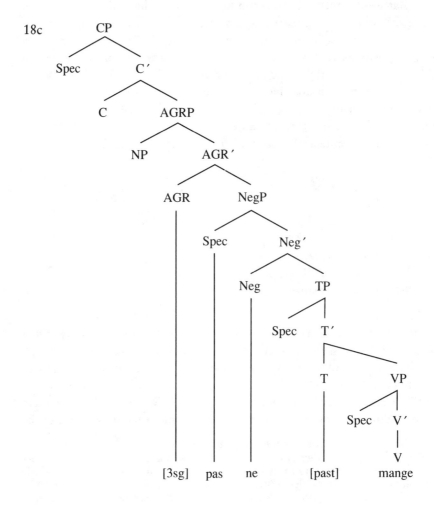

The verb (*mange*, 'eat') first moves to T to pick up the tense inflection, then it moves to the next head up, Neg, to pick up the negative head *ne*, then it moves to AGR to pick up the person/number inflection.

The reader may well wonder why we propose (contra Pollock (1989) and with Belletti (1990)) that AGRP dominates TP, i.e. that AGR is to the left of T. Consider what the kind of representation in (18c) is trying to show: on the basis of (18c) we expect that the tense inflection is more closely associated with V than the AGR inflection, in that V first picks up T and then AGR. This sequencing of the movements has a syntactic reflex: within the inflected V the T inflection is inside the person inflection. In (22a)–(22c) we see that the past T inflection is inside the person/number inflection, in (22d)–(22f) the future T inflection is inside the person/number inflection.

22	*NP*	*V*	*T*	*AGR*
22a	je	mange	ai	s
22b	tu	mange	ai	s
22c	il	mange	ai	t
		eat	Past	person + number
22d	je	mange	er	ai
22e	tu	mange	er	as
22f	il	mange	er	a
		eat	Fut	person + number

The diagram (18c) replaces the clause structure elaborated in chapter 2. IP is decomposed into two projections: AGRP and TP, where AGR selects TP. Both projections are headed by inflectional elements and thus are **functional** projections. In addition we assume that negative clauses also contain NegP. In French finite clauses all Vs, whether lexical or auxiliary, move to AGR, via T (and Neg in negative clauses); in non-finite clauses the lexical verbs may move to T but they can also remain in VP. Moreover, lexical verbs cannot move to AGR. Auxiliaries optionally move to T and to AGR. In the remainder of the book we replace IP by AGRP. In the current literature authors often use 'IP' as a shorthand representation for the clause.

The hypothesis which decomposes INFL into TP and AGRP has come to be known as the **Split INFL hypothesis**. For English the clause structure of negative sentences is (18d):

18d

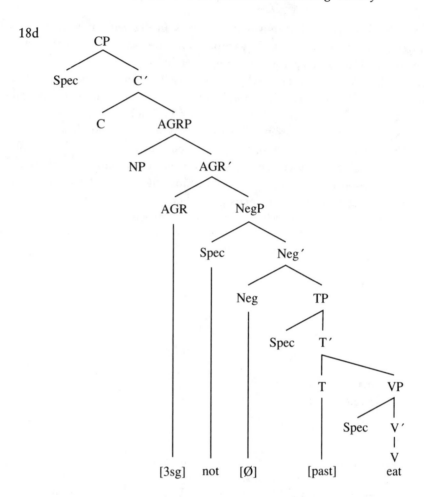

[3sg] not [Ø] [past] eat

English modal auxiliaries are base generated under AGR, other auxiliaries such as *have* and *be* originate in VP and then move to the functional heads T, Neg and AGR. We assume that lexical verbs do not leave the VP.[5]

[5] We do not go into the status of *not* and *n't* in English (i):

(ia) John has not come.
(ib) Has John not come?
(ic) John hasn't come.
(id) Hasn't John come?

For discussion the reader is referred to Haegeman (in preparation), Moritz (1989), Ouhalla (1990), Pollock (1989), Rizzi (1990a) and the references cited there.
   Another more general question that emerges is whether the ordering of AGRP, TP and NegP is universal. See for instance Ouhalla (1991) and Zanuttini (1993) for discussion.

The modification of the structure of IP which we propose here has some consequences for the theory of grammar which we are developing. We will not go into all the details. We maintain the assumption that the subject NP occupies the highest NP position in the clause, in our revised structure this is [Spec, AGRP]. We assume that AGR assigns NOMINATIVE to the subject NP. The role of T with respect to NOMINATIVE assignment is less clear (for some proposals see Chomsky, 1992). We assume that the specifier of AGRP is an A-position. It is generally assumed that the specifier of [NegP], is an A'-position;[6] it is a position which contains a negative operator (*pas*, *not*) and we have seen in chapter 9 that operators typically occupy left-peripheral A'-positions. We return to the notion A/A'-position briefly in chapter 12.

Since we propose that English Vs do not leave the VP, the question arises, of course, how English lexical verbs get associated with the agreement and tense morphology, located under AGR and T respectively. One proposal (cf. Pollock, 1989; Chomsky, 1991; Rizzi, 1990a) is that the AGR and T morphology in English are **lowered** onto the lexical V. Lowering processes in general raise problems because they leave traces which are not c-commanded by their antecedents. Various solutions have been proposed in the literature (Chomsky, 1991; Rizzi, 1990a). We shall not go in to the intricacies of the lowering process in detail here (cf. the literature cited for various accounts).

We have seen that languages vary parametrically with respect to V-movement. In present-day English (23a) lexical verbs do not move out of the VP, in French (23b) they do; lexical verbs also move in standard Dutch (23c), and in earlier forms of English (23d), too, V-movement to C was possible:[7]

23a   *Comes he tomorrow? vs. Does he come tomorrow?
23b   Vient-il demain?
23c   Komt hij morgen?
23d   (= 9c) Hwæt sægest þu, yrþlingc? Hu begæst þu weorc þin?

The question arises how to account for this type of cross-linguistic variation. An interesting indication as to the nature of the parameter regulating V-movement is that in French infinitives V-movement to AGR is restricted:

24   *Ne manger pas de chocolat. vs. Ne pas manger de chocolat.
     ne eat not chocolate   *ne* not eat chocolate

---

[6]   For a discussion of the role of specifier–head relations and negation cf. chapter 12 and Haegeman (in preparation).
[7]   For discussion of V-movement in the Scandinavian languages cf. Holmberg and Platzack (1991) and Platzack and Holmberg (1989).

Infinitives lack finite inflection, there is no person/number variation in infinitives. The nature of the inflection associated with V can be seen to play a role in determining the possibilities of V-movement. Consider the inflectional paradigms for the finite V in French, English, Dutch and Old English:

25		*French*	*English*	*Dutch*	*Old English*
	1sg	je viens	I come	ik kom	ic fremme
		I come		I come	I perform
	2sg	tu viens	you come	jij komt	þu fremest
	3sg	il vient	he comes	hij komt	he fremeð
	1pl	nous venons	we come	wij komen	we fremmað
	2pl	vous venez	you come	jullie komen	ge fremmað
	3pl	ils viennent	they come	zij komen	hi fremmað
		4 forms	2 forms	3 forms	4 forms

(Old English data from Quirk and Wrenn, 1957: 43)

It seems to be the case that V-movement correlates with the relative strength of inflection: in English the AGR inflection is weak: only the third person singular of the present tense has an overt inflectional ending, the lexical V does not move to C. In the other languages represented in (25) AGR is strong, there is more overt agreement morphology. Languages such as English with little overt agreement morphology do not allow lexical verbs to move to AGR; languages with more morphological endings do. One way of accounting for this is to argue that AGR is either **strong** or **weak**. Strong AGR attracts the V, weak AGR does not attract V.[8] In section 5 below we will briefly reconsider the V-movement parameter in terms of recent proposals by Chomsky.[9]

3   Functional Projections and the Clausal Domain

In the above discussion we have provided evidence for the decomposition of IP into AGRP and TP. The evidence for postulating a number of distinct

[8]   We have simplified the discussion for expository reasons. The reader is referred to the literature for more extensive discussion. In particular, the reader is referred to Pollock's (1989) analysis which correlates richness of AGR with theta role assignment.

[9]   Returning to our discussion of the *pro*-drop parameter in chapter 8, observe that we can retain the formulation proposed there: if AGR is rich, it can identify the features of *pro*. Note, however, that languages where strong AGR attracts the verb are not necessarily *pro*-drop languages: in French V moves to AGR but referential *pro* is not allowed. We do not go into this issue here (cf. Jaeggli and Safir, 1989).

functional heads within the IP domain derives from word-order variation. On the assumption that *pas/not* on the one hand and adverbials such as *souvent/ often* on the other, have a fixed position, we are led to postulate a functional projection in between NegP and VP. In addition, observe that T and AGR morphology can be identified as two distinct inflectional endings. If distinct inflectional endings represent distinct functional heads, then T and AGR should be kept separate and each should head a functional projection. The split INFL hypothesis first developed by Pollock (1989) has given rise to a renewed interest in the nature of the clausal projection and has led many linguists to postulate additional functional projections.

In our discussion in chapter 2, section 3.5, we discussed the nature of small clauses and on the basis of French data with overt adjectival AGR morphology we proposed that small clauses are functional projections of AGRP. We refer the reader to that discussion.

Ouhalla (1992) discusses the distribution of focused phrases in classical Arabic. In (26a) *quasiidatan* ('a poem') is focused, but it cannot receive contrastive focus, as indicated by the fact that a contrastive discourse continuation is not possible. For contrastive focus two strategies are possible: either the focused phrase is preposed (26b) or it is left *in situ* and there is a focus marker (FM) sentence-initially (26c). To account for this alternation Ouhalla (1992) proposes a structure like that in (27) where the clausal domain (here represented as IP because the internal structure is irrelevant for the point at issue) is dominated by a functional projection FP, focus phrase, whose head contains the head marking focus.

26a   ?Allaf-at Zaynabu **quasiidatan** (*laa kitaban).
      wrote-3sgfem   a-poem   not a book
      'Zaynab wrote a poem.'
26b   **Quasiidatan** ?allaf-at Zaynabu (laa kitaaban/*laa ?alquat).
      a-poem   wrote-3sgfem   not a book/not read
      'It was a poem Zaynab wrote (not a book).'
26c   (La) qad ?allaf-at Zaynabu quasiidatan.
      FM   wrote-3sg fem   a-poem
      'Zaynab did indeed write a poem.'

(27a) is the structure for (26a), with the preposed constituent in [Spec, FP], (27b) is the structure for (26b) with the focal head overtly realized and the focused phrase *in situ*:

27a
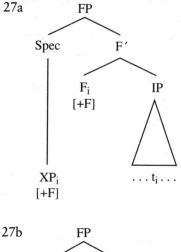

27b
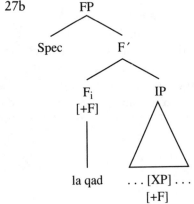

The idea that we need a focus phrase whose specifier hosts focused elements is also proposed to account for the Hungarian data in (28):

28a Jànos   szereti   Màriàt.
Janos-NOM love-Pres-3sg Mary-ACC
'Janos loves Mary.'
28b Màriàt szereti Jànos.

The sentence-initial constituents in (28) receive focal stress. Puskas (1992) proposes that this is due to the fact that they occupy [Spec, FP]. The finite verb *szereti* occupies the head of FP.

In influential work on clitics in Romance languages Kayne (1989, 1991) and Sportiche (1992) propose that clitic elements like *le* in (29) signal a head position. According to Kayne's analysis clitics move to the head AGR to which V has also moved; according to Sportiche the clitics head functional projections which he calls Clitic Phrases.

29 Jean l'a déjà vu.
    Jean him has already seen
    'Jean has already seen him.'

A full discussion of the nature of clitics is well beyond the scope of an introductory textbook. We refer the reader to Kayne (1975) for a first detailed discussion and then to the subsequent literature (cf. Sportiche (1992) for an excellent survey and a new analysis). In order to account for the distribution of subject clitics in standard Italian and in some of its dialects, Rizzi (1987) argues that the Italian AGRP should itself be decomposed into two AGR projections, one hosting the verbal agreement morphology, another one hosting the subject clitic. Shlonsky (1992) argues that following the decomposition of IP into AGRP and TP, CP should also be reinterpreted in terms of two projections: CP and an AGRP specific to the CP domain. His proposal would be able to account for the agreeing complementizers found in West Flemish, a dialect of Dutch, and which we discussed in chapter 2, section 4. Haegeman (1993) proposes that there should be a number of head initial functional projections dominating AGRP in West Flemish. The list above is by no means intended to be exhaustive: various other authors have discussed the role of functional heads in the syntax of clauses. In section 5 we turn to the relevance of functional projections for the analysis of NPs.

4   Head Movement and the ECP

So far we have argued for the need to postulate a number of functional projections which correspond to the inflectional morphology of V, specifically we propose that IP should be decomposed into AGRP and TP. In French, V moves to AGR via T. In root questions V moves to T, then to AGR, and then to C. V-movement to C is a stepwise head-to-head movement. This obligatory stepwise movement does not have to be stipulated, it follows from the theory developed so far. Consider the following data from English:

30a He could have done such a thing
30b Could you have done such a thing?
30c *Have you could done such a thing?

While we can move the highest auxiliary (*could*) to C, we cannot move a lower auxiliary to C, crossing *could*. Head movement takes place in strictly cyclic fashion. This constraint, usually referred to as the **Head Movement Constraint** (Travis, 1984), obviously calls for an explanation. Recall that we propose that movement leaves a trace and that traces are subject to the ECP (chapters 8 and 9). If we want to maintain this proposal in its full generality we must assume that V-movement, or head-to-head-movement in more general terms, also leaves a trace. On this assumption the S-structure representation of (30c) would have to be as in (30d) (we omit irrelevant structure for expository reasons):

30d　　$*[_{CP} [_C \text{Have}_i] [_{IP} \text{you} [_I \text{could}] [_{VP} t_i \text{done such a thing]]]}$?

The head movement constraint is not a primitive principle of the grammar, it derives from the ECP. The trace of *have* is separated from its antecedent by the intervening head *could*. *Could* c-commands the trace and it is itself c-commanded by *have*. *Could* will be a closer governor, hence by minimality it will block antecedent-government. This means that *have* under C cannot govern the VP-internal trace. The ECP forces head-to-head movement to apply stepwise: intervening heads cannot be skipped.

　　Schematically, head movement is forced to apply stepwise, and following the discussion above the pattern in (31a) with H representing an X^0 is grammatical, that in (31b) is ungrammatical:

31a　$[_{XP} \quad H_i \quad [_{YP} \quad t_i \quad [_{ZP} \quad t_i \quad [_{HP} \quad t_i]]]]$
31b　$*[_{XP} \quad H_i \quad [_{YP} \quad Y \quad [_{ZP} \quad t_i \quad [_{HP} \quad t_i]]]]$

In (31b) the intervening head Y blocks antecedent-government between H_i and t_i. Still, it has been argued in the literature that patterns that look like (31b) are attested. Rivero (1991) discusses a pattern which she refers to as **Long Head Movement**. She discusses, among others, the following Bulgarian examples (Rivero, 1991: 322–3):

32a　Petur e **procel** knigata.
　　　Peter has read book-the
　　　'Peter has read the book.'
32b　**Procel** e knigata.
　　　read has book-the
　　　'He has read the book.'
32c　**Procel** e knigata Petur/Procel e Petur knigata.

32d *E **procel** knigata.
32e *[**Procel** knigata] Petur e.
32f *[**Procel** knigata] e.

Rivero says:

> in Bulgarian main clauses with a lexical subject, the word order of a
> clause with a perfect construction is as in [32a], parallel to its English
> gloss ... NP1 Aux V NP2. However, the unmarked wordorder of a
> corresponding clause with a null subject is as in [32b], with (boldfaced)
> V preceding Aux ... The order Aux V NP2 is ungrammatical ... Also,
> regardless of the presence/absence of NP1, fronting of V and NP2 is
> disallowed, as shown in [32e–f]. (Rivero, 1991: 322–3)

Rivero proposes that (32b) is an example where the head V *procel* moves to
C, crossing the auxiliary *e*; in other words (32b) instantiates the pattern in
(31b). The long head movement patterns described by Rivero have given rise
to various analyses. We shall not go into the discussion here but refer the
reader to Rivero's own work (1991: 327) for an overview and references.
We return to the data briefly in chapter 12, section 3.1.

5 Functional Categories and the Projection of N: the DP Hypothesis

In chapter 2 we proposed that NPs have the structure (33):

33

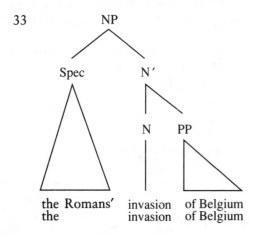

We treated the determiner *the* on a par with a GENITIVE phrase, *the Romans'*. Such an equation is rather unexpected, though. Determiners belong to a closed class, suggesting that they are non-lexical or functional elements, while GENITIVE NPs are projections of Ns, i.e. an open class. Also, determiners are typically one-word elements which one would tend to assimilate to heads, and the GENITIVE morphology is associated with a projection. That determiners are head-like functional elements is also suggested by the fact that in some languages they are realized as bound morphemes:

34a *Swedish*
 flicka -n
 girl det
 'the girl'

Similarly, in French we see that the determiner (*le, les*) sometimes is incorporated by a preposition. Incorporation is process in which one head is combined with another head to form a complex head. If P can incorporate Det, this suggests that Det is a head.

| 34b | à | la fille | | de | la fille |
| | to | the girl | | of | the girl |

| | à + le | garçon | **au** garçon | de + le | garçon | **du** garçon |
| | to the | boy | | of the | boy |

In [Spec, NP] is occupied either by functional heads such as determiners or by full phrases. This is obviously less than satisfactory.

Comparative work on the structure of NPs reveals that in many languages NP contains a functional head of the type AGR. First consider the following Hungarian data (Abney, 1987: 17):

35a az en kalap-om
 the I (NOM) hat-1sg
 'my hat'
35b a te kalap-od
 the you (NOM) hat-2sg
 'your hat'
35c a Peter kalap-ja
 the Peter (NOM) hat-3sg
 'Peter's hat'

Kalap ('hat') is a noun which agrees with its possessor, marking its person and number. The possessor phrase bears NOMINATIVE case, as would the subject of a sentence. If we maintain the idea that AGR assigns NOMINATIVE case then we conclude that the NPs in (35) contain an AGR which assigns NOMINATIVE. In Turkish (cf. Abney, 1987: 21) the possessor is assigned GENITIVE by the AGR morphology of the NP:

36a sen-in   el-in
    you-GEN   hand-2sg
    'your hand'
36b on-un   el-i
    he-GEN   hand-3sg
    'his hand'

Abney (1987) capitalizes on the symmetry between NPs and clausal projections. Clauses essentially reduce to projections of V (VP) dominated by functional projections, AGRP and TP. He proposes that in the same way that the clause is a VP dominated by the appropriate functional projections, the category which we have been referring to as NP should be seen as a projection of N dominated by a functional projection. In the Hungarian and Turkish examples we have found overt evidence for an AGRP within an NP. In English there is less direct evidence. Abney proposes that English NPs too contain an AGR head and that this head assigns GENITIVE case.

Recall that we assume that modal auxiliaries such as *will, can*, etc., are base-generated in AGR (cf. discussion in section 1.1). The question arises whether there are items which are base-generated in the AGR associated with the NP. Abney proposes that the determiners are base-generated under the nominal AGR. The following are some of the structures he proposes:

37a DP

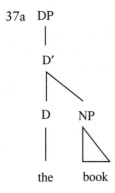

37b

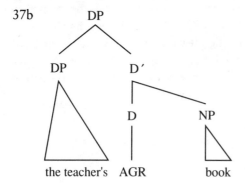

the teacher's   AGR   book

In (37a) D is realized as the determiner *the*, D selects an NP complement, here the bare N *book*. In (37b) the D-head of the DP is not realized by the determiner. D dominates the abstract nominal AGR which assigns GENI-TIVE to *the teacher*, in [Spec, DP].

Abney (1987) points out that certain realizations of D, the articles *the* and *a*, require the presence of an NP complement. Other instances of D do not require a complement. He proposes that the demonstrative *that* is a case in point: in (38a) it takes an NP complement, in (38b) it does not:

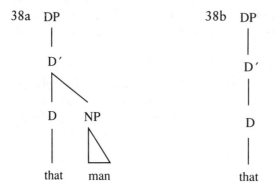

Following Postal's account for pronouns (1966) Abney proposes that pro-nouns be considered as Ds without complements as in (39).

39   DP

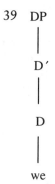

Abney's seminal proposal that noun projections be reinterpreted in terms of NPs selected by a functional head (D, AGR) has given rise to a lot of research. Further refinements of his analysis have been proposed. Ritter (1991), for instance, provides arguments for a functional projection NumP, for number phrase, in the Hebrew NP. Rouveret (1991) based on Welsh data, proposes that pronouns are NumPs. A lot of researchers are presently trying to determine the nature of the functional projections associated with NP.

It is clear that the line of argumentation discussed here will give rise to further research questions. Observe that functional projections are motivated either on the basis of data from movement or on the basis of overt morphology as displayed in some languages. The overt T and AGR morphology of the verb, for instance, has motivated the split INFL hypothesis. This analysis is then applied to languages such as English, in spite of the fact that there is very little overt inflectional morphology. One of the major developments in generative grammar over the past five years has been the identification of a large number of functional projections.

6   Extended Projections

The discussion in the current chapter focuses on a development in the theory where lexical categories such as VP and NP are associated with functional categories such as AGRP, TP on the one hand, and DP on the other. It is interesting to consider this development from a historical perspective. In traditional grammar and in earlier versions of generative grammar it had been proposed (Jackendoff (1977), for instance) that clauses were projections of V. In chapter 2 we postulate that a clause is a projection of C, which takes as its complement a projection of the functional head I, IP. In the present chapter we have refined this proposal. We will argue that in certain respects our analysis is not incompatible with the traditional idea that clauses are projections if V, after all.

We adopt the hypothesis proposed in chapter 6 and expanded in chapter 9 (section 4) that the thematic position of the subject is VP-internal, and that the subject NP moves to [Spec, AGRP] to be assigned NOMINATIVE.

40a   *D-structure*

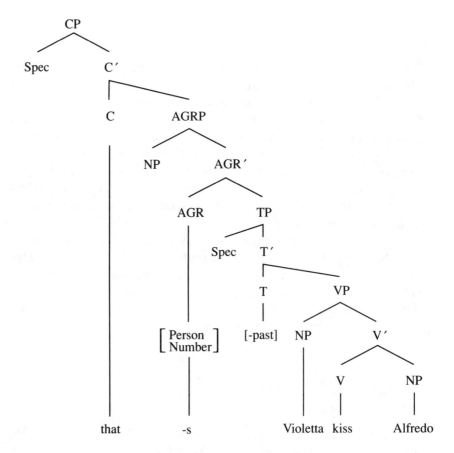

40b *S-structure*

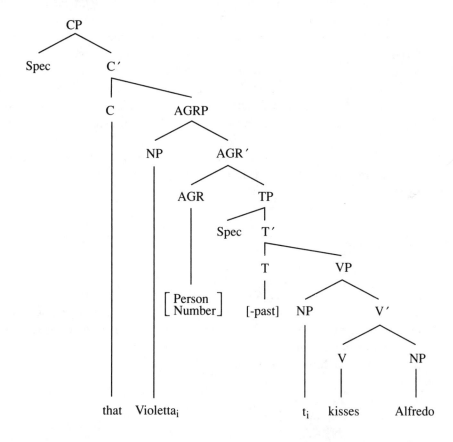

We assume that V has to associate with AGR and with Tense. AGR and T dominate the inflectional morphology associated with V, i.e. V endings. Tense morphology is typically associated with verbs, and the AGR morphology in (40) is the verb agreement for person and number. If we adopt the hypothesis (cf. chapter 6, section 5) that the thematic position of the subject is VP-internal, then the 'semantic' core of the clause is the VP: VP contains all the thematic information of the clause, i.e. the V, the predicate, which expresses the relevant state or activity, and the arguments, subject and objects, which are associated with the predicate. The functional elements in the clause do not contribute to the thematic information. TP serves to locate the event expressed by the VP with respect to time; AGR is responsible for the visibility of the external argument to which it assigns NOMINATIVE case. Similarly, the CP level does not modify the thematic information of the clause. Intuitively, the constituents of the VP, V and its arguments, encode the action described by the sentence 'Violetta's kissing Alfredo' or in the representation of formal logic K(va), and the functional projections TP, AGRP or CP do not modify the components of this action: the CP *that Violetta kisses Alfredo* describes, in some intuitive sense, the same action as the VP which it dominates, i.e. K(va). Abney (1987) suggests the following formulation: 'in the "passing on" of the descriptive content of their complements, functional heads contrast with thematic heads' (1987: 55). From a semantic point of view, then, we could say that clauses in some sense are projections of V, or rather they are **extended projections** of V, to use Grimshaw's (1991) terminology. By analogy, we can then say that the DP is an extended projection of NP.

Recall that we proposed that the lexical categories N and V could be analysed in terms of binary features, along the lines in (41):

41a N: [+N, −V]
41b V: [−N, +V]

Following Grimshaw we could propose that the categorial features of lexical heads also contain the functional feature value [F0], where F0 means that the projection is not functional. Functional heads would be associated with a specific functional value. T, for instance could be given the value [F1], AGR [F2]. Thus (41) could be extended to the following.

42 V   [−N, +V, F0]
    T   [−N, +V, F1]
    AGR   [−N, +V, F2]
    N   [+N, −V, F0]
    D   [+N, −V, F1]

Based on (42), VP is a projection of the features matrix [−N, +V, F0], the clause is a projection of AGR, i.e. of [−N, +V, F2]. VP and AGRP share the categorial features [−N, +V] and they only differ in the value of the functional feature: VP has the value 0, AGRP has the value 2. Grimshaw's work captures the intuition, also discussed by Abney (1987), that at some level clauses are indeed projections of V, though augmented with the matching functional projections. One question that remains to be debated is the relation between CP and AGRP. Grimshaw (1991) and Abney (1987) suggest that CP is an extended projection of V, Rizzi (1990b), on the other hand, suggest that the CP level is categorially distinct from IP, i.e. AGRP and TP in our new terms.

7   V-movement in the Minimalist Program

7.1   *The Minimalist Program: a Sketch*

In this book we develop an approach to generative syntax which is referrred to as the Principles and Parameters framework; within that approach we elaborate the core concepts of what is usually referred to as Government and Binding Theory. Still within the Principles and Parameters framework, Chomsky (1992) has been developing a different approach referred to as the **Minimalist Program**. It is not possible, at this stage, to provide a complete introduction to this programme, which is still being elaborated. The purpose of the present section is not to discuss the Minimalist Program in full. Rather we will illustrate a few of its concepts. We will give a comparison of the treatment of verb movement in the Minimalist Program with the Government and Binding approach sketched above.

Chomsky (1992) proposes that linguistic structure links two levels of representation, LF and PF. Linguistic structure mediates between LF and PF. The linguistic system generates abstract structures which will at some point receive an overt form, i.e. they will be **spelt out**. These abstract structures replace the traditional D-structure and S-structure levels. The **spell-out** level corresponds roughly[10] to S-structure. **Spell out** leads to the PF representation. Syntactic structures are also interpreted, i.e. they are assigned a semantic representation, corresponding to the level of LF. (43) represents the organization of the grammar in the Minimalist Program. In order to bring out the parallels with the theory developed in this book we choose a representation that is as close as possible to the T-model we have been developing.

---

[10]   The reader should be aware that the equation of S-structure and spell-out is done for expository reasons. The conception of the Minimalist Program is quite distinct from the grammar developed in this book, hence any equations are by definition inadequate.

43   Structural representations

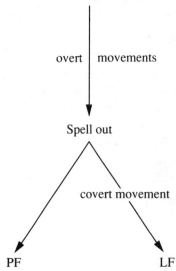

The Minimalist Program is **economy-driven**. The link between PF and LF has to be established as economically as possible. Economy, in this system, is instantiated in a number of respects. We focus on just a few.

One instantiation of the Economy Principle is that movement should only take place when necessary; this is sometimes referred to as **movement as a last resort**. This means that there should be no optional movement in the grammar. A consequence which will clearly need to be verified.[11] Recall from the

11   Examples of observed optionality come to mind. Recall that in French the non-finite lexical verb apparently optionally moves across adverbs such as *souvent*:

(ia)   Souvent manger du chocolat, c'est mauvais.
       often eat of chocolate, it is bad
       'It is bad to eat chocolate often.'
(ib)   Manger souvent du chocolat, c'est mauvais.

Another instance of apparently optional movement is what is often referred to as scrambling: the leftward movement of the object in German (cf. chapter 3, section 4, and also chapter 8 exercise 7):

(iia) dass Maria gestern diesen Roman gekauft hat.
       that Mary yesterday this novel bought has
(iib) dass Maria diesen Roman gestern gekauft hat.

(Cf. Bennis and Hoekstra (1984), Frank, Lee and Rambow (1992), Grewendorf and Sternefeld (1989), de Haan (1979), Haegeman (1992), Koster (1978a), Stechow and Sternefeld (1988: 452–77), Uszkoreit 1987: (151–60).)

discussion in this book that we assume that movement may be overt, 'in the syntax' or covert, 'at LF'. In the Minimalist Program the distinction between overt syntactic movement and covert movement is maintained. It is worth drawing attention to the distinction between the two types of movement once more. Movement which takes place before the spell-out point, i.e. at S-structure in the Government and Binding model, is overt; movement which occurs after spell-out, i.e. at LF, out is non-overt. The latter type of movement is input to the semantic representation (LF) of the sentence only, it has no bearing on the spelt out form. Chomsky proposes that overt movement is a more costly operation than covert movement. For reasons of economy, then, covert movement is preferred, or to put it differently: movement is delayed as late as possible (**Procrastinate**).

This brief and partial outline obviously only gives a small fragment of the proposals of the Minimalist Program but it will enable us to illustrate its application with respect to the topic of V-movement in French and English discussed in this chapter.

7.2 V-movement in the Minimalist Program

Recall that in the discussion developed in this book verbs are base-generated as stems under the lexical heads, and their inflectional morphology, person, number and tense endings, is base-generated separately under inflectional heads. French (44a) roughly has the D-structure (44b); English (45a) has the rough D-structure (45b). We assume now that the thematic position of the subject NP is VP internal:

44a Violetta embrassait Alfredo.
    Violetta kissed Alfredo
44b [$_{AGRP}$ [$_{AGR}$ -t] [$_{TP}$ [$_T$ -ai] [$_{VP}$ Violetta embrass Alfredo]]].

45a Violetta kissed Alfredo
45b [$_{AGRP}$ [$_{AGR}$ -∅] [$_{TP}$ [$_T$ -ed] [$_{VP}$ Violetta kiss Alfredo]]].

Finally consider the variation in word-order between (iiia) and (iiib):

(iiia) Jean mange du chocolat tous les jours.
       Jean eats chocolate all the days
       'Jean eats chocolate every day.'
(iiib) Jean mange tous les jours du chocolat.

We do not go into the issue of observed optionality here.

Following Pollock (1989) we proposed that in French finite clauses V moves to AGR via T, picking up the inflectional endings and giving rise to the structure in (44c):

44c   [$_{AGRP}$ Violetta$_j$ [$_{AGR}$ [$_T$ [$_V$ embrass]ai]t] [$_{TP}$ [$_T$ t] [$_{VP}$ t$_j$ t Alfredo]]].

In English, lexical verbs do not leave the VP. We propose that the inflectional endings AGR and T lower on to the V:

45c   [$_{AGRP}$ Violetta$_j$ [$_{AGR}$ t][$_{TP}$ [$_T$ t]   [$_{VP}$ t$_j$ kissed Alfredo].

This analysis raises the question of what happens to the traces under AGR and T. We shall not go into this issue here. For two proposals the reader is referred to Chomsky (1991) and to Rizzi (1990a).

In the Minimalist Program Chomsky (1992) adopts the split INFL clause structure which we have been developing in this chapter: clauses are extended projections of VP, VP contains the thematic material, and VP is dominated by related functional projections TP and AGRP.[12] He also proposes that verbs are base-generated *with* their inflectional endings. The functional heads AGR and T do not dominate inflectional morphology, they dominate bundles of abstract features. These features have to be eliminated in the course of the derivation. Chomsky's idea is that the morphology which is associated with the V-stem has to be **checked** by the abstract features (AGR, T). This feature-checking is a matching of the features and is done by adjoining the inflected V to the relevant functional head.[13] The feature-checking will eliminate the abstract features. Chomsky continues to assume that verbal AGR may be weak or strong. Strong AGR is **visible** at PF, weak AGR is not. Chomsky proposes that because strong features are visible at PF they have to be eliminated before PF, i.e. before spell-out. In other words: the feature-checking by adjoining V to AGR must take place before spell-out. If strong features are spelt out this leads to ungrammaticality. In Minimalist terminology: 'the derivation **crashes**'.

[12]   We omit discussion of the functional projection of object AGR (AGR$_o$P) as discussed in Chomsky (1991) and also Belletti (1990).

[13]   The same type of analysis also applies to case morphology. The idea is that NPs (or DPs, cf. the discussion above) are base-generated with their case morphology and that the case morphology is then checked by the case assigner. Moreover, in contrast with the earlier versions of the Government and Binding framework, the Minimalist Program proposes that all case is checked under specifier–head agreement. We do not go into this modification here.

Consider examples (44a) and (45a). In the new framework (44a) has the structure (46a) and (45a) has structure (47a).[14] We have used bold face for strong AGR. The abstract AGR features are represented as Fm.

46a [$_{AGRP}$ [$_{AGR}$ **Fm**]   [$_{TP}$ [$_T$ Fn] [$_{VP}$ Violetta embrass**ait** Alfredo]]].

47a [$_{AGRP}$ [$_{AGR}$ **Fm**]   [$_{TP}$ [$_T$ Fn] [$_{VP}$ Violetta kissed Alfredo]]].

The verbal AGR in French is strong; unless it is eliminated it will be visible at PF. In order to eliminate the strong AGR *embrassait* has to adjoin to **AGR**. When **AGR** has checked the agreement morphology on V it disappears.

Recall that two options are possible: overt movement, movement before spell-out, or covert movement, movement after spell out. If V-movement in French was postponed to the level of LF, i.e. if it were covert, the strong verbal AGR would remain unchecked at PF. If strong verbal **AGR** is left unchecked it is not eliminated, it remains visible and the sentence will be ungrammatical. The verb *embrassait* is forced to move: **AGR** will check the agreement morphology, strong verbal AGR will then be eliminated:

46b [$_{AGRP}$ Violetta$_j$ [$_{AGR}$[$_T$ [$_V$ embrass]ai]t]   [$_{TP}$ [$_T$ -t] [$_{VP}$ t$_j$ t Alfredo]]].

Now let us turn to English. The AGR morphology on *kissed* also has to be checked against abstract AGR features. Like Pollock (1989) Chomsky assumes that AGR is weak in English. Weak AGR is not visible at PF, even when it is unchecked. In other words the inflected verb does not have to get its features checked by moving to AGR before spell out. Since the verb need not move before spell-out it will not move before spell-out: by the Economy Principle, particularly Procrastinate, movement will be delayed to the post-spell-out level, i.e. roughly to LF in our standard terminology. Note in passing that the NP *Violetta* moves to the canonical subject position for case reasons.

47b [$_{AGRP}$ Violetta$_j$ [$_{AGR}$ Fm] [$_{TP}$ [$_T$ Fn] [$_{VP}$ t$_j$ kissed Alfredo]]].

Kissed will move to AGR to check its features after spell-out, i.e. to derive the level which we refer to as LF.

---

[14] For expository reasons we adopt a representation which is parallel to that proposed in the Government and Binding approach. In fact, in the Minimalist framework syntactic structures are built up step by step, starting from the lexical projection and extending the projection upward by means of functional projections. We cannot go into this issue here.

47c   [$_{AGRP}$ Violetta$_j$ [$_{AGR}$ [$_T$ kissed$_i$]] [$_{TP}$ [$_T$ t$_i$]   [$_{VP}$ t$_j$ t$_i$ Alfredo]]].

Obviously the very brief discussion above does in no way do justice to the Minimalist Program. At this point in time, the Minimalist Program is a research programme and it would not be possible to elaborate it in the same way that we have elaborated the Government and Binding framework in this book. However, observe that, in spite of considerable differences, many of the concepts developed in this book carry over to the Minimalist Program. The challenge for the Minimalist Program will be that of integrating the results reached by research in the Government and Binding Program over the past ten years. In the above discussion we have illustrated this point with respect to V-movement.

8   Summary

This chapter focuses on the role of functional projections. First we elaborate the structure of IP. Following Pollock (1989) we propose that IP should be decomposed into two functional projections: AGRP and TP:

1

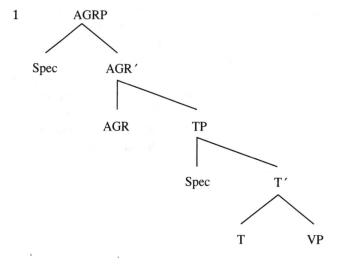

The empirical basis for this proposal is the comparative study of V-movement in French and English.

The clause is reinterpreted as an **extended projection** of V: the thematic information of the clause is contained in the projection of the lexical head V, VP is expanded by the matching functional categories (AGRP and TP). Following work by Abney (1987) it is proposed that what is usually referred to as NP is an extended projection of NP: NP is reinterpreted as DP, i.e. a projection of the functional head D which selects an NP complement:

2

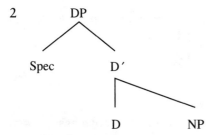

In our discussion of V-movement we also consider the Head Movement Constraint which bans movement of a head X across another head Y:

3   **The Head Movement Constraint (HMC)**
   * X^0_i Y^0 t_i

and we show how this constraint derives from the ECP. Exceptions to (3) are referred to as **Long Head Movement**.

9   Exercises

Exercise 1

Consider the following sentences. How can they be interpreted in the light of the discussion of verb movement in this chapter?

1a   *My friends love all Mary.
1b   Mes amis aiment tous Marie.
1c   My friends all love Mary.
1d   *Mes amis tous aiment Marie.
   (Pollock, 1989: 367)

2a   On imagine mal les députés tous démissionner en même temps.
     one imagines badly the representatives all resign at the same
         time
     'It is hard to imagine the representatives all resigning at the same
         time.'
2b   J'ai vu mes étudiants tous sortir en même temps de la salle.
     I have seen my students all leave at the same time from the room
     'I have seen my students all leave the room at the same time.'

For the distribution of quantifiers such as *all* and *tous* the reader should
bear in mind the discussion in chapter 6, section 5.

Exercise 2

In chapter 3 we discuss the Adjacency Constraint on case assignment.
We might wish to appeal to this constraint to exclude examples like (1):

1a   *John eats always chocolate.
1b   *The children eat all chocolate.

On the other hand, as mentioned in chapter 3, data such as (2) at
first sight seem problematic for the Adjacency Constraint on case
assignment:

2a   Jean mange toujours du chocolat.
     Jean eats always chocolate
2b   Les enfants mangent tous du chocolat.
     the children eat all chocolate
     'The children all eat chocolate.'

Discuss the sentences in (1) and (2) in the light of the analysis of V-
movement proposed in this chapter.

Exercise 3

As the reader will remember from the Introduction, one of the important
goals of linguistic theory in the generative tradition is to explain language

acquisition. A lot of recent research has been based on data from child language acquisition. One fairly popular proposal is that the so-called telegraphic speech of young children as illustrated in (1) reflects a stage where the child's grammar lacks functional projections: i.e. clauses would be VPs (cf. Lebeaux, 1989; Radford, 1990).

1a No I see truck.
    'I don't see the truck.'
1b Pas attraper papillon.
    not catch butterfly
    'I can't catch the butterfly.'
    (data from Deprez and Pierce, 1993)

The following data from the acquisition of French provide counter-evidence for this claim. Discuss why.

2a Pas manger la poupée.
    not eat the doll
2b Pas casser.
    not break
2c Pas attraper papillon.
    not catch butterfly
2d Pas rouler en vélo.
    not roll on bike

3a Veux pas lolo.
    want not milk
3b Marche pas.
    works not
3c Me plaît pas monsieur là.
    me pleases not man there
3d Ça tourne pas.
    that turns not
3e Elle roule pas.
    it doesn't roll
    (data from Deprez and Pierce, 1993: 40)

12   Relativized Minimality

Contents

Introduction and Overview

This chapter focuses on locality in syntax. The starting point is the notion minimality as developed in the *Barriers* tradition. According to the minimality condition (chapter 10) an intervening head such as the complementizer *that* blocks government by a head and it also blocks (antecedent-)government by a maximal projection. This notion of minimality is referred to as rigid minimality. Rizzi (1990a) develops an alternative framework in which minimality is relativized with respect to the type of governor: antecedent-government from X to Y can only be blocked by an intervening Z which is of the same type as X, i.e. an intervening A'-specifier blocks government by an A'-antecedent, an intervening head blocks government by a head, etc. This chapter offers an outline of the **Relativized Minimality** model.

The Relativized Minimality framework has consequences for the definition of the ECP. In this framework, the ECP is a formal licensing condition which imposes that a non-pronominal empty category, i.e. a trace, must be head-governed. Like the pronominal non-overt categories, *pro* and PRO, traces must also be identified. Traces are identified by their antecedents. Two strategies connect the trace to its antecedent: binding or government. Binding depends on coindexation, which itself is restricted to referential arguments. Selected constituents which are non-referential and adjuncts have to be related to their traces by (antecedent-)government.

Having outlined the Relativized Minimality model we turn to some further problems which it raises. These concern the Long Head Movement phenomena and the definition of A-positions and of A'-positions.

This chapter is based essentially on Rizzi's own work (1990a, 1992b).[1] Section 1 gives an overview of locality relations in syntax and introduces the notion of Relativized Minimality. Section 2 focuses on the reformulation of the ECP. Section 3 considers further ramifications of the theory developed here and outlines some general problems for future research.

---

[1] Frampton (1991) offers an excellent review of Rizzi's book (1990a). This author raises a number of problems and suggestions for revision of this particular theory. Browning (1989) also offers some further discussion of the Relativized Minimality framework.

   Some authors (Kiss, 1993; Kroch, 1989; Szabolsci and Zwarts, 1991) reinterpret Rizzi's analysis in terms of a semantic account. Rizzi (1992b) offers arguments against a purely semantic treatment.

1 Locality in Syntax: Some Examples

1.1 Head Government and Locality

In the course of the discussion we have often appealed to locality relations to restrict the domain of application of certain operations. Locality was used, for instance, in chapter 11, to restrict head-to-head movement.

1a You could have done such a thing.
1b Could you have done such a thing?
1c *Have you could done such a thing?

Recall from chapter 11 (discussion of examples (30)) that we can move the highest auxiliary (*could*) to C; we cannot move a lower auxiliary such as *have* to C, crossing *could*. The S-structure representation of the ungrammatical (1c) would have to be as in (1d) (we omit irrelevant structure for expository reasons):

1d *$[_{CP} [_C \text{Have}_i] [_{IP} \text{you} [_I \text{could}] [_{VP} t_i \text{ done such a thing}]]]$?

In chapter 11 the ungrammaticality of (1d) was explained in terms of the ECP. Like all other traces, the trace of the moved auxiliary, t_i, is subject to the ECP. In (1d) the antecedent-government relation between *have* and its trace is blocked by the intervention of *could*. The ECP forces head-to-head movement to apply stepwise: intervening heads cannot be skipped. This is represented schematically in (2a) with H representing an X^0; the pattern in (2b) where one head crosses another head is ungrammatical:

2a $[_{XP} \quad H_i \quad [_{YP} \quad t_i \quad [_{ZP} \quad t_i \quad [_{HP} \quad t_i]]]]$

2b $[_{XP} \quad H_i \quad [_{YP} \quad Y \quad [_{ZP} \quad t_i \quad [_{HP} \quad t_i]]]]$

From the discussion we conclude that head movement is strictly local: a head must move to the first c-commanding head position, it cannot skip a c-commanding head to move to a higher head. In tree diagram format we can summarize the patterns in (2a) and (2b) as in (2c):

2c

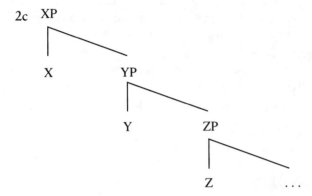

Movement from Z to X will pass through the intervening head position, Y.[2] The pattern in (2c) is reminiscent of another pattern discussed in chapter 3. Consider a sentence in which V takes a PP complement:

3

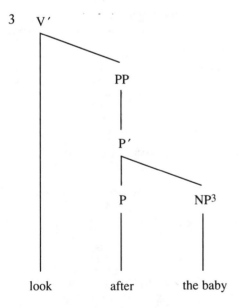

---

[2] Observe that the stepwise movement of heads is predicted also in the Minimalist framework (cf. chapter 11, section 7). In this framework economy forces the moved head to make the **shortest move**.

[3] We continue to use the label NP. Recall from chapter 11 that DP might be more accurate.

NP is selected by P and has to be case-marked. In chapter 3, section 2.1.2, we established that it is P that case-marks its object and not V, even when V itself also is a case-marker. Configurations like that in (3) highlight the role of minimality in determining government relations: by minimality the closest potential governor of a constituent will block government from a higher governor. Minimality reduces potential ambiguity with respect to government relations: for each governed element there will be one governor. In more abstract terms the configuration in (3) can be reduced to the pattern in (2c), i.e. the case-assignment relation is established between P and its complement and not between the higher head V and the NP complement of P.

Minimality effects for head government are also illustrated in (4):

4a   *John tried [$_{CP}$ C^0 [$_{AGRP}$ Bill to win]].
       (Rizzi, 1990a: 11)
4b   John tried [$_{CP}$ C^0 [$_{AGRP}$ PRO to win]].

(4a) is ungrammatical; *tried* cannot case-mark the subject of the non-finite clause *Bill*, because there is an intervening head, C^0. Conversely, (4b) is grammatical: the intervening C^0 protects PRO, the subject of the lower clause, from government by *tried* (cf. chapter 5 for the PRO theorem). C^0 has a blocking effect even though it is not itself an actual governor; what is crucial is the intervention of a *potential* governor. Any head is a potential governor, while only some heads are actual governors.

(5) captures the essence of the minimality idea:

5   ...X...Z...Y...

X cannot govern Y if there is a closer potential governor for Y (Rizzi, 1990a: 1).

1.2   A-movement

Consider the following example.

6a   [$_{AGRP1}$ John$_i$ seems [$_{AGRP2}$ t''$_i$ to be likely [$_{AGRP3}$ t'$_i$ to [$_{VP}$ t$_i$ win]]]].

In (6a) *John* is the thematic subject of *win*. The NP moves to a case position, in (6a) this will be the subject position of the matrix clause. Assuming that the thematic subject position is VP-internal (cf. discussion in chapter 6, section 5, and also in chapter 9, section 4.2), *John* moves by successive cyclic movement via the intermediate subject positions to the subject position of the matrix clause. The chain $< John_i, t''_i, t'_i, t_i>$ is licit (cf. the definition of chains in chapter 6, section 4.6, (105)): it contains one argument, it is visible, since it contains a case position, [Spec, AGRP1], and can be theta-marked by *win*. The trace in the base position of *John* and the intermediate traces in [Spec, AGRP3] and in [Spec, AGRP2] all satisfy the empty category principle (ECP), introduced in chapter 8 and repeated here for the reader's convenience in (7):

7   **ECP**
    Traces must be properly governed.
7a A properly governs B if and only if A theta-governs B or A antecedent-governs B.
7b A theta-governs B if and only if A governs B and A theta-marks B.
7c A antecedent-governs B if and only if A governs B and A is coindexed with B.

Note in passing that (7) contains a disjunction (7a): proper government is achieved either by theta-government or by antecedent-government.

(6b), corresponding to example (79a) of chapter 7, section 6.3.4, is an example of long-distance raising or **super-raising**: the NP *John* does not raise to the subject position of the immediately dominating clause, AGRP2, but it raises one clause higher, i.e. to [Spec, AGRP1]:

6b *[$_{AGRP1}$ [John$_i$ seems [$_{CP2}$ that [$_{AGRP2}$ it is likely [$_{AGRP3}$ t'_i to [$_{VP}$ t_i win]]]]]]

Super-raising gives rise to ungrammaticality. Two elements bear on this issue. In (6b) t'_i, the intermediate trace in [Spec, AGRP3], violates Principle A of the binding theory: t'_i is not bound in its governing category, AGRP2:[4] the potential antecedent *John* is too far removed (cf. chapter 7, section 6.3.4).

The distance between *John* and the intermediate trace t'_i also leads to an ECP violation. Traces have to be properly governed. Proper government is achieved by theta-government or by antecedent-government (7a). Being a subject trace, t_i cannot be theta-governed, and lacking a local binder, t_i also fails to be antecedent-governed: the coindexed antecedent *John* does

---

[4] AGRP2 is the governing category since it contains (i) the trace t_i in [Spec, AGRP3], (ii) a governor, the A *likely*, and (iii) a subject, *it* in [Spec, AGRP2].

c-command the trace but it is too far away to govern it. As shown by (6a), (6b) can be rescued by eliminating the intervening NP *it*.[5] Consider (6c):

6c   *[$_{AGRP1}$ John$_i$ seems [$_{CP2}$ that [$_{AGRP2}$ it is believed t$_i$ by everyone]]].

As discussed in chapter 7, section 6.3.4, example (79b), (6c) is like (6b) in that it also violates the binding requirement on NP-traces. In (6c) the trace of *John*, t_i, is not bound in its governing category, AGRP2. (6c) is similar to (6b). The sentence can again be saved by eliminating the intervening *it*:

6d   [$_{AGRP1}$ John$_i$ seems [$_{AGRP2}$ t$'_i$ to be believed t$_i$ by everyone]].

Recall that we interpreted (6b) as an ECP violation. By the disjunctive formulation of the ECP in (7a), though, we cannot assimilate the ungrammaticality of (6c) to an ECP violation. In this example the trace of *John* is in [NP, V′]. It is head-governed by *believed*, and it is also theta-governed by *believed*. *John* is selected by *believed*. The binding theory violation in (6b) reduces to an ECP violation, that in (6c) does not. We return to this point below.

When we compare the grammatical (6a) and (6d) to their respective ungrammatical counterparts (6b) and (6c) the following patterns emerge:

8a   John$_i$ [$_{AGRP}$ t$_i$ [$_{AGRP}$ t$_i$ (6a)
8b   *John$_i$ [$_{AGRP}$ NP   [$_{AGRP}$ t$_i$ (6b)
8c   John$_i$ [$_{AGRP}$ t$_i$ t$_i$ (6d)
8d   *John$_i$ [$_{AGRP}$ NP   t$_i$ (6c)

Or more schematically again:

8e   *NP$_i$ XP   t$_i$

In (8b) and (8d) the problem is that there is an NP, *it* in (6b) and (6c), intervening between *John* and its trace. This NP occupies the subject position of the intermediate AGRP, an A-position which itself could host an antecedent for the trace, as seen in (8a) and (8c). The intervening NP in (8b) and (8d)

---

[5]   Rizzi (1986c: 95, fn. 18) also shows that the chain in (6b) or (6c) is ill formed. The reader is referred to his discussion.

is thus a potential antecedent; it is the cause of the ungrammaticality because it blocks antecedent-government.

The parallelism between (6b) and (6c) suggests that a unified analysis is desirable: in our approach so far (6b) violates the binding theory (Principle A), a violation which can be related to the ECP, and (6c) violates the binding theory, but satisfies the disjunctive ECP in (7). In later sections we develop a unified treatment for (6b) and (6c).

It is worth pointing out here that intervening heads do not cause a problem for antecedent-government by XPs. In (6a), for instance the trace in the subject position of the lowest AGRP is antecedent-governed in spite of the fact that it is separated from its antecedent by the head *seem*. In (6d) the intervening head *believed* clearly governs the trace in [NP, V'] but it does not create a block for antecedent-government of that trace. We conclude that antecedent-government of an NP trace is blocked by intervening antecedents, not by intervening heads.[6]

1.3 Wh-*movement of Adjuncts*

Finally consider the pair of sentences in (9):

9a [$_{CP1}$ How do [$_{AGPRP1}$ you think [$_{CP2}$ that [$_{AGRP2}$ John could solve this problem t]]]]?

9b *[$_{CP1}$ How do [$_{AGRP1}$ you wonder [$_{CP2}$ what [$_{AGRP2}$ John could solve t]]]]?

In (9a) *how* is extracted from the lower clause and moves to the matrix [Spec, CP1]. By adjunctions to intermediate projections we can insure that its trace is properly governed: each intermediate trace will antecedent-govern the next trace down:

---

[6] Our discussion will depart from the analysis of A-chains proposed in chapter 10 (section 5).

Recall the discussion of chain formation in (104d), repeated here as (i), in chapter 6, section 4.6. The chain between *Gianni*$_i$ and t_i cannot skip the intervening reflexive *si*$_i$. Schematically the pattern found in (i) is as in (ii): if a potential antecedent Z intervenes between X$_i$ and t_i, Z will have to become part of the chain. The pattern in (ii) is similar to (8e) in the text. At this point, it is not obvious how (ii) could be derived from (8e), though.

(i) *Gianni$_i$ si$_i$ è stato affidato t$_i$
    Gianni to himself is been entrusted

(ii) X$_i$ Z$_i$ t$_i$

10a $[_{CP1}$ How$_i$ do $[_{AGRP1}$ you $[_{VP1}$ t'''_i think $[_{CP2}$ t''_i that $[_{AGRP2}$ John could $[_{VP2}$ t'_i $[_{VP2}$ solve this problem $t_i]]]]]]]$?

(9b) is ungrammatical: in its representation (10b) t''_i is not properly governed: the next trace up, t'''_i will not be able to antecedent-govern it, being separated from t''_i by the intervening barrier, CP2.[7]

10b *$[_{CP1}$ How$_i$ do $[_{AGRP1}$ you $[_{VP1}$ t'''_i $[_{VP1}$ wonder $[_{CP2}$ what$_j$ C^0 $[_{AGRP2}$ John could $[_{VP2}$ t''_i $[_{VP2}$ t'_j $[_{VP2}$ t'_i solve t_j $t_i]]]]]]]]]]$

Again we can look at the patterns in (10) in a slightly more abstract way and reduce them to the pattern which had already emerged from the discussion in sections 1.1 and 1.2. (11) summarizes the patterns in (10).

11a How$_i$ $[_{VP}$ t_i $[_{CP}$ t_i $[_{VP}$ t_i
11b *How$_i$ $[_{VP}$ t_i $[_{CP}$ XP $[_{VP}$ t_i

In (11a) the traces are antecedent-governed; the pattern (11b) is ungrammatical because of the intervention of an XP (*what* in (10b)) in an A'-position: the intervening element is a potential antecedent. Schematically, the configuration in (11b) is represented in (11c):

11c *XP$_i$ YP t_i

Observe that not all intervening maximal projections block antecedent-government. In (10a) for instance *you* intervenes between *how*$_i$ and t'''_i, *John* intervenes between t''_i and t'_i, but these intervening maximal projections do not block the antecedent-government relation. The question is, of course, why some XPs block the relation and others do not do so. One line to pursue is that in (10a) the intervening NPs *you* and *John* occupy A-positions, they are not potential antecedents for the trace of *how*, a *wh*-trace which should

---

[7] If *how* is base-generated VP-internally, it first adjoins to VP2, as does *what*. Next *how* crosses AGRP2 (i.e. IP), which is a BC though not a barrier, and CP2 which becomes a barrier by inheritance. Alternatively, we base-generate *how* in a VP-adjoined position, but it will still have to cross CP2, a barrier. The reader may object that we did not discuss adjunction structures for manner adjuncts in our discussion of phrase structure in chapter 2. This omission was done for expository reasons: it was felt that at that point in the discussion the introduction of adjunction structures would have complicated the picture unnecessarily.

have its antecedent in an A′-position. In (11c) YP does block the relevant relation between XP and its trace if YP is of the same kind as XP and can thus antecedent-govern it.

1.4 Summary: Locality Relations and Interventions

In the preceding sections we have considered three phenomena which, though not identical, seem to follow the same pattern.

12   . . . X . . . Z . . . Y . . .

In section 1.1 we have seen that for X a head, head government from X to Y is blocked by an intervening Z, for Z a head. In section 1.2 we have seen that antecedent-government from X, an NP in an A-position, to Y, its trace, is blocked by an intervening Z, for Z an NP in an A-position. In section 1.3 we have seen that antecedent-government from X, an adjunct in an A′-position, [Spec, CP], to Y, its trace, is blocked by an intervening Z, for Z an XP in an A′-position. The three cases, though reduced to the same pattern, cannot simply be collapsed. An intervening head, for instance, does not block antecedent-government, as illustrated in (13a):

13a   John seems [t to like it].

The intervention of the V *seems*, an X^0, does not interfere with the antecedent-government of *t* by *John*. Similarly in (13b) the intervention of an NP in an A-position cannot block antecedent-government of *t* by *how*. Nor does the intervention of the heads *solve* or *did* block antecedent-government.

13b   How did you solve the problem t?

The intuition behind (12) is clear. The blocking effect of an intervening governor is relative to the nature of the government relation involved: in (12) if Z is a potential governor of some kind for Y, it will only block government of the same kind from X. If Z is a potential head-governor, only head-government from X will be blocked. If Z is a potential antecedent-governor, only antecedent-government will be blocked (Rizzi, 1990a: 2). The hypothesis that blocking effects are not absolute, but are relative to the nature of the government relation is referred to as **Relativized Minimality,** in contrast with the **Rigid Minimality** adopted in *Barriers*. Rizzi formulates Relativized Minimality as follows:

14 **Relativized Minimality**
    X x-governs Y only if there is no Z such that
    (i) Z is a typical potential x-governor for Y;
    (ii) Z c-commands Y and Z does not c-command X.
    (Rizzi, 1990a: 7)

The notion 'a typical potential x-governor' captures the idea of relativizing minimality: an element which is a potential head-governor can block head-government, an element which is a potential antecedent for A-movement blocks antecedent-government from an A-position, and an element which is a potential antecedent for A'-movement will block antecedent-government from an A'-position.

1.5 *Further Illustrations*

1.5.1 NEGATION AND RELATIVIZED MINIMALITY

15a Why did they say that John was fired?
15b Why did they ask how John was fired?
15c Why did they not say that John was fired?

(15a) is ambiguous: *why* either bears on the matrix clause in which case it asks for the reason of them saying something, or it bears on the subordinate clause, and asks for the reason of John being fired. The latter reading is sometimes referred to in the literature as **long construal**. In either case, the trace of *why* will be antecedent-governed. We leave the reader to work this out. (15b) is grammatical but it has only one interpretation: *why* can question the motivation for them asking something, but long construal is no longer possible: *why* cannot question the reason for firing John. Under the long construal interpretation of *why*, (15b) would have to have the repre-sentation in (16a). We assume that *why* originates outside VP and we have omitted irrelevant structure, such as the traces of *John* and of *how*:

16a *$[_{CP1}$ Why did $[_{AGRP1}$ they $[_{VP1}$ t' $[_{VP1}$ ask $[_{CP2}$ how C^0 $[_{AGRP2}$ John was $[_{VP2}$ fired] t]]]]]]?

In (16a) *t*, the lowest trace of *why* has to be antecedent-governed by the VP-adjoined *t′*, but the trace, *t′*, is too far away. In the *Barriers* framework AGRP2 is a BC and CP2 will be a barrier by inheritance. In the Relativized Minimality framework the offending relation is represented schematically in (16b): *how* is a potential antecedent: it is a *wh*-phrase in [Spec, CP2] which intervenes between *why* and its trace. If we adopt VP adjunction then in fact *how* intervenes between *t′* and *t*.

16b *Why did [$_{IP1}$ they [$_{VP1}$ *t′* [$_{VP1}$ ask [$_{CP}$ how C^0 [$_{IP2}$ John was [$_{VP}$ fired] *t*]]]]]?
                       X   Z   Y

This example follows from the account sketched in section 1.4. Now let us turn to (15c). Again, and perhaps surprisingly so, *why* can only have scope over the matrix domain, it cannot question the reason for them not saying something, it can only question why John was fired. But in this case there is no intervening antecedent in the lower [Spec, CP2]. Based on the parallelism between (15b) and (15c) we would like to argue that the effect in (15c) can also be ascribed to the intervention of a potential antecedent, i.e. a constituent in an A′-position. What could this constituent be? The only element that differentiates the ambiguous (15a) from the unambiguous (15c) is *not*. Could this be the intervening Z? In chapter (11) we proposed that negative sentences contain a functional projection NegP, whose head Neg is non-overt in English and whose specifier is *not*.

17a

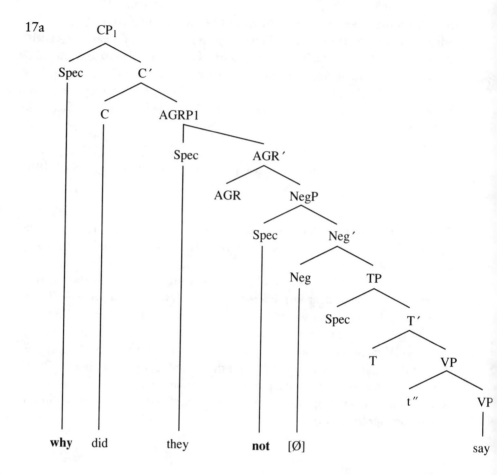

This means that *not* is a constituent in a specifier position. We assume that [Spec, NegP] is occupied by an operator: [Spec, NegP] is a scope position, hence an A′-position.[8] On the basis of these arguments we conclude that *not* is the Z which intervenes between *why* and its trace. *Not* blocks the antecedent-government relation between *why* and the VP-adjoined *t″*.

17b   *[CP1 Why did [AGRP1 they′ [NegP not [Neg] [VP t″ [VP say [CP2 t′ that [AGRP2
              X   Z   Y
       John was fired t]]]]]]]?

(15c) shows that the intervening potential antecedent may also be in its base position: by assumption, *not* is base-generated in [Spec, NegP] and functions

---

[8]   For some discussion of A and A′ positions cf. section 3.1.

as a block for antecedent-government. The same point is also clear from (15d), where the intervening A'-specifier is *whether*, by assumption base-generated in [Spec, CP]:

15d   *[$_{CP1}$ Why did [$_{AGRP1}$ they [$_{VP1}$ t' [$_{VP1}$ wonder [$_{CP2}$ whether [$_{AGRP2}$ John was fired t]]]]]]?

In (15d), as was the case in (15b) and (15c), the preposed *wh*-phrase *why* can only take scope over the matrix domain; long construal is not possible. *Whether* in [Spec, CP] is an A'-specifier and blocks antecedent-government between the VP-adjoined t' and t.[9]

15e   *[$_{CP1}$ Why did [$_{AGRP1}$ they [$_{VP1}$ t' [$_{VP1}$ wonder [$_{CP2}$ whether [$_{AGRP2}$ John was
          Y   X   Z
      fired t]]]]]]?

1.5.2 NON-REFERENTIAL COMPLEMENTS

In the following examples *wh*-movement affects a complement NP and again it gives rise to Relativized Minimality effects.

18a   What did they say he weighed last week?
      Apples.
      Sixty kilos.

---

[9]   At first glance, (ia) raises a problem for our approach:

(ia)   *[$_{CP1}$ Why do [$_{AGRP1}$ they wonder [$_{CP2}$ if [$_{AGRP2}$ John was fired t]]]]?

In (i) *why* cannot be extracted from the complement of *if*. Still, we have proposed that *if* is a head, C^0 (chapter 5). Thus at first glance, one would not expect *if* to intervene in the antecedent-government relation of *why*, an XP. Following recent proposals in the literature, though, we assume that *if* is associated with a non-overt interrogative operator in its specifier position (cf. also footnote 19). The non-overt WH operator would suffice to block antecedent-government (cf. Haegeman, in preparation).

(ib)   *[$_{CP1}$ Why do [$_{AGRP1}$ they [$_{VP}$ t' [$_{VP}$ wonder [$_{CP2}$ OP if [$_{AGRP2}$ John was fired
                                     X   Z
       t]]]]]]?
       Y

18b   What did they wonder whether he weighed last week?
      Apples.
      *Sixty kilos.
18c   What did they not say that he weighed last week?
      Apples.
      *Sixty kilos.

In (18a) *weigh* has two interpretations: it has an agentive reading in which
case the answer to (18a) could be 'Apples'; it also has a stative reading in
which case the answer could be 'Sixty kilos'. In the first interpretation the
complement of *weigh*, *what*, is a referential expression: it refers to the object
that is being weighed, the THEME, and the subject of *weigh* is the AGENT
of the action. In the second interpretation the complement of *weigh*, *what*,
is a MEASURE phrase selected by the verb *weigh*, but it does not have a
referent, and the subject of *weigh* is the THEME.

   In (18b), though, *weigh* can only have the agentive reading and *what* can
only be interpreted referentially. The non-referential reading of *what* does not
survive in this example. The difference between (18a) and (18b) is that in
(18b) the moved *wh*-phrase *what* is separated from its trace by an intervening
wh-phrase in the lower [Spec, CP]. Assuming VP-adjunction in order to void
barrierhood (18b) will be assigned the representation (19a):

19a   [$_{CP1}$ *What* did [$_{AGRP1}$ they [$_{VP1}$ t″ [$_{VP1}$ wonder [$_{CP}$ *whether* [$_{AGRP}$ he [$_{VP2}$ t′
      [$_{VP2}$ weighed t]] last week]]]]]]?

Whether blocks the relation between t″ and t′.
   If the intervening A¢-specifier is responsible for blocking one of the readings of *what* in (18b) then we predict that (18c) also has only one reading
since it contains an intervening A′-specifier that separates *what* from its trace:
not in [Spec, NegP]. Taking into account all the possibilities of VP-adjunction,
(18c) will be assigned the representation (19b). *Not* will block antecedent
government between *what* and t‴.

19b   [$_{CP1}$ *What* did [$_{AGRP1}$ they [$_{NegP}$ *not* [$_{VP1}$ t‴ [$_{VP1}$ say [$_{CP2}$ t″ that [$_{AGRP2}$ he
      [$_{VP2}$ t′ [$_{VP2}$ weighed t]] last week]]]]]]]]?

In (18c) *weigh* only has the agentive reading and *what* is referential.
   The extraction of a MEASURE phrase (*what*) gives rise to Relativized

Minimality effects similar to those associated with the extraction of adjuncts. Still, the MEASURE phrase associated with stative *weigh* cannot be simply considered an adjunct. The MEASURE phrase is selected, its presence is required by the verb; we assume that it is theta-marked. While the extraction of the MEASURE phrase associated with stative *weigh* gives rise to Relativized Minimality effects, intervening A'-specifiers do not affect extraction of the referential THEME NP argument associated with agentive *weigh*. Regardless of any intervening A'-specifiers, the examples in (20) are grammatical when *what* is referential and is assigned the THEME role by agentive *weigh*. There might be a slight degradation in (20b) due to a weak subjacency effect, but the structures are clearly not ungrammatical.

20a [$_{CP}$ What did [$_{AGRP}$ they say [$_{CP}$ that [$_{AGRP}$ he weighed t last week]]]]?

20b ?[$_{CP}$ What did [$_{AGRP}$ they wonder [$_{CP}$ whether [$_{AGRP}$ he weighed t last week]]]]?

20c [$_{CP}$ What did [$_{AGRP}$ they [$_{NegP}$ not say [$_{CP}$ that [$_{AGRP}$ he weighed t last week]]]]]?

Given that stative *weigh* selects the MEASURE phrase and that agentive *weigh* selects a THEME, it seems reasonable to say that both the MEASURE phrase and the THEME are theta-marked by *weigh*. The contrast between the two types of complements has to be established independently of theta-marking. Rizzi (1990a) suggests that the distinction to be made is that the THEME of agentive *weigh* is a referential NP, while the MEASURE phrase selected by stative *weigh* is non-referential.

In preceding sections we have first identified Relativized Minimality effects with adjunct extraction. Relativized Minimality effects are also observed with the extraction of non-referential complements. We return to this point extensively below. In the theory developed so far the asymmetry between referential complements and non-referential complements observed in this section is unexpected. The complement of *weigh* is selected, hence we assume it is theta-marked, no matter whether it has a referential or a non-referential reading. In our earlier discussion (cf. chapters 9 and 10) we assumed that theta-marked complements are gamma-marked at S-structure. In the examples in (19) the trace of *what* is theta-governed by the verb *weigh*, hence it would be assigned the feature [+γ] at S-structure. Intermediate traces are not necessary and can be deleted at LF. The theory so far offers us no way of distinguishing the referential reading of *what*, which is compatible with long extraction across intervening A'-specifiers, and the non-referential reading, which is incompatible with extraction across A'-specifiers.

1.5.3   IDIOM CHUNKS

The data in (21)–(23) confirm the asymmetry between referential and non-referential complements:

21a   What headway do you think you can make on this project?
21b   On which project do you think you can make headway?

22a   *What headway do you wonder whether you can make on this project?
22b   On which project do you wonder whether you can make headway?

23a   *What headway did they not say that they had made on this project?
23b   On which project did they not say that they had made some headway?

In all the sentences in (21)–(23) the lower clause contains the verb *make* used in the idiomatic expression *make headway on*. In this expression *what headway* is an **idiom chunk**, it is the nominal part of an idiom. This part of the idiom can be moved, witness (21a), but there are restrictions on its movement. The idiom chunk *what headway* cannot be moved across a *wh*-phrase in a scope position (22a), nor can it be moved across a negative operator in [Spec, NegP] (23a). One way of interpreting this is to say that the nominal part of the idiom, *what headway*, is non-referential. If this is true then we would predict the pattern in (22)–(23) since in this case *what headway* would behave like the non-referential selected constituents discussed in section 1.5.2.[10] Observe the sharp contrast with the extraction of the PP *on which project*, which contains the referential NP *which project*. Again extraction is possible and the intervening *wh*-phrase *whether* in [Spec, CP] in (22b) only produces a weak subjacency effect. The intervention of *not* has no effect on the extraction in (23b).

Rizzi (1990a) illustrates the contrast between nominal expressions which are parts of idioms and referential NPs also by means of data drawn from Italian (Rizzi 1990a: 80):

24a   Che libro pensi di poter dare a Gianni?
        'What book do you think you can give to Gianni?'
24b   Che credito pensi di poter dare a Gianni?

---

[10]   Chomsky (1981a: 37) distinguishes idiom chunks from arguments and proposes that the nominal parts of idioms are assigned a special, quasi-argumental theta role.

> (i) 'How much credit do you think you can give to Gianni?'
> (ii) 'What credit ('trust') do you think you can put in Gianni?'

24c Che libro non sai a chi dare?
    'Which book do you not know to whom to give?'

24d Che credito non sai a chi dare?

> (i) 'How much credit don't you know to whom to give?'
> (ii) *'What credit don't you know to whom to give?'

Italian *dare* ('give') is a ditransitive verb in (24a) and in (24c). The direct object *che libro* ('what book') is referential, it is the THEME. *Dare credito* is ambiguous. It may mean 'give financial credit to', and this reading would give a grammatical result in both (24b) and (24d). It also may mean 'trust'. In the latter interpretation *dare credito* is an idiomatic expression and *credito* is non-referential. In the latter reading (24b) is grammatical, but (24d) where the non-referential *che credito* has moved across a *wh*-phrase in the lower [Spec, CP], *a chi*, is ungrammatical.

1.6 Arguments

Let us briefly sum up the findings so far. On the basis of an analysis of various data we have formulated Relativized Minimality. In a structure like (25), where X is the antecedent of Y, a Z which c-commands Y and does not c-command X will prevent X from governing Y if Z is the same kind of governor as X.

25 X ... Z ... Y

We have seen the effect of this principle in several domains of application: head-government, A-movement and A'-movement. With respect to the latter type of movement, though, we have discovered a sharp asymmetry between referential arguments on the one hand and selected constituents which are non-referential (such as MEASURE phrases (1.5.2) and idiom chunks (1.5.3)) and adjuncts (1.5.1) on the other: while selected constituents which are non-referential and adjuncts are sensitive to Relativized Minimality effects, referential arguments which have been *wh*-moved are not, as illustrated also in (26):

26a Which woman did they think that he had met?
26b $[_{CP1}$ *Which woman$_i$* did they wonder $[_{CP2}$ *whether* he had met t_i]]?
26c $[_{CP1}$ *Which woman$_i$* did they *not* think $[_{CP2}$ t'_i that he had met t_i]]?

In preceding chapters we have seen that the argument/non-argument asymmetry usually reflects ECP effects. In the earlier discussion we also assimilated arguments with selected constituents. As already discussed in section 1.5.2 the asymmetry between referential selected constituents and non-referential ones does not follow from the theory we have been elaborating so far. In the next section we reformulate the ECP and we refine the notion of argument.

2   The ECP

2.1   Some Problems

In this section we turn to the formulation of the ECP. We consider three definitions: in (7) the ECP is formulated as a disjunction: one of two conditions has to be satisfied: theta-government or antecedent-government. This disjunctive formulation will be replaced by a conjunctive formulation of the ECP (35) where two conditions have to be satisfied: one is a formal licensing condition and the other is an identification requirement. The identification requirement itself will again be formulated as a disjunction, being satisfied either by theta government or by antecedent-government. Finally, in section 2.2.3.3, we will reduce the ECP to a formal licensing condition. The identification requirement on non-pronominal empty categories is independently required as an instantiation of the more general identification requirement on empty categories and can be satisfied by binding or by government.

2.1.1   A DISJUNCTIVE ECP: THETA GOVERNMENT OR ANTECEDENT-GOVERNMENT

In (7), repeated here as (27), we have formulated the ECP as follows:

27   **ECP** (i)
     Traces must be properly governed.
27a   A properly governs B if and only if A theta-governs B or A antecedent-governs B.
27b   A theta-governs B if and only if A governs B and A theta-marks B.
27c   A antecedent-governs B if and only if A governs B and A is coindexed with B.

As mentioned before, the formulation of the ECP which we have adopted so far contains a disjunction: according to (27a) a trace is properly governed

if it is either theta-governed or antecedent-governed. The ECP ((7) or (27))
enables us to account for the subject/object asymmetry in (28):

28a [Who do [you think [t′ that [Bill saw t]]]]?
28b *[Who do [you think [t′ that [t saw Bill]]]]?

In (28a) the trace in the base-position is theta-governed, hence obeys the
ECP. The intermediate trace is antecedent-governed. Following the *Barriers*
model we could assume that in fact the appropriate movement of the *wh*-phrase
is done via VP-adjunction. (28b) violates the ECP. The idea is that the subject
trace fails to be theta-governed: its theta role assigner, the verb, is too low
in the structure to govern it, and its antecedent, the intermediate trace is
blocked from governing the subject trace by the intervening complementizer
that.

   Though empirically fairly satisfactory the disjunctive formulation of the
ECP is conceptually unsatisfactory: introducing a disjunction means that we
are unable to capture the generalization that unites what are supposed to be
ECP effects: theta-government and antecedent-government are independent
notions.[11]

2.1.2 SUBJECT EXTRACTION AND *THAT*-TRACE EFFECTS

2.1.2.1 Head-government and antecedent-government Though (27) is satisfactory from the empirical point of view, its implementation raises considerable questions. (28b) is one problematic example (cf. Rizzi, 1990a: 29ff.).
Consider (28c), the partial structure of (28b):

28c CP

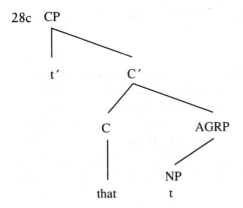

---

[11] Attempts have been made to formulate the ECP in (27) in a unitary fashion. For
     an example cf. Stowell (1981).

In a rigid minimality view, where a head can block antecedent-government by XP, the complementizer *that* blocks antecedent-government from *t'*. This would mean that we need special mechanisms to account of the fact that, for instance, in (29a), the intervening heads *does* and *seem* do not block antecedent-government:

29a   John does not seem [t to be there].

2.1.2.2   Extended chains and antecedent-government   In chapter 10 we tried to solve problems like that raised by (29a) above. We proposed an account in terms of extended chains in which the subject, the functional heads and the V of the clause are coindexed. Adopting this idea, (29a) will have the S-structure representation (29b):

29b   John$_i$ does$_i$ not seem$_i$ [t$_i$ to be there].

John is coindexed with its trace, in the usual way, and it is also coindexed with the auxiliary *does* by subject agreement. Then, in turn, INFL, i.e. AGR and T, will be coindexed with V (cf. chapter 10, section 5). In this way the trace of *John* is coindexed with and also governed by *seem* and this would count as antecedent-government.

   The extended chain proposal raises some problems, though: an extended chain approach could also rescue the violations of the Head Movement Constraint which we interpreted as ECP violations in chapter 11 and in section 1.1 above. Consider first (30a):

30a   They$_i$ would$_i$ [$_{VP}$ have$_i$ [$_{VP}$ been$_i$ [$_{VP}$ expected$_i$ [$_{AGRP}$ t$_i$ to be there]]]].

In (30a) the trace of *they* must be antecedent-governed, since it is not theta-governed. Recall that *expect* theta-marks the non-finite clause, but not its subject. The trace is separated from its antecedent *they* by the intervening heads, *have*, *been* and *expected*. We have seen that the VP-adjoined positions are not available for A-movement since VP-adjunction would lead to what is referred to as 'improper movement' (chapter 10, section 5). By the co-indexation mechanism for extended chains developed in chapter 10 we arrive at the pattern in (30a) where t$_i$ is antecedent-governed by *expected$_i$*. However, now consider (30b):

30b   *Have$_i$ they$_i$ could$_i$ t$_i$ been$_i$ expected$_i$ [t$_i$ to be there].

In (30b) the auxiliary *have* is moved to C. If we assume that functional categories, auxiliaries and the verb belonging to one extended projection (cf. discussion in chapter 11, section 6) are coindexed, the trace of *have* will be coindexed with and hence antecedent-governed by *could*, and the sentence should be grammatical (cf. Browning, 1989, cited in Rizzi, 1990a: 113).

2.1.2.3 Overt C^0 vs. non-overt C^0 Assuming that a satisfactory solution can be found to block Long Head Movement (30b), let us return to the point at issue. We have to assume that the intervening X^0 *that* can block antecedent-government. However, observe that not all C^0s block antecedent-government:

28d $[_{CP1}$ Who do $[_{AGRP1}$ you think $[_{CP2}$ t′ C^0 $[_{AGRP2}$ t saw Bill]]]].

In (28d) the subject is extracted across C^0, where C^0 is non-overt. For expository reasons we leave aside the VP-internal subject trace. In (28d) C^0 does not block antecedent-government: *who* antecedent-governs t′, t′ antecedent governs t. The partial structure for (28d) would be as in (28e):

28e

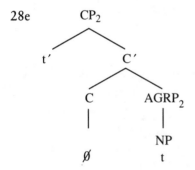

It is hard to see how to distinguish between the blocking capacities of *that* and its non-overt counterpart. Recall that non-overt C^0 has the capacity of blocking *head* government. In the discussion of (4a) above repeated here as (31) we argued that it was precisely a non-overt C^0 which prevented *try* from case-marking *Bill*.

31 *John tried $[_{CP}$ C^0 $[_{AGRP}$ Bill to win]].

We have to have recourse to an *ad hoc* device to distinguish between C^0 and *that*. The former does not intervene in antecedent-government, the latter does.

2.1.3 ADJUNCT MOVEMENT AND *THAT*-TRACE EFFECTS

Further complications arise when we consider adjunct movement:

32a $[_{CP1}$ How did $[_{AGRP1}$ they say $[_{CP2}$ t$'_i$ that $[_{AGRP2}$ John had been fired t$_i]]]]$?
32b $[_{CP1}$ How did $[_{AGRP1}$ they say $[_{CP2}$ t$'_i$ C^0 $[_{AGRP2}$ John had been fired t$_i]]]]$?

In (32) the adjunct *how* is extracted from the lower clause. The adjunct is not theta-governed by the verb, the manner adjunct (*how*) is optional, it is not selected by *fire*. So its trace has to be antecedent-governed in order to satisfy the ECP. In the case of adjunct extraction, and unlike the case of subject extraction, the intervening overt complementizer *that* apparently does not block antecedent-government. As discussed in chapter 9 the adjunct-argument asymmetry is captured in the *Barriers* framework along the lines proposed by Lasnik and Saito (1984). The idea is that the ECP is checked via gamma-marking. Gamma-marking is invariable throughout the derivation. While argument traces are gamma-marked at S-structure, adjunct traces are gamma-marked at LF. In addition, *that* can be deleted at LF. In other words, at LF, (32a) will be assimilated to (32b).

2.1.4 ADJUNCTS AND RELATIVIZED MINIMALITY

In section 1, where we introduced the concept of Relativized Minimality, we also came across an argument–adjunct asymmetry, illustrated in (33a) and (33b). We have omitted intermediate traces for expository reasons.

33a ?$[_{CP1}$ Which problem$_i$ do $[_{AGRP1}$ you wonder $[_{CP2}$ how$_j$ $[_{AGRP2}$ PRO to solve t$_i$ t$_j]]]]$?
33b *$[_{CP1}$ How$_j$ do $[_{AGRP1}$ you wonder $[_{CP2}$ which problem$_i$ $[_{AGRP2}$ PRO to solve t$_i$ t$_j]]]]$?

We have seen that adjunct movement is sensitive to Relativized Minimality effects: the intervening *wh*-phrase in (33b) renders the clause ungrammatical. In (33a) the intervening *wh*-phrase *how* does not give rise to ungrammaticality. Intuitively speaking, it would seem that adjuncts must be related to their traces in a stepwise fashion and each link in the chain that relates the trace to the antecedent must be very local: no potential antecedents must intervene. Arguments tolerate long distance relations. The same contrast is observed in (33c)–(33d) where the negative specifier *not* constitutes the blocking factor. Again, for expository reasons, we do not indicate all the intermediate traces.

33c [$_{CP1}$ Which problem$_i$ did [$_{AGRP1}$ they *not* tell us [$_{CP2}$ t$'_i$ that [$_{AGRP2}$ we should solve t$_i$]]]]?

33d *[$_{CP1}$ How$_i$ did [$_{AGRP1}$ they *not* tell us [$_{CP2}$ t$'_i$ that [$_{AGRP2}$ we should solve this problem t$_i$]]]]?

Recall that the essence of the Relativized Minimality approach is to keep different kinds of governing relations apart, in particular head-government is separate from antecedent-government. Both antecedent-government and head-government are notions which also are related to the ECP. In the next section we discuss the ECP.

2.2 A New Formulation of the ECP

2.2.1 FORMAL LICENSING AND IDENTIFICATION

In chapter 8 we discussed the empty category *pro* which occurs among other things as the subject of finite clauses in Italian. *Pro* is subject to two requirements: a licensing condition (34a) and an identification condition (34b):

34 **Pro-drop parameter**
34a Formal licensing:
   pro is governed by X^0y
34b Identification:
   Let X be the licensing head of an occurrence of *pro*: then *pro* has the grammatical specification of the features on X coindexed with it.

We will extend this double requirement of formal licensing and of identification to apply to all non-overt categories, including traces. Our first disjunctive formulation of the ECP in (27) fails to distinguish between formal licensing and identification of traces. (35) is a conjunctive formulation of the ECP: it imposes a double requirement of formal licensing (35a) and of identification (35b):

35 **ECP** (ii)
   A non-pronominal empty category must be
35a properly head-governed;   **(Formal licensing)**
35b theta-governed or antecedent-governed;   **(Identification)**
where

35c   proper head-government is government by X^0 within the immediate X';[12]
35d   theta-government is government by a theta assigner;
35e   antecedent-government is government by an antecedent, an element that governs the governee and binds it;
35f   X binds Y if and only if X c-commands Y and X and Y are coindexed; (Rizzi, 1990a: 74)

(35) contains two clauses which *both* have to be satisfied: a formal licensing condition and an identification condition. The identification requirement (35b) is formulated as a disjunction: theta-government or antecedent-government.

2.2.2   FORMAL LICENSING: HEAD-GOVERNMENT

The formal licensing clause of the ECP (35a) imposes that all non-pronominal empty categories, i.e. all traces, be head-governed. Let us examine how this clause can be implemented. Clearly the extraction of selected complements (referential or not) is unproblematic: a selected constituent will be head-governed by the verb that selects it. Consider then adjunct extraction in (36).

36   How did Bill solve the problem t?

In (36) clause (35a) of the revised ECP imposes that the trace of *how* be head-governed, where head-government is restricted to the immediate X'-domain. Roughly the relevant partial structure of (36) is as in (37):

[12]   For motivation the reader is referred to Rizzi (1990a: ch. 2).

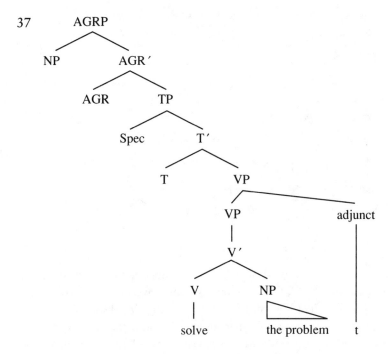

37

We assume that manner adjuncts are VP-adjoined.[13] This means that they are not dominated by VP (cf. the discussion of adjunction in chapter 7) and can be governed from the outside. In the particular case at hand we assume that T head-governs the relevant adjunct.

The next case to consider are examples of subject extraction.

38a *[CP1 Who did [AGRP1 you think [CP2 t'i that [AGRP2 ti left]]]]?

38b [CP1 Who did [AGRP1 you think [CP2 t'i Ø [AGRP2 ti left]]]]?

These examples have the structure in (38c). We omit the VP-internal subject trace which is irrelevant for our discussion.

---

[13] We assume that the base position of *how* is VP-adjoined. If *how* is base-generated VP-internally then it will first have to adjoin to VP in order to void barrierhood of VP. Cf. fn. 8.

38c

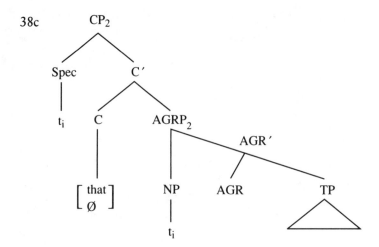

The subject trace is not governed by AGR in its immediate domain AGR': the subject trace is outside AGR'. C^0 has to ensure head-government for the subject trace. This is possible in (38a) and it is not possible in (38b). We have to distinguish between the overt complementizer *that* and its non-overt counterpart. Rizzi (1990a) proposes that in English a tensed complementizer can be realized either as *that*, which is **inert** for government, or as AGR, which belongs to the class of governors.

39   C $\longrightarrow$ $\begin{Bmatrix} \textit{that} \\ \text{AGR} \end{Bmatrix}$

In chapter 11 we saw that AGR can be an independent head with its own autonomous inflectional projection (AGRP). According to (39) AGR can also be associated with another head as a feature or a set of features (cf. Rizzi, 1990a: 52). The licensing condition on AGR is that it must be coindexed with its specifier.[14]

In (38b) AGR is associated with the non-overt C^0. AGR in C^0 is co-indexed with its specifier; (38b) can be represented as (38d):

38d $[_{CP1}$ Who$_i$ do $[_{AGRP1}$ you think $[_{CP2}$ t'$_i$ AGR$_i$ $[_{AGRP2}$ t$_i$ AGR left]]]]?

---

[14]   As mentioned in chapter 11, Shlonsky (1992) proposes that in fact AGR in C also heads its own projection. He proposes that CP should be decomposed into CP and AGRcP:

The subject trace satisfies the ECP: t_i is properly head-governed by AGR associated with C^0 and it is antecedent-governed by t'_i in [Spec, CP2].

The association of agreement features with C is not an *ad hoc* device. In chapter 2 section 4.1 (71) we illustrated the agreeing complementizer in West Flemish:

40a da den inspekteur da boek gelezen eet.
   that the inspector that book read has
   'that the inspector has read that book'.
40b dan d'inspekteurs da boek gelezen een.
   that the inspectors that book read have
   'that the inspectors have read that book'.

The complementizer *da* is third person singular form and *dan* is third person plural. In West Flemish the complementizer is fully inflected for person and number, in a way analogous to the verb inflection (Haegeman, 1992). In (41) the complementizer *da* in column (i) varies depending on the person and number of the subject in exactly the same way that the finite V *goa* varies in column (ii).

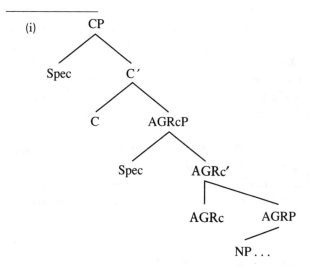

(i)

AGRcP is the AGR-projection associated with C. Shlonsky proposes that AGRc hosts the agreement features of the West Flemish complementizer (cf. text examples (40) and (41)). We do not pursue this issue here.

41 *C-agreement in West Flemish*

(i)	(ii)
41a dan-k ik noa Gent goan	Tun goan-k ik noa Gent.
that-I I to Ghent go	then go-I I to Ghent
'that I am going to Ghent'	'Then I am going to Ghent.'
41b da-j gie noa Gent goat	Tun goa-j gie noa Gent.
that-you you to Ghent go	Then go-you to Ghent
41c da-se zie noa Gent goat	Tun goa-se zie noa Gent.
that-she she to Ghent goes	then goes-she she to Ghent
41d da-me wunder noa Gent goan	Tun goan-me wunder noa Gent.
that-we we to Ghent go	Then go-we we to Ghent
41e da-j gunder noa Gent goat	Tun goa-j gunder noa Gent.
that-you you to Ghent go	then go-you you to Ghent
41f dan-ze zunder noa Gent goan	Tun goan-ze zunder noa Gent.
that-they they to Ghent go	then go-they they to Ghent

To summarize this section: we assume that the formal licensing of traces is achieved by head-government. The problematic case of subject traces can be dealt with adequately once we admit that C can be realized by AGR and that AGR belongs to the class of proper head governors.

2.2.3 IDENTIFICATION

2.3.3.1 Theta-government or antecedent-government In formulation (35) of the ECP the condition on the identification of the trace is formulated as a disjunction: identification is achieved *either* by theta-government *or* by antecedent-government. We have already discussed antecedent-government with respect to adjunct extraction. An XP is theta-governed if it is governed by a head which theta-marks it. The disjunctive formulation of the ECP in (35) implies that as soon as a trace is theta-governed it will be identified and satisfy the identification clause of the ECP. Since theta-government implies head-government, the formal licensing requirement will be fulfilled as well as the identification requirement. We expect therefore that all theta-governed traces satisfy the ECP and, crucially, do not require antecedent-government. But this prediction is not borne out by the facts. Consider (18) repeated for the reader's convenience as (42):

42a What did they say he weighed t last week?
Sixty kilos.
Apples.

42b   What did they wonder whether he weighed t last week?
      *Sixty kilos.
      Apples.
42c   What did they not say that he weighed t last week?
      *Sixty kilos.
      Apples.

Weigh has a stative reading in which case it selects, and theta-marks, a
MEASURE phrase, and it has an agentive reading in which case it selects, and
theta-marks, a THEME. As the answers show, (42a) is ambiguous between the
two readings: *what* can be interpreted either as a non-referential MEASURE
phrase or as a referential THEME. In (42b) and (42c) *what* can only have the
referential reading, the non-referential reading is lost because of the intervening
A′-specifiers. However, if theta-government suffices for the identification of
the trace then this is unexpected: whether *what* has a referential reading or
not, its trace is theta-governed by *weigh*. Apparently theta-government does
not suffice to identify the trace. A similar conclusion can be drawn from the
data in (43):

43a   [$_{AGRP1}$ It seems [$_{CP2}$ that [$_{AGRP2}$ everyone believes John]]].
43b   [$_{AGRP1}$ It seems [$_{CP2}$ that [$_{AGRP2}$ John$_i$ was believed t$_i$ by everyone]]].
43c   *[$_{AGRP1}$ John$_i$ seems [$_{CP2}$ that [$_{AGRP2}$ it is believed t$_i$ by everyone.]]].

                                                                  (cf. (6c))

Compare (43c) with (43b). In both, the trace of *John* is theta-governed by
believed. The intervening expletive subject *it* causes the problem in (43c); (43d)
is grammatical.

43d   [$_{AGRP1}$ John$_i$ seems [$_{AGRP2}$ t′$_i$ to be believed t$_i$ by everyone]].

                                                                  (cf. (6d))

This suggests that we have an effect of Relativized Minimality: *it* is a potential antecedent for the trace of *John* and it blocks antecedent-government.
If theta-government were sufficient for satisfaction of the identification
condition on traces we would not expect (43c) to have a status different from
(43b) and (43d).

2.2.3.2   *Referential indices*   In our discussion of the sentences in (18/42) we
have seen that referentiality plays an important part in determining the distance of movement:

44a   What did they say that John weighed t?
44b   What did they ask whether John weighed t?
44c   What did they not say that John weighed t?

Rizzi (1990a), referring to proposals by Aoun (1986) and Cinque (1984), proposes that referentiality is the crucial factor in determining the interpretation of (44) (cf. also Cinque, 1991). Referential arguments can be extracted regardless of the intervention of potential antecedent-governors, while non-referential complements cannot cross intervening A′-specifiers. In order to capture the distinction between referential and non-referential constituents Rizzi (1990a: 85–6) proposes a refinement of the notion argument. Following the discussion in chapter 1 we have used the term 'argument' to designate all constituents which are selected. We will continue to assume that all selected constituents are theta-marked. Among the selected (or theta-marked) constituents, only some refer to participants in the event described by the verb (*John, apples, books*, etc.); others, however, do not refer to participants but rather qualify the event (measure, manner, etc., or idiom chunks). The former type of selected constituents are referential arguments in Rizzi's more restricted interpretation, the latter are not. Rizzi's distinction between theta-marked constituents which are arguments and those which are not is similar to that proposed by Chomsky (1981a: 37, 325), who distinguishes arguments from quasi-arguments (see fn. 11). In Rizzi's approach arguments are referential expressions, i.e. they refer to participants in the event; quasi-arguments, such as the subjects of weather verbs and the nominal parts of idioms, are constituents which are theta-marked, i.e. which are selected by the predicate, but which do not refer to a participant. Selected constituents are argumental if they are referential. In other words, we distinguish two kinds of theta-roles: argumental or referential theta roles (AGENT, THEME, PATIENT, EXPERI-ENCER, GOAL, etc.) and quasi-argumental, non-referential theta roles (MANNER, MEASURE, idioms chunks, etc.) (1990a: 85–6). Rizzi proposes that the use of referential indices and coindexation be restricted to constituents which receive a referential theta role:

45a   **Referential indices:** licensing condition (i)
      A referential index must be licensed by a referential theta role.
      (Rizzi, 1990a: 86)

(45a) implies that selected constituents which are non-referential and adjuncts do not have a referential index.

2.2.3.3 The ECP as a formal licensing condition Returning once again to the ECP the following modification is proposed. We maintain the head-government requirement. We also assume that non-overt categories have to be identified, but the identification requirement is not considered part of the ECP any more. It is a general requirement on non-overt categories. The ECP is thus reduced to the formal licensing requirement (46):

46 **ECP (iii)**
A non-pronominal empty category must be properly head-governed.
(Rizzi, 1990a: 87)

What about the identification? Consider the data in (47):

47a Which problem$_i$ did he solve t$_i$?
47b How did he solve the problem t?

In (47a) we have moved a *wh*-phrase which has a referential theta role. Hence it bears an index. In (47b) we have moved a manner adjunct which does not bear an index. Rizzi proposes that the identification of the trace in (47a) is established by binding. Binding is redefined in terms of *referential* co-indexation:

48 **Binding**
X binds Y if and only if
   (i)   X c-commands Y;
   (ii) X and Y have the same referential index.
(Rizzi, 1990a: 87)

Binding (48) is not a local relation: binding relations are not sensitive to Relativized Minimality effects; they can be established across intervening potential antecedents. Apart from a slight degradation due to subjacency in (49a), the extractions in (49) raise no particular problems: *which problem$_i$* binds *t$_i$*.

49a ?Which problem$_i$ do you wonder whether he would solve t$_i$?
49b Which problem$_i$ did you not believe that he had solved t$_i$?

On the other hand, adjunct traces do not bear a referential index, hence they cannot be identified by binding. This, Rizzi argues, is the reason why such traces have to be locally antecedent-governed: a government relation has to be established between the adjunct and its trace. In (47b) above the relation can be established and *how* will antecedent-govern its trace. (47c) is ungrammatical because *which problem* blocks antecedent-government between *how* and its trace; *how* cannot be connected to its trace and the trace is unidentified. Observe that we distinguish between the A'-chain headed by *which problem*, whose members bear an index, and that headed by *how*, whose numbers cannot bear an index.

47c   *$[_{CP1}$ How do $[_{AGRP1}$ you $[_{VP1}$ t' $[_{VP1}$ wonder $[_{CP2}$ which problem$_i$ $[_{AGRP2}$ we can $[_{VP2}$ $[_{VP2}$ solve t_i]t]]]]]]]?

In (47d) a chain can be established between *how* and the lowest trace via the intermediate traces.

47d $[_{CP1}$ How do $[_{AGRP1}$ you $[_{VP1}$ t'' $[_{VP1}$ think $[_{CP2}$ t' that $[_{AGRP2}$ we can $[_{VP2}$ $[_{VP2}$ solve the problem] t]]]]]]]?

Because we now assume that only constituents which receive a referential theta role bear an index, we cannot use the notion coindexation in the definition of antecedent-government. Rizzi (1990a: 92) proposes the following alternative:

50   **Antecedent-government.**
      X antecedent-governs Y if and only if
      (i)   X and Y are non-distinct;
      (ii) X c-commands Y;
      (iii) no barrier intervenes;
      (iv) Relativized Minimality is respected.

The coindexation requirement is replaced by a more general non-distinctness requirement: two constituents are non-distinct if the features for which they are specified are non-distinct.

2.2.4 SUMMARY

Let us take stock of what we have achieved. As a first step, we have replaced the disjunctive formulation of the ECP in (7)/(27), in which proper government is ensured, (i) by theta-government *or* (ii) by antecedent-government, by a conjunctive formulation in (35) with (i) a formal licensing clause in terms of head-government *and* (ii) an identification clause. The identification clause is itself disjunctive: identification is achieved by (i) theta-government or (ii) antecedent-government. As a second step we separate the formal licensing condition from the identification requirement and we reduce the ECP to the formal licensing condition (46).

Obviously, we still need an identification requirement. Non-overt categories must be interpreted, their content must be identified. This means that independently from our newly formulated ECP, we still have to connect a moved constituent with its trace. The question is how this connection can be established and how we can capture the asymmetry between arguments, now restricted to constituents with a referential theta role, on the one hand, and adjuncts and selected constituents with a non-referential theta role, on the other hand. Rizzi (1990a) captures this distinction in terms of indexation: indices are reserved for constituents with a referential theta role. A moved constituent can be connected to its trace by one of two strategies: binding or (antecedent-)government. Binding depends on coindexation and is insensitive to Relativized Minimality effects; this means that it allows for a long distance relation. Binding is only available for referential arguments. Antecedent-government does not depend on coindexation, it is subject to a stricter locality condition: government between X and Y is blocked by intervening barriers and by potential governors.

2.3 A-chains

Consider the following contrast in the light of the newly formulated ECP.

51a ?$[_{CP1}$ Who$_i$ did $[_{AGRP1}$ you wonder $[_{CP2}$ how $[_{AGRP2}$ PRO to believe t$_i$]]]]?
51b *$[_{CP1}$ $[_{AGRP1}$ John$_i$ seems $[_{CP2}$ that $[_{AGRP2}$ it is believed t$_i$ by everyone]]]]].

(51a) is grammatical, with a weak subjacency effect. The trace of the extracted object satisfies the ECP since it is head-governed by the V *believe*. *Who* receives a theta role from *believe* and is referential, its trace is identified via binding. We have seen that binding requires coindexation and c-command, these conditions are fulfilled in (51a).

In section 2.2.3.1 we discussed (51b) as (43c). The problem with this example is that it is ungrammatical in spite of the fact the trace of *John* is head governed by *believed*. The intervening expletive subject *it* causes the problem; (43d), repeated here as (51c), is grammatical.

51c   [$_{AGRP1}$ John$_i$ seems [$_{AGRP2}$ t′$_i$ to be believed t$_i$ by everyone]].

(51b) illustrates Relativized Minimality: *it* is a potential antecedent for the trace of *John* and it blocks antecedent-government. The problem with this sentence concerns the connection of *John* to its trace. *John* is not an adjunct. In (51b) the chain <*John$_i$*, t′$_i$, t$_i$> receives an argumental theta role from *believe*. It seems natural to assume that the theta role assigned by *believed* in (51a) is the same as that assigned in (51a). The contrast in (51) is then rather unexpected: in (51a) *who* can be connected back to its trace by binding; in (51b) *John* cannot be connected back to the trace by binding and antecedent government is required.

The ungrammaticality of (51b) suggests that the use of coindexation, and hence of binding, must be even more restricted. As a first approximation let us suppose that the possibility of referential indexation is restricted to the *argument* itself, rather than extending it to any member of a *chain* receiving an argumental theta role. The trace of NP-movement as such cannot carry the referential theta role: in isolation, the NP-trace is caseless, hence it is invisible and does not bear the theta role. In (51b) the theta role is associated with the chain <*John$_i$*, t′$_i$, t$_i$>. Pursuing this line of reasoning, Rizzi proposes that NP-traces are non-arguments, they do not carry a referential index, and hence they have be connected to their antecedents via government, and would be subjected to Relativized Minimality (1992b: 4).

This approach will account for the ungrammaticality of (51b). But we must ensure that the empirical coverage of our approach remains the same, i.e. that we continue to capture the facts which we accounted for before. Notably, we must ensure that (51a) can be derived. That means that the trace of *who* must be able to be connected to its antecedent via binding. The trace of *who* is an argument: it is theta-marked and it is assigned case. In addition to permitting a referential index on the variable, though, we must permit the indexation of the operator, *who*. Based on our discussion in chapter 9 *who* is a non-argument as S-structure and at LF. But notice that in the corresponding D-structure (51d) *who* is in a thematic position. We assume that the theta criterion applies at all levels of representation and that D-structure encodes thematic relations. It follows that at D-structure *whom* receives a referential theta role and it is a referential argument:

51d   [$_{CP1}$ [$_{AGRP1}$ you did wonder [$_{CP2}$ [$_{AGRP2}$ PRO to believe whom$_i$ how]]]]?

Rizzi proposes that a constituent can carry a referential index only if it is an argument at some level of representation:

45b **Referential indices**: licensing condition (ii)
X can carry a referential index only if it bears an argumental theta role at some level of representation.
(Rizzi, 1992b: 4)

(45b) will still achieve the right result for adjunct extraction. In (47c), for instance, repeated here as (52a), the A'-chain does not contain an argument because it is not assigned an argumental theta role.

52a *$[_{CP1}$ How do $[_{AGRP1}$ you $[_{VP1}$ t' $[_{VP1}$ wonder $[_{CP2}$ which problem$_i$ $[_{AGRP2}$ we can $[_{VP2}$ $[_{VP2}$ solve t$_i$]t]]]]]]]?

Hence the trace of *how* has to be identified by antecedent-government and the intervening *which problem* gives rise to an intervention effect. In (47d), repeated here as (52b), antecedent-government between *how* and the lowest trace is achieved via the intermediate traces.

52b $[_{CP1}$ How do $[_{AGRP1}$ you $[_{VP1}$ t'' $[_{VP1}$ think $[_{CP2}$ t' that $[_{AGRP2}$ we can $[_{VP2}$ $[_{VP2}$ solve the problem]t]]]]]]]?

By restricting coindexation to constituents with a referential theta role at some level of representation we arrive at a unitary treatment for both the argument/adjunct asymmetry in A'-chains and for the strong locality conditions on A-chains.[15]

3 Further Problems

3.1 *Long Head Movement*

In section 1 above we discussed head movement to illustrate Relativized Minimality. Heads move in a stepwise fashion, and cannot cross c-commanding heads.

---

[15] Rizzi (1992b) also discusses instances of A'-chains which require antecedent-government regardless of the argument–adjunct distinction. He shows how these cases too can be made to follow from Relativized Minimality. One instance of this phenomenon is given in (i):

(ia) It was this book that John bought at the fair
(ib) Which book was it that John bought at the fair?
(ic) *Which book was it not that John bought at the fair?

53a   Could you t have done it?
53b   *Have you could t done it?

This phenomenon was initially described as the Head Movement Constraint (Travis, 1984), and ultimately reduces to the ECP. In our current format, it is obvious that the moved head is not a referential argument, hence will not bear a referential index and can only be connected to its trace by antecedent-government. Antecedent-government of *t* by *have* in (53b) is blocked by the intervening head *could*. Recall though that we pointed out certain cases of so called Long Head Movement in chapter 11, section 4. Rivero (1991) gives, among others, the following Bulgarian examples:

54a   Petur e procel knigata.
      Peter has read book the
      'Peter has read the book.'
54b   Procel e knigata.
      read has book the
      'He has read the book.'

The order (54b) in which the verb *procel* precedes the auxiliary *e* is strikingly at odds with the concept of Relativized Minimality. Schematically (54b) reduces to (54c).

54c   Procel   e   t   knigata
         X   Z   Y

where X should antecedent-govern Y across Z. One option would be to say that Relativized Minimality does not apply to head-movement: then the trace of *procel* would only be subject to the ECP, i.e. it would have to be properly head-governed, which it is.

  Let us pursue an alternative line, suggested by Rivero herself. Consider that so far we have distinguished three types of movement: head movement, i.e. X^0 movement, A-movement of XP and A'-movement of XP. There is an asymmetry between X^0 movement and XP movement: we assume that there is only one kind of X^0 movement and that there are two types of XP movement. One way of dealing with Rivero's long head movement data, and with similar phenomena in other languages, is to distinguish two types of head positions, by analogy with the A and A' distinction for maximal projections.

We could then argue that in (54c) the auxiliary *e* is of type A, and that the moved participle *procel* is of type A′. In this way *e* would not block government of *t* by *procel*. We leave the phenomenon of Long Head Movement at this point, it is a challenging one which must be subject to further research.

3.2 A-positions and A′-positions

3.2.1 INTRODUCTION

In the discussion we have been assuming that the distinction between A-positions and A′-positions is clear cut. In chapter 2 we gave a very informal definition: A-positions are positions like the subject position or the object position, while A′-positions are positions like [Spec, CP] or positions occupied by adjuncts.

Originally (Chomsky, 1981a) A-positions were equated with potential thematic positions, i.e. positions to which thematic roles *could* be assigned. In more traditional terms, A-positions are the positions to which grammatical functions such as subject or object are assigned. Such positions are, for instance, relevant for binding, the binding theory being a theory of A-binding. The canonical subject position [Spec, IP], or [Spec, AGRP] in the split INFL framework, was considered an A-position: it was generally assumed to be the base-position of subjects in transitive sentences and it also was seen to be relevant for binding. A-movement, i.e. movement of an NP to an A-position instantiated by passive structures or raising structures, is typically to the canonical subject position. In the current framework it is assumed, though, that the canonical subject position, i.e. [Spec, IP] or [Spec, AGRP], is not the thematic position of the subject (cf. chapter 6, section 5). The base-position of the thematic subject is VP-internal, the subject NP moves to [Spec, AGRP] (or [Spec, IP]) for case reasons. Hence, the canonical subject position is no longer a position to which a thematic role can be assigned, not even in transitive sentences. If we wish to continue to assume that the canonical subject position is an A-position then we cannot continue to restrict the definition of A-positions to just those positions than can be assigned a thematic role and we need another definition.

In the literature A′-positions were usually defined as the opposite of A-positions, i.e. whenever a position was not an A-position it was an A′-position. This means that depending on our definition of A-positions, the definition of A′-position also varies and that A-positions and A′-positions will be in complementary distribution: a position is either an A-position, or an A′-position.

3.2.2 THE CANONICAL SUBJECT POSITION IS AN A-POSITION

Let us first consider the canonical subject position, [Spec, IP] or [Spec, AGRP] in the Split INFL framework (chapter 11). Various arguments can be advanced that confirm the A-status of the canonical subject position.[16]

One area which throws light on the status of the subject NP is the binding theory. Consider first (55a):

55a John has invited himself.

In chapter 4 we discuss the properties of reflexives such as *himself* and we propose there that they are subject to Principle A of the binding theory: they must be bound in their governing category. For (55a) we first proposed that the relevant binder was *John*. In chapter 6, section 5 we pointed out that as a consequence of the hypothesis that the thematic position of the subject is VP-internal, the relevant local binder of *himself* will not be the actual NP *John* in [Spec, AGRP]. Rather, the relevant binder will be the VP-internal trace:

55b John$_i$ has [$_{VP}$ t$_i$ invited himself$_i$].

Examples such as (55a) do not tell us anything about the status of the canonical subject position. (56a) provides evidence that the canonical subject position is an A-position because this example shows that the canonical subject position itself is relevant for binding.

56a He$_{j/*i}$ did not come because John$_i$ was ill.

In the example, *John*, the subject of the adjunct clause of reason must not be coindexed with *he*, the subject, of the matrix clause. Consider the rough structure in (56b). We assume that reason adjuncts are TP-adjoined. In this example the VP-internal trace of *he* will be too low to c-command *John*, thus it should play no role in establishing binding relations. The NP in [Spec, AGRP], *he*, c-commands *John* and therefore should not be coindexed with it.

---

[16] This section draws from Rizzi's class lectures 1992–3.

56b

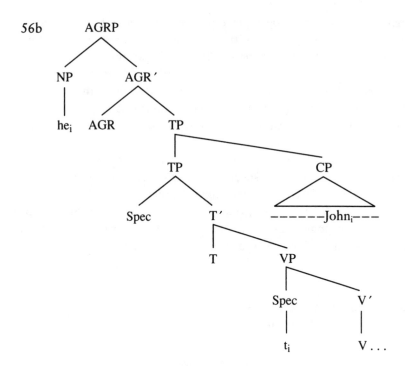

Since the coindexation of *John* and *he* gives rise to a binding theory violation we conclude that *he* occupies an A-position. If the canonical subject position occupied by *he* in (56) were an A′-position, it should not be relevant for binding and (56) would be grammatical.

Further support for distinguishing the canonical subject position from A′-positions can be obtained from data concerning parasitic gaps. Consider the examples in (57):

57a This is the book [$_{CP}$ which John filed t [without reading ec]].
57b *This is the book [$_{CP}$ which John passed the exam [without reading ec]].
57c *This book was filed t [without reading ec].

In (57a) the relative pronoun *which* has been moved from the object position of *filed* to the specifier of the relative CP. In the adjunct clause the object of *reading* is also non-overt and represented in our example as *ec*. As discussed in chapter 8, empty categories such as that in the adjunct clause of (57a) are called parasitic gaps because they depend for their acceptability on the presence of another gap. (57b), where there is no gap of movement, is ungrammatical: the *ec* in the object position of *reading* cannot be licensed by another gap. Recall also that only A'-traces are able to license parasitic gaps and traces created by NP-movement to the subject position cannot license parasitic gaps. In (57c) the gap in the object position of *filed* is A-bound by the NP *this book*. These data suggest then that movement to the canonical subject position, i.e. NP movement, differs from movement to A'-positions such as [Spec, CP]. This difference can be captured if we assume that the canonical subject position is an A-position.

Finally, we have postulated, following Rizzi (1990a), that A-movement and A'-movement are each subject to specific locality constraints: A'-movement, for instance, is not hampered by intervening A-antecedents, while A-movement is. In (58a) the A'-movement (topicalization) of *John* is not blocked by the intervention of the lower subject NP *Mary* or by the higher expletive subject *it*; in (58b) movement of *John* to [Spec, AGRP] is blocked by the intervening lower subject *Mary*.

58a   John it seems that Mary likes t.
58b   *John seems that Mary likes t.

Again these data provide grounds for distinguishing the position occupied by *John* in (58a) from that in (58b). Again we can draw the distinction by assuming that topicalization in (58a), like *wh*-movement, is A'-movement, and that NP-movement is A-movement.

3.2.3   A-POSITIONS

Rizzi (1991) proposes that A-positions are either thematic positions or specifiers of AGR. Recall that he assumes the AGR may either project its own AGRP or that AGR may also be associated with another head such as C.

In Rizzi's approach the A-status of a position is determined in configurational terms, i.e. in terms of a specifier–head relation, as well as in terms of the feature content of the position. What is relevant for the A-status of a position is not simply that it be a specifier of a projection of AGR or of a head with AGR features: the element in the specifier position shares agreement features with AGR:

59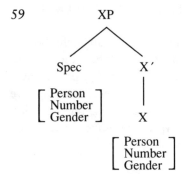

3.2.4 A'-POSITIONS

Though it is not possible to go into this issue in more detail here, consider
that the definition of A'-positions can now be reformulated analogously to
the definition of A-positions in (59). In our theory, the prototypical A'-
position is [Spec, CP]. In chapter 2 we pointed out that the head of the
clause, C, is characterized by the feature [±WH]. Moreover, there is an
agreement relation between [Spec, CP] and [C] in terms of the feature [±WH].
Recall our discussion of example (70a) repeated here as (60a):

60a I wonder what Poirot will buy.

In (60a) the direct object of *buy* is a *wh*-phrase, *what*. Such an interrogative
phrase could be said to also contain the feature [+WH]. The *wh*-phrase has
to move to [Spec, CP]. (60b) is the S-structure of (60a):

60b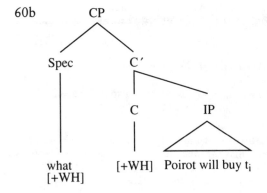

In interrogative clauses, [Spec, CP] and C agree with respect to the feature [+WH].[17]

On the basis of these observations and by analogy with our definition of A-positions, A'-positions can be defined as specifiers of XP where the relevant features that are shared are A'-features, or operator features. Typical operator features are the negative feature and the feature associated with interrogative sentences represented as [WH].[18] Much current work concerns the definition of A-positions and A'-positions (Mahajan (1990), for instance).

61   XP

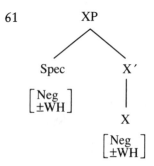

3.2.5   CONCLUSION

In this section we consider the definition of A-positions and A'-positions. A-positions are defined as either thematic positions or specifier positions which share AGR features with a head. A'-positions are specifier positions which share operator features with the head. Observe that the definition of A'-positions is no longer dependent on the definition of A-positions, both positions are defined partly in configurational terms, partly in terms of feature content. The definitions proposed here also mean that a position might meet

---

[17]   Cf. May (1985) and Rizzi (forthcoming) for discussion.

[18]   The data in (61)–(62) suggest that there is a matching requirement which imposes that a head carrying the feature [+WH] must have a matching specifier. Rizzi (forthcoming) formulates this constraint in terms of a well formedness condition:

(i)   **Wh Criterion**
   (ia)   An X^0 [+WH] must be in a specifier head relation with an operator with the feature [+WH]
   (ib)   An operator with the feature [+WH] must have a specifier head relation with an X^0 [+WH]

It is proposed in the current literature (for instance in (Chomsky, 1992; Haegeman, in preparation; Rizzi, forthcoming) that this matching requirement is an instantiation of a more general condition on the licensing of features. This issue is the topic of ongoing research. The reader is referred to the literature.

both the criteria for A-status and that for A'-status. The status of mixed positions is pursued in current research (Rizzi (1991), Haegeman (in preparation)).

4 Summary

The chapter first introduces the concept of Relativized Minimality, a locality condition on government defined in (1):

1 **Relativized Minimality**
    X x-governs Y only if there is no Z such that
    (i) Z is a typical potential x-governor for Y;
    (ii) Z c-commands Y and Z does not c-command X.
    (Rizzi, 1990a: 7)

In the chapter we have examined and reformulated the ECP. We first replace the **disjunctive** formulation in (2) by a **conjunctive** formulation of the ECP, (3), which contains a licensing condition (a) and an identification condition (b):

2 **ECP** (i)
    Traces must be properly governed.
    A properly governs B iff A theta-governs B or A antecedent-governs B

3   **ECP** (ii)
    A non-pronominal empty category must be
3a properly head-governed;   (**Formal licensing**)
3b Theta-governed or antecedent-governed;   (**Identification**)
    (Rizzi, 1990: 74)
where
3c **proper head-government** is government by X^0 within the immediate X';
3d **theta-government** is government by a theta assigner;
3e **antecedent-government** is government by an antecedent, an element that
    governs the governee and binds it;
3f X **binds** Y if and only if X c-commands Y and X and Y are coindexed.
    (Rizzi, 1990a: 74)

Finally we reduce the ECP to a formal licensing condition:

4   **ECP** (iii)
    A non-pronominal empty category must be properly head-governed.
    (Rizzi, 1990a: 87)

In order to allow for proper head-government of the trace in the canonical subject position of a finite clause we propose that C may dominate AGR in which case C can head govern:

5   $C \longrightarrow \begin{Bmatrix} that \\ AGR \end{Bmatrix}$

The relation between the moved element and its trace is established by one of the following two strategies: binding (6) or government (8).

6   **Binding**
    X binds Y if and only if
    (i)   X c-commands Y;
    (ii) X and Y have the same referential index.
    (Rizzi, 1990a: 87)

Binding is restricted to referential arguments because these are the only constituents which can bear a referential index.

7   **Licensing condition on referential indices**
    X can carry a referential index only if it bears an argumental theta role at some level of representation.
    (Rizzi, 1992b: 4)

8   **Antecedent-government**
    X antecedent-governs Y if and only if
    (i)   X and Y are non-distinct;
    (ii)   X c-commands Y;
    (iii) no barrier intervenes;
    (iv)   Relativized Minimality is respected.

5 Exercises

Exercise 1

The following examples are discussed by Rizzi (1990a: 84, (26)). Discuss their status.

1a It seems that someone told Bill that . . .
1b It seems that Bill was told t that . . .
1c *Bill seems that it was told t that . . .

(1c) shows that long distance NP-movement ('super-raising') is impossible. Does the same apply to control patterns? In your discussion consider the following example (from Rizzi (1990a: 84, his (25)).

2 John thinks that it is difficult [PRO to shave himself in public].

Exercise 2

Consider the following data,

1a How did you say that he repaired the car?
1b *How do you wonder whether he repaired the car?
1c *How didn't you say that he repaired the car?

In (1b) and in (1c) the intervening *wh* element *whether* and the intervening negation *n't* block antecedent-government between *how* and its trace. Now consider the following examples from English (2) and from Modern Greek (3) (from Agouraki (1993: 55–6)):

2a How slowly did Mary say [that Matthew gave Jared the book t]?
2b *How slowly could Mary say [that Matthew gave Jared the book t]?
2c *How slowly might Mary have said [that Matthew gave Jared the book t]?
2d *How slowly should Mary have said [that Matthew gave Jared the book t?]?

3a jatí ipe [óti me misi t]?
why said-he that me hates
'Why did he say that he hates me?'

3b *jati na pi [oti me misi t]?
why must say-he that me hates

4a jati léi [óti éftiakse to aftokínito t]?
why says that fixed-he the car
'Why does he say that he fixed the car?'

4b *jatí LEI [óti éftiakse to aftokínito t]?
why SAYS (focus) that fixed-he the car

What conclusion can we draw from the examples above with respect to the nature of elements that intervene in antecedent-government. (cf. Rizzi, 1990a: 116, fn. 16). In order to account for the contrasts above Agouraki (1993) proposes that modal elements and sentential Focus are also associated with operators (cf. Puskas (1992)).

Bibliography

Aarts, F. and J. Aarts (1982) *English Syntactic Structure*, Oxford: Pergamon.

Abney, S. (1987) 'The English noun phrase in its sentential aspects', unpublished diss., MIT Cambridge, Mass.

Abraham, W. (ed.) (1983) *On the Formal Syntax of the Westgermania*, Amsterdam: John Benjamins.

Adams, M. (1987) 'From Old French to the theory of pro-drop', *Natural Language and Linguistic Theory*, 5, 1–32.

Agouraki, Y. (1993) 'Spec-head licensing: the scope of the theory', Ph.D. diss., UCL.

Akmajian, A. and F. W. Heny (1975) *Introduction to the Principles of Transformational Syntax*, Cambridge, Mass.: MIT Press.

Akmajian, A., R. Demers and R. Harnish (1979) *Linguistics: An Introduction to Language and Communication*, Cambridge, Mass.: MIT Press.

Allwood, J., L.-G. Andersson and O. Dahl (1977) *Logic in Linguistics*, Cambridge: Cambridge University Press.

Anderson, S. (1986) 'The typology of anaphoric dependencies: Icelandic (and other) reflexives', in Hellan and Christensen (eds) *Topics in Scandinavian Syntax*, 65–88.

Aoun, J. and A. Li (1989) 'Scope and constituency', *Linguistic Inquiry*, 20, 141–72.

Aoun, Y. (1984) 'A significant generalization in Chinese', in de Geest and Putseys (eds) *Sentential Complementation*, 11–21.

Aoun, Y. (1986) *Generalized Binding, the Syntax and Logical Form of Wh-interrogatives*, Dordrecht: Foris.

Aoun, Y. and N. Hornstein (1985) 'Quantifier types', *Linguistic Inquiry*, 16, 623–36.

Aoun, Y. and D. Sportiche (1983) 'On the formal theory of government', *The Linguistic Review*, 2, 3, 211–36.

Aoun, Y., N. Hornstein and D. Sportiche (1981) 'Some aspects of wide scope quantification', *Journal of Linguistic Research*, 1, 69–95.

Ariel, M. (1988) 'Referring and accessibility', *Journal of Linguistics*, 24, 65–87.

Authier, J.-M. (1988) 'Null object constructions in Kinande', *Natural Language and Linguistic Theory*, 6, 19–37.

Authier, J.-M (1989a) 'Two types of empty operator', *Linguistic Inquiry*, 20, 117–25.

Authier, J.-M. (1989b) 'Arbitrary null objects and unselective binding', in Jaeggli and Safir (eds), *The Null Subject Parameter*, 45–67.

Authier, J.-M (1992) 'A parametric account of V-governed arbitrary null arguments', *Natural Language and Linguistic Theory*, 10, 345–74.

Bach, E. (1962) 'The order of elements in a transformational grammar of German', *Language*, 38, 263–9.

Baker, M. (1988) *Incorporation. A Theory of Grammatical Function Changing*, Chicago: University of Chicago Press.

Baker, M., K. Johnson and I. Roberts (1989) 'Passive arguments raised', *Linguistic Inquiry*, 20, 219–51.

Barss, A. (1986) 'Chains and anaphoric dependence', diss. MIT, MIT, Cambridge, Mass.

Barss, A. (1988) 'Paths, connectivity and featureless empty categories', in Cardinaletti, Cinque and Giusti (eds), *Constituent Structure*, 9–34.

Bayer, J. (1984a) 'Towards an explanation of certain *that*-t phenomena: the COMP node in Bavarian', in de Geest and Putseys (eds), *Sentential Complementation*, 23–32.

Bayer, J. (1984b) 'COMP in Bavarian syntax', *The Linguistic Review*, 3, 209–74.

Belletti, A. (1988) 'The case of unaccusatives', *Linguistic Inquiry*, 19, 1–34.

Belletti, A. (1990) *Generalized Verb Movement*, Turin: Rosenberg and Sellier.

Belletti, A. and L. Rizzi (1981) 'The syntax of *ne*: some theoretical implications', *The Linguistic Review*, 1, 117–54.

Belletti, A. and L. Rizzi (1988) 'Psych-verbs and θ-theory', *Natural Language and Linguistic Theory*, 6, 3, 291–352.

Belletti, A. and U. Shlonsky (forthcoming) 'The order of verbal complements: a comparative study', to appear in *Natural Language and Linguistic Theory*.

Bennis, H. (1986) *Gaps and Dummies*, Dordrecht: Foris.

Bennis, H. and L. Haegeman (1984) 'On the status of agreement and relative clauses in West-Flemish', in de Geest and Putseys (eds), *Sentential Complementation*, 33–53.

Bennis, H. and T. Hoekstra (1984) 'Gaps and parasitic gaps', *The Linguistic Review*, 4, 29–87.

Bertocchi, A. and C. Casadio (1980) *Conditions on Anaphora: An analysis of reflexives in Latin*, Papers on Grammar, 6, CLUE, Bologna.

Besten, H. den (1983) 'On the interaction of root transformations and lexical deletive rules', in Abraham (ed.), *On the Formal Syntax of the Westgermania*,

47–131. Also published in *Groninger Arbeiten zur Germanistischen Linguistik*, vols 1–3, pp. 1–78.

Besten, H. den (1985) 'The ergative hypothesis and free word order in Dutch and German', in Toman (ed.), *Studies in German Grammar*, pp. 23–64.

Besten, H. den and G. Webelhuth (1987) 'Remnant topicalization and the constituent structure of VP in the Germanic SOV languages', Paper presented at GLOW, Venice.

Bloomfield, L. (1935) *Language*, London: George Allen and Unwin.

Borer, H. (1980) 'Empty subjects and constraints on thematic relations', in J. T. Jensen (ed.), *Proceedings of the Tenth Annual Meeting of NELS* (*Cahiers linguistiques d'Ottawa, vol. 9*), Toronto: Department of Linguistics, University of Toronto.

Borer, H. (1983) *Parametric Syntax*, Dordrecht: Foris.

Borer, H. (1986) 'I-subjects', *Linguistic Inquiry*, 17, 375–416.

Borer, H. (1989) 'Anaphoric AGR', in Jaeggli and Safir (eds), *The Null Subject Parameter*, 69–109.

Borsley, B. (1991) *Syntactic Theory*, London: Edward Arnold.

Bouchard, D. (1984) *On the Content of Empty Categories*, Dordrecht: Foris.

Bouchard, D. (1985) 'The binding theory and the notion of accessible SUBJECT', *Linguistic Inquiry*, 16, 117–33.

Bresnan, J. (1970) 'On complementizers: toward a syntactic theory of complement types', *Foundations of Language*, 6, 297–321.

Bresnan, J. (1982) 'Control and complementation', *Linguistic Inquiry*, 13, 3, 343–434.

Brody, M. (1985) 'On the complementary distribution of empty categories', *Linguistic Inquiry*, 16, 505–64.

Brody, M. (1993a) 'θ theory and arguments', *Linguistic Inquiry*, 24, 1–24.

Brody, M. (1993b) 'Lexico-logical form – a radically minimalist theory', MS, UCL.

Browning, M. (1989) 'Comments on relativized minimality', paper presented at the Second Princeton Workshop on Comparative Grammar.

Burton-Roberts, N. (1986) *Analysing Sentences*, London: Longman.

Burzio, L. (1986) *Italian Syntax*, Dordrecht: Reidel.

Burzio, L. (1989) 'The role of the antecedent in anaphoric relations', paper presented at Geneva University, March 1989.

Burzio, L. (1991) 'The morphological basis of anaphora', *Journal of Linguistics* 27, 81–105.

Campos, H. (1986) 'Indefinite object drop', *Linguistic Inquiry*, 17, 354–9.

Cardinaletti, A., G. Cinque and G. Giusti (eds) (1988) *Constituent Structure*, Dordrecht: Foris.

Carroll, S. (1983) 'Remarks on FOR–TO Infinitives', *Linguistic Analysis*, 12, 415–54.

Chomsky, N. (1965) *Aspects of the Theory of Syntax*, Cambridge, Mass.: MIT Press.

Chomsky, N. (1970) 'Remarks on nominalisation', in Jacobs and Rosenbaum (eds), *English Transformational Grammar*, 184–221.

Chomsky, N. (1973) 'Conditions on transformations', in S. Anderson and P. Kiparsky (eds), *A Festschrift for Morris Halle*, New York: Holt, Rinehart and Winston, 232–86.

Chomsky, N. (1980) 'On binding', *Linguistic Inquiry*, 11, 1–46.

Chomsky, N. (1981a) *Lectures on Government and Binding*, Dordrecht: Foris.

Chomsky, N. (1981b) 'On the representation of form and function', *The Linguistic Review*, 1, 1, 3–40.

Chomsky, N. (1981c) 'Principles and parameters in syntactic theory', in Hornstein and Lightfoot (eds), *Explanation in Linguistics*, 123–46.

Chomsky, N. (1982) *Some Concepts and Consequences of the Theory of Government and Binding*, Cambridge, Mass.: MIT Press.

Chomsky, N. (1986a) *Knowledge of Language, its Nature, Origin, and Use*, New York: Praeger.

Chomsky, N. (1986b) *Barriers*, Cambridge, Mass.: MIT Press.

Chomsky, N. (1988) *Language and Problems of Knowledge. The Managua Lectures*, Cambridge, Mass.: MIT Press.

Chomsky, N. (1991) 'Some notes on the economy of derivation', in Freidin (ed.), *Principles and Parameters in Comparative Grammar*, 417–54.

Chomsky, N. (1992) *A Minimalist Program for Linguistic Theory*, MIT Occasional Papers in Linguistics, Cambridge, Mass: MIT.

Chomsky, N. and H. Lasnik (1977) Filters and Control. *Linguistic Inquiry*, 8: 425–504.

Chung, S. and J. McCloskey (1983) 'On the interpretation of certain island facts in GPSG', *Linguistic Inquiry*, 14, 704–13.

Cinque, G. (1984) *A-Bar Bound Pro vs. Variable*, Cambridge, Mass.: MIT Press.

Cinque, G. (1991) *Types of A'-dependencies*, Cambridge Mass.: MIT Press.

Closs-Traugott, E. (1972) *The History of English Syntax*, Transatlantic Series in Linguistics, New York, Chicago, San Francisco, Atlanta, Dallas, Montreal, Toronto, London, Sidney: Holt, Rinehart and Winston, Inc.

Cole, P. (1987) 'Null objects in universal grammar', *Linguistic Inquiry*, 18, 597–612.

Cole, P., G. Hermon and L.-M. Sung (1990) 'Principles and parameters of long distance reflexives', *Linguistic Inquiry*, 21, 1–22.

Contreras, H. (1984) 'A note on parasitic gaps', *Linguistic Inquiry*, 15, 704–13.

Contreras, H. (1993) 'On null operator structures', *Natural Language and Linguistic Theory*, 11, 1–30.

Coopmans, P. and I. Roovers (1986) 'Reconsidering some syntactic properties of PP-extraposition', in Coopmans, Bordelois and Dotson Smith (eds), *Formal Parameters of Generative Grammar*, 21–35.

Coopmans, P., I. Bordelois, and B. Dotson Smith (eds) (1986) *Formal Parameters of Generative Grammar – Going Romance*, Dordrecht: ICG Printing.

Cresti, D. (1993) 'Extraction and reconstruction', paper submitted for the Cerfiticat de Spécialisation, Geneva.

Czepluch, H. (1982) 'Case theory and the dative construction', *The Linguistic Review*, 2, 1, 1–38.

Davis, L. (1986) 'Remarks on the theta criterion and case', *Linguistic Inquiry*, 17, 564–8.

Deprez, V. and A. Pierce (1993) 'Negation and functional projections in early grammar', *Linguistic Inquiry*, 24, 25–67.

Emonds, J. (1970) 'Root and structure preserving transformations', Indiana University Linguistics Club.

Emonds, J. (1976) *A Transformational Approach to English Syntax*, New York: Academic Press.

Engdahl, E. (1983) 'Parasitic gaps', *Linguistics and Philosophy*, 6, 5–34.

Epstein, S. D. (1984) 'Quantifier pro and the LF representation of PRO arb', *Linguistic Inquiry*, 15, 499–505.

Evans, G. (1980) 'Pronouns', *Linguistic Inquiry*, 11, 337–62.

Evans, G. (1982) *The Varieties of Reference*, Oxford: Oxford University Press.

Everaert, M. (1986) *The Syntax of Reflexivization*, Dordrecht: Foris.

Flynn, S. and W. O'Neill (1988) *Linguistic Theory in Second Language Acquisition*, Dordrecht, Boston, London: Kluwer.

Frampton, J. (1991) 'Relativized minimality: a review', *The Linguistic Review*, 8, 1–46.

Frank, R., Young-Suk Lee and Owen Rambow (1992) 'Scrambling as non-operator movement and the special status of subjects', MS, University of Pennsylvania.

Freidin, R. (ed.) (1991) *Principles and Parameters in Comparative Grammar*, Cambridge, Mass.: MIT Press.

Fromkin, V. and R. Rodman (1988, 1992) *An Introduction to Language*, 4th edn, New York, etc.: Harcourt, Brace Jovanovich College Publishers, 5th edn, 1992.

Geest, W. de and Y. Putseys (eds) (1984) *Sentential Complementation*, Dordrecht: Foris.

George, L. (1980) 'Analogical generalization in natural language syntax', doctoral dissertation, MIT, Cambridge, Mass.

Gilligan, G. (1987) 'A cross-linguistic approach to the pro-drop parameter', doctoral diss., Department of Linguistics, University of Southern California.

Giorgi, A. (1984) 'Towards a theory of long distance anaphors: a GB approach', *The Linguistic Review*, 3, 4, 307–61.

Giorgi, A. (1987) 'The notion of complete functional complex: some evidence from Italian', *Linguistic Inquiry*, 18, 511–18.

Goodall, G. (1987) *Parallel Structures in Syntax*, Cambridge: Cambridge University Press.

Grange, C. and L. Haegeman (1989) 'Subordinate clauses: adjuncts or arguments', in Jaspers et al. (eds) *Sentential Complementation and the Lexicon*, 281–300.

Greenberg, J. H. (1963) 'Some universals of grammar with particular reference to the order of meaningful elements', in J. H. Greenberg (ed.), *Universals in Language*, Cambridge, Mass.: MIT Press, 33–59.

Greenberg, J. H. (ed.) (1978) *Universals of Human Language*, 4 vols, Stanford, Cal.: Stanford University Press.

Grewendorf, G. and W. Sternefeld (eds) (1989) *Scrambling and Barriers*, Amsterdam: John Benjamins.

Grimshaw, J. (1979) 'Complement selection and the lexicon', *Linguistic Inquiry*, 1, 279–326.

Grimshaw, J. (1981) 'Form function and the language acquisition device', in C. L. Baker and J. McCarthy (eds), *The Logical Problem of Language Acquisition*, Cambridge, Mass.: MIT Press, 165–82.

Grimshaw, J. (1991) 'Extended projections', MS, Brandeis University.

Guéron, J. (1980) 'On the syntax and semantics of PP extraposition', *Linguistic Inquiry*, 11, 637–78.

Guéron, J. and L. Haegeman (in preparation) *English Grammar, Syntax, Interpretation and Variation*, Oxford: Blackwell.

Haan, G. de (1979) *Conditions on Rules*, 2nd edn Dordrecht: Foris, 1981.

Haegeman, L. (1985) 'The *get*-passive and Burzio's generalization', *Lingua*, 66, 53–77.

Haegeman, L. (1986a) 'INFL, COMP and nominative case assignment in Flemish infinitivals', in Muysken and van Riemsdijk (eds), *Features and Projections*, 123–37.

Haegeman, L. (1986b) 'The double object construction in West Flemish', *The Linguistic Review*, 5, 4, 281–300.

Haegeman, L. (1987) 'Register variation in English: some theoretical observations', *Journal of English Linguistics*, 20, 2, 230–48.

Haegeman, L. (1990) 'Non-overt subjects in diary contexts', in Mascaro and Nespor (eds), *Grammar in Progress*, 167–79.

Haegeman, L. (1991) 'Adverbial positions and second language acquisition', Technical Reports, Faculty of Letters, University of Geneva.

Haegeman, L. (1992) *Theory and Description in Generative Grammar: A Case Study in West Flemish*, Cambridge: Cambridge University Press.

Haegeman, L. (1993) 'The morphology and distribution of object clitics in West Flemish', *Studia Linguistica*, 43, 57–94.

Haegeman, L. (in preparation) *The Syntax of Negation*, Cambridge: Cambridge University Press.

Haegeman, L. and H. van Riemsdijk (1986) 'Verb projection raising, scope and the typology of rules affecting verbs', *Linguistic Inquiry*, 17, 417–66.

Haider, H. (1981) 'Empty categories and some differences between English and German', *Wiener Linguistische Gazette*, 25, 13–36.

Haider, H. (1982) 'Dependenzen und Konfigurationen', *Groninger Arbeiten zur Germanistischen Linguistik*, 21, i–ii and 1–59.

Haider, H. (1985) 'The case of German', in Toman (ed.), *Studies in German Grammar*, 65–102.

Haider, H. and M. Prinzhorn (eds) (1986) *Verb Second Phenomena in Germanic Languages*, Dordrecht: Foris.

Haik, Isabelle (1983) 'Indirect binding and referential circularity', *The Linguistic Review*, 2, 2, 313–30.

Hale, K. (1983) 'Warlpiri and the grammar of non-configurational languages', *Natural Language and Linguistic Theory*, 1, 5–47.

Hale, K. and S. J. Keyser (1986) 'Some transitivity alternations in English', Lexicon Project MIT, Working Paper, 7.

Hale, K. and S. J. Keyser (1987) 'A view from the middle', Lexicon Project MIT Working Paper, 10.

Heim, I. (1982) *The Semantics of Definite and Indefinite Expressions*, GLSA.

Hellan, L. and K. Koch Christensen (1986) *Topics in Scandinavian Syntax*, Dordrecht: Reidel.

Henry, A. (1989) 'Infinitives in a *For to* dialect', MS.

Hermon, G. (1992) 'Binding theory and parameter setting', *The Linguistic Review*, 9, 145–89.

Higginbotham, J. (1980) 'Pronouns and bound variables', *Linguistic Inquiry*, 11, 679–708.

Higginbotham, J. (1983) 'Logical form, binding, and nominals', *Linguistic Inquiry*, 14, 395–420.

Higginbotham, J. (1988) 'On the varieties of cross-reference', in Cardinaletti, Cinque and Giusti (eds), *Constituent Structure*, 123–42.

Higginbotham, J. and R. May (1981) 'Questions, quantifiers and crossing', *The Linguistic Review*, 1, 1, 41–80.

Higgins, J. (1972) 'The pseudo cleft construction', Ph.D. diss., MIT, Cambridge, Mass.

Hirschbüler, P. and M. Labelle (1993) 'From *ne* V *pas* to *ne pas* V and the syntax of *pas*', MS, University of Ottawa and UQAM.

Hoekstra, T. (1984) *Transitivity*, Dordrecht: Foris.

Hoekstra, T. and R. Mulder (1990) 'Unergatives as copular verbs; locational and existential predication', *The Linguistic Review*, 7, 1–79.

Holmberg, A. and C. Platzack (1991) 'On the role of inflection in Scandinavian syntax', in W. Abraham (ed), *Issues in Germanic Syntax*, Berlin, New York: Mouton de Gruyter, 93–118.

Hornstein, N. (1977) 'S' and X' convention', *Linguistic Analysis*, 3, 137–76.

Hornstein, N. (1984) *Logic as Grammar*, Cambridge, Mass.: MIT Press.

Hornstein, N. and D. Lightfoot (1981) *Explanation in Linguistics*, London: Longman.

Hornstein, N. and D. Lightfoot (1987) 'Predication and PRO', *Language*, 63, 23–52.

Hornstein, N. and A. Weinberg (1981) 'Case theory and preposition stranding', *Linguistic Inquiry*, 12, 55–92.

Hornstein, N. and A. Weinberg (1988) '"Logical form" – its existence and its properties', in Cardinaletti, Cinque and Giusti (eds), *Constituent Structure*, 143–56.

Huang, J. (1982) 'Logical relations in Chinese and the theory of grammar', diss., MIT, Cambridge, Mass.

Huang, J. (1983) 'A note on the binding theory', *Linguistic Inquiry*, 14, 554–61.

Huang, J. (1984) 'On the distribution and reference of empty pronouns', *Linguistic Inquiry*, 15, 531–74.

Huang, J. (1989) 'Pro-drop in Chinese: a generalized control theory', in Jaeggli and Safir (eds), *The Null Subject Parameter*, 185–214.

Huang, J. (1991) 'Remarks on the status of the null object', in Freidin (ed.), *Principles and Parameters in Comparative Grammar*, 56–76.

Huang, J. (1993) 'Reconstruction and the structure of VP: some theoretical consequences', *Linguistic Inquiry*, 24, 69–102.

Huddleston, R. (1976) *An Introduction to English Transformational Grammar*, London: Longman.

Huddleston, R. (1984) *Introduction to the Grammar of English*, Cambridge: Cambridge University Press.

Hyams, N. (1986) *Language Acquisition and the Theory of Parameters*, Dordrecht: Reidel.

Hyams, N. (1989) 'The null subject parameter in language acquisition', in Jaeggli and Safir (eds), *The Null Subject Parameter*, 215–38.

Jackendoff, R. S. (1972) *Semantic Interpretation in Generative Grammar*, Cambridge, Mass.: MIT Press.

Jackendoff, R. S. (1977) *X-Syntax: A Study of Phrase Structure*, Cambridge, Mass.: MIT Press.

Jackendoff, R. (1992) 'Mme Tussaud meets the binding theory', *Natural Language and Linguistic Theory*, 10, 1–31.

Jackendoff, Ray, Joan Maling and Annie Zaenen (1993) 'Home is subject to Principle A', *Linguistic Inquiry*, 24, 173–77.

Jacobs, R. A. and P. S. Rosenbaum (1970) *English Transformational Grammar*, Waltham, Mass.: Ginn.

Jaeggli, O. (1981) *Topics in Romance Syntax*, Dordrecht: Foris.

Jaeggli, O. (1986) 'Passive', *Linguistic Inquiry*, 17, 587–633.

Jaeggli, O. and K. J. Safir (eds) (1989) *The Null Subject Parameter*, Dordrecht: Kluwer.

Jaeggli, O. and C. Silva-Corvalan (eds) (1986) *Studies in Romance Linguistics*, Dordrecht: Foris.

Jaspers, D., W. Klooster, Y. Putseys and P. Seuren (1989) *Sentential Complementation and the Lexicon. Studies in Honour of Wim de Geest*, Dordrecht: Foris.

Johnson, K. (1985) 'Subjects and θ-theory', MS, MIT, Cambridge, Mass.

Johnson, K. (1988) 'Clausal gerunds, the ECP and government', *Linguistic Inquiry*, 19, 583–610.

Jones, M. A. (1983) 'Getting *tough* with *wh*-movement', *Journal of Linguistics*, 19, 1, 129–59.

Kayne, R. (1975) *French Syntax*, Cambridge, Mass.: MIT Press.

Kayne, R. (1983) 'Chains, categories external to S, and French complex inversion', *Natural Language and Linguistic Theory*, 1, 109–37.

Kayne, R. (1984) *Connectedness and Binary Branching*, Dordrecht: Foris.

Kayne, R. (1989) 'Null subjects and clitic climbing', in Jaeggli and Safir (eds) *The Null Subject Parameter*, 239–61.

Kayne, R. (1991) 'Romance clitics, verb movement and PRO', *Linguistic Inquiry*, 22, 647–86.

Kayne, R. (1993) 'The antisymmetry of syntax', MS, CUNY.

Kemenade, A. van (1987) *Syntactic Case and Morphological Case in the History of English*, Dordrecht: Foris.

Kempson, R. (1988a) 'Grammar and conversational principles', in F. Newmeyer, (ed.), *Linguistics: the Cambridge Survey, Volume II. Linguistic Theory: Extension and Application*, Cambridge: Cambridge University Press, 139–63.

Kempson, R. (1988b) 'Logical form: the grammar cognition interface', *Journal of Linguistics*, 24, 393–431.

Keyser, S. J. (ed.) (1978) *Recent Transformational Studies in European Languages*, Cambridge, Mass.: MIT Press.

Kiss, K. E. (1981) 'Structural relations in Hungarian, a "free" word order language', *Linguistic Inquiry*, 12, 185–214.

Kiss, K. (1993) '*Wh*-movement and specificity', *Natural Language and Linguistic Theory*, 11, 85–120.

Kitagawa, Y. (1986) 'Subject in Japanese and English', Ph.D. diss., University of Massachusetts, Amherst.

Koopman, H. (1983) 'Control from COMP and comparative syntax', *The Linguistic Review*, 2, 365–91.

Koopman, H. (1984) *The Syntax of Verbs*, Dordrecht: Foris.

Koopman, H. and D. Sportiche (1982) 'Variables and the bijection principle', *The Linguistic Review*, 2, 139–60.

Koopman, H. and D. Sportiche (1991) 'The position of subjects', *Lingua*, 85, 211–58.

Koster, J. (1973) 'PP over V en de Theorie van J. Emonds', *Spectator*, 2, 294–311.

Koster, J. (1975) 'Dutch as an SOV language', *Linguistic Analysis*, 1, 111–36.

Koster, J. (1978a) *Locality Principles in Syntax*, Dordrecht: Foris.

Koster, J. (1978b) 'Why subject sentences don't exist', in Keyser (ed.), *Recent Transformational Studies in European Languages*, 53–64.

Koster, J. (1984a) 'On binding and control', *Linguistic Inquiry*, 15, 417–59.

Koster, J. (1984b) 'Infinitival complements in Dutch', in de Geest and Putseys (eds), *Sentential Complementation*, 141–50.

Koster, J. (1986) 'The Relation between pro-drop, scrambling and verb movement', Groningen Papers in Theoretical and Applied Linguistics, TTT no. 1.

Koster, J. (1987) *Domains and Dynasties*, Dordrecht: Foris.

Koster, J. and E. Reuland (eds) (1991) *Long Distance Anaphora*, Cambridge: Cambridge University Press.

Kroch, A. (1989) 'Amount quantification, referentiality and long *wh*-movement', MS, University of Pennsylviania.

Kuno, S. (1973) *The Structure of the Japanese Language*, Cambridge, Mass.: MIT Press.

Kuroda, Y. (1986) 'Whether we agree or not', MS, UCSD.

Laka, I. (1990) 'Negation in syntax: on the nature of functional categories and Projections', Ph.D. thesis, MIT, Cambridge, Mass.

Larson, R. K. (1988) 'On the double object construction', *Linguistic Inquiry*, 19, 335–91.

Lasnik, H. (1986) 'On accessibility', *Linguistic Inquiry*, 17, 126–9.

Lasnik, H. (1988) 'Subjects and the theta-criterion', *Natural Language and Linguistic Theory*, 6, 1, 1–18.

Lasnik, H. (1991) 'On the necessity of binding conditions', in Freidin (ed.), *Principles and Parameters in Comparative Grammar*, 7–28.

Lasnik, H. and J. Kupin (1977) 'A restrictive theory of transformational grammar', *Theoretical Linguistics*, 4, 173–96.

Lasnik, H. and M. Saito (1984) 'On the nature of proper government', *Linguistic Inquiry*, 15, 235–89.

Lasnik, H. and T. Stowell (1991) 'Weakest crossover', *Linguistic Inquiry*, 22, 687–720.

Lasnik, H. and J. Uriagereka (1988) *A Course in GB Syntax*, Cambridge, Mass.: MIT Press.

Lebeaux, D. (1989) 'Language acquisition and the form of the grammar', Ph.D. diss., University of Massachusetts, Amherst.

Lightfoot, D. (1979) *Principles of Diachronic Syntax*, Cambridge: Cambridge University Press.

Lightfoot, D. (1981) 'Explaining syntactic change', in Hornstein and Lightfoot (eds), *Explanation in Linguistics*, 209–39.

Lightfoot, D. (1989) 'The child's trigger experience, Degree Ø learnability', *Behavioral and Brain Sciences*, 12, 321–34.

Lightfoot, D. (1991) *How to Set Parameters: Arguments from Language Change*, Cambridge, Mass: MIT Press.

Lightfoot, D. (1982) *The Language Lottery, Towards a Biology of Grammars*, Cambridge, Mass.: MIT Press.

Lightfoot, D. (1993) 'Degree Ø Learnability', in B. Lust, J. Whitman and J. Kornfilt (eds), *Syntactic Theory and First Language Acquisition: Cross-linguistic Perspectives*, Lawrence Erlbaum.

Longobardi, G. (1987) 'Extraction from NP and the proper notion of head government', in A. Giorgi and G. Longobardi (eds), *The Syntax of Noun Phrases*, Cambridge: Cambridge University Press.

Lumšden, J. (1987) 'Parametric variation in the history of English', Ph.D. diss., MIT, Cambridge, Mass.

McCawley, J. D. (1981) *Everything that Linguists have always Wanted to Know about Logic'*, London and Chicago: Blackwell and University of Chicago Press.

Mahajan, O. (1990) 'The A/A-bar distinction and Movement Theory', Ph.D. diss, MIT, Cambridge, Mass.

Manzini, R. (1983) 'On control and control theory', *Linguistic Inquiry*, 14, 421–46.

Manzini, R. (1992) *Locality*, Cambridge, Mass.: MIT Press.

Manzini, R. (1993) 'Locality theory and parasitic gaps', MS, UCL.

Manzini, R. and K. Wexler (1987) 'Parameters, binding theory and learnability', *Linguistic Inquiry*, 18, 3, 413–44.

Maracz, L. and P. Muysken (eds) (1989) *Configurationality. The Typology of Asymmetries*, Dordrecht: Foris.

Marantz, A. (1981) *A Theory of Grammatical Relations*, Cambridge, Mass.: MIT Press.

Marantz, A. (1984) *On the Nature of Grammatical Relations*, Cambridge, Mass.: MIT Press.

Mascaro, J. and M. Nespor (eds) (1990) *Grammar in Progress, GLOW Essays for Henk van Riemsdijk*, Dordrecht: Foris.

Massam, D. and Y. Roberge (1989) 'Recipe context null objects in English', *Linguistic Inquiry*, 20, 134–9.

May, R. (1985) *Logical Form*, Cambridge, Mass.: MIT Press.

Milsark, G. (1974) 'Existential sentences in English', diss. MIT, Cambridge, Mass.

Milsark, G. (1977) 'Towards an explanation of certain peculiarities of the existential construction in English', *Linguistic Analysis*, 3, 1, 1–31.

Milsark, G. (1988) 'Singl-*ing*', *Linguistic Inquiry*, 19, 611–34.

Mohanan, K. P. (1982) 'Grammatical relations and anaphora in Malayalam', in A. Marantz and T. Stowell (eds), *Papers in Syntax*, MIT Working papers in Linguistics.

Mohanan, K. P. (1985) 'Remarks on control and control theory', *Linguistic Inquiry*, 16, 637–48.

Moritz, L. (1989) 'Aperçu de la syntaxe de la négation en français et en anglais', mémoire de licence, Université de Genève.

Moro, A. (1989) '*There, ci* as raised predicates', MIT Working papers.

Muller, C. (1991) *La Négation en Français*, Genève: Droz.

Muysken, P. (1983) 'Parametrizing the notion head', *The Journal of Linguistic Research*, 2, 57–76.

Muysken, P. and H. van Riemsdijk (1986a) 'Projecting features and feature projections', in Muysken and van Riemsdijk (eds), *Features and Projections*, 1–30.

Muysken, P. and H. van Riemsdijk (eds) (1986b) *Features and Projections*, Dordrecht: Foris.

Nakajima, H. (1984) 'COMP as subject', *The Linguistic Review*, 4, 121–52.

Newmeyer, F. (1980) *Linguistic Theory in America*, New York: Academic Press.

Newmeyer, F. (1983) *Grammatical Theory*, Chicago: University of Chicago Press.

Obenauer, H. (1985) 'On the identification of empty categories', *The Linguistic Review*, 4, 135–202.

Ouhalla, J. (1990) 'Sentential negation, relativized minimality, and the aspectual status of auxiliaries', *The Linguistic Review*, 7, 183–213.

Ouhalla, J. (1992) 'Focus in Standard Arabic: the identification requirement and the Principles of Economy', MS, Queen Mary and Westfield College.

Pankhurst, J., M. Sharwood Smith and P. van Buren (eds) (1988) *Learnability and Second Languages*, Dordrecht: Foris.

Pearce, E. (1990a) 'An analysis of negated infinitives in middle French', in *Wellington Working Papers in Linguistics*. University of Wellington. 2, 31–45.

Pearce, E. (1990b) *Parameters in Old French Syntax*, vol. 18. *Studies in Natural Language and Linguistic Theory*, Dordrecht: Kluwer.

Pearce, E. (1991) 'Tense and negation: competing analyses in Middle French', in M. Lise, L. N. Dobrin and R. M. Rodriguez (eds), *Proceedings of the Parasession on Negation*, CLS 27, University of Chicago.

Perlmutter, D. M. (1989) 'Multi-attachment and the unaccusative hypothesis: the perfect auxiliary in Italian', *Probus*, 1, 63–120.

Perlmutter, P. (1971) *Deep and Surface Structure Constraints in Syntax*, New York: Holt, Rinehart and Winston.

Pesetsky, D. (1981) 'Complementizer-Trace Phenomena and the Nominative Island Condition', *The Linguistic Review*, 1, 3, 197–344.

Pesetsky, D. (1982) 'Paths and categories', diss. MIT, Cambridge, Mass.

Pesetsky, D. (1989) 'Language particular processes and the Earliness Principle', GLOW talk, University of Utrecht.

Pica, P. (1986) 'De quelques implications théoriques de l'étude des relations à longue distance' in M. Ronat and D. Couquaux (eds) *La Grammaire modulaire*, Paris: Minuit 187–210.

Platzack, C. (1983) 'Germanic word order and the COMP/INFL parameter', Working Papers in Scandinavian Syntax, 2, University of Trondheim.

Platzack, C. (1986a) 'The position of the finite verb in Swedish', in Haider and Prinzhorn (eds), *Verb Second Phenomena in Germanic Languages*, 27–47.

Platzack, C. (1986b) 'COMP, INFL and Germanic word order', in Hellan and Christensen (eds), *Topics in Scandinavian Syntax*, 185–234.

Platzack, C. (1987) 'The Scandinavian languages and the null-subject parameter', *Natural Language and Linguistic Theory*, 5, 377–402.

Platzack, C. and A. Holmberg (1989) 'The role of AGR and finiteness in Germanic VO languages', *Working Papers in Scandinavian Syntax*, 43, 51–76.

Poggi, L. (1983) 'Implicazioni Teoretiche della Sintassi dei Pronomi Clitici Soggetto in un Dialetto Romagnolo', Tesi di laurea Universita della Calabria.

Pollock, J.-Y. (1989) 'Verb movement, UG and the structure of IP', *Linguistic Inquiry*, 20, 365–424.

Postal, P. (1966) 'On so-called pronouns in English', in D. Reibel and S. Schane (eds), *Modern Studies in English*, Englewood Cliffs, N.J.: Prentice-Hall, 201–24.

Postal, P. M. (1971) *Cross-over Phenomena*, New York: Holt, Rinehart & Winston.

Postal, P. M. (1974) *On Raising*, Cambridge Mass.: MIT Press.

Postal, P. M. and G. K. Pullum (1988) 'Expletive noun phrases in sub-categorized positions', *Linguistic Inquiry*, 19, 635–70.

Prewett, J. (1977) 'Reflexivization and *picture* noun phrase constructions', in L. Hutchinson (ed.), *Minnesota Working Papers in Linguistics and Philosophy of Language*, 4, 121–54.

Puskas, G. (1992) 'The Wh-Criterion in Hungarian', *Rivista di Grammatica Generativa*, 22, 141–186.

Quirk, R. and C. L. Wrenn (1957) *An Old English Grammar*, 2nd edn, London: Methuen.

Quirk, R., S. Greenbaum, G. Leech and J. Svartvik (1985) *A Comprehensive Grammar of the English Language*, London: Longman.

Radford, A. (1990) *Syntactic Theory and the Acquisition of English Syntax*, Oxford, UK and Cambridge, Mass.: Blackwell.

Raposo, E. (1986) 'On the null object in European Portuguese', in Jaeggli and Silva-Corvalan (eds), *Studies in Romance Linguistics*, 373–90.

Raposo, E. (1987) 'Case theory and INFL to COMP: the inflected infinitive in European Portuguese', *Linguistic Inquiry*, 18, 85–109.

Reinhart, T. (1981) 'Definite NP anaphora and c-command domains', *Linguistic Inquiry*, 12, 605–35.

Reuland, E. (1983) 'Governing *-ing*', *Linguistic Inquiry*, 14, 101–36.

Riemsdijk, H. van (1978a) *A Case Study in Syntactic Markedness*, Dordrecht: Foris.

Riemsdijk, H. van (1978b) 'On the diagnosis of *wh*-movement', in Keyser (ed.), *Recent Transformational Studies in European Languages*, 189–206.

Riemsdijk, H. van and E. Williams (1981) 'NP-structure', *The Linguistic Review*, 1, 171–217.

Riemsdijk, H. van and E. Williams (1986) *Introduction to the Theory of Grammar*, Cambridge, Mass.: MIT Press.

Ritter, E. (1991) 'Evidence for Number as a nominal head', paper delivered at the GLOW Colloquium, Leiden.

Rivero, M. L. (1991) 'Long Head Movement and negation: Serbo-Croatian vs. Slovak and Czech', *The Linguistic Review*, 8, 319–52.

Rizzi, L. (1978) 'A restructuring rule in Italian syntax', in Keyser (ed.), *Recent Tranformational Studies in European Languages*, 113–18; also in Rizzi, *Issues in Italian Syntax*, 1–48.

Rizzi, L. (1982a) *Issues in Italian Syntax*, Dordrecht: Foris.

Rizzi, L. (1982b) 'Violations of the *wh*-island constraint and the subjacency condition', in Rizzi, *Issues in Italian Syntax*, 49–76.

Rizzi, L. (1982c) 'Negation, *wh*-movement and the null subject parameter', in Rizzi *Issues in Italian Syntax*, 117–84.

Rizzi, L. (1986a) 'Null objects in Italian and the theory of *pro*', *Linguistic Inquiry*, 17, 501–58.

Rizzi, L. (1986b) 'On the status of subject clitics in Romance', in Jaeggli and Silva-Corvalan (eds), *Studies in Romance Linguistics*, 391–419.

Rizzi, L. (1986c) 'On chain formation', in H. Borer (ed.), *Syntax and Semantics*, vol. 19. *The Syntax of Pronominal Clitics*, New York: Academic Press, 65–95.

Rizzi, L. (1987) 'Three issues in Romance dialectology', paper presented at the dialectology workshop, GLOW, Venice.

Rizzi, L. (1990a) *Relativized Minimality*, Cambridge, Mass.: MIT Press.

Rizzi, L. (1990b) 'Speculation on Verb Second' in Mascaro and Nespor (eds), *Grammar in Progress, GLOW Essays for Henk van Riemsdijk*, 375–86.

Rizzi, L. (1991) 'Proper Head government and the definition of A-positions', paper presented at the GLOW conference, Leiden.

Rizzi, L. (1992a) 'Early null subjects and root null subjects', MS, University of Geneva.

Rizzi, L. (1992b) 'Argument/Adjunct (a)symmetries', paper presented at the NELS conference, Delaware; in K. Broderick (ed.), *Proceedings of the North East Linguistics Society Annual Meeting*, vol. 22.

Rizzi, L. (forthcoming) 'Residual Verb Second and the *Wh*-criterion', to appear in A. Belleti, and L. Rizzi (eds), *Parameters and Functional Heads. Essays in Comparative Syntax*, Oxford and New York: Oxford University Press.

Rizzi, L. and I. Roberts (1989) 'Complex inversion in French', *Probus*, 1, 1–30.

Roberts, I. (1983) 'Oblique case in the history of English', *Southern California Papers in Linguistics*, 10, 143–59.

Roberts, I. (1987) *The Representation of Implicit and Dethematized Subjects*, Dordrecht: Foris.

Robins, H. (1967) *A Short History of Linguistics*, 2nd edn, London: Longman, 1979.

Rochemont, M. (1978) 'A theory of stylistic rules in English', Ph.D. diss., University of Massachussets, Amherst.

Rosenbaum, P. S. (1976) *The Grammar of English Predicate Complement Constructions*, Cambridge, Mass.: MIT Press.

Ross, J. R. (1967) 'Constraints on variables in syntax', diss., MIT, Cambridge, Mass.

Ross, J. R. (1982) 'Pronoun deleting processes in German', paper presented at the Annual Meeting of the LSA, San Diego.

Rothstein, S. (1992) 'Case and NP licensing', *Natural Language and Linguistic Theory*, 10, 119–39.

Rouveret, A. (1991) 'Functional categories and agreement', *The Linguistic Review*, 8, 353–87.

Rouveret, A. and J. R. Vergnaud (1980) 'Specifying reference to the subject', *Linguistic Inquiry*, 11, 97–202.

Rowlett, P. (1993) 'On the syntactic derivation of negative sentence adverbials', *French Language Studies*, 3, 39–69.

Rudin, C. (1988) 'On multiple questions and multiple wh fronting', *Natural Language and Linguistic Theory*, 6, 445–501.

Safir, K. (1985) *Syntactic Chains*, Cambridge: Cambridge University Press.

Safir, K. (1986) 'Relative clauses in a theory of binding and levels', *Linguistic Inquiry*, 17, 663–90.

Safir, K. (1987) 'The anti-c-command condition on parasitic gaps', *Linguistic Inquiry*, 18, 678–83.

Scabolsci, A. and F. Zwarts (1991) 'Weak islands and algebraic semantics', MS.

Schwartz, B. D. and S. Vikner (1989) 'All verb second clauses are CPs', *Working Papers in Scandinavian Syntax*, 43, 27–50.

Sells, P. (1984) 'Syntax and semantics of resumptive pronouns', Ph.D. diss., University of Massachusetts, Amherst.

Shlonsky, U. (1991) 'Quantifiers as functional heads: a study of quantifier float in Hebrew', *Lingua*, 84, 159–80.

Shlonsky, U. (1992) 'Agreement in Comp', MS, University of Geneva.

Siloni, T. (1990) 'On the parallelism between CP and DP: Hebrew semi relatives', *Proceedings LCJL*, 1.

Smith, N. V. and D. Wilson (1979) *Modern Linguistics*, London: Penguin Books.

Sobin, N. (1987) 'The variable status of COMP-trace phenomena', *Natural Language and Linguistic Theory*, 5, 33–60.

Sperber, D. and D. Wilson (1986) *Relevance*, Oxford: Basil Blackwell.

Sportiche, D. (1981) 'Bounding nodes in French', *The Linguistic Review*, 1, 2, 219–46.

Sportiche, D. (1988a) 'A theory of floating quantifiers and its corollaries for constituent structure', *Linguistic Inquiry*, 19, 425–49.

Sportiche, D. (1988b) 'Conditions on silent categories', MS.

Sportiche, S. (1992) Clitic constructions, MS, UCLA.

Stechow, A. von and W. Sternefeld (1988) *Bausteine Syntaktischen Wissens*, Opladen/Wiesbaden: Westdeutschen Verlag.

Stowell, T. (1978) 'What was there before there was *there*?', in D. Farkas, W. Jacobson and K. Todrys (eds), *Papers from the Fourteenth Regional Meeting*, Chicago Linguistics Society.

Stowell, T. (1981) 'Elements of phrase structure', diss. MIT, Cambridge, Mass.

Stowell, T. (1982) 'The tense of infinitives', *Linguistic Inquiry*, 13, 561–70.

Stowell, T. (1983) 'Subjects across categories', *The Linguistic Review*, 2, 285–312.

Stowell, T. (1985) 'Null antecedents and proper government', *Proceedings of the Fifteenth Annual Meeting of NELS*, GLSA, Amherst: University of Massachusetts.

Stowell, T. (1992) 'The role of the lexicon in syntactic theory', in Stowel and Wehrli (eds), *Syntax and Semantics*, vol. 26, *Syntax and the Lexicon*, 9–18.

Stowell, T. and E. Wehrli (eds) (1992) *Syntax and Semantics*, vol. 26, *Syntax and the Lexicon*, San Diego, New York, Boston, London, Sydney, Tokyo and Toronto: Academic Press, Harcourt Brace Jovanovich.

Stuurman, F. (1985) *Phrase Structure Theory in Generative Grammar*, Dordrecht: Foris.

Taraldsen, T. (1980) 'On the nominative Island condition, vacuous application and the *that*-trace filter', distributed by the Indiana University Linguistics Club.

Taraldsen, K. T. (1981) 'The theoretical interpretation of a class of marked extractions', in A. Belletti, L. Brandi and L. Rizzi (eds), *Theory of Markedness in Generative Grammar*, proceedings of the 1979 GLOW Conference, Pisa: Scuola Normale Superiore 475–516.

Thiersch, G. (1978) 'Topics in German syntax', diss., MIT, Cambridge, Mass.

Timberlake, A. (1979) 'Reflexivization and the cycle in Russian', *Linguistic Inquiry*, 10, 1, 285–312.

Toman, J. (1981) 'Aspects of multiple *Wh*-movement', in R. May and J. Koster (eds), *Levels of Syntactic Representations*, Dordrecht: Foris, 293–302.

Toman, J. (ed.) (1985) *Studies in German Grammar*, Dordrecht: Foris.

Travis, L. (1984) 'Parameters and effects of word order variation', diss., MIT, Cambridge, Mass.

Travis, L. (1986) 'Parameters of phrase structure and V2 phenomena', MS, McGill University, presented at the Princeton Workshop on Comparative Syntax, March.

Uszkoreit, H. (1987) *Word Order and Constituent Structure in German*, Stanford: Center for the Study of Language and Information.

Valin, R. Van (1986) 'An empty category as the subject of a tensed S in English', *Linguistic Inquiry*, 17, 581–6.

Vergnaud, J.-R. (1985) *Dépendences et niveaux de représentations en syntaxe*, Amsterdam: John Benjamins.

Visser, F. Th. (1963) *An Historical Syntax of the English Language*, vol. 1, Leiden: Brill.

Visser, F. Th. (1969) *An Historical Syntax of the English Language*, vol. 2, Leiden: Brill.

Wachowicz, Kristina (1974) 'Against the universality of a single *Wh*-question movement', *Foundations of Language*, 11, 155–66.

Watanabe, A. (1992) 'S-structure Movement and *Wh* in situ', MIT paper.

Webelhuth, G. (1984/5) 'German is configurational', *The Linguistic Review*, 4, 203–46.

Weerman, F. (1989) *The V2 Conspiracy; a Synchronic and Diachronic Analysis of Verbal Positions in Germanic Languages*, Dordrecht: Foris.

Wekker, H. and L. Haegeman (1985) *A Modern Course in English Syntax*, London: Croom Helm.

Wexler, K. and P. Culicover (1980) *Formal Principles of Language Acquisition*, Cambridge: Mass.: MIT Press.

Wexler, K. and R. Manzini (1987) 'Parameters and learnability in Binding Theory', in T. Roeper and E. Williams (eds), *Parameter Setting*, Dordrecht: Reidel.

Williams, E. (1980) 'Predication', *Linguistic Inquiry*, 11, 203–38.

Williams, E. (1981) 'Argument structure and morphology', *The Linguistic Review*, 1, 1, 81–114.

Williams, E. (1982) 'The NP cycle', *Linguistic Inquiry*, 13, 277–96.

Williams, E. (1986) 'A reassignment of the functions of LF', *Linguistic Inquiry*, 17, 265–99.

Woolf, V. (1985) *The Diary of Virginia Woolf*, vol. 5 1936–41, ed. Anne Olivier Bell assisted by Andrew McNeillie, Harmondsworth: Penguin. (First published by Chalto and Windus, The Hogarth Press, 1984.)

Zagona, K. (1982) 'Government and proper government of verbal projections', Ph.D. diss., University of Washington at Seattle.

Zanuttini, R. (1991) 'Syntactic properties of sentential negation. A comparative study of Romance languages', Ph.D. diss., University of Pennsylvania.

Zanuttini, R. (1993) 'Re-examining Negative clauses', MS, University of Georgetown.

Zribi-Hertz, A. (1984) 'Orphan prepositions in French and the concept of null pronoun', *Recherches Linguistiques*, 12, 46–91.

Zubizarreta, M.-L. (1982) 'On the relationship of the Lexicon to Syntax', Ph.D. diss., MIT, Cambridge, Mass.

Zubizarreta, M.-L. (1985) 'The relationship between morphophonology and morphosyntax: the case of Romance causatives', *Linguistic Inquiry*, 16, 247–89.

Zubizarreta, M.-L. (1987) *Levels of Representation in the Lexicon and in the Syntax*, Dordrecht: Foris.

Zwart, J. W. (1993) 'SOV languages are head-initial', MS, University of Groningen.

Index